D0983024

Guide to World Commodity Markets

Physical, Futures & Options Trading

Guide to World Commodity Markets

Physical, Futures & Options Trading

Sixth edition

Consultant Editor

John Buckley

PROBUS PUBLISHING COMPANY

Chicago, Illinois

First edition published in Great Britain and in the United States of
America in 1977; second edition in 1979; third edition in 1982; fourth
edition in 1985; fifth edition in 1986.

This sixth edition first published in Great Britain in 1990 by
Kogan Page Ltd, 120 Pentonville Road, London N1 9JN

Published in the United States of America in 1989 by
Probus Publishing Company
118 N. Clinton Street, Chicago, IL 60606, USA.
ISBN 1-55738-102-X

Typeset by DP Photosetting, Aylesbury, Bucks
Printed and bound in Great Britain
by Biddles Ltd, Guildford

Contents

Part 4: Commodity Market Training Members

Appendices

List of Figures in Part 2

Introduction

The events of October 1987 have awakened renewed interest in commodity markets from the world's financial institutions. As equities end their phenomenal period of ascent with an equally startling collapse, 'tangibles' (the true raw material commodities) and 'financial instruments' (the growing range of futures and options) are becoming increasingly fashionable with investors seeking to spread portfolio risk.

Volatility in the commodity markets themselves has encouraged this process, especially in the agricultural sector. In 1988, the worst drought in the United States in 50 years wiped out at a stroke years of accumulated surplus grain stocks, driving up prices and questioning the complacent assumption of a long-term decline in the farm economies of the northern industrialized countries. The 'greenhouse effect' has also captured the public's imagination and agronomists are having a field day, struggling to divine the long-term global implications of an unstable climate for grain yields. The spectre of Third World famine lurks once again in the wings and the long-term outcome may well be a reappraisal of the need for some form of government support for food commodity crops in the 1990s and into the next century.

These events have effectively moved the goalposts for the Uruguay Round of GATT negotiations which aim to lay the framework for a more orderly world trade system for the 1990s and beyond. When the Punte del Este Round began in mid-1987, agriculture headed the list of thorny trade issues as the world faced a seemingly intractable crisis of food crop over-production. At issue was the excessive use of government support to produce surplus crops, poach rival exporters' markets and use tariff barriers to block competing imports, which had already culminated in a series of quarrels – chiefly between the United States and the European Community, but also involving Latin America and Japan.

In the ensuing battle, the United States unleashed the full force of its trade subsidy armoury, by giving away 70 million tonnes of surplus grain to exporters, thus helping to drive world wheat prices down to just US $70 per tonne. The great 1988 drought finished that stock depletion process and now, less than two years later, wheat has rocketed to US $170 per tonne and may have further yet to go as stocks become increasingly scarce. How the cash-strapped developing countries, upon whom import demand is heavily biased, will cope with the strain on their already tight foreign exchanges, only time will tell. In a worsening global debt situation, yet more trade credit can have only a limited part to play, but the other alternative of trade subsidies to bridge the gap between real grain prices and what importers can afford remains just as awkward, especially now that the world's principal grain stock holder no longer holds the stocks to fund subsidy programmes. The implications for the GATT trade talks are fascinating. In 1988, the United States was demanding the abandonment of all agricultural subsidy worldwide by the year 2000. But the currently fashionable language in Washington of 'ratcheting down subsidy' may need to be updated if global shifts in climate threaten food production.

Meanwhile, for the traditional agricultural futures markets of Chicago, Kansas City and Minneapolis and Winnipeg, the renewed volatility in grains has attracted the speculators' attention in a manner not seen since the 1970s. For example, volume on the Chicago Board of Trade soyabean market leapt 69% in 1988 to 12.5 million contracts, while maize futures rose 53% to 11.1 million and wheat by 75% to 3.37 million lots. The agricultural futures boom helped the CBOT reach record turnovers for 1988, despite the flattening tendency in many of the newer financial instrument contracts and both trends have been further extended in the first half of 1989.

Other 'soft' commodities have also experienced dramatic price movement. Coffee and cocoa have failed to rescue their ailing international stabilization pacts against a backcloth of oversupply, producer infighting and consumer resistance. This has resulted in some of the lowest prices for a decade for coffee, a 13½ year low for cocoa and an increasing threat that poor producer incomes will ultimately disrupt supply. Sugar, on the other hand, has enjoyed a series of price booms as the 20-year yawning gap between consumption and output has been finally and decisively closed by ballooning shortages in the Soviet Union and China and production shortfalls in Cuba. The hectic trading that ensued from this in the New York and London sugar futures markets was also encouraged by spillover activity from the drought-inspired grain pits.

Record-busting metals helped to burnish the investor image of the commodity sector further in 1988, as previously weighty stocks were drawn down to their lowest level for years. Copper traded at over £2000 per tonne for the first time ever, as demand boomed and output fell in the major producers of Chile, Zaire, Zambia, Peru and the Philippines. Mine labour disputes siphoned off zinc stocks, while nickel outshone all other metals with an astonishing 350% rise to US $22,200 per tonne, as stainless steel demand leapt ahead of forecasts and supplies from the Dominican Republic were also hit by strikes. Demonstrating yet again the volatility of the metals sector, aluminium prices doubled to over US $4000 per tonne on the same pattern of dwindling stocks – only to crash to under $2,000, as producers over-responded to the firm market signals.

Even the moribund tin market shrugged off the sickness that had wrecked producer incomes and ended the International Tin Agreement as the 1986 Guide was compiled. Credit should go to those producers who agreed then to limit production and sales, enabling the reduction of the buffer stock created by the ITA and the drawdown of other free market surpluses. With the tin price boom has come fresh impetus to expansion in the low-cost producing countries. The question is will they be able to resist the opportunity to gain desperately needed foreign exchange and will the bubble burst?

Despite inflation and political instability in several regions, gold was repeatedly shunned by investors, plummeting to a near 3-year low of US $360 from the high of US $490 in 1987. Again, some of that decline might be attributed to reduced world tension with the advent of the Gorbachev era and the ending of the Gulf conflict. Looking back at the post-war years, it can be seen that most of the major gold peaks occurred during periods of potential superpower conflict, for example, over Iran, Poland, Afghanistan and so on. It will be interesting to see whether the turmoil in China and East Europe might reverse the trend.

Another factor in the demise of gold has been the increasing attraction of platinum as a speculative hedge, thanks partly to the racing growth of consumption in auto-exhaust cleaners. Alternative fuel emission catalysts have now begun to compete, but these are also from the platinum group – palladium, for example – which will lend strength to the entire sector. As the 'green' fashion gathers pace, platinum prices seem unlikely to return to their old lows.

In compiling the fifth edition of the Guide we noted that the definition of a commodity as an 'article of commerce', or that which may be bought, sold or bartered, is continuing to expand to embrace not only new markets, but whole new generic fields. A decade or two ago, we might have fixed our focus exclusively on the raw material markets which were then the prime reason for the existence of most commodity trading companies and centres, but by the mid-1980s, a vastly different picture had already established itself. Commodity futures trading was no longer confined to the traditional centres of Chicago and New York and new commodity and allied futures together with financial instrument exchanges were sprouting at a truly astonishing pace. This process has continued from the Pacific Rim to Canada to South America. Some have suggested it may ultimately embrace even the Communist giants, but clearly this is now less likely for China.

We also noted that futures trading was no longer merely the domain of the giant multinational commodity firms or the corporate investors in Europe and the other wealthier parts of the world. Like their American counterparts in the early post-war years, more and more smaller European, Canadian, Asian, Australian and South American companies and private investors are learning how the commodity markets work, why they move in a given direction and what are the opportunities presented for calculated investment, outright speculation or trade and financial risk management.

One side-effect of this – augmented by the stock market crash – is the mushrooming growth of commodity funds, either as a straight investment, or as part of a broader financial portfolio. For the smaller investor, commodity funds can offer a ground floor entry into these volatile markets. Paradoxically, given the high risk image of commodity trading, the inclusion of these markets (not just metals and softs but also oil, interest rates, stock indices and currencies) can actually have a risk-levelling process as well as a potentially far higher return when included, for example, in a stock/bond-based portfolio. Many household names in the commodity world have entered this field, often offering a basket of commodities in index form.

Major bull or bear commodity markets may not, of course, occur often, but there is nearly always one going on somewhere. The rationale is that the varying performance of such commodity markets as coffee, wheat and silver can enable profit in a wide range of economic conditions which might promote relatively homogenous movement in the stock markets. In this field, the computer programme is all, ignoring the fundamentals of supply and demand and building chart patterns from the historical performance of markets. The impetus in this field is shown by the fact that global futures funds under management have grown sixfold to some US $7 billion in worth in the past five years and the services of their ancillary industry – the technical analysts – have never been in keener demand.

With the growth of market centres and participation has boomed a list of new contracts tailored to suit almost anything that can be defined, indexed, hedged or bet upon. So, the once clearly defined commodity markets like coffee, metals, soyabeans, grains and so on have had to accept first shared, then second billing to a host of larger, more active markets where the stakes and the potential rewards are vastly higher.

Heading the list have been currencies and government bonds futures and options which, in the wake of the oil crisis of the 1970s and the ensuing economic upheavals, have passed through a period of unparalleled instability. Nowhere is this more graphically illustrated than by the growth of CBOT 'T' bond futures and options markets (essentially a means of betting against the performance of the United States economy), which last year traded yet another record figure of 70.3 million contracts, a rise of 5% on 1987.

Growth in this sector may now be nudging its limits as demonstrated by the fact that, so far in 1989, 'T' bond turnover is now running level with last year. One reason for the slowdown in some of the so-called 'financial instruments', is the proliferation of often similar contracts on different markets all competing for a finite pool of investor money, which is now perhaps held more cautiously in the aftermath of 1987. So, while in the recent past the new financials tended to starve the more traditional commodity markets of liquidity, the slowing of this growth might be of eventual benefit to raw material futures trade.

Another problem for the true commodity markets and particularly the physical trade, has been the subordination of the traditional 'fundamentals' of supply and demand to the distorting effect of exchange rates. The dollar, as the international commodity trading currency, has often been the driving force in the pricing of a forward sale or purchase, in turn sucking hedging activity away from commodity futures into the more efficient currency futures.

The inter-relationship of commodities, currencies, oil, precious metals, inflation, interest rates and other indicators of global or national economic performance provide constant fodder for trader and investor alike. Not surprisingly, the economic climate within which commodities – both raw materials and financials – are traded, has remained volatile within the past five years as a constant promise of Unites States-led economic recovery has been matched by a less impressive performance, not least in the area of trade and budget deficits. Inflation has begun to rear its head yet again, suggesting dearer commodities, but as interest rates rise and the dollar again looks overvalued, the threat is renewed of stifled investment at home and overseas, industrial stagnation and a tightly lidded dollar-denominated commodity trade.

Amid this mix of mutually offsetting factors, the switchback dollar has often been blamed for robbing producers of gains from rising commodity prices. Sometimes, the currency trend confuses the price signals of the marketplace, halting the response of production and consumption to real demand and supply. For example, the strength of the dollar was one cause of the mid-1980s collapse of United States grain prices, while they were inflating in foreign currencies. Overseas buyers could not afford the grain, exports fell and internal markets subsided further. Conversely, currency movements have often had the impact of increasing production to meet depressed markets. This was typified by the gold market in the early 1980s, when the weak rand stimulated South African output when gold prices were actually falling in dollar terms on the world market.

Three years ago we were also pondering whether the dissolving influence of OPEC would begin to unwind the global inflation it had created in the 1970s. The gyrating oil price has proved an ambivalent factor, reducing oil-producer spending on commodity imports and investment, thus offsetting its invigoration of the economies of import-dependent oil consumers. In spring 1989, crude prices almost doubled from an October 1988 low of US $11 a barrel after a series of production problems and increasing co-operation between OPEC and non-member countries, but lately the market has returned to US $17.50 and forecasts of falling consumption may drive it yet lower. These fertile conditions for brisk oil futures activity have also increased uncertainty in commodity trading by effervescing the mix of economic factors governing the 'overview' from which longer-term purchase decisions must be made.

Even *perestroika* and *glasnost* are having their effect on the commodity markets, as has China's own 'revolution'. For the Soviet Union, there is the possibility of improved agrarian practices, stimulated by market incentives, but in the short to medium term, the emphasis has been on trying to keep shop shelves better filled with bread, meat and sugar at the cost of large imports. For China, the position, as one might expect, is more complex. Whether the authorities may continue to regionalize power – and thus liberalize imports into this other largest commodity-consuming block – might now be questioned by the recent upheavals in Peking.

Around the world, commodity producers continue to view with alarm the narrowing margins on their operations. On the face of things, the Third World commodity-deficit countries found themselves offered cheaper imports of many basic raw materials, but sadly, the boom in demand which this might have produced in earlier years has still been denied by the escalating debt problems of most developing countries. In this climate, the need to roll on or re-finance, has continued to give way increasingly to a call to write off some countries' debts altogether. The rationale is that a fresh slate might provide the sort of boom trade conditions which would more than offset the risks. Interestingly, the commercial banks have, in the past year, shown the first signs of preparedness to travel down this road, pushed along perhaps by the increasing readiness of even some 'model debtors' to renege on their repayments. But this problem is nowhere near solution.

As we have emphasized before, the long-term health of the markets depends on a reasonable degree of assurance that production is forthcoming. In this respect, consumers in the rich, developed northern countries have still to demonstrate a recognition that their generally poor, raw material suppliers must also earn a living.

In the United States, deregulation in the mid-1980s had the notable effect of hitting brokers' commissions, posing many intermediate-sized firms with liquidity problems. Takeovers and mergers have remained a pronounced feature, not just in the United States, but around the world and the trend will doubtless continue. At the same time, the leading commodity futures markets in the United States, Europe and Japan are coming under increasing scrutiny from the authorities who are anxious to curb insider trading and other abuses, although inevitably, the implied restrictions on trade are already being attacked by many firms as damaging to turnover.

One innovation upon which high hopes have been pinned for increased turnover is the advent of the 'global village' in electronic market communication. Increasingly, futures markets are moving away from the old system of 'open outcry' under which traders literally yell bids and offers back and forth across a market 'pit', towards orders executed by computer. More sophisticated systems are now being introduced to enable the machine to make its own trading decisions based on logged bids, offers and technical positions past and present. The cost advantages are as dramatic as the speed of order execution that cuts out intermediaries. Market 'transparency' is also vastly enhanced – everybody has a better idea what the price of a commodity is and what is being bought and sold. In the van of this movement, CBOT's AURORA system was introduced earlier this year, harnessing the latest computer technology in what is claimed to be an electronic replication of the open outcry system. The advent of the computer terminal trade has widespread implications for international competition. For example, in the battle for European white sugar futures turnover, the new British electronic ATS system has been winning hands down against the French market and may provide the blueprint for many imitators.

To sum up, political, fiscal and weather environments, trading practices and innovations will ensure that commodity markets remain in a state of high flux as the next decade approaches. Indeed, it is this very volatility that has always attracted the investor to these markets and which is yet again assisting in their revitalization.

For producers, consumers, funds and other investors, or for the academic observer, we hope that our book will help to draw the curtain back on what promises to be an interesting and exciting period for the commodity markets.

Please note that from 6 May 1990 London telephone numbers will no longer have the 01- local area code. Instead numbers will start with either 071- or 081-. Readers should check with British Telecom after 6 May 1990 if in doubt.

Part 1: Aspects of Futures Trading

Commodity Agreements

Robin Stainer,
Commodities Correspondent, The Guardian

Introduction

The United Nations Conference on Trade and Development (UNCTAD) formally established its Common Fund for Commodities on 19 June 1989. The Fund was first planned in the mid-1970s as a multi-billion dollar tool to support dozens of commodity price-stabilization agreements, but when it was finally negotiated in 1980, its scope and financing had been scaled down dramatically. It then took eight years for the minimum legal requirements for setting up the Fund to be met.

The Fund, which may not start operating until 1990 or 1991, will be armed with just over US $310 million in directly contributed capital from its 103 member governments and it will concentrate on research and development projects, not financing price-support pacts. It has been established at a time when the fortunes of such accords are at their lowest ebb for decades, with only one accord fully operational in defence of a target price range.

The International Natural Rubber Agreement (INRA)

This 32-nation accord, the second for the product, was concluded in 1987 and came into force in 1989 to defend a price range of 174–262 Malaysian/Singapore cents a kilo. These are respectively the levels at which the manager of the buffer stock – the price-control mechanism – must buy and sell. The 'may buy' level is 185 Malaysian/Singapore cents and the 'may sell' is 251. These prices can be revised every 15 months and there are provisions for automatic adjustments.

The pact's headquarters is in the Malaysian capital, Kuala Lumpur. Mr Pong Sono, the Thai nominee, was chosen as the executive director of the International Natural Rubber Organization that runs the accord.

The first INRA was negotiated in 1979, came into force in 1981 and expired on 22 October 1987. In the run-up to the entry into force of the new accord, 350,000 tonnes of the old pact's 360,000-tonne buffer stockpile (most of which was accumulated through price-defence buying during the 1981–1983 recession) was sold off.

The International Coffee Agreement (ICA)

INRA became the last price-supporting pact with the indefinite suspension on 4 July 1989 of the ICA's export quota system, which had stabilized the market since 1963, apart from an eight-year break from 1972 and a 19-month gap from February 1986. Unlike the latest suspension, which triggered a collapse in the ICO average market indicator price to a 14-year low below US $0.80 a pound, the previous suspensions had taken place when prices were rising.

The decision by the 74-nation International Coffee Organization (ICO) to remove the market's safety net followed a series of fruitless negotiations on a possible new accord to take over from 1 October 1989, or an extension of the old accord from then with its price-support provisions intact. Irreconcilable differences emerged, with the two key players – the United States and Brazil – finding themselves on opposing sides.

The United States made its support for quotas conditional on a bigger allocation being guaranteed to the mainly Latin American group producing the top quality mild arabica variety at the expense of cuts for others, including Brazil. The latter country, backed by Colombia, all African producers, the Philippines and the EEC, sought to postpone a decision on quota shares to September 1989.

These two alliances tabled separate proposals on extending the ICA for one year at the final round of negotiations in London in June 1989. A vote was postponed to 3 July, but neither was carried. The ICO decided as a fall-back to extend the ICA for two years from 1 October, but without its system of quotas, which had been defending a US $1.15–1.45 range for coffee. It also decided that as quotas would no longer be respected, they should be lifted at once.

The International Cocoa Agreement (ICCA)

Buffer stock purchases in defence of the minimum price set under the new 41-nation ICCA, which was concluded in 1986 and finally entered into force in January 1987, were indefinitely suspended in February 1988, when the stockpile reached the maximum permitted level of 250,000 tonnes; the total included 100,000 accumulated under the previous accord. The introduction of a supplementary stock withholding scheme, under which producers would receive financial help to remove up to 120,000 tonnes of surplus cocoa from the market, has been blocked by a shortage of cash and a bitter dispute between producers and consumers over the minimum price that should be defended.

This dispute is the result of differing interpretations of the wording of the ICCA article on the terms for automatic price adjustments. The consumers insist that three cuts of 115 Special Drawing Rights (SDR) a tonne have so far been triggered, taking the defended price range down from the original 1600–2270 SDR to 1255–1925; while the producers, with the Ivory Coast taking the strongest line, accept only one reduction to 1,485–2,155.

The cash shortage is the result of the failure of most producers to pass on to the International Cocoa Organization (ICCO) the US $30 a tonne levy on exports, with payment arrears – more than US $100 million by mid-1989 – expected to total US $200 million when the ICCA expires on 30 October 1990. Special provisions will have to be negotiated to stop the liquidation of the buffer stock within a maximum period of four-and-a-half years from that date.

The International Sugar Agreement (ISA)

The last ISA with powers to regulate the market through quotas expired in 1984, since when there have been two purely administrative accords. The present accord entered into force on 24 March 1988, with scope for a two-year extension on its expiry at the end of 1990. One of its four objectives is to 'provide an appropriate framework for the preparation of a possible new ISA with economic provisions'. No negotiations on such a pact have been scheduled, because of insufficient political support.

The International Sugar Organization (ISO) recently faced a possible move out of London because of the soaring cost of accommodation. In July 1989, it turned down offers of new headquarters in Paris, Amsterdam and Brussels and has instead accepted British Government and trade subsidies in order to remain London-based.

The International Wheat Agreement (IWA)

The International Wheat Council – which runs the IWA and the associated Food Aid Convention – was also included in the British offer, which is worth a total of £1.6 million over ten years. It has also decided to stay in London.

The new IWA, which, like its predecessor, has no economic clauses, was concluded in March 1986, and entered into force for five years on 1 July that year. A new three-year Food Aid Convention began operating on the same day. Under this, donors undertake to provide food grain (the target is 10 million tonnes a year) to poorer countries. Like the ISO, ICCO and ICO agreements, the IWC performs a valuable function for producers, consumers and traders of grain by collecting and disseminating data and forecasts on global supply and demand.

The International Tin Agreement (ITA)

This pact expired at the end of June 1989 but had already lost its power to influence prices in October 1985, when a cash crisis forced the indefinite suspension of buffer stock buying and left the International Tin Council (ITC) with massive debts to brokers and banks. These remain unpaid, although talks on a possible out-of-court settlement of claims of more than £500 million are continuing.

The ITC remains in being to carry out the liquidation of the ITA, but all its statistical work is likely to be taken over by a Tin Study Group, negotiated in April 1989, under the auspices of UNCTAD and expected to be operational in 1990.

The International Tropical Timber Agreement (ITTA)

This pact, whose headquarters is in Yokohama (Japan), has no economic clauses. Its administrative body provides market intelligence and oversees development and conservation projects.

Futures Markets

Izabel Grindal
Editor, Futures and Options World

By structuring commodity trading for the first time and introducing middle men into the transactions between buyers and sellers, futures and options were a logical development of nineteenth century trading methods, and it was only a matter of time before futures traders realized that the scope of their activities could be extended beyond the confines of physical commodities into the world of finance.

In comparison to their commodity predecessors, financial futures and options are a recent development, but it is the financial derivative markets, an invention of the early 1970s, which receive all the attention and most of the investment capital. In the United States, home of the world's largest exchanges, financial futures account for almost 60% of all futures trading.

Financial commodities have transformed the futures industry, acting as the driving force behind new contracts, exchanges and players. The run-up to 1992 is likely to result in every EEC member state launching its own domestic financial futures and/or options exchange, following in the footsteps of LIFFE (the London International Financial Futures Exchange) and the MATIF (*Marché à Terme International de France*), Europe's largest exchanges, which between them traded over 32 million contracts last year. Both rank among the ten largest futures exchanges in the world, although the MATIF only opened in February 1986 and LIFFE four years earlier.

Financial instruments have also had a considerable effect on the daily business of established exchanges, particularly those in the United States. The phenomenal growth in volume of Chicago's exchanges owes much to Treasury bonds, stock indices and currencies. The US Treasury bond future, the world's most active contract, accounts for nearly 50% of all business transacted on the Chicago Board of Trade (CBOT) with a 1988 volume total of over 70 million lots. In the last 5 years, volume in the 12-year-old contract has steadily risen by an average of 21% per annum.

In terms of longevity, however, these financial instruments have another hundred years or so to run if they are to prove as enduring as commodity futures and options. CBOT, the largest futures exchange in the world, having amassed over 143 million trades in 1988, started life in 1848 as a local grain exchange. Its main rival, the Chicago Mercantile (CME), came into being 26 years later as the Produce Exchange, trading butter and eggs. In London, the Metal Exchange had been around for 105 years before LIFFE was launched in 1982.

While financial futures and options continue to proliferate, the last 10 years have seen few new commodity exchanges, apart from a number of fledgling domestic markets in South America and the Far East. Several previously unlisted commodities have made it on to exchange floors, but the most significant development in commodity markets has been the launch of options. A long-standing ban on options in the United States was finally lifted from commodity exchanges in 1984. By 1987, annual volume in US agricultural options had topped 4 million contracts, while metals accounted for another 3.5 million lots and energy options 3.2 million.

As well as boosting volumes, options have brought new hedging opportunities to markets, and these factors have helped existing commodity futures exchanges to consolidate their positions. Chicago remains the centre for agricultural commodity futures trading with the CBOT listing 11 commodity futures and options, specializing in the grains, while the CME trades 8, all of them meats.

Both exchanges tried to tempt gold futures business into their pits when, in April 1987, the clearing systems of the United States' leading metals market almost ground to a halt. US metals futures and options trading, however, remains the preserve of the Commodity Exchange (COMEX), although the exchange does have to fight for its non-ferrous trade with the London Metal Exchange (LME). LME dominates the copper and aluminium markets, despite the fact that much of its aluminium business is sourced in the United States. COMEX, meanwhile, reigns supreme in gold and silver.

Often neglected in international comparisons, the Tokyo Commodity Exchange for Industry (TOCOM) could pose a serious threat to the LME/COMEX oligopoly of metals trading. In 1989, for the first time, foreign firms were allowed to trade in TOCOM's markets, which, despite their old-fashioned operating style, still traded 8.7 million contracts in precious metals in 1988, while TOCOM's platinum future amassed 4.4 million lots, making it the third most active precious contract in the world.

In the United States, platinum and palladium are traded on the same floor as COMEX, but are listed by the New York Mercantile Exchange (NYMEX). NYMEX was once considered as the poor cousin of COMEX and was almost taken over by the metals exchange after a potato futures trading scandal in 1978. However, it has remained independent and now ranks above COMEX, and is third after the Chicago giants in the league of futures exchanges. Energy and, particularly, West Texas Intermediate (WTI) crude oil futures have been the key to NYMEX's success. The WTI crude contract has become a closely scrutinized benchmark for the oil industry as OPEC loosens its tight grip on oil pricing. The popularity of the oil future which traded almost 19 million contracts in 1988 was compounded by the launch, at the end of 1987, of a crude option which traded over 5 million contracts in 1988.

New York is also home to the Coffee Sugar Cocoa Exchange (CSCE) and the New York Cotton Exchange (NYCE) which trade the United States' only cotton and frozen orange juice futures. Of the soft commodities, sugar is the most traded in terms of futures with the CSCE's raw sugar contract leading the pack. In 1988, raws traded almost 6 million lots with the option on the future adding a further 1.5 million.

New York's white sugar future, the third such contract to be listed, was launched in 1987, but it has failed to attract much interest. Physical trading is concentrated in Europe, feeding the white sugar futures of London Fox and the MATIF. Business is split fairly evenly between the two, but this is a recent development since the London Fox market only opened four months before New York's in July 1987.

Attempting to break the French monopoly in white sugar trading with the second relaunch of a London contract, Fox chose to trade the future on screen by using the Automated Trading System (ATS) as developed by the International Commodities Clearing House (ICCH). The system was an instant success and French regulators responded by bringing the Paris commodity markets under the control of the financial futures exchange, the MATIF, to encourage domestic business. Attempts to mediate a compromise with a possible merger of both markets on screen have yet to meet with any success.

In the Far East, it is Japan which boasts the largest commodity markets with 16 exchanges trading soyabeans, sugar, rubber, silk and even dried cocoons. Few of the contracts trade over 1 million lots in the year, but if the markets were to be merged, as many Japanese traders hope, they could become a powerful force in commodity trading. In Japan, however, the regulation of the markets is divided between four different ministries and the industry has, in the past, been tainted by the activities of corrupt brokers. So, the fledgling financial futures markets have disassociated themselves from the commodity exchanges, which in turn have missed out on many of the privileges accorded the financial markets.

Commodity futures generally have both benefited and suffered from their association with financial derivatives. Securities houses, banks, brokers and fund managers have all been drawn into the futures markets, expanding the potential audience for such instruments beyond the mix of trade houses, processors, refiners and merchants attracted by commodity contracts. The glamour and excitement inspired by financial markets has helped to polish up the image of commodity trading which had been tarnished by broker bankruptcies and illegal squeezes, or the attempted cornerings of various markets.

Many of the disadvantages of the commodity/financials association have been a by-product of regulation, which was itself a direct consequence of trading scandals. In the UK, for example, private client losses associated with commodity futures trading led to the Gower White Paper on which the Financial Services Act 1986 is based. The Act, which became law in 1986, treats both financial and commodity futures in the same way, introducing stringent regulations for the handling of retail business.

Despite lobbying by commodity brokers aimed at winning some exemption from the clauses of the Act, all firms which are trading futures must observe the 'compliance' and 'conduct of business' rules of the Securities and Investment Board (SIB) and the Association of Futures Brokers and Dealers (AFBD). Consequently, commodity brokers have had to change their business practices to accommodate new regulations on client handling and fund segregation to name a few. The costs of the regulatory règime have hit UK brokers badly, but regulators are not swayed by any arguments that the Act is of little relevance to the trade-oriented business of commodity brokers.

That said, the need for commodities and financials to work together is inevitable, because of the similarities between them. Both create a central, transparent market where the orders of hedgers and speculators can be matched and guaranteed. As such, both rely heavily on the principles and practices of 'open outcry' trading, although, given the 1988 United States fraud investigations which led to the indictment of 46 futures traders, both commodity and financial futures markets will have to examine the validity of open outcry for the 1990s and beyond.

Screen trading has been threatening to replace open outcry for several years, but a system has yet to be developed to convince traders and their exchanges. The CME, CBOT and LIFFE have developed their own systems – Globex, Aurora and APT – but all have been designed for off-hours trading once the normal trading day is over. In fact, the sheer volume of business transacted on these exchanges may mean that no system can ever handle peak hours trading. Yet in the commodity markets where volumes are rarely as great, screen trading may prove a cheaper, more efficient alternative. As London Fox has already shown, screen trading is a far simpler way of launching new contracts which may not be a guaranteed success.

Commodity futures traders have learnt to live in the shadow of their financial counterparts. In Chicago, in particular, many financial traders started in the commodity markets and, as illustrated by the drought-inspired surge in grain futures volumes in 1988, will eagerly move back to commodity futures when the markets are volatile. Commodity markets may lack the glamour and day-to-day excitement of financial futures, but they *have* stood the test of time.

Part 2: The Commodities

Metals

Aluminium

Emma Davey
Deputy Editor, Futures and Options World

Like nickel, aluminium is one of the youngest of the major base metals, although its mineral ore has been in use for several thousand years. In the latter half of the twentieth century it has become one of the most widely used metals in the world, with some 15 million tonnes of primary aluminium produced each year.

The potential of aluminium was only recognized after attempts in the mid-eighteeth century to process the metal itself into a useful commodity. The metal took off as the industrial revolution brought improved technology and production methods and demand. France's Pechiney, still one of the key producers today, got the ball rolling when, in the mid-nineteenth century, the company first started to produce the metal commercially.

The lightness of aluminium, its resistance to corrosion and its versatility have all helped to popularize its use. As a result of these qualities, aluminium has become essential in the manufacturing of cars, engineering and in aerospace. A more recent attraction is the metal's capacity for recycling, which in the drink can sector has brought aluminium a great deal of praise. Its re-use in other areas is now being encouraged too, and in this age of awakening environment consciousness, aluminium is being hailed as the 'environmentally friendly metal'.

Aluminium is now produced in Jamaica, Ghana, Venezuela and the Gulf States, while Canada, Norway and Switzerland remain important smelters. The main trading companies in aluminium are from the United States and Europe, including Alcoa, Alcan, Reynolds, Keiser, Pechiney and Alusuisse.

The economic climate of the industrialized world in the last decade has affected the production and price of aluminium as industry demand fell in a period of recession and rose again with improved economic conditions. By the mid-1980s, this had resulted in cuts in capacity, but demand then picked up, reversing the trends of closures and cutbacks. Indeed, increased requirements for aluminium and a sustained strong market have now prompted a number of producers to carry out those expansion plans which had been put on ice during the years of recession. Such expansion should help the industry's aim to raise its capacity to 17.25 million tonnes a year by the middle of the 1990s.

Aluminium is traded in the futures markets on the Commodity Exchange (COMEX) in New York and London's Metal Exchange (LME). The LME's planned warehouses in Japan (set to open before the end of 1989) and the

United States will improve the supply shortages which occurred in the past and help to internationalize the aluminium trading market.

The user side of the aluminium market is dominated by industrialized countries. It is expected that consumption will increase, particularly in the car and aerospace industries, despite a drop in the United States construction industry which was hurt by higher interest rates. Market observers believe that the price of aluminium will settle after a period of continued volatility. A rise in demand is expected, encouraged by the growing popularity of environmental issues.

The present picture for the future of the aluminium industry looks optimistic. Producers are witnessing record profits and output is strong. Consumption is likely to increase unabated with strong demand from Japan and Europe.

Aluminium: monthly averages of LME cash settlement price 1983-89
(£/US$ per tonne)

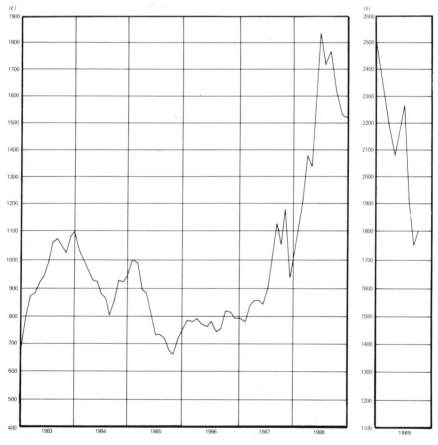

Source: London Metal Exchange

Aluminium: world refined production 1984-89 (thousand tonnes)

	1984	1985	1986	1987	1988	1989
						Jan-Mar
EUROPE						
Austria	95.8	94.1	92.5	93.4	95.5	23.4
France	341.5	293.2	321.8	322.5	327.7	82.6
Germany, F.R.	777.2	745.4	763.7	737.7	744.1	182.3
Greece	136.2	123.4	124.4	126.1	148.6	36.7
Iceland	82.4	76.8	80.0	84.6	82.5	21.7
Italy	230.2	224.1	242.6	232.6	226.3	56.0
Netherlands	247.3	244.6	258.0	268.7	270.7	68.6
Norway	760.8	724.1	729.1	797.8	826.6	210.7
Spain	380.8	370.1	354.7	341.0	293.9	87.0
Sweden	82.9	83.7	77.1	81.5	98.6	24.4
Switzerland	79.2	72.6	80.9	73.4	71.8	17.5
United Kingdom	287.9	275.4	275.9	294.4	300.2	75.6
Yugoslavia	267.5	271.1	273.2	242.6	274.9	72.5
Total	3 769.7	3 598.6	3 673.9	3 696.3	3 761.4	959.0
AFRICA						
Cameroon	73.1	81.6	81.1	71.5	80.0	20.4
Egypt	172.5	178.5	176.9	179.2	181.3	45.8
Ghana	–	48.5	124.6	150.3	163.5	42.1
South Africa	167.4	164.6	169.6	170.6	172.2	41.8
Total	413.0	473.2	552.2	571.6	597.0	150.1
ASIA						
Bahrain	177.3	174.8	178.2	180.3	182.8	45.7
India	268.5	266.2	257.1	253.4	334.5	95.1
Indonesia	199.0	216.8	218.8	201.4	185.1	49.6
Iran	42.4	43.0	40.0	45.0	40.0	10.0
Japan	286.7	226.5	140.2	40.6	35.3	8.7
South Korea	17.2	17.7	17.3	21.7	17.5	3.8
Taiwan	–	–	–	–	–	–
Turkey	37.5	54.1	60.0	41.7	56.7	15.0
United Arab Emirates	155.4	153.2	154.8	155.9	162.5	40.6
Total	1 184.0	1 152.3	1 066.4	940.0	1 014.4	268.5
AMERICA						
Canada	1 222.0	1 282.3	1 355.2	1 540.4	1 534.5	383.6
U.S.A.	4 099.0	3 499.7	3 036.5	3 342.9	3 944.5	1 005.0
Argentina	133.7	139.9	150.6	155.1	157.4	39.9
Brazil	455.0	549.2	757.4	843.5	873.5	217.8
Mexico	44.0	42.7	37.0	60.2	68.3	17.1
Surinam	23.0	28.8	28.7	1.9	9.8	6.0
Venezuela	386.0	403.1	423.0	439.6	443.4	125.2
Total	6 362.7	5 945.7	5 788.4	6 383.6	7 031.4	1 794.6
OCEANIA						
Australia	754.8	851.7	875.0	1 024.2	1 141.3	293.9
New Zealand	242.9	243.5	236.2	252.0	255.6	74.1
Total	997.7	1 095.2	1 111.2	1 276.2	1 396.9	368.0
TOTAL	**12 727.1**	**12 265.0**	**12 192.1**	**12 867.7**	**13 801.1**	**3 540.2**
Monthly Average	*1 060.6*	*1 022.1*	*1 016.0*	*1 072.3*	*1 150.1*	*1 180.1*
OTHER COUNTRIES						
Czechoslovakia	31.6	31.7	33.1	32.4	31.6	
German D.R.	58.0	60.0	61.0	62.0	61.0	
Hungary	74.2	73.8	73.9	73.5	74.7	18.5
Poland	45.9	47.0	47.5	47.5	47.7	
Romania	244.0	247.0	253.0	260.0	250.0	
U.S.S.R.	2 300.0	2 300.0	2 350.0	2 370.0	2 440.0	
China and Other Asia	460.0	490.0	520.0	550.0	610.0	
Total	3 213.7	3 249.5	3 338.5	3 395.4	3 515.0	
WORLD TOTAL	**15 940.8**	**15 514.5**	**15 530.6**	**16 263.1**	**17 316.1**	

This table shows production of primary aluminium only.

By courtesy of the World Bureau of Metal Statistics.

35

Aluminium: world refined consumption 1984–89 (thousand tonnes)

	1983	1984	1985	1986	1987	1988
						Jan-Dec
EUROPE						
Austria	123.1	127.4	127.9	129.3	133.0	137.0
Belgium	272.0	289.4	267.7	282.5	284.7	303.3
Denmark	15.7	20.9	21.7	32.3	24.9	24.0
Finland	23.5	17.4	16.5	17.8	18.0	17.3
France	613.4	579.3	586.1	592.6	615.6	650.0
Germany, F.R.	1 085.0	1 151.6	1 160.9	1 186.7	1 185.7	1 232.6
Greece	88.5	92.4	89.0	83.6	75.9	75.9
Italy	430.0	448.0	470.0	510.0	547.5	581.0
Netherlands	91.3	100.1	88.9	122.6	112.9	136.0
Norway	123.8	128.0	132.3	123.0	129.3	162.3
Spain	217.4	191.4	211.0	244.0	254.7	268.0
Sweden	94.6	87.3	93.6	95.0	77.1	98.4
Switzerland	101.1	135.0	142.9	156.4	149.2	155.7
United Kingdom	323.4	369.5	350.4	389.1	383.6	427.4
Yugoslavia	152.6	159.0	168.2	163.3	168.8	161.9
Other Europe	38.1	27.7	33.8	42.3	48.0	48.0
Total..	3 793.5	3 924.4	3 960.9	4 170.5	4 208.9	4 478.8
AFRICA						
Cameroon	27.9	24.8	29.5	27.8	24.6	24.6
Egypt	67.0	70.0	62.9	58.0	77.1	77.1
Ghana	6.0	6.0	6.0	5.0	7.8	7.7
South Africa	62.8	76.8	77.0	75.4	92.2	103.5
Other Africa	13.9	13.8	37.2	12.9	28.0	28.0
Total..	177.6	191.4	212.6	179.1	229.7	240.9
ASIA						
India	218.5	310.0	297.6	310.0	326.0	337.0
Iran	105.0	100.0	56.0	53.6	90.0	100.0
Japan	1 820.8	1 572.0	1 694.8	1 624.2	1 696.8	2 123.2
South Korea	127.6	128.8	145.6	196.8	207.9	273.0
Taiwan	136.5	96.8	147.8	150.4	177.8	158.9
Turkey	89.2	106.4	125.0	97.6	131.0	131.0
Other Asia	272.6	148.6	260.9	276.5	407.9	407.9
Total..	2 770.2	2 462.6	2 727.7	2 709.1	3 037.4	3 531.0
AMERICA						
Canada	248.0	336.0	345.0	313.0	421.6	421.6
U.S.A.	4 221.0	4 457.0	4 282.0	4 316.0	4 536.0	4 612.4
Argentina	80.4	101.2	80.9	121.3	142.0	142.4
Brazil	270.6	294.8	347.5	423.7	430.3	331.5
Mexico	49.8	69.5	78.2	50.4	66.1	65.9
Venezuela	89.0	130.3	147.0	135.0	145.0	164.2
Other America	34.9	36.0	40.0	52.0	53.6	53.6
Total..	4 993.7	5 424.8	5 320.6	5 411.4	5 794.6	5 791.6
OCEANIA						
Australia	242.2	265.4	283.5	293.6	318.7	288.5
New Zealand	26.1	32.0	34.7	29.7	33.8	30.9
Other Oceania	–	–	–	–	0.1	0.1
Total..	268.3	297.4	318.2	323.3	352.6	319.5
TOTAL..	12 003.3	12 300.6	12 540.0	12 793.4	13 623.2	14 361.8
Quarterly Average..	*3 000.8*	*3 075.1*	*3 135.0*	*3 198.4*	*3 405.8*	*3 590.4*
OTHER COUNTRIES						
Bulgaria	53.0	55.0	55.0	57.0	56.0	61.0
Czechoslovakia	124.0	121.6	111.7	111.1	108.4	106.6
German D.R.	230.0	218.0	230.0	227.0	230.0	225.0
Hungary	181.7	192.8	199.5	209.4	197.9	213.1
Poland	128.2	134.2	130.4	133.5	133.5	134.0
Romania	138.0	121.6	125.9	104.0	120.0	110.0
U.S.S.R.	1 850.0	1 750.0	1 750.0	1 750.0	1 800.0	1 800.0
China	600.0	630.0	630.0	600.0	620.0	600.0
Cuba	1.8	2.0	2.5	2.5	2.5	2.5
Other	42.0	47.5	52.5	57.5	64.3	69.3
Total..	3 348.7	3 272.7	3 287.5	3 252.0	3 332.6	3 321.5
WORLD TOTAL	**15 352.0**	**15 573.3**	**15 827.5**	**16 045.4**	**16 955.8**	**17 683.3**

This table shows consumption of primary aluminium.

By courtesy of the World Bureau of Metal Statistics.

Copper

Ruth Gardiner
Senior Assistant Editor, Futures and Options World

Traditionally a leading indicator for base metals, copper has proved an uncertain market in recent years. World distribution is wide, but production has been hit severely by strikes and debt in the developing countries, showing just how vulnerable the market is to supply disturbances.

Copper has been mined and worked since the earliest civilizations and has become one of the most traded commodities in the world. Its uses now concentrate on the capital intensive side – particularly in the electrical and construction industry. The metal's chief assets are a high electrical conductivity and good thermal properties, while it is highly ductile and easily worked. It can be found in generators, switch gears, radiators, in plumbing, cables and transformers. It is also used in construction in heating and wiring, in telecommunications for cabling under the sea and extensively in the armaments industry.

All these are traditional uses, and the market is concentrating on preserving these, particularly as the metal comes under threat from aluminium, fibre optics, and plastics. In the longer term, copper will lose out to these new materials, but they are unlikely to prove a real threat until the next century.

Copper is produced worldwide, but approximately 60% of the supply now originates in less-developed countries. The largest mine is to be found in Peru and other large producers can be found in South America, and Africa. However, Europe remains an important producer, and North America, which used to be copper's largest producer, also has important sources of the metal.

The less-developed countries producing copper have been plagued by debt and high inflation and this has been reflected in recent strikes in Peru at mines and smelters. In Papua New Guinea, the Bougainville copper mine has also been out of action for a considerable part of 1989, while an explosion at the Chuquicamata flash furnace earlier in the year also affected copper production in Chile. In the developed world, Canada too has suffered from strikes. The market continues to be vulnerable to these supply disturbances, since some high cost producers had already left the market during the recessionary period between 1980 and 1985.

Existing copper mines have now been worked for a considerable time, with the result that ore grade is falling and the recovery rate is generally not good.

Given this decline, alternative processes of mining are being examined. *In situ* leach mining, although not new, may offer an important way ahead. It offers an alternative to traditional mining, particularly where the ground has subsided. If this process, now being tested by the US Bureau of Mines, produces results, it could prove cost effective, particularly for deep deposits.

Copper consumption is dominated by the OECD countries, with the United States, Western Europe and Japan being the main consumers. However, newly emerging economies are also growing consumers of the metal, particularly those of South-East Asia (Taiwan and Malaysia) and Latin/Central America. As the demand for 'western' goods by these economies increases, so does the demand for copper. In fact, consumption in the older producing countries is increasing by only 1.5% year on year, with a decline in domestic house construction contributing to the dip. However, this decrease in demand is being offset by faster growth in the developing countries.

Copper is traded at both the London Metal Exchange (LME) and the Commodities Exchange (COMEX) in New York. In 1988, the LME overtook COMEX in copper trading volume. The LME is widely regarded as the trade centre for copper, with the new 'A' grade contract seen as more reflective of the physical market. This replaced the LME standard copper contract which was delisted in December 1988. 'A' grade copper has to be delivered in the form of either wirebars or cathodes and is used by traders both as a means to hedge, and as a reference quote when pricing their physical trade.

COMEX is still regarded as an adjunct by many to the London market to whom it retains an image of a venue for speculators, although United States producers do use COMEX for pricing. Nevertheless, as one of the first contracts to be traded at COMEX, copper is regarded as vital for the health of the exchange.

Copper: world mine production 1984–89 (thousand tonnes)

	1984	1985	1986	1987	1988	1989
						Jan-Mar
EUROPE						
Finland	30.8	28.0	25.9	19.8	20.2	4.8
France	0.2	0.2	0.3	0.3	0.3	–
Germany, F.R.	1.0	0.9	0.8	1.5	0.7	–
Greece	–	0.3	0.3	1.0	–	–
Italy	0.9	0.1	–	–	–	–
Norway	25.0	19.0	21.9	22.0	15.9	4.2
Portugal	0.4	0.3	0.2	1.1	5.2	1.9
Spain	63.6	61.0	53.5	16.3	18.1	6.8
Sweden	85.8	91.8	87.4	84.7	74.4	20.0
United Kingdom	0.7	0.6	0.6	0.8	0.7	0.1
Yugoslavia	116.2	116.7	116.7	111.0	103.5	22.5
Total..	324.6	318.9	307.6	258.5	239.0	60.3
AFRICA						
Algeria	0.2	0.2	0.2	0.2	–	–
Botswana	21.5	21.7	21.3	18.9	24.4	5.2
Congo	–	0.1	0.7	1.3	1.0	0.3
Morocco	20.9	32.8	18.0	14.3	13.1	3.3
Mozambique	–	0.1	0.1	0.2	0.1	–
Namibia	50.0	47.6	49.9	38.7	40.9	8.7
South Africa	212.0	203.9	203.2	197.1	174.6	44.8
Zaire	500.7	502.1	502.6	500.0	465.1	117.9
Zambia	576.0	510.8	512.9	527.0	480.0	120.0
Zimbabwe	23.1	20.9	18.0	18.8	16.1	4.8
Total..	1 404.4	1 340.2	1 326.9	1 316.5	1 215.3	305.0
ASIA						
Burma	12.0	16.7	8.1	9.0	9.2	2.2
Cyprus	1.3	1.1	0.6	0.1	0.4	–
India	47.0	48.0	49.2	54.1	51.5	12.9
Indonesia	85.6	88.7	95.8	105.3	125.9	31.5
Iran	43.3	40.0	50.0	40.0	51.0	24.3
Japan	43.3	43.2	34.9	23.8	16.7	3.7
Malaysia	29.2	30.5	28.3	29.9	22.0	5.8
Oman	16.2	17.6	16.7	16.9	18.1	4.2
Philippines	233.6	222.2	217.0	214.1	218.3	50.8
South Korea	1.9	2.2	1.8	1.7	0.1	–
Turkey	24.5	26.6	21.1	25.8	36.2	10.2
Total..	537.9	536.8	523.5	520.7	549.4	145.6
AMERICA						
Canada	721.8	738.6	698.5	794.1	721.6	184.8
U.S.A.	1 102.6	1 105.8	1 147.3	1 255.9	1 437.1	382.0
Argentina	0.2	0.4	0.3	0.4	0.5	0.1
Bolivia	1.6	1.7	0.3	–	0.2	–
Brazil	35.2	41.0	40.2	39.2	44.4	11.0
Chile	1 290.7	1 356.2	1 401.1	1 418.1	1 451.0	363.1
Colombia	0.2	0.1	0.2	1.4	–	0.2
Ecuador	–	0.1	–	–	–	–
Mexico	185.2	172.9	184.6	247.6	273.5	67.5
Peru	364.7	385.0	386.1	406.4	298.3	87.5
Total..	3 702.2	3 801.8	3 858.6	4 163.1	4 226.6	1 096.2
OCEANIA						
Australia	235.7	259.8	248.4	232.7	238.3	69.5
Papua New Guinea	164.4	175.0	178.6	217.7	213.7	53.5
Total..	400.1	434.8	427.0	450.4	452.0	123.0
TOTAL..	**6 369.2**	**6 432.5**	**6 443.6**	**6 709.2**	**6 682.3**	**1 730.1**
Monthly Average..	*530.8*	*536.0*	*537.0*	*559.1*	*556.8*	*576.6*
OTHER COUNTRIES						
Albania	14.1	15.0	15.5	16.4	17.0	
Bulgaria	73.0	78.0	80.0	80.0	80.0	
Czechoslovakia	10.2	10.1	8.5	9.4	10.0	
German D.R.	12.0	12.0	11.0	11.0	10.0	
Poland	431.0	432.0	435.0	438.0	441.0	
Romania	30.0	30.0	28.0	28.0	26.0	
U.S.S.R.	1 020.0	1 030.0	1 030.0	1 010.0	990.0	
China	180.0	200.0	220.0	350.0	370.0	
Mongolia	128.0	136.0	140.0	120.0	130.0	
Cuba	2.7	3.1	3.3	3.5	3.0	
Other	10.0	10.0	10.0	12.0	12.0	
Total..	1 911.0	1 956.2	1 981.3	2 078.3	2 089.0	
WORLD TOTAL	**8 280.2**	**8 388.7**	**8 424.9**	**8 787.5**	**8 771.3**	

This table shows the recoverable copper content of ores and concentrates produced.

By courtesy of the World Bureau of Metal Statistics.

Copper: world smelter production 1984–89 (thousand tonnes)

	1984	1985	1986	1987	1988	1989
						Jan-Mar
EUROPE						
Austria	24.6	25.9	25.5	38.7	38.4	9.9
Belgium	76.0	115.1	105.9	92.2	99.8	24.9
Finland	77.6	68.9	84.5	77.4	79.0	26.2
France	7.0	7.0	6.1	7.0	6.5	1.8
Germany, F.R.	225.5	247.0	238.6	207.7	207.8	51.9
Norway	37.0	38.2	35.2	29.7	31.7	8.8
Portugal	3.5	4.6	4.0	5.0	4.5	1.2
Spain	127.2	120.5	135.2	138.7	145.6	36.3
Sweden	102.7	100.7	102.5	105.6	90.3	23.2
Yugoslavia	126.1	170.9	168.5	143.5	146.5	35.1
Total..	807.2	898.8	906.0	845.5	850 1	219.3
AFRICA						
Namibia	46.4	43.3	45.7	35.5	40.0	8.7
South Africa	180.8	168.4	184.0	189.8	180.4	44.1
Uganda	–	–	–	–	–	–
Zaire [1]	465.5	470.0	476.0	472.4	436.2	116.0
Zambia [1]	531.9	544.2	514.1	523.2	459.0	115.1
Zimbabwe	24.2	24.4	29.6	30.0	27.5	6.9
Total..	1 248.8	1 250.3	1 249.4	1 250.9	1 143.1	290.8
ASIA						
India	40.4	33.6	39.3	32.9	44.3	11.3
Iran	47.9	40.0	50.0	40.0	52.0	12.9
Japan	929.0	932.6	962.1	980.2	994.0	252.0
Oman	21.3	18.8	19.6	20.6	21.7	5.1
Philippines	109.2	133.8	124.3	125.9	141.0	35.0
South Korea	100.2	112.7	123.2	143.8	111.1	27.9
Taiwan	61.7	60.6	63.8	61.5	41.8	10.5
Turkey	30.1	33.9	36.0	19.4	12.9	4.1
Total..	1 339.8	1 366.0	1 418.3	1 424.3	1 418.8	358.8
AMERICA						
Canada	494.9	520.7	477.7	503.0	480.6	109.4
U.S.A.	1 183.4	1 190.9	1 195.9	1 248.7	1 355.7	349.7
Brazil	47.3	80.6	101.0	134.0	132.0	33.0
Chile	1 098.3	1 088.4	1 123.9	1 106.9	1 189.4	276.2
Mexico	70.4	68.0	74.6	127.5	138.7	37.4
Peru	331.1	354.0	335.0	311.0	243.8	51.9
Total..	3 225.4	3 302.6	3 308.1	3 431.1	3 540.2	857.6
OCEANIA						
Australia	188.0	175.4	178.8	182.8	188.2	49.0
TOTAL..	**6 809.2**	**6 993.1**	**7 060.6**	**7 134.6**	**7 140.4**	**1 775.5**
Monthly Average..	*567.4*	*583.0*	*588.4*	*594.6*	*595.0*	*591.8*
OTHER COUNTRIES [2]						
Albania	12.6	13.0	15.0	16.2	16.5	
Bulgaria	70.0	70.0	70.0	80.0	80.0	
Czechoslovakia	10.0	10.0	10.0	10.0	10.0	
German D.R.	14.0	14.0	15.0	17.0	25.0	
Hungary	0.6	–	–	–	–	
Poland	365.0	380.0	366.4	367.3	358.0	
Romania	38.0	36.0	28.0	28.0	26.0	
U.S.S.R.	1 120.0	1 140.0	1 155.0	1 140.0	1 120.0	
China	220.0	245.0	300.0	417.0	425.0	
Other	25.0	30.0	30.0	30.0	30.0	
Total..	1 875.2	1 938.0	1 989.4	2 105.5	2 090.5	
WORLD TOTAL	**8 684.4**	**8 931.1**	**9 050.0**	**9 240.1**	**9 230.9**	

The basis of this table is metal produced in the form of blister and anode copper from ores, concentrates, other primary materials and secondary blister produced from scrup. The figures are in terms of recoverable copper content whenever possible.

Notes 1. Includes leach cathodes. 2. Primary production only.

By courtesy of the World Bureau of Metal Statistics.

Copper: world refined production 1984-89 (thousand tonnes)

	1984	1985	1986	1987	1988	1989
						Jan-Mar
EUROPE						
Austria	33.3	33.6	32.6	43.1	38.4	10.9
Belgium [1]	396.3	412.6	414.2	407.5	434.2	130.2
Finland	57.3	58.8	64.2	59.5	53.9	15.9
France	40.9	43.9	41.9	39.3	43.2	13.3
Germany, F.R.	378.8	414.4	421.9	399.8	426.5	111.7
Italy	50.3	64.3	65.4	65.0	75.4	18.9
Norway	30.3	31.1	30.5	29.4	31.7	8.8
Portugal	5.3	4.5	5.3	5.3	5.4	1.2
Spain	156.4	151.7	155.1	151.4	158.8	41.0
Sweden	63.9	64.7	84.5	91.9	90.3	23.2
United Kingdom	136.8	125.4	125.6	122.3	124.0	30.9
Yugoslavia	127.6	135.4	140.4	138.9	145.4	34.9
Total..	1 477.2	1 540.4	1 581.6	1 553.4	1 627.2	440.9
AFRICA						
Egypt	2.4	2.3	3.0	4.0	4.0	0.9
South Africa	148.4	145.5	143.2	146.5	136.6	40.3
Zaire	225.2	226.8	217.9	210.2	202.8	50.6
Zambia	521.9	510.0	487.3	508.6	445.0	110.7
Zimbabwe	22.8	22.5	25.3	23.0	27.5	6.9
Total..	920.7	907.1	876.7	892.3	815.9	209.4
ASIA						
India	33.6	28.9	36.9	30.8	40.1	10.7
Iran	5.0	12.0	12.0	30.0	32.0	7.9
Japan	935.2	936.0	943.0	980.3	955.1	238.5
Oman	15.2	14.3	14.6	15.5	16.3	4.1
Philippines	99.2	130.3	134.5	132.1	132.2	32.2
South Korea	140.6	150.0	165.0	157.9	170.4	43.6
Taiwan	47.8	46.7	50.4	47.0	43.3	9.9
Turkey	51.4	60.6	75.1	75.6	68.4	17.1
Total..	1 328.0	1 378.8	1 431.5	1 469.2	1 457.8	364.0
AMERICA						
Canada	504.3	499.6	493.4	491.1	528.7	125.3
U.S.A.	1 489.5	1 434.6	1 479.9	1 560.8	1 890.5	494.4
Brazil	86.2	120.8	146.9	176.2	150.0	37.5
Chile	879.7	884.3	942.3	970.3	1 012.8	238.3
Mexico	83.7	122.6	89.5	130.0	137.3	33.3
Peru	219.0	227.0	225.6	224.8	179.5	45.8
Total..	3 262.4	3 288.9	3 377.6	3 553.2	3 898.8	974.6
OCEANIA						
Australia	197.2	194.3	185.1	207.8	222.7	58.0
TOTAL..	7 185.5	7 309.5	7 452.5	7 675.9	8 022.4	2 046.9
Monthly Average..	*598.8*	*609.1*	*621.0*	*639.7*	*668.5*	*682.3*
OTHER COUNTRIES						
Albania	11.0	12.0	13.0	14.0	16.0	
Bulgaria	70.0	73.0	74.0	76.0	78.0	
Czechoslovakia	26.4	26.4	26.5	27.7	30.0	
German D.R.	69.0	75.0	73.0	74.0	80.0	
Hungary	25.9	23.0	22.1	23.3	15.3	
Poland	372.3	387.0	388.0	390.2	401.0	
Romania	60.0	50.0	44.0	42.0	40.0	
U.S.S.R.	1 380.0	1 400.0	1 400.0	1 410.0	1 380.0	
China	320.0	340.0	350.0	450.0	460.0	
Other	35.0	38.0	40.0	40.0	40.0	
Total..	2 369.6	2 424.4	2 430.6	2 547.2	2 540.3	
WORLD TOTAL	9 555.1	9 733.9	9 883.1	10 223.1	10 562.7	

This table shows production of refined copper, whether electrolytic or fire refined. It includes production from blister, anodes and other primary materials, together with secondary production from scrap and other similar materials. It does not include copper recovered from secondary materials by simply remelting.

Notes 1. W.B.M.S. estimate.

By courtesy of the World Bureau of Metal Statistics.

41

Copper: world refined consumption 1984–89 (thousand tonnes)

	1984	1985	1986	1987	1988	1989
						Jan-Mar
EUROPE						
Austria	21.8	14.8	18.9	26.0	26.9	6.0
Belgium	299.3	309.6	303.3	291.8	317.8	90.1
Denmark	1.4	–	–	–	0.1	–
Finland	68.0	72.0	75.0	77.0	73.7	19.5
France	411.5	397.8	401.1	399.0	408.9	114.6
Germany, F.R.	791.7	753.8	770.7	800.1	797.5	209.8
Greece	34.0	39.0	39.0	39.0	44.0	11.1
Ireland	–	–	–	–	0.3	–
Italy	348.0	362.0	394.0	420.0	445.0	111.0
Netherlands	22.1	18.0	23.5	21.9	20.1	6.2
Norway	10.0	13.0	11.0	8.0	10.0	3.2
Portugal	19.2	15.7	17.5	26.0	28.0	6.9
Spain	113.6	115.7	130.0	131.4	135.0	35.5
Sweden	116.2	110.3	103.7	98.3	104.6	27.7
Switzerland	8.1	9.0	13.6	9.5	9.0	2.3
United Kingdom	352.9	346.5	339.6	327.7	327.7	83.0
Yugoslavia	148.0	157.1	123.3	127.1	135.6	34.8
Total..	2 765.8	2 734.3	2 764.2	2 802.8	2 884.2	761.7
AFRICA						
Algeria	–	–	–	–	–	–
Egypt	6.3	4.0	5.5	6.3	6.5	1.5
South Africa	85.0	69.5	77.0	72.2	75.5	18.6
Zaire	3.3	2.7	2.5	2.1	2.4	0.6
Zambia	–	–	8.3	8.0	8.0	1.8
Zimbabwe	6.0	6.0	7.7	10.0	9.6	2.4
Other Africa	–	–	0.3	1.0	–	–
Total..	100.6	82.2	101.3	99.6	102.0	24.9
ASIA						
India	81.2	97.5	110.2	115.0	130.0	30.0
Iran	10.0	15.0	18.0	20.0	34.0	8.4
Japan	1 368.3	1 230.8	1 219.3	1 284.5	1 330.7	328.0
Philippines	11.1	4.9	9.8	10.3	8.7	3.1
South Korea	188.0	206.6	262.3	259.0	266.3	66.0
Taiwan	136.9	92.4	158.4	207.0	214.9	53.7
Turkey	54.6	76.1	77.2	75.3	75.6	18.9
Other Asia	61.4	71.3	80.7	120.2	120.0	30.0
Total..	1 911.5	1 794.6	1 935.9	2 091.3	2 180.2	538.1
AMERICA						
Canada	231.0	222.5	225.6	232.3	239.6	65.1
U.S.A.	2 122.7	1 958.0	2 100.0	2 154.3	2 268.4	560.2
Argentina	51.2	41.0	58.8	63.8	42.9	10.8
Brazil	189.4	197.1	254.9	258.8	216.0	54.0
Chile	35.3	25.7	36.4	47.8	42.7	7.0
Mexico	95.3	120.4	79.4	123.6	125.9	28.9
Peru	24.1	34.0	31.5	45.7	31.2	12.0
Other America	20.2	10.4	11.4	22.7	22.8	5.7
Total..	2 769.2	2 609.1	2 798.0	2 949.0	2 989.5	743.7
OCEANIA						
Australia	118.1	125.9	116.6	124.0	128.8	28.4
New Zealand	2.7	2.1	2.0	1.4	1.8	0.6
Total..	120.8	128.0	118.6	125.4	130.6	29.0
TOTAL..	7 667.9	7 348.2	7 718.0	8 068.1	8 286.5	2 097.4
Monthly Average..	*639.0*	*612.3*	*643.2*	*672.3*	*690.6*	*699.2*
OTHER COUNTRIES						
Albania	9.0	12.0	13.0	13.8	15.8	
Bulgaria	63.0	65.0	69.0	76.0	77.5	
Czechoslovakia	88.1	93.4	91.2	96.7	98.0	
German D.R.	122.0	133.0	122.0	131.0	130.0	
Hungary	26.0	27.8	23.5	25.8	23.5	
Poland	209.4	226.5	235.7	246.0	246.5	
Romania	60.0	50.0	44.0	42.0	40.0	
U.S.S.R.	1 280.0	1 305.0	1 300.0	1 270.0	1 250.0	
China	390.0	420.0	450.0	470.0	465.0	
Other	21.0	23.5	23.5	24.0	27.0	
Total..	2 268.5	2 356.2	2 371.9	2 395.3	2 373.3	
WORLD TOTAL	9 936.4	9 704.4	10 089.9	10 463.4	10 659.8	

This table shows consumption of unwrought refined copper whether refined from primary or secondary materials. The direct use copper in the form of scrap is excluded. Some of the data for the latest months are provisional.

By courtesy of the World Bureau of Metal Statistics.

Copper: world trade in refined copper 1984–89 (thousand tonnes)

	1984	1985	1986	1987	1988	1989
						Jan-Mar
EXPORTS						
Austria	15.5	21.1	19.5	18.2	18.2	7.2
Belgium	210.2	207.2	232.5	252.5	–	–⁴
Denmark	1.3	0.5	0.4	0.1	–	–
Finland	4.8	8.5	4.9	8.7	15.2	3.7
France	4.2	7.2	9.2	3.9	6.2	1.4
Germany, F.R.	67.7	67.6	67.8	92.9	68.0	27.7
Italy	10.6	10.8	4.7	4.0	11.8	1.7
Netherlands	0.5	1.3	0.6	2.5	1.6	0.2
Norway	29.4	28.3	29.1	30.1	29.0	7.7
Spain	66.4	69.4	62.3	40.9	35.1	7.1
Sweden	22.9	12.2	37.9	40.2	41.7	8.4
Switzerland	0.7	2.6	0.1	3.7	4.4	0.8
United Kingdom	21.2	14.6	15.0	18.6	12.9	2.9
Yugoslavia	24.5	20.0	37.3	33.0	17.7	
South Africa	67.2	75.0	72.4	64.1	64.3	22.3
Zaire	221.7	226.4	222.8	204.9	198.3	
Zambia	530.1	505.0	466.3	499.4	395.2⁶	
Japan	18.4	51.0	60.8	52.4	28.3	6.3
Oman	15.1	13.8	15.4	15.3	16.3	4.1
Philippines	91.1	130.5	124.6	119.3	124.9	28.9
Canada ¹	346.0	277.1	304.8	288.8	261.7	79.6
U.S.A.	92.3	52.8	12.5	9.2	60.6	16.8
Brazil	–	–	–	–	–⁷	
Chile	830.4	891.9	895.7	942.6	975.4	220.1
Mexico	–	–	–	–	3.0	
Peru	174.7	182.6	193.0	179.8	147.4	28.4
Australia	75.5	71.5	66.8	81.6	92.7	27.0
China ²	7.7	4.2	9.2	22.3	44.3	
Total	2 950.1	2 953.1	2 965.6	3 029.0	2 674.2	
IMPORTS						
Austria	4.1	2.3	5.8	2.8	6.0	0.7
Belgium	180.9	199.5	215.2	208.4	106.4	17.3⁴
Denmark	0.1	–	0.1	0.1	0.1	0.2
Finland	15.1	21.9	15.9	26.7	31.0	8.5
France	342.9	325.4	334.5	353.5	379.2	94.0
Germany, F.R.	465.6	442.1	447.9	396.0	433.3	102.8
Greece ²	40.1	12.1	28.3	35.5	16.7⁸	
Italy	311.9	332.8	349.1	371.8	377.4	95.6
Netherlands	23.9	19.6	23.0	24.1	22.0	6.6
Norway	0.7	0.3	0.2	0.1	0.3	–
Portugal	13.9	12.1	10.9	27.4	24.6	
Spain	24.6	23.3	31.5	13.6	8.7	2.4
Sweden	60.6	57.9	57.1	46.6	60.5	17.2
Switzerland	8.9	11.6	13.7	7.6	6.6	1.8
United Kingdom	225.9	247.7	263.5	238.8	244.3	72.6
Yugoslavia	27.3	30.1	20.2	21.2	20.2	4.0
South Africa	0.3	–	0.2	0.3	..	
India	48.6	85.6	72.5	76.9	51.2⁶	
Japan	470.2	356.1	272.4	347.7	420.8	87.1
South Korea	51.0	59.9	83.9	106.8	123.1⁶	22.6
Taiwan				161.4	172.4	29.6⁵
Canada	25.6	19.1	20.9	16.6	6.9	0.8
U.S.A.	444.7	381.1	491.7	504.9	382.3	90.4
Brazil	93.9	60.0	119.7	113.6	23.3⁷	
Mexico	–	–	–	–	5.6	
Venezuela	5.6	6.4	10.7	21.8	..	
Australia	–	–	0.1	0.6	0.1	–
China ²	254.0	355.7	171.1	75.5	84.4	
Total				3 200.3	3 007.4	

This table shows principal imports and exports of refined copper.

Notes 1. Excludes Sino-Soviet Sphere countries. 2. Primary production only. 4. January and February
5. January only 6. January to November 7. January to July 8. January to May

By courtesy of the World Bureau of Metal Statistics.

Copper (higher-grade): monthly averages of LME cash settlement price 1982-89 (£ per tonne)

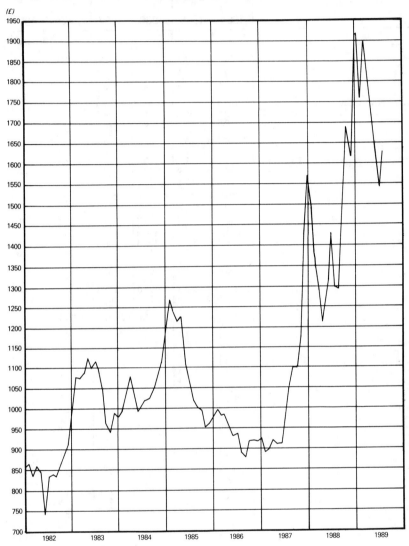

Source: London Metal Exchange

Gold

Paul Dickins

As far as most investors are concerned the gold market has lost its shine. There are two key reasons for this. First, gold prices have slumbered for several years and as an investment gold has been outperformed by virtually every other major financial market, and little is expected to change over the next 18 months or so. Secondly, it seems that gold no longer serves as the key barometer of the world economy, or as the most important store of wealth in times of chaos or ill-health in the international financial markets.

The average gold price in 1989 looks set at around $385 dollars an ounce, which is down from the 1988 average of $438, which in turn was down from the $467 average of 1987. Although today's prices are substantially higher than in January 1985 when they were stuck in a five-year low at $282, they are well below the $850 level reached in the heady days of 1979–80. And in 1988 the gold price fell in real dollar terms.

The price of gold and its volatility has been undermined in recent years by a period of stability, growth and low inflation in the leading economies, and since the turn of 1989, a strong dollar. The market's sluggishness has driven away much of the short-term speculative money. And even when there *are* periods of financial and political turmoil, the gold market has failed to react. Even the Crash of October 1987 failed to cause a swing towards gold. This shows that many investors, particularly in the United States and Europe, now treat gold like any other commodity as part of a portfolio of investments rather than an alternative home for their money in times of financial strife.

Gold is no longer the key medium of international exchange. Since the demise of the Gold Standard and the metal's debut as a freely traded commodity in 1966, with its price determined by supply and demand rather than by governments, gold has played an increasingly less important role in world financial markets.

Unlike most commodities, gold is required for few other reasons than as a medium of exchange, a perceived store of wealth, and for its decorative value. Only 15% or so of annual supplies to the west (ie non-Communist countries) is consumed by industry. This is largely absorbed by dentistry and the electronics industry, where it is mostly used to cover conductive contacts in computers. The rest of the annual world gold bullion supply is used for investment purposes, or as jewellery. In fact, jewellery absorbs approximately 75% of annual gold bullion supplies. Almost all the rest is used to make commemorative medals and coins and official coins and bars.

Possibly more than any other metal, the supply of new gold is determined by price. The supply of newly-mined gold in the west has increased throughout the 1970s and 1980s. This largely reflects gold discoveries in the 1970s and new production capacity (stimulated by the price run up in 1979–80), coming on-stream and reaching full capacity. South Africa mines more than half of all the world's gold. Other important sources of newly-mined gold are Canada (the second biggest producer, accounting for approximately 7% of western supplies), the United States, Brazil, Australia, Colombia, Papua New Guinea and the Philippines. Despite pedestrian prices in recent years, the metal trades sufficiently above the operating cost of mining gold (which is $200/oz at some mines) to stimulate continued exploration and development. However, one of the factors that has caused such flat markets has been the forward sale of gold by producers, to hedge against any price falls.

The gold market operates around-the-clock and around-the-world. The biggest trading centres are New York, London, Hong Kong, Tokyo, Singapore and Zurich. The so-called London 'fix' – which is a price agreed between the big City bullion houses and posted twice a day – is a world benchmark price for gold. However, New York is probably the most important gold trading centre, partly because the gold futures and options market at the Commodity Exchange (COMEX) is so large. In the first half of 1989, 5.2 million 100oz gold futures and 0.69 million gold options were traded at the exchange. However, a steady decrease in COMEX trading volumes in recent years indicates how gold has declined.

Mine production in the non-communist world

tonnes

	1980	1981	1982	1983	1984	1985	1986	1987	1988
Europe	11.8	11.9	12.4	14.1	15.1	26.5	15.3	16.9	18.6
North America:									
United States	30.5	44.0	45.3	62.6	66.0	79.5	118.3	154.9	205.3
Canada	51.6	53.0	66.5	73.0	86.0	90.0	105.7	116.5	128.5
Total North America	82.1	97.0	111.8	135.6	152.0	169.5	224.0	271.4	333.8
Latin America:									
Brazil	35.0	35.0	34.8	58.7	61.5	72.3	67.4	83.8	100.2
Colombia	17.0	17.7	15.5	17.7	21.2	26.4	27.1	32.5	33.4
Chile	6.5	12.2	18.9	19.0	18.0	18.2	18.9	20.0	22.7
Venezuela	1.0	1.5	2.0	6.0	9.5	12.0	15.0	16.0	16.0
Mexico	5.9	5.0	5.2	7.4	7.6	8.0	8.3	9.0	10.7
Peru	5.0	7.2	6.9	9.9	10.5	10.9	10.9	10.8	10.0
Bolivia	2.0	2.5	2.5	4.0	4.0	6.0	6.0	6.0	9.0
Dominican Republic	11.5	12.8	11.8	10.8	10.6	10.4	9.1	7.9	7.8
Other	4.8	6.0	6.7	6.5	7.0	9.5	13.0	15.1	16.1
Total Latin America	88.7	99.9	104.3	140.0	149.9	173.7	175.7	201.1	225.9
Saudi Arabia	0.0	0.0	0.0	0.0	0.0	0.0	0.0	0.0	1.7
India	2.6	2.6	2.2	2.2	2.0	1.7	2.1	1.6	1.8
Far East:									
Philippines	22.0	24.9	31.0	33.3	34.3	36.9	38.7	39.5	42.7
Japan	6.7	5.8	5.6	5.9	7.0	9.0	14.0	13.6	14.4
Other	4.5	4.6	5.2	5.3	7.4	9.6	14.9	18.7	20.4
Total Far East	33.2	35.3	41.8	44.5	48.7	55.5	67.6	71.8	77.5
Africa:									
South Africa	675.1	657.6	664.3	679.7	683.3	671.7	640.0	607.0	621.0
Zimbabwe	11.4	11.6	13.4	14.1	14.5	14.7	14.9	14.7	14.8
Zaire	3.0	3.2	4.2	6.0	10.0	8.0	8.0	12.0	12.5
Ghana	10.8	13.0	13.0	11.8	11.6	12.0	11.5	11.7	12.1
Other	8.0	12.0	15.0	15.0	15.0	17.0	18.2	25.0	27.5
Total Africa	708.3	697.4	709.9	726.6	734.4	723.4	692.6	670.4	687.9
Australasia:									
Australia	17.0	18.4	27.0	30.6	39.1	58.5	75.1	110.7	152.0
Papua New Guinea	14.3	17.2	17.8	18.4	18.7	31.3	36.1	33.9	32.6
Other	1.0	1.1	1.2	1.8	1.8	2.8	4.0	4.5	6.2
Total Australasia	32.3	36.7	46.0	50.8	59.6	92.6	115.2	149.1	190.8
Total	959.0	980.8	1028.4	1113.8	1161.7	1232.9	1292.5	1382.3	1538.0

By courtesy of Consolidated Gold Fields plc, 'Gold 1989'.

Gold fabrication in developed and developing countries

(including the use of scrap)

tonnes

	1980	1981	1982	1983	1984	1985	1986	1987	1988
Developed countries									
Jewellery	316.9	400.1	479.3	429.2	488.9	550.6	564.5	561.1	**643.7**
Electronics	93.5	91.5	87.3	104.8	128.2	111.6	119.8	118.5	**127.0**
Dentistry	62.5	63.7	59.1	50.0	51.0	51.5	49.2	45.2	**47.5**
Other industrial	57.5	57.8	54.0	49.5	52.2	49.2	51.1	51.7	**53.1**
Medals and imitation									
coins	18.1	12.4	5.8	22.3	15.7	3.4	4.2	6.7	**7.7**
Official coins	169.7	141.5	123.6	152.2	124.3	91.0	300.9	170.3	**86.1**
Sub-total	718.2	767.0	809.1	808.0	860.3	857.3	1089.7	953.5	**965.1**
Developing countries									
Jewellery	195.9	379.0	439.7	395.1	580.9	593.4	551.8	590.7	**839.8**
Electronics	1.8	1.4	1.6	1.7	2.3	2.9	4.2	6.1	**6.9**
Dentistry	1.8	1.5	1.5	0.9	1.2	1.6	1.6	3.0	**2.8**
Other industrial	4.2	4.3	3.9	3.2	3.3	5.2	5.3	4.5	**5.8**
Medals and imitation									
coins	2.6	14.9	15.9	9.3	28.3	10.9	7.5	8.4	**7.6**
Official coins	20.5	49.8	7.0	12.9	6.2	13.5	25.7	30.1	**15.6**
Sub-total	226.8	450.9	469.6	423.1	622.2	627.5	596.1	642.8	**878.5**
Total	945.0	1217.9	1278.7	1231.1	1482.5	1484.8	1685.8	1596.3	**1843.6**

Gold supply and demand in the non-communist world

tonnes

	1980	1981	1982	1983	1984	1985	1986	1987	1988
Supply (Tables 1–3)									
Mine production	959	981	1028	1114	1162	1233	1293	1382	**1538**
Net communist sales	90	280	203	93	205	210	402	303	**258**
Net official sales									
(purchases)	(230)	(276)	(85)	142	85	(132)	(145)	(72)	**(270)**
Scrap	488	239	243	294	291	304	474	405	**324**
(A) Total supply	1307	1224	1389	1643	1742	1615	2024	2018	**1850**
(B) Fabrication demand (Table 4)	945	1218	1279	1231	1483	1485	1686	1596	**1844**
(C) Net surplus (deficit) of supply over fabrication (A) – (B)	362	6	110	411	260	130	338	422	**6**
(D) Identified bar hoarding outside Europe and North America (Table 11)	23	274	294	73	332	306	214	268	**474**
(E) Net implied investment (disinvestment) in Europe and North America (C) – (D)	339	(268)	(184)	338	(72)	(176)	124	154	**(468)**

Totals may not add due to rounding. (E) includes the net impact of gold loans and forward sales

By courtesy of Consolidated Gold Fields plc, 'Gold 1989'.

48

The top 10 gold producers in the non-communist world 1988 production (tonnes)	
1 South Africa	621.0
2 United States	205.3
3 Australia	152.0
4 Canada	128.5
5 Brazil	100.2
6 Philippines	42.7
7 Colombia	33.4
8 Papua New Guinea	32.6
9 Chile	22.7
10 Venezuela	16.0

COMEX trading volumes
(100oz contracts)

	futures	options
1980	8,001,410	—
1981	10,373,706	—
1982	12,289,448	56,752
1983	10,382,805	386,501
1984	9,115,504	1,432,514
1985	7,773,834	1,395,896
1986	8,400,175	1,646,791
1987	10,239,805	2,080,067
1988	**9,496,402**	**1,698,696**

By courtesy of Consolidated Gold Fields plc, 'Gold 1989'.

Lead

Ruth Gardiner,
Senior Assistant Editor, Futures and Options World

With all the recent publicity about lead-free petrol, the prospects for the metal in the near future look unpromising. But, despite environmental worries and technological leaps which have allowed lead to be substituted by newer materials (not to mention problems with lead production), new uses are constantly being found for the metal.

Tetraethyl lead has been added to gasoline as an 'anti-knock' agent for years, but with concern about exhaust pollution growing throughout the 1980s, the move towards unleaded petrol has raced ahead of all expectations. In 1972, 370,000 tonnes of lead were used in gasoline additives, making up 11% of total consumption, but by 1987 this figure had dropped to 3%.

With the successes of the 'Green' Party in recent European elections, there must now be a strong possibility that Europe will go the way of the United States, where unleaded petrol was introduced 14 years ago and now caters for 85% of demand. Japan was the first country to complete the move to unleaded, and Canada, China and Brazil are now also well down this path. However, lead levels in petrol do remain high in Eastern Europe, and few Middle Eastern, African, Central and South American or South-East Asian countries are making the move to unleaded as yet.

Lead consumption is connected irrevocably with the motor industry and despite the decline in the petrol sector, storage batteries still constitute more than 50% of offtake. Contrary to forecasts, battery demand has remained high in Europe in recent years, although this is the only sector of lead use still increasing.

Sustained buoyancy in the motor industry in both Europe and Japan helped lead to hit an 8-year high in August 1989 at the London Metal Exchange (LME), where prices have recently exceeded £450 a tonne for cash metal after a sudden fall in LME warehouse stocks.

This buoyancy is despite two mild winters in the northern hemisphere and the consequent decrease in battery demand. In fact, the following hot summers have actually aided demand by causing increased battery deterioration.

Lead could face problems in the future if new chemical formulae for batteries are developed further, given that a majority of the metal now goes into this sector. However, despite a decline in its use in piping, cable sheathing and paints, lead continues to be used extensively in the building industry, in roofing applications and to line chemical tanks, although here too, it is being replaced by plastics. Lead is also used with tin in soldering, for protective coatings on steel, and in electric power cables, while shot and ammunition also account for a small percentage of lead consumption. Lead use has declined in printing though, as the industry moves away from hot metal and towards high technology.

The International Lead and Zinc Research Organization continues to look at new uses for this high density, inelastic, soft and malleable metal, and one big area of potential growth is in the use of lead as a container for radioactive waste. The shielding of containers for radioactive materials is usually metallic lead, and it is already used as a shield from radiation, for example from X-rays in the dentist's chair.

There are 25 countries with significant lead mines, but the production of lead has been dogged throughout the 1980s and has again recently suffered, with strikes in Peru (one of the largest lead producers) affecting the principal lead mine there. Europe has traditionally been a producer of lead, but the main sources are the United States, Australia, Canada and Mexico.

The main consumers of lead are still Europe and the United States, but Japan has now become important, accounting for 9% of world lead consumption. Africa, Asia and South America are also key consumers, with the latter alone consuming 19% of western world lead in 1987.

Following the world oil crisis, lead consumption declined, but it reached renewed highs in the 1980s. Over 4 million tonnes of lead are now consumed each year, yet while there is no doubt that the metal has been losing out to plastics and aluminium, a recent report by the Institute of Scrap Recycling Industries has forecast a strong outlook. Lead continues to have a high recovery rate in recycling.

Lead is no longer regarded as a highly speculative metal – that mantle has now passed to aluminium and copper. The market at the LME does still occasionally attract speculators into the trader's arena but the 'professional investors' themselves are disappointed that lead futures are not yet traded on a global basis.

Lead: world mine production 1984-89 (thousand tonnes)

	1984	1985	1986	1987	1988	1989
						Jan-Mar
EUROPE						
Austria	4.2	6.1	4.7	5.2	2.3	0.6
Denmark	17.7	17.8	16.2	19.4	23.5	5.7
Finland	2.6	2.4	2.0	2.4	1.9	0.5
France	2.3	2.5	2.5	2.2	2.0	0.3
Germany, F.R.	27.0	26.4	22.2	24.5	17.9	3.7
Greece	22.2	20.1	20.9	20.6	25.9	6.3
Ireland	37.2	34.6	36.4	33.8	32.5	8.6
Italy	21.5	15.6	11.1	12.2	16.5	4.2
Norway	3.5	3.3	3.2	3.1	2.8	0.9
Spain	95.6	86.9	82.1	83.2	74.9	18.6
Sweden	80.5	76.2	88.9	90.4	88.3	21.8
United Kingdom	4.0	3.6	0.6	0.7	0.6	0.2
Yugoslavia	113.6	115.1	103.0	82.0	95.5	23.5
Total..	431.9	410.6	393.8	379.7	384.6	94.9
AFRICA						
Algeria	3.6	3.8	1.0	3.5	3.6	0.9
Congo	2.5	2.5	1.0	–	–	–
Morocco	100.6	106.8	71.8	73.6	70.1	18.0
Namibia	42.6	48.6	37.1	29.5	18.9	4.2
South Africa	94.8	98.4	97.8	95.9	91.3	21.3
Tunisia	4.1	2.5	1.9	2.1	2.2	0.6
Zambia	18.8	22.5	24.3	22.8	21.4	5.4
Total..	267.0	285.1	234.9	227.4	207.5	50.4
ASIA						
Burma	8.3	7.6	6.6	4.6	6.0	1.5
India	18.6	26.0	25.0	29.0	23.3	6.3
Iran	19.9	21.6	20.0	20.0	18.0	4.5
Japan	48.7	50.0	40.3	27.9	22.7	5.2
Philippines	–	–	–	–	–	–
South Korea	9.9	8.8	10.6	13.9	14.5	3.1
Thailand	24.3	28.7	38.1	34.0	30.0	7.5
Turkey	14.6	10.0	9.6	9.1	10.1	2.7
Other Asia	0.5	0.1	0.1	–	–	–
Total..	144.8	152.8	150.3	138.5	124.6	30.8
AMERICA						
Canada	307.4	284.6	349.3	413.7	366.6	74.7
U.S.A.	334.5	424.4	348.2	318.3	395.7	101.3
Argentina	28.5	28.6	26.9	26.1	28.7	7.2
Bolivia	8.4	6.2	3.3	9.1	12.5	3.3
Brazil	19.2	18.2	17.0	13.0	19.0	4.8
Chile	4.3	2.5	1.5	0.8	1.4	0.3
Honduras	20.5	21.2	11.4	5.0	16.2	6.3
Mexico	183.3	206.7	196.9	190.0	171.2	45.9
Peru	198.4	200.6	194.4	204.0	149.0	46.0
Other America	0.2	0.5	2.0	2.4	2.4	0.6
Total..	1 104.7	1 193.5	1 150.9	1 182.4	1 162.7	290.4
OCEANIA						
Australia	440.4	497.6	447.7	489.2	465.5	115.1
TOTAL..	**2 388.8**	**2 539.6**	**2 377.6**	**2 417.2**	**2 344.9**	**581.6**
Monthly Average..	*199.1*	*211.6*	*198.1*	*201.4*	*195.4*	*193.9*
OTHER COUNTRIES						
Bulgaria	95.0	97.0	97.0	95.0	90.0	
Czechoslovakia	3.1	2.5	2.7	2.7	2.8	
Hungary	0.6	–	–	–	–	
Poland	52.8	51.3	42.5	48.8	49.5	
Romania	30.0	34.3	36.3	30.2	32.8	
U.S.S.R.	570.0	580.0	520.0	510.0	520.0	
China	210.0	220.0	226.8	267.2	311.6	
North Korea	90.0	80.0	85.0	90.0	90.0	
Total..	1 051.5	1 065.1	1 010.3	1 043.9	1 096.7	
WORLD TOTAL	**3 440.3**	**3 604.7**	**3 387.9**	**3 461.1**	**3 441.6**	

This table shows the content by analysis of lead ores and concentrates plus the lead content of mixed ores.

By courtesy of the World Bureau of Metal Statistics.

Lead: world refined production 1984-89 (thousand tonnes)

	1984	1985	1986	1987	1988	1989
						Jan-Mar
EUROPE						
Austria	26.2	25.5	25.0	22.8	25.0	6.5
Belgium	119.7	105.3	90.5	89.6	105.2	24.9
Denmark	13.0	–	–	–	–	–
Finland	4.5	4.6	1.2	–	–	–
France	205.7	223.5	230.4	245.5	255.7	70.0
Germany, F.R.	357.2	356.3	366.6	340.4	345.1	91.6
Greece	11.6	13.7	19.3	2.7	15.1	3.9
Ireland	9.1	9.0	10.2	10.0	11.7	2.9
Italy	140.5	135.0	126.4	168.3	168.4	46.2
Netherlands	33.6	37.3	35.7	40.3	39.5	9.5
Norway	–	–	–	–	–	–
Portugal	6.0	7.0	6.0	7.0	7.0	1.8
Spain	147.6	156.1	124.9	122.7	120.8	30.7
Sweden	77.5	69.1	78.9	91.4	84.7	21.7
Switzerland	2.0	2.0	2.5	2.5	1.5	0.4
United Kingdom	338.4	327.2	328.6	347.0	373.8	89.4
Yugoslavia	120.2	131.7	138.0	125.0	131.0	35.0
Total..	1 612.8	1 603.3	1 584.2	1 615.2	1 684.5	434.5
AFRICA						
Algeria	–	–	4.0	4.0	4.0	1.1
Morocco	48.3	63.5	55.3	64.9	71.0	17.7
Namibia	28.9	38.5	40.0	40.6	44.4	10.5
Nigeria	0.6	0.8	0.6	0.3	0.5	–
South Africa	24.0	34.1	29.7	34.5	36.2	10.9
Tunisia	8.4	2.0	2.2	1.7	–	–
Zambia	9.3	10.1	7.4	9.0	7.7	1.2
Other Africa	6.5	6.0	5.0	5.0	4.8	1.2
Total..	126.0	155.0	144.2	160.0	168.6	42.6
ASIA						
Burma	6.9	9.4	5.3	3.9	4.3	1.1
India	31.4	31.1	35.9	32.5	32.0	5.6
Iran	7.5	7.5	8.0	10.0	10.0	2.6
Japan	362.9	367.0	361.5	338.5	340.0	66.2
Malaysia	9.0	10.0	12.0	9.0	15.0	3.8
Philippines	4.0	7.0	7.0	7.0	7.0	1.7
South Korea	20.3	20.2	59.6	82.5	90.0	10.3
Taiwan	44.3	48.7	53.5	66.4	67.3	11.5
Thailand	6.2	7.5	15.9	11.4	12.0	3.0
Turkey	9.0	10.0	9.6	10.0	11.0	2.7
Other Asia	10.0	9.2	9.0	11.5	10.8	2.7
Total..	511.5	527.6	577.3	582.7	599.4	111.2
AMERICA						
Canada	254.4	306.8	257.7	235.6	268.1	67.8
U.S.A.	965.1	1 053.6	931.7	1 042.0	1 046.7	246.5
Argentina	28.0	28.7	30.7	32.2	28.9	4.5
Brazil	63.7	72.9	85.4	83.8	98.2	20.5
Mexico	172.4	201.9	188.6	188.6	179.4	45.4
Peru	71.2	83.3	67.4	70.8	53.6	18.7
Venezuela	17.0	20.0	19.0	18.5	18.0	4.5
Other America	3.6	6.4	6.2	6.1	6.0	1.5
Total..	1 575.4	1 773.6	1 586.7	1 677.6	1 698.9	409.4
OCEANIA						
Australia	220.3	215.7	171.0	216.7	179.9	40.5
New Zealand	6.0	6.0	4.0	4.0	4.0	1.1
Total..	226.3	221.7	175.0	220.7	183.9	41.6
TOTAL..	**4 052.0**	**4 281.2**	**4 067.4**	**4 256.2**	**4 335.3**	**1 039.3**
Monthly Average..	*337.7*	*356.8*	*339.0*	*354.7*	*361.3*	*346.4*
OTHER COUNTRIES						
Bulgaria	114.0	116.0	113.7	117.0	113.0	
Czechoslovakia	47.0	21.5	23.6	26.0	27.0	
German D.R.	35.0	55.0	44.5	49.1	55.0	
Hungary	–	–	–	–	–	
Poland	83.4	87.3	88.3	89.8	90.7	
Romania	51.0	49.0	52.0	44.0	44.0	
U.S.S.R.	800.0	810.0	790.0	775.0	795.0	
China	200.0	215.0	239.6	246.4	241.4	
North Korea	65.0	65.0	65.0	70.0	70.0	
Total..	1 395.4	1 418.8	1 416.7	1 417.3	1 436.1	
WORLD TOTAL	**5 447.4**	**5 700.0**	**5 484.1**	**5 673.5**	**5 771.4**	

This table is based on the production of refined lead including the lead content of antimonial lead from primary and secondary materials. Metal recovered from secondary material by remelting alone is excluded.

By courtesy of the World Bureau of Metal Statistics.

Lead: world refined consumption 1984-89 (thousand tonnes)

	1984	1985	1986	1987	1988	1989
						Jan-Mar
EUROPE						
Austria	62.3	61.9	63.0	54.5	49.2	5.4
Belgium	72.4	65.9	71.9	64.0	60.3	15.0
Denmark	17.0	13.4	14.6	14.8	7.2	1.8
Finland	19.5	24.1	16.9	13.1	12.8	3.3
France	209.1	208.0	205.3	207.5	215.6	59.7
Germany, F.R.	357.0	345.0	358.8	344.6	373.5	99.0
Greece	20.0	22.8	16.3	16.0	18.0	4.5
Ireland	9.4	9.4	11.7	12.0	12.4	3.0
Italy	238.0	235.0	238.0	244.0	246.0	61.5
Netherlands	47.2	45.1	49.5	51.4	50.0	12.3
Norway	14.0	14.0	14.5	13.8	10.3	4.1
Portugal	26.6	25.9	34.4	28.4	24.0	6.0
Spain	112.7	103.1	110.8	105.8	99.3	24.0
Sweden	27.0	26.5	27.8	30.2	32.3	7.8
Switzerland	9.5	10.5	10.4	11.5	10.7	1.3
United Kingdom	295.3	274.3	282.1	287.5	302.5	78.2
Yugoslavia	115.2	139.3	144.7	129.4	128.9	33.6
Other Europe	0.2	0.3	0.2	0.4	0.4	–
Total..	1 652.4	1 624.5	1 670.9	1 628.9	1 653.4	420.5
AFRICA						
Morocco	4.1	5.0	3.0	5.7	6.5	1.5
South Africa	43.9	36.8	49.4	51.4	56.1	13.8
Tunisia	3.5	2.4	3.6	4.7	2.4	0.6
Zambia	1.7	3.0	3.0	3.8	3.8	0.4
Other Africa	53.7	38.3	36.6	34.8	34.8	8.7
Total..	106.9	85.5	95.6	100.4	103.6	25.0
ASIA						
India	57.6	70.0	80.5	67.5	65.0	16.2
Japan	390.1	394.9	389.2	378.0	406.5	96.9
South Korea	46.0	63.2	88.3	112.4	146.0	36.6
Taiwan	55.8	40.4	48.6	75.6	74.8	14.0
Thailand	18.6	16.8	18.6	24.0	24.0	6.0
Turkey	19.2	26.5	22.9	22.0	21.6	5.4
Other Asia	102.5	77.5	99.3	96.0	96.0	24.0
Total..	689.8	689.3	747.4	775.5	833.9	199.1
AMERICA						
Canada	119.8	100.3	110.7	102.9	95.7	21.3
U.S.A.	1 185.3	1 141.7	1 118.5	1 216.9	1 201.0	302.4
Argentina	28.0	28.7	30.6	32.2	28.8	4.5
Brazil	64.3	74.2	87.5	92.8	95.5	19.8
Mexico	86.3	105.6	84.1	89.5	77.1	23.0
Peru	14.2	13.7	20.7	21.9	19.5	4.8
Other America	35.8	37.2	35.9	36.0	36.0	9.0
Total..	1 533.7	1 501.4	1 488.0	1 592.2	1 553.6	384.8
OCEANIA						
Australia	58.8	59.8	59.8	51.9	59.3	12.1
New Zealand	8.1	10.5	7.6	8.2	9.0	2.1
Other Oceania	–	–	–	–	–	–
Total..	66.9	70.3	67.4	60.1	68.3	14.2
TOTAL..	**4 049.7**	**3 971.0**	**4 069.3**	**4 157.1**	**4 212.8**	**1 043.6**
Monthly Average..	*337.5*	*330.9*	*339.1*	*346.4*	*351.1*	
OTHER COUNTRIES						
Albania	3.0	3.5	3.5	3.5	3.5	
Bulgaria	114.0	113.0	108.0	109.0	106.0	
Czechoslovakia	48.1	50.0	48.6	49.0	47.0	
German D.R.	90.0	95.0	79.0	79.0	82.0	
Hungary	13.2	13.5	12.8	13.8	13.0	
Poland	89.5	93.5	91.3	89.7	80.7	
Romania	51.0	49.0	52.0	44.0	44.0	
U.S.S.R.	790.0	800.0	760.0	775.0	790.0	
China	215.0	220.0	249.0	251.0	250.0	
North Korea	27.0	25.0	25.0	28.0	30.0	
Cuba	3.5	4.2	4.5	4.5	4.4	
Other	3.0	3.0	2.0	2.0	2.0	
Total..	1 447.3	1 469.7	1 435.7	1 448.5	1 452.6	
WORLD TOTAL	**5 497.0**	**5 440.7**	**5 505.0**	**5 605.6**	**5 665.4**	

This table shows the consumption of refined lead.

By courtesy of the World Bureau of Metal Statistics.

Lead: world trade in refined lead 1984-89 (thousand tonnes)

	1983	1984	1985	1986	1987	1988
						Jan-Dec
EXPORTS						
Austria	0.8	0.5	1.0	1.1	1.9	6.1
Belgium	69.8	77.8	59.4	50.4	55.9	53.0
Denmark	7.6	9.7	3.5	3.1	0.2	0.3
Finland	–	–	–	0.1	0.4	–
France	45.7	46.6	55.8	54.6	76.7	70.4
Germany, F.R.	110.4	99.3	99.3	89.2	78.2	86.3
Greece	–	2.0	..	0.5	3.1	–[4]
Netherlands	11.7	13.6	18.4	18.3	18.1	13.8
Spain	39.7	57.6	52.6	21.4	16.6	0.8
Sweden[1]	30.5	42.1	41.5	42.3	52.2	68.9
United Kingdom	56.2	82.3	64.2	60.0	70.6	67.9
Yugoslavia	18.0	13.9	15.1	24.8	21.1	10.0
Morocco	55.7	46.1	54.7	52.5	63.4	..
Namibia	23.8	9.1	14.3	12.8	15.4	..
Tunisia	3.7	6.6	0.1	2.9	1.7	0.8
South Africa	..	..	..	..	..	..
Zambia	12.7	7.6	5.0	4.6	4.4	3.7
Japan[2]	14.4	16.5	24.4	25.4	15.7	0.7
Taiwan	16.0	15.9	20.6	23.5	16.0	30.9
Canada[3]	147.3	124.1	114.0	111.9	100.2	186.7
U.S.A.[2]	17.5	4.4	24.9	9.9	4.3	7.0
Argentina	–	–	–	–	–	..
Mexico	89.8	82.2	98.9	104.0	81.7	104.9
Peru	55.0	54.4	61.2	49.4	43.0	30.4
Australia	180.6	147.3	153.7	110.8	132.9	159.4
Total..	1 006.9	959.6	982.6	873.5	873.7	902.0
IMPORTS						
Austria	31.4	39.3	37.5	38.5	31.5	32.7
Belgium	18.6	33.9	24.6	36.9	22.2	16.7
Denmark	11.8	14.0	16.9	17.7	15.0	7.5
Finland	12.1	14.9	19.6	15.8	18.0	11.9
France	44.7	51.5	39.2	33.9	32.1	37.5
Germany, F.R.	64.1	99.0	92.9	93.4	84.5	87.5
Greece	24.4	12.2	9.8	1.9	3.2	1.7[4]
Ireland[2]	0.7	0.3	0.1	1.2	0.9	1.0
Italy	112.0	103.2	107.8	134.0	103.0	111.5
Netherlands	30.8	26.8	26.2	32.3	30.1	31.3
Norway[2]	11.6	13.3	12.8	13.0	13.4	9.6
Poland	1.6	4.0	6.0	..	..	..
Portugal	16.3	13.9	20.5	17.4	21.9	0.3
Spain	6.7	4.1	2.2	6.5	10.8	7.2
Sweden	1.7	0.3	1.7	1.3	0.2	0.8
Switzerland	10.4	9.8	10.7	10.2	8.1	8.4
United Kingdom	45.5	35.8	37.3	31.0	28.8	45.8
Yugoslavia	7.1	8.9	8.0	14.4	10.4	..
South Africa	5.4	9.9	3.9	1.0	1.2	..
Hong Kong	1.4	1.4	1.6	4.8	11.7	6.0
India	12.4	38.9	39.7	16.1	28.2	11.1[5]
Japan[2]	60.7	88.7	53.8	51.1	30.9	72.8
Philippines	6.4	2.7	2.9	4.4	11.7	..
South Korea	22.2	26.0	42.1	34.9	35.5	55.4
Taiwan	17.5	12.2	12.3	16.2	20.9	18.9
Thailand	13.2	10.0	8.7	7.9	9.4	–
Canada[3]	2.6	6.3	5.5	3.9	12.3	13.8
U.S.A.	130.7	161.6	133.5	141.5	189.2	148.3
China	..	..	..	..	..	..
Total..	724.0	842.9	777.8	781.2	785.1	737.7

This table shows principal imports and exports of refined lead.

Notes 1. May include some bullion. 2. Includes alloy. 3. Includes shot. 4. January to May 5. January to November

By courtesy of the World Bureau of Metal Statistics.

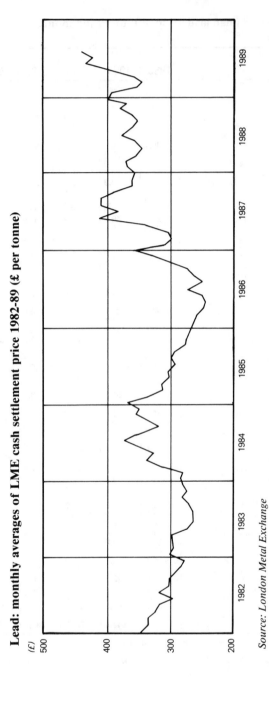

Lead: monthly averages of LME cash settlement price 1982-89 (£ per tonne)

Source: London Metal Exchange

Nickel

Emma Davey
Deputy Editor, Futures and Options World

Nickel is younger than most other base metals in terms of its applications and demand. Its primary use in the production of stainless steel links its price and supply inextricably to the demand for this product. Nickel's resistance to corrosion also makes it particularly popular in the manufacturing of steel alloys, and due to its high melting point, it is also popular in the production of heat-resistant steels and irons.

Nickel's popularity only goes back to the last century, when its use as an alloying element was recognized. Prior to that time, its use was restricted by its high melting point which had made it a difficult metal to process.

Almost all nickel is mined as nickel ore, but as a relatively expensive metal it is rarely used on its own. The main producing areas of the metal are Cuba, the Philippines, Indonesia, the United States, and South America, namely the Dominican Republic, Colombia and Brazil. Europe's nickel mines can be found in Greece, Albania, Finland and the Soviet Union.

In recent years, the economic climate of the early and mid-1980s led to a more cautious environment for the production and trading of nickel as the demand for stainless steel fell. As demand dropped so did mining output with many producers either closing down plants or reducing output. The period of supply shortage kept prices relatively high for much of the mid-1980s.

Higher spending in the industrialized world and an upswing in the call for nickel after 1987 led to demand outstripping supplies. In 1988 alone, world consumption of the metal rose by 23,000 tonnes. The resulting price rise, accompanying the increase in demand, prompted many mining companies and producers to reassess their production capacities. Some mines whose output had been reduced or which had even closed were reopened and others expanded their existing output.

Among the main nickel producers, mines have been started or reopened by Canada's Inco and Australia's Western Mining Corp. Cuba's Punta Gorda is also expected to continue to produce more nickel, and other new projects in the industry include a mine and ferro-nickel plant in Oregon. South Korea is expected to continue as a significant nickel importer with the growth of the steel firm, Posco.

Along with the growing demand and increased mining output, the more successful Soviet shipments of nickel to Europe brought greater liquidity to nickel trading on the London Metal Exchange (LME) - the accepted pricing indicator for the metal and its industry. Nickel is the most recently introduced metal to be traded on the LME, having been launched in the spring of 1979. Many at that time thought that this was an unwise move, due to the metal's political and economic connections with the stainless steel manufacturing industry. Nickel is still regarded as a highly volatile market which, spurred by supply shortages and escalating demand, has experienced huge price rises on the LME, in the recent past, causing periods of concern to the exchange.

The demand for nickel is likely to continue as long as industrial investment continues to grow. Economic growth is likely to tail off in 1989, but stainless steel consumption will probably level out with recovery in the early 1990s. Most forecasters predict that the market will move into a surplus towards the end of 1989, with supply remaining relatively tight until then. Prices will fluctuate in line with such market fundamentals as temporary shortages or boosts in production or consumption, but supply will depend to a great extent on the success of the new projects under development.

Nickel: world mine production 1984–89 (thousand tonnes)

	1984	1985	1986	1987	1988	1989
						Jan-Mar
EUROPE						
Finland	6.9	8.6	11.8	10.6	11.7	2.3
Greece	15.8	15.9	10.3	9.2	13.1	3.4
Norway	0.6	0.6	0.6	0.4	0.3	0.1
Yugoslavia	2.2	2.8	3.2	3.5	5.6	1.4
Total..	25.5	27.9	25.9	23.7	30.7	7.2
AFRICA						
Botswana	18.6	19.6	19.0	16.5	22.5	5.0
Morocco	–	–	–	–	–	–
South Africa	22.0	29.0	31.8	34.3	34.3	8.6
Zimbabwe	11.1	11.2	10.9	12.4	12.1	3.0
Total..	51.7	59.8	61.7	63.2	68.9	16.6
ASIA						
Burma	0.1	0.1	0.1	0.1	0.1	–
Indonesia	47.8	48.2	67.3	57.2	57.8	16.1
Philippines	15.6	28.2	12.7	8.5	11.1	5.1
Total..	63.5	76.5	80.1	65.8	69.0	21.2
AMERICA						
Canada	173.7	170.0	163.6	194.5	199.0	52.7
U.S.A.	8.7	5.6	1.1	–	–	–
Brazil	12.7	13.2	13.5	13.9	13.1	3.4
Colombia	16.5	14.0	19.0	19.3	16.9	4.0
Dominican Republic	24.3	25.4	24.1	32.5	29.3	8.4
Guatemala	–	–	–	–	–	–
Total..	235.9	228.2	221.3	260.2	258.3	68.5
OCEANIA						
Australia	76.9	85.8	76.7	74.6	62.4	16.2
New Caledonia	58.3	72.4	64.5	58.3	68.7	17.3
Total..	135.2	158.2	141.2	132.9	131.1	33.5
TOTAL..	**511.8**	**550.6**	**530.2**	**545.8**	**558.0**	**147.0**
Monthly Average..	*42.7*	*45.9*	*44.2*	*45.5*	*46.5*	*49.0*
OTHER COUNTRIES						
Albania	7.2	7.2	7.5	7.7	8.0	
German D.R.	2.0	2.0	2.0	2.0	2.0	
Poland	0.2	–	–	–	–	
U.S.S.R.	180.0	190.0	185.0	195.0	205.0	
China	18.3	25.8	29.4	30.4	28.6	
Cuba	33.2	33.6	32.1	35.9	43.8	
Other	0.2	0.2	0.2	0.2	0.2	
Total..	241.1	258.8	256.2	271.2	287.6	
WORLD TOTAL	**752.9**	**809.4**	**786.4**	**817.0**	**845.6**	

This table shows the nickel content of ores and concentrates produced.

By courtesy of the World Bureau of Metal Statistics.

Nickel: world refined consumption 1984-89 (thousand tonnes)

	1984	1985	1986	1987	1988	1989
						Jan-Mar
EUROPE						
Finland	15.3	15.7	17.8	15.4	15.7	3.1
France	5.2	7.0	9.3	6.7	9.0	2.7
Greece	15.8	15.9	10.3	9.2	13.1	3.4
Norway	35.6	37.5	38.3	44.6	52.5	13.8
United Kingdom	22.3	17.8	30.9	29.5	28.0	7.0
Yugoslavia	1.8	2.8	3.2	3.5	5.6	1.4
Total..	96.0	96.7	109.8	108.9	123.9	31.4
AFRICA						
South Africa	20.5	24.0	25.4	28.0	28.0	7.0
Zimbabwe	10.4	11.5	16.4	16.7	18.3	4.3
Total..	30.9	35.5	41.8	44.7	46.3	11.3
ASIA						
Indonesia	4.8	4.8	4.5	3.1	5.9	1.5
Japan	89.4	95.2	92.8	91.6	100.6	26.8
Philippines	3.5	14.8	2.6	–	–	–
Taiwan	–	2.1	8.5	8.2	10.5	2.6
Total..	97.7	116.9	108.4	102.9	117.0	30.9
AMERICA						
Canada	111.6	108.0	111.3	131.5	151.3	36.4
U.S.A.	40.8	33.0	1.5	–	–	–
Brazil	12.7	13.2	13.5	13.4	13.1	3.4
Colombia	16.5	11.4	19.0	19.3	16.9	4.0
Dominican Republic	23.0	25.4	21.8	32.5	29.3	8.4
Total..	204.6	191.0	167.1	196.7	210.6	52.2
OCEANIA						
Australia	38.7	40.8	42.1	44.4	43.4	11.6
New Caledonia	29.2	36.1	33.0	29.5	37.4	8.8
Total..	67.9	76.9	75.1	73.9	80.8	20.4
TOTAL..	**497.1**	**517.0**	**502.2**	**527.1**	**578.6**	**146.2**
Monthly Average..	*41.4*	*43.1*	*41.8*	*43.9*	*48.2*	*48.7*
OTHER COUNTRIES						
Albania	4.0	4.0	4.0	4.0	4.5	
Czechoslovakia	4.5	4.0	4.0	3.8	3.8	
German D.R.	3.0	3.0	3.2	3.2	3.5	
Poland	–	–	–	–	–	
U.S.S.R.	193.0	198.0	195.0	210.0	215.0	
China	17.5	24.6	28.0	29.0	30.0	
Cuba	17.6	16.1	16.9	17.4	25.0	
Total..	239.6	249.7	251.1	267.4	281.8	
WORLD TOTAL	**736.7**	**766.7**	**753.3**	**794.5**	**860.4**	

This table shows smelter-refinery production of electrolytic nickel, nickel pellets, briquettes, steel making powder, the nickel content of nickel salts, chemical grade nickel oxide, ferro-nickel, nickel oxide sinter and utility nickel.

By courtesy of the World Bureau of Metal Statistics.

Nickel: world refined production 1984-89 (thousand tonnes)

	1984	1985	1986	1987	1988	1989 Jan-Mar
EUROPE						
Austria	5.5	5.5	5.3	4.8	5.0	0.8
Belgium	6.0	6.6	6.8	8.5	16.0	4.4
Denmark	0.2	0.1	0.2	0.4	0.5	0.1
Finland	13.2	14.7	13.2	14.9	16.3	4.1
France	39.2	31.9	31.9	39.3	39.6	12.1
Germany, F.R.	78.0	75.0	77.3	81.1	89.4	22.6
Greece	0.1	0.1	0.1	0.2	0.2	0.1
Ireland	0.1	0.3	0.6	0.3	0.3	0.1
Italy	28.0	29.0	29.5	28.8	28.6	6.9
Netherlands	1.2	1.5	2.7	1.3	2.0	0.5
Norway	0.3	0.4	0.4	0.6	0.8	0.2
Portugal	0.2	0.3	0.2	0.2	0.2	0.1
Spain	9.3	8.2	13.7	14.2	17.0	3.8
Sweden	20.4	17.0	17.1	16.8	17.1	4.9
Switzerland	0.9	1.2	1.3	1.0	1.0	0.3
United Kingdom	26.1	24.8	27.4	33.1	26.7	8.0
Yugoslavia	3.0	5.3	5.6	3.0	2.5	0.6
Total..	231.7	221.9	233.3	248.5	263.2	69.6
AFRICA						
Total..	9.0	11.0	11.0	10.0	10.0	2.5
ASIA						
India	15.2	14.0	16.0	19.3	15.0	3.8
Japan	146.0	136.1	126.6	153.9	161.7	41.0
Other Asia	10.3	12.8	28.9	23.9	23.9	6.0
Total..	171.5	162.9	171.5	197.1	200.6	50.8
AMERICA						
Canada	9.1	8.6	9.6	11.8	11.8	3.0
U.S.A.	141.0	143.1	124.8	148.3	141.2	37.6
Argentina	0.9	0.9	0.9	0.9	0.6	0.2
Brazil	10.3	11.5	13.8	14.4	12.0	2.8
Mexico	3.6	3.4	1.4	1.4	1.4	0.4
Other America	1.6	1.6	1.5	1.1	1.1	0.3
Total..	166.5	169.1	152.0	177.9	168.1	44.3
OCEANIA						
Australia	2.9	4.0	4.0	3.1	3.0	0.8
New Zealand	0.5	0.5	0.5	0.5	0.5	0.1
Total..	3.4	4.5	4.5	3.6	3.5	0.9
TOTAL..	**582.1**	**569.4**	**572.3**	**637.1**	**645.4**	**168.1**
Monthly Average..	*48.5*	*47.5*	*47.7*	*53.1*	*53.8*	*55.9*
OTHER COUNTRIES						
Bulgaria	1.5	1.5	1.5	1.5	1.5	
Czechoslovakia	9.6	10.6	9.5	11.3	11.5	
German D.R.	10.0	12.0	12.2	12.5	13.0	
Hungary	3.0	3.2	3.5	3.5	3.8	
Poland	7.5	8.0	8.0	7.5	8.0	
Romania	8.5	10.9	10.0	9.0	9.5	
U.S.S.R.	140.0	138.0	137.0	135.0	130.0	
China	19.0	21.0	23.0	24.0	27.5	
Other	0.5	0.6	0.8	1.2	1.5	
Total..	199.6	205.8	205.5	205.5	206.3	
WORLD TOTAL	**781.7**	**775.2**	**777.8**	**842.6**	**851.7**	

This table shows consumption of unwrought nickel, to include refined nickel plus the consumption of nickel contained in other smelter-refinery products.

By courtesy of the World Bureau of Metal Statistics.

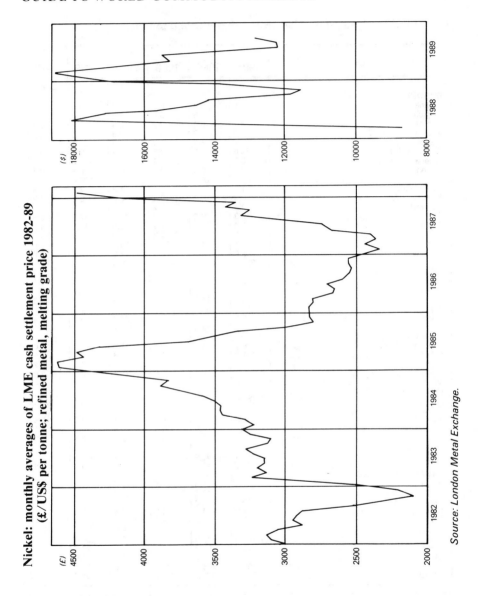

Nickel: monthly averages of LME cash settlement price 1982-89
(£/US$ per tonne; refined metal, melting grade)

Source: London Metal Exchange.

Platinum

Paul Dickins

Platinum was largely unused except for decorative purposes until the nineteenth century when the catalytic powers of this rare, silvery-white metal were discovered, and its other unique properties began to be utilized in industry. Since then, the widening use of platinum in manufacturing – mainly in catalysts for controlling air pollution from cars – and the growing popularity of platinum jewellery, particularly in Japan, has meant that demand for the metal has soared. A resistance to corrosion, a high melting point, malleability and mechanical strength have also made platinum important in such industries as glass-making, electronics and dentistry. The demand for platinum is now outstripping supply, and it has become one of the most important of all precious metals. In mid-October 1989, platinum was \$485 an ounce, making it more valuable than either gold or silver, and increasing shortages of supply and price volatility has made it rank alongside gold and silver as an investor medium and speculatively-traded commodity.

The demand for platinum is dominated by Japan and the United States, which absorb 76% of all platinum supplies to the west (ie non-Communist countries). The biggest user is Japan, which takes in half of all platinum supplies, most of it for jewellery. The Japanese fondness for platinum jewellery is long-established and 90% of all platinum jewellery – equivalent to almost one-third of all platinum supplies to the west – is made and sold in Japan. The metal's blanched colour enhances the appearance of gemstones and its strength helps in the creation of delicate settings. In the last year or so platinum has also caught the eye of influential Italian designers, who may make platinum jewellery fashionable throughout Europe.

The rising industrial demand for platinum is now dominated by its use in autocatalyst production and this is now the single biggest use of platinum, absorbing 37% of all supplies in the west. Catalysts are fitted in the exhaust systems of cars, where pollution in the form of carbon monoxide and unburnt hydrocarbons are oxidized into carbon dioxide and water, and nitrogen oxides are oxidized into nitrogen. Autocatalysts were introduced in the United States in the 1970s and are now compulsory, accounting for the absorption of almost a quarter of all platinum supplies by the United States. The demand for platinum will increase further as tighter exhaust emission controls are introduced elsewhere. United States auto emission levels are now being introduced in Europe and all new cars will have to conform to them from 1992.

The demand for platinum is increasing in virtually every area of industry, where its applications range from spark plugs to anti-cancer drugs. The chemical industry uses 5% of all platinum in the west, mostly in producing nitric acids for fertilizers. An additional 4% of platinum is used in producing silicon wafers. Another 4% is used in glass-making where platinum crucibles and moulds are used since they survive high temperatures.

In 1988, the demand for platinum rose by 10%, to a record 3.66 million ounces, while supplies grew by only 3% to 3.20 million ounces. This left a record shortfall of 360,000 ounces and was the fourth consecutive year that there had been a supply deficit, despite the fact that supplies are now higher than ever.

The world's biggest producer is South Africa, which is supplying 80% of the west's platinum. The Bushveld Complex, a 15,000 square mile area in Central Transvaal with Pretoria at its southern tip, is the heart of South African platinum production. It is worked by three key mining groups, Rustenburg (the world's largest producer), Impala and Western. South African supply increased last year, with the new supplies coming from existing mines which are believed to be now working at capacity in order to meet rising world demand.

The Soviet Union is the second most important producer, accounting for 13% of supplies for the west, 90% of which comes from the Noril'sk-Talnakh area of north-west Siberia. The Sudbury area of Ontario accounts for 90% of Canadian production of platinum group metals, and, together with South Africa and the Soviet Union, these three countries supply virtually all newly-mined platinum. Other areas of production include Stillwater, Montana, USA; the Choca area of Colombia; and Japan, but none of these contribute more than 1% of world supply. Platinum refineries do recycle at least as much metal as comes from primary sources, however, it invariably stays with industrial consumers and rarely hits the open market.

With demand for platinum growing and recently outstripping supply, platinum prices have been particularly volatile. From January to April 1989, the platinum price soared from $520/oz to $560, then from April to August tumbled back down again to $480. However, prices and price volatility are weaker now than in the market's heady days in early 1980 when it touched $1,000, and late 1986 and mid-1987 when it broke the $600 barrier several times. Although prices in dollar terms are now lower, the platinum futures market at the New York Mercantile Exchange (NYMEX) is relatively buoyant. 700,000 50oz platinum futures traded at the exchange in the first half of 1989.

Meanwhile, platinum futures business at the Tokyo Commodity Exchange has grown substantially in recent years – 4.47 million 500g platinum futures contracts were traded at the exchange in 1988, a rise of 56% on 1987. This shows the degree of speculative interest in platinum, as does the high level of investment demand for platinum coins and bars. These absorbed 17% of platinum supplies to the west in 1988, largely the result of the Koala coin launched by GoldCorp Australia and the Maple Leaf by the Royal Canadian Mint. There was also a boom in demand for large bars in Japan after the yen hit a 10-year low and tax relief on savings accounts ended.

There are five other important platinum group metals. Of these, palladium is the most important and palladium futures are traded alongside platinum at NYMEX. The other four (known as the minor PGMs) – rhodium, ruthenium, iridium and osmium – are by-products of platinum and palladium production. All the PGMs have similar qualities, but only platinum and palladium are workable in their metallic state and are therefore more widely used in industry, and, of the two, only platinum has assumed the financial attributes that rank it alongside gold and silver.

PLATINUM SUPPLY AND DEMAND: WESTERN WORLD										
Supply	1979	1980	1981	1982	1983	1984	1985	1986	1987	1988
					'000oz					
South Africa	2180	2320	1800	1960	2070	2280	2340	2350	2520	2560
Canada	130	130	130	120	80	150	150	150	140	145
Others	30	30	30	30	40	40	40	40	40	95
	2340	2480	1960	2110	2190	2470	2530	2540	2700	2800
USSR Sales	460	340	370	380	290	250	230	290	400	400
TOTAL SUPPLY	2800	2820	2330	2490	2480	2720	2760	2830	3100	3200
Demand										
By Region										
Western Europe	430	290	420	330	330	400	400	470	560	545
Japan	920	940	1150	1050	950	1140	1250	1010	1650	1915
North America	1340	980	700	710	720	910	1010	1190	900	850
Rest of Western World	160	120	160	230	180	180	170	170	180	310
	2850	2330	2430	2320	2180	2630	2830	2840	3290	3620
Western Sales to										
Comecon/China	30	30	30	30	20	30	30	40	30	40
TOTAL DEMAND	2880	2360	2460	2350	2200	2660	2860	2880	3320	3660
Movements in Stocks	(80)	460	(130)	140	280	60	(100)	(50)	(220)	(460)
	2800	2820	2330	2490	2480	2720	2760	2830	3100	3200

The supply figures are estimates of sales by the mines of primary platinum. The demand estimates shown in this table are net figures, demand in each sector being total purchases by consumers less any sales back to the market. Thus, the annual totals represent the amount of primary metal that is acquired by consumers in any particular year.

Movements in stocks in a given year reflect changes in stocks held by other than primary refiners and final consumers, such as metal in the hands of fabricators, dealers, banks, and individuals. A positive figure indicates an increase in stocks; a negative figure indicates a rundown in stocks.

By courtesy of Johnson Matthey.

PLATINUM DEMAND BY APPLICATION: REGIONS

	1979	1980	1981	1982	1983	1984	1985	1986	1987	1988
					'000oz					
Japan										
Autocatalyst: gross	200	210	190	170	170	170	210	255	310	330
recovery	(0)	(0)	(0)	(0)	(0)	(0)	(0)	(5)	(15)	(25)
Chemical	10	10	10	10	10	15	15	15	15	15
Electrical	15	15	15	20	20	30	40	45	45	45
Glass	40	40	50	45	60	75	60	30	45	45
Investment: small	0	0	0	0	5	15	35	35	60	130
large	0	160	195	115	65	150	170	(125)	275	300
Jewellery	590	440	625	620	560	625	675	740	900	1060
Petroleum	10	15	15	15	15	20	15	0	0	0
Other	55	50	50	55	45	40	30	20	15	15
TOTALS	**920**	**940**	**1150**	**1050**	**950**	**1140**	**1250**	**1010**	**1650**	**1915**
North America										
Autocatalyst: gross	670	440	430	455	450	635	700	745	690	690
recovery	(0)	(0)	(0)	(0)	(30)	(45)	(70)	(85)	(100)	(135)
Chemical	130	115	50	80	100	100	75	65	55	55
Electrical	135	145	70	70	90	95	80	65	65	65
Glass	100	50	20	10	15	30	40	25	25	25
Investment	0	0	0	40	40	30	130	300	85	70
Jewellery	15	15	15	15	15	15	15	15	15	15
Petroleum	195	140	55	20	15	15	10	10	15	15
Other	95	75	60	20	25	35	30	50	50	50
TOTALS	**1340**	**980**	**700**	**710**	**720**	**910**	**1010**	**1190**	**900**	**850**
Rest of Western World including Europe										
Autocatalyst: gross	30	30	20	20	25	35	70	140	255	305
recovery	(0)	(0)	(0)	(0)	(0)	(0)	(0)	(0)	(0)	(0)
Chemical	205	135	190	170	135	145	135	115	125	90
Electrical	90	50	100	80	65	65	80	70	70	75
Glass	110	50	30	30	30	35	40	35	50	60
Investment	0	0	0	5	45	125	95	115	70	130
Jewellery	160	105	115	130	140	135	120	95	75	105
Petroleum	(45)	(25)	70	30	(10)	(20)	(10)	10	40	35
Other	40	65	55	95	80	60	40	60	55	55
TOTALS	**590**	**410**	**580**	**560**	**510**	**580**	**570**	**640**	**740**	**855**

'Investment: small' in the above table is the long-term holding of metal in the form of bars and coins weighing 10oz or less. 'Investment: large' in the form of 500g and 1kg bars in Japan was incorporated in the 'Other' applications sector of pre-1988 reviews.

With the exception of the autocatalyst sector, the demand estimates shown are net figures, demand in each sector being total purchases by consumers less any sales back to the market. Thus, the annual totals represent the amount of primary metal that is acquired by consumers in any particular year.

Gross autocatalyst demand is purchases of platinum by the auto industry for manufacture of autocatalyst. Autocatalyst recovery is platinum recovered from scrapped catalytic converters and is allocated to the region in which the vehicle was scrapped.

By courtesy of Johnson Matthey.

PLATINUM DEMAND BY APPLICATION: WESTERN WORLD										
	1979	1980	1981	1982	1983	1984	1985	1986	1987	1988
					'000oz					
Autocatalyst: gross	900	680	640	655	645	840	980	1140	1255	1325
recovery	(0)	(0)	(0)	(10)	(30)	(45)	(70)	(90)	(115)	(160)
Chemical	345	260	250	260	245	260	225	195	195	160
Electrical	240	210	185	170	175	190	200	180	180	185
Glass	250	140	100	85	105	140	140	90	120	130
Investment: small	0	0	0	45	90	170	260	450	215	330
large	0	160	195	115	65	150	170	(125)	275	300
Jewellery	765	560	755	765	715	775	810	850	990	1180
Petroleum	160	130	140	65	20	15	15	20	55	50
Others	190	190	165	170	150	135	100	130	120	120
TOTALS	2850	2330	2430	2320	2180	2630	2830	2840	3290	3620

We define 'Investment: small' in the above table as the long-term holding of metal in the form of bars and coins weighing 10oz or less. 'Investment: large' in the form of 500g and 1kg bars in Japan was incorporated in the 'Other' applications sector of pre-1988 reviews.

With the exception of the autocatalyst sector, the demand estimates shown in this report are net figures, demand in each sector being total purchases by customers less any sales back to the market. Thus, the annual totals represent the amount of primary metal that is acquired by consumers in any particular year.

Gross autocatalyst demand is purchases of platinum by the auto industry for manufacture of autocatalyst. Autocatalyst recovery is platinum recovered from catalytic converters removed from scrapped automobiles.

By courtesy of Johnson Matthey.

Platinum and Gold: High, low and average monthly prices 1986-88

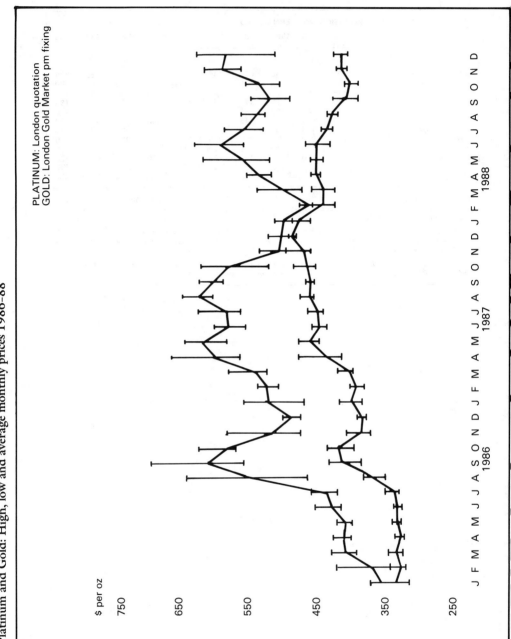

PLATINUM: London quotation
GOLD: London Gold Market pm fixing

$ per oz

750

650

550

450

350

250

J F M A M J J A S O N D J F M A M J J A S O N D J F M A M J J A S O N D
1986   1987   1988

Silver

Sarah Wilson
Assistant Editor, Futures and Options World

Silver is the most plentiful of the precious metals and, next to gold, it is the oldest investment commodity. The first producers of silver were probably Asia Minor and Syria, but the market did not really open out until the sixteenth and seventeenth centuries with the conquest of the New World. By 1700, Mexico was the world's largest silver producer and it now shares its top position with the Soviet Union. Boosted by the expansion of Australian and Canadian production at the beginning of this century, annual world production has more than doubled in the last 40 years, but western world output has increased at a slower rate than that of the Eastern Bloc.

Most people would rank the decorative qualities of silver at the top of a list of its uses, but although it is still popular with jewellers and craftworkers, its industrial and chemical uses are also on the rise. Silver is also an indispensable element in the field of electronics, photography and medicine.

Physical markets can be found in most major cities, but the western world's silver trade is dominated by the London silver market, the London Metal Exchange and Comex.

During the last 2 years, a marked lack of interest in the precious metals markets has kept silver prices stable in spite of a surplus of production. Lethargy among investors and speculators can be put down to a variety of factors. Economic developments in the United States and significantly general attempts of the industrialized world to contain inflation, have militated against interest in small bar (ingot) purchases. Unless western authorities concede defeat in the struggle against mounting prices, interest in this market is unlikely to be dramatic.

Negative sentiment has not been helped by the US Treasury's announcement that it plans to sell 7.5 million ounces of silver by the end of the fiscal year 1991. This will force the market to absorb some 2.5 million ounces, or 80 tonnes, from the US Treasury.

Political and social factors have, as always, affected consumption. *Perestroika* in the Soviet Union has boosted demand, and in spite of the volatile political situation in the aftermath of Tiananman Square, the continuing industrialization of China is opening out a new market. Similarly, Indian requirements for silver remain extremely strong as local people take advantage of increasing standards of living. However, the majority of silver investment, both in the form of coin and small bar, is still concentrated in the United States.

Since 1986, strong industrial growth has benefited suppliers in the fabrication, electrical and soldering sectors. The most promising areas for silver producers have been in jewellery and photography, the growth of which reflects an upsurge in western prosperity and an increase in time reserved for leisure.

Silver is one of the few markets in which net disinvestment has advantages, because of the supply excesses. This has been exacerbated in recent months by substantial silver deliveries to the Commodities Exchange (COMEX) in New York. COMEX inventories rose by more than 800 tonnes in the first half of 1989.

Although inflation persists behind the market, the base price of silver was still pivoting around an axis of $5.50/ounce in June 1989. In the current climate of strong industrial interest and a weakening dollar, prices could exceed $6/ounce, but further big increases seem unlikely.

Industrial bargain-hunting tends to prevent silver from steep falls in price, but it may be argued that the market is too dependent on the United States investor to sustain marked strength for any period of time. It therefore seems that silver prices may remain locked into a downtrend, with intermittent rallies.

Silver supply has tightened in 1989, but labour problems in the major producer Peru did not have the predicted impact. At full capacity, the Peruvian mining industry is responsible for approximately 17% of the western world's mined supply of silver and in 1988 25% of the country's mining output of all metals was lost due to strike action and deteriorating equipment. There was a brief repeat of the industrial action in the spring of 1989, but conditions in Peru seem settled for the moment. In fact, one might argue that any interruption in supplies from Peru may be a blessing in disguise, as it would simply slow the rise in surplus stocks.

While some new mines have opened in 1989, there have also been a number of closures, due to such factors as the depletion of ore reserves, low silver prices, high operating costs, or a shortage of skilled workers.

Taking these gains and losses into account, it is expected that mine supply will rise by some 895 tonnes in 1989, with much of the gain concentrated in the United States.

Silver: world mine production 1984–89 (thousand tonnes)

	1984	1985	1986	1987	1988	1989
						Jan-Mar
EUROPE						
Denmark	14.0	14.0	13.2	12.5	13.9	3.5
Finland	27.0	27.0	37.1	33.1	31.4	7.0
France	24.3	24.3	25.7	20.7	20.7	5.2
Germany, F.R.	38.1	38.1	27.5	30.9	30.9	7.7
Greece	57.0	57.0	53.7	51.9	51.9	13.0
Ireland	8.7	8.6	8.2	7.2	5.5	2.1
Italy	50.2	71.5	57.0	82.0	91.6	20.5
Spain	221.4	221.4	177.2	177.6	177.6	44.4
Sweden	180.2	189.8	235.0	230.6	193.2	44.4
United Kingdom	2.1	1.7	1.6	2.0	2.1	0.5
Yugoslavia	128.0	156.0	177.4	151.1	139.0	30.3
Other Europe	0.9	0.8	0.5	0.5	0.4	0.1
Total..	751.9	810.2	814.1	800.1	758.2	178.7
AFRICA						
Morocco	126.6	126.6	165.2	165.6	165.6	41.4
Namibia	105.5	105.6	117.0	82.0	118.0	29.5
South Africa	217.6	208.4	222.2	208.1	179.1	49.1
Zaire	38.0	38.0	40.0	34.0	34.0	8.5
Zambia	24.7	24.7	26.8	29.9	29.9	7.5
Zimbabwe	28.0	27.7	26.2	25.4	22.0	5.4
Other Africa '	6.9	6.0	7.2	7.2	7.2	1.8
Total..	547.3	537.0	604.6	552.2	555.8	143.2
ASIA						
Burma	17.9	17.9	13.8	26.1	26.1	6.5
India	24.9	25.4	35.3	36.2	40.7	10.2
Indonesia	34.9	34.9	40.0	47.6	47.6	11.9
Japan	323.6	339.5	351.3	281.2	251.5	41.1
Malaysia	14.6	14.6	14.1	15.5	15.5	3.9
Philippines	50.1	54.2	52.5	51.4	54.7	12.2
South Korea	69.6	69.6	80.4	71.0	83.9	13.6
Taiwan	11.3	11.4	12.6	11.6	13.2	3.3
Other Asia	37.0	37.0	40.9	40.8	40.8	10.2
Total..	583.9	604.5	640.9	581.4	574.0	112.9
AMERICA						
Canada	1 171.0	1 206.8	1 086.4	1 185.6	1 371.5	313.6
U.S.A.	1 382.2	1 224.1	1 064.4	1 237.6	1 661.1	399.7
Argentina	61.5	90.0	82.0	81.6	81.6	20.4
Bolivia	141.8	111.4	95.1	140.2	120.0	30.0
Brazil	66.8	66.5	57.6	60.6	60.6	15.2
Chile	490.4	517.6	500.1	497.2	486.2	121.4
Colombia	4.8	5.2	4.6	5.2	6.6	1.5
Dominican Republic	37.6	49.2	41.0	35.7	45.0	11.3
Honduras	80.7	80.7	50.0	50.0	50.0	12.5
Mexico	1 986.7	2 153.0	2 307.6	2 461.1	2 412.0	575.6
Nicaragua	1.5	2.0	1.0	0.8	0.8	0.2
Peru	1 662.7	1 769.8	1 925.8	2 054.5	1 551.6	455.6
Other America	1.0	1.0	1.0	1.3	1.3	0.3
Total..	7 088.7	7 277.3	7 216.6	7 811.4	7 848.3	1 957.3
OCEANIA						
Australia	972.3	1 085.9	1 009.0	1 107.0	1 115.0	270.0
Papua New Guinea	44.7	46.3	57.0	61.1	58.0	15.3
Other Oceania	0.6	0.4	0.5	0.5	0.5	0.1
Total..	1 017.6	1 132.6	1 066.5	1 168.6	1 173.5	285.4
TOTAL..	9 989.4	10 361.6	10 342.7	10 913.7	10 909.8	2 677.5
Monthly Average..	832.5	863.5	861.9			
OTHER COUNTRIES						
Bulgaria	26.0	26.0	26.0	26.0		
Czechoslovakia	32.0	32.0	33.0	34.0		
German D.R.	40.0	41.0	41.0	41.0		
Hungary	0.5	0.5	–	–		
Poland	744.0	831.0	829.0	831.0		
Romania	24.0	25.0	23.0	20.0		
U.S.S.R.	1 600.0	1 620.0	1 600.0	1 550.0		
China	80.0	100.0	120.0	150.0		
Mongolia	–	–	–	–		
North Korea	285.0	270.0	295.0	300.0		
Total..	2 831.5	2 945.5	2 967.0	2 952.0		
WORLD TOTAL	12 820.9	13 307.1	13 309.7	13 865.7		

This table shows the recoverable silver content of ores and concentrates produced.

By courtesy of the World Bureau of Metal Statistics.

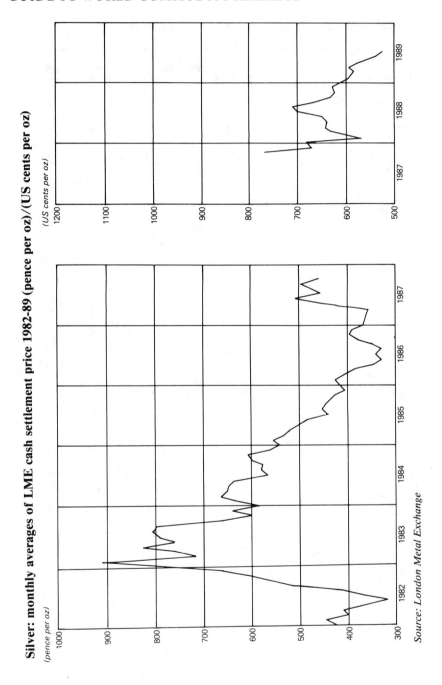

Silver: monthly averages of LME cash settlement price 1982-89 (pence per oz)/(US cents per oz)

(pence per oz)

(US cents per oz)

Source: London Metal Exchange

Tin

Paul Newman,
Independent tin consultant

The tin market is now moving into equilibrium after years of burdensome surplus culminating in the collapse of the International Tin Agreement (ITA) in 1985.

Between 1978 and 1984, the western world's output had exceeded demand by some 149,000 tonnes, forcing the ITA buffer stock manager (BSM) to mount an increasingly expensive support buying operation. But despite supplementary financing by banks and brokers, the BSM position ultimately became untenable as the value of tin continued to plummet.

Creditors owed some £900 million, less the value of tin held as collateral, have been pressing for restitution of funds owed to them through a series of court actions begun in March 1986 and likely to stretch into 1990. At the same time, some of the 22 sovereign Governments who were members of the ITA have come in for severe criticism, both from creditors and from the legal profession, for their unwillingness to honour the clearly documented debts owed by the buffer stock. Despite protracted efforts to secure an out-of-court settlement, legal action continues and what has reputedly been the biggest commercial default in history still awaits resolution.

A market crash followed the suspension of BSM operations. On the Kuala Lumpur market, prices fell from an average Malaysian $29.67 per kg in the first ten months of 1985, to just Malaysian $15.39 in 1986. The unofficial free market declined in this period to £3,876, compared with £9,475 per tonne quoted on the London Metal Exchange (LME) before dealings in tin were suspended.

Prices remained depressed throughout 1987 and 1988, but have strengthened during the course of 1989 as market forces began to assert their influence. Between 1985 and 1988, the cumulative deficit between western world mine output and primary tin metal consumption amounted to 133,500 tonnes. Over the same period, much of the buffer stock tin held as collateral by the ITC's creditors was sold and LME warehouse stocks slumped from 57,980 tonnes at end-1985 to a nominal 5 tonnes when the LME resumed trading in tin on 1 June 1989. LME stocks have since risen, but remain at relatively low levels.

The ultimate failure of the tin industry's efforts at market regulation through successive international agreements, conducted from mid-1956 to the market collapse in October 1985, has seen tin join the ranks of all other major non-ferrous metals as a hostage to the free interplay of market forces.

Tin production reached a peak of 204,600 tonnes in 1981, but slumped to under 140,000 tonnes in 1986 and 1987. Although the Kuala Lumpur-based Association of Tin Producing Countries (ATPC) imposed some restraint on production, enforcing cutbacks on exports from their members (Australia, Bolivia, Indonesia, Malaysia, Nigeria, Thailand and Zaire), the most effective rein on production was a protracted regimen of low prices, resulting in widespread mine closures.

However, Brazil, not a full member of the ATPC, expanded its output notably, to assume in 1988, the position of world's largest producer, while China, also only an observer member of the ATPC, expanded its trade in tin, particularly during 1987 and 1988. Overall, western world tin supply has been in growing deficit since the market collapse and, allied to the rapid diminution in commercial stocks, has fuelled fears of a possible price explosion.

The price collapse which severely curtailed production in the years 1986–1988 had a reverse effect on consumption, with tin's greater price competitiveness encouraging higher demand, particularly from the tinplate industry, where it began to reclaim market share lost to aluminium during the years of relatively high tin prices. Western world tin demand, which had been in decline for much of the 1980s, picked up from 166,500 tonnes in 1985 to a 12-year high of 187,400 tonnes in 1988, with all the major industrial tin consumers – USA, Japan and Federal Germany – showing notably higher consumption.

The depletion of tin stocks to around normal commercial levels, buoyant demand and a gradual expansion in mine output, albeit from a very low base, suggests that the tin market has now recovered from the price collapse, following the suspension of buffer stock operations.

The return of a free market in tin is likely to see much greater sensitivity to variations in the supply/demand balance with sharper day-to-day price movements. But with the collapse of the industry's efforts to moderate price movements through the instrument of a commodity pact, any form of market intervention is unlikely to occur for many years and market forces will be the sole determinant of the metal's price prospects.

World production of tin-in-concentrates 1980–88 (tonnes)

	1980	1981	1982	1983	1984	1985	1986	1987	1988
AFRICA									
Cameroon	24	24	24	24	24	24	–	–	–
Namibia	1000	800	800	800	900	900	710	700	700
Niger	64	55	41	50	85	109	80	80	80
Nigeria	2664	2416	1822	1560	1326	798	56	600	500
Rwanda	1490	1287	1185	1099	1124	824	29	–	–
South Africa	2913	2811	3035	2668	2301	2153	2055	1412	1400
Uganda	67	30	30	30	30	30	–	–	–
Zaire	2274	2452	2320	2163	2928	3100	1889	1900	2000
Zambia	10	–	7	16	3	4	21	24	–
Zimbabwe	926	1150	1194	1233	1219	1191	1075	997	1000
AMERICA									
Argentina	351	413	342	291	274	454	260	200	200
Bolivia	27271	29830	26773	25278	19911	16136	10479	8128	9900
Brazil	6930	8297	8218	13275	19957	26514	26405	28523	44000
Canada	243	239	135	140	209	119	2485	3466	3500
Mexico	60	28	27	50	416	380	585	369	400
Peru	1077	1519	1700	2368	2192	3807	4817	5202	5000
USA	100	100	100	100	100	100	100	100	100
ASIA									
Burma	1237	1374	1598	1573	1943	1679	1429	1200	1000
India	–	–	–	–	–	–	40	40	50
Indonesia	32527	35268	33800	26554	23223	21758	24634	26218	30500
Japan	549	562	529	599	485	510	500	86	–
Korea	9	6	–	–	–	21	–	–	–
Laos	600	600	600	600	600	600	400	400	400
Malaysia	61404	59938	52342	41367	41307	36886	29134	30388	28866
Thailand	33685	31474	26207	19942	21607	16593	16792	14765	14500
Unspecified origin	7000	6000	9850	16550	11400	11000	2500	–	–
EUROPE									
Czechoslovakia	200	200	200	200	200	200	200	500	500
EEC	3761	4794	5126	4867	5785	5911	4878	4219	4090
France	–	4	22	8	–	–	–	–	–
Portugal	296	356	411	347	321	242	199	65	40
Spain	437	564	518	444	417	465	334	70	50
United Kingdom	3028	3870	4175	4068	5047	5204	4345	4084	4000
Australia	11588	12925	12615	9578	7922	6374	8515	7651	7000
WORLD*	200000	204600	190600	173000	167500	158200	140600	137600	153000

* World totals exclude Albania, China, E Germany, Mongolia, USSR and Vietnam.

Source: International Tin Council.

World production of primary tin metal 1980-88 (tonnes)

	1980	1981	1982	1983	1984	1985	1986	1987	1988
AFRICA									
Nigeria	2684	2489	1808	1244	1334	1085	91	560	500
Rwanda	–	–	908	1100	1040	948	–	–	–
South Africa	2207	2174	2197	2200	2200	2056	1816	1608	1520
Zaire	320	450	353	201	170	85	–	–	–
Zimbabwe	917	1138	1182	1221	1207	1098	1128	999	1000
AMERICA									
Argentina	200	200	86	124	162	230	230	240	240
Bolivia	17533	19937	18980	14164	15842	12859	7673	2610	4900
Brazil	8796	7789	9298	12950	18877	24703	25147	29046	41400
Mexico	1382	866	944	1216	1531	1533	1483	1723	1700
USA	3000	2087	3500	2500	4000	3000	3213	4000	4000
ASIA									
Burma	–	–	490	500	700	510	1000	1000	1000
Indonesia	30465	32519	29755	28390	22467	20418	22080	24200	28200
Japan	1319	1313	1296	1260	1354	1391	1281	896	900
Korea	372	174	–	391	1191	1600	1266	1834	1800
Malaysia	71318	70326	62836	53338	46911	45500	43788	44363	46500
Singapore	4000	4000	4000	1800	3500	4000	500	1000	1500
Thailand	34689	32636	25479	18467	19729	17996	19672	15438	14400
EUROPE									
EEC									
Belgium	2822	65	–	–	–	–	–	–	–
Germany, FR	638	562	–	–	–	–	–	–	–
Netherlands	1148	3500	2757	5398	6188	5308	5114	3824	3463
Portugal	445	399	421	419	426	483	184	48	20
Spain	3750	3070	2750	2812	3426	3291	1725	1431	1400
United Kingdom	5829	6863	8164	6467	7105	7548	9227	12135	8300
Australia	4819	4286	3105	2878	2687	2683	1399	563	434
WORLD*	198600	196800	180300	159000	162000	158300	148000	147600	166500

* World totals exclude Albania, China, E Germany, Mongolia, USSR and Vietnam.

Source: International Tin Council.

World consumption of primary tin metal 1980-88 (tonnes)

	1980	1981	1982	1983	1984	1985	1986	1987	1988
AFRICA									
Egypt	400	400	400	400	400	400	400	400	400
Morocco	240	240	240	240	100	160	160	160	160
Nigeria	80	80	80	80	75	300	200	200	200
South Africa	2101	2018	1870	1563	1745	1900	2000	2000	2000
Zaire	120	84	65	3	6	6	7	8	8
Other	800	800	800	800	800	800	800	800	800
AMERICA									
Argentina	1200	900	1256	1179	1207	835	1593	1600	1600
Bolivia	1000	1000	1500	2400	1800	1800	1100	300	1000
Brazil	5014	3351	5061	4010	4270	4655	6019	7808	7960
Canada	4517	3766	3528	3381	4086	3781	3600	3800	3840
Chile	720	720	720	720	720	720	1000	1000	1200
Mexico	1800	1800	1400	1600	1600	1000	1200	1200	1200
USA	44342	40229	33019	34301	37819	37185	32448	35597	42000
Venezuela	500	500	500	300	600	1000	800	800	800
Other	1200	1300	1300	1200	1200	1200	1200	1200	1200
ASIA									
Hong Kong	1200	800	400	600	1100	1500	1800	2000	2000
India	2282	2787	2076	2218	2400	2200	2800	2608	2940
Indonesia	335	379	556	550	850	1012	1114	882	900
Iran	500	500	500	500	500	500	500	500	500
Israel	140	140	140	100	100	100	100	100	100
Japan	30917	30529	28705	30394	33278	31598	31521	32060	33000
Korea	1761	2207	2093	2628	3632	2600	4335	4000	4200
Malaysia	433	320	434	777	1520	1557	1944	1993	2420
Pakistan	100	100	100	100	70	70	70	70	100
Philippines	1100	1100	1000	700	700	400	500	500	400
Singapore	500	500	500	500	500	500	500	500	500
Syria	60	60	60	60	100	100	100	100	100
Taiwan	1300	1400	700	1200	1700	1200	1500	1500	1800
Thailand	734	689	598	530	631	518	1481	1860	1964
Turkey	500	700	700	1000	900	900	1100	1300	1200
Other	100	100	100	100	100	500	100	100	100
EUROPE									
Austria	537	393	434	388	453	493	506	486	460
Bulgaria	900	1000	800	800	1000	1000	1000	1000	1000
Czechoslovakia	4300	3900	3500	3200	3000	3100	3200	3200	3200
EEC	49196	46403	44736	43017	45260	42883	45249	45646	49092
Belgium/Lux	2601	2195	1889	1815	1697	920	1141	1220	1280
Denmark	123	102	70	20	6	46	45	45	50
France	10052	9024	8187	7564	7799	6900	7461	7389	7900
Germany, FR	14271	13260	13163	13792	15641	15268	16484	16947	19142
Greece	487	439	400	400	400	400	600	600	400
Ireland	3	16	6	11	37	46	59	95	100
Italy	5800	4300	4200	4500	4500	5250	5850	5050	5800
Netherlands	4764	5123	5142	4672	4842	4253	4009	4600	4720
Portugal	400	400	800	600	600	700	900	900	800
Spain	4250	4400	3900	3700	3900	3100	2600	2600	2700
United Kingdom	6445	7144	6970	5943	5838	6000	6100	6200	6200
Finland	190	140	130	108	110	101	203	109	100
Hungary	1607	1647	1585	1609	1420	1281	1353	1276	1300
Norway	422	455	379	392	396	425	398	392	310
Poland	3309	2216	4575	4351	3613	3029	3624	2485	3000
Romania	3000	2800	2500	2400	2000	2000	2000	1500	1500
Sweden	293	227	94	242	300	440	530	320	430
Switzerland	840	782	647	693	598	780	1208	912	900
Yugoslavia	1000	900	1200	1100	1100	1400	1500	1500	1400
Other	16	16	16	16	16	16	16	16	20
OCEANIA									
Australia	3100	3200	2700	2500	2500	2600	2460	2380	2480
New Zealand	250	180	170	170	170	100	100	100	100
Other	4	4	4	4	4	4	4	4	5
TOTAL*	175000	163800	153800	155100	166600	160700	165500	171800	180100

* World totals exclude Albania, China, E Germany, Mongolia, USSR and Vietnam.

Source: International Tin Council.

Trading on the London Metal Exchange, suspended on 24 October 1985, was resumed on 1 June 1989. LME quotations are for Standard Tin (99.75%). Price quotations from December 1982 to June 1989 are Reuters free market price for High Grade Tin (99.85%) and, from July 1989, "Metal Bulletin" Euro free market High Grade Tin. All prices are quoted in £ per tonne.

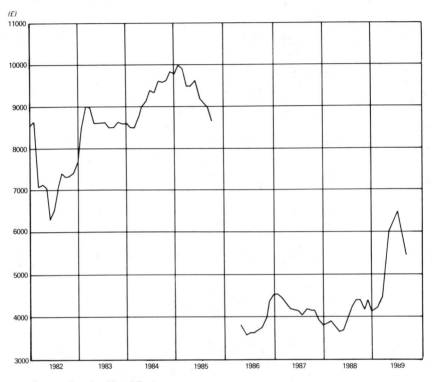

Source: London Metal Exchange.

Non Communist: World production of tin-in-concentrates

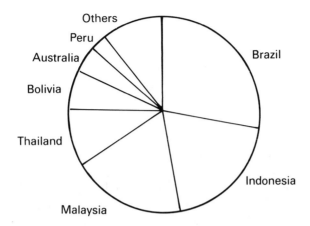

NCW consumption of tin metal

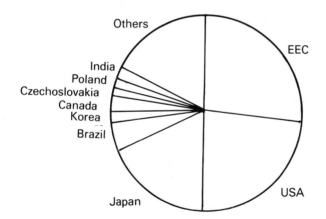

Zinc

Sarah Wilson,
Assistant Editor, Futures and Options World

The commercial production of zinc started in the fourteenth century, comparatively late considering that copper smelting began around 5000BC. India was probably the first country to produce the metal, and production techniques were developed in both India and China before being imported by the West. However, in 1746, William Champion developed an English operation at Bristol and shortly afterwards plants began to spring up all over Europe, demonstrating different solutions to the basic problem of zinc oxide reduction.

Approximately 20% of the total zinc produced is used in brass production, although in the United States, die-casting alloys of zinc/aluminium are replacing brass. Zinc is also widely used in protective coatings on sheet and strip steel, tubes and wire, and in dry battery production.

Between the beginning of 1988 and 1989, the price of zinc doubled. A drop of 25% between March and June 1989 could be put down to the strength of the dollar, and in view of restricted supplies, it is not likely to be maintained. As demand for zinc is still good, it is expected that prices will consolidate around current levels before moving upwards again.

Recent record prices have caused consumers to look for alternative metals and there have been tales of orders being lost to aluminium and magnesium on economic grounds. But on the whole, however, demand is buoyant, maintained largely by the consumption of galvanized steel, which accounts for about 45% of consumption. The forecasted downturn in general auto and housing demand will probably be offset by the use of electro-galvanized sheet in the auto industry. Die-casting, which accounts for 15% of zinc consumption, also remains strong.

Consumption appears to be expanding more quickly in newly-industrialized countries, than in those which are fully industrialized, but the four largest consumers are still West Germany, France, the United States and Japan. Demand in China is underpinned by domestic growth and shows little sign of slackening.

Supply, however, is failing to match demand and is likely to remain constrained until the mining industry manages to rebuild its ore reserve base and mining and smelting capacities. The forecast deficit for 1989 is 100,000 tonnes, which compares with a similar surplus in 1988.

Commentators are optimistic that supply will be boosted by the resolution of industrial unrest in Peruvian mines, which has tended to interrupt zinc and lead supplies faster than those of copper and silver. Extensive damage was caused to the Huarauccacca mine, near the town of Cerro de Pasco in Peru, in February 1989 when guerrillas carried out a bomb attack.

Production in many countries is already close to the limits of its capacity, but the past two years have witnessed a proliferation of new plants and improvements to old ones. The closure of Pine Point in Canada was offset by the addition of 15,000 tonnes of capacity to Canada's Trail plant this year, and by expansions at Winston Lake, Isle Dieu and Caribou. In August 1989, Australia's East West Minerals announced that it intended to step up efficiency at the Caribou mine by introducing better open slope mining techniques. Production in the United States is also expected to increase and supplies from the Red Dog plant in Alaska will begin to arrive later this year. One of the few places with a surplus is likely to be Brazil.

High prices are being supported by low zinc stocks at the London Metal Exchange (LME). While it is anticipated that production will rise in 1989, thereby allowing metal markets to retain some form of surplus and replenish inventories, supplies are extremely tight at the moment and the mildest changes in the zinc inventory still have a disproportionate effect on prices. The latest news of zinc inventories does in fact show a somewhat surprising increase, with LME stocks rising by over 5000 tonnes, and the producer inventories, in January, rising by a similar amount.

The introduction of a special high grade (SHG) zinc contract on the LME has altered trading practices and is eventually likely to end the European Producer Price (EPP). The new contract has been well received and is beginning to exert pressure on zinc stocks.

The history of zinc production is a complex one, with continually shifting trends. With a growing world energy shortage and an awareness of the need to avoid environmental pollution, a new set of problems will soon have to be tackled.

Zinc: world mine production 1984-89 (thousand tonnes)

	1984	1985	1986	1987	1988	1989
						Jan-Mar
EUROPE						
Austria	20.9	21.7	16.3	15.7	17.1	5.3
Denmark	71.3	70.4	62.1	65.9	77.2	17.1
Finland	60.2	60.6	60.3	55.1	63.9	16.3
France	36.4	40.6	39.6	31.3	31.1	6.7
Germany, F.R.	113.1	117.6	103.7	98.9	75.6	20.6
Greece	22.6	21.1	22.5	20.7	21.2	5.2
Ireland	205.9	191.6	181.7	177.0	173.2	47.8
Italy	42.3	45.4	26.3	33.2	37.9	9.9
Norway	28.7	27.8	27.5	22.2	17.8	3.4
Spain	228.1	226.8	232.6	266.0	277.0	61.1
Sweden	210.0	216.4	219.3	218.6	186.8	52.5
United Kingdom	7.2	5.0	5.6	6.5	5.4	1.5
Yugoslavia	85.8	89.3	94.6	74.0	71.2	17.8
Total..	1 132.5	1 134.3	1 092.1	1 085.1	1 055.4	265.2
AFRICA						
Algeria	14.6	13.5	14.0	13.0	12.0	3.0
Congo	–	2.0	2.0	–	–	–
Morocco	11.6	14.7	12.2	10.7	10.8	2.7
Namibia	30.6	31.2	35.4	40.1	32.4	8.1
South Africa	103.0	96.9	101.9	112.7	89.6	24.7
Tunisia	6.7	5.6	5.0	5.9	9.0	1.5
Zaire	68.4	67.9	81.3	87.5	87.6	21.9
Zambia	41.3	50.6	50.9	55.9	47.3	11.7
Total..	276.2	282.4	302.7	325.8	288.7	73.6
ASIA						
Burma	3.5	4.9	4.0	1.7	0.8	0.2
Cyprus	–	–	–	–	–	–
India	43.7	53.0	45.0	53.3	59.1	16.7
Iran	47.1	50.0	36.0	40.0	42.0	10.5
Japan	252.7	253.0	222.2	165.8	147.2	34.8
Philippines	2.2	1.9	1.6	1.1	1.4	0.4
South Korea	53.1	41.7	33.8	24.4	21.8	6.1
Thailand	39.0	48.9	70.0	73.6	80.7	20.2
Turkey	50.4	37.4	40.6	42.2	41.0	10.3
Total..	491.7	490.8	453.2	402.1	394.0	99.2
AMERICA						
Canada	1 207.1	1 172.2	1 262.1	1 504.4	1 347.4	313.6
U.S.A.	277.0	251.9	216.0	232.9	264.4	71.0
Argentina	34.9	35.7	39.5	35.6	36.3	9.1
Bolivia	37.8	38.1	33.3	39.3	32.9	8.1
Brazil	79.3	85.0	93.3	93.0	103.0	25.8
Colombia	–	–	–	0.5	0.4	0.1
Chile	19.2	22.3	10.5	19.5	19.2	4.8
Guatemala	–	–	–	–	–	–
Honduras	41.5	44.0	25.4	15.4	23.5	5.9
Mexico	303.6	291.9	278.1	271.5	261.1	63.3
Nicaragua	–	–	–	–	–	–
Peru	568.3	582.6	597.6	612.5	485.4	140.5
Other America	0.5	–	–	–	–	–
Total..	2 569.2	2 523.7	2 555.8	2 824.6	2 573.6	642.2
OCEANIA						
Australia	658.7	734.0	712.0	778.4	759.2	175.9
TOTAL..	**5 128.3**	**5 165.2**	**5 115.8**	**5 416.0**	**5 070.9**	**1 256.1**
Monthly Average..	*427.3*	*430.4*	*426.3*	*451.3*	*422.6*	*418.7*
OTHER COUNTRIES						
Bulgaria	65.0	68.0	70.0	68.0	65.0	
Czechoslovakia	7.2	7.2	6.7	6.9	7.0	
Hungary	1.9	2.0	–	–	–	
Poland	190.7	190.9	183.9	185.8	183.4	
Romania	39.0	40.0	39.0	37.0	37.0	
U.S.S.R.	980.0	1 000.0	970.0	950.0	960.0	
China	300.0	350.0	395.7	458.2	527.3	
North Korea	150.0	185.0	225.0	220.0	220.0	
Vietnam	10.0	10.0	10.0	10.0	10.0	
Total..	1 743.8	1 853.1	1 900.3	1 935.9	2 009.7	
WORLD TOTAL	**6 872.1**	**7 018.3**	**7 016.1**	**7 351.9**	**7 080.6**	

This table shows the content by analysis of zinc ores and concentrates plus the zinc content of mixed ores.

By courtesy of the World Bureau of Metal Statistics.

Zinc: world slab production 1984–89 (thousand tonnes)

	1984	1985	1986	1987	1988	1989
						Jan-Mar
EUROPE						
Austria	23.9	25.2	24.0	24.2	25.1	5.5
Belgium	270.7	271.4	268.6	284.5	298.1	72.5
Finland	158.8	160.6	155.4	151.0	156.1	32.7
France	258.8	247.2	257.4	249.3	274.1	60.6
Germany, F.R.	356.3	366.9	370.9	377.5	352.4	84.9
Italy	166.8	210.1	230.4	247.0	242.1	55.5
Netherlands	209.7	202.8	196.9	205.4	210.0	52.9
Norway	94.2	92.7	90.6	116.5	121.2	29.1
Portugal	6.4	5.9	5.7	5.8	5.5	1.4
Spain	207.4	213.3	199.3	213.6	245.4	61.4
United Kingdom	85.6	74.3	85.9	81.4	76.0	23.4
Yugoslavia	92.6	83.4	89.3	130.4	128.9	30.6
Total..	1 931.2	1 953.8	1 974.4	2 086.6	2 134.9	510.5
AFRICA						
Algeria	35.0	35.7	29.7	19.0	19.0	4.8
South Africa	90.3	93.7	80.8	96.1	84.4	20.4
Zaire	66.1	66.1	61.4	53.6	64.0	15.0
Zambia	29.2	22.8	22.0	21.0	20.2	3.2
Total..	220.6	218.3	193.9	189.7	187.6	43.4
ASIA						
India	54.3	70.9	73.8	68.9	68.9	18.9
Japan	754.4	739.6	708.0	665.6	678.2	154.9
South Korea	108.5	111.7	127.4	186.3	225.0	56.4
Thailand	4.0	60.1	58.6	66.9	68.3	17.1
Turkey	19.9	22.2	15.4	20.2	22.4	5.6
Total..	941.1	1 004.5	983.2	1 007.9	1 062.8	252.9
AMERICA						
Canada	683.2	692.4	571.0	609.9	703.9	171.0
U.S.A.	331.2	333.8	316.3	343.0	364.9	90.7
Argentina	27.7	30.4	29.2	31.9	32.7	9.0
Brazil	106.9	116.1	129.7	138.7	139.7	34.7
Colombia	–	–	–	–	–	–
Mexico	185.3	184.4	176.3	186.4	191.0	43.7
Peru	148.9	163.1	155.9	143.6	123.1	37.5
Total..	1 483.2	1 520.2	1 378.4	1 453.5	1 555.3	386.6
OCEANIA						
Australia	306.4	288.4	307.6	310.2	306.2	72.7
TOTAL..	4 882.5	4 985.2	4 837.5	5 047.9	5 246.8	1 266.1
Monthly Average..	*406.9*	*415.4*	*403.1*	*420.6*	*437.2*	*422.0*
OTHER COUNTRIES						
Bulgaria	93.0	90.0	89.0	95.0	105.0	
German D.R.	17.0	17.0	17.0	18.0	21.0	
Hungary	–	–	–	–	–	
Poland	176.1	180.0	179.2	176.5	176.6	
Romania	47.8	45.0	53.0	51.0	50.0	
U.S.S.R.	1 050.0	1 050.0	1 065.0	1 045.0	1 035.0	
China	240.0	280.0	336.2	383.1	425.4	
North Korea	130.0	180.0	210.0	225.0	225.0	
Vietnam	10.0	10.0	10.0	10.0	10.0	
Total..	1 763.9	1 852.0	1 959.4	2 003.6	2 048.0	
WORLD TOTAL	6 646.4	6 837.2	6 796.9	7 051.5	7 294.8	

This table is based on the production of slab zinc by smelters and refineries, including production on toll in the reporting country, regardless of the type of source material, i.e. whether ores, concentrates, residues, slag or scrap. Remelted zinc and zinc dust are excluded.

By courtesy of the World Bureau of Metal Statistics.

Zinc: world slab consumption 1984-89 (thousand tonnes)

	1984	1985	1986	1987	1988	1989
						Jan-Mar
EUROPE						
Austria	30.0	31.9	33.0	33.0	33.9	8.4
Belgium	171.0	169.1	172.1	163.4	174.8	44.1
Denmark	9.6	12.2	11.8	9.9	11.5	2.4
Finland	24.0	26.0	26.5	27.3	30.4	7.5
France	281.9	246.9	260.5	252.7	290.1	57.5
Germany, F.R.	424.9	408.8	433.6	452.1	445.6	105.0
Greece	13.2	15.2	15.0	13.8	15.0	3.9
Ireland	1.0	1.1	1.2	1.2	1.9	0.6
Italy	210.0	218.0	232.0	245.0	250.0	60.0
Netherlands	54.4	51.1	54.0	51.3	59.0	14.8
Norway	20.0	20.0	19.0	19.3	26.6	4.8
Portugal	10.8	8.3	9.6	12.0	10.4	2.6
Spain	99.6	100.3	104.0	99.4	103.5	25.9
Sweden	36.0	34.5	32.0	35.0	39.1	8.4
Switzerland	18.0	26.2	30.2	23.4	18.0	4.3
United Kingdom	182.2	189.3	181.9	188.1	192.5	50.5
Yugoslavia	90.0	106·9	90.0	94.9	106.3	26.6
Other Europe	–	0.2	10.2	10.8	10.8	2.7
Total..	1 676.6	1 666.0	1 716.6	1 732.6	1 819.4	430.0
AFRICA						
Nigeria	12.0	8.0	6.0	6.7	6.7	1.8
S. Africa & Namibia	85.2	84.4	83.1	92.4	87.5	23.1
Other Africa	27.6	38.3	46.8	46.8	46.8	11.7
Total..	124.8	130.7	135.9	145.9	141.0	36.6
ASIA						
Hong Kong	30.0	21.5	30.3	22.4	24.9	6.2
India	112.8	130.0	135.0	130.5	142.0	35.4
Indonesia	68.4	50.6	48.4	48.0	48.0	12.0
Japan	774.6	780.1	752.9	728.7	774.2	190.9
Philippines	24.0	13.0	18.9	20.5	27.4	6.9
Singapore	12.0	6.4	8.2	7.0	7.0	1.8
South Korea	123.0	125.0	152.2	178.5	173.0	27.6
Taiwan	34.8	49.4	69.7	74.6	74.4	18.6
Thailand	45.0	42.0	47.0	48.9	46.9	13.2
Turkey	20.4	45.9	53.0	47.6	59.6	14.9
Other Asia	50.4	44.8	56.0	56.4	56.4	14.1
Total..	1 295.4	1 308.7	1 371.6	1 363.1	1 433.8	341.6
AMERICA						
Canada	145.8	156.5	153.6	167.3	156.2	42.0
U.S.A.	980.2	961.4	998.6	1 052.2	1 110.3	279.6
Argentina	33.7	28.4	36.0	37.6	34.6	8.7
Brazil	107.8	145.4	145.6	197.5	143.1	35.8
Chile	3.6	6.3	6.0	9.1	9.1	2.4
Colombia	10.8	18.5	18.0	18.0	18.0	4.5
Mexico	100.7	106.3	91.9	109.7	116.2	29.1
Peru	15.6	41.2	50.8	60.1	64.2	16.1
Venezuela	9.6	15.4	11.8	18.6	20.9	5.1
Other America	16.8	12.9	13.0	12.0	12.0	3.0
Total..	1 424.6	1 492.3	1 525.3	1 682.1	1 684.6	426.3
OCEANIA						
Australia	77.0	86.6	86.2	82.0	77.6	24.0
New Zealand	18.0	22.0	17.9	12.1	18.0	4.5
Other Oceania	–	0.1	–	–	–	–
Total..	95.0	108.7	104.1	94.1	95.6	28.5
TOTAL..	**4 616.4**	**4 706.4**	**4 853.5**	**5 017.8**	**5 174.4**	**1 263.0**
Monthly Average..	*384.7*	*392.2*	*404.5*	*418.2*	*431.2*	*418.1*
OTHER COUNTRIES						
Bulgaria	70.0	70.0	68.0	68.0	73.0	
Czechoslovakia	59.0	60.0	61.3	57.0	58.0	
German D.R.	72.0	70.0	70.0	71.0	66.0	
Hungary	25.7	26.0	27.3	26.8	25.8	
Poland	149.4	152.8	157.0	158.4	152.3[1]	
Romania	47.0	45.0	43.0	53.0	52.0	
U.S.S.R.	1 050.0	1 000.0	990.0	1 030.0	1 080.0	
China	330.0	350.0	382.0	397.0	385.0	
North Korea	24.0	25.0	35.0	30.0	32.0	
Cuba	2.0	1.8	1.8	2.0	2.0	
Other	8.0	10.0	10.0	13.0	14.0	
Total..	1 837.1	1 810.6	1 845.4	1 906.2	1 940.1	
WORLD TOTAL	**6 453.5**	**6 517.0**	**6 698.9**	**6 924.0**	**7 114.5**	

This table shows consumption of slab zinc. Remelted zinc and zinc dust are excluded.

Notes   1. January to October

By courtesy of the World Bureau of Metal Statistics.

Zinc: world trade in slab zinc 1983-88 (thousand tonnes)

	1983	1984	1985	1986	1987	1988
						Jan-Dec
EXPORTS						
Austria	4.9	4.5	4.4	4.0	4.7	5.3
Belgium [1]	156.4	167.7	157.1	137.0	159.5	154.7
Denmark	0.2	–	–	0.1	0.3	0.1
Finland	121.0	122.8	127.1	110.9	108.2	122.7
France	50.7	93.0	68.7	59.7	70.5	66.2
Germany, F.R.	117.8	102.2	108.6	89.9	84.2	108.7
Ireland	0.2	0.2	0.1	0.1	0.1	– [4]
Italy	31.7	42.5	43.8	46.0	57.9	50.8
Netherlands	157.1	160.4	160.0	164.2	177.0	179.9
Norway	71.8	74.9	71.8	67.1	98.9	94.9
Poland	28.0	28.1	27.3	22.3	18.0	17.0 [6]
Spain [2]	96.7	105.9	127.2	94.2	105.5	146.2
United Kingdom	20.3	8.1	8.1	11.4	4.2	7.1
Yugoslavia	25.0	24.0	14.0	32.9	51.0	22.0
South Africa	1.5	0.8	7.4	1.7	0.1	..
Zaire	67.4	45.5	59.0	71.8	51.6	61.3 [4]
Zambia	36.9	31.9	21.1	21.0	19.6	19.1
Hong Kong	0.6	0.9	0.6	31.2	68.4	22.1
Japan	49.2	45.2	33.4	23.4	51.9	21.1
South Korea	–	–	0.5	1.7	37.8	69.7
Thailand	–	–	17.1	27.8	20.3	..
Canada	500.6	529.7	555.6	427.2	441.2	539.7
U.S.A.	0.6	0.8	4.0	1.9	1.5	0.5
Argentina	0.4		2.0	–	–	..
Mexico	88.1	84.3	78.0	73.9	71.3	80.5
Peru	141.5	102.0	107.0	91.3	71.8	38.8
Australia	232.7	221.0	214.5	217.4	243.1	207.0
China	2.1	1.5	2.4	56.8	95.3	13.8
Total	**2 003.4**	**1 997.9**	**2 020.8**	**1 886.9**	**2 113.9**	**2 049.2**
IMPORTS						
Austria	6.1	9.6	8.7	11.4	10.3	10.2
Belgium [1]	51.2	45.9	47.1	45.0	38.4	35.3
Denmark	8.7	10.6	12.2	11.9	10.2	12.0
Finland	–	0.1	0.1	0.1	–	..
France	55.3	64.9	61.5	64.1	70.4	88.3
Germany, F.R.	144.0	160.5	151.8	159.4	156.4	180.2
Greece [3]	12.8	11.7	17.3	16.8	15.0	2.7
Ireland [3]	1.9	1.4	1.3	1.4	1.6	1.2 [4]
Italy	84.2	90.9	63.3	54.5	63.7	58.7
Netherlands	13.9	15.8	14.0	16.9	18.7	36.1
Norway	0.2	0.4	0.4	0.1	0.3	0.3
Portugal	5.1	5.5	8.0	3.9	5.0	0.5
Spain	4.8	0.2	0.9	4.5	3.7	4.5
Sweden	32.7	35.4	32.2	32.8	36.1	39.7
Switzerland	20.3	21.4	26.4	30.2	23.4	18.3
United Kingdom	115.2	116.3	130.7	101.7	114.3	133.0
Yugoslavia	6.3	22.9	22.9	21.2	4.0	..
South Africa	2.9	2.2	–	3.2	2.3	..
Hong Kong [3]	8.3	7.5	10.4	70.3	95.7	46.1
India	28.2	57.3	68.9	48.5	63.3	32.8 [6]
Indonesia	68.9	47.8	50.6	48.4	47.7	..
Japan	41.2	56.6	64.5	92.2	105.0	112.8
Philippines	27.0	17.8	12.6	18.8	20.5	..
Singapore	15.9	12.3	9.4	11.8	26.5	45.2
South Korea	4.9	18.1	11.2	20.9	35.0	19.9
Taiwan	47.8	39.8	39.4	56.4	64.5	63.7
Thailand	37.9	38.1	13.3	2.8	4.5	..
Turkey	7.1	11.6	23.7	24.1	25.0	..
Canada	9.9	6.7	1.7	7.3	11.0	2.3
U.S.A.	617.6	639.1	609.8	667.1	712.5	740.8
Argentina	11.7	2.1	0.2	2.6	4.9	..
Brazil	3.6	5.3	28.6	22.2	49.0	..
Chile	4.0	8.8	6.3	6.9	8.3	..
Venezuela	9.9	15.9	15.4	11.8	20.6	..
China	228.7	230.2	268.6	116.9	68.2	62.0
Total	**1 738.2**	**1 830.7**	**1 833.4**	**1 808.1**	**1 936.0**	**1 746.6**

This table shows principal imports and exports of slab zinc.

Notes 1. Includes remelted zinc. 2. Includes zinc scrap. 3. Includes alloy. 4. January to September 5. January to August 6. January to November

By courtesy of the World Bureau of Metal Statistics.

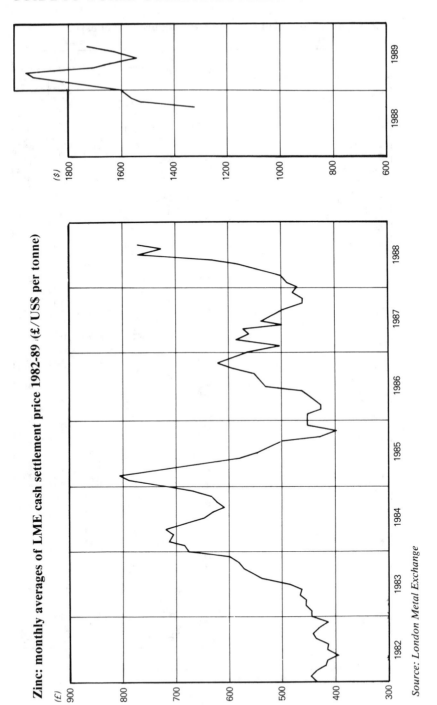

Zinc: monthly averages of LME cash settlement price 1982-89 (£/US$ per tonne)

Source: London Metal Exchange

The Commodities

Softs

Cocoa

John Buckley

Depression in the cocoa producing industry is accelerating the changing pattern of supply distribution as the 1980s draw to a close. World prices have recently hit 13½-year lows of £700 per tonne, reflecting five consecutive years of surplus, the failure of the International Cocoa Agreement (ICCA) to stabilize the market and the way that producer attempts to withhold supplies have backfired.

In the ensuing meltdown, the traditional suppliers – Brazil and the West African nations – have been faced with their worst ever cost/income squeeze. While it now seems only a matter of time before their production is affected by falling prices, there is no shortage of competition to take up their market shares. In fact, lower-costed countries like Malaysia are expanding output to record levels.

The irony underlying this turmoil is that the demand for cocoa is also growing – at a rapid 4% plus per annum – and if output could be contained just a little, producers might find many of their problems solved.

The ICCA has ceased to exert any significant stabilization effect on cocoa prices since 1986 when the Ivory Coast, the leading producer, decided to withdraw its support, but it has taken three years for participants to accept its demise as a market force. During this time, the pact has staggered from one crisis to another. Its buffer support stock has been filled to the brim without helping prices and producer members – convinced that their incomes were being manipulated by the futures markets – have shown no remorse about running up multi-million dollar arrears in their levies to support the pact. Some consuming countries have meanwhile paid lip service to the principle of a pact to safeguard future supply, while in practice applying relentless pressure to cut ICCA support prices to constantly falling 'market' levels.

All this bad feeling came to a head last year when the Ivory Coast decided to take matters into its own hands and marketed over half its crop direct through a leading French trader, *Sucres et Denrees*. This culmination of nearly two years of unilateral attempts to withhold sales and force prices up to what the Ivorians believed was a truer value, at around £1150 per tonne, was probably the straw that broke the ICCA's back.

Earlier 'withholding' schemes had been a constant cause of turbulence in cocoa futures. When they appeared to be working, the market ran up from around £900 to over £1040 per tonne in the summer of 1988. Futures turnover registered a giant blip in July 1988 (London went up 70%) as the trade sought cover and the speculators piled in, but the bubble burst in September after ICCA talks floundered yet again. The market has been on the way down ever since, apart from one or two brief remissions, for example, when the Ivorians tried to re-jig their sales by making similar bilateral deals with United States trader Phibro in the spring of 1989.

The plight of traditional cocoa producers is demonstrated by the Ivory Coast which, at the start of the decade, produced less than half the cocoa it expects for current crop. Since then, the Ivorians have come to lean on cocoa exports to earn 40% of their foreign exchange (coffee earns another 20%). The cost has been enormous to the Ivorian Government which has had to fund an ever widening gap between the market and its own high producer prices. This explains the desperate bid to raise market prices that many analysts believe will lose the Ivorians revenue by tarnishing their 'reliable supplier' image. Meanwhile, the surplus still overhangs the market; only its location has changed.

Having said that, the Ivorian/French deal gave the London markets a nasty shock. It meant that 400,000 tonnes of cocoa – equal to about 40% of London's annual trade – was cornered by one firm instead of shared by the open market. Half of this was already earmarked for customers, while the rest was to stay put in North European warehouses until prices improved, however long that took. Left with slim pickings, some London physical houses have had to make drastic staff cuts or close down physical cocoa departments altogether.

Traders say that the acrimony this caused has constantly soured fresh attempts to salvage the cocoa pact in 1989. Consumers in particular were annoyed, believing that the Ivory Coast and France had contravened the ICCA and further undermined its credibility. The ailing agreement was thus prevented from playing its last card in the form of its own withholding agreement which could have taken another 120,000 tonnes off the market.

For many in the trade that was no bad thing. For while the pact's role in the market is now academic, if it does disband, it already has 250,000 tonnes of buffer stocks – acquired through earlier price-support purchases – which will have to be sold back to the market in the next four years, providing a constant anchor to price revivals.

That prices might ultimately benefit from a disbanded pact is suggested by the effect that market forces are starting to have on producers. In the Ivory Coast, the lack of Government funds to buy from producers poses an increasing threat that cocoa pods on the trees will not be collected. However, this will be masked for a time. An expansion in Ivorian plantings carried out in the 1970s is still coming into full maturity, so there should remain an underlying trend of crop increases year-on-year.

Other producers are also feeling the pinch. The second largest supplier, Brazil's combination of several poor crops in a row and low internal prices is putting producers there in double jeopardy. Crippled by debt, smaller farmers are cutting back on their inputs and only those largest farmers with cost economies of scale are making enough profit to fund sufficient labour, fertilizer and so on. The Brazilian cocoa economy is in severe depression and low prices may be reflected in lower yields before long.

The combination of an uncertain future output and unilateral action by the traditional producers is a big fillip to competitors. Malaysia is the fastest up-and-coming supplier and is expected to produce yet another record of 250,000 tonnes this year – more than ten times the level of the late 1970s. Malaysia has doggedly refused to join the ICCA – which would, by its nature, limit expansion – although there are signs that even here, the message of low prices is getting through. The Malay Primary Industries Minister, for example, said recently that the country was now producing too much cocoa and that a breather was needed for prices to catch up. Like the Ivory Coast, however, Malaysia has considerable areas of new planting that have yet to come on stream, so even a slowdown in expansion of acreage will take some time to filter through to production.

If Malaysian output does slow, it is likely that the expansionary standard will be taken up by lower-costed Indonesia. With huge areas of virgin land to plant, it has already mirrored Malaysia's boom in palm oil, timber and tin, and since none has offered a safe haven, cocoa seems a useful diversification. The fact that Indonesian cocoa will become tenderable on the UK cocoa futures market at a discount later this year will further promote growth in Indonesia and help London become a principal outlet.

Stretched between unreliable production cycles and relatively inelastic demand, the cocoa market is typically subject to extreme and often violent fluctuations in value. But these up-and-coming producers mean that production will be more widespread geographically, so big variations in supply and swings of price may become less and less likely.

Consumers, then, may continue to have things their own way for some time yet, unless of course there is a big interruption to global supply, for example from some unforeseen weather catastrophe in one or more of the major producing regions.

Barring that, the bright aspect of low prices is the strong growth of consumption, both in traditional markets like Europe and developing countries, including Brazil itself.

The fact that increased origin grinding of beans is not displacing growth of consumption in importing countries is significant and it could promise more volatility for the cocoa market in the long term. Many analysts are convinced that there will come a point when consumption takes over and outpaces the increase in supply. If this occurs when yields are reacting to low prices or bad weather, the scene could be set for a major reversal of producer fortunes.

The cocoa market has been characterized by a swing towards trade in downstream value-added products in recent years, for example, cocoa butter, liquor, powder and so on. However, with the time-lag irregularities which can occur between purchase, manufacture and finished product sales, there is often confusion over the true performance of offtake of these in some countries.

Cocoa has also faced an increasing threat of substitution from products like shea nut butter and cheap vegetable fats like palm kernel oil, especially in the confectionary bar outlets of Europe and the United States.

Some producers are pinning their hopes increasingly on output of better quality cocoa to consolidate markets. For, like coffee, cocoa frequently responds quickly with sharply higher prices to shortages of premium grades, but quality in turn, by the very nature of the crop's growing climate and fermentation process, can often be tough to achieve.

The big price movements in cocoa in the past year have helped to generate speculative use of the new FOX options facilities to manage price volatility. Rather than using futures alone, many traders have found it better to hedge a futures position with an option, or to trade options to play the option volatility. This has helped futures turnover in a year when it has often been difficult to use them as a straight hedge because of market distortions caused by Ivorian withholding, or delivery of different quality Malaysian cocoa against certain contracts.

Cocoa beans: production by country, 1979/80-1988-89 (000 tonnes)

Country		1979/80	1980/81	1981/82	1982/83	1983/84	1984/85	1985/86	1986/87	1987/88	1988/89 Forecast
					(thousand tonnes)						
AFRICA											
Angola		0.2	0.2	0.2	0.2	0.2	0.1	0.1	0.1	0.1	0.1
Cameroon	m	123.2	117.1	122.0	105.0	108.9	120.0	118.0	123.1	130.0	125.0
Congo		2.3	1.8	2.2	1.6	1.7	1.8	1.8	1.8	2.1	2.1
Côte d'Ivoire	m	401.0	417.2	464.8	360.4	411.1	565.0	580.0	619.8	673.9	790.0
Equatorial Guinea		5.6	8.7	9.9	7.0	6.9	8.7	6.5	7.5	8.0	7.0
Gabon	m	3.7	2.9	3.4	2.5	1.6	1.6	2.0	2.0	1.6	1.8
Ghana	m	296.4	258.0	225.0	178.0	158.9	175.0	219.0	228.0	188.2	305.0
Liberia		3.7	4.0	5.5	5.0	6.0	6.0	4.5	3.0	3.0	3.5
Madagascar		2.1	2.1	1.1	1.8	2.9	1.7	1.9	2.8	2.1	2.8
Nigeria	m	170.4	155.9	181.0	160.0	118.0	154.7	110.0	100.0	150.0	155.0
Sao Tome & Principe	m	5.7	6.5	5.1	4.7	3.5	3.5	3.5	3.0	4.5	4.0
Sierra Leone	m	9.3	9.2	9.3	9.1	8.0	10.9	11.2	10.5	10.5	10.5
Tanzania		1.1	1.0	1.2	1.3	1.4	1.5	1.0	1.5	1.5	1.5
Togo	m	15.3	16.3	11.0	9.8	16.6	9.9	14.0	13.5	10.0	9.0
Uganda		0.1	0.1	0.2	0.1	0.2	0.3	0.2	0.3	0.3	0.2
Zaire		4.5	5.5	4.2	4.2	4.4	4.6	5.9	5.0	5.8	6.0
Other Africa		6.1	0.3	0.4	2.9	7.9	20.1	26.1	7.7	2.0	1.0
Total		1050.7	1006.8	1046.5	853.6	858.2	1085.4	1105.7	1129.6	1193.6	1424.5
NORTH, CENTRAL AND SOUTH AMERICA											
Bolivia		2.5	2.5	2.5	2.5	2.5	2.5	2.5	2.5	2.5	2.5
Brazil	m	295.2	353.0	310.5	334.3	296.1	406.4	366.2	357.6	402.0	340.0
Colombia		35.7	38.3	42.5	40.0	40.0	41.0	48.1	52.3	52.3	52.3
Costa Rica		10.0	4.8	6.0	5.0	5.0	5.0	6.5	7.0	8.0	8.0
Cuba		1.7	1.5	1.6	1.7	1.9	2.0	2.4	2.4	2.4	2.2
Dominican Republic		28.5	34.5	38.0	36.7	38.1	36.1	39.7	41.7	53.0	50.0
Ecuador	m	98.0	86.7	85.0	42.0	38.9	128.2	105.0	85.0	83.0	85.0
Greneda	m	1.8	4.0	2.2	2.3	2.2	1.5	1.7	1.6	1.6	2.0
Guatemala	m	1.1	1.0	1.1	1.2	1.6	2.1	1.9	1.8	1.9	1.9
Haiti	m	2.5	2.8	2.0	3.9	3.0	3.6	3.0	3.0	3.0	3.0
Honduras		0.5	0.5	0.5	0.5	0.5	1.1	1.9	1.9	1.9	1.9
Jamaica	m	1.2	1.6	1.5	2.8	2.8	2.7	2.6	2.5	2.5	2.5
Mexico	m	34.2	30.2	41.3	33.7	35.1	42.1	43.0	39.0	44.0	40.0
Nicaragua		0.2	0.3	0.3	0.3	0.3	0.3	0.3	0.3	0.2	0.2
Panama		1.2	1.2	1.2	1.0	1.0	1.0	1.0	1.0	1.0	1.0
Peru		6.9	7.0	9.0	10.0	10.0	10.0	10.0	10.0	10.0	10.0
Saint Lucia		0.1	0.1	0.1	0.1	0.1	0.1	0.1	0.1	0.1	0.1
Trinidad & Tobago	m	2.0	2.8	2.5	2.1	1.8	1.5	1.5	1.8	1.8	1.5
Venezuela	m	12.6	14.3	13.0	17.0	10.0	10.3	9.7	12.2	14.0	14.0
Other America		0.5	0.5	0.5	0.5	0.6	0.9	1.1	1.2	0.5	.1.2
Total		536.4	587.6	561.3	537.6	491.5	698.4	648.2	624.9	685.7	619.3
ASIA AND OCEANIA											
Fiji		0.2	0.1	0.2	0.2	0.2	0.2	0.2	0.2	0.2	0.2
India		0.8	1.6	2.2	3.0	3.5	4.0	6.0	6.0	6.0	6.0
Indonesia		9.8	12.4	16.2	21.0	26.0	31.0	37.0	45.0	53.0	60.0
Malaysia		34.0	47.0	61.8	69.3	83.3	97.0	118.8	167.0	227.0	240.0
Papua New Guinea	m	31.2	26.5	29.0	29.0	28.4	32.4	32.3	31.9	31.8	36.0
Philippines		4.0	4.2	5.0	5.0	5.0	5.0	5.0	6.0	7.0	7.0
Samoa	m	1.5	1.5	1.5	1.5	1.5	1.0	1.0	0.5	0.6	0.6
Solomon Islands		0.4	0.4	0.8	1.0	1.3	1.3	1.8	1.5	2.5	2.5
Sri Lanka		2.4	2.7	3.0	2.5	2.5	2.5	2.5	2.5	2.5	2.5
Vanuatu		0.7	0.7	0.8	1.1	1.0	1.0	1.3	1.3	1.0	1.0
Other Asia & Oceania		0.3	0.5	0.5	0.5	0.5	0.5	0.5	0.5	0.5	0.5
Total		85.3	97.6	121.0	134.1	153.2	175.9	206.4	262.4	332.1	356.3
World total		1672.4	1692.0	1728.8	1525.3	1502.9	1959.7	1960.3	2016.9	2211.4	2400.1
Total for members		1506.3	1507.5	1511.2	1299.3	1248.0	1672.4	1625 .6	1636.8	1754.9	1926.8
Share of members		90.1%	89.1%	87.4%	85.2%	83.0%	85.3%	82.9%	81.2%	79.4%	80.3%

Notes: m   Member of International Cocoa Agreement, 1986.

By courtesy of the International Cocoa Organisation

Cocoa beans: consumption of cocoa beans and cocoa products by country, 1981/82-1987/88 (000 tonnes)

Country		1981/82	1982/83	1983/84	1984/85	1985/86	1986/87	1987/88
				(thousand tonnes)				
WESTERN EUROPE								
Austria		22.2	22.0	22.9	24.2	24.1	23.1	21.8
Belgium/Luxembourg	m	29.2	25.4	34.7	30.1	36.7	35.8	36.7
Denmark	m	9.5	8.2	8.1	7.8	7.7	7.0	9.8
Finland	m	4.6	4.6	5.1	4.1	5.0	5.0	4.5
France	m	106.1	103.6	112.7	106.3	112.4	118.3	124.9
Germany, Fed. Rep. of	m	159.7	158.4	176.5	177.8	158.1	167.0	186.0
Greece	m	10.0	10.7	9.5	10.1	9.7	10.5	11.2
Italy	m	39.2	46.1	38.7	64.0	65.6	57.6	61.5
Netherlands	m	21.0	15.0	14.0	17.6	20.2	16.5	23.9
Norway	m	11.4	10.6	11.5	11.3	12.4	12.5	12.5
Spain	m	30.2	32.6	27.5	25.6	30.4	37.4	51.2
Sweden	m	14.4	13.2	14.3	14.1	14.4	15.2	16.2
Switzerland	m	26.3	24.8	26.7	25.9	28.5	29.3	28.5
United Kingdom	m	111.8	116.1	120.0	128.9	136.0	134.4	140.8
Yugoslavia	m	13.5	7.4	7.9	16.6	14.7	13.8	17.1
Total		609	599	630	664	676	683	747
EASTERN EUROPE								
Bulgaria	m	3.7	6.1	7.9	9.5	6.1	9.4	7.4
Czechoslovakia	m	18.0	18.8	19.1	18.1	19.3	20.4	17.3
German Democratic Rep.	m	21.4	21.0	24.3	28.7	24.2	25.8	26.9
Hungary	m	14.8	13.3	15.5	16.3	16.4	17.1	17.7
Poland		25.3	14.4	11.4	19.9	13.8	23.7	18.8
Romania		6.0	6.9	5.2	4.0	4.7	7.2	3.7
USSR	m	145.4	169.9	189.4	216.3	185.6	200.3	159.6
Total		235	250	273	313	270	304	251
NORTH, CENTRAL AND SOUTH AMERICA								
Argentina		13.6	11.3	16.6	14.1	13.3	12.6	12.0
Brazil	m	39.2	48.3	28.7	50.7	43.2	53.6	55.8
Canada		35.6	39.6	41.7	45.8	42.3	51.4	52.0
Colombia		40.5	38.8	32.1	35.4	46.8	53.1	52.5
Dominican Rep		2.7	3.7	2.9	3.6	2.2	2.4	2.5
Ecuador	m	7.1	6.2	8.8	7.4	7.3	5.0	4.6
Mexico	m	27.4	23.6	25.8	27.7	33.2	28.8	28.1
United States		353.1	407.5	457.2	462.0	483.8	505.8	524.2
Venezuela	m	7.4	3.9	6.1	7.0	4.6	3.8	6.2
Total		527	583	620	654	677	717	738
ASIA AND OCEANIA								
Australia		18.4	21.8	19.1	27.7	25.8	27.6	29.2
China		13.4	7.4	7.5	10.8	13.3	20.9	16.0
Indonesia		5.3	2.6	3.0	4.1	5.9	8.1	10.3
Israel		6.0	5.7	5.5	5.9	8.8	7.3	8.0
Japan	m	75.1	74.6	76.3	75.5	79.7	89.1	104.1
Korea, Republic of		4.0	4.7	4.8	4.8	5.4	8.2	8.0
Malaysia		5.1	2.3	3.0	3.8	0.3	0.4	0.2
New Zealand		3.6	4.3	4.4	3.1	4.8	3.2	4.2
Papua New Guinea	m	0.1	0.1	0.1	0.1	0.1	0.1	0.1
Philippines		12.4	6.1	3.8	3.4	1.9	2.4	1.4
Sri Lanka		2.4	1.7	1.8	1.6	1.7	1.7	1.7
Total		146	131	129	141	148	169	183
World Total (of above) b/		1516	1564	1652	1772	1770	1873	1919

Notes:

a/ Calculated as grindings of cocoa beans plus net imports of cocoa products and of chocolate and chocolate products in beans equivalent, using the following conversion factors:
cocoa butter 1.33; cocoa paste/liquor 1.25; cocoa powder and cake 1.18; chocolate and chocolate products 0.40
(0.20 is used in those cases where chocolate products are identified as containing only half the normal quantity of cocoa)

b/ Totals/averages for listed countries only. Some cocoa producing countries and cocoa importing countries are not included because of data problems and additional complications associated with changes in stocks and appropriateness of conversion factors.

By courtesy of the International Cocoa Organisation

Cocoa beans: grindings of cocoa beans by country, 1979/80-1988/89 (000 tonnes)

Country		1979/80	1980/81	1981/82	1982/83	1983/84	1984/85	1985/86	1986/87	1987/88	1988/89 Forecast
						(thousand tonnes)					
WESTERN EUROPE											
Austria		10.8	10.5	12.7	10.9	10.9	10.9	9.6	10.6	12.1	13.0
Belgium/Luxembourg	m	21.7	27.6	27.6	29.8	34.0	35.5	33.6	34.2	35.5	37.0
Denmark	m	2.7	2.7	2.8	2.5	2.6	2.5	2.4	2.4	2.5	2.5
Finland	m	1.4	1.4	1.0	1.1	0.8	0.8	0.3	0.1	0.2	0.2
France	m	48.0	48.0	49.0	46.4	51.0	43.0	40.9	37.8	37.0	45.0
Germany, Fed.Rep.of	m	158.5	160.0	165.4	176.0	190.6	205.4	200.9	205.0	224.9	244.0
Greece	m	5.2	5.0	5.0	6.1	4.9	5.3	5.0	5.1	5.0	5.5
Ireland	m	5.2	5.0	6.1	6.2	6.4	9.0	8.0	8.3	7.9	8.0
Italy	m	34.0	32.0	38.3	38.0	35.0	46.9	44.8	43.0	46.4	48.0
Netherlands	m	129.0	139.6	145.0	154.9	162.7	165.4	175.6	190.3	214.6	230.0
Norway	m	5.0	4.9	4.5	4.8	5.3	5.1	5.1	4.4	3.8	4.0
Portugal	m	0.1	0.1	0.2	0.2	0.2	0.2	0.3	0.3	0.2	0.2
Spain	m	37.0	36.8	37.0	33.0	31.9	30.0	29.5	32.5	42.9	45.0
Sweden	m	5.1	3.0	3.7	3.3	4.3	3.3	4.1	4.5	4.8	5.0
Switzerland	m	17.1	16.6	18.6	18.7	19.1	20.0	18.6	21.5	19.3	23.0
United Kingdom	m	61.8	80.1	89.1	77.5	86.6	95.2	83.5	93.8	99.1	110.0
Yugoslavia	m	12.5	17.0	12.0	7.0	6.4	14.4	13.6	14.0	12.1	14.0
Total		555.1	590.3	618.0	616.4	652.7	692.9	675.8	707.8	768.3	834.4
EASTERN EUROPE											
Bulgaria	m	5.4	4.5	3.2	5.7	7.0	8.7	4.0	6.0	4.9	6.0
Czechoslovakia	m	18.3	15.0	18.1	17.0	18.1	16.5	17.1	17.7	15.5	18.0
German Dem.Rep.of	m	17.0	20.0	17.9	12.2	14.5	19.2	16.9	19.8	19.9	21.0
Hungary	m	10.3	11.0	10.7	9.5	12.6	12.0	10.5	11.8	12.5	12.5
Poland		6.0	8.0	3.0	17.8	15.6	20.9	17.1	27.5	20.2	25.0
Romania		7.7	12.0	5.7	6.7	5.0	4.0	4.0	4.0	1.2	1.2
USSR	m	125.0	114.0	132.0	149.0	143.9	165.1	143.7	164.2	131.7	155.0
Total		189.7	184.5	190.6	217.9	216.7	246.4	213.3	251.0	205.9	238.7
AFRICA											
Algeria		0.4	0.3	0.2	0.2	0.2	0.2	0.1	0.1	0.1	0.1
Cameroon	m	32.0	21.0	15.7	16.4	17.0	20.0	21.0	25.0	28.0	25.0
Côte d'Ivoire	m	55.0	60.0	70.0	72.0	80.0	97.1	107.3	99.3	100.0	105.0
Egypt		0.5	1.1	1.1	1.4	1.5	2.5	2.0	1.5	1.5	1.5
Ghana	m	31.0	27.0	21.5	15.8	14.6	20.8	22.0	23.4	25.2	33.2
Nigeria	m	20.0	20.0	22.5	30.0	30.0	35.7	30.0	12.0	15.0	15.0
South Africa		2.2	3.0	4.1	4.3	4.3	2.6	2.5	2.1	3.0	2.0
Other Africa		2.0	2.0	2.0	2.0	2.0	2.0	2.0	2.0	2.0	2.0
Total		143.1	134.4	137.1	142.3	149.4	180.9	186.9	165.4	174.8	183.8

By courtesy of the International Cocoa Organisation

95

Cocoa beans: grindings of cocoa beans by country, 1979/80-1988/89 – continued

Country		1979/80	1980/81	1981/82	1982/83	1983/84	1984/85	1985/86	1986/87	1987/88	1988/89 Forecast
					(thousand tonnes)						
NORTH, CENTRAL AND SOUTH AMERICA											
Argentina		0.1	0.3	2.0	2.0	2.5	2.5	3.3	3.0	2.5	2.5
Bolivia		2.5	2.5	2.5	2.5	2.5	2.5	2.5	2.5	2.5	2.5
Brazil	m	180.4	191.3	164.8	181.0	210.0	238.4	232.8	230.2	247.1	230.0
Canada		12.4	14.4	16.4	16.2	20.4	21.5	20.4	19.0	20.5	21.0
Chile		1.5	0.5	0.1	0.1	0.1	0.1	0.1	0.1	0.1	0.1
Colombia		35.7	38.3	38.7	40.0	36.5	39.4	50.8	56.8	56.8	57.0
Costa Rica		3.5	3.5	3.5	4.0	4.0	4.0	4.0	4.0	3.1	4.0
Cuba		1.7	1.5	1.6	1.7	1.9	2.0	4.0	4.0	3.5	3.5
Dominican Republic		6.1	8.0	5.0	6.0	5.0	6.0	5.1	5.3	4.9	6.0
Ecuador	m	85.0	65.0	40.0	29.0	20.0	38.1	51.8	29.3	35.1	42.0
Guatemala	m	0.4	0.4	0.4	0.4	0.4	0.4	0.4	0.4	0.4	0.4
Honduras		0.1	0.1	0.3	0.3	0.3	0.3	0.3	0.3	0.3	0.3
Jamaica	m	0.2	0.2	0.2	0.4	0.8	0.6	0.6	0.8	0.7	0.8
Mexico	m	32.3	30.0	30.0	30.1	30.8	34.0	41.3	36.4	40.3	40.0
Panama		0.1	0.5	0.5	0.9	0.9	0.9	0.9	0.9	0.9	0.9
Peru		6.0	6.4	8.0	9.0	9.0	9.0	9.0	9.0	9.0	9.0
Trinidad and Tobago	m	0.1	0.1	0.2	0.1	0.1	0.1	0.1	0.1	0.1	0.1
United States		132.7	185.6	195.5	191.1	211.7	205.0	193.0	227.0	242.0	245.0
Uruguay		0.7	0.5	0.3	0.2	0.2	0.2	0.2	0.2	0.2	0.2
Venezuela	m	4.9	6.3	7.6	4.4	8.0	8.0	5.2	5.5	7.2	8.0
Other Americas		3.4	0.5	0.5	0.5	0.5	0.5	0.5	0.5	0.5	0.5
Total		**509.8**	**555.9**	**518.1**	**519.9**	**565.6**	**613.5**	**626.3**	**635.3**	**677.7**	**673.8**
ASIA AND OCEANIA											
Australia		10.6	11.6	9.0	7.0	5.2	2.0	0.5	1.1	0.5	0.5
China		15.0	15.0	16.0	12.9	11.7	15.0	18.0	24.5	19.5	20.0
India		1.8	1.8	2.5	3.3	3.8	4.0	5.8	5.8	5.8	5.8
Indonesia		11.0	13.0	14.0	13.0	6.0	5.0	8.0	12.0	13.0	18.0
Israel		1.1	1.3	1.2	1.3	0.9	1.3	0.9	1.1	1.5	1.5
Japan	m	24.3	27.8	31.4	33.2	34.0	34.2	35.4	35.8	38.9	42.0
Korea, Republic of		1.7	1.1	1.3	1.8	2.4	1.8	2.1	2.0	1.2	2.0
Malaysia		5.4	7.2	11.4	12.3	19.3	22.6	24.0	30.0	34.5	35.0
New Zealand		4.0	4.0	4.5	5.0	4.9	4.4	5.0	1.0	1.0	1.0
Philippines		7.0	12.0	17.0	13.0	7.0	5.7	3.7	4.0	4.0	4.0
Singapore		6.4	4.2	10.7	23.6	18.9	28.0	28.4	38.2	44.9	45.0
Sri Lanka		1.7	1.8	2.5	1.8	1.8	1.6	1.7	1.7	1.7	1.7
Turkey		0.6	2.0	2.8	3.8	3.2	2.6	3.0	5.0	5.5	5.5
Other Asia and Oceania		0.4	0.6	0.4	0.4	0.5	0.4	0.4	0.4	0.4	0.4
Total		**91.0**	**103.4**	**124.7**	**132.4**	**119.6**	**128.4**	**136.9**	**162.6**	**172.4**	**182.4**
World total		**1488.7**	**1568.5**	**1588.5**	**1628.9**	**1704.0**	**1862.1**	**1839.2**	**1922.1**	**1999.1**	**2113.1**
Total for members		1185.9	1193.4	1191.5	1211.7	1283.6	1430.9	1406.3	1414.9	1478.7	1575.4
Share of members		79.7%	76.1%	75.0%	74.4%	75.3%	76.8%	76.5%	73.6%	74.0%	74.6%
Producer country grindings		526.8	519.5	481.9	488.9	511.2	597.7	633.8	600.2	640.6	648.7
Share of producer grindings		35.4%	33.1%	30.3%	30.0%	30.0%	32.1%	34.5%	31.2%	32.0%	30.7%

Notes: m Member of International Cocoa Agreement, 1986.

By courtesy of the International Cocoa Organization.

Cocoa world production

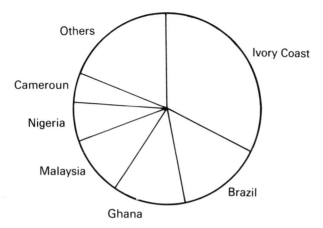

World grindings

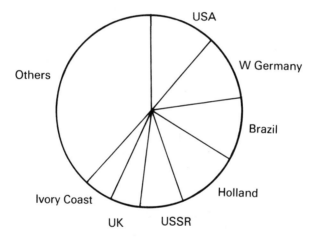

Cocoa beans: monthly averages of daily futures prices of cocoa beans 1977-1989 (US cents per lb)*

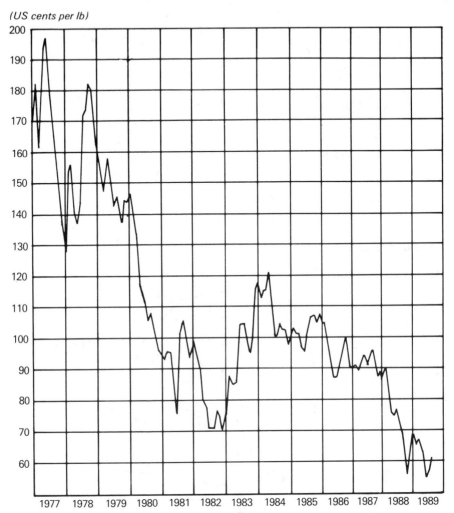

*The daily price for cocoa beans is the average of the quotations of the nearest three active future trading months on the New York Cocoa Exchange at noon and on the London Cocoa Terminal Market at closing time. The London prices are converted to United States cents per lb by using the current six months forward rate of exchange published in London at closing time. The time for shift to the next three months' period is the fifteenth of the month immediately preceding the nearest active maturing month.

Source: International Cocoa Organization

Coffee

Patrick Kelly,
Knight-Ridder Unicom

Once resilient to all but the most severe supply shocks, the global coffee market has become increasingly unstable in the late 1980s.

Output has been growing much faster than demand for some years, resulting in stock accumulation and increasing disillusionment with the export quota system of the International Coffee Organization's support pact (ICA). Now that the pact has been forced to suspend operations, open market forces will have a far greater say in the price at which coffee is to be sold, which types are produced and – ultimately perhaps – who can afford to produce the commodity at all. Without doubt, 1989 can be said to mark a turning point in the coffee market's history that will shape trading for the next decade.

Coffee originated in tropical Africa and is now grown in 80 countries across four continents, of which 50 are exporters. Producing countries earn around US $10 billion a year from the sale of coffee-beans, but these earnings could dwindle by around US $2 billion if an expected flood of coffee into a now-free market prompts a steep fall in prices.

Gone, for the time being at least, are the heady days of 1976-1977, when a disastrously low crop in key producing country Brazil, led to soaring prices in the two main trading centres of New York and London. In July 1977, prices for top quality coffees were about 240 US cents per pound, and for lesser quality types about 210 US cents; whereas in July 1989 prices were about 90 and 63 US cents respectively.

World exportable production for 1990-1991 (October–September) is likely to reach around 75 million 60-kilo bags and net exports about 70 million; but much depends on the extent to which major exporting countries expand their output in the battle to retain market share.

There are two main types of coffee: arabicas and robustas, each of which requires slightly different environments in order to thrive. Arabicas grow best at altitudes of between 600 and 2000m above sea-level in sub-tropical, almost temperate climatic conditions. Robustas, which are indigenous to tropical rainforest areas, thrive at altitudes of up to 800m. However, both do best in well-drained soil in areas where rainfall averages between 1500 and 2200mm annually.

Although susceptible to diseases such as coffee rust, both species are hardy plants. In dry processing, as used in Brazil and Ethiopia, the beans are sun-dried, either before or after they are separated from the coffee cherry. The finished product is known as 'hard' or 'unwashed' coffee. In wet processing, the outer part of the fruit is removed in water, leaving the bean in an enclosed husk known as 'parchment' which is discarded mechanically, and the beans then dried. The end product is known as 'soft' or 'mild' coffee and is of a higher quality.

Traditionally, the size of the Brazilian coffee crop has been a major determinant of world coffee supply and demand, and therefore of prices. In recent years, the country has produced an average 25 million bags a year, but has a capacity to produce up to 40 million bags. The crop is prone to frost and drought; indeed it was frost that reduced the 1976 crop to little more than 6.6 million bags. Brazil produces mostly unwashed arabicas and robustas and has been striving to maintain its near 30% share of the global export market against stiff competition from mild arabica producers.

Consumer tastes in coffee have undergone a discernible shift in recent years. Coffee drinkers in the main importing nations of the United States and West Germany (with nearly 50% of the consumer market), prefer mild arabica coffees. These types are produced in Colombia, Central America, Tanzania and Kenya and expanding demand has led growers in these nations to seek a proportionately larger share of the export market.

The shift in consumer demand was in part responsible for the suspension, in July 1989, of ICA export quotas which were regarded as too inflexible to reflect changes in consumer tastes.

Stocks have always been a major factor in coffee and have often exacerbated overproduction. At the end of September 1990, world coffee stocks are forecast at 71 million bags (gross) compared with an estimated 66 million at the end of 1988–1989.

Much depends on the speed with which countries such as Brazil, with 17 million bags stockpiled in July 1989, sell off their stocks in response to a free market. Indonesia, a major producer of robustas, had accumulated nearly 2 million bags in stocks by July 1989.

Coffee producing countries have special government-owned or controlled agencies to assist growers in obtaining money from coffee. These bodies also handle exports, either by working directly with buyers, or by regulating the activities of private traders selling on world markets. In Brazil, for example, the Brazilian Coffee Institute maintains the entire market by controlling price levels and taxes and the *Federacion de Cafeteros* performs a similar function in Colombia.

Arabica coffee futures are traded on the New York Coffee, Sugar and Cocoa Exchange (NYCSCE). Known as the 'C' contract, futures are traded in cents per pound and in lots of 37,500 pounds. A record daily high volume of 14,211 lots was recorded on 14 May 1980. Robusta futures are traded in London in sterling per tonne, each lot being 5 tonnes. There are also forward trading operations in Le Havre and Hamburg, but these are on a much smaller scale than in New York and London. Additionally, green coffee physicals are traded in Marseilles (West African robustas) and in Bremen (mainly high quality arabicas from Colombia and East Africa).

Prices in all these centres run in tandem at least in the long term, but wide short-term divergencies in price can occur. Demand from coffee roasters is often sporadic and highly specific and can cause major price fluctuations, particularly if there is uncertainty over supplies.

Because a free market now obtains, European roasters face a period of strenuous price competition as they aim to achieve the best deal on unrestricted supplies.

Coffee: total production 1980-88 (000 bags)

Crop year commencing		1980	1981	1982	1983	1984	1985	1986	1987	1988[1]
		(1)	(2)	(3)	(4)	(5)	(6)	(7)	(8)	(9)
ALL MEMBERS		80,654	100,268	84,824	89,149	83,774	90,011	81,089	1,008,321	87,463
MEMBERS ENTITLED TO A BASIC QUOTA		76,982	95,763	80,118	84,524	78,961	85,347	76,244	102,579	81,745
MEMBERS EXEMPT FROM BASIC QUOTAS		3,672	4,505	4,706	4,625	4,813	4,664	4,845	5,742	5,718
1 April		28,943	47,573	29,743	40,674	33,842	43,060	28,371	56,976	33,778
Members entitled to a basic quota		27,744	45,880	28,466	38,948	32,232	41,147	26,575	54,634	31,760
Angola	(R)	721	345	290	217	254	190	231	232	250*
Brazil	(A)	17,308	34,585	18,744	28,076	21,408	30,339	15,276	43,044	20,600
Ecuador	(A)	1,439	1,914	1,950	1,533	1,388	1,990	2,174	1,850	1,660*
Indonesia	(R)	5,044	5,895	4,787	5,900	6,206	5,629	5,935	6,202	5,800*
Madagascar @	(R)	1,203	1,165	1,042	953	1,074	896	983	1,151	1,100*
Papua New Guinea	(A)	869	907	634	932	742	861	760	1,082	1,050*
Peru	(A)	1,160	1,069	1,019	1,337	1,160	1,242	1,216	1,073	1,300*
Members exempt from basic quotas		1,199	1,693	1,277	1,726	1,610	1,913	1,796	2,342	2,018
Bolivia	(A)	145	106	166	164	146	172	130	181	150*
Burundi	(A)	313	732	340	591	459	540	532	623	585
Malawi	(A)	7	14	17	19	31	58	63	83	85
Paraguay	(A)	129	254	263	266	234	256	253[2]	501[2]	325*
Rwanda	(A)	503	506	378	537	542	717	642	704	650*
Zimbabwe	(A)	102	81	113	149	198	170	176	250	225
1 July		4,029	3,818	4,505	3,486	3,936	3,149	3,188	3,934	3,980
Members entitled to a basic quote		3,217	2,908	3,339	2,555	2,985	2,238	2,314	2,967	2,935
Congo @	(R)	45	45	33	56	34	32	14	57[3]	35*
Dominican Republic	(A)	1,105	813	1,159	871	913	433[4]	799	1,204	900*
Philippines	(R)	993	1,095	1,156	789	1,214	940	827	955	1,150*
Tanzania	(A)	1,074	955	991	839	824	833	674	751	850*
Members exempt from basic quotas		812	910	1,166	931	951	911	874	967	1,045
Cuba	(A)	313	394	469	342	352	400	430	447	480
Haiti	(A)	499	516	697	584	592	506	431	515	550*
Zambia	(A)				5	7	5	13	5	15*
1 October		47,682	48,877	50,576	44,989	45,996	43,802	49,530	47,411	49,705
Members entitled to a basic quota		46,021	46,975	48,313	43,021	43,744	41,962	47,355	44,978	47,050
Benin @	(R)	35	36	42	55	56	12	18	31	50
Cameroon @	(R)	2,006	1,959	1,959	1,034	1,587	1,667	2,201	1,372[5]	2,000
Central African Rep @	(R)	221	254	334	257	328	232	251	251[5]	250*
Colombia	(A)	13,070	14,522	12,319	12,969	11,035	11,764	10,754	13,200[1]	12,200
Costa Rica	(A)	2,156	1,617	2,639	2,230	2,523	1,324	2,639	2,300[1]	2,550*
Cote d'Ivoire @	(R)	6,275	4,201	4,959	1,952	4,831	4,682	4,566	3,278[5]	4,167
El Salvador	(A)	2,750	2,988	3,230	3,153	2,240	1,782[6]	2,343	2,494[5]	2,100*
Equatorial Guinea @	(R)	0	0	0	0	22	13	31	9	12
Ethiopia	(A)	3,304	3,214	3,725	3,888	2,322	2,833	2,973	2,883[5]	3,000*
Gabon @	(R)	13	13	30	41	41	37	13	28	40*
Guatemala	(A)	2,770	2,661	2,518	2,361	2,833	2,634	2,942	3,082[5]	2,600*
Honduras	(A)	1,304	1,330	1,899	13,367	1,425	872	1,554	1,450[1]*	1,550*
India	(A)	1,963	2,696	2,212	1,452	3,262	1,570	3,668	2,000[1]*	3,250
Kenya	(A)	1,722	1,474	1,550	1,992	1,557	2,031	1,855	2,090[5]	1,830*
Mexico	(A)	3,870	4,046	4,611	4,788	4,333	4,940	5,603	4,497[5]	5,100*
Nicaragua	(A)	970	939	1,460	812	850	708	766	649[5]	700*
Togo @	(R)	168	244	287	277	252	253	258	291[5]	248
Uganda	(R)	1,926	3,351	3,201	2,891[7]	2,551[7]	2,758[7]	2,850	3,100[1]*	3,500*
Zaire	(R)	1,498	1,430	1,338	1,480	1,705	1,832	2,092	1,970[1]*	1,900*
Members exempt from basic quotes		1,661	1,902	2,263	1,968	2,252	1,840	2,175	2,433	2,544
Ghana	(R)	25	17	9	8	8	10	12	9[5]	25*
Guinea	(R)	90	28	87	50	40	48	108	115[1]*	120*
Jamaica	(A)	24	29	27	29	20	22	22	32	45
Liberia	(R)	147	157	148	89	217	62	71	62	100*
Nigeria	(R)	3	65	37	40	22	14	20	60	80
Panama	(A)	143	122	167	158	169	147	196	194[5]	220*
Sierra Leone	(R)	154	153	252	178	185	112	98	145	100*
Sri Lanka	(R)	53	97	106	117	101	103	39	93[5]	75*
Thailand	(R)	201	277	325	328	469	526	463	614[5]	530*
Trinidad & Tobago	(R)	53	47	31	14	35	25	31	13	30*
Venezuela	(A)	768	910	1,074	957	986	771	1,115	1,096[5]	1,330

@ Member of the OAMCAF group.

[1] Based on the lower of the estimates made by the Member and the USDA (August 1988) unless otherwise indicated. When the USDA figures are used this is denoted by an asterisk (*).

[2] Under correspondence.

[3] To be adjusted according to the results of the verification of stocks as at 30 September 1988. See paragraph 39 of Decisions Adopted number 189, document EB-3048/88.

[4] See paragraph 13 of Decisions Adopted number 176, document EB-2842/87.

[5] Provisional estimate based on the preliminary results of the verification of stocks as at 30 September 1988.

[6] See paragraph 19 of Decisions Adopted number 177, document EB-2857/87.

[7] See paragraph 19 of Decisions Adopted number 178, document EB-2887/87.

(A) Arabica.
(R) Robusta.

Source: International Coffee Organization.

Coffee: imports by importing members from all sources 1983–88 (000 bags)

Importing Member	January–December					
	1983	1984	1985	1986	1987	1988
TOTAL	61,797	62,629	64,528	66,978	70,468	
USA	17,859	19,186	20,040	20,781	21,185	16,785
EEC	30,606	29,580	31,111	31,150	33,312	
Belgium/Luxembourg	1,863	1,905	2,187	1,979	2,086	
Denmark	1,029	986	983	996	982	961
France	5,924	5,557	5,711	5,658	5,942	6,019
Germany, FR of	9,227	9,005	9,190	9,855	10,621	11,065
Greece	466	501	496	368	506	
Ireland	82	102	113	126	114	
Italy	4,183	3,800	4,812	4,307	4,481	4,419
Netherlands	2,710	2,787	2,819	2,752	3,062	3,006
Portugal	295	325	362	292	457	
Spain	2,275	1,888	1,796	2,195	2,282	2,443
United Kingdom	2,552	2,724	2,642	2,621	2,779	2,811[1]
Other importing Members	13,331	13,862	13,377	15,047	15,971	
Australia	678	691	667	686	806	712
Austria	1,193	1,000	1,121	1,135	1,164	1,274
Canada	1,785	1,867	1,912	1,966	2,164	2,097
Cyprus	77	50	36	34	38	
Fiji	2	2	1	1	1	
Finland	1,064	1,156	897	978	1,251	957
Japan	3,854	4,186	4,288	4,579	5,099	5,094
Norway	755	744	716	729	728	661
Singapore	629[2]	1,152	745	1,282[2]	768[2]	464[2]
Sweden	1,665	1,632	1,601	1,663	1,671	1,599
Switzerland	1,053	1,040	1,167	1,098	1,299	1,097
Yugoslavia	576	342	226	897	982	829

A blank denotes that information was not provided by the Member.
Due to rounding the totals may not always reflect the sum of the relevant components.
[1] Provisional.
[2] Includes estimated imports from Indonesia.

Source: International Coffee Organization.

Coffee: exportable production 1979/80-1988/89 (000 bags)

Coffee year commencing	1 October:	1979	1980	1981	1982	1983	1984	1985	1986	1987[1]	1988[1]
		(1)	(2)	(3)	(4)	(5)	(6)	(7)	(8)	(9)	(10)
TOTAL		59,340	71,410	71,400	70,464	67,090	69,045	63,438	75,971	77,371	73,453
ENTITLED TO BASIC QUOTA		57,085	68,956	68,702	67,124	64,155	65,693	60,261	72,427	73,399	69,340
COLOMBIAN MILDS		12,806	14,289	15,051	12,924	14,131	11,577	12,577	11,486	14,142	12,973
Colombia	(O)	10,431	11,592	12,672	10,464	11,369	9,261	9,764	9,054	11,400	10,400
Kenya	(O)	1,601	1,654	1,438	1,500	1,941	1,507	1,931	1,755	1,990[2]	1,730*
Tanzania	(J)	774	1,043	941	960	821	809	804	677	752*	843*
OTHER MILDS		16,208	16,369	16,351	18,997	16,534	17,356	13,958	19,950	17,175	18,920
Costa Rica	(O)	1,229	1,956	1,372	2,414	2,005	2,295	1,099	2,414	2,075	2,325*
Dominican Republic	(J)	677	747	513	859	571	611	124	486	887*	582*
Ecuador	(A)	1,248	1,412	1,649	1,440	1,170	1,406	1,781	1,715	1,463*	1,774*
El Salvador	(O)	3,126	2,550	2,835	3,060	2,983	2,067	1,609	2,212	2,324[2]	1,930*
Guatemala	(O)	2,175	2,463	2,354	2,218	2,061	2,333	2,234	2,642	2,782[2]	2,300*
Honduras	(O)	1,020	1,124	1,144	1,709	1,167	1,210	657	1,394	1,285*	1,376*
India	(O)	1,684	1,130	1,619	1,295	819	2,345	1,032	2,318	1,000*	2,250
Mexico	(O)	2,304	2,370	2,446	2,911	3,288	2,603	3,040	4,003	2,897[2]	3,500*
Nicaragua	(O)	936	841	832	1,219	674	697	593	676	554[2]	605*
Papua New Guinea	(A)	838	895	711	843	795	824	787	1,051	994*	943*
Peru	(A)	971	881	876	1,029	1,001	965	1,002	1,039	914*	1,335*
BRAZILIAN & O ARABICAS		13,743	19,988	20,512	17,868	19,785	19,647	16,788	22,966	26,038	19,133
Brazil	(A)	12,190	18,284	18,915	15,760	17,492	18,873	15,808	22,160	24,322	17,300*
Ethiopia	(O)	1,553	1,704	1,597	2,108	2,293	674	980	806	1,716[2]	1,833*
ROBUSTAS		14,328	18,310	16,788	17,335	13,705	17,213	17,016	18,025	16,044	18,314
Angola	(A)	264	696	309	256	195	233	160	198	202*	218*
Indonesia	(A)	3,773	4,394	3,978	4,270	4,787	4,604	4,691	4,938	4,766*	4,736*
OAMCAF		(7,005)	(9,514)	(7,305)	(7,822)	(4,280)	(7,607)	(7,355)	(7,874)	(5,831)	(7,621)
Benin	(O)	1	35	36	42	55	56	12	18	31[3]	50
Cameroon	(O)	1,624	1,968	1,909	1,909	984	1,537	1,584	2,118	1,289[2]	1,917
Central African Rep	(O)	185	196	229	301	232	303	199	218	218[2]	217*
Congo	(J)	41	39	36	37	46	34	14	17	45*	25*
Cote d'Ivoire	(O)	3,908	6,091	3,984	4,459	1,735	4,614	4,465	4,349	3,061[2]	3,950
Equatorial Guinea	(O)	0	0	0	0	22	13	31	9	12[2]	15*
Gabon	(O)	9	13	13	29	40	39	36	12	27[3]	39*
Madagascar	(A)	1,057	1,004	854	758	889	759	761	875	858*	1,161*
Togo	(O)	180	168	244	287	277	252	253	258	290[2]	247
Philippines	(J)	295	482	633	661	307	758	480	343	445*	609*
Uganda	(O)	1,912	1,893	3,316	3,171	2,856	2,506	2,698	2,780	3,030*	3,430*
Zaire	(O)	1,079	1,331	1,247	1,155	1,280	1,505	1,632	1,892	1,770*	1,700*
EXEMPT FROM BASIC QUOTA		2,255	2,454	2,698	3,340	2,935	3,352	3,177	3,544	3,972	4,113
ARABICAS		1,790	1,906	2,048	2,561	2,311	2,495	2,495	2,929	3,092	3,300
Bolivia	(A)	111	72	121	120	102	122	77	118	93*	160*
Burundi	(A)	345	619	437	527	491	519	533	598	592	620
Cuba	(J)	160	223	288	277	146	152	193	220	237	264
Haiti	(J)	415	248	326	428	379	337	275	223	301*	322*
Jamaica	(O)	17	13	19	20	24	14	15	13	22[3]	32
Malawi	(A)	6	13	16	18	28	52	61	91	72	107
Panama	(O)	50	77	58	102	90	97	93	119	149[2]	186*
Paraguay	(A)	57	164	242	249	239	227	268	37[5]	480[5]	177*
Rwanda	(A)	500	505	423	478	540	653	668	680	669*	713*
Venezuela	(O)	59	-114	36	225	114	136	135	311	255[2]	497
Zambia	(J)					3	5	14	5	14*	10*
Zimbabwe	(A)	70	86	82	117	155	181	163	214	208	212
ROBUSTAS		465	548	650	779	624	857	682	615	880	813
Ghana	(O)	21	25	17	9	8	8	9	11	7[2]	20*
Guinea	(O)	28	53	8	67	30	10	28	85	94*	90*
Liberia	(O)	150	147	157	148	89	217	62	68	59[3]	97*
Nigeria	(O)	12	3	61	35	35	17	1	7	47[3]	67
Sierra Leone	(O)	169	154	153	234	178	176	103	96	136[3]	91*
Sri Lanka	(O)	0	44	64	71	85	69	68	4	58[2]	40*
Thailand	(O)	60	88	153	194	195	344	392	327	478[2]	390*
Trinidad & Tobago	(O)	25	34	37	21	4	16	19	19	1[3]	18*

Note: For those Members the crop year of which does not correspond to the coffee year, production which becomes available between 1 October and 30 September of the following year has been calculated by distributing the crop by quarters based on information in the Annex Table. For information on coffee years 1987/88 and 1988/89 see footnote [1].

[1] Based on the lower of the estimates of total production made by the Member and the USDA (August 1988) unless otherwise indicated. When the USDA figures are used this is denoted by an asterisk (*).
[2] Provisional estimate based on the preliminary results of the verification of stocks as at 30 September 1988.
[3] Derived.
[4] To be adjusted according to the results of the verification of stocks as at 30 September 1988.
[5] Under correspondence.

(A) Crop year commencing 1 April.
(J) Crop year commencing 1 July.
(O) Crop year commencing 1 October.

Source: International Coffee Organization.

Composite Indicator Prices

Monthly averages since 1977 in current and constant (April – June 1980) terms
1977 to 1989

(US cents per lb)

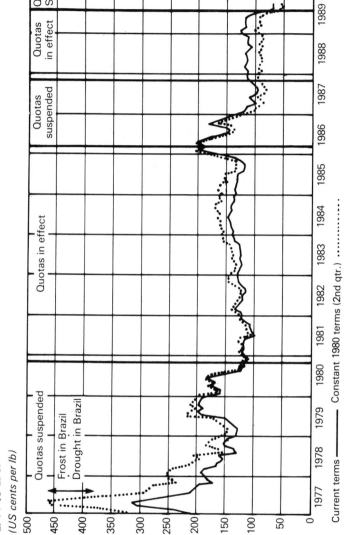

Current terms ——— Constant 1980 terms (2nd qtr.) ⋯⋯⋯⋯⋯

Prices refer to Composite Indicator Price 1976 up to September 1981; and Composite Indicator Price 1979 thereafter

Information as at September 1989

Prices in constant terms refer to prices in current terms deflated by the UN index of unit value of exports of manufactured goods from developed market economies

🅘 *By courtesy of the International Coffee Organization*

ICO Members world coffee production

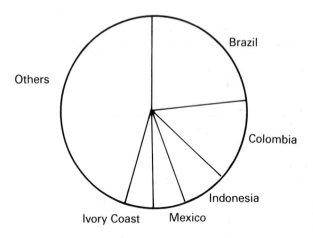

Major coffee importers (basis 1987)

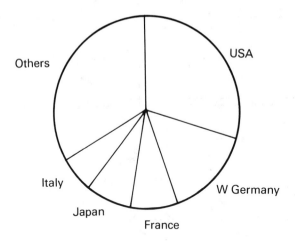

Cotton

Patrick Kelly,
Knight-Ridder Unicom

Durability and ease of drying have earned cotton its rôle as a clothing textile fibre since ancient times. Extracts from the cotton plant are also used in the chemical industry, while the seeds provide a valuable source of oil for edible and industrial uses.

During the last 30 years, the cotton market has suffered fierce and relentless competition from a succession of cheap and long-lasting man-made fibres, many of them by-products from the petrochemical industry. The cost advantages of artificial fibres and products have also been aided by the fact that they have been in the van of technological development in the weaving of both cloth and garments. Another factor has been their geographical siting in Third World countries where labour costs are low, especially in South-East Asia. As a result, textile industries have mushroomed almost overnight with a 'domino effect' – one country after another attempting to produce yet cheaper fibre products. The proliferation of supply has also contributed to downward pressure on the market for garments and cloth made from both natural and artificial fibres.

Perhaps the most interesting aspect of the current cotton market is the fashion for natural fibre whose traditional appeal of comfort, feel and hang have taken on renewed attraction for the consumers of the industrialized world.

To meet this heightened demand, production of cotton leapt in the past decade from 59.5 million bales (480lb each = 12.96 million tonnes) to a record peak of 88 million bales (19.17 million tonnes) in the 1984/85 (Aug/July) cotton marketing year.

Since then, the crop has dropped back somewhat to a forecast 84 million bales (18.29 million tonnes) in 1988/89, but consumption has gone from strength to strength. Indeed offtake is predicted to reach 83.4 million bales in 1988/89, rising to 85 million in the 1989/90 season. World stocks will have to be drawn upon to realize this need and the global international trade in cotton will probably boom to its best level in 10 years at a forecast 25 million bales.

While the cotton renaissance has buoyed its value on world markets, the progress of prices has shown violent fluctuation, recently due almost invariably to changing fortunes among the world's leading producer countries rather than events in the competing artificial fibres.

This has been graphically shown in the 1980s. Taking the New York Cotton Exchange (NYCE) (the only active futures market in the raw material) as a benchmark, prices plummeted from a high of 88 cents per lb in March 1981, to 30 cents in July 86, but have recently staged an equally spectacular recovery to around 77 cents.

One of the main reasons for this volatility has been the Chinese cotton crop which has rocketed since the 1970s in response to growing export and domestic demand. From 1976 to 1984, output in fact grew threefold, easily surpassing that of the United States and the Soviet Union. But demand could not hope to keep pace, so stocks accumulated and only a dramatic reversal in China's crop in 1986/87 brought about the necessary correction.

Currently China produces 19.3 million bales (4.23 million tonnes), around 700,000 bales (152,450 tonnes) less than it needs and is likely to revert to being a net importer, thereby boosting world exports and underpinning cotton prices.

Other big cotton exporting countries include the United States and the Soviet Union, which, together with China, provide about 50% of world production.

United States production and exports have been heavily influenced in recent years by government attempts to reduce agricultural surpluses and market support and to increase the commodity's export share.

During the 1986/87 crop year, exports more than trebled as the measure worked, while mill usage rose by around 17%. Tight world supplies and competitive prices have continued to strengthen United States export demand estimated at around 7.8 million bales in 1989/90 (1.70 million tonnes), the highest for nearly 10 years.

Currently, the United States is expected to produce 11.6 million bales (2.52 million tonnes) of cotton – considerably less than in the previous 2 years after another swing back to lower plantings, now estimated at 9.5 million acres against last year's 11.9 million. Yields have been damaged by drought.

The Soviet Union is an important supplier of cotton to the COMECON countries, but its production has tended to plateau in the last decade or so due both to a capricious weather system and the drive to increase other crops such as grain and sugar. The Soviet Union's cotton crop in 1989–90 was around 11.4 million bales (2.48 million tonnes), down from the previous season. With consumption at around 10 million bales, net exports are running at 1.4 million bales well below the seasonal average of 3.0 million.

Crops and yields in the two major producing countries of India and Pakistan, are steadily increasing following favourable monsoon rains over the last two years.

India's current output is just under 9.0 million bales (1.96 million tonnes), compared with consumption at 8.28 million (1.80). Pakistan, which has boosted its exports to meet accelerating world demand, currently produces 5.71 million bales (1.45 million tonnes) compared with consumption at 4.37 million bales (950,000 tonnes).

Countries with an annual production in excess of 1 million bales include the French-speaking nations of West Africa, Brazil, Mexico, Greece, Egypt and Turkey.

Internationally, cotton is traded in several centres. In Europe, Bremen and Milan are active trading centres, while in the Asian sub-continent, Bombay features strongly. There are also trading centres in Pakistan, Japan, and in Taiwan, while in the UK, the Liverpool Cotton Association perform an important arbitral function (see section on LCA).

During the next 4 years, world fibre consumption is expected to grow annually by 2.3% and cotton is likely to keep the large share of the textile market which it seized in the 1980s. Rising incomes will allow consumers in developed countries to trade up to cotton if they feel it is a better product.

Cotton: production 1988/89-1989/90 (bales and tonnes)

	August Estimate			
	1988/89		1989/90	
	bales	tonnes	bales	tonnes
Northern belt:				
USA:				
Memphis Terr	4,707	1,025	3,575	778
Tex/Okla	5,585	1,216	3,050	664
Far West	4,059	684	3,875	844
S. East etc	1,061	231	1,075	234
	15,412	3,355	11,575	2,520
Mexico	1,417	309	841	183
Greece	1,084	236	1,148	250
Spain	507	110	326	71
Egypt	1,427	311	1,743	379
Turkey:				
Izmir	1,401	305	1,263	275
Southern	1,378	300	1,350	294
Antalys etc	211	45	243	53
	2,990	651	2,856	622
Afghanistan	184	40	92	20
China	19,290	4,200	19,405	4,225
India	8,120	1,768	8,979	1,955
Iran	390	85	505	110
Israel	287	62	203	44
Pakistan	6,405	1,395	5,715	1,462
Russia	12,771	2,781	11,400	2,482
Syria	637	117		
Others:				
Europe	65	12	65	12
Asia	91	20	108	24
Africa	35	8	35	8
Northern Belt	71,001	15,459	66,583	14,497

Cotton production 1988/89-1989/90 (bales and tonnes) – *continued*

	August Estimate			
	1988/89		*1989/90*	
	bales	*tonnes*	*bales*	*tonnes*
Equatorial belt:				
Salvador	42	9	33	7
Guatemala	192	42	196	43
Nicaragua	121	26	121	26
Colombia	588	128	588	128
African Fr Zne	2,356	513	2,241	488
Uganda	20	4	26	6
Nigeria	209	46	251	55
Tanzania	316	69	214	47
Sudan	741	161	728	159
Thailand	147	32	161	35
*Peru	432	94	519	113
Others:				
CenAm/Carib	35	8	29	6
S. America	144	31	187	41
Africa	190	41	201	44
Asia/Oceania	262	57	235	51
Equatorial Belt	5,796	1,262	5,730	1,248
Southern belt:				
Argentina	873	190	974	212
Brazil:				
South	2,503	545	2,962	645
Bahia	220	48	335	73
**North-East	400	87	413	90
	3,123	680	3,710	808
Paraguay	1,001	218	1,010	220
South Africa	322	70	344	75
Zimbabwe	436	95	431	94
Australia	1,343	292	1,381	301
Others:	0	0	0	0
S. America	15	3	15	3
S. Africa	282	61	331	72
Southern belt	7,395	1,610	8,195	1,784
World Total	84,193	18,331	80,508	17,529

* Tanquis included to maintain country total.
** Included in zone, to maintain country total.

By courtesy of Cotton Outlook.

Cotton: consumption 1988/89-1989/90 (bales and tonnes)

	August Estimate			
	1988/89		1989/90	
	bales	tonnes	bales	tonnes
America:				
USA	7,500	1,633	7,600	1,655
Brazil	3,560	775	3,881	845
Mexico	768	167	758	165
Argentina	505	110	528	115
Colombia	409	89	409	89
Peru	294	64	308	67
Canada	215	47	225	49
Others	869	189	896	195
	14,119	3,074	14,605	3,180
Europe:				
Italy	1,240	270	1,309	285
W. Germany	918	200	955	208
Portugal	827	180	827	180
Greece	795	173	808	176
France	629	137	648	141
Yugoslavia	539	117	544	118
Spain	528	115	551	120
UK	175	38	160	39
Switzerland	280	61	288	63
Belgium	191	42	196	43
Netherlands	51	11	51	11
Austria	95	21	97	21
E. Europe	3,008	655	3,106	676
Others	183	40	191	42
	9,457	2,059	9,752	2,123
Asia/Oceania:				
China	19,000	4,132	30,000	4,354
Russia	9,000	1,980	9,100	1,941
India	8,120	1,768	8,277	1,802
Japan	3,206	698	3,197	696
Pakistan	3,924	854	4,372	952
Turkey	2,388	520	2,480	540
Korea	1,998	435	2,018	439
Taiwan	1,700	370	1,500	327
Hong Kong	1,079	235	1,079	235
Indonesia	925	202	1,100	239
Thailand	1,300	283	1,350	294
Iran	505	110	528	115
Syria	310	68	294	64
Bangladesh	257	56	297	65
Philippines	225	49	275	60
Australia	82	18	83	18

Cotton consumption 1988/89-1989/90 (bales and tonnes) - *continued*

	August Estimate			
	1988/89		*1989/90*	
	bales	*tonnes*	*bales*	*tonnes*
Israel	45	10	55	12
Others	1,051	229	1,083	236
	55,117	12,000	57,087	12,429
Africa:				
Egypt	1,332	290	1,378	300
S. Africa	344	75	357	80
Nigeria	291	53	295	64
Sudan	70	15	75	16
Others	1,254	273	1,341	292
	3,291	717	3,456	752
Total	81,985	17,850	84,900	18,484

By courtesy of Cotton Outlook.

Cotton: world stock – in millions of 480lb bales

	World Total (excl. China)	China	World Total
Stock Aug 1, 1988 (ICAC)	26.6	6.4	33.0
Production 1988/89	64.9	19.3	84.2
Net trade with China 88/89	−0.5	0.5*	—
Supply 1988/89	91.0	26.2	117.2
Consumption 1988/89	63.0	19.0	82.0
Stock Aug 1, 1989	28.0	7.2	35.2
Production 1989/90	61.1	19.4	80.5
Net trade with China 89/90	−1.0	1.0**	—
Supply 1989/90	88.1	27.6	115.7
Consumption 1989/90	64.9	20.0	84.9
Stock Aug 1, 1990	23.2	7.6	30.6

* 1988/89 exports 1.5, imports 2.0.
** 1989/90 exports 1.0, imports 2.0.

By courtesy of Cotton Outlook.

The Cotlook 'A' Index – Cents per lb CIF N. Europe –

(US cents per lb)

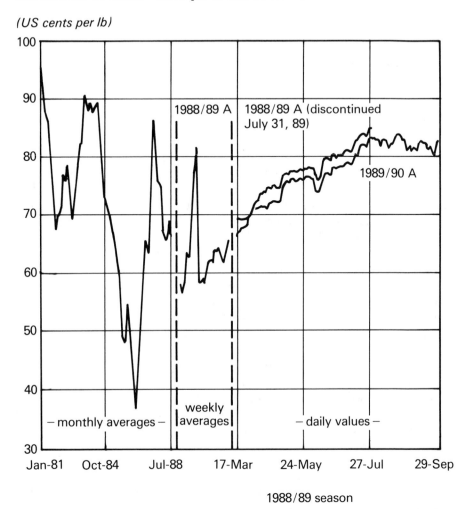

1988/89 season

By courtesy of Cotton Outlook, published by Cotlook Ltd

Grains

A W De Maria,
International Wheat Council

The 1980s saw world grain supplies swing from surplus to near scarcity. Until 1986/87, output exceeded demand, leading to the accumulation of excessive stocks. In the next two seasons consumption outpaced production, and stocks declined. In some countries, official efforts to reduce stocks coincided with bad weather, and supplies dropped rapidly.

Throughout most of the decade, policies designed to restrain production and avoid the accumulation of burdensome stocks were prominent in the United States. A series of acreage reduction programmes was enacted, and a long-term conservation reserve was introduced. The Food Security Act of 1985 covered the 1986–1990 crops, and sought to make United States agriculture more export-oriented by lowering export prices, while supporting farm incomes with deficiency payments. In the EEC, a co-responsibility levy was introduced to penalize excess output of cereals. This was supplemented by a system of 'stabilizers', which automatically triggered a further reduction in support prices if output exceeded 160 million tonnes. Voluntary set-aside provisions were also offered, but attracted only limited interest from producers. Intervention standards became progressively stricter.

Favourable weather and better official prices to producers resulted in a succession of record harvests in China, but grains then had to compete with numerous, more profitable vegetable crops. In the Soviet Union, however, production targets were rarely fulfilled. Underlying adverse factors in that country include severe climatic variations, and the high rate of post-harvest losses. Greater emphasis has been given to the intensification of grain production methods. Special incentives were announced to encourage more private, as opposed to state farming. Consistency of domestic output is recognized as the major element in expanding the livestock industry and limiting imports.

Supplies of wheat entering the world market originate mainly in the five major exporting countries (see Table 4), although as many as a dozen others have emerged as regular small exporters. Because of its huge output of maize (corn), the United States ranks first as a source of coarse grains. The Soviet Union, Canada and the EEC are the main producers of barley. Output of rice is concentrated in Asia, with China and India the major sources. Maize and sorghum account for the greater proportion of total output of cereals in Africa.

World trade in wheat rose sharply in the 1970s, largely as a consequence of rising demand in the centrally-planned countries, especially China and the Soviet Union. Subsequently, trade fluctuated in response to variations in the import requirements of these two countries. Nevertheless, there was an underlying increase in demand from developing countries due to urbanization, rising incomes and consumer subsidies.

While wheat is primarily a food grain, large quantities are used as animal feed in economically advanced countries. Feed use is also rising in newly industrialized countries with expanding livestock industries, such as the Republic of Korea. Coarse grains serve a variety of purposes. Most are traded as animal feed, although they are imported as staple foods in some developing countries. Other uses include brewing, starch extraction and ethanol production. For reasons of price, and because of lower tariffs and levies, imports of coarse grains into the EEC have, to some extent, been replaced by non-cereal feed ingredients such as manioc, corn gluten feed and citrus pulp. Only small amounts of rice enter world trade; most is consumed where it is grown. The United States and Thailand are the main sources of supply.

World grain prices are determined largely by the movement of futures on commodity markets in the United States. Options trading is also gaining popularity. Quotations at Chicago, Kansas City and Minneapolis are based on different classes of wheat (Soft Red Winter, Hard Red Winter and Dark Northern Spring, respectively), while maize is traded at Chicago. Prices may be set for forward delivery by quoting a price in relation to a particular contract month. Sales may be covered by hedging on other markets or for other delivery months.

The United States markets are open to all who wish to participate. Countries competing with the United States also trade in futures, even though they operate different systems in their own markets. In Australia and Canada for example, wheat exports remain the responsibility of wheat boards, but both may deal with approved private traders who then act as sellers. The EEC exporting system is based on export refunds or levies, designed to bring internal prices down to world market levels. Changes in market conditions for a particular grain can influence prices for others. These inter-relationships are especially evident when grains are readily substitutable. A good example is the competition between wheat and maize for use in livestock rations.

The international grain market is subject to a whole range of political, financial and economic influences. At times these can function in direct opposition to the underlying trends of supply and demand, known as the 'fundamental factors'. The main potential growth for grain consumption is concentrated within developing countries. Since the early 1980s, their rising indebtedness has inhibited their ability to finance imports of grain. Their position has worsened with high interest rates, and with the fluctuation of the US dollar in which most grain transactions are denominated.

As world trade in grain stagnated, exporting nations, in order to maintain their respective market shares, began to offer extended credit terms. Gradually, the availability and type of credit became as important as price in concluding sales with some importing countries. The United States Export Enhancement Programme (EEP) was introduced in May 1985, with the declared intention of regaining markets from countries considered to indulge in unfair trade practices. It offered traders subsidies or bonuses in the form of commodities held in government stocks. These were sometimes equivalent to as much as US $40 per tonne for wheat, but in 1989 were as low as US $5 per tonne as world prices rose. Other exporters were obliged to compete by dropping prices. The EEP applied to wheat and barley, but not to maize (corn). Other factors which have tended to impede the expansion in world trade in grains include inadequate port, transportation and storage facilities in developing countries.

Food aid shipments of grain now exceed 10 million tonnes annually. This form of assistance is regarded by many as harmful to the interests of recipients, since it could discourage domestic production. However, it is also recognized that it will be some years before developing countries will be able to meet their food requirements from their own resources. Furthermore, it is likely that some form of emergency aid will be necessary to offset crop failures, which occur with distressing frequency in some of the world's poorest countries.

Table 1 World production of wheat (including durum)

Million tonnes

COUNTRY	1984		1985		1986		1987		1988	
EUROPE	128.2		112.4		115.5		114.1		121.9	
WESTERN EUROPE	92.7		80.2		81.1		80.7		84.9	
EEC (12)		82.6		71.2		72.0		71.4		74.8
Yugoslavia		5.6		4.9		4.8		5.3		6.3
EASTERN EUROPE	36.5		32.2		34.4		33.4		37.0	
Hungary		7.4		6.6		5.8		5.7		7.0
Romania		7.6		5.7		6.7		6.0		8.5
USSR	68.6		78.1		92.3		83.3		84.5	
NORTH & CENTRAL AMERICA	96.4		95.5		93.1		87.0		68.2	
Canada		21.2		24.3		31.4		26.0		15.7
Mexico		4.5		5.2		4.8		3.7		3.2
USA		70.6		66.0		56.9		57.3		49.3
SOUTH AMERICA	17.4		15.2		17.4		17.5		16.0	
Argentina		13.6		8.7		9.0		8.8		7.6
Brazil		2.0		4.3		5.8		6.1		5.8
NEAR EAST ASIA	27.0		28.6		32.6		32.9		31.4	
Iran		6.7		6.5		7.6		8.0		6.5
Saudi Arabia		1.3		1.7		2.5		2.8		3.0
Turkey		17.2		17.0		19.0		18.9		18.5
FAR EAST ASIA	150.8		148.1		158.0		152.0		152.5	
China		87.8		85.8		90.3		87.8		87.5
India		45.5		44.1		47.1		45.6		45.1
Pakistan		10.9		11.7		13.9		12.0		13.0
AFRICA	9.4		10.4		11.6		12.4		13.6	
Algeria		1.2		1.6		1.2		1.2		1.2
Egypt (Arab Rep of)		1.8		1.9		1.9		2.4		2.8
Morocco		2.0		2.4		3.8		2.4		4.0
South Africa		2.3		1.7		2.3		3.1		3.5
Tunisia		0.7		1.4		0.5		1.4		0.2
OCEANIA	18.9		16.6		17.2		12.8		14.6	
Australia		18.6		16.2		16.8		12.4		14.4
WORLD TOTAL	**517.6**		**504.9**		**537.8**		**512.1**		**503.3**	

Source: International Wheat Council.

**Table 2   Exports of wheat and wheat flour 1984/85 to 1988/89
(million tonnes grain equivalent)**

DESTINATION	1984/85	1985/86	1986/87	1987/88	1988/89 (estimated)
Argentina	8.0	6.2	4.4	3.8	3.3
Australia	15.1	16.0	15.0	12.2	11.0
Canada	19.3	16.8	20.9	23.7	13.6
EEC	17.2	14.3	15.3	14.7	20.0
USA	36.7	23.5	27.3	44.4	40.0
Total Five Major Exporting Countries	**96.3**	**76.8**	**82.8**	**98.8**	**87.9**
Austria	0.6	0.7	0.5	0.6	0.6
Hungary	1.8	2.3	1.2	0.8	2.0
Saudi Arabia	–	0.3	1.6	2.4	2.1
Sweden	0.8	0.6	0.8	0.5	0.4
Turkey	0.1	0.1	0.1	1.1	1.9
USSR	0.7	0.5	0.3	0.3	0.5
Others	2.4	0.8	1.5	1.1	3.6
Total	**102.6**	**82.0**	**88.8**	**105.8**	**99.0**

Source: International Wheat Council.

Table 3 Coarse grains: world production and trade 1984/85 to 1988/89 (million tonnes)

COUNTRY	1984/85	1985/86	1986/87	1987/88	1988/89
PRODUCTION					
Western Europe	116.7	113.2	107.9	102.5	108.7
Eastern Europe	60.8	59.0	61.6	54.3	53.2
USSR	90.5	100.0	106.2	114.0	97.6
Canada	22.0	24.9	25.5	25.5	19.6
USA	237.7	274.9	252.9	215.9	149.6
Argentina	18.5	18.1	12.8	13.4	7.2
China	98.4	84.2	88.3	97.7	93.4
Thailand	4.6	5.3	4.6	3.0	4.8
South Africa	8.6	8.8	7.9	7.9	11.2
Australia	8.8	8.2	6.9	7.1	7.0
Others	154.5	168.8	170.7	155.9	175.3
WORLD TOTAL	**821.1**	**865.4**	**845.3**	**797.2**	**727.6**
EXPORTS					
Argentina	10.6	9.5	6.9	4.5	4.9
Australia	6.2	5.6	3.3	2.2	2.5
Canada	3.6	4.2	7.2	5.4	4.1
EEC	7.8	8.2	8.1	8.5	11.5
South Africa	–	1.1	2.6	1.6	1.1
Thailand	3.4	4.4	3.1	1.2	1.8
USA	58.2	38.5	41.7	51.6	62.3
Others	13.2	14.1	14.1	11.7	13.1
WORLD TOTAL	**103.0**	**85.6**	**87.0**	**86.7**	**101.3**
IMPORTS					
Western Europe	9.8	7.8	4.6	6.2	5.6
Eastern Europe	2.8	5.4	4.0	5.3	5.7
USSR	26.4	12.8	12.3	9.1	24.6
China	0.2	0.5	2.0	0.7	0.6
Japan	23.4	21.9	21.5	22.1	22.0
Others	40.4	37.2	42.6	43.4	42.8
WORLD TOTAL	**103.0**	**85.6**	**87.0**	**86.7**	**101.3**

Source: International Wheat Council.

Table 4   Imports of wheat and flour, including durum

Million tonnes (wheat equivalent)

DESTINATION	1984/85		1985/86		1986/87		1987/88		1988/89 estimated	
WESTERN EUROPE	3.2		3.4		4.4		3.4		3.1	
EEC		2.7		2.7		2.8		2.4		2.2
EASTERN EUROPE	3.0		2.4		3.3		3.2		2.7	
Poland		2.1		1.7		2.2		2.1		2.0
USSR	28.2		16.5		15.9		22.2		16.0	
N & C AMERICA	3.3		3.2		3.8		4.1		4.7	
Cuba		1.3		1.4		1.4		1.5		1.4
Mexico		0.4		0.1		0.5		0.6		0.2
SOUTH AMERICA	9.0		6.2		6.8		5.8		4.9	
Brazil		4.9		2.5		2.9		2.0		1.0
Chile		0.6		0.5		0.2		0.1		0.1
Colombia		0.6		0.6		0.7		0.7		0.8
Peru		1.0		1.0		1.1		1.1		1.0
Venezuela		1.1		0.9		1.1		1.2		1.2
NEAR EAST ASIA	11.2		8.7		9.4		12.2		10.6	
Iran		2.6		2.1		2.4		4.5		3.2
Iraq		2.9		2.0		2.9		2.9		3.1
Israel		0.7		0.5		0.7		0.8		0.6
Jordan		0.4		0.4		0.5		0.5		0.5
Lebanon		0.3		0.4		0.3		0.4		0.3
Syrian Arab Rep		1.3		0.7		0.5		1.2		0.6
Turkey		0.9		1.0		0.4		T		0.3
Yemen Arab Rep		0.9		0.8		0.8		0.9		0.9
FAR EAST ASIA	24.1		23.99		26.7		35.5		38.3	
Bangladesh		1.9		1.1		1.7		2.0		2.1
China		7.5		6.9		8.9		15.5		16.1
India		0.1		T		T		0.2		2.1
Indonesia		1.3		1.6		1.6		1.7		1.8
Japan		5.7		5.6		5.6		5.7		5.5
Korea, Rep of		3.0		3.0		4.1		4.6		3.0
Malaysia		0.6		0.6		0.6		0.6		0.7
Pakistan		1.0		1.9		0.4		0.6		2.5
Philippines		0.7		0.9		0.9		1.1		1.2
Singapore		0.2		0.2		0.2		0.3		0.2
Sri Lanka		0.6		0.6		0.6		0.6		0.8
Taiwan		0.8		0.8		0.9		1.0		1.0
Vietnam		0.1		0.2		0.3		0.3		0.3
AFRICA	19.7		17.2		18.0		18.9		17.9	
Algeria		2.2		2.5		2.3		3.5		3.3
Egypt (AR)		6.6		6.4		7.3		7.0		7.0
Ethiopia		1.1		0.8		0.6		0.9		0.7
Libyan AJ		0.5		0.7		0.7		0.7		0.7
Morocco		2.5		1.8		1.6		1.9		1.4
Nigeria		1.8		1.1		1.0		0.1		0.2
Sudan		1.0		1.6		0.5		0.7		0.6
Tunisia		0.8		0.7		1.0		1.0		1.1
WORLD TOTAL	**102.6**		**82.0**		**88.8**		**105.8**		**99.0**	

T – Less than 50,000 tons.

Source: International Wheat Council.

Table 5 Rice: production and trade 1984–1988 (million tonnes)

COUNTRY	CALENDAR YEARS				
	1984	1985	1986	1987	1988 (estimated)
PRODUCTION a)					
Bangladesh	21.7	21.9	22.6	23.1	23.1
China*	181.0	178.3	168.6	172.2	174.4
India	90.0	87.5	95.7	90.6	84.6
Indonesia	38.0	38.1	39.0	39.0	41.5
Japan	14.8	14.8	14.6	14.6	13.3
Thailand	19.0	19.9	20.3	18.9	17.8
Egypt AR	2.2	2.2	2.3	2.4	2.2
Brazil	9.0	9.0	10.3	10.4	11.8
USA	6.2	6.3	6.1	6.0	5.9
EEC	1.2	1.7	2.0	1.9	1.9
USSR	2.6	2.5	2.6	2.4	2.9
Australia	0.7	0.9	0.7	0.5	0.8
Others	84.6	85.1	83.6	85.5	80.8
WORLD TOTAL	**471.0**	**468.2**	**468.4**	**467.5**	**461.0**
EXPORTS b)					
Burma	0.7	0.5	0.6	0.5	0.4
China*	1.4	1.0	1.0	1.1	0.8
Pakistan	1.1	1.0	1.1	1.3	1.0
Thailand	4.7	4.0	4.3	4.4	4.8
USA	2.1	1.9	2.4	2.4	2.2
Australia	0.4	0.5	0.4	0.3	0.4
Others	1.7	2.5	2.8	2.8	2.2
WORLD TOTAL	**12.1**	**11.4**	**12.6**	**12.8**	**11.8**
IMPORTS b)					
India	0.6	–	–	0.1	0.8
Indonesia	0.4	–	–	0.2	0.1
Iran	0.7	0.6	0.5	0.9	0.4
Iraq	0.4	0.5	0.5	0.7	0.6
Saudi Arabia	0.5	0.4	0.6	0.5	0.4
Nigeria	0.7	0.4	0.3	0.4	0.3
EEC	0.5	1.3	1.3	1.2	1.2
USSR	0.5	0.1	0.4	0.5	0.2
Others	8.2	8.1	9.0	8.3	7.8
WORLD TOTAL	**12.1**	**11.4**	**12.6**	**12.8**	**11.8**

a) Rough basis (paddy)
b) Milled
* Excluding Taiwan province.

Source: International Wheat Council and US Department of Agriculture (USDA).

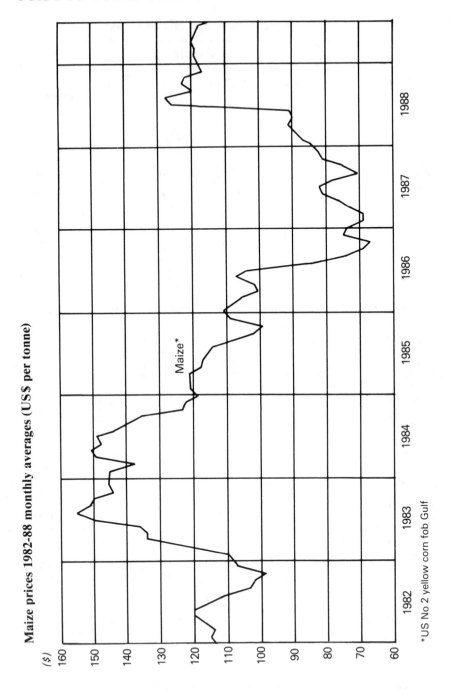

Maize prices 1982-88 monthly averages (US$ per tonne)

Maize*

*US No 2 yellow corn fob Gulf

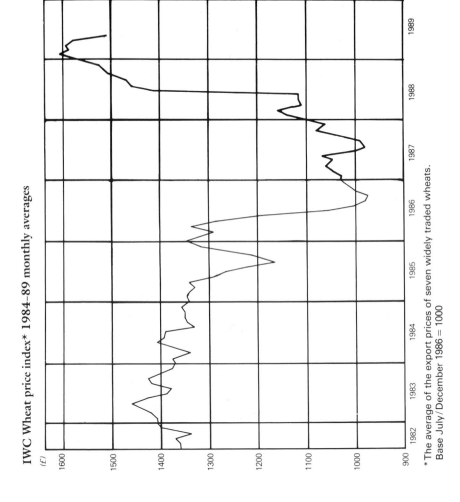

IWC Wheat price index* 1984–89 monthly averages

*The average of the export prices of seven widely traded wheats.
Base July/December 1986 = 1000

World wheat production 1988

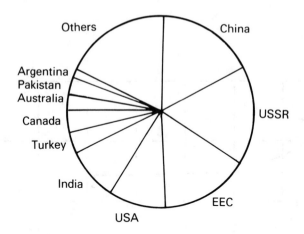

World wheat imports 1988/89

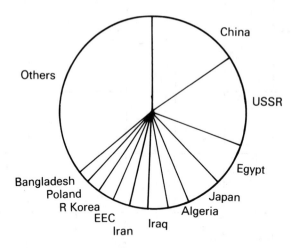

World coarse grain output 1988/89

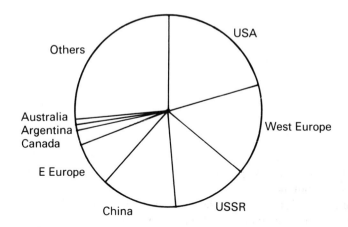

World coarse grain imports

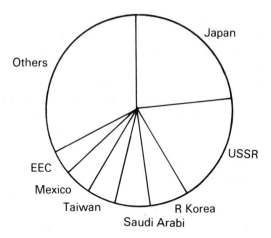

Meat

Few commodities markets rival the meat market for inherent volatility –a result of complex and overlapping forces constantly at work on the supply chain from farm gate to butcher's shelf.

Meat production is not only seasonal, in terms of when livestock breed or can best be pastured, but also cyclical. Trends which can range from 12 years in beef to four years for hogs are also subject to influence by the farmers' tradition of selling herds into market troughs and reducing slaughter into price peaks. This can lead to exaggerated fluctuations in supply over long periods during which the windows of speculative opportunity may frequently – if temporarily – be opened for the speculator.

Profitability of meat production in turn depends on several additional variables, including the price of grain and other inputs. The effect of weather on pasture quality and length of grazing season and the death rate of outwintered stock can all subvert the best-laid plans in the supply chain.

On the consumer side of the market, meat is one of the more price-elastic of commodities, providing a swift response to economic factors. The level of disposable income, particularly in the developed countries, has a direct correlation to demand for meat in preference to other protein sources. Inflation, however, can have a positive impact in making meat cheaper in real terms, so either consumer demand – or price – must rise.

This sensitivity to economic factors tends to place currency values and interest rates high on the list of priorities of meat market movers, especially in the United States. However, consumption trends can be complicated by the interrelation of the various meats. When seasonal or other factors reduce supply and squeeze up prices of beef or lamb, for example, substitution by pork or poultry is likely to take place.

These are some of the more general influences on meat markets where sentiment can become yet further tangled by government policies such as support prices, for example, where the government intervenes to buy and store surplus. Although theoretically cushioning producers from lower international prices, these can require costly subsidy when the country concerned is also dependent upon exports.

Arbitrary and sudden government policy changes on production can occur

126

when the cost of support is too great. A good example of this is the EEC's policy of quotas on milk output which reduced incentives to keep and intensively feed large dairy herds, effectively cutting the market's residual volume of beef and ultimately causing greater price volatility.

Finally, between the various links of the supply chain, profit margins may vary, especially between raw material prices for abbattoirs or meat packers and retail outlets. The relationship of cattle carcass to beef retail prices will influence the farmers' decision to keep cattle on feed or sell into a prospective decline.

Consumer demand for meat can also be influenced by fashion, the most important of which in recent years has been a growth of anti-fat and anti-meat health campaigns, particularly in the United States and Europe.

This complex mesh of supply and demand uncertainties has historically made meat a high-risk commodity for all involved in its supply, which is one of the principal factors behind the growth of futures markets around the major producer/exporter centres of the United States, Australasia and South America. Meat's volatility has also tended to attract massive speculator interest, far in excess of trade physical hedging.

In the early 1980s, investor money dwindled and with it trading volumes, due not so much to reduced speculative opportunities in meat itself, as to the far greater potential rewards offered by the new financial instrument contracts.

At the end of the 1980s, things are looking up for most meat futures contracts. On the Chicago Mercantile Exchange (CME) where financial futures provide stiff competition, turnover in CME live cattle futures has recovered by over 50% between 1984 and 1988 to 5.477 million contracts. The CME 'feeder cattle' contract has also risen sharply in volume from 316,985 lots four years ago, to 702,438 in 1988. The improvement was sparked off by expectations that the depressed prices of the mid-1980s would encourage herd cutbacks and was furthered last year as the worst drought in 50 years promised further livestock losses. But while options on cattle futures showed strong growth in 1987, the trend flattened last year at just over the 1 million lot mark. The CME also trades two important markets in pig products, live hogs and pork bellies. Both markets have traded less in the 1980s, due to the switch of speculative money into financials and to frequently depressed margins in the hog industry where intensive and less-economical feeding requires a good end product price. Live hogs are the most active market trading some 2 million lots a year, with pork bellies at about half that level.

The declining role of traditional physical trading centres and increasing emphasis on direct contract trade between producer, processor and wholesaler has also accompanied the growth of consumer interest in meat futures markets on both sides of the Atlantic.

The United States cattle industry tends to work on the 'feedlot' system, an intensive, relatively short-term/high-profit cattle fattening scheme which goes hand-in-hand with standardization and centralization of marketing. Ultimately dependent on a peak, but often increasingly uncertain return, the feedlot system embodies considerable unhedged risk which futures can help spread.

On the CME the feeder cattle contract is mainly traded against live cattle futures to give producers a guide to the profits on fattening up livestock. However, the CME live cattle contract is the most heavily used in the United States for pricing and risk management.

Generally, United States and Australian systems favour 'on the hoof' or live pricing to which futures contracts are tailored. The New York frozen beef futures contract went into demise for this reason, while on the Sydney meat futures market, 'trade steers' similarly eclipsed export beef. Amsterdam also has a live pig contract although this started out in 1977 with carcasses.

The London Meat Futures Exchange (LMFE) was launched by the United Kingdom Grain and Feed Trade Association in 1984, initially to attract trade hedging in pigmeat, but later adding a live pig contract. The Exchange has also experimented with beef futures, but most of the meats have proved a hard sell to more conservative and less futures-orientated United Kingdom trade audiences. Only the live pigs now run, and on a relatively small turnover.

World beef markets have been tightened in the past year by a drop in cattle numbers, falling meat production and exports at a time when import demand has been rising, but the ensuing rise in international beef prices – by some 20% since 1986 – has been good news for producers who were earlier struggling with low profits and surpluses.

This squeeze has been exacerbated by a shortage of exports from Argentina where economic problems have also encouraged farmers to hold their animals back from the market. Exports have also dropped from the EC, normally a major exporter of cheap beef to processing countries like Brazil and to the Eastern bloc.

OECD countries' beef exports in the medium term are expected to remain well below the level of recent years. This in turn suggests yet higher beef prices, although the opposite situation of surplus and lower prices in the pig and poultry sectors may encourage more substitution, eventually limiting the beef price upturn.

Looking further forward, the OECD expects cattle numbers to show a cyclical increase from 1990 onwards, as herds are rebuilt in the United States, Canada and Australia. These countries are expected to raise their slaughter rate and – with cheaper feed costs – their animal weights also. EC and other European countries are expected to continue a gradual reduction in herds, but this could be partly offset in the Community by a switch from veal to beef production which could raise animal weights. The net effect may be a 1% to 2% per annum rise in OECD beef output from 1990/93.

A major factor in the renewed increase in pig/poultry output has been the lower cost of feed as the effects of last year's drought in the United States pass. Reduced profitability is expected to slow the poultry growth rate in 1989 and cause a small drop in pigmeat, but higher production levels are expected to return again after 1990.

The main development in poultry markets in the last decade was the explosion of demand in the Middle East, following the rise in the region's oil export earnings. However, the increasing self-sufficiency of these and other developing countries has more recently begun to hit major exporters like Brazil and the EC. The EC itself experienced a poultry consumption boom in the late 1980s, helped by adverse publicity regarding red meats as well as cheap poultry prices, but this now appears to be levelling. Poultry has also shown a sharp consumption increase in other OECD countries, mainly the United States, Canada and Australia.

More recently, both the Soviet Union and China have shown keen interest in building up their domestic meat producing industries with a keen emphasis on poultry. However, their grain deficit problems have proved a constant restraint, as has the lack of hard currency to expand grain imports.

Sheep meat production in selected countries (a)

		1987	1988	(For) 1989	(For) 1990	1990/89 % change
		000 tonnes				
Australia:	mutton	297	257	303	325	+10
	lamb	295	286	300	303	+ 1
New Zealand:	mutton (b)	203	160	151	155	+ 3
	lamb (b)	407	416	376	354	− 6
Argentina		82	83	86	88	+ 2
China		690	800	880	920	+ 5
USSR (c)		905	910	915	920	− 1
United States (c)		143	151	155	157	+ 1
EEC-12 (c)		1,001	1,043	1,082	1,106	+ 2
Total		4,022	4,106	4,248	4,328	+ 2

(a) Carcass weight equivalent.
(b) Year ended September.
(c) Including goat meat.

Source: USDA, AMLC, NZ MAF, MLC.

Beef and veal production in selected countries (a)

	1987	1988	(For) 1989	(For) 1990	1990/89 % change
		000 tonnes			
United States	10,808	10,801	10,503	10,354	− 1
Canada	999	980	978	998	+ 2
Australia	1,546	1,526	1,560	1,585	+ 2
New Zealand (b)	554	562	486	498	+ 2
Argentina	2,700	2,590	2,460	2,350	− 4
Brazil	2,150	2,350	2,120	2,350	+11
USSR	8,288	8,400	8,550	8,465	− 1
Eastern Europe	2,435	2,340	2,340	2,330	−
Japan	564	569	583	595	+ 2
EEC-12	8,086	7,604	7,422	7,374	− 1
Total	38,130	37,160	37,002	36,899	−

(a) Carcass weight equivalent.
(b) Year ended September.

Source: USDA, SOEC, AMLC, NZ MAF, MLC.

EEC-12 sheep and goat meat production and consumption (a)

		1986	1987	1988(b)	1989(c)	% change 1989/88
			'000 tonnes			
Belgium/Luxembourg	Production	8	7	5	5	–
	Consumption	18	18	18	19	+ 5
	Net Imports	10	11	13	14	+ 8
Denmark	Production	1	1	1	1	–
	Consumption	3	3	3	3	–
	Net Imports	2	2	2	2	–
West Germany	Production	26	29	28	29	+ 4
	Consumption	51	53	53	56	+ 6
	Net Imports	25	24	25	27	+ 8
Greece	Production	107	124	128	131	+ 2
	Consumption	124	140	143	144	+ 1
	Net Imports	17	16	20	13	–35
France	Production	162	158	151	148	– 2
	Consumption	248	258	263	269	+ 2
	Net Imports	86	100	112	121	+ 8
Irish Republic	Production	46	48	49	54	+10
	Consumption	24	24	24	24	–
	Net Exports	22	24	25	30	+20
Italy	Production	67	70	47	48	+ 2
	Consumption	86	89	90	94	+ 4
	Net Imports	19	19	43	46	+ 7
Netherlands	Production	11	13	22	22	–
	Consumption	8	10	10	10	–
	Net Exports	2	3	12	12	–
Portugal	Production	25	27	29	31	+ 7
	Consumption	25	31	34	34	–
	Net Imports	–	4	5	3	–40
Spain	Production	211	224	235	242	+ 3
	Consumption	212	225	228	230	–
	Net Imports	1	1	7(d)	12(d)	+71
United Kingdom	Production	302	319	340	350	+ 3
	Consumption	383	383	383	387	+ 1
	Net Imports	81	64	43	37	+14
EEC-12	Production	944	1,001	1,043	1,082	+ 4
	Consumption	1,182	1,233	1,249	1,270	+ 2
	Net Imports	238	232	206	188	+ 9
Self Sufficiency (%)		80.1	81.2	82.1	83.2	

(a) Carcass weight equivalent. Indigenous Production. Consumption figures allow for changes in stocks.
(b) Provisional/estimate.
(c) Forecast.
(d) Net Export Value.

Source: SOEC, National Organisations and MLC.

EEC-12 pig meat production, consumption and net trade (a)

		1986	1987	1988(b)	1989(c)	% change 1989/88
			'000 tonnes			
Belgium/Luxembourg	Production	701	753	774	770	– 1
	Consumption	482	466	450	450	–
	Net Exports	219	287	324	320	– 1
Denmark	Production	1,146	1,150	1,165	1,170	–
	Consumption	325	340	337	337	–
	Net Exports	821	810	828	833	+ 1
West Germany	Production	3,288	3,286	3,200	3,010	– 6
	Consumption	3,730	3,792	3,826	3,630	– 5
	Net Imports	442	506	626	620	+ 1
Greece	Production	153	164	166	172	+ 4
	Consumption	220	246	245	251	+ 2
	Net Imports	67	82	79	79	–
Spain	Production	1,342	1,448	1,636	1,555	– 5
	Consumption	1,443	1,515	1,622	1,575	– 3
	Net Imports	101	67	14(d)	20	– 5
France	Production	1,591	1,646	1,732	1,600	– 8
	Consumption	1,964	2,032	2,051	1,963	– 4
	Net Imports	373	386	319	363	+14
Irish Republic	Production	138	137	136	137	+ 1
	Consumption	121	116	117	118	+ 1
	Net Imports	17	21	19	19	–
Italy	Production	1,053	1,121	1,130	1,130	–
	Consumption	1,604	1,668	1,669	1,629	– 2
	Net Imports	551	547	539	499	– 7
Netherlands	Production	1,736	1,846	1,948	1,890	– 3
	Consumption	624	641	663	644	– 3
	Net Exports	1,112	1,205	1,285	1,246	– 3
Portugal	Production	223	259	263	255	– 3
	Consumption	230	260	274	267	– 3
	Net Imports	7	1	11	12	+ 9
United Kingdom	Production	993	1,015	1,030	980	– 5
	Consumption	1,382	1,433	1,457	1,436	– 2
	Net Imports	389	418	427	456	+ 7
EEC-12	Production	12,364	12,825	13,180	12,672	– 4
	Consumption	12,125	12,509	12,711	12,300	– 3
	Net Exports	239	316	469	372	+21
Self Sufficiency (%)		102.0	102.5	103.7	103.0	

(a) Carcass weight equivalent. Indigenous Production.
(b) Provisional/estimate.
(c) Forecast.
(d) Net Export Value.

EEC-12 beef and veal situation

	1987	1988	(For) 1989	(For) 1990
	000 tonnes			
Production (a)	8,086	7,604	7,422	7,373
of which: Belgium/Luxembourg	336	319	315	317
Denmark	235	220	207	203
West Germany	1,704	1,622	1,590	1,575
Greece	70	70	69	69
Spain	438	450	446	442
France	2,129	2,019	1,900	1,845
Irish Republic	532	485	461	470
Italy	912	915	915	920
Netherlands	526	463	449	452
Portugal	99	102	104	104
United Kingdom	1,105	939	966	977
Consumption (b)	7,550	7,450	7,400	7,390
Trade (b)				
Imports	496	490	500	505
Exports	909	850	680	600
Intervention				
Purchases (b)	535	390	175	190
Stocks (c)	687	379	250	240
Self-sufficiency (%)	107.1	102.1	100.3	99.8

(a) Indigenous. No allowance has been made for illegal livestock movements.
(b) Carcass weight equivalent.
(c) Product weight at end of year.

Source: SOEC, MLC.

Pig meat production in selected countries

	1987	1988	(For) 1989	(For) 1990	1990/89 % change
	000 tonnes				
China	17,800	18,200	18,400	18,500	+1
Canada	937	995	980	1,020	+4
Eastern Europe	6,846	6,675	6,740	6,750	–
Japan	1,582	1,615	1,647	1,680	+2
United States	6,491	7,090	7,040	7,200	+2
USSR	6,300	6,500	6,600	6,700	+2
EEC-12	12,825	13,180	12,672	12,969	+2
Total	52,781	54,255	54,079	54,819	+1

Source: USDA, SOEC, MLC.

Meat: Smithfield prices 1982-88 (monthly averages of maximum quotations, pence per lb)

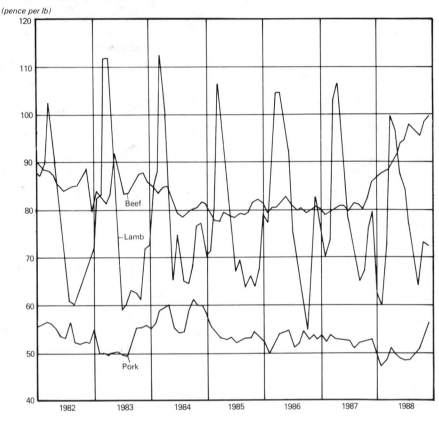

Beef: Scottish sides   Lamb: English medium   Pork: English under 100lb

Source: Meet and Livestock Commission

Oil

Sally Clubley

Oil futures and options markets have continued to increase in size and number as the oil industry has incorporated them in almost all of its activities. The futures and options markets have also led indirectly to some major changes in the industry itself as the (primarily) United States investment banks and their oil trading groups have utilized financial instruments and applied them to crude oil and products.

In essence, oil has now been accepted, even by the industry itself, who proved the most reluctant convert, as a commodity or even as a financial instrument. This has been facilitated by changes in the market, beginning with the removal of production from the major oil companies and the transfer of power to the Organization of Petroleum Exporting Countries (OPEC) during the 1960s. This in turn opened up the trading possibilities and enabled the rapid growth of oil trading companies during the late 1970s and early 1980s.

More recently, some of the OPEC countries have become involved in oil refining and distribution in the consuming countries, although even Kuwait, the most integrated so far, does not yet have the market presence of a major.

To match these changes the trading companies have had to adapt and the pure trading role that they filled a few years ago has declined sharply. Transparent prices, the tying up of crude oil supply to refineries, and the financial controls now applied to all the larger market participants have taken away the speculative trading opportunities on which many companies were founded.

In addition, the rapid and severe price swings seen in recent years have caused financial distress to a number of companies. After the price falls of early 1986, when crude oil (as measured by West Texas Intermediate (WTI)) prices fell below US $10/bbl, the market has been on a roller-coaster, with prices showing both sharp upward as well as downward moves.

Various OPEC agreements on production have helped to boost the price, although the agreements mostly failed until late 1988. In effect, every agreement led to a price rally and every failure to a fall in prices. Netback pricing was introduced for a while, with OPEC pricing crude on the basis of the price received for products by the refiner, plus a refinery margin. But this led to weaker product prices, which pushed the crude price down. It now seems, however, that most OPEC countries are prepared to limit production to keep prices steady in the knowledge that non-OPEC production, which rose from 47% of total (including CPEs) world output in 1973, to 83% in 1985 will decline in the coming years. OPEC is therefore likely to increase in power during the next decade or two.

The end of the Iran/Iraq war, various production problems in the North Sea, a gradual increase in demand and other external events have generally led to a firmer underlying tone in the market in recent months, but there are likely to be more falls yet.

There are now seven futures and five options contracts trading, with a number of others planned. By far the largest exchange is the New York Mercantile Exchange (NYMEX) which trades light sweet crude, unleaded gasoline, heating oil and propane, with options on the first three contracts. The crude contract, based on WTI crude is the most active, trading around 80,000 contracts a day on average and often more than 130,000. Although WTI is a United States domestic crude oil, and as such cannot be exported from the United States, the success of the futures contract has made it an international benchmark crude.

NYMEX also has highly successful contracts in two oil products: heating oil launched in 1978 and gasoline, which together trade around 20,000 contracts a day on average. Heating oil is the same product as the gas oil contract traded on the International Petroleum Exchange (IPE) in London and is used for diesel fuel and space heating. The gasoline contract was initially a leaded premium product, but has been changed to unleaded to reflect the shift in the balance of the physical market. The propane contract is less successful, trading only a few hundred contracts at the most.

The IPE in London is the second largest oil futures exchange, with successful contracts in gas oil and Brent Blend crude oil, the main product of the UK sector of the North Sea. Brent is unique among the oil contracts, operating by cash settlement rather than physical delivery. It was introduced in June 1988 and traded more than one million contracts in its first year, becoming the fastest growing of the oil futures contracts. The two IPE contracts trade around 8000 contracts a day each on average.

Finally, the Singapore International Monetary Exchange (SIMEX) started its first oil contract in February 1989, trading a heavy fuel oil. This has had a steady volume in its first few months and, with the support of the industry, will probably become an established contract in the near future.

The prosperity of these contracts has encouraged the introduction of a number of less successful imitators and there are still a number of new contracts planned for the future. These include a natural gas contract on NYMEX and fuel oil (a new contract) on the IPE. A new exchange trading gas oil and heavy fuel oil has been opened in Brent, Rotterdam. All three existing exchanges have other longer-term plans, and it seems likely that in another few years there will be futures contracts operating throughout the 24 hours and across the barrel, ie covering all oil products from light gasoline to heavy fuel oil.

Overall, it seems likely that the next few years will see a readjustment of the participants in the market, with the OPEC countries moving further down-stream and the financial companies playing a larger part. Prices will probably remain unstable, although the very low prices seen three years ago are unlikely to return. Many people now see US $15/bbl as the lowest price attractive even to consumers as cheaper prices tend to invite instability.

Gasoil: world production 1978–88 (million tonnes)

	1978	1979	1980	1981	1982	1983	1984	1985	1986	1987	1988
North America											
USA	488.1	480.9	484.1	482.8	484.5	486.8	500.2	500.8	486.1	471.2	462.5
Canada	74.4	83.8	81.7	72.9	70.0	71.7	78.2	85.0	86.1	80.0	83.4
Total North America	562.5	564.7	565.8	555.7	554.5	558.5	578.4	585.8	572.2	551.2	545.9
Latin America											
Argentina	23.6	24.5	25.7	25.5	25.6	24.9	24.4	24.0	22.5	23.3	23.4
Brazil	8.0	8.3	9.4	10.7	13.4	17.6	22.2	28.1	28.7	28.7	29.2
Colombia	6.6	7.5	6.3	6.8	7.4	7.8	8.6	8.9	15.3	19.6	19.0
Ecuador	10.0	10.5	10.0	10.3	9.7	11.6	12.6	13.5	13.6	8.2	14.7
Mexico	66.0	80.8	107.3	128.3	149.4	146.6	150.4	149.7	135.6	141.8	141.0
Trinidad	11.6	10.8	10.6	10.1	8.9	8.2	8.4	8.8	8.4	8.3	7.6
Venezuela	115.4	125.4	115.9	112.5	101.3	97.0	97.5	87.6	92.9	89.0	96.4
Others	10.2	12.2	13.3	13.3	14.1	12.4	12.8	12.7	12.0	11.1	9.7
Total Latin America	251.4	280.0	298.5	317.5	329.8	326.1	336.9	333.3	329.0	330.0	341.0
Western Europe											
Austria	1.8	1.8	1.5	1.4	1.3	1.3	1.2	1.2	1.1	1.1	1.1
Denmark	0.4	0.4	0.3	0.8	1.7	2.2	2.3	2.9	3.6	4.6	4.7
France	1.1	1.2	1.4	1.7	2.4	2.3	2.7	3.3	3.5	3.6	3.7
Italy	1.5	1.8	1.8	1.5	1.8	2.2	2.3	2.4	2.8	3.9	4.9
Norway	17.2	18.8	25.8	24.9	25.7	32.0	36.8	40.3	44.1	48.5	56.0
Turkey	2.7	2.8	2.3	2.4	2.3	2.2	2.1	2.1	2.4	2.6	2.6
United Kingdom	53.3	77.9	80.5	89.4	103.4	114.9	125.9	128.2	128.6	123.3	114.2
West Germany	5.1	4.8	4.6	4.5	4.3	4.1	4.1	4.1	4.0	3.8	3.9
Others	2.4	2.9	3.2	3.0	4.6	7.2	7.0	7.6	7.9	7.5	6.9
Total Western Europe	85.5	112.4	121.4	129.6	147.5	168.4	184.4	192.1	198.0	198.9	198.0
Middle East											
Abu Dhabi	69.7	70.3	64.7	54.5	42.5	39.3	38.9	41.6	50.4	57.7	61.8
Dubai	18.0	17.6	17.4	17.8	17.8	16.9	18.3	18.8	18.9	19.6	19.3
Iran	262.3	158.1	73.7	65.8	119.8	122.4	109.3	110.0	94.5	114.7	113.2
Iraq	125.7	170.6	130.2	44.0	49.6	54.1	60.3	70.6	85.5	102.4	127.7
Kuwait	97.0	113.2	71.5	48.2	34.9	44.7	48.9	45.7	62.3	53.5	66.8
Neutral Zone	23.9	29.4	28.4	19.4	16.4	16.2	21.1	17.0	17.9	20.2	16.6
Oman	15.8	14.8	14.4	16.4	16.2	19.6	21.0	25.4	28.0	29.1	30.4
Qatar	23.6	24.7	22.4	20.2	16.3	14.7	20.1	15.9	16.6	15.9	17.0
Saudi Arabia	409.8	469.9	493.0	491.3	327.9	255.8	233.0	173.1	251.2	212.2	257.1
Others	13.0	12.4	11.7	11.6	11.8	11.9	12.3	15.2	16.2	18.5	29.4
Total Middle East	1 058.8	1 081.0	927.4	789.2	653.2	595.6	583.2	533.3	641.5	643.8	739.3
Africa											
Algeria	57.2	58.5	52.2	46.3	45.8	42.9	46.1	41.6	45.7	44.8	46.0
Angola	6.6	7.6	7.7	7.1	6.4	8.1	9.5	11.8	14.4	17.9	23.0
Egypt	24.2	26.5	29.8	34.1	34.9	35.7	42.5	45.3	41.7	45.9	44.2
Gabon	10.5	10.2	8.8	7.6	7.7	7.8	7.6	7.7	8.1	7.8	8.5
Libya	95.5	100.7	88.4	58.7	54.7	53.0	53.0	52.7	49.9	47.9	50.6
Nigeria	93.9	114.2	102.3	71.0	63.5	61.0	68.6	72.9	72.2	63.7	67.6
Other Africa	8.0	10.8	12.5	14.9	16.7	18.5	21.4	22.0	22.6	22.2	22.6
Total Africa	295.9	328.5	301.7	239.7	229.7	227.0	248.7	254.0	254.6	250.2	262.5
Asia and Australasia											
Japan	0.5	0.5	0.4	0.4	0.4	0.4	0.4	0.5	0.7	0.6	0.7
Brunei	10.1	11.9	11.5	8.6	8.1	8.6	7.9	7.4	8.2	7.0	6.9
India	11.2	12.8	9.4	14.9	19.7	25.1	27.9	29.9	31.0	30.1	31.6
Indonesia	81.0	78.8	78.3	82.2	69.0	65.3	68.5	63.9	67.3	63.3	63.3
Malaysia	10.7	14.0	13.7	12.4	14.6	20.2	21.7	21.3	26.2	24.6	26.7
Other Asia	2.1	2.5	2.8	2.6	2.8	3.3	4.1	4.8	5.7	5.7	5.9
Australasia	21.4	21.9	19.2	19.0	19.5	21.8	25.8	29.6	28.3	28.8	27.7
Total Asia and Australasia	137.0	142.4	135.3	140.1	134.1	144.7	156.3	157.4	167.4	160.1	162.8
Total NCW	2 391.1	2 509.0	2 350.1	2 171.8	2 048.8	2 020.3	2 087.9	2 055.9	2 162.7	2 134.2	2 249.5
Socialist Countries											
China	104.1	106.1	105.8	101.0	101.7	106.0	114.5	124.9	130.7	132.9	136.1
USSR	572.5	586.0	603.0	609.0	612.2	616.3	612.7	595.0	615.0	624.2	624.0
Others	25.2	24.2	23.0	21.9	24.6	23.8	23.7	22.6	23.0	21.9	21.2
Total Socialist Countries	701.8	716.3	731.8	731.9	738.5	746.1	750.9	742.5	768.7	779.0	781.3
Total World	3 092.9	3 225.3	3 081.9	2 903.7	2 787.3	2 766.4	2 838.8	2 798.4	2 931.4	2 913.2	3 030.8
Of which OPEC	1 494.7	1 552.7	1 357.6	1 150.4	977.3	903.0	904.9	836.2	950.7	924.6	1 030.5

* Includes crude oil, shale oil, oil sands and NGLs (natural gas liquids – the liquid content of natural gas, where this is recovered separately).
Excludes liquid fuels from other sources such as coal derivatives
† Less than 0.05

Source: BP Statistical Review of World Energy.

Gasoil: world consumption 1978-88 (million tonnes)

	1978	1979	1980	1981	1982	1983	1984	1985	1986	1987	1988
North America											
USA	888.8	868.0	794.1	746.0	705.5	704.9	726.9	721.7	751.3	763.4	**789.2**
Canada	86.9	90.1	87.6	81.7	72.9	68.2	66.7	68.5	68.1	71.4	**74.7**
Total North America	975.7	958.1	881.7	827.7	778.4	773.1	793.6	790.2	819.4	834.8	**863.9**
Western Europe											
Austria	12.0	12.5	12.2	11.0	10.5	10.1	9.8	9.8	10.4	10.7	**10.6**
Belgium & Luxembourg	29.0	27.6	26.6	24.5	23.3	21.1	20.4	20.8	23.5	23.7	**24.3**
Denmark	16.1	15.9	13.6	12.8	11.0	10.4	10.4	10.7	10.5	9.6	**9.5**
Finland	12.5	13.3	12.8	12.3	11.3	10.5	10.6	10.8	11.3	11.2	**11.0**
France	119.0	118.3	109.9	99.0	91.5	89.4	85.9	84.3	86.0	86.6	**85.7**
Greece	11.7	12.4	12.4	11.9	11.9	11.4	11.7	12.0	12.2	13.2	**14.1**
Iceland	0.6	0.6	0.6	0.5	0.5	0.5	0.5	0.5	0.5	0.6	**0.6**
Republic of Ireland	6.0	6.4	5.9	5.1	4.6	4.2	4.1	4.0	4.8	4.1	**3.8**
Italy	99.8	103.2	97.9	95.7	90.7	89.2	84.9	84.4	86.5	90.1	**91.7**
Netherlands	38.4	41.3	38.6	35.7	31.0	29.1	28.7	29.2	32.4	32.4	**34.4**
Norway	9.3	9.6	9.3	8.7	8.3	8.3	8.6	9.0	9.3	9.7	**9.3**
Portugal	7.4	8.1	8.5	8.8	9.5	9.5	9.5	8.5	9.5	8.9	**8.0**
Spain	46.4	49.1	52.2	50.4	47.8	47.8	44.8	42.9	42.7	43.8	**45.0**
Sweden	26.4	27.3	24.8	22.4	20.5	18.4	17.5	18.3	18.7	17.1	**16.6**
Switzerland	13.4	12.9	12.8	11.9	11.2	12.3	11.8	12.0	13.2	12.4	**12.4**
Turkey	15.3	14.7	14.8	15.4	16.5	16.2	17.0	16.8	18.3	21.0	**22.3**
United Kingdom	94.0	94.5	80.8	74.7	75.6	72.5	89.6	77.4	77.4	75.2	**80.0**
West Germany	142.7	147.0	131.1	117.6	112.2	110.8	110.6	112.9	119.9	115.2	**114.8**
Total Western Europe	700.0	714.7	664.8	618.4	587.9	571.7	576.4	564.6	587.1	585.5	**594.1**
Australasia											
Australia	30.8	31.3	29.7	29.2	28.4	27.3	28.5	27.0	28.2	28.7	**29.9**
New Zealand	4.4	4.3	4.2	4.0	3.9	3.8	3.9	3.8	4.0	4.3	**4.4**
Total Australasia	35.2	35.6	33.9	33.2	32.3	31.1	32.4	30.8	32.2	33.0	**34.3**
Japan	262.7	265.1	237.7	223.9	207.8	207.2	215.1	203.4	205.3	205.7	**222.2**
Total OECD	**1 973.6**	**1 973.5**	**1 818.1**	**1 703.2**	**1 606.4**	**1 583.1**	**1 617.5**	**1 589.0**	**1 644.0**	**1 659.0**	**1 714.5**
South East Asia											
Korea	21.9	24.7	24.4	24.3	24.1	25.2	25.2	24.7	27.4	29.0	**34.7**
Taiwan	11.9	13.3	14.3	13.5	13.3	14.6	15.2	15.9	18.1	19.0	**22.9**
Other South East Asia	64.7	74.1	75.4	78.3	74.4	72.3	71.7	67.4	70.7	75.4	**83.0**
Total South East Asia	98.5	112.1	114.1	116.1	111.8	112.1	112.1	108.0	116.2	123.4	**140.6**
Rest of NCW											
Cyprus/Gibraltar/Malta	1.4	1.5	1.5	1.5	1.6	1.6	1.7	1.8	2.0	2.2	**2.5**
Latin America	191.2	203.6	211.8	212.6	216.5	211.0	210.0	209.7	215.3	224.1	**228.1**
Middle East	85.5	95.1	99.8	104.9	107.0	118.0	123.9	129.4	127.8	130.1	**135.4**
Africa	62.8	65.9	70.4	73.8	77.9	78.9	78.9	82.1	81.8	85.3	**86.2**
South Asia	37.1	37.7	40.4	43.4	45.6	46.4	50.4	56.4	58.5	61.0	**66.3**
Total Rest of NCW	378.0	403.8	423.9	436.2	448.6	455.9	464.9	479.4	485.4	502.7	**518.5**
Total NCW	**2 450.1**	**2 489.4**	**2 356.1**	**2 255.5**	**2 166.8**	**2 151.1**	**2 194.5**	**2 176.4**	**2 245.6**	**2 285.1**	**2 373.6**
Socialist Countries											
China	84.7	91.1	88.0	84.8	82.4	84.7	86.5	86.9	89.7	95.2	**100.7**
USSR	419.2	427.0	448.1	452.4	449.5	443.4	443.8	442.4	444.7	444.2	**439.1**
Others	130.4	134.2	131.9	125.6	121.6	118.1	118.2	120.8	125.2	123.9	**125.1**
Total Socialist Countries	634.3	652.3	668.0	662.8	653.5	646.2	648.5	650.1	659.6	663.3	**664.9**
Total World	**3 084.4**	**3 141.7**	**3 024.1**	**2 918.3**	**2 820.3**	**2 797.3**	**2 843.0**	**2 826.5**	**2 905.2**	**2 948.4**	**3 038.5**

* Inland demand plus international aviation and marine bunkers and refinery fuel and loss
† Less than 0.05
Note:
Differences between world production and consumption are accounted for by stock changes and oil 'Destination not known'

Source: BP Statistical Review of World Energy.

World oil production (basis 1988)

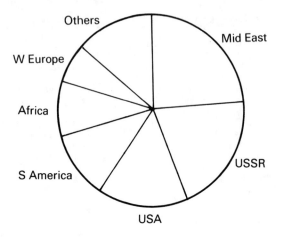

World oil consumption

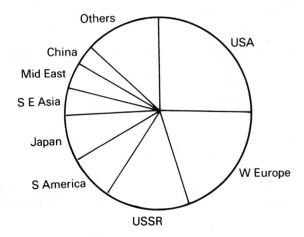

Rubber

Mr J M Hobbs,
A Runge & Company Limited

Elastomer consumption comprises two quite different commodities: synthetic and natural rubber. Synthetic rubber (which makes up approximately two-thirds of usage) is a by-product of mineral oil, on whose value in world markets its own price is ultimately dependent, and is made primarily in the industrial countries of the temperate zone. It is an industrial product, manufactured by known chemical practices to chemical formulae. Natural rubber, on the other hand (the remaining one-third), is collected in cupfuls from individual trees growing under widely differing conditions in tropical countries. The manufacturing processes are not always carefully controlled, and it is only in the last 30 years that any serious attempts have been made to understand rubber chemistry or to present the product in a form acceptable to modern industry. Nevertheless, despite frequent prophecies of impending doom, natural rubber has survived, and year by year sets new records for consumption.

Since more than 70% of world rubber output is consumed by the tyre industry and there is considerable over-capacity in synthetic rubber production, it is clear that the natural material has properties which render it attractive to large users. However, it has also become evident in the last two decades that each material has established its own area of the market in which it cannot easily be challenged, although from time to time significant ground has been gained by one side or the other. The radial-ply tyre, for instance, has greatly aided the consumption levels of natural rubber in recent years, although this has since been counterbalanced by the increase in the life of the tyre.

Competition from synthetic rubber has mainly been disappointing for natural rubber producers in terms of price. In 1984 and 1985, for instance, consumption exceeded all previous annual tonnages, but the market fell steadily, and the surplus had to be absorbed by aggressive buying for the buffer stock established under the International Natural Rubber Agreement (INRA). In 1986 and 1987, this situation gradually corrected itself, with the spread of AIDS beginning to emerge as a new feature. In the first half of 1988, fuelled by exploding demand for concentrate latex to make surgical gloves and condoms, the market embarked on a buying spree which took prices to levels not even seen during the Korean War boom. In a few months, 370,000 tonnes of stockpiled rubber disappeared, new glove manufacturers sprouted like mushrooms, and trees which had lain dormant for years were hastily brought back into the tapping round. This euphoria proved short-lived, however, as production rose unexpectedly fast, and the price differential between natural and synthetic provided a rapid incentive to consumers to change their formulations. At the time of writing, prices are at only a fraction of their early 1988 levels, and the prospect of renewed buying by INRA looks not far away.

At the lower price levels, producers in Malaysia, the world's largest and most progressive growers of rubber, have found themselves faced with negligible profit margins, and the growth in annual output has virtually ceased. The lower-cost producers, however (especially Indonesia and Thailand, although West Africa is becoming increasingly important), have found themselves still able to compete profitably, and have become more and more significant in the total picture of world consumption.

Paradoxically, these territories have tended in the past to exert less influence on the actual price level than would have been expected. Produce of Indonesia has historically found its way to the United States (the world's largest consumer) while that of Thailand went to the factories of the second largest user, Japan, without affecting world prices to a significant extent. On the other hand, smaller tonnages of rubber sold through the trading markets of Singapore, Kuala Lumpur, and London have often moved the price quite sharply. There are signs that this is changing, as increased sophistication in the market has begun to inspire worldwide interest in trading contracts based on SIR 20 (Standard Indonesian Rubber), and Thai Ribbed Smoked Sheet 3, the grades chiefly produced by these two countries.

Efficient marketing of natural rubber is greatly assisted by the fact that there is an intricate broker and dealer mechanism in the Singapore, Kuala Lumpur, and EEC markets (the EEC market traditionally has been based on London, but includes brokers and dealers in other EEC countries). These markets exist not only to service the consumers in their own countries, which is the prime function of the rubber dealer in the United States or Japan, but also to act as entrepreneurs in the world trade in natural rubber. They also cover consuming areas such as Eastern Europe, South America, and the Middle and Near East, where the needs of the user may be not only to receive the raw material, but also to be given extended finance, or other facilities which are not normally extended to the consumer in the traditional markets of Western Europe or North America.

To carry out this entrepreneurial function, sophisticated techniques are needed whereby buyers and sellers can hedge their purchases and sales. It is also helpful that a part of the risks inherent in changing prices should be taken by operators who are not professionally involved in the movement of physical rubber. Regrettably, however, the existence of a large buffer stock, and a succession of years of depressed trading conditions, combined to erode the interest previously shown in natural rubber by the outside speculator. Consequently, the Singapore paper market and the London terminal market (both based on No 1 Ribbed Smoked Sheet) have declined in importance and activity – the latter to the point of extinction, although strenuous attempts are being made to promote a revival, possibly on the basis of some other grade. This lack of a satisfactory hedging facility has undoubtedly added to the problems facing dealers during the past two years of widely fluctuating prices, when the risk factor has been unusually high.

As we prepare to enter the 1990s, natural rubber faces several challenges the largest of which is the continuing lack of market equilibrium caused by the wild excesses of 1988. Fundamentally, however, its position is sound, since consumption continues to be good, research into natural rubber usage, both potential and actual, proceeds apace, stocks in consuming areas are low, and the raw material itself is again cheap in price and remains unique in its technical characteristics. It therefore seems reasonable to expect a fair return for the producer over the next year or two, given a healthy level of world business activity and, particularly, a less expensive cost of money.

Natural rubber: production in 1988, with estimates for 1989 and forecasts for 1990 (000 tonnes)

	1988	1989	1990
Malaysia	1660	1620	1650
Indonesia	1230	1260	1290
Thailand	975	1000	1060
Sri Lanka	122	125	126
Vietnam	50	55	60
Kampuchea	27	28	28
India	255	280	305
Burma	15	15	15
China	240	245	255
Philippines	85	85	87
TOTAL ASIA	4659	4713	4876
Liberia	89	91	93
Nigeria	68	70	70
Zaire	19	19	19
Cameroon	32	36	39
Côte d'Ivoire	63	68	72
Other Africa	3	3	4
TOTAL AFRICA	274	287	297
Brazil	33	36	39
Mexico	5	5	5
Other Lat.Am.	21	21	22
TOTAL LAT.AM.	59	62	66
Papua New Guinea	5	5	5
TOTAL WORLD (a) (rounded)	4995	5070	5245

(a) Including statistical discrepancies

By courtesy of the International Rubber Study Group.

Synthetic rubber: production in 1988, with estimates for 1989 and forecasts for 1990 (000 tonnes)

	1988	1989	1990
U.S A.	2325	2325	2295
Canada	203	200	200
TOTAL N.Am.	2528	2525	2495
F.R. of Germany	493	505	510
U.K.	313	321	328
France	568	579	590
Italy	260	275	290
Netherlands	188	205	210
Belgium	126	128	130
Spain	78	81	84
TOTAL E.E.C.	2026	2094	2142
Sweden	31	32	33
Turkey	38	40	42
Finland	10	11	12
Austria	5	5	5
Yugoslavia	24	25	25
TOTAL O.W.E.	108	113	117
Bulgaria	25	26	27
Czechoslovakia	76	79	80
Germany D.R.	160	160	165
Poland	128	131	133
Romania	155	150	150
U.S.S.R.	2435	2500	2550
TOTAL E.Europe	2979	3046	3105
Japan	1299	1290	1301
China	252	267	278
India	51	57	63
S. Korea	169	198	230
Taiwan	137	145	156
TOTAL Asia	1908	1957	2028
Brazil	283	321	338
Argentina	54	55	58
Mexico	146	147	152
TOTAL Lat.Am.	483	523	548
Australia	49	52	54
S. Africa	50	51	52
TOTAL WORLD (rounded)	10130	10360	10540

By courtesy of the International Rubber Study Group.

Natural and synthetic rubber: consumption in 1988, with estimates for 1989 and forecasts for 1990 (000 tonnes)

	1988				1989				1990			
	NR	SR	Total	%SR	NR	SR	Total	%SR	NR	SR	Total	%SR
U.S.A.	833	2010	2843	71	850	2040	2890	71	845	2015	2860	70
Canada	88	202	290	70	87	200	287	70	88	205	293	70
E.E.C.:-												
France	181	315	496	64	186	326	512	64	189	331	520	64
F.R. of Germany	203	471	674	70	207	485	692	70	208	495	703	70
Italy	140	312	452	69	145	325	470	69	150	335	485	69
Netherlands	13	65	78	83	13	67	80	84	13	69	82	84
U.K.	140	226	366	62	144	232	376	62	145	235	380	62
Other E.E.C.	197	308	505	61	205	322	527	61	211	330	541	61
TOTAL E.E.C.	874	1697	2571	66	900	1757	2657	66	916	1795	2711	66
Other W. Europe	145	311	456	68	150	321	471	68	155	331	486	68
Eastern Europe	289	2887	3176	91	325	2965	3290	90	358	3025	3383	89
Africa	114	110	224	49	117	113	230	49	121	114	235	49
Australia	42	63	105	60	44	65	109	60	47	70	117	60
China	602	293	895	33	620	310	930	33	637	323	960	34
India	311	82	393	21	334	86	420	20	358	92	450	20
Japan	623	1042	1665	63	633	1078	1711	63	639	1089	1728	63
Other Asia	870	585	1455	40	926	622	1548	40	1008	682	1690	40
Brazil	125	284	409	69	135	321	456	70	148	364	512	71
Other L. America	181	283	464	61	186	293	479	61	192	308	500	62
GRAND TOTAL (rounded)	5095	9850	14945	65.9	5310	10170	15480	65.7	5510	10415	15925	65.4

By courtesy of the International Rubber Study Group.

Natural rubber: London spot prices 1977-88
(RSS1; annual averages, £ per tonne)

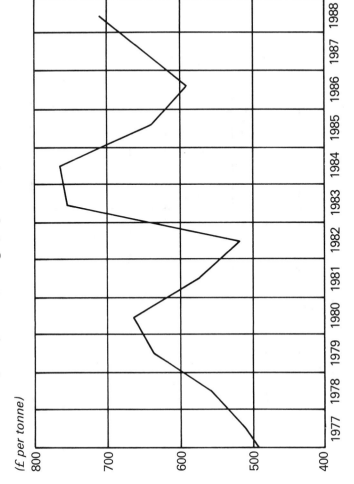

(£ per tonne)

Source: International Rubber Study Group

Natural rubber: New York prices* 1977-88 (RSS1; annual averages, US$ per tonne)

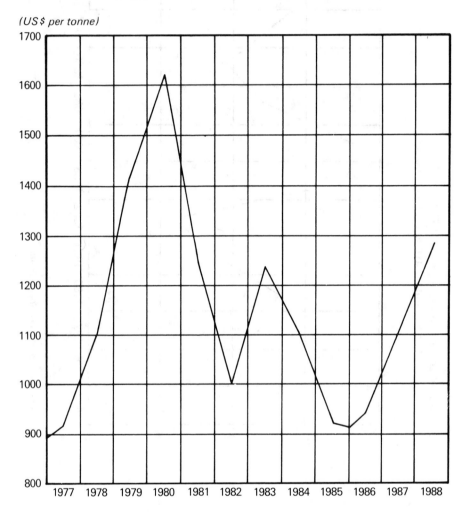

(US$ per tonne)

*New York quotations refer to sellers' asking prices for delivery during the current month.

Source: International Rubber Study Group.

Soyabeans and the oilseed 'complex'

John Buckley

The great North American drought of 1988 was a stark reminder of the world oilseed market's dependence on soyabeans. With crops averaging some 53 million tonnes in the first half of this decade, the United States normally produces about half the world's soyabeans and about one-quarter of global oilseed supply. Last year's harvest, however, fell to only 42 million tonnes in dustbowl conditions reminiscent of the 1930s. Fortunately for the world's consumers of oilseeds, meals and oils – commonly known as the oilseed 'complex' – the dominating role of the United States has been softened considerably in recent years.

The main change has emanated from Latin America, as Brazil and Argentina, who with residual producers in neighbouring Paraguay and Uruguay, now account for well in excess of 30 million tonnes of soyabean output a year. In the mid-1970s, the region's aggregate output was less than one-third of this, or about 17% of world production, and the trebling of these alternative supplies has been a major influence restraining soya prices.

Just as important as the more geographically widespread nature of production, has been the more even flow of crops to market. Those harvested in the southern hemisphere now start to arrive from February/March onwards, halfway through the traditional North American/European marketing season. This tends to reduce the impact of American shortfalls, as witnessed not only in the current season, but also during the lesser droughts of 1980 and 1983.

The soyabean market, and with it the entire complex, has also been affected in the 1980s by the development of other competing sources of supply. In the Far East, Malaysian palm oil production has leapt from a mere 1 million tonnes in 1975, to 4.5 million in 1988 and further increases are scheduled for the 1990s, as new plantations come to maturity. Added to that is a boom in palm oil supply from neighbouring Indonesia from 400,000 to over 2 million tonnes. Both countries are geared primarily towards exporting their expanding output, which is coming into increasing competition with soya oil from the United States, Brazil and Argentina.

The third new force in the complex has been the European Community which multiplied production of rapeseed and sunflowerseed from less than 1 million tonnes in the 1970s to over 10 million tonnes in 1987.

All this extra supply has taken a heavy toll on production and crushing margins for oilseeds in the last ten years, halting expansion in the United States and Europe and slowing it down in Latin America and the Far East. However, the effect has been complicated by the varying degree to which individual oilseeds have been hit by the recession.

Soyabeans, for example, are crushed primarily for their value as animal feed. The soyabean yields about 18–19% of its weight to oil and the rest mainly to meal for livestock compounds. Of a world crush of around 83 million tonnes (the rest of the crop is either fed directly to animals or used in edible human outlets, or made into products like soya milk and soy sauce), the United States alone is responsible for around 30 million tonnes. The bulk of this is consumed by domestic livestock industries, but the United States still manages to export around 4.5 million tonnes of meal and in a normal year about 20 million tonnes of beans. Its biggest customer by far is the European Community, but millions of tonnes go to countries like Japan and Taiwan and, increasingly, the Soviet Union, where soya is used to feed huge and expanding meat-producing industries.

The remaining oil product of the crush goes to a host of downstream industries supplying oilseed meals for animal feed and vegetable oils for cooking, food manufacture, margarine and technical/industrial uses. However, since the crush motive is for meal, the oil is produced as a by-product and in the United States in particular, it frequently piles up with no relation to demand, providing a constant restraint on global vegoil prices generally.

The balance of soya's dual use frequently disadvantages it against its newer competitors. European rapeseed, for example, contains 42% oil and can be grown for that market primarily, with the meal as a loss-leader. The palm tree goes even further. Most of its fruit is crushed into oil, so there is little meal by-product and virtually no secondary disposal to worry about.

This equation has favoured the so-called 'oil-rich' oilseeds in the last 10 to 15 years during which the once-dominant soyabean has undergone a series of adjustments from the boom conditions of the previous two decades. Even as recently as the five years leading up to 1982/83, world consumption of soyabeans grew by over 22%, while export growth in soyabeans was even steeper – 50% up over the period. But in the middle 1980s growth flattened as poor operating profits, smaller crops and foreign competition forced many crushing plants to close in the United States or switch to other oilseed sources in Europe.

In the late-1980s, the South Americans have resumed their expansion as demand has begun to respond to the low soyabean prices caused by several years of surplus. Whether that can continue for more than a season or two is questioned however, by the Latin nations' escalating debt problems, compounded by currency turmoil that has robbed farmers of profits and could prevent them from affording sufficient crop inputs like fertilizer.

Until last year, retrenchment in the physical markets was mirrored on the Chicago futures market, where depressed and predictable conditions replaced the volatility which hitherto had made soya the most active of the agricultural terminals. In 1985, soyabean turnover fell 35% to just 7.39 million contracts, but last year's drought caused a startling comeback. As the United States crop wilted, the futures market experienced an unprecedented 70% rise in trade to 12.5 million lots. Soya meal rallied 40% to 5.3 million and oil by 25% to 4.9 million.

World consumption of oilseed products has been on a fairly steep upward curve for many years as populations have expanded and developing countries have raised their per capita offtake levels. An aggregate 28% growth rate was achieved in meal trade alone between 1979/80 and 1985/86. However, since then the market has grown at a declining pace, down to 3.4% per annum as debt problems have begun to slow the ability of some countries to import.

Third World demand for proteins has also been restrained by the steep rise in feedgrain surpluses in the United States and Europe in the mid-1980s which, combined with increased self-sufficiency in many big traditional grain-importing countries, thrust a massive and progressively cheaper grain mountain into competition with oilmeals. The EC was also cutting its dairy surpluses with production quotas which reduced compound feed offtake and consumption of soya meal, at a time of expanding output of rapeseed meal.

Despite the increase in South American supplies, soyabean oil consumption has levelled off at just under 15 million tonnes per annum with a decline in its market share from nearly 29% of world trade in 1979/80, to just 20% in the current season. Growth in total vegoil consumption has been quickly soaked up by the other expanding oil sources: palm oil, up from 29% to 34% of trade; sunflower; rapeseed; coconut and fish oil up from 20% to an aggregate 34%.

The United States seems likely to decrease further as a world force in soya and oilseed markets in years to come, although the process will be a slow one. As the GATT Uruguay Round demands a tightening of unfair trade competition, pressure will be increased on the Latin American countries to reduce preferential export taxes and domestic consumption supports that have helped them to gain market share from the United States. So Brazil, which exports mostly oil and meal, and Argentina may find that the path to expansion gets stonier.

Brazil now crushes most of its soyabeans and dominates product export markets with 37% of world meal trade and 25% of soyabean oil sales, against the United States' 16%, where only seven years ago, the United States was the main supplier. Argentina, meanwhile, tends to concentrate on sales of beans and oil. The United States is, however, still the largest consumer, accounting for about 34% of world crush, 27% of world meal consumption and 32% of soya oil offtake.

The outlook for the soya industry in the next few years will continue to be steered by rationalization and retrenchment, not least because of the nature and diversity of competition. United States and Latin American meal exports, however, may at least come under less pressure from grain surpluses now that global grain stocks have been reduced to the minimum level required for security against famines.

In real terms, both meal and oil are at historically cheap levels and, if they can be kept there, developing countries may be able to continue some degree of expansion in imports. Chief oil importers are India, Pakistan, the Soviet Union and China and – political turmoil aside – it is the centrally planned economies which now promise the greatest growth area for the 1990s.

Another interesting development in the soya market in the latter half of the 1980s has been the growth of options trade in United States and European futures markets. Options offer another form of 'price insurance' with a more limited risk compared with the potentially huge margin calls or deposits that traders have to make when the futures market moves against them. By offering the opportunity to trade futures only when they reach a given 'strike price', the option lets the farmer protect against a falling market without giving up the opportunity to benefit from a rise. Similarly, crushers and livestock feed manufacturers can hedge against dearer raw material costs without missing the chance to buy more cheaply should the market reverse a strong upturn. From 840,786 contracts in their first full year of trading in 1985, CBOT options rose to 3.24 million lots last year and Chicago also trades options on meal and oil. A flourishing options trade has also sprung up on other United States exchanges, including MIDAM, and also on the London-based Baltic Futures Exchange meal futures market (SOMFA).

Soyabeans: world production, trade and consumption (million tonnes)

	1984/85	1985/86	1986/87	1987/88	1988/89
Production					
United States	50.64	57.11	52.80	52.33	41.88
Brazil	18.28	14.10	17.30	18.05	21.70
Argentina	6.75	7.30	7.00	9.70	7.80
China	9.70	10.51	11.61	12.18	11.00
EC-12	0.15	0.34	0.90	1.79	1.55
Paraguay	0.95	0.60	0.95	1.10	1.20
Other	6.68	7.08	7.42	7.92	8.36
Total	93.14	97.03	97.98	103.07	93.49
Exports					
United States	16.28	20.16	20.60	21.83	14.97
Brazil	3.48	1.19	3.29	2.71	5.00
Argentina	3.29	2.54	1.35	2.09	1.50
Paraguay	0.85	0.48	1.08	1.28	1.17
China	1.08	1.26	1.75	1.48	1.10
Other	0.30	0.45	0.49	0.66	0.68
Total	25.27	26.07	28.56	30.05	24.42

Soyabeans: world production, trade and consumption (million tonnes) - *continued*

	1984/85	1985/86	1986/87	1987/88	1988/89
Imports					
EC-12	12.89	13.22	14.42	13.33	11.26
Germany, Fed Rep	2.88	2.93	3.33	2.92	2.29
Netherlands	2.83	2.70	3.24	3.79	3.35
Spain	1.94	2.13	2.73	2.37	1.95
Italy	1.50	1.62	1.12	0.40	0.65
Bel-Lux	1.31	1.35	1.48	1.35	1.08
Portugal	1.01	0.92	0.96	0.85	0.73
Other W Europe	0.51	0.50	0.54	0.52	0.57
USSR	0.85	2.24	1.48	1.42	1.25
Eastern Europe	0.58	0.79	0.77	0.74	0.74
Romania	0.20	0.42	0.44	0.40	0.30
Yugoslavia	0.27	0.29	0.21	0.24	0.30
Poland	0.04	0.00	0.01	0.00	0.00
China	0.00	0.28	0.19	0.21	0.00
Japan	4.61	4.80	4.87	4.85	4.50
Korea, Rep of	0.81	1.01	1.01	1.10	1.02
Taiwan	1.47	1.59	2.01	2.12	1.80
Indonesia	0.32	0.38	0.32	0.63	0.50
Mexico	1.43	1.00	1.09	0.95	1.25
Brazil	0.38	0.29	0.29	0.47	0.08
Other	1.61	1.48	2.18	2.40	2.18
Total	25.45	27.57	29.18	28.74	25.16
Crush					
United States	28.03	28.66	32.09	31.95	28.85
Latin America	19.71	19.30	22.14	21.02	24.83
Brazil	13.13	12.46	14.48	12.84	15.20
Argentina	3.86	4.37	4.89	5.40	6.80
Mexico	2.00	1.773	1.70	1.70	1.55
EC-12	12.33	12.80	13.49	12.88	10.99
Other W Europe	0.50	0.51	0.52	0.50	0.56
USSR	1.14	2.47	1.97	1.93	1.93
Eastern Europe	1.21	1.28	1.44	1.34	1.32
Asia	8.81	10.43	11.60	13.05	12.88
Japan	3,79	3.91	3.82	3.80	3.70
China	1.72	2.69	3.64	4.74	4.21
Taiwan	1.20	1.38	1.65	1.70	1.65
Other	2.15	2.00	2.30	2.21	2.21
Total	73.86	77.45	85.55	84.88	83.56
Ending Stocks					
United States	8.60	14.60	11.87	8.22	3.67
Brazil	4.74	4.43	3.03	4.65	4.83
Argentina	1.80	1.82	2.17	3.86	2.81
Other	2.44	2.35	2.49	2.91	2.42
Total	17.58	23.20	19.56	19.65	13.73
US Season Avg Price	5.84	5.05	4.78	5.88	7.35

By courtesy of the US Department of Agriculture.

Soyabean meal: world production, trade and consumption (million tonnes)

	1984/85	1985/86	1986/87	1987/88	1988/89
Production					
United States	22.25	22.64	25.18	25.46	22.59
Latin America	15.30	15.02	17.21	16.41	19.42
Brazil	10.19	9.69	11.28	10.04	11.89
Argentina	3.08	3.49	3.87	4.29	5.40
Mexico	1.46	1.27	1.23	1.23	1.13
EC-12	9.79	10.22	10.74	10.31	8.75
Other W Europe	0.39	0.41	0.40	0.44	0.39
USSR	0.87	1.93	1.54	1.56	1.53
Eastern Europe	0.97	1.03	1.16	1.08	1.06
Asia	6.95	8.27	9.24	10.45	10.29
Japan	2.92	3.04	2.97	2.97	2.87
China	1.41	2.19	3.00	3.91	3.44
Taiwan	0.95	1.09	1.30	1.34	1.30
Other	1.68	1.56	1.79	1.72	1.73
Total	58.20	61.07	67.26	67.42	65.75
Exports					
United States	4.46	5.48	6.66	6.23	4.76
Brazil	8.44	7.38	8.37	7.35	9.60
Argentina	2.88	3.16	3.47	4.10	5.00
EC-12	5.15	5.08	5.08	4.31	4.37
China	0.65	1.11	1.54	2.42	1.50
Other	0.74	0.93	0.83	0.83	1.36
Total	22.31	23.13	25.95	25.24	26.59
Imports					
EC-12	13.34	13.79	13.60	12.15	12.49
France	3.29	3.67	3.66	3.11	3.10
Germany, Fed Rep	2.58	2.61	2.56	1.99	2.20
Netherlands	1.62	1.48	1.27	1.10	1.20
Italy	1.18	1.59	1.55	1.35	1.40
Other W Europe	0.64	0.63	0.65	0.70	0.62
USSR	0.55	0.48	2.90	3.00	4.00
Eastern Europe	3.50	3.69	3.90	3.71	3.64
Asia & Oceania	1.20	1.68	1.85	2.26	2.18
Mid-East & N Afr	1.52	1.68	1.68	1.85	1.93
Latin America	1.33	1.24	1.35	1.46	1.43
Other	0.76	0.74	0.71	0.72	0.68
Total	22.84	23.93	26.64	25.84	26.96
Consumption					
United States	17.67	17.32	18.50	19.30	17.69
Latin America	5.45	5.79	6.49	6.02	6.18
Brazil	2.01	2.41	3.01	2.39	2.50
Argentina	0.27	0.40	0.20	0.27	0.35
Mexico	1.50	1.35	1.29	1.40	1.31
EC-12	17.97	18.73	19.23	18.21	16.98
France	3.74	4.09	4.09	3.44	3.25

Soyabean meal: world production, trade and consumption (million tonnes)
- *continued*

	1984/85	1985/86	1986/87	1987/88	1988/89
Germany, Fed Rep	3.00	2.83	2.88	2.70	2.50
Netherlands	2.07	1.90	1.85	1.80	1.63
Italy	2.31	2.67	2.79	2.80	2.67
Spain	2.25	2.65	2.84	2.75	2.67
Other W Europe	0.87	0.87	0.92	1.01	0.87
USSR	1.42	2.41	4.44	4.56	5.53
Eastern Europe	4.41	4.69	4.98	4.83	4.72
German Dem Rep	0.98	1.12	1.05	0.94	0.95
Poland	0.86	0.75	1.02	1.00	1.00
Asia & Oceania	7.43	8.12	9.14	9.76	10.25
Japan	3.12	3.21	3.19	3.39	3.44
China	0.76	1.07	1.47	1.50	1.96
Taiwan	0.94	1.07	1.28	1.25	1.28
Korea, Rep of	0.70	0.78	0.93	1.02	1.15
Mid-East & N Afr	2.24	2.32	2.42	2.59	2.68
Other	1.54	1.54	1.61	1.53	1.51
Total	59.00	61.78	67.73	67.79	66.43
Ending Stocks					
United States	0.35	0.19	0.22	0.14	0.27
Brazil	0.72	0.61	0.52	0.83	0.61
Argentina	0.19	0.13	0.33	0.25	0.30
Other	1.51	1.92	2.00	2.09	1.81
Total	2.78	2.86	3.08	3.31	2.99
US Season Avg Price	125.40	154.90	162.70	221.90	230.00

By courtesy of the US Department of Agriculture.

Soyabean oil: world production, trade and consumption (million tonnes)

	1984/85	1985/86	1986/87	1987/88	1988/89
Production					
United States	5.20	5.27	5.80	5.89	5.29
Latin America	3.59	3.52	4.05	3.85	4.55
Brazil	2.46	2.35	2.73	2.42	2.86
Argentina	0.64	0.73	0.83	0.93	1.18
Mexico	0.36	0.31	0.31	0.31	0.28
EC-12	2.21	2.25	2.36	2.28	1.89
Other W Europe	0.09	0.09	0.09	0.10	0.09
USSR	0.19	0.42	0.33	0.32	0.34
Eastern Europe	0.19	0.21	0.23	0.21	0.21
Asia	1.49	1.74	1.96	2.19	2.16
Japan	0.69	0.71	0.71	0.70	0.68
China	0.24	0.38	0.55	0.71	0.63
Taiwan	0.20	0.23	0.28	0.29	0.28
Other	0.39	0.35	0.40	0.39	0.38
Total	13.34	13.85	15.22	15.22	14.90
Exports					
United States	0.75	0.57	0.54	0.85	0.59
Brazil	0.99	0.45	0.95	0.62	0.85
Argentina	0.51	0.64	0.73	0.84	1.03
EC-12	1.30	1.39	1.44	1.27	0.93
Other	0.08	0.10	0.24	0.23	0.20
Total	3.63	3.15	3.90	3.81	3.60
Imports					
United States	0.01	0.00	0.01	0.09	0.09
EC-12	0.51	0.51	0.53	0.48	0.43
USSR	0.33	0.11	0.22	0.12	0.15
Eastern Europe	0.20	0.14	0.13	0.11	0.14
China	0.02	0.13	0.41	0.14	0.25
India	0.40	0.26	0.36	0.42	0.08
Pakistan	0.19	0.32	0.19	0.40	0.38
Mid-East & N Afr	0.79	0.60	0.79	0.82	0.83
Iran	0.38	0.33	0.42	0.41	0.43
Morocco	0.12	0.07	0.12	0.06	0.08
Turkey	0.11	0.09	0.12	0.18	0.15
Tunisia	0.07	0.04	0.06	0.09	0.09
Egypt	0.04	0.01	0.01	0.01	0.01
Latin America	0.67	0.57	0.51	0.59	0.55
Brazil	0.16	0.12	0.11	0.07	0.06
Mexico	0.05	0.05	0.03	0.05	0.06
Chile	0.08	0.03	0.04	0.03	0.04
Peru	0.03	0.06	0.07	0.08	0.06
Colombia	0.05	0.07	0.04	0.06	0.05
Other	0.41	0.45	0.64	0.64	0.61
Total	3.51	3.08	3.80	3.79	3.49

Soyabean oil: world production, trade and consumption (million tonnes)
- continued

	1984/85	1985/86	1986/87	1987/88	1988/89
Consumption					
United States	4.50	4.56	4.92	4.96	4.76
Latin America	2.62	2.93	2.92	2.99	3.06
Brazil	1.55	1.94	1.93	1.91	1.98
Argentina	0.07	0.10	0.08	0.10	0.11
Mexico	0.42	0.38	0.34	0.34	0.33
EC-12	1.40	1.38	1.46	1.51	1.38
Other W Europe	0.16	0.17	0.17	0.17	0.18
USSR	0.52	0.53	0.54	0.44	0.49
Eastern Europe	0.36	0.33	0.34	0.32	0.36
Asia	2.24	2.45	3.10	3.27	3.22
Japan	0.70	0.70	0.71	0.69	0.69
China	0.25	0.50	0.96	0.85	0.88
Taiwan	0.20	0.22	0.27	0.28	0.29
Korea, Rep of	0.13	0.15	0.16	0.16	0.16
India	0.58	0.47	0.45	0.51	0.42
Pakistan	0.21	0.21	0.27	0.39	0.40
Bangladesh	0.05	0.07	0.12	0.16	0.17
Mid-East & N Afr	0.96	0.75	0.95	0.96	0.99
Iran	0.41	0.34	0.43	0.42	0.44
Morocco	0.13	0.08	0.12	0.07	0.08
Turkey	0.13	0.11	0.13	0.19	0.17
Other	0.37	0.39	0.39	0.37	0.37
Total	13.13	13.49	14.78	14.99	14.80
Ending Stocks					
United States	0.29	0.43	0.78	0.95	0.98
Brazil	0.24	0.32	0.28	0.23	0.33
Argentina	0.10	0.10	0.12	0.11	0.15
Other	0.73	0.81	0.81	0.92	0.75
Total	1.36	1.65	1.99	2.21	2.20
US Season Avg Price	29.50	18.00	15.40	22.65	21.50

By courtesy of the US Department of Agriculture.

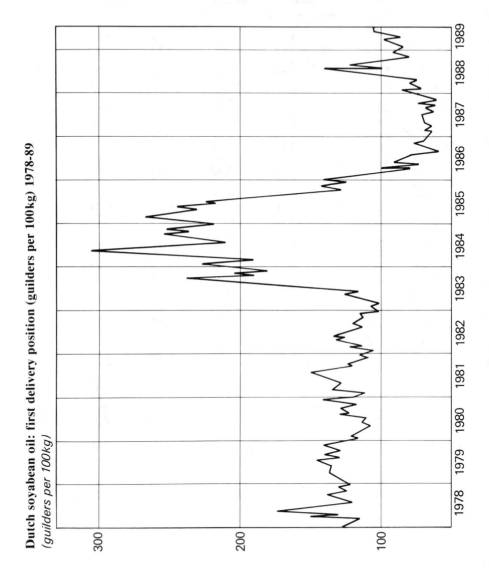

Dutch soyabean oil: first delivery position (guilders per 100kg) 1978-89
(guilders per 100kg)

Chicago soyabeans: first position ($ per bushel) 1981-89

($ per bushel)

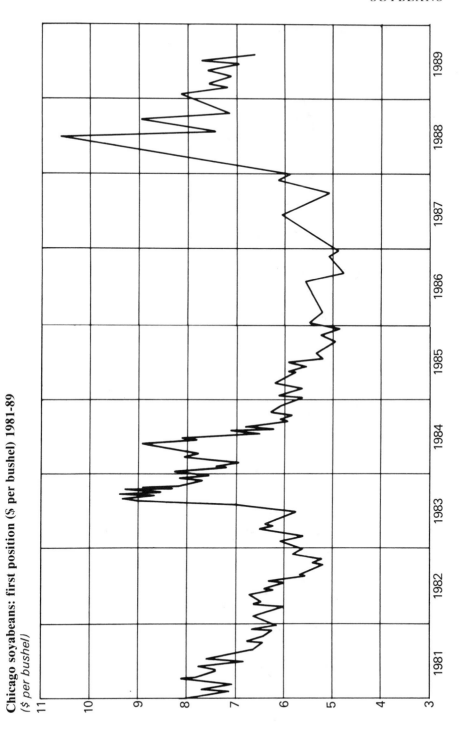

Soyabeans: world production (basis 1988/89)

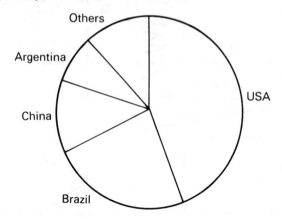

Soyabean oil: world producers (basis 1988/89)

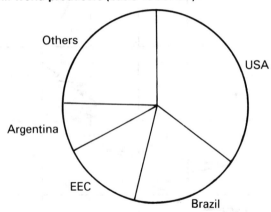

Oilseed market shares (basis 1988/89)

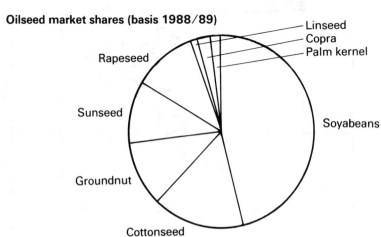

Sugar

John Buckley

Only about 15% of world sugar production is actually traded on the open market; of the remainder, the bulk is either consumed in its country of origin where many governments subsidize output, consumption or both, while the rest is sold under special cheap terms through bilateral agreements, for example between Cuba and the Comecon nations, the EC/Lomé and the US/ Caribbean.

However, that 'residual' 15% is a highly influential factor in the global sugar economy. If, for example, world sugar production falls or rises by a mere 5% to 7, the 'free' sugar market can find itself short of up to half its requirements, or alternatively with millions of tonnes of unwanted stocks to depress prices. It is this factor which explains the extraordinary volatility of sugar prices in years of surplus or short crops, a phenomenon that is enhanced by its appeal to the speculative element in the markets.

Sugar is also highly sensitive to unexpected surges in demand, as demonstrated in recent seasons when the Soviet Union and China found their sources of guaranteed cheap supplies curtailed by a series of crop shortfalls in the leading exporter Cuba. The Soviet Union's and China's resultant forays into the world market for over 3 million tonnes of sugar each, whipped up a whirlwind of panic buying. With speculators already primed by the worst United States drought in 50 years, the result was an astonishing rise in New York sugar market turnover to 5.8 million lots from only 3.85 million in 1987. The London FOX raw sugar contract meanwhile gained nearly 70% more volume, at 1.19 million lots.

In historical terms, the doubling of sugar prices in 1988 to some 15 cents a pound was a relatively low key affair, however. If one looks back to 1980/81, for example, when the ratio of stocks to consumption last fell well below 30%, the New York sugar futures market rose to a peak 46 cents a pound.

The broader significance of last year's events is the confirmation of gradual tightening in the global sugar balance. For four consecutive seasons now, sugar production has been outweighed by consumption and one need not look back beyond 1985 to locate some of the causes for this.

Then, sugar prices were in free fall, hitting just 2.67 cents a pound amid a seemingly intractible problem of surplus. (The market had in fact traded down to almost half that price in the 1960s, although in inflation-weighted terms, the 1985 low was the cheapest sugar had ever been.)

Behind that decline was the constant rise of stocks carried from one glut season to the next. Even during the 1973/74 price boom, these were estimated at 16 million tonnes, in the 1980 bull market, at 25 million tonnes and, during a late 1985 upsurge, some 40 million tonnes.

This rise had been going on for almost 20 years, as consumption failed to keep pace with production that had roughly doubled and there is no doubt the situation would not have occurred had producers been exposed more to free market forces, rather than endlessly cushioned by government subsidy.

Of course, sooner or later the reckoning has to come in such 'store or bust' situations. No government could produce sugar at the world price of 5 to 6 cents a pound in 1985/86 and many were subsidizing producer prices by between 12 and 20 cents. Production began to ease in the Far East and parts of Latin America, as well as in developing countries, including those of the European Community.

The situation was compounded by the Cuban crop shortfalls which resulted as much from poor plantation practices as from a series of unfortunate droughts, although latterly Cuba appears to be getting its act together again and a good crop is expected for the forthcoming campaign.

Another factor has been the tightening supply from Brazil, where a fierce battle has developed for cane supplies in recent seasons between the edible sugar and the alcohol fuel or ethanol industries – the latter now accounting for some 75% of the crop there. The Brazilian situation has also been compounded by muddled management following the Brazilian Government's decision to privatize the sugar industry. Export policy has fallen into disarray and Brazil's sugar trade faces an uncertain future for the next year or two at least.

About 37% of the world sugar trade of 28 million tonnes is in white form, the rest as 'raws'. Outside of the combined EC countries, Brazil is by far and away the largest supplier of whites with a market share of around 16%, so the impact of its shortfall has been profound. Recently, the premium of white over raw sugars has expanded by well over $100 per tonne, buttressed by deficits in other white producing countries including Mexico, Venezuela, India and the Eastern bloc. The premium has provided fertile trading conditions for the London FOX and the Paris white sugar futures contracts where the differentials are traded between raws/whites and market centres.

India is a major force in the sugar market, veering from either side of net importer/exporter, depending on local market conditions and on the success of the monsoon rains. Domestic consumption has soared in recent years and this has generally been matched by crop increases. However, there has recently been an overall tendency towards tighter supplies.

Elsewhere in the Far East, fortunes are mixed. Thailand has responded to the 1988 price boom by expanding production to record levels, helping to supplement shortfalls elsewhere. The other big producer in the region, the

Philippines, has tended to crop less since the 1985 price crash and the weather has tended to prevent a targeted revival more recently.

China has vastly expanded consumption and imports of sugar, as living standards have been improved and the economy liberalized. With per capita intake recently as little as 5 or 6kg per annum, there remains plenty of leeway for growth, in theory. However, the Chinese boom may come to a temporary halt because of an acute shortage of foreign exchange with which to pay for those imports that have become more expensive in the last two years. The political turmoil in Peking is a factor that may cut both ways for this, the world's largest sugar importer. Some suggest that China may need to import more to control prices and keep consumers happy, others say that imports will be made harder by greater centralization of buying and by the threat that further political instability will damage credit-backed trade.

The Soviet Union is another 'wild card' in the sugar pack. Imports have boomed in recent years, especially under the Gorbachev era. It is an interesting fact that much of this sugar has gone to feed illicit alcohol manufacture – a situation which some suppliers feared might be ending as Gorbachev attempted a crackdown on moonshine stills last year. With a variable and often harsh weather system and a need for more efficient harvesting, Russia's own crops are a key element in world sugar price-making as their season approaches each autumn.

The centrally planned economies also inject a further element of volatility into the world sugar market through their increasing use of so-called 'swap' trades in recent years. These have largely sprung from Cuba's inability to meet its preferential quotas and its consequent decision to borrow from the world sugar market. The trade itself often gets involved in these complex swap deals which can pass the sugar 'loan' through a chain of several countries or trade houses. An element of secrecy nearly always abounds, not only over timing and tonnage of such deals, but also over who is involved, giving sugar speculators yet more to feed upon.

The dynamic growth of sugar consumption in recent years has mainly emanated from developing countries, both in the socialist bloc and in the Third World. This is quite a change from the 1970s, when the northern industrialised countries dominated offtake and could be relied upon to buy on a rising market. With a more price-elastic demand, the lower income countries' offtake is constantly under threat from price rises, so the sugar market's old record prices may now be a thing of the past.

In developed countries, sugar has also suffered from a constant war of attrition from competing sweeteners like corn syrup, especially in the soft drink markets of Europe and North America. The trend appeared to be slowing as sugar presented better value, but recovery could be upset by price rises.

For these reasons, the outlook for sugar seems to be one of broad stability with steep changes of price likely to be short-lived. The low level of stocks for consumption does leave the market open to severe weather problems in one or more of the major producing or consuming countries. But the very consumption growth which has caused such deficits remains heavily dependent on an affordable sugar price and that truth has always held sway.

Sugar: world production estimates 1982-89 (000 tonnes)

	1988/89 Estimated	1987/88	1986/87	1985/86	1984/85	1983/84	1982/83	1981/82
BEET								
Europe								
Belgium	1,000	874	1,017	1,025	912	850	1,201	1,133
Denmark	550	422	542	576	595	376	584	522
France	4,395	3,973	3,734	4,297	4,303	3,870	4,833	5,576
Germany (West)	3,000	2,963	3,468	3,429	3,147	2,725	3,591	3,690
Greece	235	197	312	345	237	323	322	351
Irish Republic	215	242	202	189	241	214	242	182
Italy	1,605	1,868	1,868	1,352	1,397	1,352	1,282	2,226
Netherlands	1,075	1,064	1,325	975	1,014	807	1,228	1,135
Portugal	1	2	4	9	9	9	9	9
Spain (see also cane)	1,283	1,072	1,093	965	1,158	1,339	1,226	1,095
UK	1,420	1,335	1,438	1,316	1,440	1,157	1,542	1,187
Total EEC (Beet)	14,779	14,012	15,003	14,478	14,453	13,022	16,060	17,106
Albania	40	40	37	40	40	35	35	40
Austria	360	390	307	468	464	385	612	486
Bulgaria	90	110	175	70	115	85	150	145
Czechoslovakia	675	775	850	935	844	750	885	750
Finland	140	70	133	103	129	155	116	99
Germany (East)	450	750	790	798	776	680	813	740
Hungary	510	543	506	533	544	518	537	605
Poland	1,805	1,825	1,890	1,809	1,880	2,140	2,010	1,870
Romania	425	450	600	585	605	450	550	550
Sweden	395	274	390	345	398	298	389	370
Switzerland	150	123	129	139	131	124	120	135
Turkey	1,415	1,784	1,414	1,398	1,654	1,770	1,860	1,518
USSR	9,200	9,855	8,750	8,250	8,550	8,750	7,400	6,100
Yugoslavia	650	915	850	1,010	980	772	708	871
Total Europe	31,084	31,916	31,824	30,961	31,563	29,934	32,245	31,385
Other Beet								
Canada	114	148	122	55	113	110	126	140
Chile	425	415	437	483	350	360	230	136
China (see also cane)	1,100	830	925	983	955	1,020	815	720
Iran (see also cane)	500	575	600	545	490	515	565	439
Japan (see also cane)	675	681	685	624	647	510	667	537
Morocco (see also cane)	405	372	365	303	352	370	335	300
USA (see also cane)	3,225	3,586	3,099	2,722	2,635	2,449	2,483	3,074
Uruguay (see also cane)	30	35	37	35	25	30	45	50
Other beet	251	252	253	215	273	252	179	138
WORLD TOTAL BEET	37,809	38,810	38,347	36,926	37,403	35,550	37,690	36,919

Sugar: world production estimates - *continued*

	1988/89 Estimated	1987/88	1986/87	1985/86	1984/85	1983/84	1982/83	1981/82
CANE								
Spain (see also beet)	15	15	16	16	10	9	17	18
Argentina	1,139	1,063	1,120	1,188	1,545	1,624	1,623	1,624
Barbados	85	81	77	113	101	98	86	88
Belize	90	87	88	99	109	108	121	113
Bolivia	150	170	180	175	198	197	228	260
Brazil	8,683	8,458	8,650	8,268	9,332	9,576	9,314	8,393
Colombia	1,400	1,364	1,293	1,272	1,367	1,177	1,340	1,318
Costa Rica	230	230	229	218	234	240	200	182
Cuba	8,250	7,548	7,218	7,347	8,101	8,331	7,174	8,279
Dominican Republic	775	770	856	804	1,040	1,197	1,160	1,217
Ecuador	300	341	286	273	328	220	253	322
El Salvador	175	190	261	285	283	259	247	185
French West Indies	85	75	73	78	65	50	64	78
Guatemala	725	691	651	624	581	545	560	571
Guyana	165	177	234	261	258	256	265	305
Haiti	30	25	39	43	50	50	55	55
Hawaii	865	845	888	946	918	963	947	892
Honduras	200	175	195	224	235	226	214	221
Jamaica	210	220	189	199	209	188	202	198
Mexico	3,600	3,825	3,986	4,031	3,490	3,242	3,078	2,842
Nicaragua	200	225	199	256	240	249	275	237
Panama	108	107	123	139	160	176	206	239
Paraguay	95	85	75	80	85	80	75	77
Peru	600	565	608	585	757	605	452	622
Puerto Rico	90	90	87	87	95	88	91	103
St. Kitts	28	26	25	27	27	31	29	37
Trinidad	95	95	85	95	83	67	79	79
USA Mainland	2,200	2,136	2,030	1,833	1,765	1,711	1,887	1,619
Uruguay (see also beet)	45	55	65	55	50	60	50	50
Venezuela	500	540	565	590	496	423	377	382
Other Americas	1	1	7	7	6	7	6	6
Total Americas	**31,119**	**30,260**	**30,382**	**30,202**	**32,212**	**32,044**	**30,658**	**30,594**
Angola	13	15	20	20	23	25	28	32
Egypt (see also beet)	950	915	904	868	814	715	758	730
Ethiopia	200	205	197	191	190	202	192	160
Ivory Coast	159	151	158	144	121	125	187	166
Kenya	420	413	411	375	404	353	335	399
Malagasy	110	107	98	99	78	102	87	112
Malawi	180	181	168	154	160	187	183	177
Mauritius	672	733	748	684	610	640	729	610
Morocco (see also beet) ...	115	78	75	77	76	80	55	60
Mozambique	35	35	25	20	38	75	126	178
Nigeria	65	60	59	40	70	58	55	47
Réunion	260	240	259	242	261	236	272	266
South Africa	2,200	2,235	2,245	2,280	2,551	1,480	2,304	2,218
Sudan	500	445	525	491	542	455	375	275
Swaziland	450	461	537	396	425	408	402	368
Tanzania	105	115	100	100	110	143	114	122
Zaire	70	75	70	66	66	56	57	51
Zambia	125	130	119	143	141	132	117	102
Zimbabwe	453	454	513	456	463	433	405	391
Other Africa	388	363	325	365	342	283	280	264
Total Africa	**7,470**	**7,411**	**7,556**	**7,211**	**7,485**	**6,188**	**7,061**	**6,728**
Bangladesh	120	185	196	89	95	160	190	215
China (see also beet)	4,100	3,990	4,875	4,634	3,730	2,830	3,370	2,975
China (Taiwan)	580	650	515	575	706	661	658	771
India	10,000	9,900	9,250	7,625	6,677	6,401	8,946	9,165
Indonesia	2,085	2,300	2,195	1,875	1,856	1,790	1,769	1,359
Iran (see also beet)	150	135	175	240	200	205	202	151
Japan (see also beet)	285	258	258	298	283	296	255	236
Malaysia	95	82	90	85	82	75	45	60
Pakistan	1,995	1,895	1,365	1,198	1,430	1,225	1,180	1,375
Philippines	1,450	1,370	1,355	1,571	1,771	2,418	2,533	2,530
Thailand	4,100	2,704	2,637	2,586	2,572	2,349	2,265	2,930
Vietnam	450	425	410	415	350	310	258	125
Other Asia	87	94	122	107	110	110	92	102
Total Asia	**25,497**	**23,988**	**23,443**	**21,298**	**19,862**	**18,830**	**21,763**	**21,994**
Australia	3,771	3,510	3,444	3,439	3,624	3,254	3,634	3,527
Fiji	376	416	519	354	497	286	506	489
Other Oceania	54	24	10	33	37	36	11	—
Total Oceania	**4,201**	**3,950**	**3,973**	**3,826**	**4,158**	**3,576**	**4,151**	**4,016**
TOTAL CANE	**68,302**	**65,624**	**65,370**	**62,553**	**63,727**	**60,647**	**63,650**	**63,350**
WORLD TOTAL CANE & BEET	**106,111**	**104,434**	**103,717**	**99,479**	**101,130**	**96,197**	**101,340**	**100,269**

By courtesy of C Czarnikow Ltd.

Sugar: world consumption 1986-89 (000 tonnes)

World Consumption. Estimates of consumption in individual countries are as follows:—

000's tonnes, raw value	1989	1988	1987	1986
Asia				
Afghanistan ...	110	110	105	110
Bangladesh	300	330	325	275
Burma	60	60	63	60
China	8,150	8,150	7,750	6,850
China (Taiwan) ...	545	533	529	533
Hong Kong	135	130	130	125
India	10,750	10,545	9,645	8,855
Indonesia	2,550	2,448	2,323	2,123
Iran	1,450	1,400	1,350	1,350
Iraq	650	650	640	635
Israel	300	290	280	275
Japan	2,765	2,835	2,690	2,738
Jordan	170	163	155	148
Korea (North) ...	117	117	117	116
Korea (South) ...	700	755	788	718
Kuwait	30	30	32	35
Lebanon	85	80	75	70
Malaysia	665	650	630	615
Mongolia	52	50	49	47
Pakistan	2,200	2,100	1,950	1,800
Persian Gulf ...	95	95	94	93
Philippines	1,411	1,378	1,438	1,180
Saudi Arabia ...	375	360	350	340
Singapore	175	175	165	145
Sri Lanka	378	359	341	323
Syria	490	475	460	445
Thailand	925	886	883	744
Vietnam	525	500	475	425
Yemen (North) ...	169	161	153	145
Yemen (South) ...	66	63	60	58
Other Asia	63	60	58	57
TOTAL Asia ...	**36,456**	**35,938**	**34,103**	**31,433**
N. & C. America				
Bahamas	8	8	8	8
Barbados	13	14	13	14
Belize	6	7	7	6
Canada	1,087	1,079	1,120	1,069
Costa Rica	170	166	170	164
Cuba	765	750	773	762
Dominican Republic	345	305	351	294
El Salvador	174	173	161	176
Guatemala	350	335	320	300
Haiti	60	60	60	60
Honduras	130	126	122	114
Jamaica	113	109	108	102
Mexico	3,675	3,626	3,657	3,451
Nicaragua	171	165	151	157
Panama	80	65	80	80
St. Kitts	2	2	2	2
Trinidad	62	62	65	66
USA	7,525	7,425	7,414	7,085
Others	152	152	156	143
TOTAL N. & C. America	**14,888**	**14,629**	**14,738**	**14,053**
South America				
Argentina	1,000	1,075	1,104	1,093
Bolivia	187	186	185	184
Brazil	6,635	6,562	6,735	6,589
Chile	479	465	467	440
Colombia	1,150	1,143	1,208	1,101
Ecuador	383	372	383	353
Guyana	41	40	45	35
Paraguay	92	90	87	85
Peru	825	800	850	733
Surinam	16	16	16	15
Uruguay	85	85	83	82
Venezuela	770	755	745	735
TOTAL S. America	**11,663**	**11,589**	**11,908**	**11,445**

000's tonnes, raw value	1989	1988	1987	1986
Europe				
Albania	65	62	60	52
Austria	360	362	370	357
Bulgaria	479	472	465	459
Cyprus	21	21	21	21
Czechoslovakia ...	829	816	803	790
EEC (of twelve) ...	12,200	12,190	12,110	12,137
Finland	210	209	207	209
Germany (East) ...	839	833	826	824
Hungary	529	520	555	513
Norway	165	158	173	170
Poland	1,775	1,750	1,725	1,705
Romania	600	600	612	610
Sweden	380	380	372	387
Switzerland	301	299	287	302
Turkey	1,687	1,630	1,658	1,483
USSR	14,120	14,000	14,480	13,900
Yugoslavia	930	925	925	915
Other Europe ...	39	38	38	38
TOTAL Europe ...	**35,529**	**35,265**	**35,687**	**34,872**
Africa				
Algeria	664	655	646	637
Angola	105	105	105	105
Botswana	43	42	40	39
Burkina Faso ...	44	42	40	38
Cameroon	87	83	80	76
Chad	42	39	37	34
Egypt	1,700	1,650	1,600	1,650
Ethiopia	174	171	168	159
Ghana	63	56	48	41
Ivory Coast	145	138	131	123
Kenya	497	477	457	462
Libya	165	160	155	150
Malagasy	86	86	90	81
Malawi	114	108	89	73
Mali	50	48	47	47
Mauritania	49	47	45	43
Mauritius	41	40	40	40
Morocco	784	765	746	725
Mozambique	87	87	86	86
Nigeria	625	600	625	595
Senegal	71	72	73	71
Sierra Leone ...	19	18	17	16
Somalia	109	103	97	91
South Africa ...	1,448	1,430	1,433	1,381
Sudan	575	575	525	525
Swaziland	40	36	35	24
Tanzania	130	129	127	126
Togo	49	46	43	40
Tunisia	225	218	212	189
Uganda	45	42	39	36
Zaire	101	97	92	88
Zambia	115	110	107	99
Zimbabwe	274	265	253	238
Other Africa ...	225	210	198	199
TOTAL Africa ...	**8,991**	**8,750**	**8,526**	**8,327**
Oceania				
Australia	850	844	828	818
Fiji	37	38	36	35
New Zealand ...	173	171	169	167
Papua New Guinea ...	31	30	30	30
Other Oceania ...	16	16	15	14
TOTAL Oceania ...	**1,107**	**1,099**	**1,078**	**1,064**
WORLD TOTAL ...	**108,634**	**107,270**	**106,040**	**101,194**

By courtesy of C Czarnikow Ltd.

Sugar: London monthly averages LDP (Raws) 1981-88 (US cents per lb)

(US cents per lb)

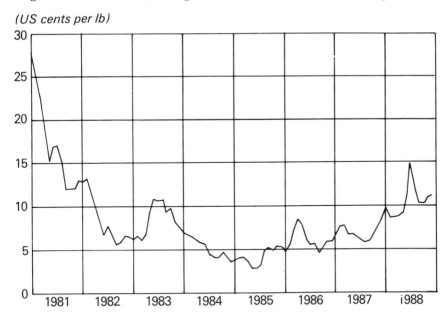

**Sugar: monthly averages New York spot price (Contract No 11) 1981-1988
(US cents per lb)**

(US cents per lb)

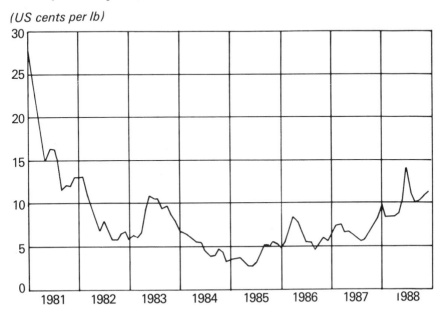

Source: International Sugar Organization

167

World sugar consumption 1988/89

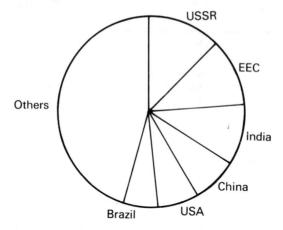

World sugar beet output 1988/89 (RMTV)

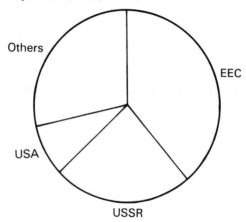

World sugar cane output 1988/89 (RMTV)

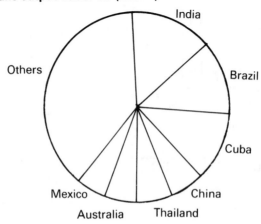

Tea

John Buckley

The shape of the international tea market is gradually changing as traditional producers are forced to adapt their operations to overcome a period of low prices and falling profits. At the same time, new buyers are rapidly emerging to boost consumption, perhaps suggesting future shortages and potentially more volatile markets.

Perhaps more than most commodities, the tea market has illustrated an old adage that 'the bull market has a short tail, the bear market a long one'. In fact, all the major price peaks of the last 40 years – in 1954, 1977 and 1984 – have been fairly transitory, just as the subsequent bear market has taken over four years to run its course.

Unlike many tropical commodities supplied by relatively few countries, tea normally maintains a superficial balance between supply and demand, but it is the longer term undercurrents which hold the key to price movement. Between 1977 and 1982, for example, world tea consumption grew by some 18%, boosted by the sudden influx of oil revenue into the Middle East and by rising demand from Eastern Europe and the Soviet Union, as well as producing/consumers including Pakistan and China. Production in the same period rose by only 8%, but because of fairly ample stocks, the global deficit only began to bite in late 1983.

Similarly, the tea trade had warned for many years that – with population growth alone adding some 20 million kg per annum to consumption – India's domestic requirements would outstrip her export capacity. But it was not until late in the winter of 1983/84 that this slow fuse burned into the powder keg.

Ostensibly, it was in an effort to conserve supplies of the crush, tear and curl varieties most sought by its own consumers, that India decided at this time to temporarily ban exports, although many trade observers suggested that the real motive was to manipulate prices before the cycle of deficit ended. If so, the move brought as many long term curses as short term blessings for producers. Panic reigned on international tea markets, especially in the key London auctions, where the CTC teas are the most sought after and, as consumers scrambled for alternative sources of supply, tea prices trebled in value, reaching the dizzy heights of 317p per kg for the first time ever.

The inability to hold firmer levels partly reflected the response of growers.

Instead of picking the time honoured 'two leaves and a bud', growers took more leaves from the tea bushes, quickly raising the volume of lower grades in the market and adding to the subsequent price depression. As production leapt well beyond the capacity of the market to absorb it, foreign buyers and blenders deserted the market in droves and by living hand-to-mouth as often as possible, bid the international market back down to an all-time low in real terms of just 80p per kg.

Interestingly, the higher prices charged for tea in the interim had mixed impact on global consumption. As the largest outlet, India's own consumers were still able to buy relatively cheap tea and, in the context of few competing beverages, had little incentive to reduce offtake. The high rate of growth in developing markets also offset the reduction of UK and other more traditional buyers' orders.

Like many of the plantation crops, profits on growing tea have been hit by low market prices, requiring a reshaping of the producing industries' growing and marketing campaigns. But it will be interesting to see whether 1989 will mark the turning point for tea producers, after one of their worst years yet in 1988. Production in the main producing region of South India is down because of dry weather, while political upheaval has hit Sri Lanka's output. There has also been concern that China's trade – which accounts for one-fifth of world exports – could be disrupted by the recent disturbances.

On the consumption front, one of the more interesting developments is the doubling of Soviet consumption in the last decade, which some analysts believe will soon put them in the position of number one importer, ahead of the UK. The Soviet Union's own production has yet to recover from setbacks after the Chernobyl disaster in 1986. Pakistan has lifted import restrictions that were holding tea prices down worldwide, while there is evidence of a dramatic 8% reversal in UK consumption after years of decline. The net effect of these developments has been to push the market back to around £1.30 per kg recently.

However, if tea prices are to be protected from future bouts of consumption-damaging volatility, there is a pressing need to continue plantation expansion against major obstacles. These include a shortage of suitable land for tea production, tangled plantation tax laws – especially on the Asian subcontinent itself, and an all-too-frequent lack of government incentive. Given that tea bushes take years to mature, growers need long-term financial backing if they are to embark on the risky venture of production for assumed future markets.

The best example has been set by the East African tea-producing nations, especially Kenya, which through irrigation practices has raised its yields per bush to up to five times the national average. Productivity and quality must, however, go hand-in-hand if consumption is to be protected in the long term. What improvement there has been in tea prices recently has been at the quality end of the market and it is there that producers can reap their best rewards.

Tea: production in main producer countries 1977-89 (tonnes)

	1977	1978	1979	1980	1981	1982	1983	1984	1985	1986	1987	1988
India (a)												
Assam Bengal Bihar Tripura	426,514	432,188	403,319	437,593	435,765	435,821	464,986	490,110	513,161	480,206	527,424	529,315
Punjab U P & H P	1,280	1,212	1,097	862	1,181	1,380	1,273	1,318	1,134	1,093		
South India	128,473	130,446	139,360	131,095	122,637	123,531	115,225	148,436	141,867	139,504	146,878	171,772
Total	556,267	563,846	543,776	569,550	559,583	560,732	581,484	639,864	656,162	620,803	674,302	701,087
Bangladesh (b)	38,115	37,914	36,128	40,037	41,316	40,938	43,729	38,211	43,285	37,593	40,611	42,550
Sri Lanka												
High-grown	78,675	71,816	76,541	72,570	80,492	71,665	67,761	79,331	78,755	77,068	73,410	76,829
Medium-grown	66,628	61,143	62,451	55,564	59,345	52,460	49,131	55,818	56,406	54,742	54,813	55,544
Low-grown	63,269	66,021	67,426	63,242	70,311	64,506	63,068	74,067	80,144	80,895	86,379	95,817
Total	208,572	198,981	206,417	191,375	210,148	188,631	179,960	209,216	215,305	212,705	214,602	228,190
Indonesia (c)												
Estates (Java) (d)	43,993	51,558	53,658	56,874	62,062	51,759	64,220	76,131	78,978	72,861	70,376	78,101
(Sumatra)	18,772	20,178	18,115	21,334	22,908	21,888	24,454	26,006	26,125	25,496	27,075	27,451
Smallholders (Java) (e)	*	*	*	*	*	*	*	*	*			
Smlhdrs (Java & Sum) (f)	17,303	17,424	19,069	20,489	23,769	16,511	22,858	24,040	27,244	31,130	30,000	30,000
Total	80,068	89,160	90,842	98,697	108,739	90,158	111,532	126,177	132,347	129,487	127,451	135,552
China (Mainland) (g) (q)	252,000	268,000	277,000	303,750	342,500	397,000	400,550	414,150	432,337	460,468	508,000	530,000
Taiwan	26,303†	25,854†	27,055†	24,479†	25,223†	24,051†	24,308†	24,365†	23,203†	23,890†	25,578†	25,000
Iran	24,000	23,000	21,000	20,000	22,500	23,500	23,500	22,000	24,000	24,000	24,000	25,000
Japan	102,301	104,737	98,000	102,305	102,304	98,503	102,700	92,500	95,500	93,601	96,301	95,000
Malaya (h)	3,542	3,451	3,171	3,281	3,438	3,188	3,328	3,650	3,784	4,463	4,500	4,500
Turkey	77,592	86,206	101,955	95,889	41,165	68,038	100,782	113,701	137,116	143,849	138,878	145,000
Viet Nam (j)	16,200	19,300	21,000	21,500	22,000	22,000	22,500	22,000	22,500	22,500	23,000	24,000
Total Asia	1,384,960	1,420,449	1,426,344	1,470,863	1,478,916	1,516,739	1,594,373	1,705,834	1,785,539	1,773,359	1,877,223	1,955,879
Burundi	1,470	1,454	1,612	1,455	2,226	2,164	2,293	3,500	4,145	3,600	4,000	4,000
Cameroon	1,003	2,015	1,950	1,878	2,130	1,799	2,097	2,290	3,205	2,797	2,876	3,000
Kenya	86,291	93,373	99,275	89,893	90,941	96,033	119,738	116,172	147,094	143,317	155,808	164,030
Malawi	31,628	31,690	32,609	29,915	31,965	38,482	32,010	37,530	39,954	38,976	31,908	40,157
Mauritius	4,727	5,128	5,072	4,386	5,052	5,354	6,142	8,021	8,115	7,876	7,149	6,856
Mozambique	17,000	18,069	19,675	19,500	22,190	21,000	14,000	11,000	7,000	5,000	3,000	1,500
Rwanda	5,356	5,341	5,770	6,627	6,845	7,050	7,508	8,669	11,320	10,418	11,677	12,500
South Africa	4,400	5,300	6,200	6,300	6,807	6,770	6,800	8,387	8,845	9,600	9,900	10,000
Tanzania	16,701	17,337	17,894	17,087	15,898	16,230	15,620	16,455	16,535	15,079	14,515	14,629
Uganda	15,179	10,910	1,832	1,533	1,672	2,580	3,169	5,223	5,599	3,228	3,332	3,000
Zaire	5,210	4,774	4,456	2,461	3,089	4,036	4,725	4,951	4,950	4,700	4,300	4,500
Zimbabwe (k)	6,649	8,749	10,262	9,954	10,296	10,799	10,808	13,941	14,994	15,679	15,081	16,612
Total Africa	195,614	204,140	206,607	190,989	199,111	212,297	224,910	236,139	271,756	260,270	263,546	280,784
U S S R (l)	106,400	111,200	117,600	129,800	136,500	139,800	145,600	151,100	152,100	146,600	140,000	140,000
Argentina (m)	21,630	26,250	32,130	20,580	29,820	36,855	37,464	42,000	28,980	40,920	35,000	35,000
Brazil	7,741	9,196	9,398	9,707	10,081	11,272	10,880	10,703	10,833	10,000	10,000	10,000
Ecuador	2,500	2,500	2,600	2,600	2,000	1,800	1,800	1,900	1,800	2,000	2,000	2,000
Peru	3,000	3,000	3,000	3,000	3,000	3,000	3,000	3,000	3,000	3,000	3,000	3,000
Total S America	34,871	40,946	47,128	35,887	44,901	52,927	53,144	57,603	44,613	55,920	50,000	50,000
Australia	149	239	276	249	306	409	376	551	605	624	703	761
Papua New Guinea	5,442	6,319	8,038	8,361	8,691	8,487	10,160	9,845	8,080	8,000	8,000	8,000
Total Oceania	5,591	6,558	8,314	8,610	8,997	8,896	10,536	10,396	8,685	8,624	8,703	8,761
Grand Total	1,727,436	1,783,293	1,805,993	1,836,149	1,868,425	1,930,659	2,028,563	2,161,072	2,262,693	2,244,773	2,339,472	2,435,424

☐ Figures of these countries relate to years other than calendar years, ending on the following dates:–
Iran — 20th or 21st March of the year following that indicated; Cameroon — calendar years up to 1977, 30th June of the following year thereafter; South Africa — 31st March of the year following that indicated; Argentina — 30th April of the year following that indicated; Australia — 30th June; Papua New Guinea — 30th June up to 1977, calendar years thereafter.

† These figures represent "crude tea"; the official figures for "finished" or "refined" tea appear to contain an element of double-counting.

(a) Figures of the Tea Board, Calcutta.

(b) Figures of the Bangladesh Tea Board.

(c) Figures of the Central Bureau of Statistics, Jakarta.

(d) Including tea manufactured by estate factories from leaf grown by "small agricultural estates".

(e) Black tea manufactured by factories from leaf grown by Smallholders ("individual farmers").

(f) Mainly Green Tea.

(g) Official figures, cover Black, Green and Other teas.

(h) Estates only. No tea is recorded in Singapore, Sabah or Sarawak.

(j) The figures are for the Socialist Republic of Viet Nam.

(k) Figures of the Zimbabwe Tea Growers' Association.

(l) Official figures given in terms of green leaf converted at 4.08 kg. green leaf to manufactured tea.

(m) Estimates of the Secretaria de Estado de Agricultura y Ganaderia, Buenos Aires, converted from figures given in terms of green leaf.

(n) Figures relate to 20% of Total USSR production – based on Trade Information.

Tea: imports for consumption in principal consumer countries 1977-89 (tonnes)

	1977	1978	1979	1980	1981	1982	1983	1984	1985	1986	1987	1988
I Europe												
West Europe												
United Kingdom (a)	208,134	149,030	173,712	186,133	135,302	183,587	155,190	184,204	155,359	171,066	142,579	162,699
Austria	930	831	1,046	1,199	1,182	1,213	1,196	1,418	1,065	1,192	1,165	1,200
Belgium & Luxembourg	1,118	1,116	1,078	1,096	1,202	1,379	1,286	1,293	1,295	1,498	1,214	1,300
Denmark	2,493	1,863	2,279	2,380	2,374	2,292	2,410	2,319	2,317	2,432	2,155	2,200
Faeroe Islands	123	80	132	108	133	140	101	114	119	111	115	115
Finland	971	723	720	900	843	1,007	915	789	875	891	1,060	1,000
France	6,431	6,097	7,105	8,742	8,278	7,579	8,944	8,439	9,154	10,036	9,148	10,155
Germany Fed Rep (b)	12,200	11,800	14,040	14,891	15,300	15,500	14,100	17,100	15,500	15,500	14,700	14,800
Gibraltar (c)	75	70	80	70	75	80	80	80	80	80	80	80
Greece	289	269	279	279	476	276	238	300	300	300	300	300
Iceland	60	57	46	54	61	47	50	46	55	71	58	60
Ireland (Republic)	14,951	9,747	10,910	14,149	11,274	8,808	10,865	10,364	10,656	11,295	10,885	10,376
Italy	3,779	2,879	3,657	3,551	3,195	3,415	3,212	3,108	3,876	3,295	3,489	3,500
Malta	623	461	549	429	618	240	530	575	616	465	530	530
Netherlands (d)	9,617	8,673	8,909	9,300	9,402	9,598	9,438	9,229	9,361	9,429	9,725	9,500
Norway	966	579	746	775	774	846	820	855	894	865	1,019	834
Portugal	269	164	310	364	240	220	177	220	285	232	217	230
Spain (e)	1,009	689	832	838	710	892	691	688	734	719	730	740
Sweden	3,491	2,555	2,972	2,879	2,795	2,859	2,856	3,075	2,797	3,061	3,104	2,800
Switzerland	1,839	1,344	1,614	1,702	1,887	1,996	1,761	2,018	1,956	1,703	1,725	1,501
Yugoslavia	4,413	1,946	1,135	146	2,622	2,358	1,181	1,581	1,727	2,514	1,640	1,700
Total W Europe (Exc UK)	65,647	51,943	58,439	63,852	63,441	60,745	60,851	63,611	63,662	65,689	63,059	62,921
East Europe												
Bulgaria	220	796	612	579	501	520	1,205	477	410	341	873	500
Czechoslovakia	1,864	1,767	2,403	2,346	2,517	2,544	2,023	2,619	1,882	2,235	2,500	2,300
Germany Dem Rep	2,019	1,878	2,098	2,135	2,901	1,751	1,818	2,965	2,876	2,050	2,600	2,500
Hungary	1,451	1,369	1,585	1,515	986	1,312	1,744	1,640	1,763	1,059	1,450	1,500
Poland	13,952	18,857	22,755	23,770	24,547	26,764	25,908	25,522	34,697	29,945	32,100	33,000
Romania	300	300	300	300	300	300	300	300	300	300	300	300
U S S R (f)	43,800	34,200	37,500	56,400	71,600	61,000	55,800	70,000	95,800	109,900	134,800	136,000
Total E Europe	63,606	59,167	67,253	87,045	103,352	94,191	88,798	103,728	137,728	145,830	174,623	176,100
II N America/W Indies												
Canada	22,117	19,810	18,991	20,323	18,866	17,695	17,467	18,430	15,739	17,483	14,159	15,200
U S A (g)	91,784	68,720	79,103	83,481	86,110	82,706	77,140	88,153	79,136	89,529	77,253	85,000
Bahamas	99	56	80	75	96	106	111	113	120	120	120	120
Barbados	159	137	140	130	126	130	130	130	130	130	130	130
Bermuda	59	63	77	49	58	66	65	60	52	60	60	60
Belize	34	50	48	34	54	21	45	28	56	30	30	30
Jamaica	96	138	172	100	166	129	110	104	181	94	107	100
Trinidad & Tobago	132	152	269	177	204	192	239	250	250	310	271	300
Netherlands Antilies	95	90	100	100	100	105	100	100	100	100	100	100
Other Countries	440	420	450	450	460	450	500	500	500	500	500	500
Total	115,015	89,636	99,430	104,949	106,240	101,600	95,907	107,868	96,264	108,356	92,730	101,540

(a) "Net Imports", including Channel Islands.

(b) The consumption figures have been calculated by the Government on the basis of the tea yield from tea tax.

(c) Recorded exports from the United Kingdom and producing countries. No import figures are compiled.

(d) Quantities delivered by Dutch tea-packers for consumption.

(e) Peninsula and Balearic Islands only.

(f) As separate import figures are not available for Mongolia, these figures include U S S R re-exports to Mongolia. See also notes to Table D 21, page 79.

(g) Including Alaska and Hawaii throughout; also including Puerto Rico and other US Possessions.

– continued

	1977	1978	1979	1980	1981	1982	1983	1984	1985	1986	1987	1988
III Latin America												
Mexico	100	78	82	120	125	100	130	120	120	120	110	120
Central America (j)	160	160	150	150	160	160	180	170	170	170	175	170
Argentina	24	81	63	60	60	43	50	50	50	50	50	50
Bolivia	440	400	400	400	462	187	203	163	200	200	200	200
Brazil	5	4	9	5	3	5	5	5	5	5	8	10
Chile	10,298	11,452	15,440	11,288	10,679	10,462	12,215	10,022	12,453	10,540	11,303	10,800
Peru	10	11	10	10	10	10	5	5	5	5	5	5
Uruguay	781	975	829	771	524	605	567	533	651	720	700	700
Other Countries	600	650	650	600	600	600	650	675	650	650	650	650
Total	12,418	13,811	17,633	13,404	12,623	12,172	14,005	11,743	14,304	12,460	13,201	12,705
IV Asia (k)												
Abu Dhabi	764	1,092	1,723	1,813	1,853	1,460	1,353	519	345	323	400	400
Bahrain	607	1,091	576	539	494	586	476	722	665	534	500	500
Dubai	5,996	9,519	13,637	12,336	12,718	4,149	3,248	5,303	6,991	9,446	8,000	8,000
Kuwait	5,219	6,452	7,142	7,332	5,549	2,427	4,044	4,596	4,000	4,500	4,500	4,500
Oman	1,194	956	1,604	1,238	996	1,319	1,436	1,987	1,766	1,472	1,500	1,500
Qatar	942	1,023	1,541	1,542	800	623	1,182	1,172	1,101	948	932	1,000
Saudi Arabia	7,441	16,723	14,136	15,274	16,236	15,060	17,955	20,463	20,562	17,600	19,000	19,000
Other Arabian States (l)	8,803	8,878	8,136	6,779	8,174	8,000	8,500	8,300	8,500	8,500	8,500	8,500
Afghanistan	15,198	17,588	12,697	15,015	13,262	10,730	9,301	9,000	8,778	9,090	9,500	9,500
Hong Kong	8,873	8,168	7,244	8,313	7,649	8,752	8,820	10,045	9,144	8,466	9,811	9,699
Iran ø	12,337	19,717	17,200	21,000	16,800	11,800	23,400	35,100	27,900	21,600	49,400	32,800
Iraq ‡	31,600	28,300	34,000	37,200	29,700	36,500	37,800	45,500	34,600	44,700	41,800	55,400
Israel	2,800	3,480	3,692	2,950	2,085	1,990	2,213	1,900	2,200	2,100	2,200	2,200
Jordan	2,834	3,200	3,122	3,019	3,465	3,227	3,335	3,640	3,766	4,348	4,098	4,000
Lebanon	969	1,000	1,500	1,800	2,200	2,500	2,600	2,600	2,500	2,000	1,800	1,800
Malaya (m)	3,106	3,333	3,000	3,500	4,000	4,000	4,000	4,000	4,500	4,300	4,400	4,500
Nepal (n)	700	700	600	700	700	700	800	800	700	800	1,000	1,000
Pakistan	60,672	57,528	66,012	64,051	76,471	72,459	86,654	85,722	89,125	84,825	90,097	85,452
Philippines	347	358	175	320	456	278	311	107	231	186	223	230
Sabah	168	223	250	280	332	243	350	300	350	350	350	350
Sarawak	277	421	352	366	350	353	384	370	400	400	400	400
Singapore	*	541	512	500	500	500	600	600	600	600	600	600
Syria	4,736	11,833	10,522	9,309	7,812	11,034	10,575	14,663	15,000	14,500	12,000	13,000
Thailand	686	899	710	555	647	553	669	585	531	502	550	500
Other Countries	900	900	1,000	900	900	1,000	1,100	1,200	1,200	1,200	1,200	1,200
Total	177,169	203,923	211,083	216,631	214,149	200,243	231,106	259,194	245,455	243,290	272,761	266,031

*   This country had no separate existence in the years indicated.

▢   Figures for these countries relate to years other than calendar years – Afghanistan – years beginning 22nd March; Iran – years beginning 21st or 22nd March.

(j)   Costa Rica, El Salvador, Guatemala, Honduras Republic, Nicaragua, Panama Republic and Canal Zone.

(k)   Excluding the major producing countries, for which see section VII of this Table.

(l)   Including Yemen and D R Yemen – estimated from recorded exports thereto. Also includes estimated figures for named Arabian Countries for the years where trade returns are not available.

(m)   Singapore and the former Federation of Malaya combined up to 1977.

(n)   Estimated from recorded exports thereto.

ø   From 1979, ITC estimates based on recorded exports to Iran.

‡   From 1977, ITC estimates based on recorded exports to Iraq.

– continued

	1977	1978	1979	1980	1981	1982	1983	1984	1985	1986	1987	1988
V Africa												
Algeria	4,117	4,253	8,476	9,945	8,032	8,495	5,576	5,850	4,687	5,000	5,000	5,000
Benin	2	2	2	2	2	2	2	2	2	2	2	2
Cameroon	3	3	3	2	3	3	3	3	3	3	3	3
Canary Islands	300	452	400	350	400	400	450	420	430	420	420	420
Central African Rep	1	1	1	1	1	1	1	1	1	1	1	1
Ceuta	294	304	125	20	23	20	46	33	30	30	30	33
Chad	790	750	800	800	800	800	825	800	800	800	800	800
Congo	4	4	4	9	11	10	10	10	17	15	15	15
Egypt †	47,400	54,200	53,900	54,400	53,000	57,300	65,500	75,000	76,200	72,900	64,900	76,400
Ethiopia	742	1,226	1,109	950	1,000	1,000	952	1,000	1,000	1,000	1,000	1,000
Gabon	5	5	5	3	4	10	10	8	12	15	15	17
Ghana	220	200	180	200	200	170	170	180	200	150	150	150
Guinea	2	2	3	3	3	3	3	3	3	3	3	3
Ivory Coast	180	200	246	213	260	200	231	422	300	300	300	300
Kenya	–934	–313	–2,850	–3,410	247	–2,765	2,520	–7,533	–4,858	–4,000	–565	–600
Libya (s)	7,156	12,928	9,652	12,969	6,083	7,392	11,300	15,700	12,900	6,100	11,000	9,500
Mali	1,106	1,000	862	800	850	850	900	900	900	1,000	1,000	1,000
Mauritania	660	630	1,000	1,000	1,000	1,200	1,200	1,200	1,300	1,500	1,600	1,800
Mauritius	7	10	10	8	4	8	10	10	10	10	10	10
Melilla	246	293	165	303	250	79	161	108	150	150	140	150
Morocco	12,355	19,515	23,859	17,551	22,622	13,866	16,593	22,586	22,256	20,402	23,426	22,000
Niger	500	550	550	1,287	1,107	1,200	1,200	1,100	1,200	1,300	1,100	1,100
Nigeria	940	1,300	1,200	1,600	1,800	2,000	2,200	2,200	2,300	2,200	2,200	2,200
Senegal	600	600	1,347	1,110	957	1,000	1,314	1,620	461	1,000	1,000	1,200
Somalia	1,896	3,692	3,063	2,649	1,474	1,000	879	1,000	1,000	1,000	1,000	1,100
South Africa (t)	18,940	15,014	15,521	17,779	14,811	12,923	15,252	13,802	11,248	11,000	11,000	11,000
Sudan	11,546	22,472	6,535	9,209	7,916	13,115	12,872	10,672	17,970	11,050	13,030	13,000
Tanzania	7	18	—	—	—	—	—	—	—	—	—	—
Togo	10	11	11	10	12	15	20	18	20	30	30	30
Tunisia	7,421	7,402	11,747	7,505	9,296	9,926	11,617	11,635	12,893	14,783	13,000	13,000
Uganda	—	—	—	—	—	—	—	—	—	—	—	—
Upper Volta	120	100	77	278	428	304	231	197	200	200	200	200
Zaire	13	20	20	15	12	10	10	10	10	10	10	10
Zambia	473	500	524	379	217	300	300	250	250	200	200	200
Zimbabwe (u)	483	164	—	458	318	37	9	3	10	10	8	10
Other Countries	800	800	900	1,000	900	1,000	1,200	1,000	1,100	1,100	1,100	1,100
Total	118,405	148,308	139,447	139,398	134,043	131,874	153,567	160,217	165,003	149,684	153,128	162,154
VI Oceania (v)												
Australia	25,129	22,138	23,765	22,146	23,145	21,647	21,767	20,562	20,706	20,646	18,214	19,367
Fiji	638	580	644	647	742	709	656	700	720	700	700	700
New Zealand	8,913	6,270	7,046	6,507	6,665	6,239	6,253	5,943	5,777	5,571	5,494	5,283
Papua New Guinea □	300	300	330	300	350	350	350	330	350	350	350	350
Other Countries	300	300	330	350	330	330	300	300	300	300	300	300
Total	35,280	29,588	32,115	29,950	31,232	29,275	29,326	27,835	27,853	27,567	25,058	26,000

□   Figures relate to years beginning 1st July.

(s)   The figures include unreported re-exports for which details are not available.

(t)   Including Botswana, Lesotho, Namibia and Swaziland.

(u)   Formerly Rhodesia.

(v)   Excluding Hawaii and US possessions, included with the United States in Section II.

†   ITC estimates based on recorded exports to Egypt.

– continued

	1977	1978	1979	1980	1981	1982	1983	1984	1985	1986	1987	1988
VII Major Producing Countries in Asia												
India	—	—	—	—	—	—	—	—	—	—	—	—
Sri Lanka	—	—	—	—	—	—	—	—	—	—	—	—
China									7,000	7,000	2,600	7,500
Japan	13,831	12,174	14,329	16,228	13,889	11,536	11,984	15,588	22,870	26,276	26,306	27,000
Total	15,000	13,000	15,500	17,400	15,400	13,100	13,500	17,100	31,000	35,000	30,000	35,500
VIII Summary												
U K and Ireland *(aa)*	223,100	158,800	184,600	200,300	146,600	192,400	166,000	194,600	166,000	182,400	153,400	173,100
Rest of Western Europe	50,700	42,200	47,500	49,700	52,200	51,900	50,000	53,200	53,000	54,400	52,200	52,500
U S S R	43,800	34,200	37,500	56,400	71,600	61,000	55,800	70,000	95,800	109,900	134,800	136,000
Rest of Eastern Europe	19,800	25,000	29,800	30,600	31,800	33,200	33,000	33,500	41,900	35,900	39,800	40,100
N America & W Indies	115,000	89,700	99,400	104,900	106,200	101,600	95,900	107,800	96,200	108,300	92,700	101,500
Latin America	12,400	13,800	17,600	13,400	12,600	12,200	14,000	11,700	14,300	12,500	13,200	12,700
Asia	177,200	203,800	211,000	216,500	214,100	200,200	231,100	259,200	245,500	243,300	272,800	266,000
Africa	118,400	148,300	139,500	139,400	134,000	131,900	153,600	160,200	165,000	149,600	153,100	162,200
Oceania	35,300	29,600	32,100	30,000	31,200	29,300	29,300	27,800	27,900	27,600	25,100	26,000
Major Producing Countries	15,000	13,000	15,500	17,400	15,400	13,100	13,500	17,100	31,000	35,000	30,000	35,500
Grand Total	810,700	758,400	814,500	858,600	815,700	826,800	842,200	935,200	936,600	958,900	967,100	1,005,600

(aa) Including Channel Islands.

By courtesy of the International Tea Committee

Medium and low medium tea: monthly price quotations at London auctions 1983-88 (pence per kg)

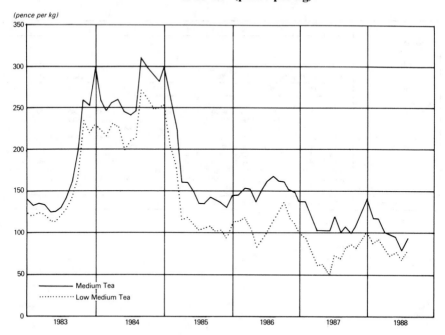

Source: The Tea Brokers' Association of London (Weekly Tea Market Report)

Part 3: World Directory of Commodity Markets

AUSTRALIA

SYDNEY

Sydney Futures Exchange Ltd

13–15 O'Connell Street, Sydney, New South Wales 2000
Telephone: 233 7633   *Telex:* AA 126713   *Cables:* SYDFUTUREX
Chairman: A Oliver
Chief Executive: L V Hosking
Manager of Education & Publications: S L Calder

Hours of trading (Sydney time):

All Ordinaries Share Price Index –	09.30–12.30, 14.00–15.45
90-day Bank Accepted bills –	08.30–12.30, 14.00–16.30
Three- and Ten-year Commonwealth Treasury bonds –	08.30–12.30, 14.00–16.30
US Treasury bonds –	08.35–16.15 (no lunch break)
Australian dollars –	08.30–16.30 (no lunch break)
Euro dollars –	08.35–16.15 (no lunch break)
Gold –	08.35–16.00 (no lunch break)
Wool –	10.30–12.30, 14.00–16.00
Live cattle –	10.30–12.30, 14.00–16.00

Contract details:

Commodities: All Ordinaries Share Price Index, 90-day bank accepted bills, three- and ten-year Commonwealth Treasury bonds, US Treasury bonds, Australian dollars, eurodollars, Comex gold, wool, live cattle

Trading units (minimum lot size):

All Ordinaries Share Price Index –	a sum of money equal to one hundred times the Australian Stock Exchange's All Ordinaries Share Price Index expressed as Australian dollars
90-day Bank Accepted bills –	A $500,000 face value of 90-day bank accepted bills of exchange

179

<table>
<tr><td>Three- and Ten-year Commonwealth Treasury bonds</td><td>–</td><td>Commonwealth Government with a face value of $100,000, a nominal coupon rate of 12% per annum and a term to maturity of three and ten years respectively – no tax rebate allowed</td></tr>
<tr><td>Eurodollars</td><td>–</td><td>US $1,000,000</td></tr>
<tr><td>Australian dollars</td><td>–</td><td>A$100,000</td></tr>
<tr><td>Comex Gold</td><td>–</td><td>100 fine troy ounces</td></tr>
<tr><td>Wool</td><td>–</td><td>2500kg clean weight of combing wool (approximately 23 bales of greasy wool)</td></tr>
<tr><td>Live cattle</td><td>–</td><td>10,000kg liveweight of cattle</td></tr>
</table>

Futures contract specifications:

All Ordinaries Share Price Index

Cash settlement price: The closing quotation for the Australian Stock Exchange's All Ordinaries Share Price Index on the last day of trading, calculated to one decimal place, provided by the ASE at 12.00 noon on the business day following the last day of trading.

Mandatory cash settlement: All bought and sold contracts in existence at the close of trading in the contract month shall be settled by the clearing house at the Index value for cash settlement.

Quotations: Prices shall be quoted in the same form as the ASE All Ordinaries Share Price Index expressed to one decimal place, with a minimum fluctuation of 0.1 Index point (equal to $10.00 per contract).

Contract months: March, June, September, and December up to 18 months ahead.

Termination of trading: The last business day of the contract month. Trading ceases at 17.10, or such other time as determined by the Board.

Settlement day: The second business day following the last permitted day of trading.

90-day Bank Accepted Bills

Standard delivery: Five 90-day bank accepted bills, or five bank-negotiable certificates of deposit (NCDs), each of face value $100,000, or one 90-day bank accepted bill, or NCD, of face value $500,000, maturing 85–95 days from settlement day.

Quotations: One hundred minus annual percentage yield to second decimal place. (The minimum fluctuation of 0.01% equals approximately $11 per contract, varying with the level of interest rates.)

Delivery months: March, June, September and December up to three years ahead.

Termination of trading: 12.00 noon on the business day immediately prior to settlement day.

Settlement day: The second Friday of the delivery month.

Ten-year Commonwealth Treasury Bonds

Cash settlement price: The arithmetic mean taken at 11.30 on the last day of trading of yields to two decimal places provided by 12 dealers, brokers and banks, at which they would buy and sell Treasury bonds in a basket of maturities set down in advance by the Exchange, excluding the two highest buying and the two lowest selling quotations.

Mandatory cash settlement: All bought and sold contracts in existence as at the close of trading in the contract month shall be settled by the clearing house at the cash settlement price.

Quotations: Prices shall be quoted in yield per annum per 100 dollars face value in multiples of 0.005%. For quotation purposes the yield shall be deducted from 100 (the minimum fluctuation of 0.005% equals approximately $30 per contract, varying with the level of interest rates).

Contract months: March, June, September and December up to 12 months ahead.

Termination of trading: The fifteenth day of the cash settlement month (or the next succeeding business day where the fifteenth day is not a business day). Trading ceases at 12.00 noon.

Settlement day: The business day following the last permitted day of trading.

Three-year Commonwealth Treasury Bonds

Cash settlement price: The arithmetic mean, taken at 11.30 on the last day of trading, of yields to two decimal places provided by 12 dealers, brokers and banks at which they would buy and sell not less than three series of Treasury bonds, details of which have been declared by the Board for each contract month. The two highest buying and the two lowest selling quotations for each series are excluded.

Mandatory cash settlement: All bought and sold contracts in existence as at the close of trading in the contract month shall be settled by the clearing house at the cash settlement price.

Quotations: Prices shall be quoted in yield per annum per 100 dollars face value in multiples of 0.01 per cent. For quotation purposes the yield shall be deducted from 100.00 (the minimum fluctuation of 0.01 per cent equals approximately $23 per contract, varying with the level of interest rates).

Contract months: March, June, September and December as determined by Board.

Termination of trading: The fifteenth day of the contract month (or the next succeeding business day where the fifteenth day is not a business day). Trading ceases at 12.00 noon.

Settlement day: The business day following the last permitted day of trading.

Australian Dollar

Quotations: Prices shall be quoted in US dollars per Australian dollar in multiples of 0.0001 US dollars (the minimum fluctuation of 0.0001 US dollars is equal to US $10.00 per contract).

Contract months: March, June, September and December up to six months ahead.

Termination of trading: Two business days prior to the third Wednesday of the contract month. Trading ceases at 15.00.

Settlement day: The third Wednesday of the contract month.

Comex Gold

(This contract will not begin trading until the implementation of the trading link with Comex in mid-1986.)

Standard delivery: Bar of 100 troy ounces (5% more or less) or three one-kilogram bars, minimum 995 fineness, and bearing serial number and identifying stamp of an approved refiner listed by the Exchange.

Quotations: In US dollars per troy ounce, with a minimum price fluctuation of 10 cents per troy ounce (equal to $10 per contract).

Maximum price fluctuation: US $25 per ounce ($2500 per contract) above or below previous trading session's settlement price, subject to variation limits. No limit in current month on day preceding the first notice day and thereafter.

Speculative position limit: 6000 contracts net; 3000 in spot month (gross).

Delivery months: February, April, June, August, October and December out 23 months, plus the current and two nearby months.

Termination of trading: The third last business day of a maturing delivery month.

Wool

Cash settlement price: 22 micron clean wool price indicator published by the Australian Wool Corporation on the business day prior to the last trading day calculated to the nearest whole cent per kilogram.

Mandatory cash settlement: All bought and sold contracts in existence at the close of trading in the contract month shall be settled by the clearing house at the cash settlement price.

Quotations: Australian cents per kilogram clean with a minimum fluctuation of 1 cent per kilogram.

Contract months: February, April, June, August, October and December up to 18 months ahead.

Termination of trading: The business day following the last day of wool auction sales as promulgated by the Joint Wool Settling Organisation in the cash settlement month. Trading ceases at 12.00 noon.

Settlement day: The business day following the last permitted day of trading.

Live Cattle

Cash settlement price: From Live Cattle Indicator published on last day of trading, calculated to nearest 0.1 cent per kilogram.

Mandatory cash settlement: All bought and sold contracts in existence at the close of trading in the contract month shall be settled by the clearing house at the cash settlement price.

Quotations: In cents per kilogram live weight (with a minimum fluctuation of $10 per contract).

Contract months: Each successive calendar month up to 12 months ahead.

Termination of trading: The second Wednesday of the contract month of the next succeeding business day where Wednesday is not a business day. Trading ceases at 16.00.

Settlement day: The second business day following the last permitted day of trading.

Three-month Eurodollar Interest Rate
(It is planned to introduce this contract during 1986.)

Cash settlement price: 100 minus the average on the last day of trading of 10 interest rates for three-month Eurodollar deposits drawn from a random sample of 16 banks from a list of designated banks, excluding the three highest and the three lowest quotes.

Mandatory cash settlement: All bought and sold contracts in existence, as at the close of trading in the contract month, shall be settled by the clearing house at the cash settlement price.

Quotations: 100 minus the annual percentage yield to second decimal place. (The minimum price movement of 0.01% equals US $25.)

Contract months: March, June, September and December.

Termination of trading: Trading ceases at 12.00 noon, two business days prior to the third Wednesday of the contract month.

Options contract specifications:

Options on 90-day Bank Accepted Bill Futures
Contract unit: One A $500,000 face value 90-day bank accepted bill futures contract for a specified contract month on the Sydney Futures Exchange.

Exercise prices: Set at intervals of 0.05% per annum yield. New option exercise prices created automatically as the underlying futures contract price moves.

Premiums: Quoted in yield per cent per annum.

Contract months: Put and call options available on the four nearest months of the 'major' calendar cycle (March, June, September and December).

Expiry: At the close of trading on the Friday one week prior to the settlement day for the underlying futures contract.

Exercise of options: Options may be exercised on any business day up to and including the day of expiry. In-the-money options are automatically exercised at expiry unless abandoned.

Options on Ten-Year Treasury Bond Futures

Contract unit: One A $100,000 face value, 12% coupon, ten-year Treasury bond futures contract for a specified contract month on the Sydney Futures Exchange.

Exercise prices: Set at intervals of 0.25% per annum yield. New option exercise prices created automatically as the underlying futures contract price moves.

Premiums: Quoted in yield per cent per annum.

Contract months: Put and call options available on the two nearest months of the 'major' calendar cycle (March, June, September and December).

Expiry: At 12.00 noon on the last day of trading in the underlying futures contract (the fifteenth day of the month or the next succeeding business day).

Exercise of options: Options may be exercised on any business day up to and including the day of expiry. In-the-money options are automatically exercised at expiry unless abandoned.

Options on Three-Year Treasury Bond Futures

Exercise prices: Set at intervals of 0.25% per annum yield. New option exercise prices created automatically as the underlying futures contract price moves.

Premium: Quoted in yield per cent per annum.

Contract months: Put and call options available on for the two nearest futures contract months, or as determined by the Board.

Expiry: At 12.00 noon on the last day of trading in the underlying futures contract (the fifteenth day of the month or the next succeeding business day).

Exercise of options: Options may be exercised on any business day up to and including the day of expiry. In-the-money options are automatically exercised at expiry unless abandoned.

Options on All Ordinary Share Price Index Futures

Contract unit: One All Ordinaries Index futures contract with a value of $100 times the Australian Stock Exchange's All Ordinaries Index for a specified contract month on the Sydney Futures Exchange.

Exercise prices: Set at intervals of 25.0 All Ordinaries Share Index points. New option exercise prices created automatically as the underlying futures contract price moves.

Premiums: Quoted in the same form as the All Ordinaries Share Index to one decimal place.

Contract months: Put and call options available on the two nearest futures contract months (March, June, September and December).

Expiry: At 12.00 noon on the last day of trading in the underlying futures contract (the last business day of the contract month).

Exercise of options: Options may be exercised on any business day up to and including the day of expiry. In-the-money options are automatically exercised at expiry unless abandoned.

Options on Australian Dollar Futures

Contract unit: One A $100,000 Australian dollar futures contract for a specified contract month on the SFE.

Exercise prices: Set at intervals of US $0.0100 per Australian dollar.

Contract months: Put and call options available on the two nearest futures contract months (March, June, September and December).

Expiry: At close of trading on the second Friday immediately preceding the third Wednesday of the underlying contract month.

Exercise of options: Options may be exercised on any business day up to and including the day of expiry. In-the-money options are automatically exercised at expiry unless abandoned.

Minimum contract deposits:
(as from 22 February 1989)

Contract	Standard deposit (A$)	Spread deposit* (A$)
All Ordinaries Share Price Index	6000	500
90-day Bank Accepted bills	750	350
Ten-year Commonwealth Treasury bonds	1500	200
Three-year Commonwealth Treasury bonds	650	200
Wool	1500	100
Live cattle	200	150
	(US$)	*(US$)*
US Treasury bonds	2000	–
Australian dollars	1500	200
Eurodollar	500	150
Gold	2700	180

* A spread consists of a bought contract in one contract month and a sold contract in another delivery month for the same commodity. The spread deposit covers both the bought and sold position.

Commission: Commission rates on futures and options contracts are negotiable between brokers and their clients.

Exchange fee: The Exchange fee covers exchange and clearing charges for both futures and options contracts and is included in the brokerage fee.

Inter Commodity spread: A spread deposit of A $500 applies to spread positions where one contract is in Ten-year Treasury bond futures and the other in Three-year Treasury bond futures.

GUIDE TO WORLD COMMODITY MARKETS

Trading limits:

Contract	Minimum price fluctuation	Value of minimum move
All Ordinaries Index	0.1 index point	$10.00
90-Day Bank bills	0.01% p.a.	$11.50*
Ten-year Treasury bonds	0.005% p.a.	$25.00*
3-year Treasury bonds	0.01%	$25.00*
Australian dollars	US $0.0001 per A $1	US $10.00
Gold	US 10c/troy ounce	US $10.00
US Treasury bonds	US $1/32	US $31.25
Eurodollar interest rates	0.01% p.a.	US $25.00
Wool	1c./kg	$25.00
Live cattle	0.1c/kg	$10.00

* The value of the minimum move (also called a point move) in the 90-day Bank bill and bond futures fluctuates with changes in the level of interest rates. The table below indicates the values of point moves in these contracts at various yields:

Value of one-point move at this yield in % p.a.

Yield	90-day Bank bills	3-year Treasury bonds	Ten-year Treasury bonds	
	0.01%	0.01%	0.01%	0.005%
10.00	$11.74	$26.18	$67.57	$33.79
11.00	$11.69	$25.37	$62.21	$31.11
12.00	$11.63	$24.58	$57.33	$28.67
13.00	$11.57	$23.82	$52.88	$26.45
14.00	$11.52	$23.09	$48.83	$24.43
15.00	$11.46	$22.39	$45.14	$22.57
16.00	$11.41	$21.71	$41.77	$20.89
17.00	$11.36	$21.05	$38.99	$19.35
18.00	$11.30	$20.42	$35.87	$17.94
19.00	$11.25	$19.81	$33.29	$16.65
20.00	$11.20	$19.22	$30.93	$15.48

Membership: Membership of the Exchange is divided into three main categories:

(a) **Floor members** – may deal on the trading floor either for themselves or for their clients. They must have minimum net tangible assets of at least A $250,000 and must be members of the Exchange's clearing house. They agree to be bound by the Exchange's rules and regulations which, among other things, require certain procedures to be followed with regard to clients' funds, participation in a Professional Indemnity Scheme, adherence to a code of ethics and trading behaviour set down by the Exchange and the filing of quarterly reports stating the member's current financial position.

Floor membership of the Exchange may be obtained by acquisition from an existing holder, although the Exchange does consider from time to time the creation and issuing of new floor memberships.

(b) **Local members** – may deal on the floor of the Exchange for their own account or for floor members, but not on behalf of clients. They must be nominated by a floor member and any business which they transact on the floor of the Exchange must be cleared through the nominating floor member. Local membership must be held either by an individual or a corporation or firm over which an individual exercises effective control.

(c) **Full associate members** – may deal either on their own behalf or on behalf of clients, but are not permitted to operate on the trading floor. Where they deal on behalf of clients they are required to maintain net tangible assets of at least A $50,000. They must deal through a floor member or floor members, but may be members of the clearing house in their own right. They are bound by the Exchange's rules and regulations and if dealing for clients must file quarterly financial statements with the Exchange. Among the advantages of full associate membership are the status that this confers on the member, the fact that such members are subject to Exchange regulations which makes them more attractive to clients and the fact that they are kept informed of new developments on the Exchange, including any amendments to its regulations. Full associate members who deal with the public are also required to participate in a Professional Indemnity Scheme.

In addition to the above classes, those who wish to maintain a trade association with the Exchange may become **market associate members**, which will allow them to be kept informed of new developments at the Exchange.

Non-residents of Australia may become associate members or local members of the Exchange, but firms or corporations which are not registered and carrying on business in Australia may not become floor members.

Applications for associate membership and local membership are invited from overseas individuals and corporations. There is no restriction on trading on the Sydney Futures Exchange by non-residents except where transactions originate from a country designated by the Australian Government as a tax haven in which a Tax Clearance Certificate is necessary.

Volumes of trading

Futures and options contracts traded:

Contract	Mar 1988	Mar 1989	Jan–Mar 1988	Jan–Mar 1989
		Monthly volumes		
All Ordinaries Index	35,720	24,180	67,544	66,622
90-day Bank Accepted bills	236,035	373,640	562,080	1,169,243
3-yr Commonwealth T-bonds*	–	73,750	–	221,294
10-yr Commonwealth T-bonds	320,975	238,892	631,349	739,702
US T-bonds**	20	–	20	–
Eurodollars**	25	40	205	90
Australian dollars***	2,205	243	3,132	1,479
Gold**	470	7	503	200
Wool	63	–	80	17
Live cattle	56	123	215	318
90-day Bank bill options	10,726	24,345	24,168	87,160
Australian dollar options***	21	1	21	1
All Ordinaries Index options	6,650	7,361	13,847	20,353
3-yr T-bond options*	–	3,572	–	8,687
10-yr T-bond options	79,295	44,342	158,579	174,726
Totals	692,761	790,503	1,462,246	2,490,092

Contract	*Yearly volumes*		
	1986	*1987*	*1988*
All Ordinaries Index	464,475	624,699	285,027
90-day Bank Accepted bills	1,071,546	2,094,696	2,988,923
3-yr Commonwealth T-bonds*	–	–	499,792
10-yr Commonwealth T-bonds	1,431,595	2,063,903	2,712,365
US T-bonds**	7,262	2,176	20
Eurodollars**	1,627	1,568	215
Australian dollars***	–	–	22,017
Gold**	3,983	3,606	664
Wool	363	551	305
Live cattle	2,666	1,427	1,998
90-day Bank bill options	31,633	58,033	191,799
Australian dollar options***	–	–	2,596
All Ordinaries Index options	27,091	137,078	82,180
3-yr T-bond options*	–	–	18,402
10-yr T-bond options	183,197	373,416	721,810
Totals	3,225,438	5,361,153	7,528,113

* Three-year Australian Government Treasury bond futures commenced trading on 17 May 1988. Options on the futures contract commenced trading on 16 June 1988.

** US Treasury bond and Eurodollar futures are fungible with the London International Financial Futures Exchange.

COMEX Gold is fungible with Commodity Exchange Inc., New York.

*** Australian dollar futures commenced trading on 24 February 1988. Options on the futures contract commenced trading on 15 March 1988.

AUSTRIA

VIENNA

Vienna Commodity Exchange

Commodity Section of the Vienna Stock and Commodity Exchange
Wipplingerstrasse 34, A-1011 Vienna
Telephone: 222 534 99   *Telex:* 13 2447 wbk a
Cables: Börsekammer, Wien Stock Exchange, Wien   *Fax:* 222 535 6857
President: Dkfm. G Wagner
Secretary General: Dr K Neuteufel
Vice President: C H Schönbichler

Hours of trading:
Skins, leather and technical leather – every Tuesday 12.00–13.00
Timber – every Wednesday 11.00–13.00
Colonial products, textiles and other
goods – every Thursday 11.00–13.00

Contract details:

Commodities: Timber, colonial products (imported food and spices), textiles, skins, leather and technical leather and other commodities.

Trading limits: None.

Quality: Described in the Special Rules and Usages for each commodity traded. Such usages today exist for trading of timber, yarns and twisted threads, textiles (rear from the loom or already worked), and waste made of cotton and/or chemical fibres, yarns and twisted threads, textiles and waste of lambswool or mixtures of lambswool and other fibres, sugar (cane and white sugar) and molasses, paper and rice.

Trading currency and unit (manner of price quotation): Austrian schilling; there is a weekly fixing of prices by a committee consisting of Official Brokers and experts from member firms. These experts announce their bid and ask prices during trading hours for each commodity quoted and thus reach general quotations. The prices are published in the weekly Official List and reflect the situation on Austria's wholesale market.

Membership: Membership is only granted to firms trading, producing or dealing in other ways with commodities traded on the Exchange. At the end of 1988 the Vienna Commodity Exchange had 338 member firms (timber – 248, food – 27, leather – 16, textiles – 27, others – 20).

Commission rates and margins: 2%; for other agreements each part of the business transaction has to pay half.

Date of establishment of the market: 1873, since 1 August 1876 as commodity section of the Vienna Stock and Commodity Exchange.

BRAZIL

SÃO PAULO

Bolsa de Mercadorias de São Paulo

Rua Libero Badaró, 471 -4° andar, São Paulo, 01009
Telephone: 011 32 3101   *Telex:* 011 22955   *Cables:* BOSP BR   *Fax:* 011 32 4244
President: N C Alves
Vice Presidents: J C de Toledo Piza Jnr
                   J A Esteve
Manging Director: F Esperante

Hours of trading:

Cotton	11.00–12.00
Coffee	10.30–15.30
Soybeans	11.30–15.15
Soybean meal	11.30–15.15
Soybean oil	11.30–15.15
Live cattle	15.00–16.00
Corn	10.15–16.00
Cocoa	14.00–15.00
Frozen chicken	10.15–16.00
Feeder cattle	10.15–16.00
Gold	10.00–15.50
American dollars	10.15–16.00
Deutschmark	10.15–16.00
Japanese yen	10.15–16.00
Pounds sterling	10.15–16.00

Contract details:
Commodities: Cotton,* coffee,* soybeans,* soybean meal, soybean oil, live cattle,*
corn, cocoa,* frozen chicken, feeder cattle, gold,* American dollars, Deutschmark,
Japanese yen, pounds sterling, Stock Index Future FGV-100.

* Also in Adjusted Futures market.

Trading currency and unit (manner of price quotation):

Cotton*	Cr $/bale of 15kg
Coffee*	Cr $/bag of 60kg
Soybeans*	Cr $/bag of 60kg
Soybean oil	Cr $/tonnes
Soybean meal	Cr $/tonnes
Live cattle*	Cr $/arrobas of 15kg

192

Cocoa* – Cr $/bag of 60kg
Frozen chicken – Cr $/tonne
Feeder cattle – Cr $/head
Corn – Cr $/bag of 60kg
Gold* – Cr $/gramme
American dollars – Cr $/US $1
Deutschmarks – Cr $/DM10
Japanese yen – Cr $/¥1000
Pounds sterling – Cr $/£1
Stock Index Future FGV-100 – Points of Index FGV-100

* In Adjusted Futures market, quotations adjusted daily as a function of the official mean rate of the American dollar, as established by the Central Bank of Brazil.

Trading units (minimum lot size):

Cotton – 500 bales of 15kg
Coffee – 100 bags of 60kg
Soybeans – 30 tonnes
Soybean meal – 25 tonnes
Soybean oil – 12.5 tonnes
Live cattle – 330 arrobas of 15kg
Corn – 60 tonnes
Cocoa – 50 bags of 60kg
Frozen chicken – 12 tons
Feeder cattle – 27 heads
Gold – 250 grammes
American dollars – US $5000
Deutschmark – DM10,000
Japanese yen – ¥1,000,000
Pounds sterling – £5000
Stock Index Future FGV-100 – one portfolio equivalent to five portfolios of Stock Index FGV-100

Trading limits:
(Considering that 1 US dollar = Cr $11.545 (22/01/86))

Cotton – Cr $0.01/15kg unit
Coffee – Cr $0.01/bag of 60kg
Soybeans – Cr $0.01/60kg
Soybean oil – (not quoted)
Soybean meal – (not quoted)
Live cattle – Cr $0.01/arroba of 15kg
Corn – (not quoted)
Cocoa – Cr $0.01/bag
Frozen chicken – (not quoted)
Feeder cattle – Cr $0.01/head
Gold – Cr $0.01/bag
American dollars – Cr $0.01/US $100
Deutschmark – (not quoted)
Japanese yen – (not quoted)

Pounds sterling – (not quoted)
Stock Index Future FGV-100 – 10 points

Quality:

Cotton – type 6; fibre of 30mm/32mm minimum
Coffee – type 6; without Rio and Rio Zona taste
Soybeans – common type
Soybean oil – common type
Soybean meal – common type
Live cattle – age limit: 60 months
– weight: minimum 450kg
maximum 550kg
Cocoa – type 11
Frozen chicken – age limit: 50 days
– weight: minimum 1000kg
maximum 1900kg
Feeder cattle – age limit: 24 months
– weight: minimum 240kg
Corn – common type No 3, halfhard, yellow as established
by the resolution No 103 from CONCEX
Gold – 995 parts of fine gold on each 1000 parts of the
metal

Deliverable tolerances:

Cotton – 5% of weight
– maximum of 3 consecutive types of the type 6/7
until type 5 inclusive
Coffee – maximum of 30% of bolting No 14 with leakage of
5% of bolting No 13
– 10% of moka coffee
– 1% of weight
– 10% of flat grains
– maximum of 8% of brocades or wormy grains
Soybeans – maximum of $% of beans damaged with maximum
of 5% of beans burnt *or* 14% of beans damaged
with maximum of 10% beans burnt
– maximum of 2% impurities
– maximum of 0.005% of drops of caster oil plant
– 30% of broken beans
– 14% of humidity
Soybean meal – maximum of 3% of compound proteins
Soybean oil – 0.25% of broken per contract
– acidity: base 1%, maximum 2% with index
reduction on the acidity excess between 1 and 2%
Live cattle – 5% of weight
Cocoa – 1% of weight
Frozen chicken – 5% of weight
Feeder cattle – (none)
Corn – 14.5% of humidity
Gold – 1% of weight

Delivery points:

Cotton	São Paulo
Coffee	São Paulo, Santos, Catanduva, Espírito Santo do Pinhal, Londrina, Maringá, Rio de Janeiro, Varginha, Trés Pontas, Guaxupé and Poços de Caldas
Soybeans	Ponta Grossa
Soybean meal	Ports of Paranaguá and Rio Grande
Soybean oil	São Paulo
Live cattle	Araçatuba, Barretos, Presidente Prudente and São Paulo
Cocoa	Ilhéus and Itabuna
Frozen chicken	São Paulo
Feeder cattle	Araçatuba, Barretos, Presidente Prudente and São Paulo
Corn	Port of Paranaguá
Gold	São Paulo
American dollars	São Paulo
Deutschmark	São Paulo
Japanese yen	São Paulo
Pounds sterling	São Paulo
Stock Index Future FGV-100	São Paulo

Delivery months:

Cotton	Mar, May, July, Oct, Dec
Coffee	Mar, May, July, Sept, Dec
Soybeans, soybean oil, soybean meal	Jan, Mar, May, Jul, Sept, Nov
Live cattle	Feb, April, June, Aug, Oct, Dec
Cocoa	Mar, May, July, Sept, Dec
Frozen chicken	Feb, April, June, Aug, Oct, Dec
Feeder cattle, corn	Jan, Mar, May, July, Sept, Nov
Gold	Feb, April, June, Aug, Oct, Dec
Australian dollars, Deutschmarks, Japanese yen, pounds sterling	at any moment delivery months will be the first six months of the year, followed by the first or third month of the next trimestrial period
Stock Index Future FGV-100	all calendar months

Clearing house: Caixa Nacional de Liquidaçaõ de Negócios a Termo e Dispnível S/A.

Termination of trading: Trading is terminated on the 13th business day before the end of the delivery month.

Currency dealt in: Cruzeiros (Cr $).

Membership: If approved for membership the candidate has to pay 100 OTN which corresponds approximately to US $7700. 613 titles of effective membership are available.

Commission rates and margins:

Types of contracts	Associated				Non-associated			
	(1)	(2)	(3)	(4)	(1)	(2)	(3)	(4)
Ordinary	0.25%	0.125%	0.10%	0.20%	0.30%	0.150%	0.12%	0.25%
Hedge	0.20%	0.100%	0.07%	0.15%	0.25%	0.125%	0.10%	0.20%
Straddle	0.15%	0.075%	0.04%	0.10%	0.20%	0.100%	0.06%	0.15%
Change of month	0.10%	0.050%	0.05%	0.05%	0.14%	0.070%	0.08%	0.08%
Day Trade	0.05%	0.025%	0.04%	0.10%	0.07%	0.035%	0.06%	0.15%

(1) Live cattle, cotton, coffee, soybean meal, soybean oil, gold, cocoa, corn, frozen chicken, feeder cattle
(2) Soybeans
(3) American dollar, Japanese yen, Deutschmark, pounds sterling
(4) Stock Index Future FGV-100

Delivery for	Associated			Non-associated		
	(1)	(2)	(3)	(1)	(2)	(3)
Ordinary	0.375%	0.185%	0.75%	0.45%	0.225%	0.90%
Hedge	0.30%	0.150%	0.60%	0.375%	0.185%	0.75%

(1) Live cattle, cotton, coffee, soybean meal, soybean oil, gold, frozen chicken, feeder cattle
(2) Soybeans
(3) Cocoa

Date of establishment of the market: 26 October 1917.

Volume of trading since 1988:

Commodity	Number of contracts	
	1987	1988
Cotton	11	7
Coffee	90,388	54,658
Soybeans	–	6,227
Live cattle	15,183	78,261
Cocoa	3,937	–
Frozen chicken	1,764	–
Gold	614,872	265,973
American dollars	88,943	60,229
Stock Index Future FGV-100	–	85,901
Totals	815,048	551,256

Date of establishment of contracts:

Cotton – 18 August 1980
Coffee – 4 April 1978
Soybeans – 4 April 1978
Soybean oil, soybean meal – 12 May 1981
Live cattle – 22 September 1980
Cocoa – 21 November 1986
Frozen chicken – 27 February 1978
Feeder cattle – 24 July 1986
Corn – 4 April 1979
Gold – 20 December 1980
American dollars,
Deutschmarks, Japanese yen – 16 May 1986
Pounds sterling – 15 August 1986
Stock Index Future FGV-100 – 15 April 1988

Further information: BMSP has established new market modalities such as the Premium market and the Adjusted Futures market, as well as a new share index, the FGV-100.

There are 137 brokers active in BMSP, responsible for a total transaction of US $6.75 billion. In the Futures market a total of 620,000 contracts were negotiated in the various operational modalities, which represented a total of US $5.37 billion (79.5% of total volume negotiated in the BMSP during 1988); in the Cash market the total was US $694,600,000 (10.3%); the Classifications Service produced an income of US $415,000,000 (6.2%) and the Auctions Department (special cash auctions of products belonging to Government Agencies or enterprises) was responsible for US $271,200,000 (4%).

The BMSP Classification Department, as official cotton classification entity for São Paulo State, certified over 1,600,000 bales in 1988, corresponding to 307,800 tons of cotton and sub-products.

Bolsa Mercantil & de Futoros

Praca Antonio Prado 48, São Paulo 01010
Telephone: 5511 239 5511   *Telex:* 11 26 928   *Fax:* 5511 35 2541
Chief Executive Officer: D R Alves
Managing Director: L F Forbes
Settlements and Custody Director: E Pinto
Operations Director: A C M Barbosa
Economic Affairs Consultant: A Kulaif

Hours of trading:

Stock Index – 09.30–13.15
Gold – 10.00–16.00
Broilers – 14.15–14.35
Live cattle – 15.30–16.30
Live hogs – 14.15–14.35
Foreign currency – 10.00–15.45

                    Coffee – 10.45–16.00
          Interest rates – 11.45–12.30, 15.15–16.00 (CD), 10.30–15.45
                    (GTB)

Contract details:

Commodities: Stock Index, gold, broilers, live cattle, live hogs, foreign currency, coffee, interest rates (Government Treasury Bonuses, GTBs and Certificates of Deposit, CDs)

Trading currency and unit (manner of price quotation):

                Stock Index – points of index
                       Gold – Cr $/grammes
                   Broilers – Cr $/kg
                Live cattle – Cr $/arroba of 15kg
                  Live hogs – Cr $/net kg
          Foreign currency – Cr $/US $1000
                            – Cr $/DM1000
                            – Cr $/¥100,000
                     Coffee – Cr $/bag of 60kg
             Interest rates – points/face value (1 point = Cr $1)
                            – Cr $/1000 GTB

Trading units (minimum lot size):

                Stock Index – index × Cr $0.50
                       Gold – 250 grammes (0.25 grammes for odd lot)
                   Broilers – 12 tonnes
                Live cattle – 330 arrobas
                  Live hogs – 8000 net kg
          Foreign currency – US $5000
                            – DM10,000
                            – ¥1,000,000
                     Coffee – 100 bags
             Interest rates – Cr $10,000 (face value)
                            – 5000 GTBs

Trading limits:
Minimum:

                Stock Index – 5 points
                       Gold – Cr $/0.01 gramme
                   Broilers – Cr $0.01/kg
                Live cattle – Cr $0.10/arroba
                  Live hogs – Cr $0.01/kg
          Foreign currency – Cr $/US $1
                            – Cr $/DM1000
                            – Cr $/¥100,000
                     Coffee – Cr $0.01/bag
             Interest rates – 1 point
                            – Cr $/1000 GTBs

Maximum:
5% on the third month (except for gold spot, forward and options, foreign currency options, and domestic CD futures).

Quality:

Stock Index –	São Paulo Stock Exchange Index
Gold –	pure gold, in bar form, melted by refining company and kept under custody in a depository bank, both authorized and qualified by the BM&F
Broilers –	slaughtered and chilled or frozen
Live cattle –	ready for slaughter
Live hogs –	ready for slaughter
Foreign currency –	the exchange rate for Cruzados per American dollar, Deutschmark or Japanese yen
Coffee –	type 6 or better, 'bebida duro' or better
Interest rates –	60- or 90-day domestic CD issued by investment and commercial banks, bearing prefixed interest and payable upon redemption
–	the nominal value of the GTB for the delivery month

Deliverable tolerances:

Gold –	250 and 1000 gramme gross bars, assaying 999 fineness or better; 100 and 400 troy ounce bars, assaying 995 fineness or better
Live cattle –	330 arrobas +/- 5%, equivalent to a 17 to 20 head lot
Live hogs –	8000 net kilogrammes +/- 5%, equivalent to an 86 to 117 head lot
Coffee –	besides proper characteristics previously determined in the contract, variation of up to +/- 1% in the weight of the bag

Delivery points:

Broilers –	establishments under federal inspection, located in the states of São Paulo, Parana, Santa Catarina and Rio Grande do Sul, authorized and qualified by the BM&F and the commodities exchange of Parana
Live cattle –	Aracatuba, Barretos, Presidente Prudente and São Paulo
Live hogs –	Campinas, Ribeiro Preto and Sorocaba in the State of São Paulo; Cascavel, Francisco Beltrao, Maringa, Pato Branco, Ponta Grossa and Toledo in the State of Parana

Termination of trading:

Stock Index –	Wednesday closest to the fifteenth day of the delivery month
Gold –	futures, last business day of the previous month
–	options, third Friday of the delivery month or previous business day

Broilers, live cattle, live hogs – last business day of delivery month
Foreign currency – first business day of delivery month
Coffee – last business day of delivery month
Interest rates – third Wednesday of the delivery month or the
following business day (CD)
– first business day of the delivery month (GTB)

Delivery months:

Stock Exchange – even months
Gold – futures, even months
– options, odd months
– forward, five days and multiples of five
Broilers, live cattle, live hogs – even months
Foreign currency – all months
Coffee – March, May, July, September, December

Membership: Effective members must be engaged in the following professions: agriculture, trade, industry or capital market. They are represented on the Board of Governors, enjoy discounts in their transactions, and are permanently entitled to receive technical material and information issued by the Exchange.

Types of membership: Commodities brokerage houses, including commercial companies having the right to intermediate purchase and sale operations on the BM&F's markets, in their own name or on behalf of others, maintaining for this purpose licensed representatives on the Exchange's trading floor, represented on the Exchange's Board of Governors; clearing agents, including brokerage firms responsible for the register and liquidation of transactions effected on the floor, represented on the Exchange's Board of Governors; floor trader trading on his or her own, directly on the trading floor, or for commodities brokerage houses; specialist licensees or market makers, that is brokerage institutions (selectively admitted) not holding titles of commodities brokerage houses and which, at the sole discretion of the Board of Governors, are authorized to operate independently, directly on the trading floor, for a limited time, transacting an agreed minimum number of contracts per month.

Commission rates and margins: Margins are a fixed value per contract, due the day after trade is executed on the floor, and adjusted whenever deemed necessary by the Exchange.

Commodity	*operations (%)*	
	common	*day trade*
(Futures unless otherwise stated)		
Stock Index	0.25	0.10
Gold (round lot)	0.25	0.80
	0.40	0.10 (spot)
	0.40	– (forward)
	0.40	0.20 (options on actuals)
Gold (odd lot)	0.40	0.10 (spot)
Broilers	0.15	0.06

Live cattle	0.25	0.10
Live hogs	0.25	0.10
Foreign currency	0.15	0.06
	0.40	0.20 (options on actuals)
'Brazil' coffee	0.20	0.06
Interest rates – CD	0.06	0.025
– GTB	0.08	0.025

Date of establishment of the market: 31 January 1986.

Date of establishment of contracts:

Stock Index – 14 February 1986

Gold – spot (round lot), forward, call options on actuals, 31 January 1986
- spot (odd lot), 8 November 1988
- futures, 4 March 1986
- put options on actuals, 27 November 1987

Broilers – 20 March 1987

Live cattle – 6 May 1987

Live hogs – 25 September 1987

Foreign currency – American dollar futures, 11 June 1986
- American dollar call options on actuals, 9 March 1988
- American dollar put options on actuals, 19 May 1988
- Deutschmark and Japanese yen futures, 19 May 1986

Coffee – 26 August 1988

Interest rates – domestic CD futures, 11 June 1986
- GTB futures, 14 July 1989

Membership of other organisations: Founder member of the São Paulo Stock Exchange.

Further information: The GTB futures contract was introduced recently in order to replace the futures contract on the Brazilian T-bond (extinguished by the 'summer plan' on 16 January 1989). The GTB futures contract aims at providing an hedge against the risk of variations in the increase rate of price levels.

The BM&F will soon be introducing the American dollar denominated coffee futures contract to complement the existing 'Brazil' coffee futures contract. This is an attempt to avoid speculation over inflation and make the price of coffee in the Brazilian market equivalent to that of the international market.

The BM&F trades an average of 65,000 contracts daily – 95% of the overall volume of futures exchanged in Brazil – and averages 150,000 open contracts per day.

Volume of trading since 1987

Commodity	Number of contracts 1987
Gold spot 250g	253,292
spot 1000g	798
call options	177,828
options exercise	5,190
futures	117,870
forward 250g	10,060
forward 1000g	1,790
Ibovespa futures	5,339,126
Unindexed domestic CD futures	46,577
Indexed domestic CD futures	44
Nominal T-bond futures	113,701
futures (March/87)	0
US dollar futures	2,786
Japanese yen futures	106
Coffee futures	1,706
Frozen broilers futures	8,653
Chilled broilers futures	3,565
Live cattle futures	5,685
Live hogs futures	816
Total	6,087,982

Commodity	Number of contracts 1988
Gold spot 250g	710,840
spot 1000g	48
fractionary	151,658
call options	1,327,896
put options	75,878
call options exercise	69,847
put options exercise	6,432
futures	31,599
forward 250g	10,717
forward 1000g	0
Ibovespa futures	8,931,080
Nominal T-bond futures	459,846
call options	9,807
put options	1,070
US dollar futures	25,202
call options	487
put options	164
call options exercise	10
Coffee futures	10
Live cattle futures	145
Brazil coffee futures	1,236
Total	11,813,962

1988

Commodity	JANUARY		FEBRUARY		MARCH		APRIL		MAY	
	V.C.	O.I.	V.C.	O.I.	V.C.	O.I.	V.C.	O.I.	V.C.	O.I.
Gold spot 250g	33,467	0	22,140	0	46,750	0	37,678	0	62,809	0
spot 1,000g	0	0	4	0	3	0	0	0	1	0
fractionary	0	0	0	0	0	0	0	0	0	0
call options	35,376	9,311	22,477	14,720	61,850	11,264	57,223	18,110	85,287	10,673
put options	2,201	1,238	3,854	1,922	1,099	247	966	995	1,197	0
call options exercise	2,613	0	0	0	1,561	0	0	0	12,693	0
put options exercise	22	0	0	0	1,593	0	0	0	25	0
futures	2,065	723	1,034	404	4,275	1,185	9,062	2,978	5,317	2,183
forward 250g	690	330	694	538	1,830	1,295	565	109	40	40
forward 1,000g	0	0	0	0	0	0	0	0	0	0
Ibovespa futures	511,620	18,590	816,696	22,403	1,080,259	23,219	682,034	31,945	629,741	27,665
Nominal T-bond futures	14,780	9,573	24,617	11,732	35,620	13,761	46,919	15,920	45,715	15,081
call options	0	0	0	0	2,500	2,092	2,320	2,220	2,308	2,203
put options	0	0	0	0	170	0	530	700	170	0
call options exercise	0	0	0	0	0	0	0	0	0	0
US dollar futures	0	0	0	0	4,715	2,741	7,011	5,080	3,095	5,481
call options	0	0	0	0	373	137	92	77	22	42
put options	0	0	0	0	0	0	132	132	0	132
call options exercise	0	0	0	0	0	0	10	0	0	0
Coffee futures	10	0	0	0	0	0	0	0	0	0
Live cattle futures	0	0	0	0	0	0	68	55	55	55
Brazil coffee futures	0	0	0	0	0	0	0	0	0	0
Total	602,844	39,765	891,486	51,719	1,232,598	55,941	844,710	78,321	848,475	63,500

JUNE V.C.	JUNE O.I.	JULY V.C.	JULY O.I.	AUGUST V.C.	AUGUST O.I.	SEPTEMBER V.C.	SEPTEMBER O.I.	OCTOBER V.C.	OCTOBER O.I.	NOVEMBER V.C.	NOVEMBER O.I.	DECEMBER V.C.	DECEMBER O.I.	GRAND TOTAL V.C.
56,443	0	44,548	0	47,327	0	64,446	0	78,296	0	108,664	0	108,272	0	710,840
0	0	0	0	38	0	0	0	1	0	1	0	0	0	48
0	0	0	0	0	0	0	0	0	0	34,409	0	117,249	0	151,658
113,768	23,795	99,008	15,805	152,213	32,953	134,746	18,643	189,262	41,417	172,253	16,467	214,463	39,930	1,327,896
8,586	3,425	9,561	6,024	21,364	13,677	9,579	778	2,539	2,244	5,628	2,203	9,304	8,066	75,878
0	0	9,758	0	0	0	19,182	0	0	0	24,040	0	0	0	69,847
0	0	1,639	0	0	0	2,903	0	0	0	250	0	0	0	6,432
1,855	747	1,975	1,106	504	349	648	518	299	205	1,972	987	2,693	1,173	31,599
554	164	191	120	746	326	549	234	443	171	182	21	4,133	727	10,717
0	0	0	0	0	0	0	0	0	0	0	0	0	0	0
625,954	22,605	662,512	17,600	771,680	21,240	764,603	25,761	667,454	24,815	366,410	22,785	852,117	17,460	8,931,080
63,873	17,515	61,181	15,788	60,195	19,500	50,924	16,426	13,555	6,990	24,471	9,277	17,996	9,158	459,846
555	575	110	5	120	120	304	0	316	100	874	281	400	18	9,807
0	0	200	0	0	0	0	0	0	0	0	0	0	0	1,070
227	3,513	3,307	3,402	3,201	4,576	1,170	3,627	519	2,904	549	2,207	1,408	2,337	25,202
0	0	0	0	0	0	0	0	0	0	0	0	0	0	487
22	132	0	132	0	0	0	0	0	0	0	0	0	0	164
0	0	0	0	0	0	0	0	0	0	0	0	0	0	10
0	0	0	0	0	0	0	0	0	0	0	0	0	0	10
0	0	0	0	0	0	0	0	0	0	20	10	2	2	145
0	0	0	0	217	129	291	153	82	120	496	344	150	342	1,236
871,837	72,471	893,990	59,982	1,067,605	92,870	1,049,345	66,140	952,766	78,966	1,240,219	54,582	1,328,087	79,376	11,813,962

CANADA

MONTREAL

The Montreal Exchange

PO Box 61, 800 Square Victoria, Montreal, Quebec H4Z 1A9
Telephone: 514 871 2424   *Telex:* 055 60586   *Fax:* 514 871 3559
President: B Riverin
Executive Vice-president: G Giarusso
Senior Vice-president, Corporate Development: L Lachapelle
Director, Derivative products: B Pham

Hours of trading: North American Lumber futures contract – 10.00–14.30 (Eastern time) and on the last day of trading from 10.00–13.30 (Eastern time)
North American Woodpulp futures – 09.30–13.35 (Eastern time) and on the last day of trading for the contract month from 09.30–12.35 (Eastern time), or such other times as may be determined by the Exchange.

Hours of trading (EST/EDT time):

IOCC Gold options –	09.00–14.30
IOCC Platinum options –	09.00–14.30
Gold certificates –	09.00–16.00
Silver certificates –	09.00–16.00
Platinum certificates –	09.00–16.00
Canadian Bankers' Acceptance futures –	08.30–15.00
Canadian Government Bond futures –	08.20–15.00

Contract details:
Commodities: IOCC Gold options, IOCC Platinum options, Gold certificates, Silver certificates, Platinum certificates, Canadian Bankers' Acceptance futures, Canadian Government bond futures.

Trading currency and unit (manner of price quotation):

IOCC Gold & Platinum options –	Premiums and exercise prices quoted in American dollars and cents per ounce
Gold certificates –	American dollars and cents per troy ounce
Silver certificates –	American dollars and cents per troy ounce
Platinum certificates –	American dollars and cents per troy ounce
Canadian Bankers' Acceptance futures –	C $1,000,000 unit
Canadian Government bond futures –	C $100,000 nominal value notional Canadian government bond with 9% coupon

Trading units (minimum lot size):

IOCC Gold options	– 10 troy ounces of fine gold bullion of minimum .995 fineness acceptable for good London delivery
IOCC Platinum options	– 10 troy ounces of platinum of minimum .9995 fineness
Gold certificate	– 5 troy ounces minimum
Silver certificate	– 250 troy ounces minimum
Platinum certificate	– 10 troy ounces minimum
Canadian Bankers' Acceptance futures	– C $1,000,000
Canadian Government bond futures	– C $100,000 nominal value notional Canadian Government bond with 9% coupon

Trading limits:

IOCC Gold options	–
Position limit	– 5000 contracts on same side of market
Premium quotations	– increments of US $0.10 per troy ounce (US $1.00 per contract)
Exercise price	– minimum intervals set at $10.00 per ounce
IOCC Platinum options	–
Position limit	– 500 contracts on same side of market
Premium quotations	– increments of US $0.10 per troy ounce (US $1.00 per contract)
Certificates	– minimum quotation fraction per troy ounce
Gold	– US $0.05 no trading limit
Platinum	– US $0.05 no trading limit
Silver	– US $0.005 no trading limit
Canadian Bankers' Acceptance futures	– reporting limit 300 contracts
Position limit	– 5000 contracts

Tick size & Value 0.01% (1 basic point = $25 per contract)

Canadian Government bond futures

Reporting limit	– 250 contracts Position limit – 4000 contracts

Tick size & Value 0.01 = C $10.00 per contract

Quality and deliverable tolerances:

IOCC Gold options	– minimum .995 fineness acceptable for good London delivery
IOCC Platinum options	– minimum .9995 fineness acceptable for good London delivery
Gold certificate	– minimum fineness of 995 parts per 1000 acceptable for good London delivery
Silver certificate	– minimum fineness of 999 parts per 1000 acceptable for good London delivery
Platinum certificate	– minimum fineness of 9995 parts for 10,000 acceptable for good London delivery

Canadian Bankers' Acceptance futures – 3-month Canadian Bankers' Acceptance
Canadian Government bond futures – Eligible bonds must be deliverable during the delivery month and they must not mature or be callable for at least $6\frac{1}{2}$ years and no more than 10 years from the date of delivery with C $1 billion in circulation

Delivery points:

IOCC Gold options – deposit of good London deliverable gold in IOCC's account with institution acting as its delivery depot. MOCATTA Gold in London
IOCC Platinum options – deposit of good London deliverable gold in IOCC's account with institution acting as its delivery depot. MOCATTA in London
Precious metal certificates – N/A
Canadian Bankers' Acceptance futures – N/A
Canadian Government bond futures – N/A

Termination of trading:

IOCC Gold & Platinum options – 14.30 in Montreal (EST/EDT time) on the third Friday in expiry month
Certificates – no set date
Canadian Bankers' Acceptance futures – trading terminates at 10.00 (EST/EDT time) on the second London business day prior to the third Wednesday of the delivery month
Canadian Government bond futures – on the seventh business day preceding the last business day of the delivery month

Delivery months:

IOCC Gold options – expiry months are the next 3 months falling on the February, May, August, November cycle
IOCC Platinum options – next 3 months falling on March, June, September, December cycle
Gold certificates – deliverable at any time upon request
Silver certificates – deliverable at any time upon request
Platinum certificates – deliverable at any time upon request
Canadian Bankers' Acceptance futures – March, June, September, December for a total of 2 years
Canadian Government Bond futures – March, June, September, December

Clearing house:

IOCC Gold & Platinum options – IOCC
Gold certificates – Canadian Depository for Securities Ltd
Silver certificates – Canadian Depository for Securities Ltd
Platinum certificates – Canadian Depository for Securities Ltd

Canadian Bankers' Acceptance futures – Trans Canada Options
Canadian Government bond futures – Trans Canada Options

Membership: Full-fledged or 'local'.

Commission rates and margins:

IOCC Gold options – premium plus 10%
IOCC Platinum options – premium plus 15%
For both the minimum is 3% of premium
Precious metals certificates – 25% of market minus portion out
Canadian Bankers' Acceptance futures – spec. C $1500
hedge C $1000
spread C $625
Canadian Government bond futures – spec. C $1500 per contract
hedge C $1000 per contract
spread C $625 per contract

Date of establishment contracts:

IOCC Gold options – March 1982
IOCC Platinum options – 19 May 1987
Gold certificates – 29 April 1983
Silver certificates – 29 April 1983
Platinum certificates – 12 December 1986
Canadian Bankers' Acceptance futures – April 1988
Canadian Government bond futures – 15 September 1989

Volume of trading since 1988:

	Total volume	
	1987	*1988*
IOCC Gold options	446,585	289,399
IOCC Platinum options	3,793	1,773
Gold certificates	19,760 oz	10,644 oz
Silver certificates	992,452 oz	559,305 oz
Platinum certificates	1,525	1,585
Canadian Bankers' Acceptance	–	10,099

Further information: The Montreal Exchange is Canada's leading futures and options market. The Exchange trades Canadian equity options, Canada Bond options, International Options Clearing Corp. (IOCC) gold and platinum options and Canadian Bankers' Acceptance Futures. On 15 September 1989 it will launch its new Canadian Government Bond Futures contract. Its options and futures are cleared by Trans Canada Options Inc, except its precious metal options which are cleared by the IOCC.

Clearing house: International Commodities Clearing House.

TORONTO

The Toronto Futures Exchange

The Exchange Tower, 2 First Canadian Place, Ontario M5X 1J2
Telephone: 416 947 4487   *Fax:* 947 4788
Chairman: T Lett
President: A Clademenos
Retail Marketing: S Kokal
Institutional Marketing: J McDonald

Hours of trading (Eastern):

                Toronto 35 options – 09.30–16.15
                Toronto 35 futures – 09.30–16.15
                   Silver options – 09.05–16.00
                    TSE 300 spot – 09.20–16.10
   91-day Canada treasury bill futures – 09.00–15.15
    Long-term Canada bond futures – 09.00–15.15
    Mid-term Canada bond futures – 09.00–15.15

Contract details:

*Commodities:*Toronto 35 index options (TXO) Toronto 35 index futures (TXF), silver options, TSE 300 composite spot index, 91-day Government of Canada treasury bill futures, TFE long-term bond futures, TFE mid-term bond futures.

Toronto 35 index options

Trading unit (minimum lot size): Each option contract represents $100 times the value of the Toronto 35 index.

Trading limits:
Aggregate exercise price: the exercise price times $100.

Exercise price intervals: set at five point intervals to bracket the value of the Toronto 35 index. New exercise prices are added when the value of the Toronto 35 index closes at or beyond the last exercise price.

Premium quotations: premiums under $0.10 = $0.01; premiums under $5.0 = $0.05; premiums at $5.00 and above = $0.125.

Position and exercise limits: 8000 contracts.

Expiration: Third Friday of the expiry month. The expiry months are three consecutive near months.

Termination of trading: Thursday before the third Friday of the month.

Exercise and settlement: Cash settlement. European-style option, exercisable only on day after last trading day. Upon exercise an option holder will receive the amount equal to the difference between the official opening level of the Toronto 35 index on the expiration date and the exercise price of the option. Settlement is through the facilities of Trans-Canada options two business days after the last trading day.

GUIDE TO WORLD COMMODITY MARKETS

Exercise and settlement: Cash settlement. European-style option, exercisable only on day after last trading day. Upon exercise an option holder will receive the amount equal to the difference between the official opening level of the Toronto 35 index on the expiration date and the exercise price of the option. Settlement is through the facilities of Trans-Canada options two business days after the last trading day.

Toronto 35 index futures
Trading unit (minimum lot size): Values at $500 times the Toronto 35 index futures price.

Trading limits:
Minimum price fluctuation: multiples of 0.02 of a point, equivalent to $10 per contract.

Price quotation: index points rounded to two decimal places.

Daily price limit: 13.50 index points or $6750 per contract.

Position limits: hedgers – 2200 contracts in total; speculators – 1000 contracts in total.

Reporting levels: 500 contracts in total.

Termination of trading: Thursday before the third Friday of the month.

Delivery months: Three consecutive near months.

Settlement: On the third Friday of the month, all open positions will be marked to the market using the official opening level of the Toronto 35 index on Friday and terminated by cash settlement. The value of the TSE 35 index to two decimal places will be used as the cash settlement price.

Silver
Trading unit (minimum lot size): 100 ounces of .999 fineness silver bullion.

Trading limits:
Price multiples: one cent for all premium levels.

Exercise price: below $5 = $0.25 interval; $5 to $15 = $0.5 interval; above $15 = $1 interval.

Position limits: 20,000 puts and calls on the same side of the market.

Reporting levels: 500 or more aggregate long or short positions of any single class.

Exercise limits: 20,000 contracts over a five day period. Exercise notice can be tendered any business day, the delivery day being the fifth business day following receipt of the exercise notice.

Expiration: The Saturday following the third Friday of each expiry month.

Settlement: In the form of a silver certificate issued by an approved depository. Holders should refer to the individual certificate for the conditions of delivery.

TSE 300 spot
Trading unit (minimum lot size): Valued at $10 times the TSE 300 composite index.

Trading limits:
Minimum price fluctuation: one index point or $10 per contract.

Price quotation: index points rounded to the nearest whole number (except at settlement).

No daily price limit.

Position limits: 2000 contracts in total (spec and hedge).

Reporting levels: 300 contracts in total (spec and hedge).

Settlement: At the end of each day of trading all open positions will be marked to market and terminated by cash settlement. The actual value of the TSE 300 composite index (to two decimal places) times $10 will be used as the cash settlement price.

Settlement day is next day of gains and losses in cash by 09.00.

91-day treasury bill futures
Trading unit (minimum lot size): $1,000,000 face value.

Trading limits: Minimum price fluctuation: 0.01 or $24 per contract.

Daily price limit: 0.6 or $1440 per contract, with an expanded price limit of 0.9 or $2160 per contract.

Position limits: 300 contracts in total (spec); 3000 in total, 750 per month (hedge).

Reporting levels: 100 contracts in total (spec); 300 in total (hedge).

Termination of trading: 11.00 on the day of the Bank of Canada auction preceding the last Friday of the delivery month.

Delivery: March, June, September and December, in addition to the current month.

Delivery notices may be tendered on any of the last three Bank of Canada auction days immediately preceding the last Friday of the delivery month.

Delivery days are any of the last three Fridays of the delivery month, provided a delivery notice is submitted on the previous business day. In the event that the Friday is a holiday the Exchange will name another day for delivery.

Deliverable issues: the seller may substitute bills with maturities ranging from 89 to 93 days with a discounted value of $1,000,000 at maturity.

Long-term bond futures
Trading unit (minimum lot size): $100,000 face value, 9% theoretical coupon rate.

Trading limits:
Minimum price fluctuation: 1/32 or $31.25 per contract.

Daily price limit: 2 points or $2000 per contract, with an expanded price limit of 3 points or $3000 per contract.

Position limits: 1200 contracts in total (spec); 6000 in total (hedge).

Reporting levels: 400 contracts in total (spec); 600 in total (hedge).

Termination of trading: 11.00 on the sixth last business day of the delivery month.

Delivery:

Delivery notice may be tendered any business day from five business days prior to the first business day of the delivery month up to and including the last trading day.

Delivery day is the fifth business day following tender of a delivery notice.

Deliverable issues: eligible bonds must not mature or be callable for at least fifteen years from the date of delivery with a face value of $100,000. The Exchange will determine from time to time which issues are deliverable.

Mid-term bond futures

Trading unit (minimum lot size): $50,000 face value, 9% coupon rate, maturity no less than four years and no greater than six from the date of delivery.

Trading limit:

Minimum price fluctuation: 1/32 or $15.625 per contract.

Daily price limit: 2 points or $1000 per contract, with an expanded limit of 3 points or $1500 per contract.

Position limits: the Exchange may set limits on the maximum net long or net short mid-term bond futures positions held by individuals and organizations. Currently, investors are subject to a position limit of 500 bond contracts for delivery in any one month, or 1200 in total.

Reporting levels: currently, all accounts with positions of 380 or more contracts for delivery in any one month, or 900 in total, are required to report to the Exchange in such form as prescribed.

Termination of trading: the sixth last business day of the delivery month.

At the seller's discretion delivery may be effected on the fifth business day following tender of a delivery notice during the contract month.

Deliverable issues: the Exchange will allow the seller to substitute Canada bonds with a coupon rate other than 9%, at a discount for bonds with coupons less than 9%, and at a premium for bonds with coupons more than 9%. The Exchange will publish a list of acceptable issues at the time a contract begins trading and will update the list as new issues become available. All bonds in a delivery unit (a unit meaning one contract) must be of the same issue.

Margins:

	speculative	hedge	spread
		(US dollars)	
Toronto 35 futures	9000	5000	1200
TSE 300 spot	1500	1000	–
91-day treasury bills	1500	1000	625
Long-term bond futures	2000	1000	625
Mid-term bond futures	1000	500	300

Membership: A total of 260 TFE seats are held by over 190 members including individuals, banks, trust companies, security and commodity dealers and other corporations. There are three types of TFE membership:

Dealer, must be registered as either a futures commission merchant under the Commodity Futures Act, or a securities dealer under the Securities Act. Dealer members are the only class permitted to solicit and accept orders from the public with regard to commodity futures or options trading.

Trader, able to trade for themselves or for any other member. A trader member may be an individual, financial institution or other organization not carrying on business in Canada as a futures commission merchant or securities dealer.

Sponsor, not entitled to trade, but provides management and administrative support for the Exchange. The sponsor member of the TFE is the Toronto Stock Exchange (TSE). Although the TFE is sponsored by the TSE, it operates as a separate entity with its own by-laws, membership and Board of Governors.

Date of establishment of market: 16 January 1984.

Further information: In May 1987 the TSE introduced the Toronto 35 index comprised of 35 of the largest and most liquid stocks in Canada. The index is updated every 15 seconds. The initial purpose of the Index was to trade derivative products specifically designed to meet the trading and hedging needs of investors and fund managers.

WINNIPEG

The Winnipeg Commodity Exchange

500 Commodity Exchange Tower, 360 Main Street, Winnipeg, Manitoba R3C 3Z4
Telephone: 204 949 0495   *Telex:* 07 587778   *Fax:* 204 943 5448
President: R P Purves
Director of Special Projects: P K Huffman
Director of Compliance: F V Siemens
Secretary: T Condra

Hours of trading:
> All commodities – 09.30–13.15 (central time)

Contract details:
Commodities: Domestic feed barley, Western domestic feed barley, feed oats, feed wheat, rapeseed/canola, flaxseed, rye and canola cash call.

Trading units:
> Board lot – 100 tonnes
> Job lot – 20 tonnes
> For canola cash call – one railcar lot 66.5 to 73.5 net tonnes

Trading limits:

	Price fluctuation units	Daily limits up or down from previous close
	(cents per tonne)	(dollars per tonne)
Feed wheat	10	5
Feed oats	10	5
Feed barley	10	5
Western domestic feed barley	10	5
Rye	10	5
Rapeseed	10	10
Flaxseed	10	10
Canola cash call	10	–

After two consecutive limit closes in the same direction in two out of three nearest contract months, limit increases $1\frac{1}{2}$ times normal; if trend continues for two more consecutive days, 2 times normal limit.

Quality:

Feed wheat – No 3 CWRS, alternatively No 2 Prairie Spring, No 1 CW utility, No 2 CW utility, or CW feed wheat may be delivered at a $5.00/tonne discount

Feed oats – No 3 Canada Western, or, until December 1989, No 4 CW at a $5.00/tonne discount

Feed barley – No 1 CW, or No 2 CW $5.00/tonne discount

Western domestic feed barley – 48lbs per bushel (59.9kg/bl) maximum moisture 14.5% and maximum dockage 2%. All other specifications to meet standards of No 1 CW barley

Rye – No 1 CW, or No 2 CW $2.00/tonne discount

Rapeseed – No 1 Canola, or No 2 C $13.00/tonne discount

Flaxseed – No 1 CW, or No 2 CW $2.00/tonne discount

Canola cash call – No 1 C, or No 2 C $13.00/tonne discount (alternative discount may be named in bid or offer for acceptance)

Delivery points:

Feed wheat – Thunder Bay
Feed oats – Thunder Bay
Feed barley – Thunder Bay
Western domestic feed barley – Lethbridge, Alberta
Rye – Thunder Bay

Rapeseed – Vancouver (alternative delivery at
Saskatoon, Winnipeg, Edmonton,
Calgary, Lethbridge and Moose Jaw
permitted until eighth business day before
end of contract month)

Flaxseed – Thunder Bay (alternative delivery at
Moose Jaw, Saskatoon, Calgary and
Winnipeg permitted until eighth business
day before end of contract month)

Canola cash call – Vancouver

Termination of trading: Last trading day is the last business day of the delivery month.

Delivery months:

Feed barley, oats and wheat – October, November, December, March,
May and July

Rye and flaxseed – October, December, March, May and July

Rapeseed – September, November, January, March
and June

Western domestic feed barley – August, November, February and May

Canola cash call – any calendar month named at time and
date of sale

Manner of price quotation: Canadian dollars and cents per tonne.

Clearing house: Winnipeg Commodity Clearing Ltd.

Commission rates and margins:

Customer minimum margins (dollars per unit of trade)

	Regular	Hedge	Spread both sides
Wheat	*i* – $120	*i* – $100	*i* – $ 50
	m – $100	*m* – $100	*m* – $ 50
Oats	*i* – $120	*i* – $100	*i* – $ 50
	m – $100	*m* – $100	*m* – $ 50
Barley	*i* – $120	*i* – $100	*i* – $ 50
	m – $100	*m* – $100	*m* – $ 50
Western barley	*i* – $120	*i* – $100	*i* – $ 50
	m – $100	*m* – $100	*m* – $ 50
Rye	*i* – $120	*i* – $100	*i* – $ 50
	m – $100	*m* – $100	*m* – $ 50
Rapeseed	*i* – $300	*i* – $200	*i* – $100
	m – $200	*m* – $200	*m* – $100
Flaxseed	*i* – $300	*i* – $200	*i* – $100
	m – $200	*m* – $200	*m* – $100

i – initial
m – maintenance

Commission rates: $10.00 a round tonne per visit of trade (20 tonnes),
$ 8.00 per unit of trade for day trades and spreads.

Membership: The Exchange is a voluntary, non-profit association with 278 members, including terminal elevator companies, domestic merchants, exporters, oilseed crushers, feed manufacturers, maltsters, futures commission merchants (brokerage firms), banks and individuals. Each member has one vote. Firms and corporations may be registered annually for trading privileges. The Exchange is a self-regulating institution with an elected Board of Governors.

Date of establishment of the markets:

Feed wheat and oats	1904
Barley	1913
Western domestic feed barley (once Alberta barley)	1983
Rye	1917
Rapeseed/canola	1963
Flaxseed	1904
Canola cash call	1988

Volume of trading:
1987–88 – 2,791,073 contracts, with an estimated gross value of 12.4 billion dollars.

Membership of other organizations: Canada Grains Council; Canola Council of Canada; Conference Board of Canada; Canadian Chamber of Commerce; Western Canadian Wheat Growers Association, Western Barley Growers Association, Flaxgrowers Western Canada, Inter-Exchange Technical Committee, Futures Industry Association, Swiss Commodities and Futures Association.

Further information: The WCE has created a canola cash call contract in response to the development, by the Canadian Grain Commission (CGC), of a new policy for canola producer cars which will allot all such rail cars on a ship to sales basis in the same way rail cars are allotted to other shippers. The trading procedures of the contract provide canola producers with a way to make their own sales into the export market under conditions of improved access to producer cars. As is the case with other markets, Exchange members will carry out all of the floor trading in the new market. Non-members, as usual, will be able to engage members to conduct trading for them on a commission agency basis.

An intensive study is currently in progress to determine the feasibility of offering options on canola futures.

FRANCE

PARIS

Chambre de Compensation du Marche a Terme International de France (MATIF)

176 Rue Montmatre, Paris 75002
Telephone: 40 28 82 74   *Telex:* 218 362   *Fax:* 40 28 80 01
President: G Pfauwadel
General Manager: G Durieux

Hours of trading:

90-day Treasury bill	– 09.30–15.00
Three-month Pibor	– 09.30–16.00
Option on Notional bond future	– 10.05–16.00
Long-term Notional bond	– 10.00–16.00
Stock Index future	– 10.00–17.00
White sugar	– 10.45–13.00, 15.00–19.00
Cocoa beans	– 10.30–13.00, 15.00–18.30
Robusta coffee	– 10.15–13.00, 15.00–18.30
Options on white sugar futures	– 10.45–13.00, 15.00–19.00

Contract details:

Commodities: 90-day Treasury bill, three-month Pibor (Paris Interbank offer related), option on Notional bond future, long-term Notional bond, Stock Index future (CAC 40 future), white sugar, cocoa beans, Robusta coffee, options on white sugar futures.

Trading currency and unit (manner of price quotation):

90-day Treasury bill and three-month Pibor	– 0.01% of FF 5,000,000 × 90/360, ie FF 125
Option on Notional bond future	– premium by multiples of 0.01%, ie FF 50
Long-term Notional bond	– 0.02% of FF 500,000, ie FF 100
Stock Index future	– CAC 40 index to one decimal number, 0.1, × FF 200, ie FF 20
White sugar	– FF per tonne
Cocoa beans	– FF per 100kg on a CIF basis (FF 0.5)
Robusta coffee	– FF per 100kg
Options on white sugar futures	– FF per tonne

Trading units (minimum lot size):

90-day Treasury bill and three-month Pibor –	FF 5,000,000 nominal value
Option on Notional bond future –	one notional bond
Long-term Notional bond –	FF 500,000 nominal value, with 10% coupon and 10 year maturity
Stock Index future –	FF 200 per full index point
White sugar –	50 tonnes in bags of 50kg
Cocoa beans –	10 tonnes in bags
Robusta coffee –	5 tonnes in bags
Options on white sugar futures –	1 Paris white sugar contract

Trading limits:

90-day Treasury bill and three-month Pibor –	60 basis points of prior clearing price
Option on Notional bond future –	none
Long-term Notional bond –	200 basis points of prior clearing price
Stock Index future –	initially 50 index points, to be reviewed by the CCIFP depending on index value
White sugar –	do not apply to two nearest delivery months from 30 days prior to liquidation of nearest month. For others, see rules
Cocoa beans –	see rules
Robusta coffee –	see rules
Options on white sugar futures –	none

Quality:

Long-term Notional bond –	7 to 10 year eligible bond, 10% rate, redeemable at maturity
White sugar –	white crystal sugar of any origin, with a maximum polarization of 99.8°, and maximum moisture of 0.06%
Cocoa beans –	good fermented maincrop Ivory Coast beans. Other origins and qualities deliverable as per technical committee decisions
Robusta coffee –	of Ivory Coast origin. Other origins and qualities deliverable as per technical committee decisions

Exercise prices:

Option on Notional bond future –	at least five, equivalent to even strike prices 'bracketing' the current notional bond futures prices
Options on white sugar futures –	intervals of at least FF 100 per tonne. Five exercise prices will be listed for new series;

additional prices will be introduced if none of the options are above or below the contract settlement price

Delivery points:

White sugar –	FOB in a port approved by the technical committee
Cocoa beans –	authorized warehouses in the ports of Amsterdam and Dunkirk
Robusta coffee –	authorized warehouses in delivery ports approved by the technical committee

Termination of trading:

90-day Treasury bill and three-month

Pibor –	at 11.00, two business days prior to the eleventh Thursday of the quarter
Option on Notional bond future –	last Friday prior to delivery month of the notional
Long-term Notional bond –	at 13.00 on the last business day of delivery month
Stock Index future –	at 16.00 on the last business day of delivery month
Options on white sugar futures –	last trading day of the penultimate month before delivery month

Delivery months:

90-day Treasury bond, three-month Pibor, option on Notional bond future and long-term Notional bond –

and long-term Notional bond –	March, June, September and December
Stock Index future –	three spot months plus one quarterly expiry month
Options on white sugar futures –	March, May, August and October, for a total period of 16 months including delivery month
White sugar –	March, May, August, October and December
Cocoa beans –	March, May, July, September and December
Robusta coffee –	January, March, May, July, September and November

Commission rates and margins:

Initial margins:

90-day Treasury bill and three-month

Pibor –	0.3% of FF 5,000,000 nominal value
Option on Notional bond future –	put up by the writer and based on notional and optional portfolio liquidation value
Long-term Notional bond –	4% of FF 500,000 nominal value

Stock Index future – 100 index points or FF 20,000, to be reviewed by the CCIFP depending on index value

Options on white sugar futures – buyer: none
seller: same deposit as for future

Date of establishment of contracts:

White sugar – 1964
Cocoa beans – 1962
Robusta coffee – 1972
Financial futures – 11 July 1985
Option on Notional bond future, three-month Pibor and Stock Index future – 1988

Volume of trading:

1987 – 11.99 million contracts
1988 – 16.3 million contracts
Up to 20 February 1989 – more than 33 million contracts

Further information:
MATIF was formed in February 1986, and is now the leading financial futures exchange in Europe.

In the first half of 1989 the first individual floor traders were admitted. This period also saw the creation of a futures contract for the five-year BTAN (as complement to the option on the Notional bond) and an option on the three-month Pibor.

A currency futures contract and a currency option are soon to be introduced.

TOURCOING

Syndicat des Courtiers Agrees au Marche a Terme de la Pomme de Terre

445 Boulevard Gambetta, Tourcoing, 59976
Telephone: 20 26 22 13   *Telex:* 110153   *Fax:* 20 36 55 83
Secretary: P Lucien

Hours of trading: 11.00–12.45, 15.00–16.30.

Contract details:
Commodities: potato futures.

Trading currency: Francs per 100kgs.

Trading unit (minimum lot size): One lot is 20 tonnes, in new poly bags of 25kgs loaded on exchangeable pallets of 100kgs.

Trading limits: 15 FF/100kgs, with a minimum price fluctuation of 0.25 FF/100kgs.

Quality: Bintje variety of grades 40+ and 50+. According to R.U.C.I.P. regulations a maximum of twelve tubers is permitted for grade 40+, eight for 50+.

Delivery points: Warehouses agreed in tender. Most are located in the north of France, around Calais and in the Somme counties.

Termination of trading: Fourth Tuesday of the delivery month.

Delivery months: November, February, April and May.

Clearing house: Banque Centrale de Compensation.

Membership:
Professional, with a yearly fee of 1000 FF (3000 FF in the first year).
Private, no fee.
Affiliated, for example foreign brokers, 1000 FF yearly fee (4000 FF first year).

Commission rates:
Professional, 135 FF, 20 FF for lower commissions.
Private, 172.50 FF and 23.72 FF.
Affiliate, 48.75 FF and 20 FF.

Date of establishment of the market: May 1984.

Volume of trading:
1987 – 23,752 contracts of 20 tonnes.
1988 – 27,319.

GERMANY, WEST

FRANKFURT

Frankfurt Corn and Produce Exchange

(Frankfurter Getreide-und Produktenbörse), Börsenplatz 6, D 6000 Frankfurt am Main
Telephone: 69 2197338   *Telex:* 411255 ihkf d   *Fax:* 069 2197 424
Chief Executive: H-M Nowak

Hours of trading:
Eggs – every Tuesday 14.00–14.30
All other listed products below – every Wednesday 15.15–17.00

Contract details:
Commodities: Coarse fodder, eggs, home-grown and foreign fodder, home-grown and foreign grain, milling products, peat, potatoes, specially light fuel oil.

Trading units:
Coarse fodder, corn, milling products, peat, potatoes – 100kg or 1000kg.
Eggs – 30 cartons of 360 eggs, equivalent to 10,800 eggs.
Specially light fuel oil – 100 litres.

Quality: The qualities traded are basically determined by the appropriate regulations of the German Federal Republic as well as by EEC standards.

Delivery points: Frankfurt.

Currency dealt in: Deutschmark.

Membership: (a) Principals, managers or persons who according to law, statute or contract are appointed to carry out business transactions and are entitled to conclude business transactions independently at the Exchange; (b) employees who are not entitled to conclude business transactions independently.

Date of establishment of the market: 1862.

Membership of other organizations: Study Group of the German Produce Exchanges, Mannheim; Consortium of European Commodity Exchanges.

Branches and affiliates: Quotation Commission for Specially Light Fuel Oil at the Chamber of Industry and Commerce, Wiesbaden.

OSTHOFEN

Worms Grain and Produce Exchange

(Wormser Getreide und Produktenbörse eV)
Mälzerei Schill, PO Box 1453, 6522 Osthofen, Rheinland-Pfalz
Telephone: 06242 860   *Telex:* 04 67839   *Fax:* 06242 4854

Hours of trading: Every Friday 16.00–18.00.

Contract details:
Commodities: Grain (especially brewing barley), mill products, feed products, fertilizers, seeds.

Date of establishment of the market: 1907.

HONG KONG

The Chinese Gold and Silver Exchange Society

Gold & Silver Commercial Building, 12–18 Mercer Street, Hong Kong
Telephone: 5 441945, 5 439158   *Cables:* GOLDEXCHA   *Fax:* 5-8540869
President: S M Yip
Manager: M O Lai

Hours of trading: Monday to Friday 09.30–12.30; 14.30–16.30; Saturday 09.30–12.00.

Contract details:
Commodities: Gold.

Trading units: 100 taels (1 tael = 37.429 grammes).

Quality: 99% fineness.

Delivery points: Hong Kong.

Clearing house: The Chinese Gold and Silver Exchange Society.

Currency dealt in: Hong Kong dollars.

Membership: Ordinary member (total of 192 members).

Date of establishment of the market: 1910.

The Hong Kong Futures Exchange Ltd

Rm 911, New World Tower, 16–18 Queen's Road, Central, Hong Kong

Telephone: 5-251005   *Telex:* 65326 HKFE HX   *Cables:* COMXCHANGE
Fax: 5-8105089

Chairman: E McMillan

Chief Executive: D Ford

Hours of trading:
  Hang Seng Index – Monday to Friday 10.00–12.30, 14.30–15.30
               Sugar – Monday to Friday 10.30–12.00, 14.25–16.00
          Soybeans – Monday to Friday 09.05–10.50, 12.50–14.50
               Gold – Monday to Friday 09.00–12.00, 14.30–17.30

Contract details:
Commodities: Hang Seng Index, sugar, soybean and gold futures.

Trading unit (minimum lot size):
Hang Seng Index - 1 lot
        Sugar - 112,000 lbs
     Soybeans - 500 bags of 60kg each
         Gold - 100 troy ounces

Trading currency and unit (manner of price quotation):
Hang Seng Index - index point, HK $50 per point
        Sugar - US cents per lb
     Soybeans - HK dollars per bag
         Gold - US dollars per troy ounce

Trading limits:
Hang Seng Index - 300 points per trading session. The limit will be calculated by reference to the previous sessions settlement price
        Sugar - US $0.01
     Soybeans - none
         Gold - US $40

Minimum fluctuations:
Hang Seng Index - one index point
        Sugar - 1/100 cents per lb
     Soybeans - 20 cents per bag
         Gold - 10 cents per troy ounce

Quality:
        Sugar - raw cane sugar of 96° polarization
     Soybeans - unselected China Yellow soybeans
         Gold - refined gold of not less than 995 fineness

Deliverable tolerances:
        Sugar - 2% more or less
     Soybeans - 5% more or less
         Gold - bars of 100 troy ounces, 50 troy ounces and 1 kilogram

Delivery points:
        Sugar - FOB & SE Asian countries
     Soybeans - Tokyo or Kanagawa, Japan
         Gold - Hong Kong

Termination of trading:
Hang Seng Index - the business day preceding the last business day of the month
        Sugar - the business day prior to the first day of the delivery month
     Soybeans - second session on the 15th of the spot month
         Gold - morning session on the last business day of the spot month

Delivery months:
Hang Seng Index - four consecutive, even months
        Sugar - January, March, May, July, September, October

Soybeans - consecutive months up to six months ahead
Gold - even months, spot months and the following two months

Clearing house: HKFE Clearing Corporation Ltd.

Membership:
Full membership: open to residents of Hong Kong and corporations limited by shares and incorporated in Hong Kong, who hold at least one ordinary share of the exchange company, with minimum paid-up capital of $2,000,000.

Market membership: open to residents of Hong Kong and corporations limited by shares and incorporated in Hong Kong, who hold at least one standard share of the exchange company, with minimum paid-up capital of $1,000,000.

Individual and affiliated membership also available.

Recommended commission rates and margins:
Original margin:
Hang Leng Index - HK $18,750 per lot
Sugar - US $1350 per lot
Soybeans - HK $7500 per lot
Gold - US $1000 per lot

Date of establishment of the market: 9 May 1977.

Date of establishment of contracts:
Hang Seng Index - 6 May 1986
Sugar - November 1977
Soybeans - November 1979
Gold - August 1980

Volume of trading:
Yearly turnovers for 1988:
Hang Seng Index - 140,155 lots
Sugar - 201,461 lots
Soybeans - 356,642 lots
Gold - 1984 lots

INDIA

BANGALORE

Coffee Board of India

PO Box 5359, No 1, Dr B R Ambedkar Veedhi, Bangalore 560 001
Telephone: 76991   *Telex:* 845221 COFI IN 8081-COF IN
Cables: COFIPOOL, BANGALORE
Chairman: G Y Krishnan
Director of sales: N Jayarami Reddy
Chief Coffee Marketing Officer: K M Shivakumar

Hours of trading: Monday to Friday 10.00–18.00.

Contract details:
Commodities: Raw and instant coffee.

Trading unit: 50kg/1 tonne.

Trading limits: None.

Trading positions: Physical trading only.

Quality: Coffee offered must be of fair to average quality for the season.

Delivery points: Ex-bags, ex-curing works to exporters and on FOB basis against direct sales.

Clearing house: State Bank of India.

Currencies dealt in: American dollars, pounds sterling, Swiss francs, Deutschmarks and rupees.

Membership: Only exporters of coffee who are registered with the Board are allowed to participate in the Coffee Export Open Auctions conducted by the Board twice a month.

Date of establishment of the market: 2 March 1942.

Volume of trading:

Fiscal year	Quantity (tonnes)	Value (R's in crores)
1986–87	86,666	362,82
1987–88	92,461	259.84
1988–89	93,452	316.93 (provisional)

Further information: The Coffee Board of India is a statutory Government body. Its functions include promotion of agricultural and technological research, assisting in the development of coffee estates and the improvement of working conditions and amenities for workers in the industry.

IRELAND

DUBLIN

Irish Futures and Options Exchange (IFOX)

Segrave House, Earlsfort Terrace, Dublin 2
Telephone: 01 767413   *Fax:* 01 614 645
Chief Executive: D Bradley
Operations Director: K Luddy
Guarantee and Compliance Officer: M Whelan
Financial Controller: P Morris

Hours of trading: Monday to Friday 10.30–15.30.

Contract details:
Commodities: 20-year long gilt, three-month Dibor (Dublin Interbank offer rated), Irish pound/American dollar exchange rate quotation.

Trading currency and unit (manner of price quotation):
 20-year long gilt – IR £
 Three-month Dibor – IR £
Pound/dollar quotation – IR £/US $ (up to four decimal places)

Trading units (minimum lot size):
 20-year long gilt – IR £50,000, notional 8% coupon
 Three-month Dibor – IR £100,000
Pound/dollar quotation – US $50,000

Trading limits:
Minimum price fluctuation:
 20-year long gilt – IR £0.01
 Three-month Dibor – IR £0.01
Pound/dollar quotation – IR £0.0001/US $

Price limits:
 20-year long gilt – 2.0%
 Three-month Dibor – 1.2%
Pound/dollar quotation – 2.0%

Quality:
 20-year long gilt – any deliverable, non-variable, non-convertible, non-index linked, non-partly paid, non-dual date, semi-annual Irish Government security of 15–25 years maturity
 Three-month Dibor – cash settlement based on the Exchange settlement price

Pound/dollar quotation – futures contract quoted using the Direct method. Also operated via cash settlement

Termination of trading:
20-year long gilt – at 11.00, two business days before delivery/settlement day
Three-month Dibor – at 11.00, two business days before delivery/settlement day
Pound/dollar quotation – at 15.00, two business days before delivery/settlement day

Delivery/settlement:
20-year long gilt – third Wednesday of settlement month (date to be published at least three months in advance by IFOX)
Three-month Dibor – third Wednesday of settlement month
Pound/dollar quotation – third Wednesday of settlement month

Delivery months: for all three contracts: March, June, September and December.

Membership: The Exchange is made up of 24 members, each having subscribed IR £60,000, drawn from leading Irish banks, stockbrokers, fund managers and treasury operations. All have equal status.

Commission rates and margins:

	Exchange fees	*Clearing fees*	*Initial deposit*
20-year long gilt	100	150	2500
Three-month Dibor	50	50	300
Pound/dollar quotation	50	50	1250

Date of establishment of market: 29 May 1989.

Membership of other organisations: ECOFEX.

Further information: Trading on the Exchange occurs via a computerised trading system, with dealers entering orders and match prices via screens in their own offices, linked to the central IFOX computer. There is therefore no central Exchange floor.

IFOX is a self-regulatory body, under the formal supervision of the Central Bank of Ireland.

The long-term plans of the Exchange are to list other contracts such as futures for Irish pound/pounds sterling, five-year gilts, futures and options for Irish equity index and individual Irish equities, and options on 20-year gilts.

ITALY

BOLOGNA

Borsa Merci di Bologna

Associazione Granaria Emiliana Romagnola (AGER), Piazza Costituzione 8,
Bologna 40128
Telephone: 051 501958   *Telex:* 521 568 AGER I   *Cables:* AGER BOLOGNA
Fax: 051 501043
President: A Pasquale
Secretary: Z Giampaolo

Hours of trading: Every Friday 09.00–17.00.

Contract details:
Commodities: Grains and animal feed.

Trading unit: 100kg.

Trading limits: None.

Quality: Contract No 3 corn; Contract No 8 dry vegetables; Contract No 11 cereals
imported; Contract No 101 soft wheat; Contract No 102 durum wheat; Contract No
104 barley, oats, rye; Contract No 105 sorghum; Contract No 121 flour soft wheat;
Contract No 122 flour durum wheat; Contract No 129 flour dehydrate lucern;
Contract No 131 bran wheat; Contract No 133 corn germ; Contract No 136 vegetal
extraction flour; Contract No 140 seeds oil.

Delivery points: Docks and private stores.

Currency dealt in: Lira.

Membership: Farmers, traders, manufacturers, brokers – individuals or representative
corporations.

Date of establishment of the market: 1949.

Membership of other organizations: Italian Arbitration Association, Rome.

Further information: There being no commodity exchanges in Italy, only commodity
markets, members conduct only physical trading without monetary control or
agreement registrations.

JAPAN

HOKKAIDO

The Hokkaido Grain Exchange

3 Odori Nishi 5-chrome, Chuo-ku Sapporo, Hokkaido 060
Telephone: 011 221 9131
President: Minoru Ito
Managing Director: Masao Moroto

Hours of trading:

	March to October	November to April
1st session –	08.50–12.50	09.00–13.00
2nd session –	09.50–13.50	10.00–14.00
3rd session –	10.50–14.50	11.00–15.00

Contract details:
Commodities: Potato starch, red beans, soybeans (domestic and imported) and white beans.

Trading unit:

Potato starch –	2500kg
Red beans –	2400kg
Soybeans (domestic) –	2400kg
Soybeans (imported) –	15,000kg
White beans –	2400 kg

Trading limits: For the closing price on the previous day of business – potato starch – 7%; soybeans (domestic) – 7%; soybeans (imported), red beans, white beans – less than 7% (these figures are defined by the governing board).

Minimum fluctuation: potato starch – 1 yen per 25kg; soybeans (domestic and imported), white beans – 10 yen per 60kg; red beans – 10 yen per 30kg.

Quality: Domestic soybeans – No 2 small soybeans produced in Hokkaido; imported soybeans – yellow soybeans imported from the USA; red beans – produced in Hokkaido; white beans No 2 and potato starch are also produced in Hokkaido.

Deliverable tolerances: Domestic soybeans and other grades of soybeans produced in Hokkaido. Imported soybeans, well-screened yellow soybeans, non-screened yellow soybeans imported from the People's Republic of China. Red beans – other grades of red beans produced in Hokkaido. Red beans imported from the People's Republic of China and Taiwan. White beans – other grades of white beans produced in Hokkaido.

232

Pea beans and great northern beans imported from the USA, pea beans imported from Canada.

Delivery points: Warehouses specified by the Exchange; located at Sapporo City, Otaru City, Asahigawa City, Obihiru City and Kushiro City in Hokkaido.

Termination of trading: The delivery day of each month shall be the day preceding the last business day of the delivery month.

Delivery months: Domestic soybeans - three months; imported soybeans - six months; red beans - six months; white beans - six months; potato starch - three months.

Manner of price quotation: Domestic soybeans, imported soybeans and white beans - 60kg; red beans - 30kg; and potato starch - 25kg.

Currency dealt in: Yen.

Membership: There are now 37 members including 18 commodity commission merchants. Commodity commission merchants are able to conduct buying and selling transactions on both personal and customer accounts. In order to become a commodity commission merchant one must first obtain a licence from the Ministry. A strict qualifications check is set regarding the financial situation, knowledge and experience of the applying body. The licence is valid for four years after which it must be renewed.

Commission rates and margins:
Commission:

Commodity	Contracted price	
Red beans	New contract	
	Off Session	3000
	within the same month	2800
	within 2 months	3000
	within 3 months	3200
	within 4 months	3400
	within 5 months	3600
	within 6 months	3800
Soybeans (imported)	Off Session	3500
	within the same month	3100
	within 2 months	3300
	within 3 months	3500
	within 4 months	3700
	within 5 months	3900
	within 6 months	4100
	within 7 months	4300
	within 8 months	4500
	within 9 months	4700
	within 10 months	4900
	within 11 months	5100
	within 12 months	5300

Soybeans (domestic)	regardless of price	1900
White beans	regardless of price	3000
Potato starch	regardless of price	1900

Commodity	Contracted price		Customer	Commodity commission merchant	Member*
Red beans	Less than	14,000	3200	1600	1920
	More than	14,000	3600	1800	2160
	Less than	18,000			
	More than	18,000	4000	2000	2400
Soybeans	Less than	4000	3500	1750	2100
(imported)	Less than	6000	3750	1875	2250
	Less than	8000	4000	2000	2400
White beans	Less than	18,000	2900	1450	1740
	Less than	20,000	3100	1550	1860
	Less than	22,000	3300	1650	1980
	Less than	24,000	3500	1750	2100
	Less than	26,000	3750	1875	2250
	Less than	28,000	3900	1950	2340
	More than	28,000	4100	2050	2460
Soybeans	Less than	5000	800	400	480
(domestic)	More than	5000	900	450	540
Potato starch	Regardless of price		700	350	420

* General member excluding commodity commission merchant.

Margins:

Commodity	Level of price			Initial margin
Soybeans	Less than		3000	8000
(domestic)	More than	3000	Less than 4000	10,000
	More than	4000		12,000
Soybeans	Less than		5000	70,000
(imported)	More than	5000	Less than 6000	80,000
	More than	6000		90,000
Red beans	Less than		14,000	50,000
	More than	14,000	Less than 18,000	60,000
	More than	18,000		70,000
White beans	Less than		13,000	60,000
	More than	13,000	Less than 18,000	70,000
	More than	18,000		80,000
Potato starch	Less than		1500	8000
	More than	1500	Less than 2000	10,000
	More than	2000		12,000

Date of establishment of the market: 3 July 1951.

Volume of trading:
1987 January to December 312,081 units
1988 January to December 550,067 units

KOBE

Kobe Rubber Exchange

49 Harima-cho, Chuo-ku, Kobe 650
Telephone: 078 331 4211   *Telex:* 332 1622   *Cables:* Rubbex Kobe
Chairman: Takeshi Ohira
Senior Managing Director: Keisuke Konishi
Director: Keiichiro Hayashi

Hours of trading: First session 09.30; second session 10.30; third session 13.30; fourth session 14.30; fifth session 15.30; after-the-close session 17.00.

Contract details:
Commodities: Crude rubber, international No 3 ribbed smoked sheet.

Trading unit: 5000kg.

Trading limits:

Contract price (¥)

   less than 130 – ¥6
    130 to 159 – ¥7
    160 to 189 – ¥8
    190 to 220 – ¥9
more than 220 – ¥10

Quality: Ribbed smoked sheet RSS No 3 specified in the International Standards of Quality and Packing for Natural Rubber Grades.

Deliverable tolerances: Deliverable grade is RSS No 4 which substitutes for RSS No 3.

Delivery points: Kobe City and Osaka City.

Termination of trading: The session for current month delivery shall be closed at 10.30 on the morning of the fifth from last business day of the month.

Delivery months: Current month, ensuing three months, and two even-numbered months beyond.

Manner of price quotation: Per 1kg.

Currency dealt in: Yen.

Commission rates and margins:
Commission:

Contract price (¥ per kg)	Commission (¥ per lot)	Commission of member or associate member (equivalent to 60%)
less than 200	3310	¥1980
200 to 299	3480	¥2080
300 to 399	3650	¥2180

for each additional ¥100 in the contract price, ¥170 commission is to be charged, or ¥100 in the case of members or associate members.

Margins:

Contract price (¥ per kg)	Initial customer margin (¥)
less than 130	30,000
130 to 159	40,000
160 to 189	50,000
190 to 220	60,000
more than 220	70,000

if the customer is a member or associate member, the margin is 50% of the above.

Membership: The Kobe Rubber Exchange is a non-profit organisation with the following categories of membership available:

Regular: a person who carries out the business of importer, dealer, middleman, commission merchant or agent, or processor of rubber or rubber goods.

Commission merchant: a person licensed by the Minister of International Trade and Industry to receive commission contracts for rubber futures traded on the market of the Exchange.

Associate: a foreign rubber trader (non-resident) registered with the Exchange and carrying out the business of dealer, middleman, producer or processor of rubber. Privileges for associate members include discounts on customer margins and transaction commissions, as well as receipt of market information.

Date of establishment of the market: 16 January 1952.

Volume of trading:
1986 – 1,044,648 lots
1987 – 553,552 lots
1988 – 916,942 lots

MAEBASHI

Maebashi Dried Cocoon Exchange

1-49-1, Furuichi-Machi, Maebashi City, Gunma prefecture 371
Telephone: 0272 521401   *Telex:* 0272 521305
President: Kimiji Kurihara
Executive Director: Masao Yamamura
Managing Director: Yukio Saito

Hours of trading: 09.20–13.20, 11.20–15.20.

Contract details:
Commodities: Dried cocoon.

Trading unit: 300kg, 15 bales.

Trading limits: The fluctuation in one day is limited to be within 5% of the closing price of the preceding day (existing limits 130 yen). Minimum price fluctuation – 1 yen per kg.

Deliverable tolerances: 300kg, 15 bales.

Delivery points: Warehouses located in Maebashi specified by the Exchange. Approved delivery facilities – Jomo warehouses, Gunma Chuo warehouses and Takasaki warehouses.

Delivery months: Six months.

Currency dealt in: Yen.

Membership: The members of the Exchange select a fellow trader via an examination set by the Qualification Judging Committee.

Commission rates and margins:
Regardless of contracted price – customer 3860 yen, member 2560 yen, others 2960 yen.

Margins:

Level of price	Initial margin
Less than ¥5800	¥60,000
More than ¥5800	
Less than ¥6400	¥70,000
More than ¥6400	¥80,000

Date of establishment of the market: 10 July 1952.

Volume of trading:
1987 –   865,696 contracts
1988 – 1,109,350 contracts

Trading members: 53 (Commodity Commission Merchants – 25).

OSAKA

Osaka Textile Exchange

2-5-28 Kyutaro-Machi, Chuo-Ku, Osaka 541
Telephone: 06 253 0031   *Fax:* 06 253 0034

Hours of trading:

Cotton yarn (20's) – first session 09.45–13.45
second session 10.45–14.25
Cotton yarn (30's) – 09.45–13.45
Cotton yarn (40's) – first session 09.45–13.45
second session 10.45–14.45
Staple fibre – 09.45–13.45
Woollen yarn – first session 09.20–14.20
second session 11.20–15.20

Contract details:
Commodities: cotton yarn (20's single Z-twist, 30's single Z-twist and 40's single Z-twist), staple fibre yarn, woollen yarn.

Trading currency and unit (manner of price quotation):
Cotton yarn – 10 sen/pound (0.1 yen/pound)
Staple fibre yarn – 10 sen/pound
Woollen yarn – 1 yen/kg

Trading unit (minimum lot size):
Cotton yarn (20's and 30's) – 2000lbs
Cotton yarn (40's) – 4000lbs
Staple fibre – 5000lbs
Woollen yarn – 500kgs

Trading limits:
Cotton yarn – +/- 3% on the previous day's closing prices
Staple fibre – +/- 5%
Woollen yarn – +/- 3%

Quality:

Cotton yarn – 20, 30 and 40 count single, gray weaving yarn, Z-twist, 'Kingyo' brand by Toyoboseki
Staple fibre – 30 count single, weaving yarn, Z-twist, 'Kinkicho' brand by Daiwaboseki
Woollen yarn – 48 count double, worsted weaving yarn, Z-twist, 'A G' brand

Delivery points:

Cotton yarn – business warehouses approved by the Exchange in Osaka and Kobe city
Staple fibre and woollen yarn – Osaka, Kyoto, Hyogo, Tokyo, Kanagawa, Saitawa and Aichi

Termination of trading: Last four days, including the last business day, of the current month.

Delivery months: The current month and the following five months.

Commission rates and margins:
Commission:

	contracted price (yen)	customer	member
cotton yarn (20's)	less than 220	1910	1240
	less than 280	2080	1350
	more than 280	2250	1460
cotton yarn (40's)	less than 300	4260	2980
	less than 400	4460	3120
	more than 400	4660	3260
staple fibre	less than 220	3060	1840
	less than 280	3280	1970
	more than 280	3500	2100
woollen yarn	less than 2000	3300	2310
	less than 2500	3730	2610
	more than 2500	4160	2910

Margins:

	level of price (yen)	initial margin
cotton yarn (20's)	less than 280	15,000
	280 to 320	20,000
	more than 320	25,000
cotton yarn (30's)	less than 300	20,000
	300 to 340	25,000
	340 to 380	30,000
	more than 380	35,000
cotton yarn (40's)	less than 350	40,000
	350 to 390	45,000
	more than 390	50,000
staple fibre	less than 210	30,000
	210 to 250	37,000
	more than 250	44,000

Volume of trading:

	1987	1988
Cotton yarn (20's)	439,849	267,609
Cotton yarn (40's)	231,650	197,796
Staple fibre	7,900	7,273
Woollen yarn	386,693	257,171
Totals	1,066,092	729,849

TOKYO

Tokyo Commodity Exchange for Industry

Tosen Building, 10-8, 1-Chome, Horidome-cho, Nihonbashi, Chuo-ku, Tokyo 103
Telephone: 03 661 9191   *Fax:* 03 661 7568
Chairman: Naozo Mabuchi
Senior Managing Director: Yonosuke Ariga
Director: Shichiro Takahashi

Hours of trading:

Gold – 09.10, 10.30, 11.30, 13.10, 14.30, 15.45
Silver – traded after the gold sessions
Platinum – traded after the silver sessions
Rubber – 09.45, 10.45, 13.45, 14.45, 15.30
Cotton yarn – 08.50, 10.00, 12.50, 15.10
Woollen yarn – traded after the cotton sessions

Contract details:
Commodities: Gold, silver, platinum, rubber, cotton yarn and woollen yarn.

Trading currency and unit (manner of price quotation):
Gold – ¥1.0/1 gramme
Silver – ¥0.1 (10 sen)/10 grammes
Platinum – ¥1.0/1 gramme
Rubber – ¥0.1/1kg
Rubber – ¥0.1/1lb
Woollen yarn – ¥1.0/1kg

Trading units (minimum lot size):
Gold – 1kg
Silver – 30kg
Platinum – 500g
Rubber – 5000kg
Cotton yarn – 4000lb
Woollen yarn – 500kg

Trading limits: Daily quotations are not allowed to fluctuate beyond the prices provided by the Board of the Exchange. These are based on the following percentages above or below the previous day's closing prices:

> Gold, silver and platinum – 20%
> Rubber, cotton and woollen yarns – 10%

No limit is applicable to the current month from the first day in the precious metals market and on or after the 15th of the contract month in the rubber, cotton and woollen yarn markets.

Quality:

> Gold, silver and platinum – bars with purity above 99.99%
> Rubber – RSS No 3 of the International Standard Specification
> Cotton yarn – 40 count single gray, weaving yarn Z twist 'Marufuji' brand
> Woollen yarn – 48 count double, worsted weaving yarn Z twist 'AG' brand

Deliverable tolerances: These are designated by the Board of the Exchange.

Delivery points: At warehouses designated by the Exchange.

Termination of trading: The last day of trading in the current month is three days (in the precious metals markets) or four days (in the cotton yarn and woollen yarn markets) or five days (in the rubber market) before the delivery day.

Delivery months:
Precious metals: even-numbered month within the twelve-month period after the date of transaction in an odd-numbered current month; and also an odd-numbered month following an even-numbered month.
Rubber: every month within the six-month period after the date of transaction.
Cotton and woollen yarns: every month within the six-month period after the date of transaction.

Currency dealt in: Japanese yen.

Commission rates and margins:
Commission:

Commodity	Contract price	Type of member	
		General	*Associate*
Gold	*(¥ per gramme)*	*(¥ per unit of 1kg)*	
	less than 2800	7600	2400
	2800 to 3199	8800	2800
	3200 to 3599	10,000	3200
	33600 to 3999	11,200	3600

¥1200 general member commission and ¥400 associate member commission is to be added for each increase in the contract price of ¥400.

Silver	(¥ per gramme)	(¥ per unit of 30kg)	
	less than 250	5900	2900
	250 to 449	6500	3200
	450 to 650	7100	3500
	more than 650	7700	3800

Platinum	(¥ per gramme)	(¥ per unit of 500g)	
	less than 3000	4800	2350
	3000 to 3399	5500	2700
	3400 to 3799	6200	3050
	3800 to 4199	6900	3400

¥700 general member commission and ¥350 associate member commission is to be added for each increase in the contract price of ¥400.

Rubber	(¥ per kg)	(¥ per unit of 5000kg)	
	less than 250	3450	2050
	250 to 299	3750	2230
	300 to 349	4050	2410
	350 to 399	4350	2590

¥300 general member commission and ¥180 associate member commission is to be added for each increase in the contract price of ¥50.

Cotton yarn	(¥ per lb)	(¥ per unit of 4000lbs)	
	less than 330	4400	3000
	330 to 410	4700	3200
	more than 410	5000	3400

Woollen yarn	(¥ per kg)	(¥ per unit of 500kg)	
	less than 2000	3400	2400
	2000 to 2499	3900	2700
	more than 2500	4400	3000

Membership: The members of the Exchange are divided into two categories; (i) general members whose business activity is limited to the transaction of buying and selling on their own accounts and (ii) ring members (authorised commodity commission merchants) who take orders from customers at large on a commission basis.

The Exchange also permits individuals or firms in other countries to participate in trading on the Exchange as associate members. At the end of 1985 there were 198 general members, 72 ring members and 53 associate members.

Date of establishment of the market: 1 November 1984.

Date of establishment of contracts:

Gold – March 1983
Silver – January 1984
Platinum – January 1984
Rubber – December 1952
Cotton yarn – September 1951
Woollen yarn – October 1953

Volume of trading:

Total futures volume: 1987 –   9,205,091
                           1988 – 11,694,581
Gold physical trading volume: 1988 –   3428

Further information: The Tokyo Commodity Exchange began operating a gold spot market on 19 October 1988. The standard unit for warrant trading is 1kg.

The Tokyo Grain Exchange

1-12-5 Kakigara-cho, Chuo-ku, Tokyo, 103
Telephone: 03 668 9311   *Fax:* 668 9566

Hours of trading:
am – first session 09.00; second session 10.00; third session 11.00
pm – first session 13.00; second session 14.00; third session 15.00

Contract details:
Commodities: American soybeans, Chinese soybeans, Red beans

Trading units:

American soybeans – 15 tonnes
Chinese soybeans – 250 bags (15 tonnes)
Red beans – 80 bags (2.4 tonnes)

Trading limits:
Minimum fluctuation – American soybeans, Chinese soybeans, 10 yen per 60kg; Red beans, 10 yen per 30kg.
Daily price movement limits – American soybeans, Chinese soybeans, Red beans – sum determined by the Board of Directors within 7% above or below the previous business day's closing price.

Quality:

American soybeans – non-screened Yellow soybeans of Indiana, Ohio, and Michigan origin, imported from the USA
Chinese soybeans – non-screened Yellow soybeans imported from the People's Republic of China
Red beans – No 2 polished Red beans produced in Hokkaido

Deliverable tolerances:

American soybeans – well-screened Yellow soybeans of Indiana, Ohio, and Michigan origin, imported from the USA

243

> Chinese soybeans – well-screened Yellow soybeans imported from the People's Republic of China
>
> Red beans – other grades of Red beans produced in Hokkaido and other parts of Japan. Red beans imported from the People's Republic of China and Taiwan

Delivery points: Warehouses located in Tokyo metropolis, Kanagawa prefecture, Chiba prefecture and Saitama prefecture which are specified by the Exchange.

Termination of trading: The delivery day for each month is the day preceding the last business day of the delivery month. The third morning session of the day, two days before the last business day, is the final session for futures trading of a current delivery month, then such month expires.

Delivery months:

> American soybeans – April, June, August, October, December, February within 12 months
>
> Chinese soybeans, red beans – six consecutive months beginning with current calendar month

Currency dealt in: Yen.

Membership: There are 60 commodity commission merchants who are permitted to deal for their customers by the Ministry of Agriculture and Forestry; there are 86 general members who are admitted to affiliation by the Board of Directors of the Exchange and are able to deal only on their own account. Floor members who can execute the transaction on the trading floor are restricted to members only and floor representatives who are employees of the members and registered by the Exchange.

Commission rates and margins:
Commission:

Commodity	Passage		Rate (¥)
American soybeans	*New contract*	*Off setting*	
& Chinese soybeans	3500	Within the same month	3100
		Within the 2nd month	3300
		Within the 3rd month	3500
		Within the 4th month	3700
		Within the 5th month	3900
		Within the 6th month	4100
		Within the 7th month	4300
		Within the 8th month	4500
		Within the 9th month	4700
		Within the 10th month	4900
		Within the 11th month	5100
		Within the 12th month	5300
Red beans	3000	Within the same month	2800
		Within the 2nd month	3000
		Within the 3rd month	3200

Within the 4th month		3400
Within the 5th month		3600
Within the 6th month		3800

Margins:

Commodity	Level of price		Initial margin (¥)
American & Chinese soybeans		less than 3000	50,000
	more than 3000	less than 4000	60,000
	more than 4000	less than 5000	70,000
	more than 5000	less than 6000	80,000
	more than 6000		90,000
Red beans		less than 14,000	50,000
	more than 14,000	less than 18,000	60,000
	more than 18,000		70,000

Date of establishment of the market: 24 September 1952.

Volume of trading:
1987 – 5,200,469 units
1988 – 6,604,800 units

Tokyo Sugar Exchange

9-4 Nihonbashi Koami-cho, Chuo-ku, Tokyo 103
Telephone: 03 666 0201   *Fax:* 81 3 661 4496
Chairman: Kojiro Yada
Managing Directors: Mioya Ohashi, Teruo Kodaira

Hours of trading: 09.30, 10.30, 13.30, 14.30, 15.30

Contract details:
Commodities: refined soft white sugar futures contract, raw sugar futures contract.

Trading currency and unit (manner of price quotation):
10 sen (¥0.1)/tonne.

Trading units (minimum lot size):
Refined soft white sugar – 9 tonnes (9000kgs)
Raw sugar – 10 tonnes (10,000kgs)

Trading limits:
Minimum fluctuation: multiples of 10 sen.
Maximum: ¥3 per kilogram above or below the previous day's settlement price.

Quality:
Refined soft white sugar – domestically produced refined soft white sugar not more than three months old (including delivery month)

> Raw sugar – raw centrifugal sugar in bulk based on 96 of polarisation

(Standard product: T1, manufactured by Tokyo Sugar Refining Co Ltd)

Delivery points:
> Refined soft white sugar – ex-warehouse in bags
> Raw sugar – ex-hold of arrived vessel (CIF FO), ie loaded in bulk on board ocean vessel at country of origin and delivered to domestic ports

Termination of trading:
> Refined soft white sugar – second morning session of the business day preceding the last business day of the month
> Raw sugar – the last business day two months prior to delivery month

Delivery months:
> Refined soft white sugar – every month within a six month period
> Raw sugar – odd-numbered months within a 20 month period

Membership: Full, commodity commission merchant and associate.

Commission rates and margins:
Commission:

	Non-member	Member & Associate member
Raw sugar	¥3420	¥1710

Initial margin:

	Standard price	Non-member	Member & Associate member
Raw sugar	less than ¥50	¥50,000	¥25,000
	¥50 to ¥99	¥60,000	¥30,000
	¥100 and above	¥70,000	¥35,000

Date of establishment of contracts:
> Refined soft white sugar – 7 May 1952
> Raw sugar – 1 August 1974

Volume of trading:
1987 – 27,937,211 lots
1988 – 34,265,269 lots

KENYA

NAIROBI

East African Tea Trade Association

PO Box 42281, Nairobi
Telephone: 337521/2 and 337725   *Telex:* 22070   *Fax:* 339559
Chairman: K D Guenther
Vice Chairman: J B Low
Secretary: N G Sandys-Lumsdaine

Hours of trading: Auctions every Monday 08.30 in Mombassa.
Auctions trading conducted by broker members, Combrok Ltd, Tea Brokers
Association East Africa Ltd, and Africa Tea Brokers Ltd.
Private contracts conducted five days a week 08.30–16.30.

Contract details:
Commodity: Black Tea.

Trading currency and unit: The currency of the country in which Auction takes place
or any other mutually acceptable currency in the case of teas sold by private treaty.
Bidding at Auction advances by not less than Shs cents 0.20 on all teas.

Trading unit (minimum lot size): Lots are sold by the kilogramme. For the Main
Grade catalogue the minimum number of packages for a lot is 20. For the
Supplementary catalogue there is no minimum, except for secondary fannings for
which the minimum lot is 20 packages.

A lot may be divided provided divisions are in multiples of 20 packages and not more
than three Buyers participate in any one lot.

Quality: All teas on Estate Account must be offered 'factory bulked' and under estate
marks. Secondhand teas may only be offered for sale on condition they are described
as being 'On account of the concerned'. Damaged teas may not be offered for sale
unless they are described as 'with all faults and at Buyer's risk'.

Termination of trading: Buyers must pay the full price of Broker's invoice by 12.00
noon on the tenth business day from the date of the sale contract, called Prompt day.
Payment must be made by either a Mombassa or Nairobi standard cheque by 12.00
noon within three business days before Prompt day, or by 12.00 noon on Prompt day
if by Banker's cheque.

Brokers must pay Sellers not later than 12.00 noon on Prompt day.

Delivery points: As required by overseas buyer dependent on overseas sale or contract and availability of shipping.

Currency dealt in: Kenya shilling.

Recommended commission rates and margins: Brokerage charged 1% to seller, 0.5% to buyer. Buyer at liberty to fix own selling price to overseas client.

Membership:
Buying member: Any person, firm or company actively engaged in buying tea (at least 50,000kgs in the twelve month period 1 January to 31 December). Upon election a Buying member will remain as a Provisional Buying Member for a full calendar year.

Producer member: Any person, firm or company engaged in the growing and/or manufacture of tea, or as agents for such, in East Africa.

Broker member: Established in East Africa as negotiators for the sale or buying of tea between members of the Association.

Warehouse member: Not having the same rights and privileges as full Buyer, Broker or Producer members, paying half entrance fee and annual subscription.

Associate member: With same rights and privileges as warehouse members and paying same fees.

The business of the Association is managed by a management committee of twelve, five of whom represent Buyers, five Producers and two Brokers.

Date of establishment of the market: 1958.

MALAYSIA

KUALA LUMPUR

Kuala Lumpur Commodity Exchange

4th Floor, City Point, Dayabumi Complex, Jalan Sultan Hishamuddin,
PO Box 11260, 50740 Kuala Lumpur
*Telephone:*603 2936822   *Telex:* MA 31472 KLCE   *Fax:* 603 2742215
Chairman: T S L B Chim
Chief Executive: S A J Shahabudin

Hours of trading:

Crude palm oil –	11.00-12.30, 15.30-18.00
Tin –	12.15-13.00, 16.00-19.00
Rubber –	10.00-13.00, 16.00-18.00
Cocoa –	11.15-12.00, 16.00-19.00

Contract details:
Commodities: Crude palm oil, tin, rubber (SMR 20), cocoa.

Trading currency and unit (manner of price quotation):

Crude palm oil –	M $1.00/tonne
Tin –	US $5.00/tonne
Rubber –	M $0.0025/kg
Cocoa –	US $1.00/tonne

Trading units (minimum lot size):

Crude palm oil –	25 tonnes
Tin –	5 tonnes
Rubber –	10 tonnes (single delivery month)
	30 tonnes (delivery)
Cocoa –	10 tonnes

Crude palm oil
Trading limits: M $50 above or below the settlement prices of the preceding day for all months, except current month. Limits are expanded when on any one day the settlement prices of all three quoted months following the current month are at the limits listed below:

Day	Limits (M $)
First	50
Second	75

Third	100
Fourth	none
Fifth	50

Minimum price fluctuation: M $1.00 per tonne.

Quality: Of good merchantable quality, in bulk, unbleached and in port tank installations. Free fatty acid (FFA) content of palm oil delivered to port tank installations shall not exceed 4%, and from port tank installations 5%. Moisture and impurities shall not exceed 0.25%.

Deliverable tolerances: 25 tonnes +/- 2%.

Delivery points: Port tank installations located at the option of the seller at Port Kelang, Butterworth/Prai and Pasir Gudang (Johore).

Termination of trading: Fifteenth of the month, or the preceding business day.

Delivery months: Current month, the next five succeeding months, and thereafter alternate months up to twelve months forward.

Tin

Trading limits: Price limits for all months, except current month, are established at the opening of the market on each day at US $250 above or below the previous day's settlement prices. When prices for the first three months following the current month are being bid or offered at limits, trading in all months except the current month shall cease for fifteen minutes. When trading resumes the limits will be adjusted by US $250 up or down to form new limit prices.

In the event of settlement prices for the three consecutive months immediately following the current month reaching the new limit prices, this shall be termed a 'limit day'. In the event of there being three limit days for three consecutive business days, on the fourth business day there shall be no price limits. On the fifth business day the limit price fluctuation shall apply.

Minimum price fluctuation: US $5 per tonne.

Quality: Refined tin assaying not less than 99.85% Sn and complied with American Society for Testing and Materials (ASTM) specification B 399-86 for Banka, DKS (Escoy), Mentok, MSC and Thaisarco brands.

Deliverable tolerances: 5 tonnes +/- 2% on warrants issued by warehouses approved by the Exchange.

Delivery points: At the option of the seller, approved warehouses in Penang, Singapore, Rotterdam or such places determined by the Exchange.

Termination of trading: The business day immediately before the last two business days of the month.

Delivery months: Current month, the next three succeeding months, thereafter alternate months up to twelve months forward.

Rubber

Trading limits: Price limits, established before the opening of the market each trading day, are set at 10 sen above and below the settlement prices of the previous day, this applies for all months except the current month.

If trading for the two nearest months, excluding the current month, is transacted at established limits, trading for all months and quarters ceases for fifteen minutes, at which time limit prices are re-established.

Minimum price fluctuation: M c0.25 per kilogramme.

Quality: In accordance with the latest published technical specifications from the Rubber Research Institute of Malaysia for SMR 20.

Deliverable tolerances: Contract unit: 20 tonnes; tender unit: 19.2 tonnes (one container load).

Delivery points: FOB at the ports of Penang, Port Kelang and Singapore, at the option of the seller.

Termination of trading: The last business day of the month preceding the contract month.

Delivery months: Current month, the next three to five months forward and two distant quarters.

Cocoa

Trading limits: US $80 per tonne above or below the settlement prices of the preceding day for all months except current month. Limits are expanded when on any one day the settlement prices of all three quoted months immediately following the current month are at the limits listed below:

Day	Limits (US $)
First	80
Second	100
Third	120
Fourth	none
Fifth	80

Minimum price fluctuation: US $1 per tonne.

Quality:
Growth:
group A, Malaysia, Papua New Guinea – at par
group B, Indonesia, Thailand, Philippines – at a discount of US $45 per tonne

Grade:

moisture content – not more than 7.5% by weight
mouldy – not more than 3.0% by count
slaty – not more than 3.0% by count
insect damaged and germinated – not more than 3.0% by count

Bean count: cocoa with a bean count of up to 140 beans per 100 grammes is acceptable subject to the following scale of discounts:

Bean count	Total discount (US $/tonne)
110 and less	none
111 to 120	4.50 to 56.25
121 to 130	63.25 to 137.50
131 to 140	147.25 to 257.50

Deliverable tolerances: 10 tonnes +/- 1% on warehouse warrants.

Delivery points: Warehouses approved by the KLCE at Tawau, Pasir Gudang (Johore) and Port Kelang.

Termination of trading: Twentieth of the month or the preceding business day.

Delivery months: January, March, May, July, September, November and December.

Clearing house: Malaysian Futures Clearing Corporation Sdn Bhd (MFCC).

Membership: A corporate Member can own multiple memberships, each one entitling the Member to have a trader on the floor of the Exchange to trade in any contract market. The membership of the Exchange is limited to 130, each membership costing M $50,000 and able to be bought or sold. Before a corporate Member is allowed to trade on the floor, he or she must first have been qualified and guaranteed by a Clearing member.

The Exchange admits local or overseas companies through a restricted form of membership – Trade Affiliate – with no voting rights. A Trade Affiliate can trade for its own account or for the accounts of overseas clients at reduced brokerage. Deals with other Trade Affiliates are not allowed, all business needing to be transacted through a Member. The entrance fee for this type of membership is M $10,000.

Furthermore, the Exchange admits individual residents to trade on the Exchange floor as 'Locals'. A Local is allowed to trade only for his or her own account or for the account of his or her Clearing member.

Commission rates and margins:
Commission:

Commodity	Type of Member	Day trade	Overnight trade
		(Roundturn in M $)	
Crude palm oil	Member	26	52
	Trade Affiliate	37	72
	Non-member	51	102
Rubber	Member	31	62
	Trade Affiliate	41	82
	Non-member	51	102
Cocoa	Member	11	20
	Trade Affiliate	15	30
	Non-member	20	40

		No of 5-tonne lots transacted per month	
		1 to 50	above 50
Tin	Member	40	40
	Trade Affiliate	60	40
	Non-member	90	negotiable (but not less than 40)

Margins: Minimum initial margins are set by the clearing house and adjusted from time to time depending on market volatility. Variation margins are marked market to market.

Date of establishment of the market: July 1980.

Date of establishment of contracts:

Crude palm oil – October 1980
Tin – October 1987
Rubber – March 1986
Cocoa – August 1988

Volume of trading:

	1987		1988	
	lots	*tonnes*	*lots*	*tonnes*
Crude palm oil	131,451	3,286,275	207,185	5,179,625
Tin	1288	6441	6736	33,682
Rubber	54	540	2543	25,430
Cocoa	–	–	5772	57,720
Totals	132,793	3,293,526	222,236	5,296,457

Membership of other organisations: International member of the US Futures Industry Association (FIA).

Further information: Planned new contracts include RBD palm olein and stock index futures, based on the Kuala Lumpur Stock Exchange Composite Index.

The Kuala Lumpur Tin Market

405A, 4th Floor, City Point, Kompleks Dayabumi, Jalan Sultan Hishamuddin, Kuala Lumpur
Telephone: 03 2740341   *Telex:* MA31472   *Fax:* 03 2742215
Chairman: Ibrahim Menudin
Secretary: Amin Zahari Nordin

Hours of trading: 11.45 Monday to Friday.

Contract details:
Commodity: Refined tin of approved origin, namely DKS (Escoy), MSC, Mentok, Banka and Thaisarco.

Trading units (minimum lot size): 1 tonne.

Trading currency and unit (manner of price quotation): Malaysian ringgit per kilogram.

Quality: Refined tin ASTM Grade A, B 339.86 with minimum tin content of 99.85 Sn of approved brands.

Deliverable tolerances: Individual weight between 25kg and 50kg steel-strapped bundles, self-palleted and one tonne in weight subject to a variation of not more than 2%.

Delivery points: Approved warehouses in Penang and Singapore.

Delivery: Spot trading with prompt delivery by means of warrant within four business days of market contract. Tin for delivery by registered smelters shall be appropriated at seller's option within 45 days from date of contract.

Membership: Ordinary and associate members subject to approval by a Board of Directors. Entrance fee is MR $5000; annual subscription MR $5000 and lodge trading guarantee MR $1,000,000.

Date of establishment of the market: 1 October 1984.

Volume of trading:
1986 – 16,751 tonnes
1987 – 20,436 tonnes
1988 – 19,090 tonnes

Further information: The KLTM is the only open forum market for physical tin in the world.

KLTM was incorporated by the Malaysian Government as a Company Limited by Guarantee on 28 June 1984 to take over from the Penang Tin Market.

THE NETHERLANDS

AMSTERDAM

Amsterdam Pork Terminal Market

PO Box 252, Nes 49/Koopmansbeurs, Damrak 62a, Amsterdam 1000 AG
Telephone: 20 5504390   *Telex:* 16582 nlk nl   *Cables:* PRODUKTENBANK
Fax: 20 236659
Managing Director: M P A de Vries

Hours of trading: Monday to Friday 10.30-12.00, 13.30-16.15.

Contract details:
Commodity: Porkers.

Trading unit: 10,000kg net of live porkers.

Trading, currency and unit (manners of price quotation):
In guilders, cents and half cents per kilogramme.

Trading limits: There are no limits on daily price fluctuations.

Quality: The quality should be SEUAA and/or SEUA with a maximum of 35 porkers of a lower quality than SEUA of which a maximum of ten porkers can be of a lower quality than UB of which a maximum of three porkers can be of a quality C.
Each porker should weigh between 85 and 120kg.

Deliverable tolerances: Minimum 9700kg net (9898kg gross). A deliverable tolerance to minimum 9000kg net (9184kg gross) with a discount of Dfl 1.00 per kg net. The lot weighs less than 9700kg net. Maximum of 45 porkers of a lower quality than SEUA of which maximum 15 porkers of a lower quality than UB.

Delivery points: Warehouses nominated by the Foundation at the seller's option.

Termination of trading: The last Thursday of the month, after which must remain a minimum of five business days.

Delivery months: All calendar months, and twelve months forward.

Clearing house: NLKKAS Amsterdam Futures Clearing House.

Membership: Anyone who, in the ordinary course of his or her business, is associated with the livestock and meat industries, may, at his or her request, be admitted as an associate member of the Foundation.

	Normal contracts	Day-trade contracts	Straddle contracts
Associates	75.00	30.00	40.00
Non-associates	95.00	30.00	47.50
(in Dfl/contract)			

Deposits: The deposit must be received by the clearing house not later than noon on the working day following the day of execution of the contract. The clearing house may change the amount of the deposit at any time. The usual deposit is Dfl 2000.

Margins: Margins are required whenever the quotations show an adverse change in price in respect of the price of a registered contract, deposits not included. Margins as well as deposits may be covered by banker's guarantee.

Date of establishment of the market: November 1980.

Volume of trading:
1987 – 15,703 contracts
1988 – 16,247 contracts

Amsterdam Potato Terminal Market

PO Box 252, Nes 49/Koopmansbeurs, Damrak 62a, Amsterdam 1000 AG
Telephone: 20 5504390   *Telex:* 16582 nlk nl   *Cables:* PRODUKTENBANK
Fax: 20 236659
Managing Director: M P A de Vries

Hours of trading: Monday to Friday 10.45–12.45, 14.00–16.00.

Contract details:
Commodity: Potatoes.

Trading units: 25,000kg net.

Trading, currency and unit (manner of price quotation): In guilders and fractions thereof of 10 cents per 100kg.

Trading limits: There are no limits on daily price fluctuations.

Quality: Type, grade, crop year and type of soil are prescribed by the NLKKAS and the Potato Terminal Market Foundation. At present they are from the current crop year, from clay soil and suitable for export to West Germany.

Deliverable tolerances: None.

Delivery points: Only potato warehouses appointed by the Foundation and correspondingly admitted by the clearing house. These storehouses must be located in The Netherlands, but not in the offshore North Sea islands (Waddeneilanden).

Termination of trading: The last Monday of the month, provided that it is at least four working days before the end of the month.

Delivery months: November, February, March, April, May and June.

Manner of price quotation: In guilders and fractions thereof of 10 cents per 100kg.

Clearing house: NLKKAS Amsterdam Futures Clearing House.

Membership: Growers, dealers and other persons or firms who have established a reputation in the potato economy and are affiliated to the Foundation can be admitted by the clearing house as associate members.

Commission rates and margins:

	Normal contracts	Day-trade/straddle contracts
Members	77.50	40.00
Non-members	82.50	40.00
(in Dfl/contract)		

Deposits: The deposit must be received by the clearing house not later than noon on the working day following the day of execution of the contract. The clearing house may change the amount of the deposit at any time. The usual deposit is Dfl 750.

Margins: Margins are required whenever the quotations show an adverse change in price in respect of the price of a registered contract, deposits not included. Margins as well as deposits may be covered by banker's guarantee.

Date of establishment of the market: 10 April 1958.

Volume of trading:
1987 – 83,356 contracts
1988 – 90,285 contracts

ROTTERDAM

Rotterdam Energy Futures Exchange N.V. (ROEFEX)

Beursplein 37, PO Box 30214, 3001 de Rotterdam
Telephone: 010 405 2250   *Fax:* 010 405 5068
Project manager: P W H de Jong
Marketing: W A R M Peek

Hours of trading: 10.00–18.30.

Contract details:
Commodities: Crude oil (Brent blend), gasoil (German Din Specification 51603 and amendments), heavy fuel oil (Bunker C grade).

Trading currency and unit (manner of price quotation):
Crude oil – US $/barrel
Gasoil – US $/tonne
Heavy fuel oil – US $/tonne

Trading units (minimum lot size):
Crude oil – 1000 barrels
Gasoil – 100 tonnes, equivalent to 118.35 cubic metres
Heavy fuel oil – 100 tonnes, equivalent to 100.91 cubic metres

Trading limits:
Minimum price fluctuation:

> Crude oil – US $0.01/barrel
> Gasoil – US $0.05/tonne
> Heavy fuel oil – US $0.05/tonne

Maximum price fluctuation:

> Crude oil, 1st day – $1.00/barrel
> 2nd   – $1.50
> 3rd   – $2.00

There is a maximum daily limit of $1.00/barrel above or below the preceding day. There is no maximum daily limit on price fluctuations during the month preceding the delivery month.

> Gasoil and heavy fuel oil, 1st day – $6.00/tonne
> 2nd   – $9.00
> 3rd   – $12.00

There is no limit for the month preceding delivery month.

Quality:

> Crude oil – FOB Rotterdam ex-storage installation or refinery, current export pipeline quality Brent blend; deliverable at PAR API 38
> Gasoil – basis Din 51603 'of merchantable quality, not containing inorganic acids or halogenated hydro-carbons', 0.845 par density at 15 deg C kg/L
> Heavy fuel oil – limited to hydrocarbon mineral oils derived from petroleum and stemming from refining processes, but restricted to streams previously unused. 0.991 par density at 15 deg C kg/L

Deliverable tolerances:

> Crude oil – Forties, Ninian, Statfjord, Oseberg and Bonny Light crudes may also be delivered, with a gravity adjustment on an API 38 basis (no less than 33 degrees API). There shall be a discount on the contract price for each full degree gravity below par; above par there will be no premium on the contract price
> Gasoil – EEC origin or EEC qualified. There shall be a discount on the contract price for each full degree gravity below par; above par there will be a premium on the contract price for each full degree gravity
> Heavy fuel oil – EEC origin or EEC qualified. There shall be a discount on the contract price for each full degree gravity above par; below par there will be no premium. Delivery above gravity 0.998 is not permitted

Delivery points:

Crude oil – i) by in-tank transfer of title to the buyer without physical transfer of product; ii) by pump-over; iii) by delivery ex-storage or refinery Rotterdam into a designated pipeline; iv) FOB production terminals by sea-going vessels if mutually agreed upon by buyer and seller; exchange for physicals (EFP)

Gasoil – i) FOB storage installation/refinery in the Amsterdam/Rotterdam/Antwerp area (inclusive of Flushing); ii) by barges/coasters or sea-going vessels or pumpovers (intertank transfers). Delivery made at Flushing is not permitted in winter

Heavy fuel oil – FOB storage installation/refinery Rotterdam and environs, loading by barges/coasters or sea-going vessels or pumpovers (intertank transfers) may be made where the seller's facility permits

Termination of trading:

Crude oil – fifth business day prior to the twenty-fifth calendar day of the month preceding the delivery month

Gasoil and heavy fuel oil – last business day of the month preceding the delivery month

Delivery months: Nine consecutive months commencing with the current calendar month.

For crude oil, delivery must be initiated after the first calendar day and before the last calendar day of the delivery month. For gasoil and heavy fuel oil, delivery must be initiated after the fifth business day and completed before the last business day of the delivery month.

Alternative delivery procedure (ADP): available to buyers and sellers who have been matched by the clearing corporation subsequent to the termination of trading in the spot month contract. If buyer and seller agree to consummate delivery under terms different from those prescribed in the contract specifications, they may proceed on that basis after submitting a notice of their intention to the clearing corporation.

Exchange of futures for, or in connection with, physicals (EFP): the buyer or seller may exchange a futures position for a physical position of equal quantity by submitting a notice to the clearing corporation. EFPs may be used to either initiate or liquidate a futures position. The clearing corporation is entitled to ask for evidence of the implementation of the transaction.

Clearing house: International Petroleum Clearing Corporation.

Membership: The following participants may be admitted to the ROEFEX:
Clearing members, legal entities who shall guarantee the transactions of the members for whom they clear and who shall have a minimum net worth of Dfl 1,000,000.

Brokers, banks, brokers, agents and the like who may accept orders from other parties, and execute them on the ROEFEX. The minimum net worth requirement is Dfl 250,000.

Market makers, individuals or legal entities who may conclude contracts solely for their own account and who are obliged to maintain the market by providing bid and ask prices. The minimum net worth requirement is Dfl 100,000. Market makers will pay only a limited transaction fee.

Off-floor traders, individuals or legal entities who conclude contracts solely for their own account but who are not present on the Exchange floor. The minimum net worth requirement is Dfl 100,000.

Local traders, including traders who may be just starting out and who do not yet have sufficient financial means or who do not yet qualify for the status of market maker; a minimum net worth of Dfl 25,000 for a ROEFEX seat.

All existing members of the European Options Exchange and of the Financial Futures Market, Amsterdam and all agents authorized to trade on those agricultural futures market in Amsterdam which are affiliated with the NLLKas are in principle eligible for membership of the ROEFEX.

NEW ZEALAND

AUCKLAND

The New Zealand Futures Exchange Ltd

10th floor, Stock Exchange Centre, 191 Queen Street, PO Box 6734, Auckland
Telephone: 09 398 308   *Telex:* NZ 63359/NZ 60251   *Fax:* 09 398 817
Chairman: G Kennedy
Managing Director: L Ward
Finance and Operations Manager: W Hall
Marketing Manager: L Gould

Hours of trading:

US dollar futures –	08.15–16.45
NZ dollar futures –	08.15–16.45
NZ dollar options –	08.15–16.45
Barclays share index (BSI) –	09.00–16.50
BSI options –	09.00–16.50
5-year Government stock futures –	08.00–17.00
5-year Government stock options –	08.00–17.00
90-day bank accepted bills futures –	08.10–16.50

Contract details:
Commodities: US dollar futures contract (USD), NZ dollar futures contract (KWI), NZ dollar options (KWO), Barclays share price index futures contract (BSI), BSI share index options (BSO), Five-year Government stock futures No 2 contract (GSC), Five-year Government stock options (GSO), 90-day bank accepted bills futures contract (BBC).

US dollar futures
Trading currency and unit (manner of price quotation): NZ $/US $0.0001.

Trading unit (minimum lot size): $50,000.

Trading limits: The rate of exchange is calculated as follows: the clearing house shall obtain from any six licensed foreign exchange dealers in New Zealand (of whom at least two shall be trading banks) their buying and selling quotations for the spot exchange of US dollars against NZ dollars at 2.30pm on the last permitted day of trading. The rate to be declared shall be the average of the mid-rates after disregarding the highest and lowest of such rates.

Termination of trading: The first Wednesday after the ninth day of the cash settlement month or such other day as the Board of the Exchange shall determine.

Settlement: Two business days following the last day of trading.

Delivery months: Spot month plus next three consecutive months then financial quarters out to one year.

NZ dollar futures
Trading currency and unit (manner of price quotation): US $/NZ $0.0001.

Trading unit (minimum lot size): NZ $100,000.

Trading limits: At 11.30 on the last trading day the clearing house obtains a quote from each licensed foreign exchange dealer on the Approved Settlement List of the buying and selling quotations for the spot exchange of NZ dollars against US dollars.

After discarding those with a spread of more than 0.15 per annum, the clearing house will randomly select the quotes of ten dealers. The two highest and two lowest mid-rates will be discarded and the mean of the remaining mid-rates used as the settlement rate.

Termination of trading: At 14.30, two business days before the third Wednesday of the cash settlement month.

Settlement: One business day following the last day of trading in the cash settlement month.

Delivery months: Spot month plus the next three consecutive months then financial quarters out to one year.

NZ dollar options
Trading currency and unit (manner of price quotation): NZ $1, known as one point.

Trading unit (minimum lot size): NZ $100,000.

Trading limits: The premiums of an option shall be quoted in minimum fluctuations of US $0.0001/NZ $1.

Termination of trading: At 14.30 on the last day of trading in the underlying futures contract.

Delivery months: Financial quarters out to six months.

Exercise: Options may be exercised on any business day up to and including the day of expiry. In-the-money options are automatically exercised at expiry.

Margins: The initial margin deposit for long and short options will be the daily published risk factor multiplied by the initial margin of the underlying futures contract. The initial margin deposit cannot exceed the value of the option premium.

Initial margin deposits are reduced for all options and option futures combinations which include offsetting positions.

Barclays share index
Trading currency: NZ dollars.

Trading unit (minimum lot size): A sum of money equal to twenty times the value of the BSI.

Trading limits: The price of cash settlement shall be declared by the clearing house and shall be the closing quotation for Barclays New Zealand Limited to the clearing house at 09.00 on the business day following the last day of trading.

Termination of trading: The second to last business day of the cash settlement month.

Settlement: All bought and sold contracts in existence at the close of trading on the final day of trading shall be settled by the clearing house at the amount representing the difference between the contract value and the cash settlement value.

Settlement day is the business day following the last permitted day of trading.

BSI options
Trading currency: NZ dollars. The option premium (contract price) is payable by the buyer of a call or put to the seller on the exercise or expiry of the option, not on purchase of the option.

Trading units (minimum lot size): A sum of money equal to twenty times the value of the BSI.

Exercise: Set at intervals of fifty points of the BSI.

Termination of trading: At the close of trading on the last trading day in the underlying futures contract.

Settlement: Financial quarter out to six months.

Margins: The initial margin deposit for long and short options will be the daily published risk factor multiplied by the initial margin of the underlying futures contract. The initial margin deposit cannot exceed the value of the option premium.

Initial margin deposits are reduced for all options and option futures combinations which include offsetting positions.

Five-year Government stock futures
Trading currency and unit (manner of price quotation): 100 minus yield per annum per $100 face value in multiples of 0.01%.

Trading units (minimum lot size): NZ $100,000 – with a coupon rate of 10%, and a term to maturity of five years.

Trading limits: At 11.30 on the last day of trading in the cash settlement month, the clearing house will obtain quotes of the buying and selling yields for $1,000,000 of basis type Government stock from dealers listed on the Approved Settlement List.

After discarding those with a spread of more than 0.15 per annum, the clearing house will randomly select the quotes of ten dealers. Those of the two highest and the two lowest mid-rates will be discarded, the cash settlement price being the mean of the remaining six mid-rates.

Termination of trading: At 12.00 noon on the first Wednesday after the ninth day of the cash settlement month.

Settlement: Financial quarter out to one year.

The cash settlement price will be announced at 15.00 on the last day of trading. Settlement day is the second business day after the last day of trading.

Five-year Government stock options
Trading currency and unit (manner of price quotation): The option premium (contract price) is payable by the buyer of a call or put to the seller on exercise or expiry of the options, not on purchase.

Trading units (minimum lot size): NZ $1,000,000, 10% coupon.

Trading limits: Premiums are quoted in yield percent per annum in multiples of 0.01% multiplied by 100.

Exercise: Set at intervals of 0.25% per annum yield.

Termination of trading: At 12.00 noon on the last day of trading in the underlying futures contract.

Delivery months: Financial quarters out to six months.

Margins: The initial margin deposit for long and short options will be the daily published risk factor multiplied by the initial margin of the underlying futures contract. The initial margin deposit cannot exceed the value of the option premium.

Initial margin deposits are reduced for all options and option futures combinations which include offsetting positions.

90-day bank accepted bills futures
Trading currency and unit (manner of price quotation): 100 minus the yield per annum per $100 face value in multiples of 0.01%.

Trading units (minimum lot size): NZ $500,000.

Trading limits: At 10.00 on the last day of trading in the cash settlement month, the clearing house will obtain quotes of the buying and selling yields for $500,000 of basis type bills from dealers listed on the Approved Settlement list.

After discarding those with a spread of more than 0.25 per annum, the clearing house will randomly select the quotes of ten dealers. The two highest and the two lowest mid-rates will be discarded, and the mean of the remaining six used as the cash settlement price.

Termination of trading: At 12.30 on the first Wednesday after the ninth day of the cash settlement month.

Delivery months: Financial quarters out to two years.

Settlement: The cash settlement price is announced at 13.30 on the last day of trading. Settlement day is the first business day following.

Commission rates: By negotiation between client and Trading or Affiliate member.

Date of establishment of the contracts:
USD – 25 January 1985
KWI – 18 November 1988
KWO – 2 December 1988
BSI – 5 January 1987
BSO – 3 February 1989
GSC – 1 June 1988

GSO – 2 December 1988
BBC – 2 December 1986

Clearing house: International Commodities Clearing House Limited.

Membership: Trading members, who must be Clearing House members, operate either for themselves or on behalf of their clients. A commission is charged for this service. Affiliate members may become Clearing House members if they meet the relevant criteria.

NORWAY

OSLO

Oslo Fur Auctions Ltd

(Oslo Skinnauksjoner S/L)
Økern Torgvei 13, Oslo 5
Telephone: 02 644150   *Telex:* 76727   *Cables:* OSLOSKINN
Managing Director: H Soerenson
Export Manager: K Fjield
New York Agent: Scandinavian Fur Agency Inc, 259 West 30th Street, New York, NY
10001;   *Telephone:* 212 868 4166   *Telex:* 222094
London Agent: McMillan and Moore Ltd, 16 Queenhithe, London EC4U 3DX;
Telephone: 01-248 3063/4/5   *Telex:* 888266   *Fax:* 01 489 0264

Hours of trading: 08.00–16.00 (15.00 from 1 June to 31 August)

Contract details:
Commodities: Raw mink skins and raw fox skins.

Trading unit: Lots of skins in bundles. The skins are supplied by traders and the
Auction Company sells the skins on their instructions.

Currency dealt in: Norwegian kroner.

PAKISTAN

KARACHI

Karachi Cotton Association

The Cotton Exchange, 11 Chundrigar Road, Karachi
Telephone: 2410336 (Chairman), 2412570 (Secretary), 2416497 (Dy. Secretary),
2413025 (Assistant Secretary), 2413025 (Office)   *Cables:* COTEX, Karachi
Secretary: S Mohammad Ali

As per trade policy announced by the Government for 1988–89, the private sector has been de-linked from the Cotton Export Corporation of Pakistan (Pvt) Limited for the purchase of export sales and local cotton purchases. As such, the registered cotton exporters have been allowed to procure cotton directly from the cotton ginners to cover their export commitments. The system of Minimum Export Price and the registration of EPC with the State Bank of Pakistan has, however, continued during the season.

The target for the 1988–89 crop was fixed at 8.7 million bales (of 170kgs each). Due to severe flooding in Punjab and heavy rains in Sind the final harvest was 8.2 million bales, of which about 5.0 million have been purchased by the local textile industry and about 3.0 million have been sold abroad. The share of the private sector is in excess of 2.0 million bales.

SINGAPORE

Singapore International Monetary Exchange Limited (SIMEX)

1 Raffles Place, OUB Centre #07-00, Singapore 0104
Telephone: 535 7382   *Telex:* RS38000 SIMEX   *Fax:* 535 7282
Chairwoman: E Sam
General Manager: A S Tian
Deputy General Manager: Q K Tung
Marketing Director: L W Peng

Hours of trading:

High sulphur fuel oil futures – 09.30-12.30, 14.30-18.00
Three-month eurodollar futures – 07.45-17.20
Nikkei stock average futures – 08.00-14.15
Japanese yen futures – 08.15-17.05
Deutschmark futures – 08.20-17.10
Pound sterling futures – 08.25-17.15
Gold futures – 09.30-17.15
Eurodollar options – 08.30-17.20
Japanese yen options – 08.15-17.05
Deutschmark options – 08.20-17.10

Contract details:

Commodities: High sulphur fuel oil futures, three-month eurodollar futures, Nikkei stock average futures, Japanese yen futures, deutschmark futures, pound sterling futures, gold futures, options on eurodollar futures, options on Japanese yen futures, options on deutschmark futures.

High sulphur fuel oil

Trading currency and unit (manner of price quotation): US $/tonne.

Trading unit (minimum lot size): 100 tonnes.

Trading limits: Minimum price fluctuation: US $0.10/tonne.

When the price moves by US $5.0/tonne in either direction from the previous day's settlement price, trading within the price limit of US $5.0/tonne is allowed for the next 30 minutes. Thereafter the price limit is US $10.0/tonne.

If the settlement price reaches the maximum price limit of US $10.0/tonne (in either direction) for two consecutive business days, there shall be no price limit on the third day. On the fourth day the price limits are reinstated.

During the month prior to the contract month there shall be no price limits.

Termination of trading: Between 09.30 and 12.30 (Singapore time) on the last business day of the month preceding the delivery month.

Delivery: Six consecutive months.

Delivery shall be between the day after the fifth business day and the twenty-fifth calendar day of the delivery month.

Delivery method is F.O.B. seller's ex-tank, in-tank transfer, or ex-ship (in exceptional circumstances and subject to the Exchange's approval), with all duties, entitlements, taxes, fees and other charges imposed prior to delivery on or in respect to the product paid by the seller. For small lots (less than 10 lots) delivery may be made by cash settlement.

Margins:

	Prior to the month preceding delivery month	During month preceding delivery month	From 5th business day prior to last trading day
Initial	US $700	US $1100	US $1400
Maintenance	US $500	US $800	US $1000

(Margin requirements are subject to change)

Three-month eurodollar

Trading unit (minimum lot size): US $1,000,000.

Trading limits:
Minimum price fluctuation: 0.01%
Value of one tick: US $25.0
No daily price limit.

Termination of trading: Second London business day immediately preceding the third Wednesday of the contract month.

Delivery day is the third Wednesday of the contract month.

Contract months: March, June, September and December.

Margins:

	Delivery month	Non-delivery month
Initial	US $1050	US $1050
Maintenance	US $750	US $750

(Margin requirements are subject to change)

Nikkei stock average

Trading currency: Japanese yen.

Trading unit (minimum lot size): ¥500 times Nikkei stock average futures price.

Trading limits:
Minimum price fluctuation: 5.0 points
Value of one tick: ¥2500
Daily price limit is 10%, or an expanded limit of 15% depending on specified circumstances.

Termination of trading: Third Wednesday of the contract month.

Delivery day is the last trading day.

Contract months: March, June, September and December. (Spot months will be listed after the third Wednesday of the preceding month.)

Margins:

	Delivery month	Non-delivery month
Initial	¥1,000,000	¥1,000,000
Maintenance	¥850,000	¥850,000
	(Margin requirements are subject to change)	

Japanese yen
Trading unit (minimum lot size): ¥12,500,000.

Trading limits:
Minimum price fluctuation: US $0.000001/¥
Value of one tick: US $12.50
No daily price limit.

Termination of trading: Second business day immediately preceding the third Wednesday of the contract month.

Delivery day is the third Wednesday of the contract month.

Contract months: March, June, September, December and the spot month.

Margins:

	Delivery month	Non-delivery month
Initial	US $1700	US $1700
Maintenance	US $1300	US $1300
	(Margin requirements are subject to change)	

Deutschmark
Trading unit (minimum lot size): DM125,000.

Trading limits:
Minimum price fluctuation: US $0.0001/DM
Value of one tick: US $12.50
No daily price limit.

Termination of trading: Second business day immediately preceding the third Wednesday of the contract month.

Delivery day is the third Wednesday of the contract month.

Contract months: March, June, September, December and the spot month.

Margins:

	Delivery month	Non-delivery month
Initial	US $1400	US $1400
Maintenance	US $1000	US $1000
	(Margin requirements are subject to change)	

Pound sterling
Trading unit (minimum lot size): £62,500.

Trading limits:
Minimum price fluctuation: US $0.0002/£
Value of one tick: US $12.50
No daily price limit.

Termination of trading: Second business day immediately preceding the third Wednesday of the contract month.

Delivery day is the third Wednesday of the contract month.

Contract months: March, June, September, December and the spot month.

Margins:

	Delivery month	Non-delivery month
Initial	US $1650	US $1650
Maintenance	US $1200	US $1200

(Margin requirements are subject to change)

Gold
Trading unit (minimum lot size): 100 fine troy ounces.

Trading limits:
Minimum price fluctuation: US $0.10/oz
Value of one tick: US $10.00
Daily price limit: 250 ticks (US $25/troy oz).

Termination of trading: The business day preceding the fifth last business day of the delivery month.

The delivery month is the last business day of the contract month.

Contract months: February, March, April, June, August, September, October and December.

Margins:

	Delivery month	Non-delivery month
Initial	US $1600	US $1600
Maintenance	US $1200	US $1200

(Margin requirements are subject to change)

Options on eurodollar futures
Trading unit (minimum lot size): One eurodollar futures contract (covering three-month, US $1,000,000 principal).

Trading limits:
Minimum price fluctuation: 0.01 eurodollar point (US $25) except that trade may occur at a price of US $1/- if such trades result in the liquidation of positions for both parties to the trade.

Strike price: Fifty point intervals for eurodollar levels below 88.00. Twenty five point intervals for eurodollar levels above 88.00.

No daily price limit.

Termination of trading: Second London business day immediately preceding the third Wednesday of the contract month.

Contract months: March, June, September and December.

Options on Japanese yen futures

Trading unit (minimum lot size): One Japanese yen futures contract (covering ¥12,500,000).

Trading limits:
Minimum price fluctuation: US $0.000001 (US c0.0001) equivalent to US $12.50, except that trades may occur at a price of US $1/– if such trades result in the liquidation of positions for both parties to the trade.

Strike price: Intervals of US c0.01.

Premium quotations: Quotations are cents/Japanese yen. A quote of US c0.005 represents an option price of $625 ($0.00005 × ¥12,500,000).

No daily price limit.

Termination of trading: Two Fridays before the third Wednesday of the contract month. If that Friday is an Exchange holiday, the last trading day will be the business day immediately preceding.

Contract months: March, June, September, December. In addition, serial months are listed including the spot month, the first deferred and second deferred months.

Options on Deutschmark futures

Trading unit (minimum lot size): One Deutschmark futures contract (covering DM125,000).

Trading limits:
Minimum price fluctuation: US $0.0001 (US c0.01) equivalent to US $12.50, except that trades may occur at a price of US $1/– if such trades result in the liquidation of positions for both parties to the trade.

Strike price: Intervals of one cent.

Premium quotations: Quotations are cents/Deutschmark. A quote of c0.50 represents an option price of $625 ($0.005 × DM125,000).

No daily price limit.

Termination of trading: Two Fridays before the third Wednesday of the contract month. If that Friday is an Exchange holiday, the last trading day will be the business day immediately preceding.

Contract months: March, June, September, December. In addition, serial months are listed including the spot month, the first deferred and second deferred months.

Membership: The Exchange has five classes of membership: *Corporate clearing member*, of which there are 36 (as of 30 April 1989). Entitlements include full trading rights on the trading floor, authority to accept customer business, authority to clear trades, ownership of one share priced at S $40,000, ownership of three seats priced at S $75,000.

Such members have a minimum paid-up capital of S $2,000,000, minimum adjusted net capital of S $3,000,000, or 10% customer funds, and security deposits of US $250,000 cash or standing letter of credit.

Corporate non-clearing member, 43 in number. Entitlements include full trading rights on the trading floor, authority to accept customer business, no authority to clear trades, ownership of three seats priced at S $75,000.

Must have minimum paid-up capital of S $1,000,000, and minimum adjusted net capital of S $500,000 or 10% customer funds.

Commercial associate member, 9 in number. Trading rights limited to energy futures contract(s), may trade only for own account and that of their related and associated companies, no authority to clear trades, ownership of one seat priced at S $75,000. Must have minimum net adjusted capital of S $25,000 and a standing letter of credit for S $1,000,000.

Individual non-clearing member, 355 in number. Full trading rights on the trading floor, may trade only for own account, ownership or lease of one seat on the Exchange.

Individual trading permit holder, 21 in number. Trading rights limited to energy futures contract(s), may trade only for own account, hold one trading permit.

Date of establishment of contracts: Originally established as the Gold Exchange of Singapore, SIMEX was inaugurated in 1984 as the first financial futures exchange in Asia. Trading in gold futures commended on 5 July 1984. Eurodollar and Deutschmark futures were listed on 7 September 1984 in conjunction with the establishment of a mutual offset system with the Chicago Mercantile Exchange whereby positions established at one exchange can be liquidated in or transferred to the other. Currently, the eurodollar, Deutschmark, Japanese yen and pound sterling are on the mutual offset system.

Volume of trading:
SIMEX trading statistics of key contracts:

	1987	*1988*	*1988 (Jan–Apr)*
Eurodollar	1,519,630	1,881,132	1,219,303
Nikkei	363,439	586,921	328,126
Japanese yen	93,573	221,046	150,406
High sulphur fuel	–	–	539,139 (Feb–Apr)
Totals	2,141,983	2,872,668	2,273,217

UNITED KINGDOM

LIVERPOOL

The Liverpool Cotton Association

620 Cotton Exchange Building, Edmund Street, Liverpool, Merseyside L3 9LH
Telephone: 051 236 6041   *Telex:* 627849   *Cables:* COTTEX   *Fax:* 051 253 0174
Director General: J A C Read
President: P Southworth
Vice President: D G Smith
Treasurer: P J M Stern

Contract details:
Commodity: Raw cotton.

Quality* Liverpool Official Standards:
South Brazilian: Types 4,4/5,5,5/6,6,6/7,7,7/8,8,9
Ugandan: BPA – UNWE, UNUG, SS, UNFA, SATU – ANWE, ENUG, SS, INFA
Greek: Grades 3,4,5,6,7
Indian: DCH-32: Superfine, Fine, Fully Good
MCU-5: Superfine, Fine, Fully Good
Varalaxmi (A): Superfine, Fine, Fully Good
Shankar 6: Superfine, Fine, Fully Good
Argentine: Grades A,B,C,C-1/2,D,E,F
Pakistan: Saw-Ginned: Grades A,B,C,D
Punjab – Superfine, Fine to Superfine, Fully Good/Fine
BHP Desi – Superfine, Fine, Fully Good/Fine
Sind Desi – Choice, Superfine, Fine/Superfine
Paraguayan – Grades 1,2,3,4,5,6,7
Peruvian: TANGUIS – Grades 2,2½,3,3½,4,5,6,7; PIMA BLANCO – Grades Extra
    1,1¼,1½,1¾
Russian: Grades A,B,C,D,E,F
Sudan: BARAKAT – Grades 1,2,3,4,5,6,C6; VS – Grades 2,3,4,5,6,C6; SHAMBAT
    – Grades GSH,2,3,4,5
Syrian: Saw-Ginned – Extra, zero, 1,2,3
Tanzanian: Tang, Gany, Yika
Turkish: Roller-Ginned EGE – Extra 1,2,3,4; Cukurova – Extra 1,2; Saw-Ginned
    Upland – Extra 1,2

---

* Trading under 'Liverpool Rules' is not confined to cotton as described above. The list indicates only those standards which have been officially adopted by the Association.

Date of establishment of the market: 1841.

Membership of other organizations: International Textile Manufacturers Federation (ITMF), Zürich; Federation of Commodity Associations, London; British Federation of Commodity Associations, London; Merseyside Chamber of Commerce and Industry (Council and Port Users Committee); Textile Industry Support Campaign, Oldham; Incorporated Liverpool School of Tropical Medicine (Council); Committee for International Co-operation between Cotton Associations (CICCA); International Chamber of Commerce – International Maritime Bureau.

Further information: In spite of the contraction of the British cotton textile industry, the volume of trading in recent years has risen very significantly and the international influence of the Liverpool Cotton Association has become increasingly important because, whereas in earlier days a large proportion of the world's cotton supply was shipped to Liverpool for resale to the Lancashire industry, much of this cotton is now traded through members and associate members of the Association for shipment to all parts of the world.

Some 19.5 million bales of raw cotton were traded internationally during the 1983–84 season at a value in excess of US $7500 million. It has been estimated that over 50% of all contracts for international trade are made subject to Liverpool Rules and are therefore ultimately dependent upon Liverpool Arbitration in the event of dispute concerning performance of contracts. The Liverpool Cotton Association consequently provides a vital service to the international marketing and movement of cotton between producers, traders and consumers throughout the world.

The Association is under the direction of a Board of 16 Directors, including the President and Vice-President, who each hold office for a period of one year. Various committees are elected annually or are appointed by the Board of Directors to deal with Association matters and a large proportion of the membership gives freely of its time to serve on these committees and in other ways in the interests of the Association, the functions of which can be divided into four main categories, namely: (a) maintenance of uniform trade practices and upholding the sanctity of contracts; (b) centralized negotiation and liaison with other organizations in the United Kingdom and elsewhere; (c) maintenance of a set of By-laws and Rules and organization of international services, including arbitration and laboratory cotton testing services; (d) provision of statistics and information.

LONDON

The Baltic Futures Exchange

Baltic Exchange Chambers, 24–28 St Mary Axe, London EC3A 8EP
Telephone: 01 626 7985 *Telex:* 916434 BALFUT G *Fax:* 01 623 2917
Chairman: P Elmer
Secretary General: S M Carter
Director of Futures Markets: W J Englebright
Futures Markets Manager: Jeremy Wall
Company Secretary: R P S Neave

On 1 December 1987 the Baltic Futures Exchange took over the running of the BIFFEX, Meat, Potato and Soya markets, with its own staff taken on from the secretariats of BIFFEX and GAFTA. In April 1988 a Grain market was established by the BFE to take over from the GAFTA grain market. On 28 April 1988 the BFE was declared a Recognised Investment Exchange by the Securities and Investment Board (SIB). The constituent markets of the BFE are, therefore, the Baltic International Freight Futures Market (BIFFEX), London Grain Futures Market (LGFM), London Meat Futures Market (LMFM), London Potato Futures Market (LPFM), Soya Bean Meal Futures Market (SOMFA).

Market details:

The Baltic International Freight Futures Market (BIFFEX)

Chairman: John Wheeler
Information: P Neave

Hours of trading: 10.15–12.30, 14.30–16.15.

Contract details:
Commodity: Dry cargo Baltic Freight Index.

Trading currency and unit (manner of price quotation): US dollars per index point.

Trading unit: Baltic Freight Index valued at $10 per full index point.

Trading limits:
Minimum price fluctuation: one full index point, equivalent to $10 per lot.
Price limit: fifty points on near positions.

Settlement price: The average of the index of the last trading day and preceding four market days.

Settlement day: The first business day after the last trading day.

Termination of trading: Last trading day is the last business day in the delivery month with the exception of December which will be 20 December, and if that day is not a business day then nearest preceding business day.

Delivery months: The current month, the following month and January, April, July, October for two years ahead.

Margin: Initial minimum of $500 per contract.

The Baltic Freight Index (BFI) is based upon the following routes:

Route no	Cargo size	Voyage	Weighting %
1	55,000 grain	US Gulf to N Continent	20.0
2	52,000 grain	US Gulf to S Japan	20.0
3	52,000 grain	US N Pacific to S Japan	15.0
4	21,000 grain	US Gulf to Venezuela	5.0
5	35,000 barley	Antwerp to Jeddah	5.0

6	120,000 coal	Hampton Roads/Richards Bay to	
		S Japan	7.5
7	65,000 coal	H Roads to N Continent	5.0
8	110,000 coal	Queensland to Rotterdam	5.0
9	55,000 pet coke	Vancouver/San Diego to Rotterdam	5.0
10	90,000 iron ore	Monrovia to Rotterdam	5.0
11	15/25,000 phosrock	Casablanca to W Coast India	2.5
12	14,000 phosrock	Aqaba to W Coast India	5.0

Clearing house: International Commodities Clearing House Ltd (ICCH).

Membership: Clearing and floor members representing the leading shipping, chartering and freight broking firms, as well as major international futures and commodity trading brokerage firms.

Date of establishment of the market: 1 May 1985.

Volume of trading: 1986: 44,911 lots
1987: 84,862 lots

Further information: The BFI is published daily by the Baltic Exchange. The BFI shows the weighted average freight rate level, on that day, of the dry bulk cargo shipping market. The index (BFI) is traded on BIFFEX for specified future settlement months (up to two years ahead) by open negotiation between a willing buyer and a willing seller on the 'ring' of the market.

Substantial BFI futures positions may be held with initial cash commitments of approximately 5% of the full underlying value of the contracts bought or sold. BFI futures contracts may be liquidated (and settled in cash) by an offsetting purchase or sale any time prior to maturity.

The London Grain Futures Market
Chairman: R Moore
Information: J Wall

Hours of trading: 11.00–12.30, 14.45–16.00.

Contract details:
Commodities: EEC wheat futures, EEC barley futures, wheat traded option, barley traded option.

EEC Wheat Futures
Trading currency and unit (manner of price quotation): Pence per tonne.

Trading unit (minimum lot size): 100 tonnes.

Trading limits:
Minimum price fluctuation – £0.05/tonne
Tick value – £5.00
No price limit.

Quality:
a) Wheat to be sound and sweet and in good condition and to contain not more than 3% heat damage;

b) Natural weight to be not less than 72.50kg/hectolitre;

c) Moisture content not to exceed 16%;

d) Admixture – i) seeds and farinaceous grain (including wild oats) and dirt not to exceed 2%, of which the dirt content not to exceed 1% ii) ergot or garlic not to exceed 0.001%;

e) Sprouted grains not to exceed 8%.

All the above tests shall be calculated on a weight basis.

Delivery months: January, March, May, June, September and November.

Delivery points: At seller's option, one of 150 registered stores of the Futures market within mainland United Kingdom.

Termination of trading: The last trading day is the twenty-third day of the delivery month (twenty-second for June).

The first notice day is the seventh day prior to the contract month of delivery.

Margins: £100 per lot.

EEC Barley Futures
Trading currency and unit (manner of price quotation): Pounds sterling per tonne.

Trading unit (minimum lot size): 100 tonnes.

Trading limits:
Minimum price fluctuation – £0.05/tonne
Tick value – £5.00
No price limit.

Quality:
a) Barley to be sound and sweet and in good condition and to contain not more than 3% heat damage;

b) Natural weight to be not less than 62.50kg/hectolitre;

c) Moisture content not to exceed 16%;

d) Admixture – i) seeds and farinaceous grain (including wild oats) and dirt not to exceed 2%, of which the dirt content not to exceed 1%;

e) Sprouted grains not to exceed 8%.

All the above tests shall be calculated on a weight basis.

Delivery months: January, March, May, September and November.

Termination of trading: The last trading day is the twenty-third day of the delivery month.

The first notice day is the seventh day prior to the contract month of delivery.

Margin: £100 per lot.

Wheat traded option
Trading currency and unit (manner of price quotation): Pounds sterling per tonne.

Trading unit (minimum lot size): One EEC wheat futures contract of 100 tonnes.

Trading limits:
Minimum price fluctuation – £0.05/tonne

Tick value – increments of £0.05/tonne or £5.00 per contract
Strike prices – multiples of £1.00/tonne
No price limit.

Delivery months: November, January, March and May. Three months will be traded at any point in time, a new month will commence trading on the day following the last trading day.

Termination of trading: The last trading day is the second Thursday of the month prior to the relevant delivery month.

Expiry is automatic at 10.30 on the next market day after the last trading day unless exercised.

Margin: Initial minimum of one futures deposit for granters.

Barley traded option
Trading currency and unit (manner of price quotation): Pence per tonne.

Trading unit (minimum lot size): One EEC barley futures contract of 100 tonnes.

Trading limits:
Minimum price quotation – £0.05/tonne
Tick value – increments of £0.05/tonne or £5.00 per contract
Strike prices – multiples of £1.00/tonne
No price limit.

Delivery months: November, January, March and May. Three months will be traded at any one point in time, a new month will commence trading on the day following the last trading day.

Termination of trading: The last trading day is the second Thursday of the month prior to the relevant delivery month.

Expiry is automatic at 10.30 on the next market day after the next unless exercised.

Margin: Initial minimum of one futures deposit for granters.

Membership: Full members must be members of the Association and the Baltic Exchange and have a genuine place of business, as approved by the committee, within a radius of five miles from the registered office of the Association. Associate members must be members of the Association and have a genuine place of business within the EEC.

Date of establishment of the market: 1929.

Volume of trading:

	Wheat futures	*Barley futures*
	(lots)	
1986	79,927	32,170
1987	67,335	24,624

Membership of other organizations: Agricultural Futures Exchange.

The London Meat Futures Exchange Ltd

Chairman: P Elmer

Hours of trading: 10.30–12.00, 14.45–16.30.

Contract details:
Commodities: Pig futures and live cattle.

Pig futures
Trading currency and unit (manner of price quotation): Pence per kilogram.

Trading uinit (minimum lot size): 3250kg.

Trading limits:
Minimum price fluctuation – 0.1p/kg
Tick value – £3.25
Price limit – £0.10/kg.

Delivery months: There is no physical delivery. The settlement months are as follows: February, April, June, August, October and November.

Termination of trading: Last Tuesday of the delivery month.

Settlement: First market day after the last trading day.

The settlement basis is in cash against the UK Average All Pigs Price (AAPP) as published by the Exchange on the Wednesday following the last trading day. The UK AAPP is calculated by the Meat and Livestock Commission for the week ending on the Saturday before the last trading day.

Margin: Initial minimum of £65 per lot.

Live cattle
Trading currency and unit (manner of price quotation): Pence per kilogram.

Trading unit (minimum lot size): 5000kg.

Trading limits:
Minimum price fluctuation – 0.1p/kg
Tick value – £5.00
Price limit – £0.1/kg.

Delivery months: There is no physical delivery. Settlement months are as follows: January, February, April, June, August, October and November.

Termination of trading: Last Friday of the delivery month.

Settlement: In cash against the Meat and Livestock Commission (MLC) England and Wales All Centres Medium Steer Price as published by the Exchange on the Monday following the last trading day. The price is calculated by the MLC for the week ending on the Saturday following the last trading day.

Margin: Initial minimum of £100 per lot.

Clearing house: International Commodities Clearing House Ltd (ICCH).

Membership: There are two types of members – full members and associate members who must have a continuing interest in the production, consumption, processing or trading of meat. The minimum net worth for a full member is £250,000 and for an associate member is £100,000.

Date of establishment of the market: 16 March 1984.

Volume of trading:

	Pig futures	*Live cattle*
1986	1073	–
1987	1641	286

Membership: IMTA, ICCH, Agricultural Futures Exchange.

The London Potato Futures Market

Chairman: R Harris
Information: W J Englebright

Hours of trading: 11.00–12.30, 14.45–16.00.

Contract details:

Potatoes (deliverable)
Trading currency and unit (manner of price quotation): Pounds sterling per tonne.

Trading unit (minimum lot size): 40 tonnes.

Trading limits:
Minimum price fluctuation – £0.10/tonne
Tick value – £4.00
Price limit – £10.00/tonne.

Quality:
a) Unwashed and of EEC origin;
b) Delivered in closed 25kg bags on standard pallets from a registered futures store;
c) Of the following varieties: Desiree, Pentlend Dell, King Edward VII, Pentlend Hawk, Maris Piper, Pentlend Squire, Bintje, Romano, Pentlend Crown, Cara, Red King, Wilja, Estima;
d) Of such quality and condition as to satisfy the Ware Standard Description of the Potato Marketing Board (PMB) in force at the time delivery is made.

Delivery months: February, April, May and November.

Termination of trading: The last trading day is the tenth calendar day of the delivery month or the next business day.

The first notice day is the first business day of the contract month of delivery.

Margin: Initial minimum of £400 per lot.

Potatoes (cash settled)
Trading currency and unit (manner of price quotation): Pounds sterling per tonne.

Trading unit (minimum lot size): 40 tonnes.

Trading limits:
Minimum price fluctuation – £0.10/tonne
Tick value – £4.00
No price limit.

Delivery months: July, August, September and March.

Termination of trading: The last Friday of the delivery month.

The contract basis is the PMB weekly average ex-farm price.

Margin: Initial minimum of £400 per lot.

Potato traded options
Trading currency and unit (manner of price quotation): Pence per tonne.

Trading unit (minimum lot size): One LPFA potato (deliverable) futures contract of 40 tonnes.

Trading limits:
Minimum price fluctuation – £0.10/tonne
Tick value – increments of £0.10/tonne or £4.00 per contract
Strike price – below £100/tonne – intervals at £5.00 integers; between £100 and £200 – intervals at £10 integers; above £200 – intervals at £15 integers
No price limit.

Delivery month: April.

Termination of trading: At 17.00 on the second Wednesday of the month prior to delivery month of underlying contract.

Expiry is the next business day after the last trading day.

Margins: All margins calculated on delta.

Clearing house: International Commodities Clearing House Ltd (ICCH).

Membership: Floor membership is limited to firms or companies who are clearing members of the Baltic Mercantile and Shipping Exchange Limited and clearing members of the Clearing House. They must satisfy the committee that they are actively interested in the trading of potatoes.
Associate membership is open to those companies or firms who have a continuing interest in the production, trading or consumption of physical potatoes, or trading in the London Potato Futures market.

Date of establishment of the market: 16 June 1980.

Volume of trading:

	Potatoes	
	deliverable	cash settled
1986	259,783	–
1987	206,850	2480

Membership of other organizations: Agricultural Futures Exchange, International Commodities Clearing House Ltd.

London Soyabean Meal Futures Market

Chairman: D Wilkins
Information: J Wall

Hours of trading: 10.30–12.00, 14.45–16.45.

Contract details:
Commodities: Toasted extracted soybean meal/pellets.

Trading currency and unit (manner of price quotation): Pound sterling per tonne.

Trading unit (minimum lot size): 20 tonnes (options on the contract).

Trading limits: £0.10 per tonne minimum price fluctuation.

Quality:
Quality 'A': The quality of the toasted soybean meal/pellets to be warranted by the storekeeper shall be in accordance with the following specifications:

Minimum 48% protein and oil combined	Maximum 2.5% sand and/or silica
Maximum 7% fibre	Maximum 12.5% moisture

Quality 'B': Sellers shall have the option of delivering toasted soybean meal/pellets warranted by the storekeeper to be in accordance with the following specifications, at a discount of 1.5% as defined in Rule 27.5:

Minimum 45.5% protein and oil combined	Maximum 2.5% sand and/or silica
Maximum 7% fibre	Maximum 13.5% moisture

Quality 'C': Sellers shall have the option of delivering toasted soybean meal/pellets warranted by the storekeeper to be in accordance with the following specifications, at a discount of 3% as defined in Rule 27.5:

Minimum 44% protein and oil combined	Maximum 2.5% sand and/or silica
Maximum 8.5% fibre	Maximum 13.5% moisture

Delivery points: Approved stores in the Federal Republic of Germany, Belgium, Netherlands and the United Kingdom.

Delivery months: February, April, June, August, October and December.

Tenderable origins: Europe, United States, Canada, Brazil, Argentina, Paraguay and Uruguay.

Contract basis: Seventh calendar day before the contract month of delivery. The first notice day is the twenty-second calendar day of the delivery month.

Clearing house: ICCH.

Membership: There are two categories of membership:
Floor membership – floor membership of the market is limited to firms or companies who are members of the Grain and Feed Trade Association, who are carrying on business from a properly established office in London, and who satisfy the Committee

that they are actively interested in the trading of soybean meal. Firms and companies whose principal place of business is not within the member countries of the EEC shall not be eligible for floor membership.

Associate membership – trade associate membership shall consist of companies or firms who have a continuing interest in the production, trading or consumption of physical soybean meal, and who are elected by a majority of the committee.

Commission rates and margins:
Initial minimum margin – £100 per lot; initial deposit – approximately 10% of the Contract value.

Volume of trading:
1986 – 78,304 lots
1987 – 54,063 lots

Membership of other organizations: Agricultural Futures Exchange.

The European Federation of Commodity Associations

1 Commodity Quay, St Katharine Docks, London E1 9AX
Telephone: 01 481 2080   *Fax:* 01 702 9924

EEC Office: Avenue de Cortenberg 79–81, Bte 7, B 1040 Brussels, Belgium
Telephone: 02 736 2058   *Telex:* 23895 dhsb
Director (UK): J H Farr
Manager (France): D Magada

Status:
The Federation of Commodity Associations (FCA) is a non-profit organization, recognized by the Commission of the European Community, whose purpose is to represent European Commodity businesses.

The commodities represented are cocoa, coffee, sugar, oils and fats, energy, general produce (tapioca, rice, spices), cotton, metal and grain.

The FCA has observer status at UNCTAD, an organization set up by the United Nations to promote trade and development, mainly in the production and trade of raw materials.

Objectives:
– To promote and protect the commercial interests of various European commodity associations, companies and firms.
– To promote or oppose European legislation and EEC directives affecting the interests of the Federation's members.
– To act as a link for the exchange of views and information between different European commodity associations and relevant international organizations.

Membership:
Full members – trade associations or other similar organizations; may be represented on the council and special sub-committee, their representatives having full voting powers.

Associate – companies, firms or individual traders in commodities; may be invited to provide representatives who can be co-opted on to the council or special sub-committee and granted voting rights.

The Grain and Feed Trade Association (GAFTA)

Baltic Exchange Chambers, 24–28 St Mary Axe, London EC3A 8EP
Telephone: 01 283 5146   *Telex:* 886984   *Fax:* 01 626 4449
Director General: J C S Mackie
Secretary: P K Johnson

GAFTA is the world's leading association promoting the international trade in grain and feeding stuffs. In addition to representing the interests of its members in terms of trade policy, the Association also provides an arbitration and contract service which is accepted worldwide.

GAFTA has about 80 standard contract forms, all for physical goods. These include grains – cereals, legumes, pulses and feedstuffs – oilseed derivatives, cereal by-products, rootcrops, fishmeal.

List of contracts:

1. General Contract
2. Chinese (other than wheat) – Parcels
3. East Indian Pulse or Grain, Other than wheat – Parcels
4. Home Produced Cakes and/or Meal
6. Imported Feedingstuffs in Bags (CIF terms)
8. Locust Beans (CIF terms)
9. Imported Feeding Meat Meal and Meat and Bone Meal (CIF terms)
10. Feeding Fish Meal (CIF terms)
12. Australian Grain TQ – Cargoes
13. Australian Offals TQ – Parcels
14. Australian Grain TQ – Parcels
14A. Australian and New Zealand Pea TQ – Parcels
15. Imported Feedingstuffs in Bags (CIF terms)
16. Australian Seed – Parcels
17. General Contract Short Form for use between Continental Buyers and Sellers
22. Rice Bran (CIF terms)
27. Canadian and USA Grain TQ – Cargoes
28. Canadian and USA Grain TQ – Parcels
30. Canadian and USA Grain in Bulk
31. Canadian Pacific Coast TQ – Parcels
32. La Plata Grain RT – Cargoes
35. La Plata Grain TQ – Parcels
36. La Plata Grain RT – Parcels
41. La Plata Grain RT – Parcels – to Continent
43. South American Offal RT – Parcels
54A. Baltic Grain RT – Cargoes or Parcels
59. South African Grain TQ – Cargoes
60. South African Grain TQ – Parcels
61. Mediterranean and Morocco TQ – Cargoes
62. Mediterranean and Morocco TQ – Parcels
64. FOB
75. Madagascar TQ – Parcels
77. Brazilian RT – Parcels
78. Contract for Bulk Grain by rail within the EEC Rye Terms
79. United Kingdom and Eire Grain (CIF terms) RT
79A. United Kingdom and Eire Grain (FOB terms)
79B. UK/Republic of Ireland Grain – Delivered/Collected
80. French Grain RT – Cargoes or Parcels

80A. EEC Grain – Parcels or Cargoes
83. Transhipment/Re-Shipment Grain TQ – Cargoes or Parcels
84. Contract of Sale (For Mechanised Accounting)
85. Contract Addendum (For Transhipments)
86. Contract for Full Container Loads (FCLs) – Cereals
86A. Contract for Full Container Loads Short Form
95. Contract for Sales for Arrival of Feedingstuffs in Bulk
96. Contract for Shipment of Tapioca, Manioc, and Cassava Products in Bulk (TQ, CIF terms)
97. Contract for Shipment of North American Soyabean Meal and/or Pellets in Bulk. Taie Quaie. CIF Terms
98. Contract for Shipment of North American Soyabean Meal and/or Pellets in Bulk. Taie Quaie. CIF Terms
99. Contract for North American HIPRO (High Protein) Soyabean Meal and/or Pellets in Bulk
100. Feedingstuffs in Bulk (TQ, CIF terms)
100A. Contracts for Shipment of Feedingstuffs in full lash barge loads

101. Feedingstuffs in Bulk (Rye Terms CIF)
102. Transhipment of Feedingstuffs in Bulk to the UK (CIF/FOB terms)
103. Shipment of Feedingstuffs in Bulk to the UK (CIF terms)
104. Feeding Fishmeal in Bulk (CIF terms)
107. Contract for Full Container Loads (FCLs) – Proteins
108. Short Form Contract for Full Container Loads (FCLs) – Proteins
109. Ex-Store/Silo Contract for Proteins/Feedingstuffs in Bulk
110. Ex-Store/Silo Contracts for Cereals in Bulk
111. Contract for EEC Grain – Delivered Premises
112. Contract for Feedingstuffs in Bulk TQ Freeout Alongside Buyers Berth (to Denmark)
113. Contract for UK Produced Feedingstuffs of Marine and Animal Origin
116. Sales Note
118. Contract for Feeding Fish Meal FOB Terms for Goods in bags or bulk
119. General Contract (FOB terms)

Terms of trade: Include cost, insurance and freight (CIF), free on board (FOB), sales for arrival, ex-store, ex-farm or delivered.

Quality: For most of the cereals and pulses contracts GAFTA provides standards known as Fair Average Quality Standards (FAQ) for the season's shipments. One of the contractual conditions is that an extra set of samples should be drawn at discharge and sent to GAFTA for the purpose of making up standards. Samples above or below the average standard are excluded. The remainder are mixed in proportion to the quantity they represent, resulting in a mix which represents a fair average quality of the goods shipped in that particular month from the origin concerned.

Membership: GAFTA has more than 500 members in more than 40 countries. Members may purchase GAFTA contracts at preferential prices and, if involved in arbitration, pay lower arbitration fees.

Membership of other organizations:
- Comité du Commerce des Céréales et des Aliments du Betail de la CEE (COCERAL) in Brussels, which nominates trade representatives to the EC Commission's Consultative Committee for Cereals.
- Confederation Internationale du Commerce et des Industries des Legumes Secs (CICILS) in Brussels and Paris, which represents the trade in peas, beans and other pulses.
- Euromarket Federation of Animal Protein Importers and Traders (EFAPIT) in Hamburg, representing fish meal and meat meal interests.
- European Commodity Exchanges Association (ECEA), based in Strasbourg, organizer of 'annual trading days' in member countries.
- London Chamber of Commerce and Industry.

Further information: GAFTA's subsidiary company, the GAFTA Clearing House Limited, is officially recognized by the Securities and Investments Board and provides clearing facilities for the London Grain futures market.

International Commodities Clearing House Limited (ICCH)

Roman Wall House, 1-2 Crutched Friars, London EC3N 2AN
Telephone: 01 488 3200   *Telex:* 887234   *Cables:* Libonotus London EC3
Fax: 01 481 3462, 01 481 4131 (Clearing Services)

Contract details:
The ICCH clears the following exchanges in London:
London Futures and Options Exchange (FOX), International Petroleum Exchange (IPE), London International Financial Futures Exchange (LIFFE), Baltic Futures Exchange (BFE), London Metal Exchange (LME), London Traded Option Market – management only – (LTOM).

Commodities:

FOX –	cocoa*, coffee*, white sugar*, raw sugar
IPE –	gasoil*, gasoline, heavy fuel oil, crude oil
LIFFE –	financial instruments: short gilt, medium gilt, yen bond, long gilt*, US treasury bond*, German government bond*; interest rates: 90-day sterling*, 90-day eurodollar*, 90-day eurodeutschmark; the FT-SE 100 stock index; currencies: pound sterling*, Deutschmark, yen, Swiss franc, US/Deutschmark*
BFE –	potatoes*, soyabean meal, pigs, cattle, dry cargo freight index
LME –	silver, lead*, aluminium*, nickel*, copper*, zinc*

* Traded options also offered on these contracts.

Trading currencies: Pounds sterling, American dollars, French francs, Deutschmarks, Japanese Yen.

The ICCH also operates from the following overseas offices:

Sydney, Australia:
Level 9, Grosvenor Place, 225 George Street, Sydney NSW 2000
Telephone: 612 258 8000   *Telex:* 7122142   *Fax:* 612 251 5152

Commodities:

SFE – cash settled wool, cash settled cattle, 90-day bank bills*, Australian dollars*, All ordinary share index*, 10-* and 3-year treasury bonds*, gold (COMEX linked), US T bonds and eurodollars (both LIFFE linked)

Trading currency: Australian dollars.

Melbourne, Australia:
Ground Floor Bank House, 11–19 Bank Place, Melbourne, Victoria 3000
Telephone: 613 670 0307   *Telex:* 152147

Commodities:

AFFM – shares futures

Trading currency: Australian dollars.

Paris, France:
35 rue des Jeuneurs, 75002 Paris

Commodities:

MONEP – sugar, cocoa, coffee, potatoes

Trading currencies: French francs, American dollars.

Hong Kong:
1211 New World Tower, 16–18 Queen's Road Central, Hong Kong
Telephone: 852 5868 0338   *Telex:* 76375   *Fax:* 852 5868 0134

Commodities:

HKFE – gold, sugar, soyabeans, Hang Seng stock index

Trading currencies: American dollars, Hong Kong dollars.

Auckland, New Zealand:
First floor, 105 Symonds Street, Auckland
Telephone: 649 39 6281   *Telex:* 63046   *Fax:* 649 37 0031

Commodities:

NZFE – New Zealand dollars, crossbred wool, 5-year government bonds, wheat, 90-day bank-accepted bills, Barclays share price index, 90-day prime commercial paper

Trading currency: New Zealand dollars.

Date of establishment of the market: Formed in 1888 as the London Produce Clearing House Limited by a group of commodity merchants and bankers in the City of London. In 1973 the name was changed to International Commodities Clearing House Limited.

Volume of trading:
1986 – 22,951,994 lots bought and sold
1987 – 42,504,412
1988 – 59,087,442

Membership: Clearing membership is open to organizations resident in any part of the world and subject to approval by ICCH Board of Directors.

ICCH is owned by six major UK clearing banks – Barclays, Lloyds, Midland, National Westminster, Royal Bank of Scotland and Standard Chartered.

Volume of trading:
Futures contracts cleared in London by ICCH:

	1987	1988
FOX		
Cocoa	926,335	1,351,561
Cocoa traded options	281	3,374
Coffee	906,930	963,831
Coffee traded options	5,505	21,350
Sugar	762,053	1,191,079
Sugar traded options	3,457	68,660
White sugar	200,000	347,813
Totals	2,804,901	3,947,668
IPE	1,102,148	1,556,958
Gasoil traded options	7,518	16,246
Heavy fuel oil	3,019	–
Gasoline	1,584	–
Crude oil	171	291,823
Totals	1,114,440	1,865,027
BFE (not including grains)		
Potatoes	206,196	92,219
Potatoes traded options	–	525
Soyabean meal	52,310	71,857
Early potatoes	2,474	242
Biffex	84,862	106,382
Cattle	275	15
Pigs	1,591	1,967
Totals	347,709	273,207

INTEX				
FNCI			24,963	3,876
Freight			7,489	356
Totals			32,452	4,232

LME				1988
Futures:				
Silver 10,000oz	$	($ sett)		9,501
	£	($ sett)		302
	$	(£ sett)		192
	£	(£ sett)		31
Aluminium 99.7%	$			672,710
	£			517
Aluminium 99.5%	$			1,479,903
	£			558,799
Copper 'A'	$			1,599,798
	£			1,736,608
Copper standard	$			28
	£			1,137
Nickel	$			328,699
	£			14,522
Lead	$			56,408
	£			428,754
Silver 2000oz	$	($ sett)		23
	$	(£ sett)		11
Zinc	$			404,689
	£			309,133
Zinc special HG	$			13,178
	£			12
Totals				7,614,955

Options:			
Aluminium 99.7%	$		50,053
99.5%	$		85,072
Copper 'A'	$		48,512
Nickel	$		448
Lead	$		62
	£		202
Zinc	$		8,754
Totals			193,103

The International Petroleum Exchange

International House, 1st Katharine's Way, London E1 9UN
Telephone: 01 481 0643 *Telex:* 927479 *Fax:* 01 481 8485
Chairman: D Whiting
Chief Executive: P Wildblood
Deputy Chief Executive: G Wright
Marketing Manageress: C Denton

Hours of trading:
Gasoil futures and options – 09.15–17.24
Brent crude oil futures and options – 09.25–17.30

Contract details:
Commodities: Gasoil futures (GOF), Brent crude oil futures (BCOF), gasoil options (GOO), Brent crude oil options (BCOO).

Trading units (minimum lot size):
Gasoil futures – 100 tonnes
Brent crude oil futures – 1000 barrels
Gasoil options – one lot of gasoil futures
Brent crude oil options – one lot of crude oil futures

Trading limits:

	Price fluctuation	
	minimum (cents)	*maximum* (dollars)
Gasoil futures	25	15.00
Brent crude oil futures	1	no limit
Gasoil options	5	–
Brent crude oil options	1	–

Quality:
Gasoil contract: Gasoil shall be delivered in the month specified under the contract in bulk and free of all liens and claims conforming to the following specification:

			Test method
Density at 15°C	kg/litre	max 0.855 min 0.820	ASTM D 1298 (in a vacuum)
Distillation			
Evaporated at 250°C	% vol	max 64	ASTM D 86
Evaporated at 350°C		min 85	
Colour		max 1.5	ASTM D 1500
Flash point			
Pensky Martens			
'Closed Cup'	°C	min 60	ASTM D 93
Total sulphur	% wt	max 0.3	ASTM D 1552
Kinematic viscosity	Cst at 20°C	max 6.0	ASTM D 445

Cloud point	°C		
	(for delivery in calendar months April/September)		
		max + 2	
	(for delivery in calendar months October/March)		
		max - 2	ASTM D 2500
Cold filter plugging point	°C		
	(for delivery in calendar months April/September)		
		max - 7	
	(for delivery in calendar months October/March)		
		max - 11	IP 309
Oxidation stability	mg/100ml	max 3	ASTM D 2274
Cetane index		min 45	ASTM D 976/80
Sediment	% wt	max 0.05	ASTM D 473
Water	% vol	max 0.05	ASTM D 95

It is to be understood that Gasoil shall be of merchantable quality and accordingly shall not contain inorganic acids or halogenated hydrocarbons.

Crude oil contract: The crude oil shall be current pipeline export quality Brent Blend for delivery at the Sullom Voe Delivery Area in the delivery month.

Deliverable tolerances: Gasoil contract: Plus or minus 0.5% of the contract volume.

Delivery points:
Gasoil contract: Antwerp, Amsterdam or Rotterdam (or in accordance with agreed alternative delivery procedure).

Crude oil contract: There is cash settlement of outstanding contracts. Physical delivery may only take place if contract is exchanged for physicals (EFP).

Termination of trading:

Gasoil futures – three business days prior to thirteenth calendar day
Brent crude oil futures – tenth calendar day of preceding month
Gasoil options – third Wednesday of month
Brent crude oil captions – third business day prior to cessation of trading in underlying future

Delivery months:

Gasoil futures – nine consecutive months
Brent crude oil futures – six consecutive months following current month
Gasoil options and Brent crude oil options – first three months of underlying contract

Clearing house: ICCH.

Membership:

Floor members, 35 in number. Entitled to one share and one vote, and the right to trade with other Floor members free of commission. A Floor member may put as many traders on the floor as s/he wishes, and may trade for clients (members or non-members, including members of the public).

Floor members must be registered under the Financial Services Act, ie registered by the AFBD or the SIB. Since Floor members are limited in number such membership can be bought or sold, the fee being privately negotiated between the two parties and a transfer fee paid to the Exchange. A Floor member may lease his or her trading rights. The lessee (known as a tenant) does not have voting rights but may clear and register contracts in their own names, or through an existing clearing member. Criteria for Floor membership and clearing lessee include a net worth requirement of £500,000, and offices in or near the City of London. If trading rights have been leased the requirement for Floor members falls to £25,000.

General Associate members, unlimited in number. GA members are not entitled to trade on the floor, but may transact business on behalf of clients. All the business of the GA must be put through a Floor member for execution on the Exchange. The commissions charged by a Floor member to a GA are fully negotiable. Must have a net worth requirement of £175,000 and possess a banker's reference.

Trade Associate members are companies having a bona fide continuing interest in the production, manufacture or distribution of physical oil or oil products. No minimum net worth requirement but must possess a banker's reference. Should Associate members wish to clear contracts in their own name they must become members of the Clearing House and conform to the House's criteria as well as those of the Exchange.

Local members, limited to 50. Available to individuals who may trade on the market floor of the Exchange for themselves or for other locals or Floor members. They may not, however, transact business for any client in any way be they a member or non-member.

Local members must be registered by the AFBD and have their contracts cleared by a Floor member company of the Exchange with a clearing agreement approved by the Exchange. Local membership may be transferred or leased to another individual acceptable to the Exchange. No minimum net worth requirement for Local members. Locals (or tenants) may also appoint an alternate to operate their trading rights on the floor of the Exchange in their stead. An alternate must be a qualified registered trader and all or any of his or her actions are deemed to be those of the Local or tenant.

Commission rates and margins:

Commission: 40p each side Exchange fee; 15p each side clearing house fee.
Margins: US $1000 per lot basic initial; US $350 spread.

Brokerage rates are freely negotiable between broker and customer.

Date of establishment of contracts:

Gasoil futures – 6 April 1981
Brent crude oil futures – 23 June 1988
Gasoil options – 20 July 1987
Brent crude oil options – 11 May 1989

Volume of trading:

	Gasoil	*Crude (revised contract)*
1987	1,102,148	–
1988	1,546,958	284,460
1989 (up to May)	703,718	575,294

The London Futures and Options Exchange (FOX)

1 Commodity Quay, St Katharine Docks, London E1 9AX
Telephone: 01 481 2080   *Telex:* 884370   *Fax:* 01 702 9923
Chairman: S Tate
Executive Director: P A S Rucker
Business Development Director: C Kennedy
Finance and Administrative Director: J Rodda
Marketing Services Manager: B Eatough
Compliance Officer: J P B Hecks

London FOX was launched on 10 June 1987. It succeeds the London Commodity Exchange (LCE) which emerged after the war as an umbrella organization bringing together the major soft commodity futures market associations. During 1986 the LCE underwent dramatic restructuring, changing from a trade association to a marketing organization.

London FOX incorporates the London Sugar futures Market, the London Cocoa Terminal Market and the Coffee Terminal Market of London, details of which are given below.

Clearing House: ICCH.

Membership:
Authorized Floor members: shareholders and/or member companies trading on the Exchange floor.

Exchange Associate members: companies not having access to the trading floor, nor entitled to own shares in the Exchange.

Traded Options Authorized Floor members: companies allowed to deal on the floor of the traded options market only.

Local Floor membership: allowing individuals to take advantage of direct trading, for their own account, other local members or AFM's, on all the floors of the London FOX and International Petroleum Exchange (LPE).

Membership of other organizations: The European Federation of Commodity Associations.

The London Cocoa Terminal Market Ltd

Telephone: 01 481 2080   *Telex:* 884370   *Fax:* 01 702 9924
Secretary: H R Dauncey

Hours of trading: 10.00–13.00, 14.30–16.45

294

Contract details:

Commodity: No 67 cocoa contract.

Trading currency and unit (manner of price quotation): pounds sterling per tonne.

Trading unit (minimum lot size): 10 tonnes.

Trading limits: Minimum price fluctuation £1 per tonne.

Termination of trading: Last trading day of delivery month.

Delivery months: March, May, July, September, December (seven months always quoted).

Delivery points: Ex-warehouse UK or in warehouse Amsterdam, Antwerp, Hamburg or Rotterdam.

Origins tenderable: West Africa, South America, West Indies and other cocoa-producing countries, as defined in LCTMA rules.

Margin: £400 per lot.

Date of establishment of the market: 1928, following on the establishment of the Cocoa Association of London two years earlier which regulated trade in physical cocoa by setting out contract rules, recognized grades and arbitration machinery.

Volume of trading:
1987   926,335 lots
1988   1,351,561 lots

The Coffee Terminal Market of London Ltd

Telephone: 01 481 2080   *Telex:* 884370   *Fax:* 01 702 9924
Secretary: H R Dauncey

Hours of trading: 09.45–12.32, 14.30–17.02.

Contract details:

Commodity: Robusta coffee.

Trading currency and unit (manner of price quotation): Pounds sterling per tonne.

Trading unit (minimum lot size): 5 tonnes.

Trading limit: Minimum price fluctuation £1 per tonne.

Termination of trading: Last trading day of delivery month.

Delivery points: London, Home Counties, Bristol, Hull, Amsterdam, Rotterdam, Le Havre, Hamburg, Bremen and Antwerp.

Origins tenderable: Africa, India, West Indies and other coffee-producing countries, as defined in the CTMAL Rules.

Delivery months: January, March, May, July, September and November (seven months always quoted).

Clearing house: International Commodities Clearing House.

Margin: £250 per lot.

Date of establishment of the market: 1 July 1958.

Volume traded:
1987   906,930 lots
1988   963,831 lots

The London Sugar Futures Market Ltd

Telephone: 01 481 2080   *Telex:* 884370   *Fax:* 01 702 9924
Secretary: P I King

Hours of trading: Monday to Friday 10.30 until the close of the 12.30 call and 14.30 until the close of the 19.00 call. Calls at 10.30, 12.30, 14.30, 16.40 and 19.00 hours.

Contract details:
Commodities: Raw sugar (contract No 6) and white sugar (contract No 5).

Trading currency and unit (manner of price quotation): American dollars per tonne.

Trading unit: 50 tonnes.

Trading limits:
>   Raw sugar – $0.20/tonne minimum lot size
>   White sugar – $0.10/tonne minimum lot size

Quality: White sugar – white beet or cane crystal sugar or refined sugar of any origin. Raw sugar – raw cane sugar minimum 96° polarization at time of shipment from a producing country as defined in the Rules.

Termination of trading:
>   Raw sugar – last trading day of month preceding delivery
>   month
>   White sugar – fifteenth day of month preceding delivery
>   month

Delivery months: March, May, August, October, December (seven months always quoted).

Margin: £600 per lot.

Membership: The voting membership comprises 30 full members. Full membership is corporate. The non-voting membership comprises companies or persons who may be elected to associate or overseas affiliate membership.

Date of establishment of the market: The market reopened in 1957 after the Second World War. Earlier historical records are no longer available.

Volume of trading:

	Raw sugar	White sugar
	(lots)	
1987	762,053	200,340
1988	1,191,079	347,813

The London Jute Association

Artillery House, 4th Floor, Artillery Row, London SW1P 1RT
Telephone: 01 222 0940   *Telex:* 8812939 COMMET G   *Fax:* 01 799 1852
Secretary: R Shimell

Hours of trading: Monday to Friday. Market holidays are fixed by the Committee.

Contract details:
Commodities: Raw jute, kenaf and allied fibres.

Trading unit: With Bangladesh, India, Nepal and Thailand a bale of Pucca press-packed jute weighing 180kg. Price is quoted per metric tonne.

Trading currency: Any.

Quality: Jute shipped under LJA contract is guaranteed of average quality of the grade specified. If the jute is inferior an allowance is fixed either by amicable settlement or by arbitration in London.

Delivery points: Worldwide.

Membership: Membership is in a personal capacity. Members represent merchant houses engaged in the international raw jute trade. Members conduct their business on the appropriate LJA contract form. The Association is not a marketing body but only administers the contract, which it does through its officials and annually elected committee.

Date of establishment of the market: 1875.

The London International Financial Futures Exchange (LIFFE)

The Royal Exchange, London EC3V 3PJ
Telephone: 01 623 0444   *Telex:* 8938994 LIFFE G   *Fax:* 01 588 3624
Chairman: D Burton
Chief Executive: M N H Jenkins

Hours of trading:
Futures:

Long gilt	09.00–16.15
Medium gilt	08.55–16.10
Short gilt	09.05–16.20
US treasury bond	08.15–16.10
German government bond	08.10–16.00
Japanese government bond	08.10–16.05
Three-month euromark	08.15–16.10
Three-month eurodollar	08.30–16.00
Three-month sterling	08.20–16.02
Pounds sterling	08.32–16.02
Dollar-mark	08.34–16.04
Deutschmark	08.34–16.04
Swiss franc	08.36–16.06

Japanese yen – 08.30–16.00
FT-SE 100 – 09.05–16.05

Options:

Long gilt – 09.02–16.15
US treasury bond – 08.17–16.10
German government bond – 08.12–16.00
Three-month eurodollar – 08.32–16.00
Three-month sterling – 08.22–16.02
Pounds sterling – 08.34–16.02
Dollar-mark – 08.36–16.04

Contract details: *(see pages 299–302).*

Commodities: Interest rate and currency futures and options contracts, Stock Index futures contract, gilts and government bonds.

Trading limits: None, except for JGB: i) ¥1.00 from Tokyo SE closing price. If limit is hit price limits are removed one hour later for remainder of day; ii) no limit during last hour of trading on each day.

Date of establishment of contracts:
Futures:

Long gilt – 18 November 1982
Medium gilt – 7 January 1988
Short gilt – 10 September 1985
US treasury bond – 21 June 1984
German government bond – 29 September 1988
Japanese government bond – 13 July 1987
Three-month euromark – 20 April 1989
Three-month eurodollar – 30 September 1982
Three-month sterling – 4 November 1982
Pounds sterling – 30 September 1982
Dollar-mark – 30 January 1986
Deutschmark – 14 October 1982
Swiss franc – 30 November 1982
Japanese yen – 1 December 1982
FT-SE 100 – 3 May 1984

Options:

Long gilt – 13 March 1986
US treasury bond – 13 March 1986
German government bond – 20 April 1989
Three-month eurodollar – 27 June 1985
Three-month sterling – 5 November 1987
Pounds sterling – 27 June 1985
Dollar-mark – 30 January 1986

Date of establishment of the market: 30 September 1982.

Contract details

Contract	Unit of trading	Contract standard	Delivery months	Delivery day
Futures:				
Long gilt	£50,000 nominal value notional gilt with 9% coupon	Any gilt stock with a life of between 15–25 years, as listed by LIFFE	March June September December	Any business day in delivery month (at seller's choice)
Medium gilt	£50,000 nominal value notional gilt with 9% coupon	Any gilt stock with a life of 7–10 years	March June September December	Any business day in delivery month (at seller's option)
Short gilt	£100,000 nominal value notional gilt with 9% coupon	Any gilt stock with a life of 3–4½ years	March June September December	Any business day in delivery month (at seller's choice)
German government bond (bund)	DM250,000 nominal value notional bond with 6% coupon	Any Bundesanleihe with a life of 81/2–10 years	March June September December	Tenth calendar day of delivery month
Japanese government bond (JGB)	¥100 million face value notional long-term JGB with 6% coupon	Cash settlement based on price of Tokyo SE JGB futures	March June September December	First business day after last trading day of TSE
Three-month eurodeutsch-mark (euromark)	DM1 million	Cash settlement based on Exchange Delivery Price	March June September December	First business day after last trading day
US Treasury bond	US $100,000 par value notional US Treasury bond with 8% coupon	Any US Treasury bond with a life of at least 15 years	March June September December	Any business day in delivery month (at seller's choice)*

* For the US Treasury Bond contract, a business day in the delivery process is defined as a day when banks in New York and Chicago are open for business as well as LIFFE. The last trading day is defined to coincide with the last trading day for the Chicago Board of Trade US Treasury Bond futures contract, where this is a LIFFE trading day.

Last trading day	Quotation	Minimum price movement (Tick size & value)	Initial margin (Straddle)
11.00 Two business days prior to last business day in delivery month	Per £100 nominal	£1/32 (£15.625)	£500 (£125)
11.00 Two business days prior to last business day in delivery month	Per £100 nominal	£1/32 (£15.625	£500 (£125)
11.00 Two business days prior to last business day in delivery month	Per £100 nominal	£1/64 (£15.625)	£500 (£125)
11.00 Three business days prior to delivery day	Per DM100 nominal	DM0.01 (DM25)	DM1500 (DM250)
16.05 One business day prior to last trading day of TSE	Per ¥100 face value	¥0.01 (¥10,000	¥1,000,000 (¥250,000)
11.00 Two days prior to third Wednesday of delivery month	DM100 minus rate of interest	DM0.01 (DM25)	DM750 (DM500) provisional
16.10 Seven CBOT business days prior to last business day in delivery month*	Per $100 par value	$1/32 ($31.25)	$1250 ($125)

Contract	Unit of trading	Contract standard	Delivery months	Delivery day
Three-month sterling interest rate	£500,000	Cash settlement based on the Exchange Delivery Price	March June September December	First business day after the last trading day
Three-month eurodollar interest rate	US $1,000,000	Cash settlement based on the Exchange Delivery Price	March June September December	First business day after the last trading day

Options:

Contract	Unit of trading	Contract standard	Delivery months	Delivery day
Sterling currency	£25,000**	Currency deliverable in country of issue	March June September December	Third Wednesday of delivery month
Dollar-mark currency	$50,000 traded against DM	Currency deliverable in country of issue	March June September December	Third Wednesday of delivery month
Deutschmark	DM125,000**	Currency deliverable in country of issue	March June September December	Third Wednesday of delivery month
Swiss franc	SFr125,000**	Currency deliverable in country of issue	March June September December	Third Wednesday of delivery month
Japanese yen	¥12,500,000**	Currency deliverable in country of issue	March June September December	Third Wednesday of delivery month
FT-SE 100	Valued at £25 per full index point	Cash settlement at Exchange Delivery Price	March June September December	First business day after the last trading day

** All currencies are traded against American dollars.

Last trading day	Quotation	Minimum price movement (Tick size & value)	Initial margin (Straddle)
11.00 Third Wednesday of delivery month	100.00 minus rate of interest	0.01 (£12.50)	£500 (£125)
11.00 Two business days prior to the third Wednesday of delivery month	100.00 minus rate of interest	0.01 ($25.00)	$500 ($100)
10.30 Second business day prior to delivery	US $ per £	0.01 cents per £ ($2.50)	$750 ($100)
10.32 Two business days prior to delivery	DM per US $	DM0.0001 per US $ (DM5)	DM1250 (DM100)
10.32 Second business day prior to delivery	US $ per DM	0.01 cents per DM ($12.50)	$1000 ($100)
10.33 Second business day prior to delivery	US $ per SFr	0.01 cents per SFr ($12.50)	$1000 ($100)
10.30 Second business day prior to delivery	US $ per ¥100	0.01 cents per ¥100 ($12.50)	$1000 ($100)
11.20 The last business day in the delivery month	FT-SE 100 Index ÷ 10	0.05 (£12.50)	£1250 (£100)

Volume of trading:

	1988	% increase on 1987
Futures	13,787,184	11.36
Options	1,759,426	50.02
Totals	15,546,610	14.71

Clearing house: ICCH.

Membership: Full membership – under this category a member may apply for (a) general clearing membership (minimum net worth £1,000,000 +); (b) individual clearing membership (minimum net worth £500,000 +); (c) non-clearing 'public order' membership (minimum net worth £100,000 +) or 'non public order' (minimum net worth £25,000). Associate membership (ie where an individual or corporation has leased a seat from a full member) may only apply for 'public order' or 'non public order' status.

The criteria for full and associate membership are identical. Both are governed by the regulations of the exchange as detailed in the Rules and Memorandum & Articles of Association.

The London Metal Exchange Limited

Plantation House, Fenchurch Street, London EC3M 2AP
Telephone: 01 626 3311   *Telex:* 8951367   *Fax:* 01 626 1703
President: J K Lion
Chairman: C J B Green
Vice-Chairman: J P A Wolff
Chief Executive: M E Brown

Hours of trading: 11.50-13.25, 15.20-17.00.

The two floor trading sessions are broken down into two rings made up of five minutes trading in each contract. Each session is followed by a short period of open-outcry dealing in all metals simultaneously (known as kerb trading). After the second ring of the first session the official prices for the day are announced. The trading times for the contracts are as follows:

> Copper – 12.00-12.05, 12.30-12.35, 15.30-15.35, 16.15-16.20
> Aluminium – 11.55-12.00, 12.55-13.00, 15.35-15.40, 16.20-16.25
> Zinc (special high) – 12.10-12.15, 12.50-12.55, 15.25-15.30, 16.10-16.15
> (high) – 12.10-12.15, 12.45-12.50, 15.25-15.30, 16.05-16.10
> Lead – 12.05-12.10, 12.40-12.45, 15.25-15.30, 16.00-16.05
> Nickel – 12.15-12.20, 13.00-13.05, 15.45-15.50, 16.30-16.35

Tin - 11.50-11.55, 12.35-12.40, 15.40-15.45,
16.25-16.30

Contract details:
Commodities: Electrolytic copper, high grade primary aluminium, special high grade zinc, high grade zinc, refined pig lead, primary nickel and refined tin futures contracts.

Traded options contracts are also available for the above metals with the exception of tin.

Futures:
Trading currency and unit (manner of price quotation):

Copper and lead - Pounds sterling per tonne
Aluminium, zinc, nickel and tin - American dollars per tonne

Trading unit (minimum lot size):

Copper, aluminium, zinc, lead - 25 tonnes
Nickel - 6 tonnes
Tin - 5 tonnes

Trading limits:

Copper - £0.50/tonne
Aluminium - US $1.00/tonne
Zinc - US $0.50/tonne
Lead - £0.25/tonne
Nickel - US $1.00/tonne
Tin - US $1.00/tonne

Quality:

Copper – electrolytic, in the form of either grade A cathodes or wirebars; of standard dimensions in the weight range 110-125kg in seller's option; of brands listed in the LME approved list of copper; of British Standard 6017-1981

Aluminium – high grade primary of minimum 99.70% purity in the form of ingots in the range of 12-26kg, T bars of maximum 675kg or sows of maximum 750kg

Zinc – special high grade of minimum 99.995% purity in the form of slabs, plates or ingots weighing not more than 55kg each; of brands listed in the LME approved list of special high grade zinc brands

– high grade of minimum 99.95% purity in the form of slabs, plates or ingots weighing not more than 55kg each; of brands listed in the LME approved list of high grade zinc brands

Lead – refined pig assaying not less than 99.97% purity in pigs weighing not more than 55kg each; of brands listed in the LME approved list of lead brands

Nickel – primary, of minimum 99.80% purity with chemical analysis conforming to the current ASTM specification; in the form of cathodes, pellets or briquettes; of production of producers named in the LME approved nickel list

Tin – refined, of minimum 99.85% purity, conforming to BS 3252-1986 in ingots or slabs weighing not less than 12kg or not more than about 50kg each; of brands listed in the LME approved list of tin brands

Delivery: Daily for three months forward, then the third Wednesday of the month for the next twelve months.

Delivery points:
UK – Avonmouth, Birmingham, Glasgow, Goole, Hull, Liverpool, London and Newcastle.

Europe – Antwerp, Gothenberg, Helsingborg, Rotterdam, Genoa, Leghorn, Trieste, Bremen, Hamburg and Dunkirk.

Far East – Singapore, Djakata, Kobe, Moji, Nagoya, Osaka and Yokohama (Japanese warehouses are registered for high grade primary aluminium storage only).

Options:
Trading currency and unit (manner of price quotation): Pounds sterling and American dollars per tonne for each traded option.

Trading months:
Copper and Aluminium – January and every second month thereafter. The nearest six designated months only are tradeable in American dollars, the nearest three months only are tradeable in pounds sterling

Zinc – February and every second month thereafter. The nearest three months only are tradeable in either currency

Lead – February and every second month thereafter. The nearest two months only are tradeable in either currency

Nickel – February and every second month thereafter. The nearest three months only are tradeable in American dollars, the nearest two in pounds sterling

Strike price:
Copper and Aluminium – £25/$25 per tonne gradation. Where the strike price is between $1750 and $2950 the gradation increases to $50/tonne, and where the price rises to $3000 or above the gradation increases to $100/tonne

> Zinc – £20/$20 per tonne. Where the strike price is
> $2000 or above the gradation is $50/tonne
> Lead – £20/$20 per tonne
> Nickel – £50/$100 per tonne

Delivery (prompt date): The third Wednesday of the relevant month.

Declaration date (the last date that an option can be exercised or abandoned) is the first Wednesday of each trading month. If either Wednesday is a holiday the next business day will prevail.

Clearing house: ICCH.

Membership: Members may be representative or individual subscribers. Persons eligible for election as representative subscribers must be connected with the metal industry or trade; over the age of 21; and a director of the company represented which must be incorporated in the UK. Alternatively, the representative subscriber could be a partner in the company represented, the majority of which partners must be British subjects domiciled in the UK. Individual subscribers are nominees of trade organizations or associations connected with the metal trade; directors or partners, the status of whose company does not qualify them to become representative subscribers; and persons who have ceased to be representative subscribers but retain an active interest in the London Metal Exchange. A candidate for election as a subscriber must be proposed by one subscriber and seconded by another and election of individual subscribers and honorary members is the exclusive province of the directors. Applications for membership in the category of representative subscribers are dealt with jointly by the Board and Committee, and in all cases a decision is taken by a majority of votes. Subscribers are elected until 31 December each year and in the absence of a notification to the contrary it is assumed that the subscriber is eligible for re-election. Ring membership is granted jointly by the directors and the Committee of the LME and only representative subscribers of firms and companies are eligible. A subscriber who wishes to become a ring dealer must apply to both the directors and the Committee for permission. Two sponsors who are themselves subscribers are needed, and two referees who must be persons engaged in the metal trade. There is an entrance fee for subscribers plus a subscription, and each candidate for election is required to purchase two qualification shares in the company. A subscriber is entitled to be admitted to the Exchange in accordance with the rules and regulations.

Date of establishment of market: Established as a company in 1877.

Date of establishment of contracts:

> Copper – 1899
> Aluminium – 1978
> Zinc – 1920
> Lead – 1920
> Nickel – 1979
> Tin – 1899

Further information: The LME is now subject to the Financial Services Act (FSA) of 1986, and the regulations of the Securities and Investment Board (SIB) created in 1987. In order to qualify as a Recognized Investment Exchange (RIE) the LME had to incorporate a clearing house system with price transparency and audit trails. With the introduction of a clearing system the LME extended its trading period from three to fifteen months.

The London Metal Exchange Limited was formed in July 1987, with a new constitution and with a single tier Managing Board made up of ten drawn from the membership, one appointee (the chief executive) and up to four invited directors.

The Tea Broker's Association of London

Sir John Lyon House, Upper Thames Street, London EC4A 3LA
Telephone: 01 236 3368/3369
Chairman: L N J Leefe
Vice Chairman: M J Bunston
Secretary: D Mayne

Hours of trading: Auction sales are held each Monday from 10.30 am.

Contract details:
Commodity: Tea.

Trading currency and unit (manner of price quotation): Pence per kilogram.

Trading unit: Auction lot size may vary, minimum normally 20 packages, approximately 1000kg landed weight.

Quality: Sales are against sample of each individual lot.

Delivery points: Landed auctions - ex UK warehouses; CIF auctions - UK ports.

Clearing house: Tea Auction Services Limited.

Membership: Full - auctioneers; associate - others.

Commission rates and margins: Landed auctions - 1.75%; CIF auctions - 2.00%.

Date of establishment of market: 18 April 1890.

Volume of trading:
1987 - 56,800,000kg
1988 - 45,900,000kg

Membership of other organizations: United Kingdom Tea Association.

UNITED STATES OF AMERICA

CHICAGO

Chicago Board of Trade

141 West Jackson Boulevard, Chicago, Illinois 60604
Telephone: 312 435 3500   *Telex:* (100) 253223   *Fax:* 312 435 7170
Chairman: K Mahlman
President: T R Donovan

European office:
52–54 Gracechurch Street, London EC3V 0EH
Telephone: 01 929 0021   *Telex:* 941 3558   *Fax:* 01 929 0558
Vice-President and Managing Director: P F Donnelly

Asia-Pacific office:
Imperial Tower 6-A-12, 1-1-1 Uchisaiwaicho, Chiyoda-ku, Tokyo 100
Telephone: 03 593 2600   *Fax:* 03 593 8013
Vice-President and General Manager: W D Grossman

Hours of trading:
Futures:

Corn –	09.30–13.15
Oats –	09.30–13.15
Soybean –	09.30–13.15
Soybean meal –	09.30–13.15
Soybean oil –	09.30–13.15
Wheat –	09.30–13.15
Kilo gold –	07.20–13.40
100oz gold –	07.20–13.40*
100oz silver –	07.25–13.25
5000oz silver –	07.25–13.25*
CBOE 250 index –	08.30–15.15
Major market index –	08.15–15.15
Municipal bond index –	07.20–14.00
US treasury bond –	07.20–14.00**
US treasury note –	07.20–14.00**
Five-year treasury note –	07.20–14.00
30-day interest rate –	07.20–14.00 (Central standard time)

Options:

Corn	- 09.30–13.15
Soybean	- 09.30–13.15
Soybean meal	- 09.30–13.15
Soybean oil	- 09.30–13.15
Wheat	- 09.30–13.15
1000oz silver	- 07.25–13.25
Municipal bond index	- 07.20–14.00
US treasury bond	- 07.20–14.00**
US treasury note	- 07.20–14.00**

* Evening trading hours are 17.00–20.30 (CST) or 18.00–21.00 (CST) Sunday to Thursday.
** Evening trading hours are 17.00–20.30 (CST) or 18.00–21.30 (CST) Sunday to Thursday.

Contract details:
Commodities: Corn, oat, soybean, soybean meal, soybean oil, wheat, kilo gold, 100oz gold, 1000oz silver, 5000oz silver, CBOE 250 index, major market index, municipal bond index, US treasury bond, US treasury note, five-year treasury note and 30-day interest rate futures contracts; options on the corn, soybean, soybean meal, soybean oil, wheat, 1000oz silver, municipal bond index, US treasury bond and US treasury note futures contracts.

Clearing house: Board of trade clearing corporation.

Membership:
Full memberships: 1402; provide individual access to all CBOT markets.

Associate memberships: 722; provide access to financial instruments, and gold futures.

Delegates: Persons who qualify may obtain the trading privileges of full members or associate members through leasing as delegates.

Membership interests: Provide access to the following markets:
Government Instruments Market (GIM; 245) – bonds, GNMA, notes;
Index, Debt and Energy Market (IDEM; 565) – gold and stock indexes;
Commodity Options Market (COM; 583) – Treasury bond options and soybean futures options, corn futures options, Treasury note options and silver futures options. Membership interests confer trading privileges on the holders but no voting rights.

Agricultural futures contracts:

Contract details

Contract	Unit of trading	Contract standard	Delivery months	Delivery day
Corn	5000 bushels	No 2 yellow at par	Dec, Mar, May, July, Sept	Last business day of delivery month
Oats	5000 bushels	No 2 heavy and no 1 at par	July, Sept, Dec, Mar, May	Last business day of delivery month
Soybeans	5000 bushels	No 2 yellow at par	Sept, Nov, Jan, Mar, May, July, Aug	Last business day of delivery month
Soybean meal	100 tons (2000lbs/ton)	One grade only with 44% min protein	Oct, Dec, Jan, Mar, May, July, Aug, Sept	Fifth business day preceding last business day
Soybean oil	60,000lbs	One grade crude only	Oct, Dec, Jan, Mar, May, July, Aug, Sept	Last business day of delivery month
Wheat	5000 bushels	No 2 soft red, no 2 hard red winter, no 2 dark northern spring, no 1 northern spring at par	July, Sept, Dec, Mar, May	Last business day of delivery month

Last trading day	Quotation	Minimum price movement	Tick size and value
Seven business days before last business day	Cents and quarter cents per bushel	10 cents per bushel ($500 per contract)	1/4 cent per bushel ($12.50 per contract)
Same	Cents and quarter cents per bushel	10 cents per bushel ($500 per contract)	1/4 cent per bushel ($12.50 per contract)
Same	Cents and quarter cents per bushel	30 cents per bushel ($1500 per contract)	1/4 cent per bushel ($12.50 per contract)
Same	Dollars and cents per ton	$10 per ton ($1000 per contract)	10 cents per ton ($10 per contract)
Same	Dollars and cents per hundredweight	1 cent per lb ($600 per contract)	1/100 cent per lb ($6 per contract)
Same	Cents and quarter cents per bushel	20 cents per bushel ($1000 per contract)	1/4 cent per bushel ($12.50 per contract)

Metals futures contracts:

Contract	Unit of trading	Contract standard	Contract months	Delivery method
Kilo gold	1kg (32.15 troy ounces)	One bar, refined, 995 fineness, of approved brand	Current month, next two calendar months, Feb, April, June, Aug, Oct, Dec	By receipt issued by approved vault in Chicago or New York
100oz gold	100 troy ounces	One 100oz bar or three 1kg bars assaying not less than 995 fineness, not more than 5% variation in weight	Same	By receipt issued by approved vault in Chicago or New York
1000oz silver	1000 troy ounces	Refined, assaying not less than 999 fineness, not more than 12% variation in weight	Same	By receipt drawn on deposits in approved vaults in Chicago
5000oz silver	5000 troy ounces	Refined, in four or five bars of 1000 or 1100oz (10% tolerance), of not less than 999 fineness, not more than 6% variation in weight	Same	By receipt issued by approved vault in Chicago or New York

UNITED STATES OF AMERICA

Last trading day	Quotation	Minimum price movement	Tick size and value
No trades deliverable in current month shall be made during last three business days of that month	Dollars and cents per troy ounce	$50 per troy ounce ($1607.50 per contract)	10 cents per troy ounce ($3.22 per contract)
Same	Same	$50 per troy ounce ($5000 per contract)	10 cents per troy ounce ($10 per contract)
Same	Same	$1 per troy ounce ($1000 per contract)	10/100 cent per troy ounce ($1 per contract)
Same	Same	$1 per troy ounce ($5000 per contract)	1/10 cent per troy ounce ($5 per contract)

Financial futures contracts:

Contract	Unit of trading	Settlement	Contract months
CBOE 250 index	$500 times the value of the CBOE	Marked-to-market daily according to closing prices. At expiration positions are cash settled according to value of underlying index	First three consecutive months and next three in Mar, June, Sept, Dec quarterly cycle
Major market index (MMI)	$250 times the value of the MMI	Marked-to-market daily according to closing MMI futures prices, settled in cash at closing value of MMI on last trading day	Monthly
Municipal bond index	$1000 times 'Bond Buyer' Municipal bond index	Cash equal to 'Bond Buyer' index value on last trading day	Mar, June, Sept, Dec
30-day interest rate	$5,000,000	Cash settled against average daily Fed Funds Rate for delivery month	First seven calendar months in Mar, June, Sept, Dec cycle following last spot month

Contract	Unit of trading	Contract standard	Delivery method
US treasury bonds	$100,000 face value	Maturing at least 15 years from first day of delivery month, 8% coupon	Federal Reserve book-entry wire transfer system
US treasury notes	$100,000 face value	Maturing at least 6½, but not more than 10, years from first day of delivery month, 8% coupon	Same
Five-year treasury note	$100,000 face value	Any of the four most recently auctioned notes of original maturity not more than 5 years and 3 months, not less than 4 years and 3 months remaining	Same

Last trading day	Quotation	Minimum price movement	Tick size and value
First business day prior to first Saturday following third Friday of month	Points ($500) and increments of 0.05 of a point	50 index points above previous days price; initial limit of 30 index points below*	0.05 of an index point ($25 per contract)
Third Friday of delivery month	Points ($250) and increments of 0.05 of a point	—	0.05 of an index point ($12.50 per contract)
Eighth to last business day of delivery month	Points ($1000) and thirty-seconds of a point	Three points ($3000) per contract	1/32 of a point ($31.25 per contract)
Last business day of delivery month	$41.67 per basis point, daily price limit of 150 basis points	1/100 of 1% of $5 million	100 minus the monthly average overnight FF Rate
Seven business days prior to last business day of delivery month	Points ($1000) and thirty-seconds of a point	Three points ($3000) per contract)	1/32 of a point ($31.25 per contract)
Seven business days prior to last business day of delivery month	Points ($1000) and thirty-seconds of a point	Three points ($3000) per contract	1/32 of a point ($31.25 per contract)
Eighth to last business day of delivery month	Percent of par in increments of 1/32 of a point	Three points ($3000) per contract (expandable to $4\frac{1}{2}$ points)	1/64 of a point ($15.625 per contract)

* For prices below the previous day's settlement price, coordinated price limits and trading halts will be based on 250- and 400-point declines in the Dow Jones Industrial Average.

Agricultural Options:

Contract	Unit of trading	Contract months	Expiration
Corn	One futures contract of 5000 bushels	Mar, May, July, Sept, Dec	Unexercised options expire at 10.00 on first Saturday following last day of trading
Soybeans	One soybean futures contract of 5000 bushels	Jan, Mar, May, July, Aug, Sept, Nov	Same
Soybean meal	One soybean meal futures contract of 100 tons	Jan, Mar, May, July, Aug, Sept, Oct, Dec	Same
Soybean oil	One soybean oil futures contract of 60,000lbs	Jan, Mar, May, July, Aug, Sept, Oct, Dec	Same
Wheat	One wheat futures contract of 5000 bushels	Mar, May, July, Sept, Dec	Same

Last trading day	Strike price	Minimum price movement	Tick size and value
Last Friday preceding first notice day of corresponding contract by at least 5 business days	Integral multiples of 10 cents per bushel	10 cents per bushel ($500 per contract)	1/8 cent per bushel ($6.25 per contract)
Same	Integral multiples of 25 cents per bushel	30 cents per bushel ($1500 per contract)	1/8 cent per bushel ($6.25 per contract)
Same	Integral multiples of $5 per ton if futures price less than $200 per ton; $10 if price equal to or greater than $200	$10 per ton ($1000 per contract)	5 cents per ton ($5 per contract)
Same	Integral multiples of 1 cent per lb	1 cent per lb ($600 per contract)	5/1000 of a cent per lb ($3 per contract)
Same	Integral multiples of 10 cents per bushel	20 cents per bushel ($1000 per contract)	1/8 cent per bushel ($6.25 per contract)

Contract details: metals and financial options

Contract	Unit of trading	Quotation	Contract months	Expiration
1000oz silver	One silver futures contract of 1000oz	Multiples of 1/10 cent per troy ounce ($1 per contract)	Feb, April, June, Aug, Oct, Dec	10.00 first Saturday following last day of trading
Municipal bond index	One municipal bond index futures contract	Points ($1000) and 1/64 of a point	Mar, June, Sept, Dec	Unexercised options expire 20.00 last day of trading
US treasury bonds	$100,000 face value US treasury bond futures	Same	Same	10.00 first Saturday following last day of trading
US treasury notes	$100,000 face value US treasury note futures	Same	Same	Same

Last trading day	Strike price	Exercise	Minimum price movement	Tick size and value
Last Friday preceding first notice day of corresponding futures contract	Integral multiples of 1/4 cent per ounce for prices of less than $8; 1/2 cent for $8 to $20; $1 for $20 or more	—	1/10 cent per troy ounce ($1 per contract)	10/100 cent per ounce ($1 per contract)
14.00 on last trading day of corresponding futures contract	Integral multiples of 2 points ($2000) to bracket current Muni-bond futures price	20.00 any business day up to and including expiration day	3 points ($3000) per contract	1/64 of a point ($15.63 per contract)
Noon on last Friday preceding by at least 5 business days the first notice day of corresponding futures	Integral multiples of 2 points per contract to bracket current futures price	Same	Same	Same
Same	Integral multiples of 1 point per contract to bracket current futures price	Same	Same	Same

Margins:

Futures contract	Initial		Maintenance		Hedge	
			($ per contract)			
Corn	600	(900)	400	(600)	400	(600)
Oats	700	(1050)	500	(750)	500	(750)
Soybean	1500	(2250)	1250	(1875)	1250	(1875)
Soybean meal	1000	(1500)	800	(1200)	800	(1200)
Soybean oil	600	(900)	500	(750)	500	(750)
Wheat	800	(1200)	500	(750)	500	(750)
Kilo gold	500	(750)	300	(450)	300	(450)
100oz gold	1250	(1875)	1000	(1500)	1000	(1500)
1000oz silver	350	(525)	250	(375)	250	(375)
5000oz silver	1750	(2625)	1250	(1875)	1250	(1875)
CBOE 250 index	4000	–	2000	–	2000	–
Major market index	4000	–	2000	–	2000	–
Municipal bond index	1250	(1875)	750	(750)	750	(1125)
US treasury bond	2000	(3000)	1500	(2250)	1500	(2250)
US treasury note	1500	(2250)	1000	(1500)	1000	(1500)
Five-year treasury note	1250	(1875)	1000	(1500)	1000	(1500)
30-day interest rate	800	(1200)	600	(900)	600	(900)

(Figures in parentheses are the minimum margin requirements which go into effect when variable limits are imposed.)

Date of establishment of contracts:
Futures:

Corn – 2 January 1877
Oats – 2 January 1877
Soybean – 5 October 1936
Soybean meal – 19 August 1951
Soybean oil – 17 July 1950
Wheat – 2 January 1877
Kilo gold – 12 April 1983
100oz gold – 14 September 1987
1000oz silver – 16 March 1981
5000oz silver – 14 September 1987
CBOE 250 index – 11 November 1988
Major market index – 6 August 1985
Municipal bond index – 11 June 1985
US treasury bond – 22 August 1977
US treasury note – 3 May 1982
Five-year treasury note – 20 May 1988
30-day interest rate – 3 October 1988

Options:

Corn – 27 February 1985
Soybean – 31 October 1984

Soybean meal - 19 February 1987
Soybean oil - 19 February 1987
Wheat - 17 November 1986
1000oz silver - 29 March 1985
Municipal bond index - 11 June 1987
US treasury bond - 1 October 1982
US treasury note - 1 May 1985

Date of establishment of the market: 1848.

Volume of trading:

	1987	1988	% change
Futures			
Corn	7,253,212	11,105,516	+ 75.1
Oats	291,108	354,578	+ 21.8
Soybean	7,378,760	12,497,096	+ 69.4
Soybean meal	3,797,970	5,313,081	+ 39.9
Soybean oil	3,912,417	4,896,194	+ 25.1
Wheat	1,929,306	3,377,738	+ 75.1
Kilo gold	159,627	103,335	- 35.3
100oz gold	24,893	84,965	+241.3
1000oz silver	509,965	481,566	- 5.6
5000oz silver	12,092	4,165	- 65.6
CBOE 250 index	-	55,840	-
Major market index	2,630,887	1,175,531	- 55.3
Municipal bond index	1,613,107	1,274,316	- 21.0
US treasury bond	66,841,474	70,307,872	+ 5.2
US treasury note	5,253,791	5,200,949	- 1.0
Five-year treasury note	-	505,595	-
30-day interest rate	-	19,476	-
GNMA (CDR)	7,583	-	-
Corporate bond index	10,591	49	- 99.5
Institutional	175	-	-
Options			
Corn	661,519	1,591,223	+140.5
Soybean	1,242,072	3,245,134	+161.3
Soybean meal	81,213	172,428	+112.3
Soybean oil	85,735	124,131	+ 44.8
Wheat	124,598	445,575	+257.6
1000oz silver	10,009	8,303	- 17.0
Municipal bond index	118,632	171,788	+ 44.8
US treasury bond	21,720,402	19,509,425	- 10.2
US treasury note	1,421,852	1,011,626	- 28.9
Totals	127,092,990	143,038,495	+ 12.5

Further information: Discussions with the Tokyo Stock Exchange (TSE) have led to an agreement for mutual assistance by each of the respective exchanges in introducing new contracts. For the CBOT it means that the TSE will assist in opening a Japanese government bond contract and a TOPIX stock index futures contract based on the first tier of companies listed on the TSE. Final agreement is still pending with the London International Financial Futures Exchange (LIFFE) on ways the two exchanges can better serve customer and member needs together.

Chicago Mercantile Exchange (International Monetary Market, Index and Options Market)

30 South Wacker Drive, Chicago, Illinois 60606
Telephone: 312 930 1000   *Telex:* 210214   *Fax:* 312 930 3439
President & Chief Executive Officer: W J Broksky
Chairman, Executive Committee: Leo Melamed
PR/Information: Andrew Yemma

Hours of trading:

Commodity	Hours	Months
Live cattle	9.05–13.00	Feb and alt months
Feeder cattle	9.05–13.00	Jan, Mar, Apr, May, Aug, Sept, Oct, Nov
Live hogs	9.10–13.00	Feb, Apr, Jun, Jul, Aug, Oct, Dec
Pork bellies	9.10–13.00	Feb, Mar, May, Jul, Aug
Standard & Poor 500 Index	8.30–15.15	Mar, Jun, Sep, Dec
US Treasury Bills	7.20–14.00	Mar, Jun, Sept, Dec
Eurodollars	7.20–14.00	Mar, Jun, Sept, Dec
Australian dollars	7.20–14.00	Jan, Mar, Apr, Jun, Jul, Sept, Oct, Dec
Swiss franc	7.20–14.00	Jan, Mar, Apr, Jun, Jul, Sept, Oct, Dec
Deutschmark	7.20–14.00	Jan, Mar, Apr, Jun, Jul, Sept, Oct, Dec
Canadian dollar	7.20–14.00	Jan, Mar, Apr, Jun, Jul, Sept, Oct, Dec
British pound	7.20–14.00	Jan, Mar, Apr, Jun, Jul, Sept, Oct, Dec
Japanese yen	7.20–14.00	Jan, Mar, Apr, Jun, Jul, Sept, Oct, Dec
French franc	7.20–14.00	Jan, Mar, Apr, Jun, Jul, Sept, Oct, Dec

Lumber	9.00–13.05	Jan and alt months
Gold	7.20–14.00	Jan, Mar, May, Jul, Sept, Dec
US Treasury bills	7.20–14.00	Mar, Jun, Sept, Dec
Standard & Poor's 500	8.30–15.15	Mar, June, Sept, Dec/Serial months
Deutschmark options	7.20–14.00	Mar, Jun, Sept, Dec/Serial months
Live cattle options	9.05–13.00	Feb and alt months
British pound options	7.20–14.00	Mar, Jun, Sept, Dec/Serial months
Swiss franc options	7.20–13.16	Mar, Jun, Sept, Dec
Live hog options	9.10–13.00	Feb, Apr, Jun, Jul, Aug, Oct, Dec
Eurodollar options	7.20–14.00	Mar, Jun, Sept, Dec
Pork bellies options	9.10–13.00	Feb, Mar, May, Jul
Feeder cattle options	9.05–13.00	Jan, Mar, Apr, May, Aug, Sep, Oct, Nov
Canadian dollar options	7.20–14.00	Mar, Jun, Sep, Dec/Serial months
Japanese yen options	7.20–14.00	Mar, Jun, Sept, Dec/Serial months
Lumber options	9.00–13.05	Jan and serial months

* Currency and Eurodollar futures also traded on spot month.

Contract details:

Commodities: Chicago Mercantile Exchange: pork bellies, live hogs, live cattle, feeder cattle, lumber.

International Monetary Market (IMM): British pound, Canadian dollar, Deutschmark, French franc, Japanese yen, Swiss franc, US Treasury bill, Eurodollar, Australian dollar

Index and Option Market (IOM): S&P 500 Stock Index futures, live cattle options, live hog options, pork bellies options, feeder cattle options, Canadian dollar options, British pound options, Deutschmark options, Swiss franc options, Japanese yen options, Eurodollar options, S&P 500 options, US Treasury Bill options, lumber options.

Singapore International Monetary Exchange (SIMEX): Deutschmark, Japanese yen, gold bullion, Eurodollar.

Trading unit and tick size:

Commodity	Size	Tick size
Live cattle	40,000lbs	$10.00
Feeder cattle	44,000lbs	$11.00
Live hogs	30,000lbs	$ 7.50
Pork bellies	40,000lbs	$10.00
Standard and Poor 500 Index	$500 × Index	$25.00

US Treasury Bills	$1,000,000	$25.00
Eurodollars	$1,000,000	$25.00
Australian dollars	A$100,000	$10.00
Swiss franc	Swf125,000	$12.50
Deutschmark	DM125,000	$12.50
Canadian dollar	C$100,000	$10.00
British pound	£25,000	$12.50
Japanese yen	¥12,500,000	$12.50
French franc	FF250,000	$12.50
Lumber	$150,000bd/ft	$15.00
Gold	$100 troy oz	$10.00
US Treasury bills options	$1,000,000	$25.00
Deutschmark options	DM125,000	$12.50
Live cattle options	40,000lbs	$10.00
British pound options	£25.000**	$12.50
Swiss franc options	Swf125,000	$12.50
Live hog options	30,000lbs	$ 7.50
Eurodollar options	$1,000,000	$25.00
Pork bellies options	40,000lbs	$10.00
Feeder cattle options	44,000lbs	$11.00
Canadian dollar options	C$100,000	$10.00
Japanese yen options	¥12,500,000	$12.50
Lumber options	$150,000bd/ft	$15.00

** Effective with September 1988 contract, size if £62,500.

Membership: The 24-member Board of Governors establishes and maintains policy for the Exchange. The Board comprises six public members and 18 members of the Exchange and its two divisions, the International Monetary Market and the Index and Option Market.

In the early part of 1986 the Exchange had more than 2724 full individual members comprising CME 625; IMM 812; and the IOM 1287. On 7 September 1984, the CME and SIMEX began trading operations under a mutual offset system with the 3-month Eurodollar deposit, Japanese yen and Deutschmark futures contract being mutually offsetable. Further details on membership can be obtained by writing to the Membership Department or phoning 01-920 0722.

Date of establishment of the market: The Chicago Mercantile Exchange was founded in 1919. The Exchange pioneered trading in livestock futures and financial futures, two of the industry's most active areas.

MidAmerica Commodity Exchange

141 West Jackson Boulevard, Chicago, Illinois 60606
Telephone: 312 341 3000
President: T R Donovan

The MidAmerica Commodity Exchange is affiliated to the Chicago Board of Trade. The MidAm futures and options contracts listed below are traded on the floor of the CBOT.

Hours of trading:
Futures:

Live hogs – 09.10-13.15
Live cattle – 09.05-13.15
Corn – 09.30-13.45
Wheat – 09.30-13.45
Oats – 09.30-13.45
Soybeans – 09.30-13.45
Soybean meal – 09.30-13.45
NY Gold – 07.20-13.40
NY Silver – 07.25-13.40
Platinum – 07.20-13.40
Treasury bonds – 07.20-15.15
Treasury bills – 07.20-14.15
Treasury notes – 07.20-15.15
Deutschmark – 07.20-14.15
Pound sterling – 07.20-14.15
Swiss franc – 07.20-14.15
Japanese yen – 07.20-14.15
Canadian dollar – 07.20-14.15

Options:

Soybeans – 09.30-13.45
Wheat – 09.30-13.45
Gold – 07.20-13.40

Contract details:
Commodities: Corn, oats, soybeans, wheat, soybean meal, options on wheat futures, options on soybean futures, live cattle, live hogs, gold, options on gold futures, silver, copper, platinum, Treasury bonds, Treasury bills, Pounds sterling, Canadian dollars, Swiss francs, Japanese yen and Deutschmarks, Treasury notes.

Live hogs
Trading unit (minimum lot size): 15,000lbs.

Trading limits:
Minimum price fluctuation – $0.00025 (1/4000 cent) per lb ($3.75 per contract).
Daily price limit – 1-1/2 cent per lb ($225 per contract).
Speculative position limits – 400 contracts in any one month, 800 contracts in all months combined.

Quality: USDA No 1-3, barrows and gilts. Average weight of delivery unit and at least 45 hogs must fall into the 210-240lb weight range. Hogs under 210 but not 200 and over 240 but not 250 are deliverable at a 50 cent discount/cwt. Hogs under 200 or over 250 shall not be deliverable. (Effective 8/86 and subsequent contracts.)

Delivery points: Stockyards at par: Peoria, IL.
Stockyards at a discount:

$0.25	*$0.50*	*$0.75*
Omaha, NE	Kansas City, MO	S St Paul, MO

E St Louis, IL   St Joseph, MO
Sioux City, IA   Sioux Falls, SD

Delivery months: February, April, June, July, August, October, December.

Live cattle
Trading unit (minimum lot size): 20,000lbs.

Trading limits:
Minimum price fluctuation – $0.00025 cent per lb ($5.00 per contract).
Daily price limit – 1-1/2 cent per lb ($300 per contract).
Speculative position limits – 600 contracts in any delivery month. Limits do not apply to bona fide hedging transactions.

Quality: USDA choice steers yield Nos 1, 2, 3, 4. A maximum of two head of No 4 choice steers are deliverable at par. Yield No 4 choice steers in excess of two through a maximum of four head are deliverable at a 15% discount. Up to four head of good grade steers may be included at a 3 cents per lb discount. Cattle must average between 1050 and 1200lbs. Steers weighing between 100–200lbs over or under the average are deliverable at a 3 cent per lb discount; no animal may weigh more than 200lbs over or under average, and no animal weighing less than 950lbs or more than 1300lbs is deliverable.

Par delivery units containing steers with average weight between 1050 and 1125.5lbs must have an estimated average hot yield of 62%, while units averaging between 1125.6 and 1200lbs must have a hot yield 63%. Units with average hot yield under par are deliverable at a 1/2 cent per lb discount for each 0.5% or less by which the estimated yield is under par, provided that no units with an average hot yield of less than 60% are deliverable.

Delivery points: Stockyards at par: Peoria, IL, Amarillo, TX, Sious City, IA, Greeley, CO, Omaha, NE, Dodge City, KS.

Delivery months: February, April, June, August, September, October, December.

Corn
Trading unit (minimum lot size): 1000 bushels.

Trading limits:
Minimum price fluctuation – 1/8 cent per bushel ($1.25 per contract).
Daily price limit – $0.10 per bushel ($100 per contract).
Speculative position limits – 3 million bushels in any one month, net 3 million in all delivery months combined.

Quality: No 2 yellow corn is deliverable at par. No 1 yellow corn is deliverable at a 1/2 cent per bushel premium. No 3 yellow corn is deliverable at a 1-1/2 cent per bushel discount.

Delivery points: By warehouse receipt issued by an Exchange-approved elevator in Chicago or Burns Harbor, IN at par, and at St Louis, MO, Toledo, OH, East St Louis, IL and Alton, IL at a 4 cent per bushel discount.

Delivery months: March, May, July, September, December.

Wheat
Trading unit (minimum lot size): 1000 bushels.

Trading limits:
Minimum price fluctuation – 1/8 cent per bushel ($1.25 per contract).
Daily price limit – $0.20 per bushel ($200 per contract).
Speculative position limits – 3 million bushels in any one month, net 3 million in all delivery months combined.

Quality: No 2 soft red, No 2 hard red winter, No 2 dark northern spring and No 1 northern spring wheat is deliverable at par. No 1 soft red, No 1 hard red winter, and No 1 dark northern spring is deliverable at a 1 cent per bushel premium. No 3 soft red, No 3 hard red winter, No 3 dark northern spring and No 2 northern spring is deliverable at a 1 cent per bushel discount. Wheat containing moisture in excess of 13.5% is not deliverable.

Delivery points: By warehouse receipt issued by an Exchange-approved elevator in Chicago or Burns Harbor, IN at par, and at Toledo, OH at a 2 cent per bushel discount.

Delivery months: March, May, July, September, December.

Oats
Trading unit (minimum lot size): 1000 bushels.

Trading limits:
Minimum price fluctuation – 1/8 cent per bushel ($1.25 per contract).
Daily price limit – $0.10 per bushel ($100 per contract).
Speculative position limits – 2 million bushels in any one month, net 2 million in all delivery months combined.

Quality: No 2 heavy and NO 1 at par; No 1 heavy at 3 cents premium; No 2 extra heavy at 4 cents premium; No 1 extra heavy at 7 cents premium; No 2 34lb minimum test weight at 6 cents discount; No 2 36lb minimum test weight at 3 cents discount.

Delivery points: By warehouse receipt issued by an Exchange-approved elevator in Chicago or Burns Harbor, IN at par, and at Minneapolis or St Paul, MN, at a 7-1/2 cent per bushel discount.

Delivery months: March, May, July, September, December.

Soybeans
Trading unit (minimum lot size): 1000 bushels.

Trading limits:
Minimum price fluctuation – 1/8 cent per bushel ($1.25 per contract).
Daily price limits – $0.30 per bushel ($300 per contract).
Speculative position limits – 3 million bushels in any one month, net 3 million in all delivery months combined.

Quality: US No 2 yellow soybeans are deliverable at par. US No 1 yellow soybeans are deliverable at a 3 cent per bushel premium. US No 3 yellow soybeans (all factors equal to No 2 or better except foreign material) are deliverable at a 4 cent per bushel discount and US No 3 yellow soybeans (14% or less moisture) at an 8 cent per bushel discount.

Delivery points: By warehouse receipt issued by an Exchange-approved elevator in Chicago or Burns Harbor, Indiana at par, and at Toledo at an 8 cent per bushel discount.

Delivery months: January, March, May, July, August, September, November.

Soybean meal

Trading unit (minimum lot size): 20 tons of 44% protein soybean meal, basis bulk, Decatur, IL.

Trading limits:
Minimum price fluctuation – Prices are quoted in dollars per ton, in multiples of ten cents per ton ($2 per contract).
Daily price limits – $10 per ton ($200 per contract). No daily limits in the spot month.
Speculative position limits – 2000 contracts prior to the spot month.
Spot month limits for hedge and speculative accounts – 600 contracts effective one business day prior to the spot month and extending through the eighth from the last trading day; thereafter, 200 contracts until the close of business on the fourth from last trading day in the spot month, when such position limits shall be 50 contracts until contract expiration.

Termination of trading: No trading in soybean meal, deliverable in the current month, shall be conducted during the last 12 business days of that month.

Delivery: Each contract which is not offset prior to the expiration of trading shall be offset with the clearing house on the day following the last day of trading at a settlement price calculated by averaging the settlement prices from the last three days of the contract.

Delivery months: January, March, May, July, August, September, October, and December.

Soybean options

Trading unit (minimum lot size): One MidAmerica 1000 bushel soybean futures contract.

Trading limits:
Minimum price fluctuation – 1/8 cent per bushel ($1.25 per contract).
Daily price limit – $0.30 per bushel ($300 per contract).
Speculative position limits – 3000 contracts long or short of the same type (put or call), and 6000 contracts of the same type where excess contracts are components of conversion or reverse-conversion positions.

Termination of trading: 12.15 on the last Friday which precedes by at least ten business days the first notice day for the underlying soybean futures contract.

Exercise: Until 18.00 (Central time) on the last trading day.

Deep-out-of-the-money option: An option whose strike price is more than two plus the number of calendar months remaining until option expiration strike prices distant from the strike price closest to the underlying futures settlement.

Contract months: January, March, May, July, August, September, and November.

Wheat options
Trading unit (minimum lot size): Five MidAmerica wheat futures contracts.

Trading limits:
Minimum price fluctuation – 1/8 cent per bushel ($6.25 per contract).
Strike price increments – $0.10 per bushel. On the first day of trading for any option month, there will be seven stroke prices listed for puts and seven strike prices listed for calls, bracketing the underlying futures price. Strike prices will be added as required according to a predetermined formula.
Prime limits – $0.20 per bushel (same as underlying futures).
Speculative position limits – 600 contracts long or short of the same type (put or call), and 1200 contracts of the same type where excess contracts are components of conversion or reverse-conversion positions.

Termination of trading: The last Friday which precedes by at least ten business days the first notice day for the underlying wheat futures contract.

Exercise: Until 18.00 (Central time) on the last trading day. Upon exercise, option holders receive the appropriate short or long MidAmerica wheat futures contracts by way of a book entry. Writers of options who receive a notice of exercise are assigned the opposite futures position.

Contract months: March, May, July, September, December.

New York gold
Trading unit (minimum lot size): 33.2 fine troy ounces.

Trading limits:
Minimum price fluctuation – $0.10 per fine troy ounce or $3.32 per contract.
Daily price limit – $25 per ounce ($830 per contract). No limit in the spot month. Limit expands after two successive limit days in any contract month.
Speculative position limits – 50,000 troy ounces in any one month, 100,000 troy ounces in all months combined.

Quality: One bar of .995 fineness weight variance of 10%, bearing brands and markings officially approved by the Exchange.

Delivery: By warehouse receipt issued by depositories in New York, as approved by the Exchange.

Delivery months: The current month and any subsequent months, generally up to 12 months in the future. The most frequently traded are February, April, June, August, October, and December.

Gold options
Trading unit (minimum lot size): One MidAmerica gold futures contract.

Trading limits:
Minimum price fluctuation – 10 cents per troy ounce ($3.32 per contract).
Strike price increments –
$10/oz apart for strike prices below $300
$20/oz apart for strike prices between $300–$500
$30/oz apart for strike prices between $500–$800
$40/oz apart for strike prices above $800

On the first day of trading for any option, there will be five strike prices listed each for puts and calls, bracketing the underlying futures price. Strike prices will be added as required according to a predetermined formula.

Speculative position limits – 2000 contracts long or short of same type (put or call), and 4000 contracts of the same type where the excess contracts are components of conversion or reverse-conversion positions.

Termination of trading: Noon on the second Friday of the month prior to expiration of underlying futures contract.

Exercise: Until 18.00 (Central time) on any business day for which the option is listed for trading. Upon exercise, option holders receive the appropriate short or long MidAmerica gold futures contract(s) by way of a book entry. Writers of options who receive a notice of exercise are assigned the opposite futures position.

Delivery months: February, April, June, August, October, December.

New York silver
Trading unit (minimum lot size): 1000 troy ounces.

Trading limits:
Minimum price fluctuation – 10/100 cents per troy ounce ($1.00 per 1000 ounce contract).
Daily price limit – $0.50 per ounce ($500 per contract), except during the current or spot month, when daily price limits are removed.
Speculative position limits – 1.5 million troy ounces in any one month, 3 million in all months combined.

Quality: Refined silver in a bar cast in a basic weight of either 1000 or 1100 troy ounces (varying in weight no more than plus or minus 10%), assaying in weight not less than .999 fineness, and bearing one of the brands and markings officially listed by the Exchange.

Delivery: By warehouse receipt issued by depositories in New York, as approved by the Exchange.

Delivery months: Current month and any subsequent months.

Platinum
Trading unit (minimum lot size): 25 fine troy ounces.

Trading limits:
Minimum price fluctuation – $0.10 per fine troy ounce ($2.50 per contract).
Maximum daily price fluctuation – $25 per ounce ($625 per contract). No limit in the spot month.
Speculative position limits – 500 contracts in the spot month, 3000 in any one month and 3000 in all months combined.

Quality: One ingot or plate of .999 fineness, weight variance of 4%, bearing brands and markings officially approved by the Exchange.

Delivery: By warehouse receipt issued by depositories in New York as approved by the Exchange.

Delivery notices of intention to deliver must be tendered to the Clearing House by 12.00 noon on the day immediately prior to delivery.

Termination of trading: There shall be no trading during the last three days of the contract month.

First notice day: First business day of the contract month.

Last notice day: Second business day prior to the end of the contract month.

Delivery months: The spot month and cycle months of January, April, July and October.

Treasury bonds
Trading unit (minimum lot size): US Treasury bonds with a face value at maturity of $50,000.

Trading limits:
Minimum price fluctuation – 1/32 of a percentage point ($15.62 per contract).
Daily price limit – 64/32 of a percentage point ($1000 per contract). No limit in the spot month.
Speculative position limits – $100 million face value net long or short.

Quality: US Treasury bonds maturing at least 15 years from the date of delivery if not callable; if callable, not callable for at least 15 years from date of delivery.

Delivery: Federal Reserve book entry wire transfer system. Invoice is adjusted for coupon rates and term to maturity or call.

Delivery months: March, June, September, December.

Treasury bills
Trading unit (minimum lot size): $500,000 face value US Treasury bills with 90 days until maturity.

Trading limits:
Minimum price fluctuation – One basis point ($12.50 per contract).
Speculative position limits – $200 million face value in any one month, and $400 million face value in all months combined.

Delivery: Contracts outstanding as of the expiration of trading shall be settled in cash at the settlement price of the corresponding International Monetary Market T-bill contract.

Delivery months: March, June, September, December.

Treasury notes
Trading unit (minimum lot size): $50,000 face value US treasury note.

Trading limits:
Minimum price fluctuation – 1/32 of one point ($15.62 per contract).
Speculative position limits – $100 million face value net long or short.

Quality: US treasury notes maturing not less than 61/2 years, not more than 10 years, from first day of delivery month.

Delivery: Federal Reserve book-entry wire transfer system. Invoice price on delivery is adjusted to a standard 8% and actual term to maturity.

Delivery months: March, June, September, December.

Deutschmark
Trading unit (minimum lot size): 62,500 Deutschmarks.

Trading limits:
Minimum price fluctuation – $0.0001 per Deutschmark ($6.25 per contract).
Speculative position limits – Net position of 6000 contracts in one or all months combined.

Delivery: The currency shall be deliverable in the country of issue at a bank approved by the Exchange.

Delivery months: March, June, September, December.

Pound sterling
Trading unit (minimum lot size): £12,500.

Trading limits:
Minimum price fluctuation – $0.0002 per British pound ($2.50 per contract).
Speculative position limits – Net position of 6000 contracts in one or all months combined.

Delivery: The currency shall be deliverable in the country of issue at a bank approved by the Exchange.

Delivery months: March, June, September, December.

Swiss franc
Trading unit (minimum lot size): 62,500 Swiss francs.

Trading limits:
Minimum price fluctuation – $0.0001 per Swiss franc ($6.25 per contract).
Speculative position limits – Net position of 6000 contracts in one or all months combined.

Delivery: The currency shall be deliverable in the country of issue at a bank approved by the Exchange.

Delivery months: March, June, September, December.

Japanese yen
Trading unit (minimum lot size): ¥6,250,000.

Trading limits:
Minimum price fluctuation – $0.000001 per Japanese yen ($6.25 per contract).
Speculative position limits – Net position of 6000 contracts in one or all months combined.

Delivery: The currency shall be deliverable in the country of issue at a bank approved by the Exchange.

Delivery months: March, June, September, December.

Canadian dollar

Trading unit (minimum lot size): 50,000 Canadian dollars.

Trading limits:
Minimum price fluctuation – $0.0001 per Canadian dollar ($5.00 per contract).
Speculative position limits – Net position of 6000 contracts in one or all months combined.

Delivery: The currency shall be deliverable in the country of issue at a bank approved by the Exchange.

Delivery months: March, June, September, December.

Volume of trading:

	1987	1988	% change
Futures			
Live hogs	44,364	34,230	– 22.8
Live cattle	44,112	48,349	+ 9.6
Corn	311,722	429,219	+ 37.7
Wheat	189,610	294,236	+ 55.2
Oats	6,958	12,917	+ 85.6
Soybeans	417,620	863,934	+106.9
Soybean meal	17	—	—
New soybean meal	3,191	8,558	+168.2
Rice	31,114	47,627	+ 53.1
Gold	17,957	14,652	– 18.4
Silver	9,578	12,063	+ 25.9
Platinum	4,342	2,874	– 33.8
Copper	2	—	—
New copper	29	—	—
Treasury bonds	1,015,454	1,414,390	+ 39.3
Treasury bills	25,592	22,203	– 13.2
Treasury notes	—	4,159	—
Deutschmark	85,009	49,993	– 41.2
Pound sterling	10,979	28,240	+157.2
Swiss franc	97,571	77,176	– 20.9
Japanese yen	58,836	44,257	– 24.8
Canadian dollar	7,749	9,282	+ 19.8
Options			
Soybeans	12,317	21,043	+ 70.8
Wheat	530	533	+ 0.6
Gold	74	77	+ 4.1
Totals	2,394,727	3,440,012	+ 43.6

Chicago Rice and Cotton Exchange

The Chicago Rice and Cotton Exchange (CRCE) is affiliated with the MidAmerica Commodity Exchange, therefore the CRCE rough rice futures contract also trades on the floor of the Chicago Board of Trade.

Hours of trading: 09.15–13.30.

Contract details:
Commodity: Rough rice futures.

Trading unit (minimum lot size): 2000 hundredweight.

Trading currency and unit (manner of price quotation): Dollars and cents per hundredweight.

Trading limits:
Minimum price fluctuation – $0.005 per hundredweight ($10 per contract).
Daily price limit – 30 cents per hundredweight ($600 per contract).

Quality: American no 2 or better long grain rough rice with a total milling yield of not less than 65%, including head rice of not less than 48%. Premiums and discounts are provided for each percent of head rice above or below 55% and for each percent of broken rice above or below 15%.

Termination of trading: Noon on the eighth to last business day of delivery month.

Delivery: Last business day of delivery month.

Delivery months: September, November, January, March, May.

Volume of trading: See figures for MidAmerica Commodity Exchange.

KANSAS CITY

Kansas City Board of Trade

4800 Main Street, Suite 303, Kansas City, Missouri 64112
Telephone: 816 753 7500   *Fax:* 816 753 3944
President: M Braude
Chairman: R Stover

Hours of trading:
Wheat – 09.30–13.15
Options on wheat futures – 09.30–13.20
Grain sorghum – 09.30–13.15
Value line – 08.30–15.15
Mini value line – 08.30–15.15

Contract details:
Commodities: Hard red winter wheat futures, hard red winter wheat options, Value Line stock index futures, mini Value Line stock index futures, grain sorghum futures.

Wheat futures
Trading currency and unit (manner of price quotation): cents and quarter cents per bushel.

Trading unit (minimum lot size): 5000 bushels.

Trading limits:
Minimum price fluctuation - 1/4 cent per bushel ($12.50 per contract).
Daily price limit - 25 cents per bushel ($1250 per contract) above and below previous settlement.

Quality: No 2 hard red winter; No 1 and No 3 deliverable at differentials established by the Exchange.

Delivery point: Kansas City.

Delivery instrument: Registered warehouse receipts issued by regular elevators.

Termination of trading: The day prior to the last seven trading days in the delivery month.

Delivery months: March, May, July, September, December.

Wheat options
Trading unit: The option is for one Kansas City wheat futures contract of 5000 bushels hard red winter wheat.

Trading limits:
Minimum price fluctuation - 1/8 cent ($6.25 per contract).
Daily price limit - 25 cents per bushel ($1250 per contract).
Strike price intervals - 10 cents per bushel. List new strikes to maintain 3 above and 3 below futures settlement prices for each contract month. No new strikes added during expiration month. Delist strikes with no trading activity or open interest for ten consecutive days.

Termination of trading: Trading shall end at 13.00 Central time on the Friday which is at least 7 business days prior to the first notice day of the underlying futures contract. (The first notice day for Kansas City wheat futures is the last business day of the month preceding the contract month. For example, the first notice day for July Kansas City wheat futures is the last business day of June.)

Expiration day: 10.00 Central time on the first Saturday following the last trading day.

Exercise procedures: Kansas City wheat options may be exercised at any time during the life of the contract by giving notice to the clearing corporation by 16.00 on any regular business day. Options may be exercised until 10.00 Central time on the expiration date. There is no automatic exercise at expiration.

Reportable positions: A position of 25 puts or 25 calls in a contract month, regardless of the strike price.

Position limits:
Calls: No more than 600 long and 600 short.
Puts: No more than 600 long and 600 short.

Contract months: March, May, July, September, December (same as the underlying futures contract).

Margin: There is no margin required for long option positions, but the full premium must be paid in cash. Margin for short options positions will be the outright margin for the underlying future and the value of the option premium marked to the market.

Grain sorghum
Trading currency and unit (manner and price quotation): Dollars, cents and quarter cents per bushel.

Trading unit (minimum lot size): One 5000 bushel sorghum futures contract of a specified month.

Trading limits:
Minimum price fluctuation - 1/4 cent per bushel ($12.50 per contract).
Daily price limit - 15 cents per bushel ($750 per contract).

Quality: No 1 and no 2 yellow sorghum at contract price; no 3 yellow sorghum at a 5 cent discount, subject to 7% maximum total damage and 10% maximum foreign material.

Delivery points: Kansas City, Topeka, Atchison, St Joseph.

Delivery instrument will be a registered warehouse receipt issued by regular elevators.

Delivery months: March, May, July, September, December.

Termination of trading: The business day prior to the last seven business days of contract month.

KC Value line stock index futures
Trading unit (minimum lot size): $500 × futures price for Maxi futures, $100 × futures price for mini.

Trading limits:
Minimum price fluctuation - 0.05 point.
Daily price limit - 50 points.

Termination of trading: Third Friday of contract month.

Delivery: Settlement price is the actual Value line composite index at the close on last trading day of contract month.

Delivery date is the first business day following the last trading day of contract month.

Delivery months: March, June, September, December.

Margins:

	Maxi	Mini
Hedge		
Initial	$3000	$600
Maintenance	$3000	$600
Speculative		
Initial	$5000	$1000
Maintenance	$3000	$600
Spread – Intramarket		
Initial	$400	$80
Maintenance	$200	$40

Significant dates for futures contracts – 1990:

	Contract month	First notice day	First delivery day	Last trading day	Last notice day	Last delivery day
Hard	March	Feb 28	March 1	March 1	March 29	March 30
winter	May	April 30	May 1	May 1	May 30	May 31
wheat	July	June 29	July 2	July 20	July 30	July 31
	Sept	Aug 31	Sept 4	Sept 19	Sept 27	Sept 28
	Dec	Nov 30	Dec 3	Dec 19	Dec 28	Dec 31
Grain	March	Feb 28	March 1	March 21	March 29	March 30
sorghum	May	April 30	May 1	May 21	May 30	May 31
	July	June 29	July 2	July 20	July 30	July 31
	Sept	Aug 31	Sept 4	Sept 19	Sept 27	Sept 28
	Dec	Nov 30	Dec 3	Dec 19	Dec 28	Dec 31
Value Line	March	—	—	March 16	—	March 16
and mini	June	—	—	June 15	—	June 15
	Sept	—	—	Sept 21	—	Sept 21
	Dec	—	—	Dec 21	—	Dec 21

	Contract month	First notice day	First delivery day	Last trading day	Last notice day	Expiration day
KC wheat	March	—	—	Feb 16	—	Feb 17
options	May	—	—	April 20	—	April 21
	July	—	—	June 22	—	June 23
	Sept	—	—	Aug 24	—	Aug 25
	Dec	—	—	Nov 23	—	Nov 24

Volume of trading:
1986 – 1,729,638
1987 – 1,538,402
1988 – 1,462,932

Membership: To become a member, a person must make an application ($500 fee) and be approved by the Board of Directors. Trading opportunities are available through i) Class 'A' membership – full membership, can trade all futures contracts; ii) Class 'B' membership – limited membership, can only trade in Value Line Stock Index futures contracts and other contracts as specified by the Board of Directors.

Leasing a Class 'A' or 'B' membership allows an individual or firm with limited capital to take advantage of the opportunities provided by membership and work towards full ownership of a Class 'A' or 'B' membership. The lessee is granted all the privileges of membership except voting rights.

Date of establishment of the market:
Corporation – 1856
Wheat futures – 1876
Value Line stock index futures – February 1982
Wheat options – October 1984
Sorghum futures – May 1989

Membership of other organizations: Board of Trade Investment Company; Grain Clearing Company.

MINNEAPOLIS

Minneapolis Grain Exchange

400 South 4th Street, Room 150, 150 Grain Exchange Building, Minneapolis, Hennepin, Minnesota 55415
Telephone: 612 338 6212   *Fax:* 612 339 1155
President: J H Lindow
Chairman of the Board: D E Brummer
Vice-President, treasury: G B Wollan
Vice-President, marketing: J P Wood

Hours of trading:
Spring wheat – 09.30–13.15
White wheat – 09.30–13.15
Oats – 09.00–13.25
Corn syrup – 09.00–13.25
Spring wheat options – 09.35–13.25

Contract details:
Commodities: Spring and white wheat, oats and high fructose corn syrup futures contracts, spring wheat options.

Trading currency and unit (manner of price quotation): Grains futures and spring wheat options – American dollars and cents per bushel; corn syrup – dollars and cents per hundredweight.

Trading unit (minimum lot size): Grains futures and spring wheat options – 5000 bushels (1000 bushel lots of spring wheat are sometimes permissible); corn syrup – 37,000lbs.

Trading limits:

Spring wheat – $0.00125 per bushel minimum price fluctuation; $0.20 maximum

White wheat – $0.0025 per bushel; $0.20

Corn syrup – $0.02 per cwt; $1.00

Spring wheat options – $0.00125 per bushel; $0.20

Quality:

Spring wheat – No 2 northern spring, no 1 dark northern spring or no 1 northern spring, 13.5% pro or better at par, with scale of disc to 13% pro and premium for above 60lb test weight

White wheat – No 1 soft white at par, with no 2 soft white deliverable at $0.01 per bushel disc

Oats – No 2 heavy oats or no 1 oats at par, with scale of premiums and discs for other grades

Corn syrup – 55 HFCS strictly conforming to Society of Soft Drink's technologist's standards for bottlers

Delivery points:

Spring wheat – Minneapolis/St Paul, Duluth, Superior, Red Wing

White wheat – delivered to the Columbia River district, as defined in Exchange rules

Corn syrup – delivered to Chicago within the county of Cook

Oats – Minneapolis/St Paul rail and barge switching district elevators

Delivery months: March, May, July, September, December trading cycle.

Termination of trading: All futures – maturing futures contracts may not be traded during the last seven business days of the delivery month; spring wheat options – trading in an option class shall terminate on the last Friday that precedes by at least five business days the first notice day for the underlying futures contract in spring wheat.

Clearing house: Minneapolis Grain Exchange Clearing House.

Membership: Any person of legal age whose character, credit and reputation for fair dealing are such as to satisfy the directors' membership committee and Board of Directors that the applicant will be a suitable person to entrust with the privileges and responsibilities of membership, and only such persons, shall be eligible to membership in this Association.

Date of establishment of contracts:

Spring wheat – 3 January 1893

Oats – 25 May 1917 (re-established October 1988)

Corn syrup – 6 April 1987

Spring wheat options – October 1984

Date of establishment of the market: 19 October 1881.

Volume of trading:
>Spring wheat futures – 1987 – 1,552,998,000 bushels
>1988 – 2,117,712,000 bushels

Membership of other organizations: National Grain and Feed Association, National Grain Trade Council, Futures Industry Association, National Association of Wheat Growers, National Soft Drinks Association.

NEW YORK

Coffee, Sugar and Cocoa Exchange, Inc

4 World Trade Center, New York, NY 10048
Telephone: 212 938 2800   *Telex:* 12-7066   *Cables:* COSUCOEX
President: B J Corn
Chairman of the Board: C P Nastro
First Vice Chairman: C S Evans
Treasurer: J G Apuzzo

Hours of trading:
>Coffee 'C' – 09.45–14.30
>Sugar no 11 – 10.00–13.45
>Sugar no 14 – 09.40–13.35
>World white sugar – 09.45–13.45
>Cocoa – 09.30–14.15
>International market index – 09.30–16.15
>Coffee options – 09.45–14.45
>Sugar no 11 options – 10.00–14.00
>Cocoa options – 09.30–14.15

Contract details:
Commodities: Coffee 'C', sugar no 11 (world), sugar no 14 (domestic), world white sugar (refined), cocoa, international market index futures, coffee options, sugar options, cocoa options.

Trading currency and unit (manner of price quotation):
>Coffee 'C' – cents per pound
>Sugar no 11 – cents per pound
>Sugar no 14 – cents per pound
>World white sugar – cents per pound
>Cocoa – dollars per ton
>International market index – quoted in points and hundredths of a point. One point equals $250
>Coffee 'C' options – same as futures
>Sugar no 11 options – same as futures
>Cocoa options – same as futures

Trading units (minimum lot size):

Coffee 'C'	- 37,500lbs in approximately 250 bags
Sugar no 11	- 112,000lbs (50 long tons)
Sugar no 14	- 112,000lbs (50 long tons)
World white sugar	- 110,230lbs (50 tonnes)
Cocoa	- 10 tonnes
International market index	- $250 multiplied by the index value
Coffee 'C' option	- one coffee 'C' futures contract
Sugar no 11 option	- one sugar no 11 futures contract
Cocoa option	- one cocoa futures contract

Trading limits:

Coffee 'C' - no daily trading limits. Minimum fluctuation 1/100 cents per pound ($3.75 per contract)

Sugar no 11 - no daily trading limits. Minimum fluctuation 1/100 or 0.01 cents per pound ($11.20 per lot)

Sugar no 14 - no daily trading limits. Minimum fluctuation 1/100 or 0.01 cents per pound ($11.20 per lot)

World white sugar - no daily trading limits. Minimum fluctuations are 20 cents per tonne ($10.00 per contract)

Cocoa - no daily trading limits. Minimum fluctuations are $1.00 tonne ($10.00 per lot)

International market index - no daily limits. Daily prime limit, initial limit of 30 points below and 50 points above the previous day's settlement price

Coffee 'C' option - minimum fluctuation same as the future

Sugar no 11 option - minimum fluctuation same as the future

Cocoa option - minimum fluctuation same as the future

Quality:

Coffee 'C' - determined on the basis of the grade of beans and by dup testing for flavour. If found deliverable, a certificate of Grade and Quality is issued. Since not all coffees are of equal value, the Exchange has established certain differentials when delivery occurs. Certain coffees are used to establish the 'basis'. Coffees judged better than the basis are deliverable at a premium; those judged inferior are deliverable at a discount

Sugar no 11 and Sugar no 14 - raw centrifugal cane sugar based on 96° average polarization

World white sugar - refined or white, beet cane sugar based on minimum 99.8° polarization

Cocoa - grades are established by the Exchange-licensed graders in accordance with specified tolerances or defects, bean count and other standards

Deliverable tolerances:

Coffee 'C'
Growths deliverable at basis: Mexico, Salvador, Guatemala, Costa Rica, New Guinea, Nicaragua, Kenya, Tanzania, and Uganda.

Growths deliverable plus 200 points: Colombia.
Growths deliverable minus 100 points: Honduras, Venezuela.
Growths deliverable minus 300 points: Burundi, India, Rwanda.
Growths deliverable minus 400 points: Dominican Republic, Ecuador.
Growths deliverable minus 700 points: Ethiopia.

The delivery must consist of one growth and must be in sound condition, the soundness requirement meaning that the coffee being delivered has not been damaged by any external cause resulting from, but not limited to, improper storage, shipping or handling.

Imperfections: the foregoing is the basis, or standard, deliverable for these growths. Each growth, however, is allowed a maximum of 23 imperfections, with a differential in deliverable price of 10 points for each full imperfection below basis.

Basis: Colombian coffee (13); Ethiopian coffee (50) and other growths (8).
Maximum below basis: Colombian coffee (10); Ethiopian coffee (10) and other growths (15).
Total imperfections permitted: Colombian coffee (23); Ethiopian coffee (60) and other growths (23).

Sugar no 11
Growths of Argentina, Australia, Barbados, Belize, Brazil, Colombia, Costa Rica, Dominican Republic, El Salvador, Ecuador, Fiji Islands, French Antilles, Guatemala, Honduras, India, Jamaica, Malawi, Mauritius, Mexico, Nicaragua, Peru, Republic of the Philippines, South Africa, Swaziland, Taiwan, Thailand, Trinidad, United States and Zimbabwe delivered FOB and stowed in bulk.

Sugar no 14
Cane sugars of the United States, duty free, foreign origin, duty paid and delivered in bulk.

World white sugar
Sugars manufactured in the country of the delivery port, except in EEC nations where the sugar may be of any EEC manufacturer.

Cocoa
The growth of any country or clime, including new or yet unknown growths. Growths are divided into three classifications: Group A, deliverable at a premium of $160 per ton (including Ghana, Nigeria, Ivory Coast, among others); Group B, deliverable at a premium of $80 per tonne (includes Bahia, Central America, Venezuela, among others) Group C, deliverable at par (includes Sanchez, Haiti, Malaysia and all others). Deliveries are discounted for subnormal size beans.

Delivery points:
> Coffee 'C' – at Exchange-licensed warehouses in port of New York District, and the Port of New Orleans

Sugar no 11 – a port in the country of origin in the case of landlocked countries, at the berth or anchorage in the customary port of export, FOB and stowed in bulk

Sugar no 14 – New York, Galveston, Baltimore, New Orleans, Savannah

World white sugar – Ports of Rotterdam and Flushing (Netherlands), Antwerp (Belgium), Hamburg (Federal Republic of Germany), Dunkirk and Rouen (France), Immingham (United Kingdom), Galveston, New Orleans, Savannah, Baltimore and New York (including Yonkers) (United States), and Recife/Maceio, Imbituba/Itajai and Santos (Brazil), Pusan, Inchon and Ulson (Republic of Korea), and Gdansk/Gdynia (Poland)

Cocoa – at licensed warehouses in the port of New York District, Delaware River Port District, or Port of Hampton Roads

Termination of trading:

Coffee 'C' – the business day that is one day prior to the seven business days prior to the last business day of the business month

Sugar no 11 – the last full business day of the month preceding the delivery month

Sugar no 14 – the eighth calendar day of the month preceding the delivery month. If this day is not a business day then the last trading day shall be the next succeeding business day

World white sugar – fifteenth calendar day of the month preceding the delivery month, or next succeeding business day if 15th calendar day is not a business day

Cocoa – the business day one day prior to the ten business days prior to the last business day of the delivery month

International market index – business day prior to the third Friday of the contract month

Coffee 'C' option – first Friday of the month preceding the contract month

Sugar no 11 option – second Friday of the month preceding the contract month. The one exception is the December/March option, which expires on the second Friday of December

Cocoa option – first Friday of the month preceding the contract month

Delivery months:

Coffee 'C' – March, May, July, September, December

Sugar no 11 – January, March, May, July, October

Sugar no 14 – January, March, May, July, September, November

World white sugar – January, March, May, July, October

Cocoa – March, May, July, September, December

International market index – the current calendar month, immediately following two calendar months, and every March, June, September and December thereafter in a 14-month period from the current calendar month

Coffee 'C' option – same as future

Sugar no 11 – March, May, July, October and first of these months in next year for which futures trading has begun, as well as an options which futures trading had begun, as well as an option which expires in December and calls for delivery of March futures

Cocoa – same as future

Clearing house: CSC Clearing Corporation.

Membership:
527 full memberships – eligible to trade all futures and options contracts listed with the Exchange. Minimum financial requirements (net liquid assets) – $25,000 without floor trading privileges; $125,000 with floor trading privileges. 250 associate memberships – eligible to trade options listed with the Exchange. Minimum financial requirements (net liquid assets) – $25,000 without floor trading privileges; $50,000 with floor trading privileges. Member firms must have minimum net liquid assets of $100,000; associate member firms must have minimum net liquid assets of $50,000. Individuals may be guaranteed by the Exchange members in lieu of meeting the above requirements for individuals.

Date of establishment of the markets:
Coffee, Sugar of the City of New York – 1882
New York Coffee & Sugar Exchange, Inc – 1916
New York Cocoa Exchange – 1925
Coffee, Sugar & cocoa Exchange, Inc – 1979

Volume of trading:
1987 – 6,256,859
1988 – 10,019,644

Membership of other organizations: The CSCE is a member of the Futures Industry Association and the National Futures Association.

Commodity Exchange, Inc (COMEX)

4 World Trade Center, New York, NY 10048
Telephone: 212 938 2900 *Telex:* 12 7066 *Fax:* 212 432 1154
President and Chief Executive Officer: A F Staloff

Hours of trading:
Gold – 08.20–14.30
Silver – 08.25–14.25
Copper – 09.28–14.00
Aluminium – 09.30–14.10

Contract details:

Commodities: Gold, silver, copper and aluminium futures contracts, gold, silver and copper options.

Gold

Trading unit (minimum lot size): 100 troy ounces.

Trading limits:
Minimum price fluctuation – 10 cents per troy ounce ($10 per contract).
Tick size – $0.10.

Quality: Refined gold assaying not less than 995 fineness, cast either in one bar or three 1kg bars (varying in weight by not more than 5%), bearing a serial number and identifying stamp of a refiner approved and listed by COMEX.

Termination of trading: The third last business day of the maturing delivery month.

Delivery months: Current calendar month, next two calendar months, any February April, June, August, October, and December falling within a 23-month period beginning with the current month.

Delivery: The first notice day is the last business day of the month prior to a maturing delivery month.

The last notice day is the penultimate business day of the maturing delivery month.

Silver

Trading unit (minimum lot size): 5000 troy ounces.

Trading limits:
Minimum price fluctuation – 1/10 cent per troy ounce ($5 per contract).
Tick size – $0.001 per troy ounce.

Quality: Refined silver assaying not less than 999 fineness, cast in bars weighing 1000 – 1100 troy ounces each (varying in weight by not more than 6%), bearing a serial number and identifying stamp of a refiner approved and listed by COMEX.

Delivery months: Current calendar month, next two calendar months, any January, March, May, July, September and December falling within a 23-month period beginning with the current month.

Copper

Trading unit (minimum lot size): 25,000lbs.

Trading limits:
Tick size – $0.0005 ($12.50 per contract).

Quality: ASTM-certified grade 1 electrolytic copper cathodes.

COMEX is phasing out the currently traded copper contract by not newly listing any contract months after December 1989, and by delisting any 1989 or later contract months for which open interest is zero.

Termination of trading: Third last business day of the contract month.

Delivery months: January, March, May, July, September, December.

Delivery: First notice day is the last business day of the month, the last notice day the penultimate business day of the month.

Aluminium
Trading unit (minimum lot size): 44,000lbs.

Trading limits:
Minimum price fluctuation – 5/100 cent per lb ($20 per contract).
Tick size – $0.0005.

Quality: Ingots, sows or T-bars of virgin primary aluminium grade P1020A with 99.7% minimum purity, weight varying by not less than 2%.

All deliverable aluminium must either i) bear the brand or distinguishable mark of an approved smelter, or ii) be accompanied by a declaration of a COMEX clearing member as to the origin of the aluminium. Each lot of deliverable aluminium must be accompanied by the producer's heat analysis or by a certificate of analysis from a COMEX-approved assayer.

Termination of trading: Third last business day of a maturing delivery month.

Delivery months: Current calendar month, the next two calendar months, and any January, March, May, July, September and December falling within a 23-month period beginning with the current month.

Delivery: The first notice day is the last business day of a maturing delivery month.

The last notice day is the penultimate business day of a maturing business day.

Gold options
Trading limits:
Minimum price fluctuation – 10 cents per troy ounce ($10 per contract).
Strike price intervals – $10 increments for strike prices below $500; $20 between $501 and $1000; $50 for prices above $1000.

On the first trading day for any option contract month there will be nine strike prices available each for puts and calls. Strike prices will be added on futures price movements.

Expiration: Second Friday of the month prior to the delivery month of the underlying futures contract.

Silver options
Trading limits:
Minimum price fluctuation – 1/10 cent per troy ounce ($5 per contract).
Strike price intervals – 25 cent increments for strike prices below $8; 50 cents between $8 and $15; $1 for prices above $15.

On the first trading day for any option contract month there will be nine strike prices available for puts and calls. Strike prices will be added based on futures price movements.

Expiration: Second Friday of month prior to the delivery month of the underlying futures contract.

Copper options
Trading limits:
Minimum price fluctuation – $0.0005 per lb ($12.50 per contract).
Strike price intervals – $0.01/lb apart for strike prices below $0.40; $0.02/lb
between $0.40 and $1.0; $0.05/lb for prices above $1.0.

Expiration: Second Friday of the month prior to the delivery month of the underlying
futures contract.

Membership: Requirements for full membership are as follows:
i) all applicants must be guaranteed by a PCM in order to execute transactions on the
Exchange floor;
ii) an applicant may become a member through individual seat purchase without a
member firm affiliation;
iii) firms may become members through conferring individuals;
iv) an applicant for membership employed by a member firm may purchase a seat
directly or obtain an ABC agreement through the firm;
v) an applicant may lease a seat from a full member.

Member numbers are: 72 full, 238 option, 148 licensees and 13 aluminium.

Date of establishment of contracts:
Gold – 31 December 1974
Silver – 5 July 1933
Copper – 5 July 1933
Aluminium – 8 December 1983
Gold options – 4 October 1982
Silver options – 4 October 1984

Date of establishment of the market: 5 July 1933.

Volume of trading:
Futures:

Gold	9,496,402
Silver	4,664,655
Copper	2,112,459
High grade copper	924
Aluminium	2,610

Options:

Gold	1,698,696
Silver	872,106
Copper	402,790
High grade copper	2
Total	19,250,644

Further information: COMEX policy is set by a 25 member Board of Governors. In
addition to the Chairman and President, the Board is made up of seven
representatives from each of the Exchange's primary constituencies: commission
houses, trade houses and floor members. Currently, two general or non-member
governors also sit on the Board to represent the public interest.

New York Cotton Exchange

4 World Trade Center, New York, NY 10048
Telephone: 212 938 2702   *Telex:* 961 312   *Fax:* 212 839 8061
President: J J O'Neill
Chairman: D B Conlin
Vice-Chairman: J P Hirsch
Treasurer: P T Jones

Hours of trading: 10.30–15.00.

Contract details:
Commodities: Cotton futures and options.

Trading currency and unit (manner of price quotation): Cents and 1/100 cent per lb.

Trading unit (minimum lot size): 50,000lbs.

Trading limits:
Minimum price fluctuation – 1/100 cent per lb.
Maximum price fluctuation – 2 cents above or below previous day's settlement price.

Quality: Strict low middling 1-1/16 inch.

Delivery months: Galveston, Houston, New Orleans, Memphis, Greenville.

Termination of trading: Last trading day for cotton futures is 17 business days from the end of the spot month; for options the first Friday of the month before delivery month.

Delivery months: March, May, July, October, December.

Clearing house: Commodity Clearing Corporation.

Membership: All seats and licences are bought and sold through a bid/offer system. There are 448 Exchange seats.

Margins:

	Initial				Maintenance			
	outright		straddle		outright		straddle	
	S	H	S	H	S	H	S	H
				(US dollars)				
Cotton	1500	750	200	100	1125	750	150	100
USDX	1000	500	200	200	750	375	150	150
ECU	2500	1250	200	200	1875	937.5	150	150
ESDX/ECU			500	500			375	375
FYTR	1000	500	200	200	750	375	150	150
2YTN	1000	500	200	200	750	375	150	150
FCOJ	1500	750	500	500	1125	563	375	375

S – spec, *H* – hedge

Date of establishment of the markets:
> Cotton futures - 10 September 1870
> Cotton options - 30 October 1984

Volume of trading:

	1987	1988	% change
	(contracts)		
Cotton futures	1,395,980	1,370,249	- 2
options	73,480	124,260	+ 69
USDX futures	403,783	446,525	+ 11
options	14,538	10,525	- 28
ECU futures	42,648	23,936	- 44
FYTR futures	—	789,630	—
options	—	13,479	—
FCOJ futures	236,223	358,039	+ 52
options	2,383	5,873	+146
Totals	2,169,035	3,142,516	+ 45

New York Futures Exchange

10th Floor, 20 Broad Street, New York, NY 10005
Telephone: 212 656 4949   *Fax:* 212 656 2925
President: L J Horowitz

NYSE Composite index futures
Trading unit (minimum lot size): $500 × NYSE Composite index.

Citrus Associates of the New York Cotton Exchange, Inc an affiliate of the New York Cotton Exchange

Hours of trading: 10.15–14.45.

Contract details:
Commodities: Frozen concentrated orange juice (FCOJ) futures and options.

Trading unit and currency (manner of price quotation): Cents and 1/100 cent per lb.

Trading unit (minimum lot size): 15,000lbs.

Trading limits:
Minimum price fluctuation – 5/100 of a cent per lb.
Daily price limit – 5 cents above or below the previous day's settlement.
Spot month limit – 10 cents during last three trading days. Higher limits can take effect under certain market conditions.

Quality: US grade A with a Brix value of not less than 57°, having a Brix value to acid ratio of not less than 13:1, not more than 19:1, with a minimum score of 94.

Termination of trading: Ninth business day prior to last delivery day, where last delivery day is the last business day of the month.

Delivery months: January, March, May, July, September and November.

Delivery points: Exchange-licensed warehouses in Florida.

Membership: Class A members who are members of the New York Cotton Exchange.

Margins: See figures for New York Cotton Exchange.

Date of establishment of the market: FCOJ futures – 26 October 1966, options – 19 December 1985.

Volume of trading: See figures for the New York Cotton Exchange.

Further information: The Citrus Associates of the New York Cotton Exchange have filed an application with the Commodity Futures Trading Commission to introduce a new frozen concentrated orange juice contract, FCOJ-2, designed to complement the existing FCOJ contract. It will provide for delivery of concentrated orange juice that meets a minimum score of 92 under official US standards for grades. Delivery can be made at one of several primary national markets where FCOJ is produced or imported in sufficient supply.

The Financial Instrument Exchange (FINEX) a Division of the New York Cotton Exchange

Hours of trading: 08.20–15.00.

Contract details:
Commodities: American dollar index (USDX) futures and options, European currency unit (ECU), five-year US treasury note (FYTR) futures and options, two-year US treasury note (2YTN) futures.

Trading currency and unit (manner of price quotation):
US dollar index – percentage of its March 1973 value
ECU futures – Cents and 1/100 cent
Base note 100 – to two decimal points

Trading unit (minimum lot sizee):
US dollar index – 500 × index
ECU futures – 100,000 ECUs
Five-year treasury notes – $100,000 face value at maturity
Two-year treasury notes – $200,000 face value

Trading limits:
US dollar index – minimum price fluctuation of 0.01 point ($5 per contract); no daily price limit
ECU futures – minimum price fluctuation of 0.01 cent per ECU ($10 per contract)

Five-year treasury notes – 1/2 of 1/32 of a point ($15.625 per contract); no daily price limit

Two-year treasury notes – 1/4 of 1/32 of a point ($15.625 per contract); no daily price limit

Quality:

Five-year treasury notes – original maturity of 41/2 to 51/2 years at delivery

Two-year treasury notes – original maturity of 1 year 9 months to 5 years 6 months at delivery of 1 year 9 months to 2 years 1 month

Termination of trading:

US dollar index futures – third Wednesday from end of expiring contract month

US dollar index options – two Fridays before the third Wednesday of expiring contract month

ECU futures – three business days prior to third Thursday of expiring contract month

FYTR futures – at 13.00 on eighth last business day of expiring month

FYTR options – the Friday at least five business days prior to the first business day of the expiring month

2YTN futures – at 13.00 on the eighth last business day of expiring month

Delivery months: March, June, September and December.

Delivery:

US dollars index – cash settlement

ECU – physical

FYTR – Federal Reserve book-entry system

2YTN – Federal Reserve book-entry system

Margins: See figures for the New York Cotton Exchange.

Date of establishment of the markets:

US dollar index futures – 20 November 1985

US dollar index options – 3 September 1986

FYTR futures – 6 May 1987

FYTR options – 23 February 1988

2YTN futures – 22 February 1989

Volume of trading: See figures for the New York Cotton Exchange.

Trading limits:
Minimum price fluctuation – 0.05, 5 basis points ($25 per contract).
Price limits – 28 points.

Termination of trading: Thursday before the third Friday of the month, unless not an Exchange or NYSE business day when the last trading day shall be the preceding business day.

Delivery months: March, June, September, December cycle.

Settlement: At maturity by cash payment; final settlement is based upon a special calculation of the third Friday's opening prices of all the stocks listed in the NYSE Composite index.

Settlement day is the business day following the third Friday of the month.

Option on NYSE Composite Index futures contract
Trading unit (minimum lot size): Call and put options on one NYSE Composite Index futures contract.

Trading limits:
Price fluctuations – 0.05 (five base points); however, if an option transaction liquidates an existing position, the minimum fluctuation can be one point if the price is less than five points.
Strike price intervals – integers evenly divisible by two. Minimum of nine exercise prices at all times: four in-the-money, one at-the-money, and four out-of-the-money.

Termination of trading: The last trading day of the underlying NYSE Composite Index futures contract.

Exercise: Open puts and calls in index options may be exercised on any Exchange business day during the life of the contract by notifying the Intermarket Clearing Corporation by 20.00 on that day. Any short position open at the end of a trading day is subject to assignment. A long call (put) that is exercised receives a long (short) position in the underlying futures contract, whereas a short call (put) that is assigned receives a short (long) position in the underlying futures contract. (Exercises on the final day of trading result in cash settlement rather than the assignment of a futures position.) At the close of business on the last trading day, all in-the-money options will be automatically exercised.

CRB futures price index futures contract
Trading unit (minimum lot size): $500 × the CRB Futures Price Index.

Trading limits:
Minimum price fluctuation – 0.05 ($25 per contract).
Position limits – 5000 contracts long or short.

Termination of trading: Third business day of expiration month.

Delivery months: March, May, July, September, December (with at least four months trading at all times).

Settlement: All contracts are marked-to-market daily. Settlement at contract maturity by cash payment.

Option on CRB futures price index futures contract
Trading unit (minimum lot size): Call and put options on one CRB index futures contract.

Trading limits:
Minimum price fluctuation – 0.05 (5 basis points); if an option transaction liquidates an existing position however, the minimum fluctuation can be 1 point if the price is less than 5 points.
Strike price intervals – 5.0 intervals at exercise values less than 300, 10.0 intervals at exercise values greater than 300. Minimum of five exercise prices at all times: two in the morning, one at the money, two out-of-the-money.
No price limits.

Termination of trading: The last day of trading of the underlying CRB index futures contract.

Exercise: On any NYFE business day the option is traded by notifying the clearing member carrying the account by 18.00 on that day. The clearing member must then notify the Intermarket Clearing Corporation by 20.00 on that day. Upon expiration, all in-the-money options will be automatically exercised, in the absence of written instructions to the contrary.

US treasury bond futures
Trading unit (minimum lot size): $100,000 face value.

Trading limits:
Minimum price fluctuation – 1/2 of 1/32 of 1% ($15.625 per contract).
Price limits – 96/32 (3 points).

Quality: T-bonds with at least 15 years to maturity and, if callable, with 15 year call protection, adjusted to 8% coupon.

Termination of trading: Eighth last business day of delivery month.

Delivery months: March, June, September, December.

Delivery: First delivery day is the first day of the delivery month, the last being the last day of the delivery month.

Settlement: Via delivery through Federal Reserve book-entry wire transfer system.

Margins:

	Initial	Maintenance
		(US dollars)
NYSE Composite index:		
Speculative	4000	1750
Members and hedgers	1750	1750
Spreads	200	100
CRB futures price index:		
Speculative	3500	2500
Members and hedgers	2500	2500
Spreads	200	100

Date of establishment of the market: 1980.

Volume of trading:

	1986	1987	1988
NYSE Composite index futures	3,123,668	2,915,915	1,668,732
options	296,303	206,631	23,304
CRB index futures	59,324	136,832	205,951
options	—	—	1,007
Totals	3,479,295	3,259,378	1,898,994

New York Mercantile Exchange

4 World Trade Center, New York, NY 10048
Telephone: 212 938 2222   *Telex:* 127 066 NYMEX NY   *Fax:* 212 938 2985
President: R T McFadden
Chairman of the Board: Z L Guttman
Vice President - Research: R Levin
Vice President - Marketing: J B Kay

Hours of trading:

Crude oil – 09.45–15.10
Heating oil – 09.50–15.10
Unleaded gasoline – 09.50–15.10
Propane – 09.50–15.10
Palladium – 08.10–14.20
Platinum – 08.20–14.30

Contract details:
Commodities: Options and futures on crude oil, no 2 heating oil and unleaded gasoline; futures on propane, palladium and platinum.

Trading currency and unit (manner of price quotation):

Crude oil – dollars and cents per barrel

Heating oil, unleaded gasoline and
propane – dollars and cents per gallon

Palladium and platinum – dollars and cents per troy ounce

Options on crude oil – dollars and cents per barrel

Options on heating oil and unleaded
gasoline – dollars and cents per gallon

Trading units (minimum lot sizes):

Crude oil – 1000 US barrels (42,000 gallons)

Heating oil, unleaded gasoline and
propane – 42,000 US gallons (1000 barrels)

Palladium – 100 troy ounces

Platinum – 50 troy ounces

Options on crude oil, heating oil and
unleaded gasoline – one underlying futures contract

Trading limits:

	Minimum lot size	*Maximum daily limit*	*Expanded limits*
Crude oil	1 cent/barrel ($10 per contract)	$1/barrel* ($1000)	$2/barrel
Heating oil	0.01 cent/gallon ($4.20)	2 cents/gallon* ($840)	4 cents/gallon
Unleaded gasoline	0.01 cent/gallon ($4.20)	2 cents/gallon* ($840)	4 cents/gallon
Propane	0.01 cent/gallon ($4.20)	2 cents/gallon* ($840)	4 cents/gallon
Palladium	5 cents/troy ounce ($5.00)	$6/troy ounce** ($600)	$12/troy ounce ($1200)
Platinum	10 cents/troy ounce ($5.00)	$25/troy ounce** ($1250)	$50/troy ounce ($2500)
Options on crude oil	1 cent/barrel ($10)	None	—
Options on heating oil	0.01 cent/barrel ($4.20)	None	—
Options on unleaded gasoline	0.01 cent/barrel ($4.20)	None	—

* There is no maximum daily limit on price fluctuations during the month preceding the delivery month.
** There is no maximum daily limit during the current delivery month and the three business days preceding it.

Strike price: Crude oil options strike prices are in increments of $1 per barrel. Heating oil and unleaded gasoline options strike prices are in increments of 2 cents per gallon. At all times at least seven strike prices are available for puts and calls on the underlying futures contract. The middle strike price is closest to the previous day's close of the underlying futures contract. Strike price boundaries are adjusted according to the futures price movements.

Quality:

Crude oil –	par crude, West Texas intermediate, 0.4% sulphur, 40° API gravity. The following streams are deliverable: Mid-Continent Sweet, Low Sweet Mix, New Mexican Sweet, North Texas Sweet, Oklahoma Sweet, South Texas Sweet, Brent blend, Brass blend, Bonny light, Ekofisk, Zarzaltine,/El Borma, Saharan blend
Heating oil –	conforming to industry standards for fungible no 2 heating oil specifications
Unleaded gasoline –	conforming to industry standards for fungible, northern grade, unleaded regular gasoline specifications
Propane –	conforming to industry standards for fungible liquified propane gas as determined by the Gas Processors Association (GPA-HD5)
Palladium –	99.9% palladium content, packaged or unpackaged
Platinum –	99.9 platinum content, packaged or unpackaged

Deliverable tolerances:

Crude oil –	other deliverable crude oil grades with 0.5% or less sulphur by weight, not less than 34°, not more than 45° API gravity
Palladium –	plates or ingots assayed before 26 March 1985 and certified as 99.8% palladium may be delivered under the 99.9 contract at a discount of $6.00 per troy ounce
Platinum –	lots of bars assayed before October 1982 and certified as a minimum PGM content of 99.8% with no less than 99.5% platinum may be delivered under the 99.9 contract at a discount of 7.50% per troy ounce

Termination of trading:

Crude oil –	third business day prior to twenty-fifth calendar day of month preceding delivery month

Heating oil, unleaded gasoline and
propane – last business day of month preceding
delivery month

Palladium and platinum – fourth business day prior to end of
delivery month

Options on crude oil – second Friday of month prior to delivery
month of underlying futures contract,
provided there are at least 5 days
remaining to trade in underlying contract

Options on heating oil and unleaded
gasoline – second Friday of month prior to delivery
month of underlying futures contract

Delivery months:

Crude oil – 18 consecutive months commencing with
current calendar month

Heating oil, unleaded gasoline and
propane – 15 consecutive months commencing with
current calendar month

Palladium – March, June, September and December,
over 15 months beginning with current
month and next two consecutive months
before moving into quarterly cycle

Platinum – January, April, July and October, over 15
months beginning with the current month
and next two consecutive months before
moving into quarterly cycle

Delivery points:

Crude oil – Cushing, Oklahoma, FOB seller's facility;
at any pipeline or storage facility with
pipeline access to Arco or Texaco, by in-
tank or in-line transfer, book-out or inter-
facility pumpover

Heating oil and unleaded gasoline – New York Harbour ex-shore, FOB seller's
facility; all duties, entitlements, taxes, fees
and other charges paid. Seller's shore
facility must have capability to deliver into
trucks (with $0.0125/gallon surcharge) or
barges at buyer's option. Delivery may also
be completed by pipeline, Tanker, book
transfer or inter- or intra-facility transfer

Propane – FOB, seller's pipeline, storage or
fractionation facility in Mont Belvieu,
Texas, with direct pipeline access to the
Texas Eastern Transmission pipeline
(TET); by in-line or in-well transfer, inter-
facility or book transfer

Delivery:

Crude oil –	all deliveries must be initiated after the first calendar day and completed before the last calendar day of the delivery month
Heating oil and unleaded gasoline –	all deliveries must be initiated after the fifth business day and completed before the last business day of the delivery month
Propane –	all deliveries must be initiated after the ninth business day and be completed before the second to last business day of the delivery month
Palladium and platinum –	notice may be submitted to the Exchange by the seller by 17.00 on the last business day preceding delivery month or any subsequent business day up to the third business day prior to end of delivery month. Delivery notices are passed to buyers the following business day

Alternative delivery procedure (ADP):
Available to buyers and sellers of energy futures who have been matched by the Exchange subsequent to the termination of trading in the spot month contract. If buyer and seller agree to consummate delivery under terms different from those prescribed in the contract specifications, they may proceed on that basis after submitting a notice of their intention to the Exchange.

Exchange of futures for, or in connection with, physicals (EFP):
Buyers and sellers of all futures contracts may exchange a futures position of equal quantity by submitting a notice to the Exchange. EFPs may be used to either initiate or liquidate a futures position.

Exercise: For crude oil, heating oil and unleaded gasoline options, exercise must be made by 16.30 on any day up to and including the option's expiration.

Membership: Regular and commercial associate (no longer open) members, 816 in total.

Margins:

	Outright	Intermarket spread (US dollars)		Intermarket spread
Crude oil	2000	500		200
Heating oil	2000	500		200
Unleaded gasoline	2000	500		200
Propane	750	1000		200
Palladium	1000		700*	
Platinum	1600		500**	

* Additional margin for delivery month: $750 on the fifth business day prior to the first business day of delivery month, $750 on the fifth business day prior to last trading day.
** Additional margin for delivery month: $1500 on the first business day of the delivery month.

Date of establishment of contracts:

Crude oil – 1983
Heating oil – 1978
Unleaded gasoline – 1981
Propane – 1987
Palladium – 1986
Platinum – 1956
Options on crude oil – 1986
Options on heating oil – 1987
Options on unleaded gasoline – 1989

Volume of trading:

	1987	*1988*	*% change*
Futures:			
Crude oil	14,581,614	18,858,948	+29
Heating oil	4,293,395	4,935,015	+15

Date of establishment of the market: 1882 (first established in 1872 as the Butter and Cheese Exchange).

Volume of trading:

	1987	*1988*	*% change*
Futures:			
Crude oil	14,581,614	18,858,948	+29
Heating oil	4,293,395	4,935,015	+15
Unleaded gasoline	2,056,238	3,292,055	+60
Propane	15,312	23,749	+55
Palladium	160,284	139,883	–13
Platinum	1,361,546	1,460,455	+ 7
Totals	22,474,629	28,710,105	+28
Options:			
Crude oil	3,117,037	5,480,281	+76
Heating oil	143,605	125,812	–12
Totals	3,260,642	5,606,093	+72
Grand totals	25,735,271	34,316,198	+33

PHILADELPHIA

Philadelphia Stock Exchange

1900 Market Street, Philadelphia, Pennsylvania 19103-3584
Telephone: 215 496 5000   *Telex:* 902 636   *Fax:* 215 496 5653/5567/6729
President: N A Giordano
Chairman: J J Wallace

European office:
39 King Street, London EC2V 8DQ
Telephone: 01 606 2348   *Telex:* 892735   *Fax:* 01 606 3548

Far Eastern office:
Kyobashi Tokiwa Building, 4th floor, 8-5 Kyobashi 2-chome, Chou-ku, Tokyo 104
Telephone: 561 2851   *Fax:* 561 2850

Hours of trading:

Canadian dollar, French franc and ECU options and futures	– 04.30–14.30
Deutschmark, Swiss franc, pound sterling, Japanese yen and Australian dollar options	– 18.00–10.00 (Mon–Thurs)
PHLX utility index options	– 09.30–16.10
S & P 500 and Blue chip CIP shares	– 09.30–16.15
Value line index options	– 09.30–16.15
Gold/silver index options	– 09.30–16.10
National over-the-counter index options and futures	– 09.30–16.15

Contract details:

Commodities: Foreign currency options – Deutschmarks, Swiss francs, Canadian dollars, pounds sterling, Japanese yen, French francs, Australian dollars, European currency units (ECU); PHLX utility index options, S & P 500 and Blue chip CIP shares, European-style Value line index options, gold/silver index options, national over-the counter index options and futures.

Foreign currency options

	Trading unit	Price quotation	Minimum price fluctuation	Exercise price interval
Deutschmark	62,500	cents/unit	0.01c ($6.25)	1.0c
Swiss franc	62,500	cents/unit	0.01c ($6.25)	1.0c
Canadian dollar	50,000	cents/unit	0.01c ($5.00)	0.5c
Pound sterling	31,250	cents/unit	0.01c ($3.125)	2.5c
Japanese yen	6,250,000	1/100 cent/unit	0.01c ($6.25)	1/100c
French franc	250,000	1/10 cent/unit	0.02c ($5.00)	1/4c
Australian dollar	50,000	cents/unit	0.01c ($5.00)	1.0c
ECU	62,500	cents/unit	0.01c ($6.25)	2.0c

Contract months: March, June, September, December and nearest-term months, in one, two, three, six, nine and twelve month expiration cycles.

Termination of trading: Friday before the third Wednesday of the month.

Expiry: The expiration day is the Saturday before the third Wednesday of the month. The expiration settlement day is the third Wednesday of the contract month.

Exercise: For American-style options, exercise may be any time until expiration; for European-style exercise is restricted until the last trading day.

Margin: Premium plus 4% of contract value less out-of-the-money amount, to a minimum of premium plus 3/4% of contract spot value, marked-to-market daily.

PHLX Utility index options
Trading currency and unit (manner of price quotation): Dollars and cents per point (1 point = $100).

Trading unit (minimum lot size): $100 × index value.

Trading limits: Position limits – 8000 contracts on same side of market.

Quality: Consisting of 20 geographically diverse NYSE electric utility stocks.

Contract months: Five expiration months – two nearby months plus three successive months from the March, June, September, December cycle.

Delivery: European-style exercises are restricted until the last day of trading prior to expiration Saturday.

S & P cash index participation (CIP) shares
Trading unit and currency (manner of price quotation): Dollars and cents per CIP.

Trading unit (minimum lot size): 1 round lot of 100 CIPs.

Trading limits:
Minimum price fluctuation – 0.01 ($1).
Position limits – 15 million or 150,000 round lots.

Quality: Based on the Standard and Poor 500 index.

Contract months: March, June, September, December.

Settlement: Cash in one business day.

Quarterly cash out is the third Friday of the contract month based on opening prices.

Ex-dividend day is the third Friday of the contract month, daily and accrued dividend.

Margin: 50% customer margin same as stock.

Blue chip CIP shares
Trading currency and unit (manner of price quotation): Dollars and cents per CIP.

Trading unit (minimum lot size): 1 round lot of 100 CIPs.

Trading limits:
Minimum price fluctuation – 0.01 ($1).
Position limits – 15 million or 150,000 round lots.

Quality: Based on the Blue chip index of 25 stocks (which correlate with the Dow Jones Industrial Average).

Contract months: March, June, September, December.

Settlement: Cash in one business day.

Quarterly cash out is the third Friday of the contract month based on opening prices.

Ex-dividend day is the third Friday of the contract month daily and accrued dividend.

Margin: 50% customer margin same as stock.

European-style Value line index options
Trading unit (minimum lot size): $100 × the index value (1 point = $100).

Trading limits:
Minimum price fluctuation – 1/16 change for a premium under 3, 1/8 change for over 3.
Strike price intervals of 5 points.

Quality: Based on the Value line Composite index, arithmetically averaged and broad-based, of approximately 1700 primarily second-tier stocks.

Contract months: Five expiration months – three from the March, June, September, December cycle plus two additional near months.

Exercise: European-style exercises are restricted until the last trading day prior to expiration Saturday.

Expiration day is the Saturday following the third Friday of the expiration month.

Gold/silver index options
Trading currency and unit (manner of price quotation): Dollars and cents per point.

Trading unit (minimum lot size): $100 × index value (1 point = $100).

Trading limits:
Exercise price intervals – 5 points.
Position limits – 6000 contracts on same side of market.

Contract months: Monthly and quarterly expiration cycles.

Delivery: Cash settlement. Exercise can be made on any business day and will be based on the closing value of the index on that day. On the Saturday of expiration the previous business day's closing value will be used. Assignments will be made on the morning of the business day after exercise, and will settle that business day.

National over-the-counter index futures
Trading unit (minimum lot size): $500 × futures price.

Trading limits: Minimum price fluctuation – 0.05 of a point ($25).

Contract months: Consecutive and cycle months such as February, March, April, June and September.

Termination of trading: At 16.00 on the third Friday of the contract month.

Settlement: Cash, based on the difference between the value of the XOC index as disseminated by the Exchange at 16.00 on the last day of trading of the OX futures contract and the closing value of the OX futures contract on the day preceding the last day of trading.

Settlement day is the first business day following the last day of trading in the contract month.

National over-the-counter index options
Trading unit (minimum lot size): $100 × the index value.

Trading limits:
Exercise price intervals – set at 5 points. An additional exercise price is added when the value of the index touches the next highest or lowest existing exercise price.
Aggregate exercise price – fund by multiplying the index multiplier ($100) by the exercise price.
Position and exercise limits – not larger than the equivalent of $300 million on the same side of the market.

Contract months: Consecutive and cycle month series, such as February, March, April, June and September.

Exercise: Instructions to exercise a long contract must be given no later than 16.10, except on the last trading day of the expiring option series. Settlement is in cash based on the difference between the closing index value and $100 times the option exercise price.

Expiration day is the Saturday following the third Friday of the expiration cycle.

Margin: An amount equal to the current market value of the option premium, plus 10% of the closing option index value, less the amount by which the option is out-of-the-money, with a minimum amount equal to the current market value of the option premium plus 2% of the closing index value.

Clearing house: Options Clearing Corporation (OCC).

Date of establishment of the markets:
ECU options – 28 August 1987
Australian dollar options – 19 January 1987
PHLX utility index options – 22 September 1987
S & P 500 and Blue chip CIP shares – 12 May 1989
Value line index options – 23 May 1988

Philadelphia Board of Trade (PBOT) a wholly-owned subsidiary of the Philadelphia Stock Exchange

Established in 1985, the PBOT trades in the foreign currency futures contracts listed below.

Hours of trading:
Canadian dollar, French franc and
ECU options and futures – 04.30–14.30
Deutschmark, Swiss franc, pound
sterling, Japanese yen and Australian
dollar futures – 18.00–10.00 (Mon–Thurs)

Contract details:
Commodities: Foreign currency futures.

Foreign currency futures:

	Trading unit	Price quotation	Minimum price fluctuation	Position limits (contracts)
Deutschmark	125,000	cents/unit	0.01c ($12.50)	6000
Swiss franc	125,000	cents/unit	0.01c ($12.50)	6000
Canadian dollar	100,000	cents/unit	0.01c ($10.00)	6000
Pound sterling	62,500	cents/unit	0.01c ($6.25)	5000
Japanese yen	12,500,000	1/100 cent/unit	0.01c ($12.50)	6000
French franc	500,000	1/10 cent/unit	0.02c ($10.00)	6000
Australian dollar	100,000	cents/unit	0.01c ($10.00)	6000
ECU	125,000	cents/unit	0.01c ($12.50)	4000

Contract months: March, June, September and December and two additional near-term months.

Termination of trading: Friday before the third Wednesday of the contract month.

Settlement: Settlement day is the third Wednesday of the contract month.

Clearing house: Intermarket Clearing Corporation (a subsidiary of the Options Clearing Corporation).

Date of establishment of contracts: 8 August 1986, except Australian dollars 22 May 1987.

Date of establishment of the market: 1985.

Part 4: Commodity Market Trading Members

Commodity Market Trading Members

Australia

Sydney Futures Exchange Ltd

Floor Members

All-States Futures Pty Ltd
1st Floor, 64 Castlereagh St
Sydney, NSW 2000
Tel: 231 5899

Bain Refco Commodities Ltd
19th Level, Grosvenor Place
225 George St, Sydney, NSW 2000
Tel: 258 1222

C A & L Bell Commodities
Corp Pty Ltd
28th Floor, 80 Collins St
Melbourne, Victoria 3000
Tel: 03 654 3677

Bisley Commodity Brokers Ltd
Level 24, Grosvenor Place
225 George St, Sydney, NSW 2000
Tel: 251 5755

BT Australia Ltd
38th Level, Australia Square Tower
Sydney, NSW 2000
Tel: 259 3555

Capel Court Corp Ltd
Level 19, 60 Margaret St
Sydney, NSW 2000
Tel: 259 5911

CitiFutures Ltd
Level 12, Citibank Centre
1 Margaret St, Sydney, NSW 2000
Tel: 239 9174

CL-Alexanders Rouse Pty Ltd
Level 10, Aussat House
54–62 Carrington St
Sydney, NSW 2000
Tel: 232 1388

Commonwealth Bank of Australia
Group Treasury
Cnr Pitt St & Martin Place
Sydney, NSW 2000
Tel: 227 5902

Elders Futures Ltd
10th Floor, 4 O'Connell St
Sydney, NSW 2000
Tel: 231 9700

Fay Richwhite Futures Australia Ltd
Level 51, MLC Centre
Sydney, NSW 2000
Tel: 232 1255

Irving Australia Ltd
15 Castlereagh St
Sydney, NSW 2000
Tel: 237 2844

Jackons Futures Ltd
9th Floor, 10 Spring St
Sydney, NSW 2000
Tel: 233 8000

LCF Limited
C/- Drake Business Centre
5th Flr, National Australia Bank
House, 255 George St, Sydney, NSW
2000
Tel: 251 3819

Macquarie Bank Ltd
Level 26, Exchange Centre
20 Bond St, Sydney, NSW 2000
Tel: 237 3333

McCaughan Dyson Futures Ltd
Level 27, Qantas International
Centre, International Square
George St, Sydney, NSW 2000
Tel: 257 6111

McIntosh Risk Management Ltd
Level 25, Rialto
525 Colins St, Melbourne, Victoria
3000
Tel: 03 618 0000

Merrill Lynch, Pierce, Fenner &
Smith (Brokers & Dealers) Ltd
Level 17, State Bank Centre
52 Martin Place, Sydney, NSW 2000
Tel: 225 6500

Midland Montagu Australia Futures Ltd
Level 8 South, Grosvenor Place
225 George St, Sydney, NSW 2000
Tel: 258 2000

J P Morgan Australia Ltd
Level 20, 52 Martin Place
Sydney, NSW 2000
Tel: 239 6111

National Australia Bank Ltd
29th Floor, National Australia Bank
House, 225 George St
Sydney, NSW 2000
Tel: 237 1090

Ord Westpac Futures Ltd
Level 25, Grosvenor Place
225 George St, Sydney, NSW 2000
Tel: 220 1555

Schroders Australia Ltd
Level 31, Grosvenor Place
225 George St, Sydney, NSW 2000
Tel: 258 9500

State Bank of New South Wales
Level 40, Grosvenor Place
225 George St, Sydney, NSW 2000
Tel: 259 4503

State Bank of Victoria trading as
SBV Futures
3rd Floor, 27 O'Connell St
Sydney, NSW 2000
Tel: 233 5533

Tricontinental Futures Pty Ltd
Level 22, 385 Bourke St
Melbourne, Victoria 3000
Tel: 03 605 0111

Tullett & Tokyo (Australia) Pty Ltd
Level 2A, Hunter Connection
7-13 Hunter St
Sydney, NSW 2000
Tel: 223 3100

Wallman Futures Pty Ltd
Level 27, Grosvenor Place
225 George St, Sydney, NSW 2000
Tel: 258 8777

Wardley Australia Futures Ltd
14th Floor, 20 Bond St
Sydney, NSW 2000
Tel: 235 9300

**Introducing Broker and
Full Associate Members**

(introducing broker: ib, full: f)

ABM Investments Pty Ltd
8th Floor, 32 Grenfell St
Adelaide, SA 5000
Tel: 08 212 6900
(f)

Australian Index Money Managers ltd
Level 66, MLC Centre
19-29 Martin Place
Sydney, NSW 2000
Tel: 238 2172
(ib)

Australian Interdealer Brokers Pty Ltd
Level 7, 114-120 Castlereagh St
Sydney, NSW 2000
Tel: 261 1455
(ib)

Baring Securities (Australia) Ltd
Level 54, Rialto Bldg
525 Collins St
Melbourne, VIC 3000
Tel: 03 612 2333
(f)

Burdett, Buckeridge & Young Ltd
2nd Floor, 405 Collins St
Melbourne, VIC 3000
Tel: 03 614 8922
(ib)

Capita Financial Management Ltd
Level 18, MSB Tower, 207 Kent St
Sydney, NSW 2000
Tel: 259 4600
(ib)

Capita Securities Ltd
Level 18, MSB Tower, 207 Kent St
Sydney, NSW 2000
Tel: 259 4600
(ib)

Chase AMP Futures Ltd
Level 33, Qantas International
Centre, International Square
George St, Sydney, NSW 2000
Tel: 250 4111
(f)

Commodity Technical Trading Ltd
Suite C Mezz, 52-62 King William St
Adelaide, SA 5000
Tel: 08 212 6088
(f)

County NatWest Australia Capital
Markets Ltd
Level 15, Grosvenor Place
225 George St, Sydney, NSW 2000
Tel: 258 0400
(f)

County NatWest Australia Investment
Management Ltd
Level 38, 385 Bourke St
Melbourne, VIC 3000
Tel: 03 670 7227
(ib)

Dominguez Barry Samuel Montagu Ltd
Level 6, Grosvenor Place
225 George St, Sydney, NSW 2000
Tel: 258 2000
(f)

EquitiLink Australia Ltd
44 Pitt St
Sydney, NSW 2000
Tel: 258 8222
(ib)

Fixed Interest Brokers (Australia) Pty
Ltd
8th Floor, 2 Castlereagh St
Sydney, NSW 2000
Tel: 231 4633
(f)

Friends' Investment Management Ltd
P O Box 142
Milsons Point, NSW 2061
Tel: 925 9255
(ib)

A C Goode & Co Ltd
10th Floor, 500 Bourke St
Melbourne, VIC 3000
Tel: 03 607 9600
(ib) (f)

Hambros Australia Investment
Management Ltd
15th Floor, 167 Macquarie St
Sydney, NSW 2000
Tel: 229 9300
(ib)

Hartley Poynton Ltd
21st Level, Allendale Square
77 St George's Terrace
Perth, WA 6000
Tel: 09 325 8104
(f)

Invia Ltd trading as Were
Commodity Services
6th Floor, 379 Collins St
Melbourne, VIC 3000
Tel: 03 614 4233
(f)

James Capel Australia Ltd
5th Floor, 20 Bond St
Sydney, NSW 2000
Tel: 232 2288
(f)

Jarden Morgan Futures Pty Ltd
Level 29, Riverside Centre
123 Eagle St
Brisbane, QLD 4000
Tel: 07 834 4111
(f)

Kleinwort Hattersley Securities Ltd
Kleinwort Benson House
55 Harrington St
Sydney, NSW 2000
Tel: 251 7311
(f)

Lewis Securities Ltd
3rd Floor, 16 Spring St
Sydney, NSW 2000
Tel: 251 7933
(ib)

Longfield Holdings Pty Ltd
Suite 2, 7 The Esplanade
Mount Pleasant, WA 6153
Tel: 09 316 1766
(f)

Merrill Lynch (Australia) Pty Ltd
Level 17, State Bank Centre
52 Martin Place, Sydney, NSW 2000
Tel: 225 6500
(ib)

Peter G Moloney & Associates
Pty Ltd
147–149 Wellington Parade
South Jolimont,
Melbourne, VIC 3002
Tel: 03 650 6789
(ib)

Mort Pty Ltd
43 McDougall St
Kirribilli, NSW 2061
Tel: 957 6929
(ib)

Mullens & Co Ltd
GPO Box 394
Sydney, NSW 2001
Tel: 233 6277
(f)

National Mutual Portfolio
Management Ltd
Level 35, Rialto North Tower
525 Collins St, Melbourne, VIC 3000
Tel: 03 616 3911
(f)

The Nikko Securities (Australia) Ltd
Level 22, State Bank Centre
52 Martin Place, Sydney, NSW 2000
Tel: 233 7166
(f)

Nomura Australia Ltd
Level 23, State Bank Centre
52 Martin Place, Sydney, NSW 2000
Tel: 221 5911
(f)

NZI Investment Services Ltd
6th Floor, 20 Bond St
Sydney, NSW 2000
Tel: 221 6444
(ib)

Oceanic Funds Management (NSW) Ltd
Level 20, 100 Miller St
North Sydney 2060
Tel: 925 0700
(ib)

Paterson Ord Minnett Ltd
7th Floor, City Centre Tower
44 St George's Terrace
Perth, WA 6000
Tel: 09 323 9222
(f)

Pembroke Securities Ltd
6th Floor, 60 Pitt St
Sydney, NSW 2000
Tel: 251 1566
(f)

PP Futures Ltd
325 Collins St
Melbourne, VIC 3000
Tel: 03 6162611
(f)

Pring Dean Ltd
Level 9, 20 O'Connell St
Sydney, NSW 2000
Tel: 233 6555
(f)

Prudential-Bache Securities
(Australia) Ltd
26th Floor, 367 Collins St
Melbourne, VIC 3000
Tel: 03 618 9666
(f)

Roach Tilley Grice & Co Ltd
7th Floor, 55 Hunter St
Sydney, NSW 2000
Tel: 232 0333
(f)

Rudolf Wolff & Co Pty Ltd
80 Collins St
Melbourne, VIC 3000
Tel: 03 654 3677
(f)

Safra Holdings Pty Ltd
Suite 1008, 10th Floor
Challis House, 10 Martin Place
Sydney, NSW 2000
Tel: 235 3833
(ib)

H Schmidhofer Pty Ltd
18 Warrimoo Ave, St Ives, NSW 2075
Tel: 235 2680
(ib)

Shearson Lehman Hutton (Aust) Ltd
Level 18, 52 Martin Place
Sydney, NSW 2000
Tel: 231 7900
(f)

G H Shin Toh (Australia) Pty Ltd
(Suspended)
Receiver & Manager
Ernst & Whinney, Accountants
35 Collins St, Melbourne
VIC 3000
Tel: 03 654 4155
(f)

South Global Industries Pty Ltd
4th Floor, Hong Kong Bldg
724–728 George St
Sydney, NSW 2000
Tel: 281 1500
(f)

Stafford Financial Ltd
Level 14, 3 Spring St
Sydney, NSW 2000
Tel: 251 4987
(ib)

Strathspey Ltd
Suite 411, 282 Victoria Ave
Chatswood, NSW 2067
Tel: 419 3266
(f)

Throgmorton Securities Pty Ltd
C/- BZW Meares Ltd
Level 24, National Aust Bank House
255 George St, Sydney, NSW 2000
Tel: 259 5711
(f)

Tricontinental Management Ltd
22nd Floor, 385 Bourke St
Melbourne, VIC 3000
Tel: 03 605 0111
(ib)

Wardley Australia Management Ltd
6th Floor, 99 William St
Melbourne, VIC 3000
Tel: 03 619 9800
(ib)

Wardley Investment Management Ltd
6th Floor, 99 William St
Melbourne, VIC 3000
Tel: 03 619 9800
(ib)

Wessex Fund Management Ltd
Level 15, 37 Bligh St
Sydney, NSW 2000
Tel: 235 3133
(ib)

Yamaichi Australia Ltd
Level 23, Qantas International
Centre, International Square
George St, Sydney, NSW 2000
Tel: 232 8600
(f)

**Local Members
(locals: l)**

Mr J Beaumont
Anaray Pty Ltd
15 Parke St
Katoombi, NSW 2780
(l)

Mr Kenneth J Anderton
57 Archbold Rd
Roseville, NSW 2069
(l)

Mr John A Hewett
Austral Pacific Nominees Pty Ltd
Trading as Austral Pacific Exports
12 Mouat St
Fremantle, WA 6160
(l)

Mr Murray E West
Balespane Pty Ltd
PO Box 197, Grosvenor Place
Sydney, NSW 2000
(l)

Mr Geoffrey Peter Ballard
2 Allambee Ave
Camberwell, VIC 3124
(1)

Mr Timothy R Bishop
c/- 27th Floor, Qantas I'national
Centre, International Square
George Street, Sydney, NSW 2000
(1)

Mr Andrew D Bloom
2020 Lincoln Part West #310
Chicago, ILL 60614 USA
(1)

Mr Graham R Brown
5 Rosetta St
Beverly Hills, NSW 2209
(1)

Mr Graham A Whiting
Burmill Pty Ltd
13 Elvina St
Dover Heights, NSW 2030
(1)

Mr Julian L Burridge
J L & R E Burridge
34 Dillon St, Paddington, NSW 2021
(1)

Mr Michael G Larkins
Capital Futures (Australia) Pty Ltd
12 Riverpark Court
22–23 Embankment Gardens
London SW3, England
(1)

Mr Rowland C Chalmers
C/- Bain Refco Commodities Ltd
Level 19, Grosvenor Place,
225 George St, Sydney 2000
(1)

Mr Raymond K T Chiu
11005 Broad Green Drive
Potomac, Maryland 20854, USA
(1)

Mr K Connolly
K & B N Connolly
22 Hale Rd, Mosman, NSW 2088
(1)

Mr R John Connolly
PO Box 1009
Neutral Bay Junction, NSW 2089
(1)

Mr W D King
Davary Pty Ltd
17 Bishopsgate Ave
Castlehill, NSW 2154
(1)

Mr Roostam Sadri
Detalee Pty Ltd
47/299 Burns Bay Road
Lane Cove, NSW 2066
(1)

Ms Barbara B Diamond
C/- Diamond Services Group
Suite 1310-A, 141 W Jackson Blvd
Chicago, Ill 60604 USA
(1)

Mr Donald K Douglas
34 Jellicoe Ave
Kingsford, NSW 2032
(1)

Mr A Graham Ducker
73/17 Wylde St
Potts Point, NSW 2011
(1)

Mr Peter Anthony Fay
159 Sutherland Street
Paddington, NSW 2021
(1)

Mr George Gero
2/591 New South Head Rd
Rose Bay, NSW 2029
(1)

Mr Graham W Gilbert
18 The Rampart,
Castlecrag, NSW 2068
(1)

Mrs Maree Frances Haldane
c/- McCaughan Dyson Futures Ltd
Level 27, Qantas International Cntr
I'national Sq, George St,
Sydney 2000
(1)

Ms Lee T Hamilton
48 Wentworth Road
Vaucluse, NSW 2030
(1)

Mr Damien James Hatfield
53A The Avenue,Newport, NSW 2106
(1)

Mr Clayton G Hitch
8 West Parade
West Chatswood, NSW 2067
(1)

Mr Kenneth Hoadley
118 Hopetoun Ave
Vaucluse, NSW 2030
(1)

Mr Henry Charles Hull
C/- Tim Bishop, McCaughan Dyson
Level 27, Qantas International Ctr
Inter'l Square, George St,
Sydney, NSW 2000
(1)

Mr J Condylis
Idameneo (No 143) Pty Ltd
184 Slade Rd, Bexley North
NSW 2204
(1)

Mr Geoffrey G Illingworth
10 Hollister Place
Carlingford, NSW 2118
(1)

Mr David A M Ireland
329 Victoria Place
Drumoyne, NSW 2047
(1)

Mr John D M Ireland
1/18 Thrupp Street
Neutral Bay, NSW 2089
(1)

Mr Terence P Jackson
29/3 Mosman Street
Mosman, NSW 2088
(1)

Mr Barry Connley
Janshore Pty Ltd
4/27 Shirley Road
Wollstonecraft, 2065
(1)

Mr R D McGregor
Juvem Investments Pty Ltd
20 Korangi Rd, St Ives, NSW 2075
(1)

Mr F J Kelly
JWK Nominees Pty Ltd
For F J Kelly Trust
Red Hill, Bowning, NSW 2583
(1)

Mr Gederts Karklins
6 Eric St, Wahroonga NSW 2076
(1)

Mr Dennis P Karp
32 Arthur Street
North Sydney, NSW 2060
(1)

Mr Stephen F Knapp
C/- McCaughan Dyson Futures Ltd
4th Floor, 360 Collins St
Melbourne, VIC 3000
(1)

Mr David Mark Kyte
13 Gordon Avenue
Stanmore, Middlesex, England
(1)

Mr Barry A Jones
Lodberry Commodities Pty Ltd
1 James Street, Hunters Hill 2110
(1)

Mr Simon S McCann
13 Warwick Place, Coxtie Green Rd
Brentwood, Essex
England CM14 5QB
(1)

Mr G Christopher McCormick
C/- McIntosh Hamson Hoare Govett
3rd Floor, 255 George St
Sydney, NSW 2000
(1)

Mr A John McDonald
35 Royalist Rd
Cremorne, NSW 2090
(1)

Mr Michael McGrath
"Neila", RMB 721
Cowra NSW 2794
(1)

Mr Stephen McShane
71 Villiers St
Rockdale, NSW 2216
(1)

Mr Robert Maher
C/- C, A & L Bell Commodities Corp
Level 33, Grosvenor Place
225 George Street, Sydney, NSW 2000
(1)

Mrs Elsie Manasseh
4/116-118 Brighton Boulevarde
North Bondi, NSW 2026
(1)

Mr Jerry Manne
327 South La Salle St
Chicago, Illinois 60604 USA
(1)

Mr David Fenwicke
Martlet Commodities Pty Ltd
2 Cambridge Street
Paddington, NSW 2021
(1)

Richard Naegele
401 S Lasalle St
Chicago, Ill 60605 USA
(1)

Mr David L Seliga
Nazko Holdings Pty Ltd
Basement Flat
42 Kensington Gardens Square
London W2, England
(1)

Mr Errol Newman
61 Henry Bull Drive
Bullcreek WA 6155
(1)

Mr Telford Conlon
Nolnoc Mosman Pty Ltd
10 Plunkett Road
Mosman, NSW 2088
(1)

Mr Allen Oayda
3/64 Wallaroy Rd
Woollahra NSW 2025
(1)

Mr T P Jackson
Olabook Pty Ltd
C/- McIntosh Hamson Hoare Govett
Ltd
255 George St, Sydney, NSW 2000
(1)

Mr Robert J Boswell
Premier Commodities Pty Ltd
108 Nicholson Parade
Cronulla, NSW 2230
(1)

Mr Hamish A Raw
75/1 Addison Rd
Manly, NSW 2095
(1)

Mrs Barbara A Pheloung
Redleaf Lodge Motel Pty Ltd
Unit 9, 114-117 North Steyne
Manly, NSW 2095
(1)

Mr Francis William Regan
PO Box 218
South Perth, WA 6151
(1)

Mr A John Reynolds
A J & J Reynolds
4th Floor, Datec House
220 George St, Sydney, NSW 2000
(1)

Mr Robert Noel Kimberley Rigg
35 Wiley St, Waverley, NSW 2024
(1)

Mr Michael Anthony Saleh
c/- Mr K Anderton
57 Archbold Rd,
Roseville, NSW 2069
(1)

Mr R Tooher
Sanolu Pty Ltd
14 Kardinia Rd, Clifton Gardens, 2088
(1)

Mr Peter H Swatridge
60 Monash Ave
Mackeral Beach via Palm Beach
NSW 2108
(1)

James John Titlow
45 Kens Road
Frenchs Forest, NSW 2086
(1)

Mr Richard J Wallace-Smith
Flat 21, 103 Kirribilli Ave
Kirribilli, 2061
(1)

Mr Kerry C Woods
3/24 Gardyne St
Bronte, NSW 2024
(1)

Mr Nicholas H Wright
3/2 Rawson St, Mosman, NSW 2088
(1)

Mr J J Jackson
York Futures Pty Ltd
C/- LCF Ltd, C/- Drake Business
Centre, 5th Flr, National Australia
Bank House, 255 George St, Sydney,
NSW 2000
(1)

**Lessees of Local Membership
(leased local: *ll*)**

Mr Frank Atkins
GPO Box 4974
Sydney, NSW 2000
(*ll*)

Mr Gordon Holland
Babnet Pty Ltd
216 Terry St
Connells Point, NSW 2221
(*ll*)

Mr Geoffrey D Lawton
Baksun Pty Ltd, 2 Dindima Place
Bangor, NSW 2234
(*ll*)

Mr Mark Brandwood
Unit 3/11 Moruben Rd
Mosman, NSW 2088
(*ll*)

Mr Julian L Burridge
34 Dillon St
Paddington, NSW 2000
(*ll*)

Mr Vincent M Cataldo
6 Parkview Place, Westleigh, NSW 2120
(*ll*)

Mr Rex A Broadbent
Chernelle Pty Ltd
907/73 Victoria St
Potts Point, 2011
(*ll*)

Mr Phillip K Cohen
25 Pine St, Manly, 2095
(*ll*)

Mr W P G Davies
Johnniefields
Marulan, NSW 2580
(*ll*)

Mr Chris Heasman
Deltavale Pty Ltd
33 Fox Valley Road
Wahroonga, NSW 2076
(*ll*)

Mr James T Fenwicke
2 Cambridge St
Paddington, NSW 2021
(*ll*)

Mr John Griggs
17 Edward St, Balmain East
NSW 2041
(*ll*)

Mr Lawrence J Hardy
35 Jannali Crescent
Jannali, NSW 2226
(*ll*)

Mr William H James
Invesco Futures Pty Ltd
Suite 703
4 Bridge Street
Sydney, NSW 2000
(*ll*)

Mr William M Irving
1/8 Kynaston Ave
Randwick, NSW 2031
(*ll*)

Mr Steven Kaposi
61 Pritchard St, Annandale
NSW 2038
(*ll*)

377

Mr Kristopher J Cherry
Laputan Pty Ltd
7/26 Manion Ave, Rose Bay, NSW 2029
(*ll*)

Mr Joseph G Maasakkers
90 Elliott St, Balmain
NSW 2041
(*ll*)

Mr Terry J Antram
Milo Minderbinder Enterprises Pty Ltd
922 Barrenjoey Rd
Palm Beach, NSW 2108
(*ll*)

Mr John Moulton
187A Whale Beach Rd
Whale Beach, NSW 2107
(*ll*)

Mr Simon O'Neill
14 Ashburner St, Manly, NSW 2095
(*ll*)

Mr Michael Dhuna
Palfos Pty Ltd
5/28 Cameron St, Balmain
NSW 2041
(*ll*)

Mr Sidney Schuyler Picht
44/3 Plunkett Street
Kirribilli, NSW 2061
(*ll*)

Mrs Jan Provan
132 Blues Point Road
McMahons Point, NSW 2060
(*ll*)

Mr Noel E Ramsden
3/17 Harriette St
Neutral Bay, NSW 2089
(*ll*)

Mr Michael Joseph Ryan
57 Windsor Street
Paddington NSW 2021
(*ll*)

Mr M P Bristow
Sigita Pty Ltd
Unit 1211, 83–85 Spring St
Bondi Junction, NSW 2022
(*ll*)

Mr S J Kessler
Sozipa Pty Ltd
4/23 Manning Road
Double Bay 2028
(*ll*)

Mr Jason Stavely-Alexander
105 Jersey Rd
Woollahra, NSW 2025
(*ll*)

Mr Michael B Hall
Upwave Investments Pty Ltd
45 Addison St, Roseville, NSW 2069
(*ll*)

Mr Graham Hammond
Yabado Pty Ltd
43 Raeburn Ave, Castecrag,
NSW 2068
(*ll*)

Mr R A Langley
Yesa Holdings Pty Ltd
9 Jellicoe St
Balgowlah Heights, NSW 2093
(*ll*)

Mr Malcolm Ian Young
PO Box N743, Grosvenor Place
NSW 2000
(*ll*)

**Associate and Local Members
(full: f; market: mkt; introducing
broker: ib; local: l; leased local: tl)**

ABM Investments Pty Ltd
8th Floor, 32 Grenfell St
Adelaide, SA 5000
(f)

ABN Australia Ltd
13th Floor, 56 Pitt St
Sydney, NSW 2000
(mkt)

Advance Bank Australia Ltd
Level 9, 182 George St
Sydney, NSW 2000
(mkt)

AEtna Life of Australia
and New Zealand Ltd
c/o Prudential Assurance Co Ltd
34–49 Martin Plce, Sydney, NSW 2067
(f)

Allied Irish Australia Ltd
Level 65, MLC Centre
19–29 Martin Place
Sydney, NSW 2000
(mkt)

Amro Australia Ltd
Level 28, MLC Centre
Martin Place, Sydney, NSW 2000
(mkt)

Anaray Pty Ltd
15 Parke St
Katoombi, NSW 2780
(l)

Mr Kenneth J Anderton
57 Archbold Rd, Roseville
NSW 2069
(l)

ANZCAP Securities Ltd
20th Floor, 60 Margaret St
Sydney, NSW 2000
(f)

A R Nominees Pty Ltd
325 Riley St
Surrey Hills, NSW 2010
(mkt)

Array Corp Pty Ltd
44 Ord St, West Perth, WA 6005
(f)

Mr Frank Atkins
GPO Box 4974, Sydney, NSW 2000
(tl)

AUSJAP Pty Ltd
c/o Mr L Wang
57 Boblynne St
Chapel Hill, Queensland 4069
(f)

Australasian Options Brokers Pty Ltd
92 Woods Rd, Sefton, NSW 2162
(f)

Australia and New Zealand Banking
Group Ltd
10th Floor, 55 Collins St
Melbourne, Victoria 3000
(f)

Australian European Finance Corp Ltd
15th Floor, 175 Pitt St
Sydney, NSW 2000
(f)

Australian Gilt International Ltd
15th Floor, Goldfields House
Circular Quay, Sydney, NSW 2000
(f)

Australian Index Money Managers Ltd
Level 66, MLC Centre
19–29 Martin Place
Sydney, NSW 2000
(ib)

Australian Industry Development Corp
212 Northbourne Ave
Canberra, ACT 2600
(mkt)

Australian Interdealer Brokers Pty Ltd
Level 7, 114–120 Castlereagh St
Sydney, NSW 2000
(ib)

Australian Mutual Provident Society
11th Floor, 1–3 Phillip St
Circular Quay, Sydney, NSW 2000
(mkt)

Australian Wheat Board
GPO Box 4562
Melbourne, Victoria 3001
(mkt)

Austral Pacific Nominees Pty Ltd
trading as Austral Pacific Exports
12 Mouat St
Fremantle, WA 6160
(l)

BA Australia Ltd
167 Macquarie St
Sydney, NSW 2000
(f)

Babnet Pty Ltd
216 Terry St
Connells Point, NSW 2221
(tl)

Bache London Ltd
9 Devonshire Square
London EC2M 4HP England
(f)

Baksun Pty Ltd
2 Dindima Place
Bangor, NSW 2234
(tl)

Balespane Pty Ltd
PO Box 197, Grosvenor Place
Sydney, NSW 2000
(l)

Mr Geoffrey Peter Ballard
2 Allambee Ave
Camberwell, Victoria 3124
(l)

Bank of New Zealand
8th Floor, BNZ House
333–339 George St, Sydney, NSW 2000
(mkt)

Bank of Tokyo Australia Ltd
Level 15
52 Martin Place, Sydney, NSW 2000
(f)

Banque Nationale de Paris
12 Castlereagh St
Sydney, NSW 2000
(mkt)

Barclays Bank Australia Ltd
25 Bligh St, Sydney, NSW 2000
(mkt)

Bardrill Finance Pty Ltd
133 Rundle St, Kent Town, SA 5067
(f)

Baring Securities (Australia) Ltd
Level 54, Rialto Bldg
525 Collins St, Melbourne,
Victoria 3000
(f)

Barrack Securities Ltd
262 St Georges Terrace
Perth, WA 6000
(mkt)

Bartinon Securities Ltd
PO Box 306
Surfers Paradise, Queensland 4217
(mkt)

BBL Australia Ltd
28th Floor, Westpac Plaza
60 Margaret St, Sydney, NSW 2000
(mkt)

BCC Australia Ltd
BCC House, 263 George St
Sydney, NSW 2000
(mkt)

Beneficial Finance Corp Ltd
33 Franklin St, Adelaide, SA 5000
(f)

Benney Partners Pty Ltd
GPO Box G420
Perth, WA 6001
(f)

Betour Pty Ltd
3-3 Carlisle St
Bondi, NSW 2026
(mkt)

BHP Finance Ltd
BHP House, 140 William St
Melbourne, Victoria 3000
(mkt)

Mr Timothy R Bishop
c/o 27th Floor, Qantas International
Centre, International Square
George St, Sydney, NSW 2000
(l)

Mr Andrew D Bloom
2020 Lincoln Part West # 310
Chicago, Illinois 60614 USA
(l)

BNP Pacific (Australia) Ltd
12 Castlereagh St
Sydney, NSW 2000
(mkt)

BNZ International Australia Ltd
333 George St
Sydney, NSW 2000
(mkt)

BNZ Norths Ltd
PO Box R527, Royal Exchange,
Sydney, NSW 2000
(f)

Boston Australia Ltd
Level 28, Qantas International
Centre, International Square
George St, Sydney, NSW 2000
(mkt)

Mr Mark Brandwood
Unit 3-11 Moruben Rd
Mosman, NSW 2088
(tl)

Broken Hill Mine Employees' Pension
Fund Custodian Ltd
162 Beryl St
Broken Hill, NSW 2880
(mkt)

Mr Graham R Brown
5 Rosetta St
Beverly Hills, NSW 2209
(l)

Bunny, McGhee & Co Ltd
405 Collins St
Melbourne, Victoria 3000
(f)

Burdett, Buckeridge & Young Ltd
2nd Floor, 405 Collins St
Melbourne, Victoria 3000
(ib)

Burmill Pty Ltd
13 Elvina St
Dover Heights, NSW 2030
(l)

J L & R E Burridge
34 Dillon St, Paddington
NSW 2021
(l)

Mr Julian L Burridge
34 Dillon St
Paddington, NSW 2000
(tl)

Canaan Investments Pty Ltd
23 Iona Ave, North Rocks, NSW 2151
(f)

Capita Financial Management Ltd
Level 18, MSB Tower
207 Kent St, Sydney, NSW 2000
(ib)

Capital Futures (Australia) Pty Ltd
12 Riverpark Court
22-23 Embankment Gardens
London SW3, England
(l)

Capita Securities Ltd
Level 18, MSB Tower
207 Kent St, Sydney, NSW 2000
(ib)

Cargill Australia Ltd
GPO Box 58A
Melbourne, Victoria 3001
(mkt)

Mr Vincent M Cataldo
6 Parkview Place
Westleigh, NSW 2120
(tl)

Challenge Bank Ltd
GPO Box P1226
Perth, WA 6001
(mkt)

Mr Rowland C Chalmers
c/o Bain Refco Commodities Ltd
Level 19, Grosvenor Place
225 George St, Sydney, NSW 2000
(l)

Chase AMP Futures Ltd
Level 33, Qantas International
Centre, International Square
George St, Sydney, NSW 2000
(f)

Chernelle Pty Ltd
907-73 Victoria St
Potts Point, NSW 2011
(tl)

Mr Raymond K T Chiu
11005 Broad Green Drive
Potomac, Maryland 20854, USA
(l)

CIBC Australia Ltd
Level 2, P & O Bldg, 55 Hunter St
Sydney, NSW 2000
(f)

Citibank Savings Ltd
Citibank Centre, 1 Margaret St
Sydney, NSW 2000
(f)

Citicorp Scrimgeour Vickers
Australia Ltd
GPO Box 1161K
Melbourne, Victoria 3001
(f)

Clayton Robard Management Ltd
Level 22, MLC Centre
Martin Place, Sydney, NSW 2000
(f)

CML Nominees Proprietary Ltd
330 Collins St
Melbourne, Victoria 3000
(mkt)

Mr Phillip K Cohen
25 Pine St, Manly, NSW 2095
(tl)

Coles Myer Finance Ltd
800 Toorak Rd
Tooronga, Victoria 3146
(f) (mkt)

The Colonial Mutual Life Assurance
Society Ltd
330 Collins St
Melbourne, Victoria 3000
(mkt)

Colonial Mutual Deposit Services Ltd
330 Collins St
Melbourne, Victoria 3000
(mkt)

Comfutures Pty Ltd
PO Box 527
Nedlands, WA 6009
(f)

Commodity Technical Trading Ltd
Suite C Mezz, 52-62 King William St
Adelaide, SA 5000
(f)

K & B N Connolly
22 Hale Rd, Mosman, NSW 2088
(l)

Mr R John Connolly
PO Box 1009
Neutral Bay Junction, NSW 2089
(l)

Consolidated Press Investments Pty Ltd
3rd Floor, 54 Park St
Sydney, NSW 2000
(f)

County NatWest Australia Capital
Markets Ltd
Level 15, Grosvenor Place
225 George St, Sydney, NSW 2000
(f)

County NatWest Australia Investment
Management Ltd
Level 38, 385 Bourke St
Melbourne, Victoria 3000
(ib)

Mr James Wright Cowan
c/o R Murrel, Masterplan Managers
4th Floor, 845 Pacific Highway
Chatswood, NSW 2067
(f)

CRA Finance Ltd
GPO Box 384D
Melbourne, Victoria 3001
(mkt)

Credit Commercial de France (Australia)
Ltd
11th Floor, 37 Pitt St
Sydney, NSW 2000
(mkt)

Dalgety Commodities Pty Ltd
4th Floor
38 Bridge St
Sydney, NSW 2000
(f)

Davary Pty Ltd
17 Bishopsgate Ave
Castlehill, NSW 2154
(l)

Mr W P G Davies
Johnniefelds
Marulan, NSW 2580
(tl)

Dean Witter Futures Ltd
1 Appold St
6th Floor, Broadgate 5
London EC2A 2AA, England
(f) (mkt)

Deltavale Pty Ltd
33 Fox Valley Rd
Wahroonga, NSW 2076
(tl)

Detalee Pty Ltd
47-299 Burns Bay Rd
Lane Cove, NSW 2066
(l)

Deutsch Bank Australia Ltd
19th Floor, Transcity House
15 Castlereagh St
Sydney, NSW 2000
(mkt)

DFC New Zealand Ltd
30 Panama St
Wellington, New Zealand
(mkt)

Ms Barbara B Diamond
c/o Diamond Services Group
Suite 1310-A, 141 W Jackson Blvd
Chicago, Illinois 60604 USA
(l)

Dominguez Barry Samuel Montagu Ltd
Level 6, Grosvenor Place
225 George St, Sydney, NSW 2000
(f)

Mr Donald K Douglas
34 Jellicoe Ave
Kingsford, NSW 2032
(l)

Drexel Burnham Lambert Ltd
Winchester House
100 Old Broad St
London EC2N 1BE, England
(mkt)

Mr A Graham Ducker
73-17 Wylde St
Potts Point, NSW 2011
(l)

Duke Pacific Securities Ltd
Level 7
38 Bridge St
Sydney, NSW 2000
(f)

Econotec Australia Pty Ltd
PO Box 68
St Ives, NSW 2075
(f)

Elders Bullion & Futures Ltd
18th Floor, Hong Kong Club Bldg
3A Chater Rd, Central
Hong Kong
(f)

Engelhard Industries Pty Ltd
PO Box 8
Thomastown, Victoria 3074
(mkt)

EquitiLink Australia Ltd
44 Pitt St
Sydney, NSW 2000
(ib)

Euro-National Investment Corp Ltd
Level 17, 60 Margaret St
Sydney, NSW 2000
(f)

Mr Peter Anthony Fay
159 Sutherland St
Paddington, NSW 2021
(l)

Fay, Richwhite Financial Services Ltd
Level 51, MLC Centre
19-21 Martin Place
Sydney, NSW 2000
(mkt)

Mr James T Fenwicke
2 Cambridge St
Paddington, NSW 2021
(tl)

First Boston Australia Ltd
Level 21, 60 Margaret St
Sydney, NSW 2000
(f)

First Chicago Australia Ltd
5th Level, 33 Pitt St
Sydney, NSW 2000
(mkt)

First Federation Discount Co Ltd
50 Bridge St
Sydney, NSW 2000
(mkt)

First Pilgrim Enterprise Pty Ltd
c/o Gillon, Derham & Co
351 Collins St
Melbourne, Victoria 3000
(f)

Fixed Interest Brokers (Australia) Pty Ltd
8th Floor, 2 Castlereagh St
Sydney, NSW 2000
(f)

Friends' Investment Management Ltd
PO Box 142
Milsons Point, NSW 2061
(ib)

Fujichu Co Ltd
2-48 Funakoshi-Cho, Higashi-Ku
Osaka-Shi, Osaka, Japan
(mkt)

Fuji Shohin Co Ltd
1-8-6 Nihonbashi-Muromachi
Chuoku
Tokyo, Japan
(mkt)

Futaba Shoji Kaisha Ltd
5-25 Kita-Kyohoji-Machi
Higashi-Ku
Osaka 541, Japan
(mkt)

Mr George Gero
2-591 New South Head Rd
Rose Bay, NSW 2029
(l)

Mr Graham W Gilbert
18 The Rampart
Castlecrag, NSW 2068
(l)

GNI Ltd
Colechurch House
1 London Bridge Walk
London SE1 2SX, England
(f)

A C Goode & Co Ltd
10th Floor, 500 Bourke St
Melbourne, Victoria 3000
(ib) (f)

Goodman Fielder Industries Ltd
Level 42, Grosvenor Place
225 George St
Sydney, NSW 2000
(mkt)

Government Insurance Office of New South Wales
c/o GIO Investments
PO Box A136,
Sydney South, NSW 2000
(mkt)

Mr John Griggs
17 Edward St
Balmain East, NSW 2041
(tl)

Grosvenor Pirie Management Ltd
GPO Box 263
Sydney, NSW 2000
(f)

Guthrie Brokers Ltd
PO Box 4388
Auckland 1, New Zealand
(f)

Mrs Maree Frances Haldane
c/o McCaughan Dyson Futures Ltd
Level 27, Qantas International Cntr
I'national Sq, George St
Sydney, NSW 2000
(l)

Hambro Australia Ltd
15th Floor, 167 Macquarie St
Sydney, NSW 2000
(mkt)

Hambros Australia Investment Management Ltd
15th Floor, 167 Macquarie St
Sydney, NSW 2000
(ib)

Ms Lee T Hamilton
48 Wentworth Rd
Vaucluse, NSW 2030
(l)

Mr Lawrence J Hardy
35 Jannali Crescent
Jannali, NSW 226
(tl)

Harlow Butler (Australia) Pty Ltd
Level 4
33-35A York St
Sydney, NSW 2000
(f)

Harringtons Metallurgists Pty Ltd
3rd Floor, 12–14 O'Connell St
Sydney, NSW 2000
(f)

B T Hart & Associates
PO Box 36
Broadway, Queensland 4006
(mkt)

Hartley Poynton Ltd
21st Level, Allendale Square
77 St George's Terrace
Perth, WA 6000
(f)

Mr Damien James Hatfield
53A The Ave
Newport, NSW 2106
(l)

Hiro-Shoji Co Ltd
10–14, 1-Chome, Awaza
Nishi-Ku, Osaka
Japan
(mkt)

Mr Clayton G Hitch
8 West Parade
West Chatswood, NSW 2067
(l)

Mr Kenneth Hoadley
118 Hopetoun Ave
Vaucluse, NSW 2030
(l)

Hoei Pty Ltd
PO Box 698
Richmond, Victoria 3121
(f)

Mr Henry Charles Hull
c/o Tim Bishop, McCaughan Dyson
Level 27, Qantas International Ctr
Inter'l Square, George St
Sydney, NSW 2000
(l)

H W H Commodity Consultants Ltd
Plantation House, 5–8 Mincing Lane
London EC3M 3DX, England
(f)

Ian Laycock Pty ltd
55 Lower Fort St, The Rocks
Sydney, NSW 2000
(f)

IBJ Australia Bank Ltd
Level 29, Qantas I'national Centre
Cnr George & Jamison Sts
Sydney, NSW 2000
(mkt)

ICLE Finance Corp Ltd
ICLE House, 73 York St
Sydney, NSW 2000
(mkt)

Idameneo (No 143) Pty Ltd
184 Slade Rd
Bexley North, NSW 2204
(l)

Mr Geoffrey G Illingworth
10 Hollister Place
Carlingford, NSW 2118
(l)

Indosuez Australia Ltd
29th Floor, 20 Bond St
Syndey, NSW 2000
(f)

International Option Investment BV
Oudezyds Voorburgwal ZD2
1012 GL Amsterdam
Nederlands
(f)

International Commodities Services Pty
Ltd
GPO Box 182
Sydney, NSW 2001
(mkt)

Invesco Futures Pty Ltd
Suite 703, 4 Bridge St
Sydney, NSW 2000
(tl)

Invia Ltd trading as Were Commodity
Services
6th Floor, 379 Collins St
Melbourne, Victoria 3000
(f)

Mr David A M Ireland
329 Victoria Place
Drumoyne, NSW 2047
(l)

Mr John D M Ireland 1–18 Thrupp St
Neutral Bay, NSW 2089
(l)

Mr William M Irving
1-8 Kynaston Ave
Randwick, NSW 2031
(tl)

C Itoh & Co (Australia) Ltd
29th Level Grosvenor Place
225 George St
Sydney, NSW 2000
(mkt)

Mr Terence P Jackson
29-3 Mosman St
Mosman, NSW 2088
(l)

Jaggard Commodity Futures (Aust) Pty
Ltd
PO Box 646
North Sydney, NSW 2060
(f)

James Capel Australia Ltd
5th Floor, 20 Bond St
Sydney, NSW 2000
(f)

Janshore Pty Ltd
4-27 Shirley Rd
Wollstonecraft 2065
(l)

Jarden Morgan Futures Pty Ltd
Level 29, Riverside Centre
123 Eagle St
Brisbane, Queensland 4000
(f)

Jardine Fleming Australia Ltd
Jardine Fleming House, 19 Pitt St
Sydney, NSW 2000
(mkt)

Jenex Commodities Pty Ltd
9th Floor, 15 Young St
Sydney, NSW 2000
(f)

John Dee (Export) Pty Ltd
PO Box 222
Broadway, Queensland 4006
(f)

Johnson Matthey Ltd
160 Rocky Point Rd
Kogarah, NSW 2217
(mkt)

Johnston Investments Trust
PO Box 531
Bundaberg, Queensland
4670
(f)

G W Joynson & Co Ltd
14 Trinity Square
London EC3N 4AA, UK
(mkt)

Juvem Investments Pty Ltd
20 Korangi Rd
St Ives NSW 2075
(l)

JWK Nominees Pty Ltd
For F J Kelly Trust
Red Hill
Browning, NSW 2583
(l)

Kaladbro Pastoral Co
Kaladbro Private Bag 104
Casterton, Victoria 3311
(f)

Mr Steven Kaposi
61 Pritchard St
Annandale, NSW 2038
(tl)

Mr Gederts Karklins
6 Eric St
Wahroonga, NSW 2076
(l)

Mr Dennis P Karp
32 Arthur St
North Sydney, NSW 2060
(l)

KBA Discount Ltd
Kleinwort Benson House
55 Harrington St
Sydney, NSW 2000
(mkt)

A J & M Kikuts
6 Bellevue Rd
North Balwyn, Victoria 3104
(mkt)

Killara (Quirindi) Pty Ltd
PO Box 197
Quirindi, NSW 2343
(mkt)

Kleinwort Benson Australia Ltd
Kleinwort Benson House
55 Harrington St
Sydney, NSW 2000
(f)

Kleinwort Hattersley Securities Ltd
Kleinwort Benson House
55 Harrington St
Sydney, NSW 2000
(f)

Mr Stephen F Knapp
c/o McCaughan Dyson Futures Ltd
4th Floor, 360 Collins St
Melbourne, Victoria 3000
(l)

Kojima & Co Ltd
39-2 Chome Kitakyuhoji-Machi
Higashi-Ku
Osaka 541, Japan
(mkt)

Chan Chan Kong
GPO Box 8437
Hong Kong
(mkt)

Kyoei Bussan Co Ltd
1-6-1 Hatchobori
Chuo-Ku
Tokyo, Japan
(mkt)

Mr David Mark Kyte
13 Gordon Ave
Stanmore
Middlesex, England
(l)

Laputan Pty Ltd
7-26 Manion Ave
Rose Bay, NSW 2029
(tl)

Lewis Securities Ltd
3rd Floor, 16 Spring St
Sydney, NSW 2000
(ib)

LIT Futures Ltd
International House
1 St Katharine's Way
London E1 9UN England
(mkt)

Lloyds Bank NZA Ltd
35 Pitt St
Sydney, NSW 2000
(f)

Lodberry Commodities Pty Ltd
1 James St
Hunters Hill 2110
(l)

M Loftus, D L Washington & J R
Farrington
Suite 27-209, Toorak Rd
South Yarra, Victoria 3141
(f)

Longfield Holdings Pty Ltd
Suite 2, 7 The Esplanade
Mount Pleasant, WA 6153
(f)

Louis Dreyfus Australia Pty Ltd
505 St Kilda Rd
Melbourne, Victoria 3000
(mkt)

LTCB Australia Ltd
19th Level, 255 George St
Sydney, NSW 2000
(mkt)

Mr Joseph G Maasakkers
90 Elliott St
Balmain, NSW 2041
(tl)

Mr Simon S McCann
13 Warwick Place, Coxtie Green Rd
Brentwood, Essex
England CM14 5QB
(l)

Mr G Christopher McCormick
c/o McIntosh Hamson Hoare Govett
3rd Floor, 255 George St
Sydney, NSW 2000
(l)

Mr A John McDonald
35 Royalist Rd
Cremorne, NSW 2090
(l)

R A McGee & Co Pty Ltd
21 Euryalus St
Beauty Point, NSW 2088
(mkt)

Mr Michael McGrath
"Neila", RMB 721
Cowra, NSW 2794
(l)

J W McGregor & Co
GPO Box 2507
Adelaide, SA 5001
(mkt)

McKinley Wilson & Co Ltd
1st Floor
34 Queen St
Melbourne, Victoria 3000
(f)

Mr I S Macnee
GPO Box 3426
Sydney, NSW 2001
(f)

Mr Stephen McShane
71 Villiers St
Rockdale, NSW 2216
(l)

MAFG Ltd
4th Floor, 55 Clarence St
Sydney, NSW 2000
(mkt)

Mr Robert Maher
c/o C, A & L Bell Commodities Corp
Level 33, Grosvenor Place
225 George St, Sydney, NSW 2000
(l)

Mair Astley Ltd
PO Box 1477
Christchurch, New Zealand
(mkt)

Mrs Elsie Manasseh
4-116-118 Brighton Blvd
North Bondi, NSW 2026
(l)

Manhill Pty Ltd
PO Box 271
Claremont, WA 6010
(f)

Mr Jerry Manne
327 South La Salle St
Chicago, Illinois 60604, USA
(l)

Manufacturers Hanover Australia Ltd
Level 14, State Bank Centre
52 Martin Place, Sydney, NSW 2000
(f)

Maresa Pty Ltd
61 Bambra Rd
Caulfield North, Victoria 3161
(f)

Mr David Marina
23 Depper St
Sunshine Beach, Queensland 4567
(mkt)

Martin Securities Pty Ltd
Suite 1, 13 Stephen St
Paddington, NSW 2021
(f)

Martlet Commodities Pty Ltd
2 Cambridge St
Paddington, NSW 2021
(l)

Marubeni Australia Ltd
PO Box R1000, Royal Exchange
Sydney, NSW 2000
(mkt)

Mase Westpac Australia Ltd
Level 6, AMP Centre
50 Bridge St
Sydney, NSW 2000
(f)

Ma Valor Commodities (Aust) Pty Ltd
297 Warringah Rd
Beacon Hill, NSW 2100
(mkt)

Maynard Commodities Pty Ltd
c/o J G Salvetti
11 Quambi St
Edgecliff, NSW 2027
(f)

Mercantile Mutual Life Insurance Co
Ltd
8th Floor, 55 Clarence St
Sydney, NSW 2000
(mkt)

Merchant Capital Ltd
Level 10, 2 Bligh St
Sydney, NSW 2000
(f)

Merrill Lynch (Australia) Pty Ltd
Level 17, State Bank Centre
52 Martin Place, Sydney, NSW 2000
(ib)

Michell Futures Pty Ltd
GPO Box 1739
Adelaide, SA 5001
(f)

Milo Minderbinder Enterprises Pty Ltd
922 Barrenjoey Rd
Palm Beach, NSW 2108
(tl)

Mitsui Finance Australia Ltd
Level 43, 50 Bridge St
Sydney, NSW 2000
(mkt)

Mitsui Trust Finance (Australia) Ltd
Level 8, NAB House
255 George St, Sydney, NSW 2000
(mkt)

The MLC Ltd
Level 42, Australia Square
Sydney, NSW 2000
(mkt)

Peter G Moloney and Associates Pty Ltd
147–149 Wellington Parade
South Jolimont, Melbourne, Victoria
3002
(ib)

Moorgate Finance Pty Ltd
PO Box 69
Red Hill, Queensland 4059
(mkt)

Morgan Pacific Finance Pty Ltd
17th Floor, 56 Pitt St
Sydney, NSW 2000
(f)

Morgan Grenfell Australia Ltd
4th Floor, 70 Phillip St
Sydney, NSW 2000
(mkt)

Mort Pty Ltd
43 McDougall St
Kirribilli, NSW 2061
(ib)

Mr John Moulton
187A Whale Beach Rd
Whale Beach, NSW 2107
(tl)

Mullens & Co Ltd
GPO Box 394
Sydney, NSW 2001
(f)

Richard Naegele
401 S Lasalle St
Chicago, Illinois 60605 USA
(l)

Nam-Bee (Australia) Pty Ltd
c/o 8 Jessica Garden
St Ives, NSW 2075
(f)

The National Mutual Life
Association of Australasia Ltd
447 Collins St
Melbourne, Victoria 3000
(mkt)

National Mutual Portfolio
Management Ltd
Level 35, Rialto North Tower
525 Collins St
Melbourne, Victoria 3000
(f)

National Australia Ltd
526 Bourke St
Melbourne, Victoria 3000
(mkt)

NatWest Australia Bank Ltd
Level 41, Qantas International Centre
International Square
Sydney, NSW 2000
(f)

Nazko Holdings Pty Ltd
Basement Flat
42 Kensington Gardens Square
London W-2, England
(l)

NCNB Australia Ltd
Level 55, MLC Centre
Martin Place
Sydney, NSW 2000
(mkt)

Mr Errol Newman
61 Henry Bull Drive
Bullcreek, WA 6155
(l)

New South Wales Treasury Corp
Level 8, 130 Pitt St
Sydney, NSW 2000
(mkt)

The Nikko Securities (Australia) Ltd
Level 22, State Bank Centre
52 Martin Place, Sydney, NSW 2000
(f)

Nolnoc Mosman Pty Ltd
10 Plunkett Rd
Mosman, NSW 2088
(l)

Nomura Australia Ltd
Level 23, State Bank Centre
52 Martin Place
Sydney, NSW 2000
(f)

NZ Equities Futures Ltd
Level 15, Tower 2, The Shortland Centre
55-59 Shortland St
Auckland, New Zealand
(f)

NZI Investment Services Ltd
6th Floor, 20 Bond St
Sydney, NSW 2000
(ib)

NZI Securities Australia Ltd
1 Castlereagh St
Sydney, NSW 2000
(mkt)

Mr Allen Oayda
3-64 Wallaroy Rd
Woollahra, NSW 2025
(l)

Oceanic Funds Management (NSW) Ltd
Level 20, 100 Miller St
North Sydney, NSW 2060
(ib)

Okachi & Co Ltd
Okachi Bldg
3-7-29 Chome Sakae
Naka-Ku, Nagoya, Japan
(mkt)

Okato Shoji Co Ltd
International Dpt
3-9 Shinkawa 2-Chome Chuo-Ku
Tokyo, Japan 104
(mkt)

Okayasu Shoji Co Ltd
53-2 Kitahama, Higashi-Ku
Osaka, Japan
(mkt)

Olabook Pty Ltd
c/o McIntosh Hamson Hoare Govett
Ltd
255 George St
Sydney, NSW 2000
(l)

Mr Simon O'Neill
14 Ashburner St
Manly, NSW 2095
(tl)

Option Technology Pty Ltd
Level 60, MLC Centre, Martin Place
Sydney, NSW 2000
(f)

Pacific Commodities Pty Ltd
PO Box 27
Glebe, NSW 2037
(f)

Palfos Pty Ltd
5-28 Cameron St
Balmain, NSW 2041
(tl)

Partnership Pacific Ltd
Level 28, 52 Martin Place
State Bank Centre, Sydney, NSW 2000
(f)

Paterson Ord Minnett Ltd
7th Floor, City Centre Tower
44 St George's Terrace
Perth, WA 6000
(f)

Paul Morgan & Co (NSW) Pty Ltd
Trading as Jarden Morgan Securities
Level 9, 345 George St
Sydney, NSW 2000
(mkt)

Pembroke Securities Ltd
6th Floor, 60 Pitt St
Sydney, NSW 2000
(f)

Phibro Energy (Australia) Pty Ltd
1 York St
Sydney, NSW 2000
(mkt)

Mr Sidney Schuyler Picht
44-3 Plunkett St
Kirribilli, NSW 2061
(tl)

Mr Tony G Piliotis
4-82 Drumalbyn Rd
Bellevue Hill, NSW 2023
(f)

PP Futures Ltd
325 Collins St
Melbourne, Victoria 3000
(f)

Premier Commodities Pty Ltd
108 Nicholson Parade
Cronulla, NSW 2230
(l)

Pring Dean Ltd
Level 9, 20 O'Connell St
Sydney, NSW 2000
(f)

Project Redeployment Pty Ltd
GPO Box 4796
Sydney, NSW 2001
(f)

Proulefco SA
Level 9, The Chelsea, 110 Sussex St
Sydney, NSW 2000
(mkt)

Mrs Jan Provan
132 Blues Point Rd
McMahons Point, NSW 2060
(tl)

The Prudential Assurance Co Ltd
Prudential Bldg
39-49 Martin Place, Sydney, NSW 2000
(mkt)

Prudential-Bache Securities (Australia) Ltd
26th Floor, 367 Collins St
Melbourne, Victoria 3000
(f)

Mr Noel E Ramsden
3-17 Harriette St
Neutral Bay, NSW 2089
(tl)

Mr Hamish A Raw
75-1 Addison Rd
Manly, NSW 2095
(l)

Redleaf Lodge Motel Pty Ltd
Unit 9, 114-117 North Steyne
Manly, NSW 2095
(l)

Mr Francis William Regan
PO Box 218
South Perth, WA 6151
(l)

Renouf Underwriters Pty Ltd
c/o Price Waterhouse
GPO Box 3509
Sydney, NSW 2001
(f)

RESI-Statewide Building Society
108 Flinders St
Melbourne, Victoria 3000
(mkt)

A J & J Reynolds
4th Floor, Datec House
220 George St
Sydney, NSW 2000
(l)

Rezzonico Weekes Pty Ltd
PO Box 109
Homebush, NSW 2140
(f)

Richardson Mann Futures Pty Ltd
c/o Mr Adrian Dunn, Love & Rodgers
Chartered Accountants, 31st Level
31 Market St, Sydney, NSW 2000
(f)

Mr Robert Noel Kimberley Rigg
35 Wiley St
Waverley, NSW 2024
(l)

Roach Tilley Grice & Co Ltd
7th Floor, 55 Hunter St
Sydney, NSW 2000
(f)

Geoff Robson-Scott & Partners
18 Smith St
Balmain, NSW 2041
(f)

Rothmetal Trading Ltd
PO Box 1549
Argus Insurance Bldg
Wesley St, Hamilton, Bermuda
(mkt)

Rothschild Australia Ltd
6th Floor, 17 Bridge St
Sydney, NSW 2000
(f)

Rudolf Wolff & Co Pty Ltd
80 Collins St
Melbourne, Victoria 3000
(f)

Rural & Industries Bank of Western
Australia
GPO Box E237
Perth, WA 6001
(mkt)

Mr Michael Joseph Ryan
57 Windsor St
Paddington, NSW 2021
(tl)

Safra Holdings Pty Ltd
Suite 1008, 10th Floor
Challis House, 10 Martin Place
Sydney, NSW 2000
(ib)

Saitama Australia Finance Ltd
5th Floor
25 Bligh St
Sydney, NSW 2000
(f)

Mr Michael Anthony Saleh
c/o Mr K Anderton
57 Archbold Rd
Roseville, NSW 2069
(l)

Sanger Australia Pty Ltd
"Archway Terraces"
Suite 3, 2nd Floor, 26 Market St
Sydney, NSW 2000
(f)

Sanolu Pty Ltd
14 Kardinia Rd
Clifton Gardens 2088
(l)

Sanwa Australia Ltd
10 Spring St
Sydney, NSW 2000
(f)

SBC Australia Ltd
PO Box H173, Australia Square
Sydney, NSW 2000
(f)

Scandinavian Pacific Ltd
Level 3, 17-19 Bridge St
Sydney, NSW 2000
(mkt)

H Schmidhofer Pty Ltd
18 Warrimoo Ave
St Ives, NSW 2075
(ib)

Security Deposits Ltd
10th Floor, 50 Bridge St
Sydney, NSW 2000
(mkt)

Security Pacific Australia Ltd
Level 4, 255 George St
Sydney, NSW 2000
(mkt)

Seiyu Shoji Co Ltd
1-10-11 Horidome-cho Nihonbashi
Chuo-ku, Tokyo 123, Japan
(mkt)

Shared Technology (Futures) Pty Ltd
596 Goodwood Rd
Daw Park SA 5041
(f)

Shearson Lehman Brothers Ltd
Winchester House
100 Old Broad St
London EC2N 1AP, England
(f)

Shearson Lehman Hutton (Aust) Ltd
Level 18, 52 Martin Place
Sydney, NSW 2000
(f)

N C Shierlaw & Associates
28 Grenfell St
Adelaide, SA 5000
(f)

G H Shin Toh (Australia) Pty Ltd
(suspended)
Receiver & Manager
Ernst & Whinney, Accountants
35 Collins St, Melbourne
Victoria 3000
(f)

Short Term Investments Ltd
Level 4, 175 Macquarie St
Sydney, NSW 2000
(mkt)

Sigita Pty Ltd
Unit 1211, 83-85 Spring St
Bondi Junction, NSW 2022
(tl)

R & B Smith (Aust) Pty Ltd
7 Lloyds Rd
Bathurst, NSW 2795
(mkt)

South Global Industries Pty Ltd
4th Floor, Hong Kong Bldg
724-728 George St
Sydney, NSW 2000
(f)

Sozipa Pty Ltd
4-23 Manning Rd
Double Bay, NSW 2028
(tl)

Spedley Securities Ltd
10th Floor, AMP Centre, 50 Bridge St
Sydney, NSW 2000
(f)

Stafford Financial Ltd
Level 14, 3 Spring St
Sydney, NSW 2000
(ib)

Standard Chartered Bank
Australia Ltd
GPO Box 2633
Adelaide, SA 5001
(f)

State Authorities Superannuation Board
15th Floor, 1 Margaret St
Sydney, NSW 2000
(mkt)

State Building Society Ltd
Level 22, 1 Oxford St
Whitlam Square
Sydney, NSW 2000
(mkt)

State Electricity Commission of Victoria
15 William St
Melbourne, Victoria 3000
(mkt)

State Insurance Office, 480 Collins St
Melbourne, Victoria 3000
(mkt)

Mr Jason Stavely-Alexander
105 Jersey Rd
Woollahra, NSW 2025
(tl)

Strathspey Ltd
Suite 411, 282 Victoria Ave
Chatswood, NSW 2067
(f)

Sumitomo International Finance
Australia Ltd
Level 26, 56 Pitt St
Sydney, NSW 2000
(mkt)

Sumitomo Trust Finance (Australia) Ltd
Level 61, MLC Centre, 19-29 Martin Pl
Sydney, NSW 2000
(f)

Superannuation Fund Investment Trust
5th Floor, Hobart Place
Canberra City, ACT 2600
(mkt)

Mr Peter H Swatridge
60 Monash Ave
Mackeral Beach via Palm Beach, NSW
2108
(l)

Taiyo Kobe Australia Ltd
Level 57, MLC Centre
19-29 Martin Place
Sydney, NSW 2000
(f)

J P Tarlinton
PO Box 8
Cobargo, NSW 2547
(f)

Throgmorton Securities Pty Ltd
c/o BZW Meares Ltd
Level 24, National Aust Bank House
255 George St, Sydney, NSW 2000
(f)

James John Titlow
45 Kens Rd, Frenchs Forest
NSW 2086
(l)

Tokyo Commodity Ltd
16F Parkview Commercial Bld
9-11 Shelter St, Causeway Bay
Hong Kong
(f)

Toronto Dominion Australia Ltd
385 Bourke St
Melbourne, Victoria 3000
(mkt)

Toyomenka (Australia) Pty Ltd
9th Floor, St Martins Tower
31 Market St
Sydney, NSW 2000
(mkt)

Toyoshima Australia Pty Ltd
American Express Tower
Suite 1008, 10th Floor
388 George St, Sydney, NSW 2000
(mkt)

Trans Pacific Petroleum NL
Lufthansa House
143 Macquarie St
Sydney, NSW 2000
(f)

Tricontinental Corp Ltd
23rd Floor, 385 Bourke St
Melbourne, Victoria 3000
(f) (mkt)

Tricontinental Management Ltd
22nd Floor, 385 Bourke St
Melbourne, Victoria 3000
(ib)

Twynam Cotton Pty Ltd
Level 10, 17-19 Bridge St
Sydney, NSW 2000
(f)

UBS Australia Ltd
Level 36, 8-18 Bent St
Sydney, NSW 2000
(mkt)

Upwave Investments Pty Ltd
45 Addison St
Roseville, NSW 2069
(tl)

D J C Urquhart
RMB 5006D
Wodonga, Victoria 3690
(f)

Vanimo Nominees Pty Ltd
18 The Esplanade
Perth, WA 6000
(f)

Victorian Development Fund
Level 12, 303 Collins St
Melbourne, Victoria 3000
(mkt)

Victorian Public Authorities
Finance Agency
20th Floor, 385 Bourke St
Melbourne, Victoria 3000
(mkt)

Wales Meat Pty Ltd
Suite 54, 110 Sussex St
Sydney, NSW 2000
(f)

Mr Richard J Wallace-Smith
Flat 21, 103 Kirribilli Ave
Kirribilli, NSW 2061
(l)

W A Meat Exports Pty Ltd
30 Cliff St
Fremantle, WA 6160
(mkt)

Wardley Australia Management Ltd
6th Floor, 99 William St
Melbourne, Victoria 3000
(ib)

Wardley Investment Management
Limited
6th Floor, 99 William St
Melbourne, Victoria 3000
(ib)

Wessex Fund Management Ltd
Level 15, 37 Bligh St
Sydney, NSW 2000
(ib)

Westpac Banking Corp
Treasury Division
18th Floor, 60 Martin Place
Sydney, NSW 2000
(f)

Westpac Investments Management Pty
Ltd
Endeavour House
Cnr Pitt & Bridge St
Sydney, NSW 2000
(f)

W & J Whitehead (Australia) Pty Ltd
PO Box 340, New Lane Mills
Laisterdyke, Bradford BD4 8BD,
England, UK
(mkt)

Wilson Commodities Pty Ltd
GPO Box 1361
Brisbane, Queensland 4001
(f)

Mr Kerry C Woods
3-24 Gardyne St
Bronte, NSW 2024
(l)

Mr Nicholas H Wright
3-2 Rawson St
Mosman, NSW 2088
(l)

Yabado Pty Ltd
43 Raeburn Ave
Castecrag, NSW 2068
(tl)

Yamaichi Australia Ltd
Level 23, Qantas International Centre,
International Square, George St
Sydney, NSW 2000
(f)

Yesa Holdings Pty ltd
9 Jellicoe St
Balgowlah Heights, NSW 2093
(tl)

York Futures Pty Ltd
c/o LCF Ltd, c/o Drake Business
Centre
5th Flr, National Australia Bank House
255 George St, Sydney, NSW 2000
(l)

Mr Malcolm Ian Young
PO Box N743, Grosvenor Place
NSW 2000
(tl)

Yutaka Shoji Co Ltd
16-12 Kakigaracho, 1-Chome
Nihonbashi, Chuoku
Tokyo 103, Japan
(mkt)

The following Floor Members also have Associate Memberships

Bain Refco Commodities Ltd
Level 19, Grosvenor Place
225 George Street, Sydney, NSW 2000
(f)

Commonwealth Bank of Australia
Cnr Pitt Street & Martin Place
Sydney, NSW 2000
(f)

State Bank of New South Wales
Level 40, Grosvenor Place
225 George St, Sydney, NSW 2000
(f)

State Bank of Victoria trading as SBV
Futures
3rd Floor, 17 O'Connell Street
Sydney, NSW 2000
(f)

Wallman Futures Pty Ltd
Level 27, Grosvenor Place
225 George St, Sydney, NSW 2000
(f)

Austria

Vienna Commodity Exchange

Members

Allinger – Mattner Holzindustrie –
Gesellschaft mbH
8641 St Marein im Mürztal,
Mattnerstraße 8

Herbert Aschbacher jun
Holzhandel – Commercio Legnami
9861 Eisentratten, Innernöring 7

Atex-Verkaufsbüro österreichischer
Waldbesitzer
Gesellschaft mbH
8665 Langenwang

Attco Holzhandelsgesellschaft mbH
1010 Wien, Stubenring 14-2-4

Augustiner Chorherrenstift
Klosterneuburg –
Forstamt
3400 Klosterneuburg, Stiftsplatz 3

prot Fa Aurachthaler Holzwerk
Stockhammer & Co
4812 Pinsdorf 106

Baillou Holzhandelsgesellschaft mbH
2351 Wiener Neudorf, Industriezentrum
Nö-Süd
Straße 13-47

prot FA Karl Banyai, Holzgroßhandlung
1182 Wien, Sternwartestraße 25

prot Fa Bauer & Grossmann OHG
Holzhandel
1212 Wien, Schillgasse 9

A Baumgartner Gesellschaft mbH
2340 Mödling, Friedrich-Schiller-Straße
96

R Baumgartner Gesellschaft mbH & Co
KG
Holzgroßhandel und Export
3580 Horn, Muschingergasse 5

prot Fa Franz Bayerl
Sägewerk und Holzexport
D-8441 Obermiethnach 1

Bäuerlicher Waldbesitzerverband
Oberösterreichs
4021 Linz, Bergschlößlgasse 7

Benediktinerstift St Lambrecht
Forst-und Sägebetrieb
8813 St Lambrecht

Sägewerk Bernhard Gesellschaft mbH
3525 Sallingberg, Lugendorf 31

Hans Bichler
Sägewerk und Holzexport
8720 Knittelfeld, Unterfarrach 19

prot Fa Franz Binder Gesellschaft mbH
6263 Fügen 283

Franz Bock Gesellschaft mbH
Säge und Holzhandel
3912 Grafenschlag
Langschlag 15

Lorenz Böhm
Holzhandel und Holzschlägerei
2453 Sommerein, Hauptstraße 21

Holzwerke Karl Brandstätter
Gesellschaft mbH
2020 Hollabrunn, Mühlgasse 39

prot Fa Michael Brandstätter Sägewerk
und Holzhandlung Oberweissburg
5582 St Michael im Lungau

Konrad Brunner Gesellschaft mbH
Sägewerk, Kisten-und Palettenerzeugung
3910 Zwetti, Gradnitztalweg 6

Otto Brüstle
Holzgroßhandlung
5010 Salzburg, Bayernstraße 21

Buben & Fried Gesellschaft mbH & Co
KG
Holzhandel und Sägewerk
4810 Gmunden

Buben & Fried Laubholz Gesellschaft
mbH & Co KG
4451 Garsten

Josef Bugelnig
Säge- und Hobelwerk, Holzhandel
9815 Kolbnitz

Christian Burger
Holz-Handel-Agentur – Import–Export
9503 Villach, Heizhausstraße 60

prot Fa Cappellari & Co KG
9400 Wolfsberg, Schoßbach 5

Cistercienserstift Heiligenkreuz
2532 Heiligenkreuz bei Baden

Ignaz De Colle Holzindustrie
Gesellschaft mbH
9462 Bad St Leonhard

Degginger & Hess Klöpferholz
Gesellschaft mbH
Holzgroßhandel
D-8000 München 2, Barthstraße 22

prot Fa Rupert Deisl, Sägewerk und
Kunstmühle in Adnet (Land Salzburg)
5421 Adnet Nr 67

Ing Franz Dier
Holzhandel, Sägewerk
3441 Freundorf, Hauptstraße

prot Fa Ludwig Dirmayer KG
4951 Polling 71

Donausäge Rudolf Rumplmayr
Gesellschaft mbH & Co KG
4813 Altmünster

DOWA Holzhandel- und
Beteiligungsges mbH
9371 Brückl, St Veiter Straße 7

Dr. Karl Draskovich
Forst-und Gutsverwaltung,
Holzgroßhandel
Sägewerk, 7540 Güssing, Schloßgasse 12

prot Fa Hermann Eberhard Inhaber
Gerald Eberhard
9413 St Gertraud bei Wolfsberg,
Teichweg 2

Eberstein – Holz Gebrüder Neuper
9372 Eberstein, Klagenfurter Straße 1

Johann Edlinger Gesellschaft
mbH & Co KG
Sägewerk und Holzhandel
9815 Kolbnitz

Engel Gesellschaft mbH
1016 Wien, Babenbergerstraße 9

prot Fa Entacher Sägewerk und
Gastwirtschaft KG Großarl
5611 Großarl, Markt 43

Dr Paul Esterházy'sche Güterdirektion
7000 Eisenstadt, Esterházyplatz 5

Etablissement Südholztrans
FL-9490 Vaduz
Josef-Rheinberger-Straße 29

Eurospan Kranebitter Gesellschaft mbH
6405 Pfaffenhofen Nr 87

Fensterholzwerk Ebensee Gesellschaft
mbH & Co KG
4802 Ebensee, Langwies 167

prot Fa Gebrüder Feroli, Sägewerk und
Holzhandel in Dienten
5652 Dienten am Hochkönig
Schwarzenbach 1

Johann Fischer
Sägewerk un Holzhandel
8230 Penzendorf 76 bei Hartberg

FORESTA Holzgroßhandel Gesellschaft
mbH
4020 Linz an der Donau, Bürgerstraße 1

Forstbetriebe Fronsburg, Marianne Pilati
Ida Bongart, Ferdinand Melichar
2084 Fronsburg 1

prot Fa Eligius Frewein, Inh Dipl -Ing
Karl Frewein
Sägewerk und Holzhandel
8741 Weißkirchen, Allersdorf 26

prot Fa Robert Frey, Holzgroßhandel-
Holzexport
1010 Wien, Franz-Josefs-Kai 27

J u A Frischeis Gesellschaft mbH
200 Stockerau, Gerbergasse 2

prot Fa Franz Germuth, Eibiswald
Sägewerk und Holzhandel
8552 Eibiswald 10

Germuth –
Konstruktionsholzgesellschaft mbH
8552 Eibiswald 10

Fritz Gerrard
Holzexport
1030 Wien, Untere Weißgerberstraße 17

prot Fa Thomas Geyer
9363 Metnitz-Metnitztal, Untermarkt 73

prot Fa Willibald Glanzer Sägewerk und
Holzhandel
9853 Gmünd, Waschanger Nr 4

prot Fa Anton Goller KG
Sägewerk und Holzhandel
9942 Obertilliach/Bergen 35

Wilhelm Gottschligg Gesellschaft mbH
& Co KG
Holzgroßhandel – Paletten
2340 Mödling, Neugasse 22

Gottschligg Holzexport Gesellschaft
mbH & Co
2372 Gießhübl, Hauptstraße 19

Johann Grimas Gesellschaft
mbH & Co Kg
2331 Vösendorf bei Wein
Treister Straße 3

Ing Franz Berthold Gruber
Sägewerk
3681 Weins-Isperdorf

J & S Gruber, Julius und Susanne
Gruber
Sägewerk und Holzhandel
3663 Laimbach am Ostrong

H & H Hackenberg Gesellschaft mbH
Holzgroßhandel und Holzexport
1010 Wien, Falkestraße 6

Otto Haingartner
Sägewerk in Bretstein
8763 Möderbrugg, Bretstein 15

H C Handels-Contor Gesellschaft mbH
& Co KG
8565 St Johann o H, Köppling 99

Helmut Hanger ehemals Leopold
Hanger
Säge- und Hobelwerk
4442 Kleinraming

prot Fa Martin Hartl, Säge und
Hobelwerk
Leogang – Salzburg
5771 Leogang, Rain 17

Ing Thomas Hasler
Säge- und Hobelwerk Fertighäuserbau
8762 Oberzeiring, Katzling

Hasslacher Holzwerke Gesellschaft mbH
9640 Kötschach

prot Fa J Hasslacher
9751 Sachsenburg, Feistritz 7

prot Fa Brüder Hasslacher
Holzindustrie
9620 Hermagor, Eggerstraße 15

Hans Peter Hassler Sägewerk –
Holzhandel
9761 Greifenburg

prot Fa Theresia Häupl OHG, Sägewerk
und Holzhandlung
4880 St Georgen im Attergau

Friederike Heider
Holzgroßhandlung
9062 Moosburg, Tuderschitz 60

Ferdinand Heindl
Säge- und Hobelwerk
3193 St Aegyd am Neuwalde,
Mitterbach 2

Hermann & Müller Gesellschaft mbH
& Co KG
Holzhandlung und Sägewerk
5671 Bruck an der Großglocknerstraße

prot Fa Ing Edwin Hochwimmer & Co
3743 Röschitz 173

prot Fa Holz-Export Dipl-Ing
Carl Anton Goess-Saurau
8707 Leoben-Göß

prot Fa Holzimpex Holzhandel
Blumenfeld & Co
1100 Wien, Laaerbergstraße 110

prot Fa Holzkontor Etablissement
Holzhandel
FL-9490 Vaduz, Altenbachstraße 8

prot Fa Holzwerk A Paul
3343 Hollenstein an der Ybbs,
Dornleiten 8

Holzwerke Stingl Gesellschaft mbH
& Co KG
9334 Guttaring, Hollersberg 28

prot Fa Gebrüder Hoppichler
Sägewerk
4871 Zipf, Langwies 15

prot Fa Kistenfabrik und Spaltwerk
Hoppichler & Co
4870 Vöcklamarkt 179

Leopold Hubegger Gesellschaft mbH
3264 Gresten, Unterer Markt 13

prot Fa Jörg Hutter
Sägewerk & Holzexport
5722 Niedernsill

Franz Jannach
Sägewerk
8754 Thalheim bei Pöls

prot Fa Ing Georg Jung KG
Holzexport
5700 Zell am See

Jung-Holz Export-und
Handelsgesellschaft mbH
5700 Zell am See,
Brucker Bundesstraße 20a

Kaml & Huber Gesellschaft mbH & Co
KG
8630 Rasing bei Mariazell

KANZIAN-HOLZ
Gesellschaft mbH
9761 Greifenburg, Eben 1

Kaufmann Holzbauwerk Gesellschaft
mbH
6870 Bezau, Reuthe 57

Kämtner Holzindustrie Villach F X
Wirth
Gesellschaft mbH & Co KG
9500 Villach, Klagenfurter Straße 26

Karntner Montanindustrie Gesellschaft
mbH
Forstgut und Sägewerk Gleiß
3343 Hollenstein an der Ybbs

Alfred Kemptner Säge- und Holzexport
4710 Grieskirchen, Tollet 4

Friedrich Kern
Holzwerk – Holzexport
8243 Pinggau 301

Adolf Kernmaier
Sägewerk
9556 Liebenfels, Glantschach 4

Ing Ilse Kilches
Holzhandel aller Art – Export
8020 Graz, Quergasse 3

prot Fa Rudolf Kirchner Sägewerk
5541 Altemmarkt im Pongau,
Sinnhub 50

prot Fa Ludwig Klausbauer OHG
Sägewerk
8921 Lainbach bei Hieflau

Dieter Manfred Klinger Gesellschaft
mbH
3631 Ottenschlag/Armschlag 3

Koch Holz Gesellschaft mbH
5020 Salzburg, Franz-Sauer-Strasse 42

prot Fa Hermann Kofler & Co
9551 Bodensdorf, Bundesstraße 18

Josef Kogler Gesellschaft mbH & Co KG
9556 Liebenfels 34

Sägewerk Gebr Kolbitsch KG
6262 Schlitters 98

George Koller Sägewerk Zackermühle
D-8496 Lam'/ Thürnstein

prot Fa Johann Kollmann
Sägewerk und Holzhandel
8153 Geistthal 7

Karl Kopp
Holzhandel, Export
1160 Wien, Gallitzinstraße 108

prot Fa Franz Kreps Holzgroßhandel-
Export
8430 Leibnitz-Kaindorf
Grazer Straße 154

Alfred Kreuzer
Sägewerk – Holzexport
3663 Laimbach am Ostrong 88

prot Fa Industrieholz Krieger
6332 Kufstein, Schützenstraße 16

Johann Kumer
Holzhandel und
Holzschlägerungsunternehmen
9020 Klagenfurt, Siebenhügelstraße 126

Dkfm F Lackenschweiger KG
Holzgroßhandlung
2331 Vösendorf, Triester Straß 347

prot Fa Alois Lackner
5542 Flachau, Reitdorf 22

Landhaus-Bau Gesellschaft mbH
Holzhandel
8225 Pöllau, Grazer Straße 164

prot Fa Lanner & Kaltenbrunner
Sägewerk
5310 Mondsee-Teufelmühle

Herbert Leberbauer
Sägewerk und Holzhandel
4643 Pettenbach, Mitterndorf 11

prot Fa Jakob Lederer Holzhandel und
Sägewerke
9642 Mauthen Nr 77 Gailtal

prot Fa Alfred Leeb, Holzexport
9563 Gnesau

Karl Leitner
Export – Import – Holzhandel
D-8358 Vilshofen, Stadtplatz 42

Leitner Holzindustrie Gesellschaft mbH
3261 Steinakirchen am Forst, Edla

Andreas Lenzhofer
Sägewerk,Export
9634 Gundersheim

Liechtenstein Holzhandelsges mbH
1232 Wien, Lamezanstraße 7

Franz Lohninger
Säge Holzwerk
4870 Vöcklamarkt, Fornacherstraße 18

Friedegund Loitzl
Holzhandel – Holzexport
8983 Bad Mitterndorf 130

Hans Löscher
Sagewerk – Holzexport – Holzhandel
9500 Villach, Obere Fellacher Straße 6

Gustav Lukanz, Sägewerk und
Hotelbetrieb
Gesellschaft mbH
8820 Neumarkt, Bahnhofstraße 14

prot Fa Franz Lummerstorfer
Holzhandlung
4201 Gramastetten, Aschlberg 10

Franz Lusser
Sägewerk – Holzexport
9941 Kartitsch 110

Hans O Lütkens Gesellschaft mbH & Co
D-2000 Hamburg 76, Armgartstraße 2

Alois Maier
Sägewerk – Hobelwerk
5580 Tamsweg, Mörtelsdorf 44

Ernst und Hermine Maier
Säge- und Hobelwerk
3800 Göpfritz an der Wild
Nordrandweg 30

prot Fa Karl und Ernst Maier OHG
Sägewerk und Holzexport Taxwirt
9463 Reichenfels

Erich Maislinger
Sägewerk – Holzhandel
5120 St Pantaleon, Mühlach 3

Holzbau Maresch Gesellschaft mbH &
Co KG
2081 Nieder-Fladnitz 116

Dipl-Ing Friedrich Marso
Holzgroßhandel
1092 Wien, Porzellangasse 20

prot Fa Fritz Mauthner
Import – Export
1010 Wien, Parkring 12

prot Fa Barthl Mayer-Zeiner OHG
Sägewerk und Holzexport
8741 Weißkirchen, Baumkirchen

prot Fa Franz Mayr-Melnhof
Säge- und Hobelwerke
8707 Leoben-Göß, Turmgasse 57

Sägewerk Gertrud Meinhart
4880 St Georgen im Attergau, Im
Weidach 16

MELINZ Gesellschaft mbH
Holzhandel und Export
9184 St Jakob im Rosental, Längdorf 11

Holzgroßhandel Dkfm Dr Eugen Milota
Gesellschaft mbH
1050 Wien, Franzensgasse 12/3/13

prot Fa Leopold Mittendorfer-Edlmayr
Alleininhaber Peter Mittendorfer
Säge- und Hobelwerk
Spirituosenerzeugung
4271 St Oswald bei Friestadt, Wippl 35

Hans Moidl Laubholz-Sägewerk und
Holzhandel
Gesellschaft mbH
4407 Dietach, Steyr-Gleink
Ennser Straße 76

Moosbrugger Sägewerk – Holzhandel –
Export KG
8911 Admont 97, Postfach 23

Ing Hans Moser
Sägewerk/Holzexport/Hobelware/
Imprägnierungen/Techn Trocknungen
9712 Fresach, Mitterberg

MOSSER Holzindustrie Gesellschaft
mbH
3263 Randegg, Mitterberg 25

Josef Mosser
Säge und Holzhandel
9771 Berg im Drautal

Mösenbacher & Sohn
Holzgroßhandelsgesellschaft
mbH & Co KG
Holzgroßhandel und Holzexport
5020 Salzburg, Bergstraße 22/V

prot Fa Josef Mühlberger
Sägewerk – Holzexport
6345 Kössen Nr 260a

Dkfm Dr Fritz Nagele
Gebrüder Nagele
Gutsbesitz, Säge- und Hobelwerk,
Holzexport, 8862 Stadl an der Mur

Nettingsdorfer Papierfabrik AG
4045 Nettingsdorf

Johann Neubauer Gesellschaft mbH
7411 Loipersdorf 99

Holzhandlung Karl Neulinger & Co KG
1220 Wien, Stadlauer Straße 41

Josef Neumann Gesellschaft mbH
Holzhandel – Sägewerk – Transporte
2761 Miesenbach, Reichental 200

Neumayr Gesellschaft mbH
Holz- und Baustoffhandel, Holzexport –
Holzimport
5722 Niedernsill 12

prot Fa Sägewerk Neuschmied Hansjörg
Sägewerk – Holzexport
6361 Hopfgarten

Neusiedler AG
1120 Wien, Schönbrunner Schloßstraße
42

Hans Niedermeier
Import – Holzgroßhandel – Export
D-8300 Landshut, Maistraße 4

Anton Niklasch Holz –
Handelsgesellschaft mbH
Handel mit Holz, Drogen und
Chemikalien
Parfumeriewaren, 1190 Wien,
Heiligenstädter Lände 13

prot Fa Ernst Nussbaumer & Co
Sägewerk
6932 Langen bei Bregenz

Helmut Oberlojer
Holzexport
9781 Oberdrauburg

Johann Offner Holzindustrie
Gesellschaft mbH
9400 Wolfsberg

Generaldirektion der Österreichischen
Bundesforste
1030 Wien, Marxergasse 2

prot Fa G A Pap KG
Holzgroßhandel
1030 Wien, Reisnerstraße 41

Papierholz Gesellschaft mbH,
Niederlassung Pöls
8761 Pöls ob Judenburg, Burgogasse 10

PHi Paletten- und Holzindustrie
Rohrbach an der Lafnitz Gesellschaft
mbH
8234 Rohrbach an der Lafnitz

prot Fa Rudolf Pisec, Holzgroßhandel
Export – Import
1010 Wien, Göttweihergasse 1

Robert Placzek AG
1010 Wien, Trattnerhof 1

Konrad Planegger
Sägewerk, Holzexport
Schotter- und Splitterwerk
Land- und Forstwirtschaft
9314 St Sebastian-Launsdorf

Johann Posch
Sägewerk, Holzexport
8224 Kaindorf, Kopfing 79

E u A u G Prein Gesellschaft mbH
Sägewerk und Holzhandel
8793 Trofaiach, Leintal 37

Alois Pretzl
Säge- und Hobelwerk
4785 Haibach, Hareth 30

prot Fa Kaml & Huber OHG
8786 Rottenmann, Bärndorf 87

Franz Pungg
Sägewerk
6271 Uderns, Kapfing 41

prot Fa Alois Pürrer OHG
Holzgroßhandel
5322 Hof bei Salzburg, Seestraße 20

prot Fa Hans Rainer Sägewerk –
Holzindustrie
8831 Niederwölz, Fresen bei Niederwölz

Othmar Ramsbacher
Sägewerk
9863 Rennweg 62

Michel Rauter
Holzhandel und Holzexport
9360 Friesach, 10-Oktober-Straße 3

Raimund Regensburger
Sägewerk und Holzhandel
8943 Aigen im Ennstal

Hans Reischer
Sägewerk – Hobelwerk – Holzhandel
2564 Weißenbach an der Triesting,
Hauptstraße 61

prot Fa Georg Reschreiter, Sägewerk,
Rußbachsaag
5442 Rußbach am Paß Gschütt
Gseng 30

Rieder-Holzhandelsgesellschaft mbH
3372 Blindenmarkt, Lindenstraße 16

Joh Riedlinger Söhne KG
Sägewerk – Holzhandlung
D-7700 Singen/Hohentwiel 14, Zur
Mühle 7

Hans Rochol
Gut Gstettenhof, Forstwirtschaft
3184 Türnitz

Herbert Roth
Sägewerk und Holzexport
9560 Feldkirchen

Franz Salzger
Holzindustrie
8530 Deutschlandsberg
Grazer Straße 55

Johann Santner, Sägewerk, Gesellschaft
mbH
5580 Unternberg bei Tamsweg

Johann Santner's Erben, Sägewerk in
Weißbriach
9622 Weißbriach

prot Fa Sägewerk Tamsweg Johann
Graggaber
5580 Tamsweg, Wölting Nr 42

prot Fa Franz Schachl Sägewerk
5441 Abtenau, Döllerhof 23

prot Fa Gotthard Schaffer Sägewerk und
Holzexport
8741 Eppenstein 2

prot Fa A u E Schafler
Holzindustrie
8221 Hirnsdorf 1

prot Fa Hermann Schenker
2870 Mariensee 62

Andrä Schermer Gesellschaft mbH
Säge- und Hobelwerk
6364 Brixen im Thale

prot Fa Rupert Schnell Sägewerk
5541 Altenmarkt, Reitdorf

prot Fa Schößwendter & Kendlbacher
OHG
Säge-, Spalt- und Hobelwerk
5760 Saalfelden

Hermann Schuster, Holzgroßhandlung
Holzexport
Gesellschaft mbH & Co KG
6020 Innsbruch, Magtstraße 4a

Schwaiger Holzindustrie Gesellschaft
mbH
4802 Ebensee, Offenseestraße 32

HOLZINDUSTRIE Schweighofer
Gesellschaft
mbH & Co KG
3531 Niedernondorf, Brand 44

Alfred Seebacher
Sägewerk – Holzexport
9563 Gnesau

Friedrich Seier
Sägewerk, Baustoffe und
Holztrockenanlage
2833 Bromberg, Schlatten 55

Seilern – Aspang'sche Forstamts- und
Gutsleitung
Litschau
Sägewerksbetrieb
3874 Litschau, Seilerndorf 22

„Slavonia" Furnier- und
Holzhandelsgesellschaft
mbH Nfg KG
1110 Wien, Zinnergrasse 6

prot Fa Ludwig Sommer
Holzimport – Export
D-8227 Seigsdorf, Zottmayerstraße 9

Karl Soukup Gesellschaft mbH
Fabriksmäßige Erzeugung von Fumieren
und Holzwaren
1150 Wien, Flachgasse 29

Wolfgang Steiner
Forstgut Rothenfels
8832 Oberwölz

Johann und Gerhard Steininger
Sägewerk – Holzhandel
3532 Rastenfeld Nr 86

STIA – Holzindustrie Gesellschaft mbH
8911 Admont 1

Paul Stockert
3192 Hohenberg 104

Hermann Stöckl
Holzhandel
8020 Graz, Quergasse 3/V

prot Fa Karl Stöckler
Sägewerk
4300 St Valentin, Langenharter Straße 3

prot Fa Ignaz Stögmüller & Co
Sägewerk – Holzhandel
4800 Attnang-Puchheim, Wankham 40

Engelbert Franz Straubinger
Holzexport
8623 Aflenz/Kurort
Mariazeller Straße 107

Ladislaus Szapary
Forstbetrieb
3843 Dobersberg, Kautzener Straße 2

prot Fa Sägeindustrie Dipl-Ing W
Teischinger & Co
8181 St Ruprecht an der Raab
Unterfladnitz Nr 7

Teuschler Gesellschaft mbH
8271 Waltersdorf 165

Josef Thalinger
Säge- und Hobelwerk
3643 Maria Laach am Jauerling,
Zeissing 23

prot Fa Brüder Theurl, Sägewerk und
Holzhandel
9911 Thal/Aßling 101–102

prot Fa Josef Thurner
Holzvermittlung
9640 Kötschach 163

Tilly Holzindustrie Gesellschaft mbH &
Co KG
9330 Treibach, Krappfelderstraße 27

prot Fa Holz- und Kohlengroßhandlung
Hans Traninger
9020 Klagenfurt, Völkermarkter Straße
38

Tyrolignum Internationale Holzmakler
Gesellschaft mbH
6020 Innsbruck, Botanikerstraße 9

Umdasch Industriegesellschaft mbH
Ladeneinrichtungen, DOKA-Schalungen
3300 Amstetten, Reichsstraße 23

UNIHOLCO Handelsgesellschaft mbH
1070 Wien, Kandlgasse 13

„Uniholz" Sägewerk und Holzindustrie
Gesellschaft mbH
1210 Wien, Fultonstraße 24

VELOX Werk Gesellschaft mbH
9422 Maria Rojach, Dachberg 10

Verband ländlicher Genossenschaften in
Niederösterreich reg Genossenschaft
mbH
1011 Wien, Seilergasse 6–8

prot Fa Alfred Vesely
Holzhandel, Holzexport
1010 Wien, Mahlerstraße 3

Waldgenossenschaft Matrei in Osttirol
reg Genossenschaft mbH
9971 Matrei in Osttirol, Virgener Straße
20

Wallner Gesellschaft mbH
Holzindustrie
3352 St Peter/Au, Bubendorf 47

prot Fa Erich Walter Sägewerk und
Holzhandlung
6712 Thüringen, Bludesch

Robert Wegerer Gesellschaft mbH & Co
KG
Holzhandel
1235 Wien, Rudolf-Waisenhorn-Gasse
103

Seril Dr Weinberger Gesellschaft mbH
Handel mit Holz und Holzprodukten
9463 Reichenfels

Johann Weinberger Säge- und
Hobelwerk Gesellschaft mbH
Säge- und Hobelwerk
9463 Reichenfels

Paul Wieland
Holzgroßhandel, Holzexport 2601
Sollenau, Industriestraße 260

prot Fa Wieland KG
Sägewerk, Schnittholzexport,
Parkettfabrik
2601 Sollenau, Industriestraße 260

Wiener Betriebs- und Baugesellschaft
mbH
1153 Wien, Anschützgasse 1

Manfred Wiesinger
Sägewerk
3664 Martinsberg, Thumling 10

prot Fa H Willenshofer
Holz-Import-Export
8650 Kindberg

prot Fa Rupert Wimmer & Co
Sägewerk und Holzhandlung
5431 Kuchl

Franz Wittmann Gesellschaft mbH
Sägewerk und Holzhandel
3172 Ramsau, Gaupmannsgraben 1

Franz Wrodnigg Sägewerk und Kaufhaus
Gesellschaft mbH
9311 Kraig

prot Fa Johann Ziegner KG, Säge- u
Hobelwerk, Mühle
8273 Ebersdorf 60

Johann und Herta Zöchling Gesellschaft
mbH
3171 Kleinzell 62

Ludwig Zwickl
Säge- und Hobelwerk
3943 Schrems, Bahnstraße 60

Colonial products and food

A & O Großhandelshaus Kastner
Gesellschaft mbH
3910 Zwetti, Kremser Straße 35

Adeg Österreich
Handelsaktiengesellschaft
1120 Wien, Gaudenzdorfer Gürtel
41–45

Ankerbrot AG
1101 Wien, Absberggasse 35

prot Fa Joh Berger's Witwe & Söhne
Lebensmittel-Großhandel
1150 Wien, Flachgasse 24–28

Gustav Bogner Handelsagentur
1170 Wien, Hernalser Hauptstraße 167

prot Fa Bernhard Delfiner
Großhandel mit Getreide
Mahlprodukten
und Futtermitteln
1010 Wien, Rosenbursenstraße 4

Ebhart & Herout Gesellschaft mbH
Margarinefabrik
1144 Wien, Stockhammerngasse 19

prot Fa August Gamerith
Großhandel mit Nahrungs- und
Genußmitteln, Eisenhandlung
3730 Eggenburg, Rathausstraße 2

prot F Friedrich Glatz
Groß- und Außenhandel in Getriede,
Mehl, Futtermitteln, Düngemitteln etc
1015 Wien, Johannesgasse 23

Dkfm Liesbeth Hofmann Gesellschaft
mbH
Lebensmittel – Import – Export
2351 Wiener Neudorf, Straße 10
Objekt 40, Industriezentrum Nö-Süd

„Imgro" Nahrungs- und
Genußmittelgroßhandel
und Import Gesellschaft mbH
1020 Wien, Bahnhof Wien Nord

Inzersdorfer Nahrungsmittelwerke
Gesellschaft mbH, nunmehr KG
1232 Wien-Inzersdorf, Draschestraße
107

Konsum Österreich reg Genossenschaft
mbH
1120 Wien, Wolfganggasse 58–60

Josef Manner & Comp AG
1171 Wien, Wilhelminenstraße 6

Mautner Markhof und Wolfrum
Gesellschaft mbH
1110 Wien, Simmeringer Hauptstraße
101

Julius Meinl AG
Nahrungs- und Genußmittelerzeugung
1160 Wien, Julius-Meinl-Gasse 3–7

Merkur Öl- und
Fettgroßhandelsgesellschaft mbH
1020 Wien, Scherzergasse 1

Österreichische Importvereinigung
reg Genossenschaft mbH
1010 Wien, Franz-Josefs-Kai 13

Österreichische Unilever Gesellschaft
mbH
1010 Wien, Schenkenstraße 8–10

W Pregartbauer
Außenhandels-Agentur Gesellschaft
mbH
1130 Wien, Kopfgasse 7

Pretscher & Co Gesellschaft mbH
Import und Export, Großhandel mit
Kaffee sowie Kakao
1082 Wien, Friedrich-Schmidt-Platz 4

prot Fa Joh Schönbichler & Co „St
Etienne"
Spirituosenerzeugung
1010 Wien, Wollzeile 4

Sugana Zucker-Gesellschaft mbH
1020 Wien, Hollandstraße 2

Vereinigte Fettwarenindustrie
Gesellschaft mbH & Co KG
4600 Wels, Vogelweiderstraße 71–73

Vereinigte Kaffee-Großröstereien
Arabia-Mikado Kaffee
Vertriebsgesellschaft mbH
1160 Wien, Zeillergasse 3–5

„Vog" Einfuhr und Großhandel mit
Lebensmitteln
und Bedarfsgütern Gesellschaft mbH
4020 Linz, Bäckermühlweg 44

Wiking Fischhandels–AG
1200 Wien, Nordwestbahnhof

Leather goods

Arbeitsgemeinschaft Lederwirtschaft
Gesellschaft mbH
1010 Wien, Zelinkagasse 6/6

Gustav Binder
Häute – Lederhandlung,
Sportbekleidung
3720 Ravelsbach

„Conzentra"
Vertriebsgesellschaft mbH & Co KG
1232 Wien, Mosetiggasse 1

prot Fa Alois Hirsch KG
Schuh- und Lederhandel
2870 Aspang, Hauptstraße 3

HUMANIC Schuh AG
8020 Graz, Lastenstraße 11

Kraus & Co Warenhandelsgesellschaft
mbH
1040 Wien, Karolinengasse 5

Ernst Kruml
Groß- und Kleinhandel mit Schuhen,
Kleinhandel, Textilien, Handelsagentur
1170 Wien, Hernalser Hauptstraße 230

prot Fa Dr Hans Neuner
Lederfabrik Klagenfurt OHG
9020 Klagenfurt, An der Walk 6

Österreichische Leder & Gummi Co
Gesellschaft mbH
1060 Wien, Liniengasse 50

Carl Ritsch Lederfabrik Gesellschaft
mbH
6361 Hopfgarten

prot Fa Rohrbacher Lederfabrik
Jos Poeschl's Söhne
4150 Rohrbach, Postfach 46

prot Fa Karl Staudt & Co KG
Großhandel, Ex- und Import von Häuten
und Fellen
1010 Wien, Rotenturmstraße 13

Steiermärkische Fleischervereinigung
reg Gen mbH
8020 Graz, Herrgottwiesgasse 55

Rudolf Tentschert Gesellschaft mbH
Fleischhauerei, Fleischselcherei
Stechviehhändler, Rohhäute und Felle
1160 Wien, Lambertgasse 4

Wiener Fleischer –
Genossenschaft reg Gen mbH
1020 Wien, Handelskai 346

Gustav Wurm Gesellschaft mbH
Lederfabrik
4720 Neumarkt im Hausruck

Textiles

Altessa Strickwarenfabrik Gesellschaft
mbH Nfg KG
1030 Wien, Modecenterstraße 22

Brüder Baumann Gesellschaft mbH
Webwarenfabrik
3950 Gmünd, Schremser Straße 38

G Borckenstein & Sohn AG
Baumwollspinnerei
1010 Wien, Domgasse 4

Cöletex Handelsgesellschaft mbH
Textile- Transferdrucke
8010 Graz, Theodor-Köer-Straße 182

Fahnen – Gärtner Gesellschaft mbH
5730 Mittersill, Salzachdamm 135

prot Pa L Freistadtl & Comp
1010 Wien, Sterngasse 13

J M Fussenegger
Textilfabrik
6850 Dornbirn, Wallenmahd 23

Getzner Textil AG
6700 Bludenz, Bleichestraße 1

F M Hämmerle Textilwerke AG
(mit Zweigniederlassung Wien) 6850
Dornbirn

Ing Rudolf Kurt Kastner
Textilgroßhändler
1010 Wien, Gonzagagasse 14

Norbert Langer & Söhne Gesellschaft
mbH
Weberei, Tisch-, Bett-, Hotel- und
Haushaltswäsche
1011 Wien, Sterngasse 11

LINZ TEXTIL HOLDING AG
4032 Linz-Kleinmünchen, Wiener Straße
435

Österreichische Linoleum-, Wachstuch-
und
Kunstlederfabriken AG
2514 Traiskirchen, Badener Straße 9–11

POLYFILL – Handels- und Produktions-
Gesellschaft
mbH und Co KG
6060 Absam, Rhombergstraße 9

Rhomberg Textil Gesellschaft mbH
6850 Dornbirn, Färbergasse 15

Schielseide AG
1231 Wien, A-Schiel-Straße 4
(Gastgebgasse)

prot Fa Schwadorfer
Baumwollspinnerei und Bleicherei
Kantor, Pollack & Co
1010 Wien, Sterngasse 13

Seidra Textilwerke Gesellschaft mbH
9613 St Feistritz an der Gail, Draschitz

Spinnerei und Weberei Teesdorf AG
1110 Wien, Modecenterstraße 17

Martin Stapf Textilwerke Gesellschaft
mbH
6460 Imst, Auwerk 21

Stransky & Söhne
Textilproduktions- und
Handelsgesellschaft
mbH & Co KG
1013 Wien, Börsegasse 1

TAB Textilgesellschaft mbH
6500 Landeck, Bruggfeldstraße 3

Tiroler Loden AG
6020 Insbruck, General-Eccher-Straße 3

Vonwiller Gesellschaft mbH
4170 Haslach, Stelzen 13

Walek & Co Gesellschaft mbH
2700 Wiener Neustadt, Wiener Straße
125

prot Fa Franz Werner KG
Tuch- und Schafwollwaren
1010 Wien, Eßlinggasse 13/1

WMT Handelsgesellschaft mbH
1010 Wien, Rudolfsplatz 12

Miscellaneous

„ADRIA" Internationale Speditions AG
1090 Wien, Alserbachstraße 18

Arcana chem-pharm Fabrik, Gesellschaft
mbH
9800 Spittal an der Drau, Hößlgasse 20

AWT Internationale Handels- und
Finanzierungs AG
1013 Wien, Schottenring 12

BP Austria AG
1041 Wien, Schwarzenbergplatz 13

Bruckmüller Gesellschaft mbH
3970 Weitra, Rathausplatz 58

prot Fa F J Elsnerr & Co
6064 Rum, Siemensstraße 15

Elsner Gesellschaft mbH
Export, Import, Bank- und
Handelsagentur
6020 Innsbruck, Adamgasse 5

„Gallia" Mineralölprodukte-
Vertriebsgesellschaft AG
Zweigniederlassung Wien
1010 Wien, Wipplingerstraße 23

Herbert Görg
Großhandel mit Mineralölen,
Mineralölprodukten,
Treib- und Schmierstoffen
1160 Wien, Effingergasse 27–29

Leykam-Mürztaler Papier und Zellstoff
AG
8101 Gratkom

Mobil Oil Austria AG
1015 Wien, Schwarzenbergplatz 3

NEUBER Gesellschaft mbH
1061 Wien, Brückengasse 1

ÖMV Mandels-Aktiengesellschaft
1011 Wien, Julius-Raab-Platz 4

Österreichische Länderbank AG
Warenabteilung
1010 Wien, Am Hof 2

Österreichische Leasing Gesellschaft
mbH
1040 Wien, Wiedner Hauptstraße 56

prot Fa A Putz Kassen- und
Bürostahlmöbelbau
Tresore, Wandsafes, Nachttresore,
Stahlregale
1160 Wien, Effingergasse 27–29

RTH – Reedereiagentur
Transportagentur
Handelsagentur Gesellschaft mbH
1010 Wien, Wipplingerstraße 34

Schoeller Handelsbeteiligungen
Gesellschaft mbH
1230 Wien, Industriegasse 7

prot Fa Viktor Trampisch
Import-Großhandel mit Rohstoffen für
die Leder-, Gummi-
Textil- und Farbenindustrie
1020 Wien, Hollandstraße 18

Warenhandels- und Datenverarbeitungs-
Gesellschaft mbH
1013 Wien, Börsegasse 9

Brazil

Bolsa de Mercadorias de São Paulo

Omnibus Account

Intermarket Corretora de Mercadorias
S/C Ltda
Rua Dr Sodré, 106 São Paulo/SP 04535
Tel: 531 9433
Telex: 35968

SN Crefisul S/A Sociedade Corretora
Rua Henrique Schaumann, 270
Sobreloja
São Paulo/SP 05413
Tel: 874 1130/1132/1207
Telex: 21917/39878 CREF

Operadora Corretora de Mercadorias
Ltda
Rua XV de Novembro, 228, 16° andar
Ala XV de Novembro
São Paulo/SP 01013
Tel: 34 4147

Bancocidade Corretora de Valores
Mobiliários e de Cambio Ltda
Pça D José Gaspar, 134, 7° e 9° andares
São Paulo/SP 01047
Tel: 231 6322/6577/6573/6574
Telex: 36135
Fax: 2310194

Comercial S/A Corretora De Valores e
Cambio
Av Paulista, 1 439, 3° andar, cj 33
São Paulo/SP 01311
Tel: 289 5011/283 0266
Telex: 37926

FMR Corretora de Mercadorias Ltda
Rua São Bento, 470, 4° andar, conj par
São Paulo/SP 01008
Tel: 239 4066
Telex: 34976

Aplicação Administração & Serviços
Ltda
Rua Três de Dezembro, 43, 3° andar
São Paulo/SP 01014
Tel: 37 4071/36 2034 (Mesa de
Operações)
Telex: 26 294
Fax: 37 3938

Sinal S/A Sociedade Corretora de
Valores
Rua XV de Novembro, 178, SL
São Paulo/SP 01013
*Tel:*255 6544/34 7176
Telex: 60849

Spread Commodities Mercantil e
Corretora de Mercadorias Ltd a
Rua Haddock Lobo, 1 307, 5° andar,
Cj 53 e 54
São Paulo/SP 01414
Tel: 883 1011
Telex: 34154

Spinelli S/A Corretora de Valores
Mobiliários e Cambio
Rua José Bonifácio, 93, 6°/10°/11°
andares
São Paulo/SP 01003
Tel: 37 4521 até 26
Telex: 25997

Santos Corretora de Cambio e Valores
S/A
Rua Libero Badaro, 293, 24° andar, Cj
A/B
São Paulo/SP 01009
Tel: 37 9021
Telex: 24103

Schahin Cury Corretora de Cambio e
Valores Mobiliários S/A
Pça Doc José Caspar, 134, 12° até 14°
andares
São Paulo/SP 01047
Tel: 257 5922/258 0455
Telex: 32996

Termo Corretora de Mercadoria S/C
Ltda
Rua XV de Novembro, 200, 2° andar, Cj
A
São Paulo/SP 01013
Tel: 239 0099
Telex: 35785

Norchem Noroeste Chemical
Commodities Coml e Corr Mercs Ltda
Av Paulista, 1 842, 16° andar
São Paulo/SP 01310
Tel: 234 8533
Telex: 39775

Hedging Comércio e Corretagem de
Mercadorias S/A
Pça Ramos de Azevedo, 206, 13° andar
São Paulo/SP 01037
*Tel:*220 4122/223 6822
Telex: 34009

Open S/A Corretora de Cambio Valores
Mobiliários
Rua Líbero Badaró, 462, 7° andar
São Paulo/SP 01008
Tel: 239 4111
Telex: 31942

Banespa S/A Corretora de Cambio e
Titulos
Rua Álvares Penteado, 49-53
São Paulo/SP 01012
Tel: 231 7544
Telex: 23944/53300/36598/1136205/
113708

Patente S/A Corretora de Cambio e
Valores Mobiliários
Rua Líbero Badaró, 425, 31° andar
São Paulo/SP 01405
Tel: 239 2455
Telex: 24381 PATE

Brasval Distribuidora de Titulos e
Valores Mobiliários Ltda
Rua São Pento, 365, 16° andar
São Paulo/SP 01011
Tel: 35 6181/34 6171
Telex: 38273

Triplik S/A Corretora de Valores e
Cambio
Rua Libero Badaró, 613, 6° andar
São Paulo/SP 01009
Tel: 37 5564
Telex: 32787

Escritório Levy Corretora de Valores
Mobiliários Ltda
Av das Nações Unidas, 11 633, 19° e 20°
andares
São Paulo/SP 04578
Tel: 531 2022
Telex: 54630/54640

Unidade Corretora de Mercadorias S/A
Av Paulista, J 765, 15° andar, Cj 151
São Paulo/SP 01311
Tel: 251 1400
Telex: 38830

Clearing Members

Suplicy Corretora de Cambio e Titulos
Ltda
Rua Boa Vista, 254, 10° andar
São Paulo/SP 01014
Tel: 32 3181/257 6911
Telex: 23583/22175/24466

Theca S/A Distribuidora de Titulos e
Valores Mobiliários
Rua Boa Vista, 314, 2° andar
São Paulo/SP 01014
Tel: 229 2988
Telex: 26482

Boa Vista S/A Corretora de Cambio e
Valores Mobiliários
Pça Pio X, 118, 10° andar
Rio de Janeiro/RJ 20040
Tel: 021 211 1661
Telex: 021 35135

Graphus S/A Corretora de Cambio e
Valaores Mobiliários
Rua Libero Badaro, 425, Cj 213-4, 21°
andar
São Paulo/SP 01009
Tel: 32 4141
Telex: 21047

Pebb Corretora de Valores Ltda
Rua São Bento, 470, 6° andar
São Paulo/SP 01010
Tel: 354145
Telex: 23100

Criffo Corretora de Valores S/A
Rua Formosa, 367, 13° andar
São Paulo/SP 01049
Tel: 223 6822
Telex: 34009

Sigma Distribuidora de Titulos e Valores
Mobiliários Ltda
Rua Líbero Badaró, 425, Cj 42-43
São Paulo/SP 01009
Tel: 359087/88/89/80
Telex: 23215

Penfield Commodity Corretora de
Cambio e Valores Ltda
Rua Frei Gaspar, 25, 1° andar
Santos/SP 11010
Tel: 0132 329311
Telex: 013 1100 ou 2433
Fax: 0132 32 4118

Unibanco Corretora de Valores
Mibiliários S/A
Rua Líbero Badaró, 293, 6° andar
São Paulo/SP 01009
Tel: 235 4265/4267/4951/36 3181/37
5188
Telex: 39779

Cia Real de Cambio e Valores
Mobiliários
Av Paulista, 1 374, 16° andar
São Paulo/SP 01310
Tel: 285 0255 ramal 75
Telex: 011 1261177

Socopa Sociedade Corretora Paulista
S/A
Rua Líbero Badaró, 425, 29° andar
São Paulo/SP 01009
Tel: 34 6121/37 9031
Telex: 38741/25864/22947

Porto Seguro Distribuidora de Titulos e
Valores Mobiliarios Ltda
Rua Líbero Badaró, 377, 5° andar, Cj
510 à 512
São Paulo/SP 01009
Tel: 37 5071 até 5078
Telex: 30384

Kromo Distribuidora de Titulos e
Valores Mobiliários Ltda
Av Paulista, 1 765, 15° andar
São Paulo/SP 01311
Tel: 285 6511/6493
Telex: 37013

Safic Corretora de Valores e Cambio
Ltda
Rua Vergueiro, 1 883, 9° andar
São Paulo/SP 04101
Tel: 549 8266/549 7211
Telex: 36292/36295

Novo Norte S/A Corretora de Valores
Rua João Brícola, 67, 8° andar
São Paulo/SP 01014
Tel: 239 1900
Telex: 36322

Digibanco Corretora de Cambio e
Valores Mobiliários S/A
Av Paulista, 1 337, 3° andar
São Paulo/SP 01311
Tel: 284 7900
Telex: 25197/34658/36191

Econômico S/A Corretora de Cambio e
Valores Mobiliarios
Rua João Bricola, 39, 7° andar
São Paulo/SP 01014
Tel: 37 0011/37 4185
Telex: 24011/30551

Primus Corretora de Valores e Cambio
S/A
Rua da Quitanda, 113, 5° andar
São Paulo/SP 01012
Tel: 369081
Telex: 53131
Fax 344779

Corretora Souza Barros Cambio e
Titulos S/A
Rua Libero Badaro, 293, 23° andar
São Paulo/SP 01009
Tel: 239 2233/258 3211
Telex: 22659/21114

Omega S/A Corretora de Valores
Mobiliarios e Cambio
Rua da Consolação, 331, 11° andar
São Paulo/SP 01301
Tel: 258 8122
Telex: 22694

FNC Corretora de Titulos e Valores
Mobiliários S/A
Rua da Assembléia, 100 – 4° andar
Rio de Janeiro – RJ
Tel: 021 276 3543
Av Paulista, 1 111, 14° andar
São Paulo/SP
Tel: 576 2092/2240
Telex: 32228/33756

Banco do Brasil S/A
Rua Senador Dantas, 105, 5° andar
Rio de Janeiro/RJ 20031
*Tel:*021 240 5198
Telex: 021 51207

CCV Concórdia S/A Corretora de
Valores Mobiliários Cambio e Comm
Rua Líbero Badarõ, 425, 23° andar
São Paulo/SP 01009
Tel: 239 3122
Telex: 37226

Sistema S/A Corretora de Cambio e
Valores Mobiliários
Rua Libero Badaró, 386, 5° andar
São Paulo/SP 01008
Tel: 239 0077 ramal 269 à 271
Telex: 36189/36187

Santista Corretora S/A Cambio e
Valores Mobiliários
Av Maria Coelho Aguiar, 215, Bloco E
8° andar
São Paulo/SP 05804
Tel: 545 4922/2596
Telex: 70625/37885

Botujuru Distribuidora de Titulos e
Valores Mobiliários S/A
Av Brigadeiro Faria Lima, 2 020, 5°
andar, Cj 5 253
São Paulo/SP 01452
Tel: 212 4300/813 2011/814 2568/
210 9500
Telex: 81239

Walpires S/A Corretora de Cambio
Titulos e Valores Mobiliários
Pça Manuel da Nóbrega, 21, 4°, 5° e 6°
andares
São Paulo/SP 01015
Tel: 228 4122
Telex: 25953

Brokers

A Coutinho Comissaria Ltda
Rua Marconi, 31, 8° andar, Cj 82
São Paulo/SP 01047
Tel: 258 3177
Telex: 30052

A Figueiredo Mercadorias S/C Ltda
Rua Dr Sodré, 106
São Paulo/SP 04535
Tel: 35968
Telex: 531 9433

Adfinan Cor de Merc S/C Ltda
Rua XV de Novembro, 184, 8° andar, Cj
806
São Paulo/SP 01013
Tel: 372186

Adriatica Cor de Mercadorias Ltda
Rua Boa Vista, 254, 10° andar
São Paulo/SP 01014
Tel: 257 6911

Agente S A, DTVM
Al Santos, 1357, 4° andar
São Paulo/SP 01419
Tel: 284 1400

Almeida Prado Neto CM Ltda S/C
Av Nações Unidas, 11.633, 19° andar
São Paulo/SP 04578
Tel: 531 2022
Telex: 36942

Aplicação Adm e Serviços Ltda
Rua Três de Dezembro, 43, 3° andar
São Paulo/SP 01014
Tel: 37 4071
Telex: 26294

Arpafi Comm e Corretagem Ltd ME
Rua Apiacas, 869, 2° andar
São Paulo/SP 05017
Tel: 65 8466

Aval S/A CCVM
Rua Pamplona, 1001-5, 4° andar
São Paulo/SP 01405
Tel: 283 4188
Telex: 30739

Bahia CCVM S/A
Av Paulista, 1009, 12° andar
São Paulo/SP 01311
Tel: 285 6822
Telex: 25752

Bancocidade CVMC Ltda
Praça Dom Josē Gaspar, 134, 7° andar
São Paulo/SP 01047
Tel: 231 6322

Boaventura S/C Ltda
Rua Oscar Freire, 1055, Lj 6
São Paulo/SP 01426
Tel: 64 3306

Boavista S/A CCVM
Rua da Quitanda, 96, 2° andar
São Paulo/SP 01012
Tel: 239 0144
Telex: 21515

Brasval DTVM Ltda
Rua São Bento, 365, 16° andar
São Paulo/SP 01014
Tel: 346171
Telex: 38273

Buffolo Cor de Alg S/C Ltda
Av Acoce, 740
São Paulo/SP 04075
Tel: 549 9299
Telex: 31774

Capital SA Cor de Vals e Cambio
Rua Cel Xavier de Toledo, 44, 4° andar
São Paulo/SP 01048
Tel: 37 9501
Telex: 24333

Capitanea DTVM Ltda
Av Paulista, 2202, 5° andar, Cj 56
São Paulo/SP 01310
Tel: 287 1889
Telex: 31540

CCV Concordia S/A CVMCC
Rua Líbero Badaró, 425, 23° andar
São Paulo/SP 01009
Tel: 239 3122
Telex: 37226

Cofinco CCVM Ltda
Alameda Santos, 1800, 5°-9° andar
São Paulo/SP 01418
Tel: 284 9544
Telex: 25256

Rua da Quitanda, 96, 1° andar
São Paulo/SP 01012
Tel: 36 0151

Comerc Cor de Mercadorias Ltda
Rua 03 de Dezembro, 33, 6° andar
São Paulo/SP 01014
Tel: 239 5666
Telex: 39172

Comercial S/A CVC
Av Paulista, 1.439, 3° andar, Cj 33
São Paulo/SP 01311
Tel: 289 5011

Contato Commodities CM S/C Ltda
Rua Carlos Steinen, 335, apto 42
São Paulo/SP 04004
Tel: 887 8682

Convenção S/A DTVM
Av Paulista, 925, 7° andar
São Paulo/SP 01311
Tel: 289 6988
Telex: 30570

Convenção S/A CVC
Av Paulista, 925, 7° andar
São Paulo/SP 01311
Tel: 289 6988
Telex: 30570

Corretora Souza Barros CT S/A
Rua Líbero Badaró, 293, 23° andar
São Paulo/SP 01009
Tel: 239 2233
Telex: 22659

Cottonsul Cor de Merc Ltda
Rua São Bento, 279, 3° andar, Cj
311-13
São Paulo/SP 01011
Telex: 32124

Daycoval Metais Ltda
Rua Marques de Itu, 837, 6° andar, S1,
63-C
São Paulo/SP 01223
Tel: 259 5199

Economico S/A CCVM
Rua João Bricola, 39, 7° andar
São Paulo/SP 01014
Tel: 370011
Telex: 24011

Eduardo Florsheim CM S/C Ltda
Rua Líbero Badaró, 346, 10° andar
São Paulo/SP 01009
Tel: 357171
Telex: 25426

Equipe S/A DTVM
Rua Líbero Badaró, 377, 12° andar, CJ
1203
São Paulo/SP 01009
Tel: 37 3055
Telex: 26440

Esboriol Cor de Mercadorias Ltda
Praça Pe Manoel da Nóbrega, 16, 6°
andar
São Paulo/SP 01015
Tel: 352101
Telex: 26034

Esc di Franco & Gianetti CM S/C Ltda
Rua Líbero Badaró, 471, 24° andar
São Paulo/SP 01009
Tel: 37 3621

Esc Suplicy Cor e Repres Ltda
Rua Boa Vista, 254, 10° andar
São Paulo/SP 01014
Tel: 257 6911
Telex: 23583

Escritorio Lefévre Ltda
Rua Líbero Badarõ, 471, 15° andar
São Paulo/SP 01009
Tel: 37 1557
Telex: 24606

Escritorio Planalto S/C Ltda
Rua Tupi, 280
São Paulo/SP 01233
Tel: 67 1176
Telex: 32902

F Barreto CCT Ltda
Rua Direita, 32, 6° andar
São Paulo/SP 01002
Tel: 258 0333
Telex: 23519

F K Corretora de Merc S/C Ltda
Rua Líbero Badarõ, 471, 10° andar
São Paulo/SP 01009
Tel: 37 2486

Fap Almeida Prado Cor de Merc Ltda
Rua São Bento, 279, 7° andar, Cj 702-8
São Paulo/SP 0100
Tel: 37 7076
Telex: 25442

Fibra Coml e Cor de Merc Ltda
Praça Antonio Prado, 33, 14° andar, CJ 1411
São Paulo/SP 01010
Tel: 37 5137
*Telex:*36397

FMR Corretora de Merc Ltda
Rua São Bento, 470, 4° andar, Cj Par
São Paulo/SP 01010
Tel: 239 4066
Telex: 34976

FNC - CTVM S/A
Av Paulista, 1111, 11° andar
São Paulo/SP 01311
Tel: 576 1666

Fonte S/A CCV
Rua Libero Badarõ, 425, 10° andar, CJ 102
São Paulo/SP 01009
Tel: 35 7183

Forbes CM Ltda
Rua da Consolaçao, 3741, 5° andar, Cj B
São Paulo/SP 01410
Tel: 64 4963

Franco CCTVM Ltda
Rua Direita, 32, 1° andar
São Paulo/SP 01008
Tel: 228 8488

Frandis SA DTVM
Av Paulista, 1294, 3° andar
São Paulo/SP 01310
Tel: 251 4522

Front Commodities CM Ltda
Rua São Bento, 470, 15° andar
São Paulo/SP 01010
Tel: 35 6121
Telex: 25519

Rua 03 de Dezembro, 43-7° andar ao 8° andar
São Paulo/SP 01014
Tel: 35 4121

Gap Commodities Mercantil Ltda
Rua Tabapuã, 41, 4° andar, Chac Itaim
São Paulo/SP 04533
Tel: 852 3444
Telex: 36214

Goldbras Comm Cor de Merc Ltda
Rua Líbero Badarõ, 377, 5° Andar, Cj 509
São Paulo/SP 01009
Tel: 32 0312

Goldmine DTVM Ltda
Av Rio Branco, 177, 19° andar
Rio de Janeiro/RJ 20000
Tel: 240 6030

Graphus S/A CCVM
Rua Líbero Badarõ, 425, 21° andar
São Paulo/SP 01009
Tel: 32 4141
Telex: 21047

Griffo Corretora de Valores SA
Rua Formosa, 367, 13° andar
São Paulo/SP 01049
Tel: 223 6822
Telex: 34009

Grow Commodities S/C Ltda
Rua Joáo Ramalho, 766
São Paulo/SP 05008
Tel: 263 6299

H H Picchioni S/A CCVM
Rua Guajajaras, 557
Belo Horizonte/MG 30180
Tel: 212 4499
Telex: 1196

Havre Part e Empreendimentos Ltda
Rua Pascoal Segueto, 16
Rio de Janeiro/RJ 22600
Tel: 399 9896

Hedging CCM, S/A
Rua Formosa, 367, 13° andar
São Paulo/SP 01049
Telex: 34009

Indusval S/A CTVM
Rua João Bricola, 67, 1° andar
São Paulo/SP 01014
Tel: 239 4344
Telex: 34448

Inter Export Commodities Ltda
Rua Des F Franca, 40, Cj 111
São Paulo/SP 01009
Tel: 239 2699
Telex: 38729

Intermarket CM S/C Ltda
Rua Dr Sodré, 106
São Paulo/SP 04535
Tel: 531 9433
Telex: 35968

Intra Cor Merc Ltda
Rua Líbero Badaró, 377, 25° andar
São Paulo/SP 01009
Tel: 239 2699
Telex: 22592

IOB DTVM Ltda
Rua São Bento, 365, 15° andar
São Paulo/SP 01011
Tel: 239 4711
Telex: 25216

Ippolito Cor de Merc S/C Ltda
Praça Antonio Prado, 33, 16ª S/1604
São Paulo/SP 01010
Tel: 36 0722
Telex: 26926

Irmaos Almeida Prado e Cia Ltda
Rua São Bento, 279, 7° andar, Cj 702-8
São Paulo/SP 01008
Tel: 34 5195
Telex: 25464

JC Toledo Piza Mercadorias Ltda
Rua da Consolação, 374, 3ª andar, Cj, 31
São Paulo/SP 01302
Tel: 257 7760
Telex: 39762

J G Crivellente S/C Ltda
Rua Francisco Teles Dourado, 185
São Paulo/SP 04649
Tel: 37 9271
Telex: 54038

JJTO Cor de Mercadorias S/C Ltd
Av Paulista, 1499, 7° andar, Cj, 711
São Paulo/SP 01311
Tel: 289 8220

JSA Planej Partic S/C Ltda
Rua Peixoto Gomide, 671, 9° andar
São Paulo/SP 01311
Tel: 284 9679
Telex: 35401

Kontike CM S/C Ltda
Av Paulista, 1765, 17° andar
São Paulo/SP 01311
Tel: 284 4744
Telex: 30777

Kromo DTVM Ltda
Av Paulista, 1765, 15° andar
São Paulo/SP 01311
Tel: 288 8014
Telex: 37013

L Suplicy Comm CM Ltda
Rua Boa Vista, 254, 10° andar
São Paulo/SP 01014
Tel: 239 3488
Telex: 38259

LOR SADTVM
Rua Líbero Badaró, 377, 5° andar
São Paulo/SP 01009
Tel: 371431

Margem Comm CM S/C Ltda
Rua Estados Unidos, 403
São Paulo/SP 01427
Tel: 887 4423

Master Commodities CM Ltda
Av Paulista, 575, Cjs 1513-14
São Paulo/SP 01311
Tel: 285 6000

Mercantil de Descontos S/A CCVM
Rua XV de Novembro, 244, 6° andar
São Paulo/SP 01013
Tel: 35 7107
Telex: 26281

Metalcorp Cor de Merc S/C Ltda
Rua da Quitanda, 113, 6° andar, CJ 61
São Paulo/SP 01012
Tel: 35 9997

Mtr Comm Cor Merc Ltda
Rua Gabriel dos Santos, 388
São Paulo/SP 01231
Telex: 67 8854

Misasi Corretora de Valores Ltda
Rua Líbero Badaró, 377, 29° andar
São Paulo/SP 01009
Tel: 37 7151
Telex: 24574

Multinvest DTVM Ltda
Av Ipiranga, 318, 10° andar, Cj 1001
São Paulo/SP 01046
Tel: 257 7022

Natal Corretora de Mercad Ltda
Rua do Comércio, 55, Lj 01
Santo/SP 11100
Tel: 34 6852
Telex: 1376

Nieri Cor Coml Ltda
Rua Líbero Badaro, 101, 11° andar
São Paulo/SP 01009
Tel: 359022
Telex: 30699

Nilo Branco e de Paula CMS/C Ltda
Rua Estados Unidos, 86
São Paulo/SP 01427
Tel: 374451
Telex: 38475

Norchem-Noroeste Chemical CCCM
Ltda
Av Paulista, 1842, 16° andar
São Paulo/SP 01310
Tel: 284 8533
Telex: 39775

Novo Norte S/A Cor de Valores
Rua João Bricola, 67, 8° andar
São Paulo/SP 01014
Tel: 239 1900
Telex: 36322

Oldemar Santos Filho CM S/C Ltda
Rua Líbero Badaró, 346, 10° andar
São Paulo/SP 01008
Tel: 3571/1
Telex: 31848

Omega S/A CVMC
Rua da Consolação, 331, 11° andar
São Paulo/SP 01301
Tel: 258 8122
Telex: 22694

Open S/A CCVM
Rua da Assembléia, 77, 6° andar
Rio de Janeiro/RJ 20011
Tel: 297 2000

Operadora Cor de Merc Ltda
Rua XV de Novembro, 228, 16° andar
São Paulo/SP 01000
Tel: 34 4147

PA Corretora de Merc Ltda
Rua São Bento, 470, 4° andar, Cj Impar
São Paulo/SP 01010
Tel: 35 0074
Telex: 34976

Panbrasilia Comm CMIN S/C Ltda
Av São Luiz, 50, 8° andar, Cj 82 E
São Paulo/SP 01046
Tel: 255 6288
Telex: 37759

Pasternak, Baum do Brasil Ltda
Av Pacaembu, 1917
São Paulo/SP 01234
Tel: 263 1188
Telex: 31807

Patente S/A CCVM
Rua Líbero Badaró, 425, 31° andar
São Paulo/SP 01009
Tel: 239 2455
Telex: 24381

Pebb Corretora de Valores Ltda
Rua São Bento, 470, 4° andar
São Paulo/SP 01011
Tel: 35 4145
Telex: 34976/23100

Penfield Comm Assessoria e Com Ltda
Rua Frei Gaspar, 25, 1° andar
Santos/SP 11010
Tel: 32 9311
Telex: 2433/1100

Penfield Comm CCV Ltda
Rua Frei Gaspar, 25, 1° andar
Santos/SP 11010
Tel: 32 9311
Telex: 1100/2433

Planibanc CV S/A
Av Paulista, 1728, 6°, 7° e 8° andares
São Paulo/SP 01310
Tel: 283 3233
Telex: 35026

PNC International CCTVM S/A
Rua São Bento, 470, 14° andar
São Paulo/SP 01010
Tel: 37 9461

Prime S/A CCV
Rua Direita, 32, 10° andar
São Paulo/SP 01002
Tel: 37 3411
Telex: 30563

Primus CVC S/A
Rua da Quitanda, 113, 5° andar
São Paulo/SP 01012
Tel: 36 9081
Telex: 53131

Procal Cor Merc e Consultoria Ltda
Rua Manoel Guedes, 504, 5° andar
São Paulo/SP 04536
Tel: 852 3044
Telex: 33541

Representações Kaufmann Ltda
Av Duquesa de Goiás, 235
São Paulo/SP 05686
Tel: 543 3988
Telex: 30867

Reserva CVC S/A
Rua Boa Vista, 356, 10° andar
São Paulo/SP 01014
Tel: 229 1911
Telex: 21190

Reunidas Comm Rep Cor Merc Ltda
Av Prestes Maia, 220, 13° andar
São Paulo/SP 01031
Tel: 228 8711

Safic CVC Ltda
Rua Vergueiro, 1883, 9° andar
São Paulo/SP 04101
Tel: 549 8266
Telex: 53321

Sant'anna Commodities S/C Ltda
Rua Casemiro de Abreu, 636
São Paulo/SP 04624
Tel: 531 6072

Santista Corretora SA CVM
Av Maria C Aguiar, 215, BE 8 A
São Paulo/SP 05804
Tel: 545 5503
Telex: 37885

Santos CCV S/A
Rua Líbero Badaró, 293, 22°-24° andar
São Paulo/SP 01008
Tel: 37 9021
Telex: 53015

São Paulo CV Ltda
Av Paulista, 1009, 22° andar
São Paulo/SP 01311
Tel: 285 6755

Schahin Cury CCVM S/A
Praça Dom Josĕ Gaspar, 134, 12 AO 14°
andar
São Paulo/SP 01047
Tel: 257 5922
Telex: 32996

Segmento DTVM Ltda
Rua Jerônimo da Veiga, 164, 5° andar
São Paulo/SP 04536
Tel: 853 0811

Sergio Carnelosso
Rua Centelha, 288, Cj 702
Guarulhos/SP 07000
Tel: 874 1207

Sidney Pires Cor de Merc Ltda
Rua Pe Manoel da Nóbrega, 21-4 AO 6°
andar
São Paulo/SP 01015
Tel: 228 4122
Telex: 25953

Sigma DTVM Ltda
Rua Líbero Badaro, 425, 4° andar, Cj 42
São Paulo/SP 01009
Tel: 37 7561

Sinal S/A Soc Corretora de Valores
Rua XV de Novembro, 178, Sobreloja
São Paulo/SP 01013
Tel: 34 7176
Telex: 60849

Sistema S/A CCVM
Rua XV de Novembro, 317, 3° andar
São Paulo/SP 01008
Tel: 239 0077 Ramal 168
Telex: 36189

Sistema S/A DTVM
Rua XV de Novembro, 317, 3° andar
São Paulo/SP 01008
Tel: 239 0077
Telex: 36189

SN Crefisul S/A Soc Corretora
Rua Henrique Schaumann, 270
São Paulo/SP 05413
Tel: 874 1177
Telex: 29217

Socopa Soc Corretora Paulista S/A
Rua Líbero Badaró, 425, 29° andar
São Paulo/SP 01009
Tel: 346121
Telex: 34455

Spinelli S/A CVMC
Rua José Bonifácio, 93, 10° andar
São Paulo/SP 01003
Tel: 37 4521
Telex: 25997

Spread Comm CM S/C Ltda
Rua Boa Vista, 254, 10° andar, Cj 1011
São Paulo/SP 01014
Tel: 35 8141
Telex: 23583

Spread Comm Mercantil CM Ltda
Rua Hadock Lobo, 1307, 5° andar, Cj
53-54
São Paulo/SP 01414
Tel: 883 1011

Suplicy CCT Ltda
Rua Boa Vista, 254, 10° andar
São Paulo/SP 01014
Tel: 32 3181
Telex: 23583

T C Commodities S/C Ltda
Rua Líbero Badaró, 425, 29° andar
São Paulo/SP 01000
Tel: 34 6121
Telex: 34455

Tecnica Cor Planej e Asses Ltda
Rua Varnhagem, 57, 4° e 5° andares
São Paulo/SP 01022
Tel: 221 7288

Tendencia DTVM Ltda
Av Brig Faria Lima, 1383, 20° andar
São Paulo/SP 01051
Tel: 815 3500
Telex: 30020

Termo CM Ltda
Rua Líbero Badaro, 471, 11° andar
São Paulo/SP 01009
Tel: 239 0099
Telex: 35785

Theca S/A DTVM
Rua Boa Vista, 314, 2° andar
São Paulo/SP 01014
Tel: 228 4177
Telex: 26482

Ticker Cor de Merc Ltda
Rua Jerônimo da Veiga, 164-15° and, Cj
A
São Paulo/SP 04536
Tel: 881 2100

Titulo S/A CCVM
Rua Boa Vista, 254, 11° andar, Cj
1111-22
São Paulo/SP 01014
Tel: 229 2811
Telex: 22327

Trader Cor de Mercadorias Ltda
Rua Sáo Bento, 329, 2° andar, Sala 25
São Paulo/SP 01011
Tel: 364055

Trycomm Cor de Merc S/C Ltda
Rua da Consolação, 3741, 12° andar
São Paulo/SP 01416
Tel: 881 6083
Telex: 38520

Unibanco CVM S/A
Rua Líbero Badaró, 293, 6° andar
São Paulo/SP 01009
Tel: 235 4911
Telex: 39780

Unidade Cor de Mercadorias S/A
Av Paulista, 1765, 15° and, Cj 151
São Paulo/SP 01311
Tel: 251 1400
Telex: 38830

Vetor CVC S/A
Rua do Mercado, 11, 6° AO 8° andar
Rio de Janeiro/RJ 20010
Tel: 297 5115
Telex: 35145

Vitoria Cor de Mercadorias Ltda
Av Senador Queiroz, 605, 14° and, Cj
1421-23
São Paulo/SP 01026
Tel: 255 9904
Telex: 35076

Walpires S/A CCTVM
Rua Pe Manoel da Nobrega, 21, 5° andar
São Paulo/SP 01015
Tel: 228 4122
Telex: 25953

Winner DTVM Ltda
Rua Haddock lobo, 1307, 17° andar
São Paulo/SP 01414
Tel: 881 7166

Bolsa Mercantil & de Futuros

Commodities Brokerage Houses and Clearing Members

(* Commodities Brokerage House
 **** Commodities Brokerage House and Clearing Member**
 ***** Clearing Member)**

* A Coutinho Comissária Ltda
Rua Marconi, 31, 8 andar, São Paulo/SP
01047
Tel: 5511 258 3177
Telex: 11 30052

* Agente S/A DTVM
Al Santos, 1357, 4 andar
São Paulo/SP 01419
Tel: 5511 284 1400
Telex: 11 22444

* Aplicação Adm & Serviços Ltda
Rua 3 de Dezembro, 43, 3 andar
São Paulo/SP 01014
Tel: 5511 37 4071
Telex: 11 1126294

** Arbi S/A SCCTVM
Alameda Santos, 1787, 5 andar
São Paulo/SP 01419
Tel: 5511 287 7977
Telex: 11 34692

* Ativa Commodities Ltda
Rua Líbero Badaró, 425, 16 andar, cj
163
São Paulo/SP 01009
Tel: 5511 35 8131

*** Attual CCTVM Ltda
Rua Líbero Badaró, 377, 22 andar, cj
2210
São Paulo/SP 01009
Tel: 5511 34 7101

** Bahia CCVM S/A
Av Paulista, 1842, 10 andar
São Paulo/SP 01311
Tel: 5511 284 9144

** Baluarte S/A CTVM
Rua Boa Vista, 356, 15 andar
São Paulo/SP 01014
Tel: 5511 227 2111
Telex: 11 21787

* Bancap Mercantile e Part Ltda
Av Brig Luiz Antonio, 487, 10 andar
São Paulo/SP 01317
Tel: 5511 239 0866
Telex: 11 36413

* Banco HM De Inv S/A
Rua Líbero Badaró, 425, 9 andar
São Paulo/SP 01009
Tel: 5511 258 9322

** Bancocidade CVMC Ltda
Pça Dom José Gaspar, 134, 7 andar
São Paulo/SP 01047
Tel: 5511 231 3399
Telex: 11 53993

* Bandeirantes CCVM S/A
Rua Boa Vista, 162, 2 andar
São Paulo/SP 01014
Tel: 5511 239 5622

** Banespa S/A CCT
Rua Alvares Penteado, 49
São Paulo/SP 01012
Tel: 5511 231 7544
Telex: 11 23944

* Banorte DTVM S/A
Rua 15 de Novembro, 140, 2 andar
São Paulo/SP 01013
Tel: 5511 239 5222/257 7522
Telex: 11 23640

** BCN S/A VM
Rua Boa Vista, 208, 12 andar, cj C
São Paulo/SP 01014
Tel: 5511 37 0710

** BMG Corretora S/A
Largo da Misericórdia, 20, 3 e 4 andares
São Paulo/SP 01012
Tel: 5511 258 9811
Telex: 11 22090

** Boa Vista S/A CCVM
Rua da Quitanda, 96, 2 andar
São Paulo/SP 01012
Tel: 5511 239 0144

** Bozano Simonsen S/A CCVM
Rua Boa Vista, 84, sobreloja A
São Paulo/SP 01014
Tel: 5511 252 8133
Telex: 11 21194

** Brasval CV Ltda
Rua São Bento, 365, 16 andar
São Paulo/SP 01011
Tel: 5511 34 6171
Telex: 11 38273

* Cacique DTVM Ltda
Av das Naçóes Unidas, 10989, 9 andar
São Paulo/SP 04101
Tel: 5511 531 4922
Telex: 11 21891

** Cambial S/A CCTVM
Rua Líbero Badaró, 425, 10 andar
São Paulo/SP 01009
Tel: 5511 37 8564/5/6

* CCV Concordia S/A CVMCC
Rua Líbero Badaró, 425, 23 andar
São Paulo/SP 01009
Tel: 5511 239 3122
Telex: 11 37226

** Celtec S/A CCVM
Rua Fomosa, 367, 14 andar
São Paulo/SP 01049
Tel: 5511 223 7222
Telex: 11 22657

* Chase Manhattan S/A DTVM
Rua Alvares Penteado, 131, 2 andar
São Paulo/SP 01012
Tel: 5511 239 0633
Telex: 11 21479

** Cia America Do Sui CCTVM
Largo São Francisco, 34, 5 andar
São Paulo/SP 01005
Tel: 5511 37 0101
Telex: 11 31845

*** Cia Real CCVM
Av Paulista, 1374, 16 andar
São Paulo/SP 01310
Tel: 5511 287 1205

* Cia Real De Commodities
Av Paulista, 1374, 16 andar
São Paulo/SP 01310
Tel: 5511 287 1205

** Citibank CCTVM S/A
Av Paulista, 1111, 10 andar
São Paulo/SP 01311
Tel: 5511 576 2211

** Cobansa S/A CCTVM
Rua Alvares Penteado, 97, 2 andar
São Paulo/SP 01012
Tel: 551 37 5576
Telex: 11 53161

* Coinvalores DTVM Ltda
Rua da Quitanda, 96, 1 e 2 andares
São Paulo/SP 01012
Tel: 5511 36 0151

** Comercial S/A CVC
Av Paulista, 1439, 3 andar, cj 33
São Paulo/SP 01311
Tel: 5511 289 5011

* Com Tec Commodities SC Ltda
Rua São Bento, 389, 6 andar, cj 62
São Paulo/SP 01011
Tel: 5511 36 8533

** Convençao S/A CVC
Av Paulista, 925, 7 andar
São Paulo/SP 01311
Tel: 5511 289 6988
Telex: 11 24870

* Copercom Mercadorias Ltda
Rua São Bento, 470, 7 andar, cj impar
São Paulo/SP 01010
Tel: 5511 34 9874
Telex: 11 11540

* Correção Coml CM Ltda
Rua São Bento, 365, 8 andar, s/86
São Paulo/SP 01010
Tel: 5511 37 1131

** Cotibra S/A CCTM
Rua Líbero Badaró, 471, 12 andar
São Paulo/SP 01009
Tel: 5511 35 2115/6

* Credit Commercial de France S/A
DTVM
Av Paulista, 1106, 4 e 5 andares
São Paulo/SP 01310
Tel: 5511 251 1877/3722

*** DC CCTVM S/A
Rua 3 de Dezembro, 43, 2 andar
São Paulo/SP 01014
Tel: 5511 36 1003

* DC CM S/A
Rua Ridrigo Silva, 26, 19 andar
Rio de Janeiro/RJ 20000
Tel: 5521 292 7722

** Dias De Souza Valores SC Ltda
Rua Líbero Badaró, 471, 16 andar
São Paulo/SP 01009
Tel: 5511 37 7506

* Dibran DTVM Ltda
Av Ipiranga, 318, Bloco A, 14 andar
São Paulo/SP 01046
Tel: 5511 256 6188

* Dig S/A Distr irm Guimaráes TV
Rua Líbero Badaró, 377, 27 andar, cj
2710/2712
São Paulo/SP 01009
Tel: 5511 37 0121/3114

** Digibanco CCVM S/A
Av Paulista, 1337, 3 andar
São Paulo/SP 01311
Tel: 5511 284 7900
Telex: 11 25197

* Distribank Ass Com Ltda
Rua São Bento, 44, sobreloja
São Paulo/SP 01010
Tel: 5511 36 9669

** Doria & Atherino S/A CCVM
Rua Líbero Badaró, 377, 24 andar, cj
2402
São Paulo/SP 01009
Tel: 5511 228 8466
Telex: 11 24727

** Economico S/A CCVM
Rua João Bricola, 39, 7 andar
São Paulo/SP 01014
Tel: 5511 37 4185
Telex: 11 22342

* Equipe S/A DTVM
Rua Líbero Badaró, 377, 12 andar, cj
1203
São Paulo/SP 01009
Tel: 5511 37 3055

* Esboriol SM Ltda
Pça Pe Manoel da Nóbrega, 16, 6 andar
São Paulo/SP 01015
Tel: 5511 35 2101
Telex: 11 34915

** Escritório Lerosa S/A CV
Pça Pe Manoel da Nóbrega, 21, 7 andar
São Paulo/SP 01015
Tel: 5511 258 8422
Telex: 11 34736

** Escritório Levy CVM Ltda
Av das Nações Unidas, 11633, 19 andar
São Paulo/SP 04578
Tel: 5511 531 2022
Telex: 11 36942

* Fator S/A CVC
Rua do Carmo, 57 3-4-5 andares
Rio de Janeiro/RJ 20011
Tel: 5521 221 2997
Telex: 21 34551

* Fenicia DTVM Ltda
Rua João Bricola, 59-67, 3 andar
São Paulo/SP 01014
Tel: 5511 256 6211
Telex: 11 37150

* Fiat Distribuidora S/A TVM
Av Paulista, 967, 14 andar
São Paulo/SP 01311
Tel: 5511 251 3133
Telex: 11 24524

** Finasa CCVM Ltda
Rua Líbero Badaró, 377, 3 andar
São Paulo/SP 01009
Tel: 5511 37 1171
Telex: 11 23181

* Fininvest S/A DTVM
Rua Líbero Badaró, 282, 3 andar
São Paulo/SP 01008
Tel: 5511 234 9011
Telex: 11 24274/36285

* Fonte S/A CCV
Rua Líbero Badaró, 425, 10 andar, cj
102
São Paulo/SP 01009
Tel: 5511 35 7183/37 9763
Telex: 11 54394

* Forbes CM Ltda
Rua da Consolação, 3741, 5 andar cj B
São Paulo/SP 01416
Tel: 5511 64 4963

* Front Comm CM Ltda
Rua São Bento, 470, 17 andar
São Paulo/SP 01010
Tel: 5511 35 4034/5
Telex: 11 25519

* Futura Comm CM Ltda
Rua Boa Vista, 254, 10 andar
São Paulo/SP 01014
Tel: 5511 239 3488
Telex: 11 38259

* Gap Commodities Mercantil Ltda
Rua Tabapuã, 41 4 andar
São Paulo/SP 04533
Tel: 5511 852 3444
Telex: 11 36214

** Garantia S/A CTVM
Av Paulista, 1106, 17 andar
São Paulo/SP 01310
Tel: 5511 283 9133/3233
Telex: 11 24844

** Geral do Comércio S/A CCVM
Rua Funchal, 160, 2 andar
São Paulo/SP 04551
Tel: 5511 833 4434
Telex: 11 70755

** Graphus S/A CCVM
Rua Líbero Badaró, 425, 21 andar, cj
213
São Paulo/SP 01009
Tel: 5511 32 4141
Telex: 11 21047

** Griffo CV S/A
Rua Formosa, 367, 13 andar
São Paulo/SP 01049
Tel: 5511 223 6822
Telex: 11 34009

* Guilder CCT S/A
Rua Líbero Badaró, 425, 12 andar
São Paulo/SP 01009
Tel: 5511 258 8711/34 7761

* Hedging CCM Ltda
Pça Ramos de Azevedo, 206, 13 andar, cj
1330
São Paulo/SP 01037
Tel: 5511 220 4122
Telex: 11 34009

* Incentivo S/A CCTVM
Rua Alvares Penteado, 65, 1 andar
São Paulo/SP 01012
Tel: 5511 37 8081
Telex: 11 23604

* Indice CM Ltda
Av Paulista, 1009, cj 20001
São Paulo/SP 01311
Tel: 5511 251 5222

** Indusval S/A CTVM
Rua João Bricola, 67, 1 e 2 andares
São Paulo/SP 01014
Tel: 5511 239 4344

* Intermarket CM S/C Ltda
Rua Dr Sodré, 106
São Paulo/SP 04535
Tel: 5511 531 9433
Telex: 11 35968

* Intra CM Ltda
Rua Líbero Badaró, 377, 25 andar
São Paulo/SP 01009
Tel: 5511 239 2699

*** Intra S/A CCVM
Rua Líbero Badaró, 377, 25 andar
São Paulo/SP 01009
Tel: 5511 239 2699
Telex: 11 22592

* Investor S/A CCTM
Rua São José, 20, 13 e 14 andares
Rio de Janeiro/RJ 20010
Tel: 5521 221 2277
Telex: 21 37406

** Isoldi S/A CVM
Pça Antonio Prado, 33, 15 andar
São Paulo/SP 01010
Tel: 5511 37 4021
Telex: 11 32695

* Itamarati S/A DTVM
Av Pres Juscelino Kubitschek, 1830, T 1
10 andar
São Paulo/SP 04543
Tel: 5511 241 9433
Telex: 11 21216

* Itau CV S/A
Rua São Bento, 413
São Paulo/SP 01011
Tel: 5511 239 4611
Telex: 11 21281

* Liberal CCVM Ltda
Rua Formosa, 367, 15 andar, cj 1550
São Paulo/SP 01049
Tel: 5511 220 2388
Telex: 11 80103

* Libor DTVM Ltda
Rua da Quitanda, 113, 1 andar
São Paulo/SP 01012
Tel: 5511 35 1131

* Lider CM&F Ltda
Av Paulista, 2073, ed Horsa 2, 11 andar
cj 1
São Paulo/SP 01311
Tel: 5511 285 3458

* Lor S/A DTVM
Rua Líbero Badaró, 377, 5 andar, jc 503
São Paulo/SP 01009
Tel: 5511 35 9795/37 1431
Telex: 11 23083

** Magliano S/A CCVM
Rua Formosa, 367, 29 e 30 andares
São Paulo/SP 01049
Tel: 5511 222 8211
Telex: 11 31764

** Mercantil De Descontos S/A CCVM
Rua 15 de Novembro, 244, 6 andar
São Paulo/SP 01013
Tel: 5511 36 8098
Telex: 11 38197

* Mercantil Do Brasil Cor S/A CTVM
Rua São Bento, 366, 1 andar
São Paulo/SP 01011
Tel: 5511 37 4333/13
Telex: 11 39157

* Merimpex S/A CCV
Pça Pe Manoel da Nóbrega, 21, 20 andar
São Paulo/SP 01015
Tel: 5511 228 5122

* Merrill Lynch Repr Ltda
Rua São Bento, 365, 2 andar
São Paulo/SP 01011
Tel: 5511 36 9191
Telex: 11 34193

* Mesa MTVM Ltda
Rua Dr Miguel Couto, 53, 2 andar
São Paulo/SP 01009
Tel: 5511 229 4322

** Misasi CV Ltda
Rua Líbero Badaró, 377, 2 e 29 andares
São Paulo/SP 01009
Tel: 5511 37 7151
Telex: 11 24574

* Money CM Ltda
Rua Boa Vista, 254, 15 andar, cj 1510
São Paulo/SP 01014
Tel: 5511 37 8614/8367/7786

* Montreal Bank S/A DTVM
Av Paulista, 1842, 15 andar
São Paulo/SP 01310
Tel: 5511 283 0309
Telex: 11 83450

* Multiplic CVM S/A
Av Jurubatuba, 73, 4 ao 11 andar
São Paulo/SP 04583
Tel: 5511 534 6855
Telex: 11 54211 668

** Noroeste S/A CCTVM
Rua Alvares Penteado, 216, 5 andar
São Paulo/SP 01012
Tel: 5511 259 2233
Telex: 11 37011

** Novação S/A CCVM
Rua Floréncio de Abreu, 157, 8 andar
São Paulo/SP 01029
Tel: 5511 228 8811
Telex: 11 34509

** Novinvest S/A CVM
Rua Boa Vista, 63, 10 andar
São Paulo/SP 01014
Tel: 5511 37 2161
Telex: 11 34070

** Novo Norte S/A CV
Rua João Bricola, 67, 7 e 8 andares
São Paulo/SP 01014
Tel: 5511 239 1900
Telex: 11 36322

** Omega S/A CVMC
Rua da Consolaçáo, 331, 11 andar
São Paulo/SP 01301
Tel: 5511 258 8122
Telex: 11 22694

* Open S/A CCVM
Rua Líbero Badaró, 462, 7 andar
São Paulo/SP 01008
Tel: 5511 239 4111
Telex: 11 31942

* Operadora CM Ltda
Rua XV de Novembro, 228, 16 andar
São Paulo/SP 01013
Tel: 5511 34 4147

* P A Cm Ltda
Rua São Bento, 470, 4 andar, cj impar
São Paulo/SP 01010
Tel: 5511 35 0074
Telex: 11 34976

* Panbrasilia CCM Int Neg S/A
Av São Luiz, 50, 8 andar, cj 82E
São Paulo/SP 01046
Tel: 5511 255 6288
Telex: 11 37759

** Patente S/A CCVM
Rua Líbero Badaró, 425, 31 andar
São Paulo/SP 01009
Tel: 5511 239 2455
Telex: 11 24381

** Pebb CV Ltda
Rua São Bento, 470, 6 andar, cj impar
São Paulo/SP 01010
Tel: 5511 35 4145
Telex: 11 23100

* Pirelli Fintec S/A DTVM
Av Paulista, 1842, 7 andar, cj 75
São Paulo/SP 01310
Tel: 5511 289 7499
Telex: 11 33519

* Planibanc CV S/A
Av Paulista, 1728, 6 ao 8 andar
São Paulo/SP 01310
Tel: 5511 283 3233
Telex: 11 38741

** PNC International CCTVM S/A
Rua São Bento, 470, 14 andar
São Paulo/SP 01010
Tel: 5511 37 9461

* Portobello Repres Empr Ltda
Av Brig Faria Lima, 2020, 8 andar, cj 83
São Paulo/SP 01452
Telex: 5511 813 4113/8069
Telex: 11 81209

* Prime S/A CCV
Rua Direita, 32, 10 andar
São Paulo/SP 01002
Tel: 5511 37 3411
Telex: 11 30563

** Primus CVC S/A
Rua da Quitanda, 113, 5 e 6 andares
São Paulo/SP 01012
Tel: 5511 36 9081
Telex: 11 53131

* Procal CM e Cons Ltda
Rua Manuel Guedes, 504, 5 andar
São Paulo/SP 04536
Tel: 5511 852 3044
Telex: 11 33541

** Prosper S/A CVC
Rua São Bento, 470, 2 andar
São Paulo/SP 01010
Tel: 5511 239 1311

** Reserva CVC S/A
Rua Boa Vista, 344, 4 andar
São Paulo/SP 01014
Tel: 5511 229 2966/228 4366
Telex: 11 21190

* Safra CVC Ltda
Av Paulista, 2100, piso Augusta
São Paulo/SP 01310
Tel: 5511 251 7297/7029/7329
Telex: 11 37742

** Santista Corretora S/A CVM
Av Maria Coelho Aguiar, 215, Bl D, 5
andar
São Paulo/SP 05804
Tel: 5511 545 5913

** Santos CCV S/A
Rua Líbero Badaró, 293, 24 andar, cj A/B
São Paulo/SP 01009
Tel: 5511 37 9021
Telex: 11 24103

** São Paulo CV Ltda
Av Paulista, 1009, 17 ao 22 andar
São Paulo/SP 01311
Tel: 5511 285 6755
Telex: 11 35878

** Schahin Cury CCVM S/A
Pça D José Gaspar, 134, salas 12-13-14
São Paulo/SP 01047
Tel: 5511 257 5922
Telex: 11 32996

* Senior DTVM S/A
Rua Sete de Setembro, 99, 17 andar
Rio de Janeiro/RJ 20050
Tel: 5521 224 2077
Telex: 21 38022

** Silex CCVM Ltda
Al Santos, 1800, 5 e 9 andares
São Paulo/SP 01419
Tel: 5511 284 9544
Telex: 11 25256

* Simpex CM Futuros Ltda
Rua Líbero Badaró, 377, 28 andar
São Paulo/SP 01009
Tel: 5511 35 3524
Telex: 11 22936

** Sinal S/A SCV
Rua 15 de Novembro, 178, sobreloja
São Paulo/SP 01013
Tel: 5511 255 6544

** Sistema S/A CCVM
Rua Líbero Badaró, 386, 1 ao 6 andar
São Paulo/SP 01009
Tel: 5511 239 0077
Telex: 11 36189

** SLW CVC Ltda
Rua Emílio de Menezes, 38
São Paulo/SP 01231
Tel: 5511 826 2311
Telex: 11 31372

** SN Crefisul S/A SC
Rua Henrique Schaumann, 270
sobreloja
São Paulo/SP 05413
Tel: 5511 874 1207
Telex: 11 21917

** Socopa SC Paulista S/A
Rua Líbero Badaró, 425, 29 andar
São Paulo/SP 01009
Tel: 5511 34 6121
Telex: 11 34455

* Sodril S/A CTV
Rua Líbero Badaró, 501, 12 andar
São Paulo/SP 01009
Tel: 5511 37 6131
Telex: 11 31679

* Sogeral S/A CCTVM
Av Paulista, 1355, 10 andar
São Paulo/SP 01311
Tel: 5511 251 5533
Telex: 11 25049

** Souza Barros CT S/A
Rua Líbero Badaró, 23 andar
São Paulo/SP 01009
Tel: 5511 239 2233
Telex: 11 22659

** Spinelli S/A CVMC
Rua José Bonifácio, 93, 6-10-11 andares
São Paulo/SP 01003
Tel: 5511 37 4521
Telex: 11 25997

* Spread Comm Merc CM Ltda
Rua Haddock Lobo, 1307, 5 andar, cj 53
São Paulo/SP 01414
Tel: 5511 883 1011
Telex: 11 34154

* Stotler-Dime S/A DTVM
Rua São Bento, 470, 1 andar
São Paulo/SP 01010
Tel: 5511 37 0992

** Sudameris CCVM S/A
Av Paulista, 1000, 7 andar
São Paulo/SP 01310
Tel: 5511 289 8066/ 285 6444
Telex: 11 38088

* Suplicy CCT Ltda
Rua Boa Vista, 254, 10 andar
São Paulo/SP 01014
Tel: 5511 32 3181
Telex: 11 23583

** Talarico CCTM Ltda
Rua Boa Vista, 254, 7 andar, cj 712-3
São Paulo/SP 01014
Tel: 5511 34 8126

* Telles CCM Ltda
Rua 125 de Novembro, 269, 8 andar
cjs 801
São Paulo/SP 01013
Tel: 5511 35 2450

** Tendência DTVM S/A
Av Brig Faria Lima, 1383, 20 andar
São Paulo/SP 04551
Tel: 5511 815 3500

* Termo CM Ltda
Rua 15 de Novembro, 200, 2 andar, cj A
São Paulo/SP 01013
Tel: 5511 239 0099
Telex: 11 35785

** Theca CCTVM Ltda
Rua Boa Vista, 314, 2 andar
São Paulo/SP 01014
Tel: 5511 229 2988

* Ticker Merc Ltda
Rua Jerônimo da Veiga, 164, 15 andar
São Paulo/SP 04536
Tel: 5511 883 1599/881 2100

** Titulo S/A CCVM
Rua Boa Vista, 254, 11 andar
São Paulo/SP 01014
Tel: 5511 229 2811
Telex: 11 22327

* Torre DTVM Ltda
Av Paulista, 2240, 3 andar
São Paulo/SP 01310
Tel: 5511 284 5811
Telex: 11 21412

** Triplik S/A CVC
Rua Líbero Badaró, 613, 5 andar
São Paulo/SP 01009
Tel: 5511 37 5564
Telex: 11 32787

* Umuarama S/A CTVM
Rua São Bento, 470, 3 andar
São Paulo/SP 01010
Tel: 5511 36 7034/35 4743
Telex: 11 35183

** Unibanco CVM S/A
Rua Líbero Badaró, 293, 6 andar
São Paulo/SP 01009
*Tel:*5511 37 1071/5181
Telex: 11 36498

* Vaz Guimaraes, Braga S/A CCT
Rua Boa Vista, 63, 7 e 8 andares
São Paulo/SP 01014
Tel: 5511 34 8191

* Vereda Futuros Ltda
Rua Jerônimo da Veiga, 164, 12 andar
São Paulo/SP 04536
Tel: 5511 852 6274/8549/2045
Telex: 11 23387

* Veritas Adm e Part Ltda
Rua Joáo Bricola, 67, 1 andar
São Paulo/SP 01014
Tel: 5511 221 7288

** Walpires S/A CCTVM
Pça Pe Manoel da Nóbrega, 21, 4 ao 6
andar
São Paulo/SP 01015
Tel: 5511 2288 4122
Telex: 11 25953

Canada

The Montreal Exchange

Full Members

Ais Securities
250 Bloor St East, Suite 301, Toronto
Ontario M4Y 1E6
Tel: 416 925 2512

Allenvest Group Ltd
8 King St East, Suite 700, Toronto
Ontario M5C 1B5
Tel: 416 364 9000
Fax: 416 364 6710

Amsterdam Options Traders (Canada)
Inc
1080 Côte du Beaver Hall, Bureau 200
Montreal, Quebec H2Z 1S8
Tel: 514 875 7093

Andras Research Capital Inc
The Exchange Tower, 2 First Canadian
Place, PO Box 449, 7th Floor, Toronto
Ontario M5X 1J7
Tel: 416 860 7600
Telex: 065 24584
Fax: 416 860 1179

Andras Recherche Capital Inc
1555 rue Peel, Bureau 900, Montréal
Québec H3A 3X6
Tel: 514 281 6780

Bekhor Securities Canada Ltd
Bekhor, Valeurs Mobilières du Canada
Ltée
1255 rue Université, Bureau 1000,
Montréal
Québec H3B 3W6
Tel: 514 878 3110
Fax: 514 878 3109

Brault, Guy, O'Brien Inc
1155 rue Université, Bureau 1000,
Montreal
Québec H3B 3A7
Tel: 514 871 1175
Telex: 05 24599
Fax: 514 876 8894

65 Queen St West
PO Box 29, Suite 1410, Toronto
Ontario M5H 2M5
Tel: 416 869 1373

L A Brenzel Securities Ltd
10 Temperance St, Toronto
Ontario M5H 1Y4
Tel: 416 863 1655

Brockhouse & Cooper Inc
800 bout René-Lévesque ouest
Bureau 2750, Montréal
Québec H3B 1X9
Tel: 514 871 1250
Telex: 05 25412
Fax: 514 397 9349

Brown Baldwin Nisker James Capel Inc
390 Bay St, 19th Floor, Toronto
Ontario M5H 2Y2
Tel: 416 947 2700
Telex: 065 24433

Bunting, Warburg Inc
130 Adelaide St West
Suite 3000, Toronto
Ontario M5H 3V4
Tel: 416 364 3293
Telex: 06 217587

1110 rue Sherbrooke ouest
Bureau 2606, Montréal
Québec H3A 1G8
Tel: 514 842 8726

Burns Fry Ltd
1 First Canadian Place
Suite 5000, PO Box 150, Toronto
Ontario M5X 1H3
Tel: 416 365 4000
514 875 5014
Telex: 065 24138
Fax: 416 365 4311

Burns Fry Ltée
770 rue Sherbrooke ouest
Bureau 2100, Montréal
Québec H3A 1G1
Tel: 514 286 7200

Canarim Investment Corp Ltd
700 Georgia St West
PO Box 10337, Pacific Center
Vancouver, BC V7Y 1H2
Tel: 604 643 7300
Telex: 04 54496
Fax: 604 687 7620

Capital Group Securities Ltd
141 Adelaide St West
Suite 1810, Toronto
Ontario M5H 3L5
Tel: 416 860 7800
Telex: 06 218236
Fax: 416 860 7850

Le Groupe Capital Ltée
1200 ave McGill-College
Bureau 1520, Montréal
Québec H3B 4G7
Tel: 514 866 8811

Casgrain & Compagnie Ltée
625 boul René-Lévesque ouest
Bureau 905, Montréal
Québec H3B 1R2
Tel: 514 871 8080
Telex: 055 61353
Fax: 514 871 1943

Hector M Chisholm & Co Ltd
Suite 300, 330 Bay St, Toronto
Ontario M5H 3T5
Tel: 416 362 4731

Continental Securities (Quebec) Ltd
Investissements Continental (Québec)
Ltée
10th Floor, Four Bentall Center
PO Box 49333, 1055 Dunsmuir St
Vancouver, BC V7X 1C4
Tel: 604 682 4450

Deacon Morgan McEwen Easson Ltd
PO Box 72, North Tower
Royal Bank Plaza, Toronto
Ontario M5J 2J2
Tel: 416 865 0303
Telex: 06217826
Fax: 416 865 9513

Deacon Morgan McEwen Easson Ltée
600 de Maisonneuve ouest, Bureau 750
Montréal, Québec H3A 3J4
Tel: 514 499 0099

Dean Witter Reynolds (Canada) Inc
Scotia Plaza, 40 King St West, Suite
3300
Toronto, Ontario M5H 1B5
Tel: 416 369 8900

2000 ave McGill-College, Bureau 250
Montréal, Québec H3A 3H3
Tel: 514 282 7100

Deragon Langlois Ltée
Edifice Sun Life
1155 rue Metcalfe, Bureau 920
Montréal, Québec H3A 3J4
Tel: 514 861 2771

Dominick & Dominick Securities Inc
55 University Ave, Suite 500, Toronto
Ontario M5J 2H7
Tel: 416 363 0201
Telex: 062 19659
Fax: 416 366 8279

Dominick & Dominick Valeurs Inc
5 Place Ville-Marie, Bureau 1417
Montréal, Québec H3B 2H1
Tel: 514 871 8111

Drapeau Capital Inc
800 Square Victoria, Bureau 310
Montréal, Québec H4Z 1A9
Tel: 514 878 3200

Euro Canadian Securities Ltd
347 Bay St, Suite 700, Toronto
Ontario M5H 2R7
Tel: 416 365 3040
Telex: 06 218013
Fax: 416 365 9903

FCG Securities Corp
1210 Sheppard Ave East, Suite 305
Willowdale, Ontario M2K 1E3
Tel: 416 494 8600

First Boston Canada Ltd
121 King St West
PO Box 111, Suite 2500, Toronto
Ontario M5H 3T9
Tel: 416 365 1330

First Canada Securities International Ltd
Bureau 816, 1155 boul René-Lévesque
ouest
Montréal, Québec H3B 2H7
Tel: 514 397 9073
Fax: 514 397 9073

Standard Life Centre
121 King St West, Suite 2100
PO Box 117, Toronto
Ontario M5H 3T9
Tel: 416 947 7200
Telex: 06 219894
Fax: 416 947 7213

First Marathon Securities Ltd
PO Box 21, 31st Floor
The Stock Exchange Tower
2, First Canadian Place, Toronto
Ontario M5X 1J9
Tel: 416 869 3707

Société de Valeurs First Marathon Ltée
1155 rue Metcalfe, Bureau 2160
Montréal, Québec H3B 2X8
Tel: 514 875 5060

Geoffrion, Leclerc Inc
5 Place Ville-Marie, Bureau 900
Montréal, Québec H3B 2G2
Tel: 514 871 9000
Fax: 514 875 9213

60 Yonge St, Suite 1200
Toronto, Ontario M5E 1S1
Tel: 416 364 0264

Gordon Capital Corp
PO Box 67, Suite 5401
Toronto-Dominion Centre
Toronto, Ontario M5K 1E7
Tel: 416 364 9393
Telex: 06 22118

Corporation Gordon Capital
1 Place Ville-Marie, Bureau 4130
Montréal, Québec H3B 3P9
Tel: 514 861 9751

Great Pacific Management Co Ltd
Suite 300, 1190 Hornby St
Vancouver, BC, V6Z 2K5
Tel: 604 669 1143
Fax: 604 669 0310

Green Line Investor Services Inc
17th Floor, Royal Trust Tower
PO Box 1, Toronto-Dominion Center
Toronto, Ontario M5K 1A2
Tel: 416 982 7800

Services d'Investissement Ligne Verte Inc
2001 rue Université, Bureau 1900
Montréal, Québec H3A 1A6
Tel: 514 289 8458

Société de Courtage Guardinvest Inc
Guardinvest Securities Inc
55 boul René-Lévesques ouest
12ième étage, Montréal
Québec H2Z 1B1
Tel: 514 842 7161

Hamilton Edward Holdings Inc
249 Bruton St, Beaconsfield
Québec H9W 1N1
Tel: 514 694 7282

Invescourt, Courtier en Valeurs
Mobilières Inc
Invescourt, Stockbroker Inc
625 boul René-Lévesque ouest
3ième étage, Montréal
Québec H3B 1R1
Tel: 514 397 1881
Fax: 514 874 4090

Les Investissements Disnat Inc
2020 rue Université, 9e étage
Montréal, Québec H3A 2A5
Tel: 514 842 8471
Fax: 514 842 3137

Disnat Investment Inc
330 Bay St, Suite 711
Toronto, Ontario M5H 2S8
Tel: 416 868 0698

John Graham & Co Ltd
100 Sparks St, Ottawa
Ontario K1P 5B7
Tel: 613 237 0590
Telex: 053 4204
Fax: 613 237 0299

Lafferty, Harwood & Partners Ltd
Lafferty, Harwood & Associés Ltée
500 St-Jacques, Bureau 600
Montréal, Québec H2Y 3R3
Tel: 514 845 3166
Fax: 514 281 1383

W D Latimer Co Ltd
PO Box 96
Toronto-dominion Centre
Toronto, Ontario M5K 1G8
Tel: 416 363 5631
Telex: 06 22285
Fax: 416 363 8022

2020 rue Université, Bureau 1623
Montréal, Québec H3A 2A5
Tel: 514 845 5235

Leduc & Associés Valeurs Mobilières Inc
1801 ave McGill-College, Bureau 870
Montréal, Québec H3A 2N4
Tel: 514 499 1066

Levesque, Beaubien Inc
Edifice Sun Life
1155 rue Metcalfe, 5e étage
Montréal, Québec H3B 4S9
Tel: 514 879 2222
Telex: 055 61048
Fax: 514 875 7914

121 King St West, Suite 600
Toronto, Ontario M5H 3T9
Tel: 416 865 7400

Loewen, Ondaatje, McCutcheon & Co
Ltd
40 King St West, Suite 5500
Toronto, Ontario M5H 3Y2
Tel: 416 869 7211
Telex: 06 219767

Loewen, Ondaatje, McCutcheon & Cie
Ltée
1200 ave McGill-College, Bureau 2010
Montréal, Québec H3B 4G2
Tel: 514 393 4600

MacDougall, MacDougall & MacTier
Inc
Place du Canada, Bureau 2000, Montréal
Québec H3B 4J1
Tel: 514 871 9611
Telex: 055 60578
Fax: 514 871 1481

PO Box 13, 150 King St West
Toronto, Ontario M5H 1J9
Tel: 416 977 0663

J D Mack Ltd
Suite 1204, Purdy's Wharf
1959 Upper Water St, Halifax
N S B3J 2N2
Tel: 902 420 0077
Fax: 902 422 9515

Maison Placements Canada Inc
Place du Canada, Bureau 1130
Montréal, Québec H3B 2P7
Tel: 514 879 1662
Fax: 416 947 6046

130 Adelaide St West, Suite 906
PO Box 99, Toronto
Ontario M5H 3P5
Tel: 416 947 6040

McCarthy Securities Ltd
55 Yonge St, Suite 1200
Toronto, Ontario M5E 1J4
Tel: 416 863 2307
Telex: 06 218437
Fax: 416 862 8053

Valeurs McCarthy Ltée
1981 ave McGill-College, Bureau 460
Montréal, Québec H3A 2W9
Tel: 514 845 4262
Telex: 514 845 2375

McDermid St Lawrence Ltd
601 West Hastings St, Suite 1000
PO Box 90, Vancouver, BC V6B 5E2
Tel: 604 654 9111
Telex: 04 54491
Fax: 604 654 1224

McLean McCarthy Ltd
11 King St West, Toronto
Ontario M5H 1A3
Tel: 416 368 2751
Telex: 06 23852

McNeil, Mantha, Inc
1080 Beaver Hall, Bureau 200
Montréal, Québec H2Z 1S8
Tel: 514 875 4810
Telex: 055 61261
Fax: 514 397 0827

Standard Life Centre
121 King St West, Suite 110
Toronto, Ontario M5H 3T9
Tel: 416 369 2500

Merit Investment Corp
55 University Ave, Suite 1000
Toronto, Ontario M5J 2P8
Tel: 416 867 6000
Telex: 06 217773

Merrill Lynch Canada Inc
Merrill Lynch Canada Tower
200 King St West, Toronto
Ontario M5H 3W3
Tel: 416 586 6000
Telex: 06 23221.
Fax: 416 586 6076

Place Montréal Trust
25e et 26e étage
1800 ave McGill-College
Montréal, Québec H3A 3J6
Tel: 514 982 2600

Midland Doherty Ltd
121 King St West, Toronto
Ontario M5Y 3W6
Tel: 416 369 7400
Telex: 06 219592
Fax: 416 369 7680

Midland Doherty Ltée
1 Place Ville-Marie, Bureau 2300
Montréal, Québec H3B 3M5
Tel: 514 879 1050

Nesbitt Thomson Deacon Ltée
355 St-Jacques ouest
Rez-de-chaussée, Montréal
Québec H2Y 1P1
Tel: 514 282 5800

Nesbitt Thomson Deacon Inc
150 King St West, Toronto
Ontario M5H 3W2
Tel: 416 586 3600

Odlum Brown Ltd
1800–609 Granvill St, PO Box 10012
Pacific Centre, Vancouver
BC V7Y 1A3
Tel: 604 669 1600

C M Oliver & Co Ltd
750 Pender St West, 2nd Floor
Vancouver, BC V6C 1B5
Tel: 604 668 6700
Telex: 04 51215
Fax: 604 681 8964

Ouimet Hubbs Inc
1 Place Ville Marie, Bureau 1535
Montréal, Québec H3B 2B5
Tel: 514 866 2121
Telex: 514 866 2140

95 Wellington West, Suite 702
Toronto, Ontario M5J 2N7
Tel: 416 368 8900

John Pasztor & Associates Inc
330 Bay St, Suite 201, Toronto
Ontario M5H 2S8
Tel: 416 369 0162

Pemberton Securities Inc
Suite 2400 Park Place, 666 Burrard St
Vancouver, BC V6C 3C7
Tel: 604 688 8411
Telex: 04 54331
Fax: 604 688 3084

Valeurs Mobilières Pemberton Inc
1 Place Ville Marie, Bureau 2101
Montréal, Québec H3B 4H5
Tel: 514 875 2180

Placements Banque Nationale Inc
National Bank Securities Inc
600 de la Gauchetière ouest, 6e étage
Montréal, Québec H3B 4L2
Tel: 514 394 8670

Pollitt, Bertrand, Hart & Co Inc
11 King St West, Suite 1500, Toronto
Ontario M5H 1A7
Tel: 416 365 3313

625, boul René-Lévesque ouest
Bureau 115, Montréal
Québec H3B 1R2
Tel: 04 395 8910

Pope & Co
15 Duncan St, Toronto
Ontario M5H 3P9
Tel: 416 593 5535
Telex: 065 24418
Fax: 416 593 5099

Prudential-Bache Securities Canada Ltd
33 Yonge St, 5th Floor, Toronto
Ontario M5H 1V7
Tel: 416 860 3000
Telex: 065 24262
Fax: 416 860 3193

La Societe de Courtage Prudential-Bache
Canada Ltée
1080 Beaver Hall, Bureau 400
Montréal, Québec H27 1Y8
Tel: 514 879 9649

RBC Dominion Securities Inc
PO Box 21, Commerce Court South
Toronto, Ontario M5L 1A7
Tel: 416 864 4000
Telex: 065 24114
Fax: 416 864 8816

2000 ave McGill-College, Bureau 300
Montréal, Québec H3A 3H5
Tel: 514 282 5200

Rasmussen, Sharp & Co Ltd
Rasmussen, Sharp & Cie Ltée
1010 rue Sherbrooke ouest, Bureau 2408
Montréal, Québec H3A 2R7
Tel: 514 284 2420

Refco, Valeurs Mobilières (Canada) Ltée
2000 rue Mansfield, Bureau 920
Montréal, Quéec H3A 2Z6
Tel: 514 843 1000

Refco Futures (Canada) Ltd
150 York St, Suite 1600, Toronto
Ontario M5H 3S5
Tel: 416 862 7000 (64-65)
Fax: 416 862 0576

Richardson Greenshields of Canada Ltd
One Lombard Place, Minnipeg
Manitoba R3B 0Y2
Tel: 204 934 5858
Telex: 065 24133
Fax: 204 934 5875

Richardson Greenshields du Canada Ltée
4 Place Ville-Marie, Montréal
Québec H3B 2E8
Tel: 514 397 2000

Royal Oak Securities Corp
55 University Ave, Suite 320
Toronto, Ontario M5J 2H7
Tel: 416 862 0066 (62-63)
Fax: 416 862 7737

Scotia Bond Co Ltd
1809 Barrington St, Suite 1100
Halifax, NS B3J 2T3
Tel: 902 425 6900
Telex: 019 21861
Fax: 902 429 8323

Scotia McLeod Inc
PO Box 433, Commercial Union Tower
Toronto-Dominion Centre
Toronto, Ontario M5K 1M2
Tel: 416 863 7411
Telex: 065 24250
Fax: 416 863 7748

760 rue Sherbrooke ouest
Montréal, Québec H3A 1G1
Tel: 514 287 3600
Telex: 055 61106

Tassé & Associés Ltée
630 boul René-Lévesque ouest
Bureau 1200, Montréal
Québec H3B 1S6
Tel: 514 879 2100
Telex: 055 61249
Fax: 514 879 3931

181 University Ave, Suite 1118
Toronto, Ontario M5H 3M7
Tel: 416 868 6200

Valeurs Mobilières SMC Inc
SMC Securities Inc
1155 rue Metcalfe, Bureau 820
Montréal, Québec H3B 2V6
Tel: 514 875 9040
Telex: 055 61525

Walwyn Stodgell Cochran Murray Ltd
70 University Ave, Suite 800
Toronto, Ontario M5J 2M5
Tel: 416 591 6000
Telex: 06 217807
Fax: 416 591 6250

Walwyn Stodgell Cochran Murray Ltée
2000 ave McGill-College, Bureau 900
Montréal, Québec H3A 3H3
Tel: 514 842 2818

Wood Gundy Inc
PO Box 274, Royal Trust Tower
Toronto-Dominion Centre, Toronto
Ontarion M5X 1M7
Tel: 416 869 8100
Telex: 06 219508
Fax: 416 869 8330

600 boul de Maisonneuve ouest, 30e
étage
Montréal, Quebec H3A 3J2
Tel: 514 843 2800

Yamaichi International (Canada) Ltd
150 King St West, Suite 2400
Toronto, Ontario M5H 1J9
Tel: 416 597 2730

Yamaichi International (Canada) Ltée
600 de Maisonneuve ouest, Bureau 2300
Montréal, Québec H3A 3J2
Tel: 514 499 1110

Yorkton Securities Inc
Suite 2700 – PO Box 379
1 First Canadian Place
Toronto, Ontario M5X 1J8
Tel: 416 864 3500
Telex: 06 217596

Individual Members

Biron, Ronald
939 Des Mésanges
Longueuil, Québec J4G 1X1
Tel: 514 646 1055

Brunet, Jacques
415 Saraguay, Pierrefonds
Québec H8Y 2G3
Tel: 514 684 3937
Bur. 514 684 1443

Costa, Remo
7870 Croissant Du beau Bois, Montréal
Quebec H4K 9Z7
Tel: 514 332 9947

Scott, John
251 Ballantyne nord
Montréal ouest, Québec H4X 2C3
Tel: 514 482 7045

Membres Jitney
Casey, Gerald P
4368 ave Melrose
Montréal, Québec H4A 2S6
Tel: 514 486 4408

Cavanagh, Frank
8204 Levis Sauvé
LaSalle, Québec H8P 3J7
Tel: 514 363 7464

Membres du Marché International D'Options
Bank of America Canada
4 King St West, 18th Floor
Toronto, Ontario M5H 1B6
Tel: 416 863 5481

Banque Nationale du Canada
600 rue de la Gauchetière ouest
6ième étage, Montréal
Québec H3B 4L8
Tel: 514 394 6398

Banque Royale du Canada
Investment Banking and Treasury
200 Bay St, 16th floor, South Tower
Toronto, Ontario M5J 2J5
Tel: 416 974 5151

Compagnie de Fiducie Guardian
618 rue St-Jacques, Montréal
Québec H3C 1E3
Tel: 514 842 7161

Discount Corp of New York Futures
200 West Madison, Second Floor
Chicago, Illinois 60606
Tel: 312 368 2200

Membres de la Division Mercantile
Alco-Canada Commodities Services Inc
800 Square Victoria, Bureau 4708
Montréal, Québec H4Z 1K2
Tel: 514 871 8323

Donaldson Lufkin and Jenrette Acli
Futures Ltd
140 Broadway, New York
NY 10005
Tel: 212 902 2000

Mathieu, Jr, Arthur James
2413 Bayshore Blvd, Apt 2205
Tampa, Florida 33629

Universal Commodities Ltd
PO Box 839
6600 Highland Rd
Pontiac, Michigan 48056
Tel: 313 666 3000

Membres-Accès Électronique
Darier Canada Inc
3655 Redpath, Montréal
Québec H3G 2G9
Tel: 514 288 2991/92

Pictet (Canada) Société en Commandite
2020 rue Université, Bureau 1544
Montréal, Québec H3A 2A5
Tel: 514 288 8161

Transatlantic Securities Co
1155 rue Sherbrooke ouest, Bureau 1401
Montréal, Québec H3A 2W1
Tel: 514 288 5261

Membres Correspondants Pour les Options
Algemene Bank Nederland NV
Vijzelstraat, PO Box 669
1000 EG, Amsterdam

Bank Der Bondsspaarbanken NV
Singel 236, 1016 AB Amsterdam

James Capel & Co Inc
James Capel House, 6 Bevis Marks
London, England EC3A 7JQ

Crediet en Effectenbakk NV
PO Box 35100, 3508 AC Utrecht

Effectenkantoor A Strating and Co BV
Herengracht 130, 1015 BV Amsterdam

Effectenkantoor E Van Wijngaarden &
Co BV
NZ Voorburgwal 48–50
1015 SC Amsterdam

Effectenbank Van Meer and Co NV
PO Box 19553, 1000 GV Amsterdam

Europtions BV
Rokin 65, 1012 KK Amsterdam

F Van Lanschot Bankiers NV
Damrak 62A
1012 LM Amsterdam

GW and H Van Ophoven & Co BV
c/o Ottervanger Effectenkantoor BV
Rokin 9–15, 1012 KK Amsterdam

Hambros Bank Ltd
41 Bishopsgate
London, England EC2P 2AA

Kredietbank NV
Arembergstraat 7
B-1000 Brussels, Belgium

Lentjes en Drossaerts NV
PO Box 1036
5200 BA S-Hertogenbosch

Nederlandsche Middenstandsbank NV
Amstelstraat 21
1017 DA Amsterdam

Paine Webber International Futures Ltd
1 Finsbury Ave
London, England EC2M 2PA

Phillips & Drew
120 Moorgate, London
England EC2M 6XP

Pierson, Heldring and Pierson NV
Herengracht 206–214
1016 BS Amsterdam

Rabobank Nederland
PO Box 17100
3500 HG Utrecht

Sheppards
1 London Bridge
London, England SE1 904

CLN Oyens & Van Eeghen·NV
PO Box 956
1000 AZ Amsterdam

Van Der Hoop and Co NV
Prins Hendrikkade 123
1011 Am Amsterdam

Van Kollem & Zoon BV
Rokin 91, 1012 KL Amsterdam

Titulaires de Permis Restreints

Belanger, Serge
9150 Emile-Legault
Anjou, Québec H1K 4Y7
Tel: 514 354 5313

Boudreau, Gilbert
1927 Doucet
Varennes, Québec J0L 2P0
Tel: 514 652 2814

Calvo, Fernando
1790 boul des Laurentides
Laval, Québec H7M 2P6
Tel: 514 667 1226

Cusson, Yves
655 rue Claude
Beloeil, Québec J3G 4X3
Tel: 514 467 3976

Du Sablon-Bullock, Huguette
Chemin de la Montagne
Bolton Sud, Québec J0E 2H0
Tel: 514 292 5721

Fefer, Hervé
6745 ave Monkland
Montréal, Québec H4B 1H9
Tel: 514 489 1484

Gervais, Guy
2445 rue Marquette
Longueuil, Québec J4K 4K1
Tel: 514 674 4487

Guevremont, Eddy
5261 6e ave, Montréal
Québec H1Y 2P5
Tel: 514 721 3515

Lachapelle, René
5 Deblois, Joliette, Québec J6E 4H5
Tel: 514 756 8688

Lapointe, Louis
7570 Tétrault, Brossard
Québec J4W 2V3
Tel: 514 466 2816

Mizrahi, Michael David
4521 Notre-Dame
Laval, Québec H7W 1T7
Tel: 514 688 5922

Muttalib, Abdul
173 Trenton, Ville Mont-Royal
Québec H3P 1Z3
Tel: 514 735 9407

Pereira, Arthur R
5773 ave Smart, Côte St-Luc
Québec H4W 2M8
Tel: 514 489 9084

Perras, François
398 Colombine, St-Bruno
Québec J3V 5T8
Tel: 514 653 3264

Ricciardo, Stefano
8406 Casgrain
Montréal, Québec H2P 2K8
Tel: 514 387 1880

Therrien, Jean-Pierre
10,202 Basile-Routhier
Montréal, Québec H2C 2C4
Tel: 514 382 3959

The Toronto Stock Exchange

Andras Research Capital Inc (83)
7th Floor
2 First Canadian Place
Box 449, M5X 1J7
Tel: 860 7600

Arachnae Securities Ltd
Buttonville Airport
Markham, L3P 3J9
Tel: 477 7150

Begg Securities Ltd
90 Adelaide St West
2nd Floor, M5H 1P6
Tel: 869 1721

R Brant Securities Ltd
Suite 301
4 King St West, M5H 1B6
Tel: 865 1090

Brault, Guy, O'Brien Inc (47)
Suite 1410
PO Box 29
65 Queen St West, M5H 2M5
Tel: 869 1373

Brawley Cathers Ltd (17)
11 King St West, M5H 1A7
Tel: 363 5821

L A Brenzel Securities Ltd (57)
10 Temperance St, M5H 1Y4
Tel: 863 1655

Brink, Hudson & Lefever Ltd (14)
1500 Park Place
666 Burrard St
Vancouver, British Columbia, V6C 3C4
Tel: 0604 688 0133

Brockhouse & Cooper Inc
Suite 2750
800 Dorchester Blvd West
Montreal, Quebec, H3B 1X9
Tel: 514 871 1250

Brown Baldwin Nisker James Capel Inc
(99)
19th Floor
390 Bay St, M5H 2Y2
Tel: 947 2700

Bunting Warburg Inc (15)
130 Adelaide St West
Suite 3000, M5H 3V4
Tel: 364 3293

Burns Fry Ltd (12)
Suite 5000
PO Box 150
First Canadian Place, M5X 1H3
Tel: 365 4000

Caldwell Gundy Inc (43)
55 University Ave
Suite 340, M5J 2H7
Tel: 862 7755

Canarim Investment Corporation Ltd
(33)
2 First Canadian Place
36th Floor, PO Box 27, Suite 3640
Toronto, Ontario, M5X 1A9
Tel: 869 1900

Capital Group Securities Ltd (88)
Suite 1810
141 Adelaide St West, M5H 3L5
Tel: 860 7800

Cassels Blaikie & Co Ltd (35)
33 Yonge St
Suite 200, M5E 1S8
Tel: 362 6531

Hector M Chisholm & Co Ltd (57)
330 Bay St
Suite 300, M5H 3T5
Tel: 362 4731

Connor, Clark & Co Ltd (50)
Scotia Plaza
40 King St West
Suite 5110, PO Box 125, M5H 3Y2
Tel: 360 0006

Daiwa Securities Canada Ltd
1 First Canadian Place
Suite 650, PO Box 194, M5X 1A6
Tel: 863 6560

Deacon Morgan McEwen Easson Ltd
(27)
Suite 1330
North Tower, Royal Bank Plaza
Box 72, M5J 2J2
Tel: 865 0303

Dean Witter Reynolds (Canada) Inc (40)
Scotia Plaza
40 King St West, Suite 3300, M5H 1B5
Tel: 369 8900

Dominick & Dominick Securities Inc (31)
55 University Ave, Suite 500
5th Floor, M5J 2H7
Tel: 363 0201

First Boston Canada Ltd (72)
Standard Life Centre
121 King St West
Suite 2500, PO Box 111, M5H 3T9
Tel: 947 2600

First Canada Securities International Ltd
(90)
Standard Life Centre
121 King St West, Suite 2100
PO Box 117, M5H 3T9
Tel: 947 7200

First Marathon Securities Ltd (80)
2 First Canadian Place
The Exchange Tower
Suite 3100, M5X 1J9
Tel: 869 3707

Fraser Dingman Ltd (68)
Royal Bank Plaza
South Tower
PO Box 24, Suite 2950, M5J 2J1
Tel: 365 2365

Geoffrion, Leclerc & Co Ltd (61)
PO Box 175
Suite 2400, Royal Bank Plaza
South Tower, M5J 2J4
Tel: 865 1060

Geoffrion, Leclerc Inc (61)
5 Place Ville Marie
Suite 900
Montreal, Quebec, H3B 2G2
Tel: 514 871 9000

Gordon Capital Corporation (81)
Suite 5401
PO Box 67
Toronto-Dominion Centre, M5K 1E7
Tel: 364 9393

Green Line Investor Services Inc (7)
17th Floor, Royal Trust Tower
PO Box 1
Toronto-Dominion Centre, M5K 1A2
Tel: 982 7980

Haywood Securities Inc
11th Floor, Commerce Place
400 Burrard St
Vancouver, British Columbia, V6C 3A6
Tel: 604 643 1100

Jones, Gable & Co Ltd (44)
110 Yonge St, M5C 1T6
Tel: 362 5454

Kingwest and Co
86 Avenue Rd, M5R 2H2
Tel: 927 7740

Lafferty, Harwood & Partners Ltd (5)
500 St Jacques St
Suite 600
Montreal, Quebec, H2Y 3R3
Tel: 514 845 3166

W D Latimer Co Ltd (36)
PO Box 96, 25th Floor
Bank Tower
Toronto-Dominion Centre, M5K 1G8
Tel: 363 5631

Levesque, Beaubien Inc (63)
121 King St West
Suite 600, M5H 3T9
Tel: 865 7400

Loewen, Ondaatje, McCutcheon & Co
Ltd (45)
40 King St West
Suite 5500, M5H 3Y2
Tel: 869 7211

MacDougall, MacDougall & Mactier Inc
(37)
150 King St West, Suite 1305
PO Box 13, M5H 1J9
Tel: 977 0663

J D Mack Ltd
PO Box 2052
1204 Purdy's Wharf
1959 Upper Water St
Halifax, Nova Scotia, B3J 2Z1
Tel: 902 420 0077

Maison Placements Canada Inc (34)
130 Adelaide St West
Suite 906, M5H 3P5
Tel: 947 6040

Majendie Securities Ltd (3)
20 Queen St W
Suite 2208, PO Box 28, M5H 3R3
Tel: 366 1980

McCarthy Securities Ltd (28)
55 Yonge St
Suite 1200, N5E 1J4
Tel: 862 9160

McConnell & Co Ltd (4)
390 Bay St
Suite 1400, M5H 2Y2
Tel: 364 4461

McDermid St Lawrence Ltd (70)
401 Bay St
Suite 2315, M5H 2Y4
Tel: 368 3811

McLean McCarthy Ltd (51)
Suite 1300
11 King St West, M5H 1A3
Tel: 368 2751

McNeil, Mantha Inc (64)
Standard Life Centre
Suite 1010, PO Box 110
121 King St West, M5H 3T9
Tel: 369 2500

Merit Investment Corp (87)
55 University Ave
Suite 1000, M5J 2P8
Tel: 867 6000

Merrill Lynch Canada Inc (24)
Merrill Lynch Canada Tower
200 King St West, M5H 3W3
Tel: 586 6000

Midland Doherty Ltd (39)
Standard Life Tower
121 King St West, M5H 3W6
Tel: 369 7400

Moss, Lawson & Co Ltd (76)
48 Yonge St, M5E 1G7
Tel: 864 2700

Nesbitt Thomson Deacon Inc (9)
150 King St West
Suite 1900
Sun Life Tower
Sun Life Centre, M5H 3W2
Tel: 586 3600

The Nikko Securities Co Canada, Ltd
Suite 3808, PO Box 84
Toronto-Dominion Bank Tower
Toronto Dominion Centre, M5K 1G8
Tel: 366 2600

Nomura Canada Inc
1 First Canadian Place
Suite 5830, M5X 1E3
Tel: 868 1683

Odlum Brown Ltd (25)
8 King St East, M5C 1B5
Tel: 363 8443

Ouimet Hubbs Inc (21)
95 Wellington St West
Suite 702, PO Box 9, M5J 2N7
Tel: 368 8900

Pemberton Securities Inc (89)
Suite 3600, PO Box 110
1 First Canadian Place, M5X 1B6
Tel: 364 2231

Peters & Co Ltd (77)
200 Sun Life Plaza
North Tower
140-4th Ave SW
Calgary, Alberta, T2P 3M3
Tel: 403 261 4850

Pollitt, Bertrand, Hart & Co Inc (92)
Suite 1500
11 King St West, M5H 1A7
Tel: 365 3313

Pope & Co (66)
15 Duncan St, M5H 3P9
Tel: 593 5535

Prudential-Bache Securities Canada Ltd
(18)
4th Floor
33 Yong St, M5E 1V7
Tel: 860 3000

RBC Dominion Securities Inc (2)
PO Box 21
Commerce Court South, M5L 1A7
Tel: 864 4000

Richardson Greenshields of Canada Ltd
(46)
130 Adelaide St West, M5H 1T8
Tel: 860 3400

Scotia Bond Co Ltd (10)
Suite 1100
1809 Barrington St
PO Box 666
Halifax, Nova Scotia, B3J 2T3
Tel: 902 425 6900

Scotiamcleod Inc (85)
PO Box 433
Commercial Union Tower
Toronto-Dominion Centre, M5K 1M2
Tel: 863 7411

Security Trading Inc
Suite 220
145 Wellington St West, M5J 1H8
Tel: 586 0333

Sprott Securities Ltd (73)
1 University Ave
Suite 702, M5J 2P1
Tel: 362 7485

Standard Securities Ltd (41)
Suite 1202, Metropolitan Place
1 University Ave, M5J 2P1
Tel: 363 5911

Tasse & Associates Ltd (75)
181 University Ave
Suite 1118, M5H 3M7
Tel: 868 6200

Thomson Kernaghan & Co Ltd (22)
365 Bay St, M5H 2V2
Tel: 860 8800

Walwyn Stodgell Cochran Murray Ltd
(20)
Suite 800
70 University Ave, M5J 2M5
Tel: 591 6000

Wardley Canada Inc
Suite 103
3650 Victoria Park Ave
North York, Ontario, M2H 3P7
Tel: 756 8888

Wood Gundy Inc (79)
PO Box 274
Royal Trust Tower
Toronto-Dominion Centre, M5K 1M7
Tel: 869 8100

Yamaichi International (Canada) Ltd
(23)
150 King St West
Suite 2400, Sun Life Tower
Sun Life Centre, PO Box 62, M5H 1J9
Tel: 597 2730

Yorkton Securities Inc (11)
Suite 2700
PO Box 379
1 First Canadian Place, M5X 1J8
Tel: 864 3500

France

Courtage et Terme International SA
Quai Georges V
Centre Havrais de Commerce
International
7660 Le Havre
Tel: 35 43 61 71

Sarl Bryonterme
Centre d'Affaires Mercure
445, boulevard Gambetta
59200 Roubaix
Tel: 20 24 17 18

Eurocafe SA
132, bd de Strasbourg
76600 Le Havre
Tel: 35 42 09 67

Franceca SA
Quai Georges V
Centre de Commerce International
76600 Le Havre
Tel: 35 22 48 61

Frank Cavanagh SA
Quai Georges V
Centre de Commerce International
76600 Le Havre
Tel: 35 42 51 42

Jacques Louis Delamare SA
5, Place Léon Meyer
BP 103, 76600 Le Havre Cedex
Tel: 35 21 07 77

Jean Baron SA
BP 224, 76054 Le Havre Cedex
Tel: 35 21 08 80

Sarl Micauterme
445, boulevard Gambetta
59220 Tourcoing
Tel: 20 25 45 45

Sarl Guy Lemaire
445, boulevard Gambetta
59220 Tourcoing
Tel: 20 24 22 23

Sarl Gilterme
37 bd Serurier
75019 Paris
Tel: 42 08 84 40

Raoul Duval et Cie
7 place Léon Meyer
BP 1414, 76067 Le Havre Cedex
Tel: 35 43 60 34

Adherents Compensateurs Generaux
Banques et Establissements de Credit

Banque Federative du Credit Mutuel
34 rue du Wacken
67000 Strasbourg
Tel: 88 35 90 35

Banque Financiere Parisienne (BAFIP)
48 rue la Pérouse
75116 Paris
Tel: 45 01 52 50

Banque Regionale d'Escompte et de
Depots (BRED)
21 rue le Boëtle
75008 Paris
Tel: 48 98 60 00

Caisse Centrale des Banques Populaires
(CCBP)
115 rue Montmartre
75002 Paris
Tel: 40 39 30 00

Caisse Centrale de Credit Cooperatif
(CCCC)
Parc de la Défense, BP 211
33 rue des 3-Fontanot
92002 Nantérré Cedex
Tel: 47 24 85 00

Caisse des Depots et Consignations
(CDC)
56 rue de Lille
75007 Paris
Tel: 40 49 56 78

Midland Bank SA
6 rue Piccini, 75116 Paris
Tel: 45 02 80 80

Gie Solidaires et Societes en Nom
Collectif

Carr Futures International (GIE)
11 rue Marsollier
75002 Paris
Tel: 49 27 07 37

AO Carr Futures International (Art 99)
11 rue Marsollier, 75002 Paris
Tel: 49 27 07 37

Amm Banque Indosuez
Service Option MATIF
96 bld Haussmann, 75008 Paris
Tel: 45 61 20 20

Financiere des marches a a term (SNC)
(FIMAT)

Societe Generale
29 bld Haussmann, 75009 Paris

Societe Generale
Alsacienne de Banque (Sogenal)
8 rue du Dôme, 67035 Strasbourg

Banque de Placement et de Reescompte
(BAREP)
16 avenue de Messine, 75008 Paris

Tuffier Ravier
8 rue Saint-Flacre, 75002 Paris

Printemps SA
102 rue de Provence, 75009 Paris

Societe Centrale de Banque
5 bld de Madeleine, 75001 Paris

Delahaye-Ripault
178, rue Montmartre, 75002 Paris

Kuwaiti French Bank
17 rue de Caumartin, 75009 Paris

Interfutur (GIE)
6 rue des Petits-Péres
75002 Paris
Tel: 40 20 20 00

Via Banque
10 rue Volney, 75002 Paris
Tel: 42 61 50 27

Caisse de Gestion Mobiliere
6 rue Petits-Pères, 75002 Paris
Tel: 40 20 20 00

Grel (art 69)
11 avenue Delcassé
BP 625 75367, Paris Cedex 08
Tel: 42 89 27 27

Nord Futures (GIE)
6/8 bd Haussmann, 75009 Paris
Tel: 48 24 20 02

Banque Arjil
138 av des Champs-Elysées
78008 Paris
Tel: 42 25 27 57

BBT SA (art 69)
1 rue des Italiens, 75009 Paris
Tel: 45 23 50 13

Credit du Nord
6/8 bd Haussmann, 75009 Paris
Tel: 40 22 40 22

Gerance Parisienne Privee (art 99)
225 rue Saint-Honoré
75001 Paris
Tel: 40 15 05 75

Societe Lyonnaise de Compensation sur les Marches a Terme (SNC) *(SLICOMAT)*
19 bd des Italiens
75009 Paris
Tel: 42 95 01 58

Credit Lyonnais
19 bd des Italiens, 75009 Paris

Societe Rhodanienne Mobiliere et
Immobiliere
95 avenue des Champs Elysées
75008 Paris

Nouveau Gie X a constituer entre
9 rue Auber, 75009 Paris
Tel: 42 66 92 93

Societe Marseillaise de Credit
4 rue Auber, 75009 Paris
Tel: 42 66 92 13

Generale de Placement Banque
4 rue Auber, 75009 Paris
Tel: 42 66 68 70

Securite Futures (GIE)
15 rue de Berrl
75008 Paris
Tel: 42 89 22 36

Banque de L'Union Europeenne
4/6 rue Gaillon, 75002 Paris
Tel: 42 66 70 00

Societe Liaud Courtage (art 69)
15 rue de Berri 75008 Paris
Tel: 42 89 34 91

Adherents Compensateurs Individuels

Banques et Establissements de Credit

American Express Bank
12-14 Rond Point des Champs-Elysées
75008 Paris
Tel: 42 25 15 16

Banque D'Arbitrage et de Credit (BAC)
21 av George V, 75008 Paris
Tel: 47 23 01 40

Banque D'Arbitrage de Tresorerie et
D'Instruments Financiers (BATIF)
34/36 av. de Friedland
75008 Paris
Tel: 47 54 80 00

Banque D'Escompte
Secrétariat général
13 bd Haussmann, 75009 Paris
Tel: 48 24 85 44

Banque Francaise du Commerce
Exterieur (BFCE)
21 bd Haussmann, 75008 Paris
Tel: 42 47 41 21

Banque Francaise D'Investissement (BFI)
46 rue Lauriston, 75116 Paris
Tel: 47 27 24 00

Banque Francaise Standard Chartered
(BFSC)
34 rue du Wacken
67000 Strasbourg
Tel: 1688359035

Banque de Gestion Privee – SIB (BGP
SIB)
26 rue de la Baume
75008 Paris
Tel: 40 75 62 62

Banque Internationale de Placement
(BIP)
108 bd Haussmann, 75008 Paris
Tel: 42 93 14 14

Banque Louis Dreyfus
6 rue Rabelais, 75008 Paris
Tel: 43 59 07 59

Banque Nationale de Paris (BNP)
1 bd Haussmann, 75009 Paris
Tel: 40 14 67 58

Banque Pallas France
61 rue de Monceau, 75009 Paris
Tel: 40 74 20 00

Banque Paribas
3 rue d'Antin, 75002 Paris
Tel: 42 98 12 34

Banque Shearson Lehman Hutton
56 rue Fbg St-Honoré
75008 Paris
Tel: 42 65 50 70

Banque Worms
Service MATIF – Bureau 1876
Tour Voltaire
1 Place des Degrés
92059 Paris la Defense, Cedex 58
Tel: 49 07 50 50

Barclays Bank SA
33 rue du 4-septembre
75002 Paris
Tel: 40 06 85 85

Caisse Centrale de Reescompte (CCR)
32–34 rue Marbeuf
75008 Paris
Tel: 42 89 22 92

Citibank SA
19 Parvis de la Défense
La Defense 7
92073 Paris la Defense
Tel: 49 06 10 10

Compagnie Parisienne de Reescompte
(CPR)
59/61 rue La Fayette
75428 Paris, Cedex 09
Tel: 40 23 24 25

Credit Chimique
20 rue Treilhard
75383 Paris, Cedex 08
Tel: 45 61 94 00

Credit Commercial de France (CCF)
103 av des Champs-Elysées
75008 Paris
Tel: 40 70 70 40

Deltabanque – Banque International
d'Arbitrage et de Marche
42 rue d'Anjou, 75008 Paris
Tel: 42 65 06 30

Deutsche Bank
10 place Vendôme, 75001 Paris
Tel: 42 61 82 02

Istituto Bancario San Paolo di Torino
42 rue d'Anjou, 75008 Paris
Tel: 42 65 50 50

J P Morgan & Cie SA
21 pl Marché St-Honoré
75001 Paris
Tel: 40 15 45 00

Societe de Banque Occidentale (SDBO)
8 rue de la Rochefoucault
75009 Paris
Tel: 42 81 91 61

Societe Generale
59 rue de Provence
75009 Paris
Tel: 40 98 20 00

Direction des Marchés de Capitaux
Changes – Trésorerie
2–4 Cité d'Antin 75009 Paris

Lyonnaise de Banque
24 rue de la Banque
75002 Paris
Tel: 49 27 68 68

**Establissements de L'Article 99 de La
Loi Bancaire**

Bankers Trust Finance et Marches SA
12/14 Rond-Point des Champs-Elysées
75386 Paris Cedex 08
Tel: 43 59 62 62

Drexel, Burnham, Lambert France SA
17 avenue George V
75008 Paris
Tel: 47 20 41 42

Goldman Sachs International Limited et
Cie
8 rue Halévy, 75009 Paris
Tel: 42 66 94 71

L'Lione Finance
36 rue du Louvre
75001 Paris
Tel: 40 26 02 89

Merrill Lynch Capital Markets (France)
SA
96 avenue d'Iéna
75116 Paris
Tel: 47 20 59 16

Options Financieres et Matif (OFM)
9 bd des Italiens
75002 Paris
Tel: 47 03 47 29

Pallas Equation SA
61 rue de Monceau
75008 Paris
Tel: 40 74 20 00

Plus X Futures (en constitution et en
substitution de Tuffier Ravier PY &
Associés SA)
8 rue St Fiacre
75002 Paris
Tel: 40 28 85 86

Tuffier Ravier PY et Associes SA
8 rue St Fiacre, 75002 Paris

Banque Finance Plus
26 rue de Lisbonne, 75008 Paris

Caisse Centrale des Banques Populaires
115 rue Montmartre, 75002 Paris

Refco SA
9 rue Royale, 75008 Paris
Tel: 47 42 23 25

Salomon Brothers International Ltd
Victoria Plaza
111 Buckingham Place Road
London SW1W 0SB England
Tel: 01 721 2571

Societe de Transactions et d'Arbitrage
sur Futurs Finnciers (STAFF)
15 avenue Matignon
75008 Paris
Tel: 42 56 46 67

Gie Solidaires

BIF-Lavandeyra
10 bd Haussmann, 75009 Paris
Tel: 42 47 70 00

Banque Pour L'Industrie Francaise
26 rue Laffitte, 75009 Paris
Tel: 42 47 54 76

Sté de bourse
Eric de Lavandeyra
10 bd Haussman, 75009 Paris
Tel: 42 47 70 00

Cofutures
Services Administratifs
14 bd Malesherbes
75008 Paris
Tel: 47 42 37 60

Caisse Federale du Credit Mutuel de
Bretagne
B 351 – 29074 Brest Cedex
Tel: 16 98 00 22 22 ou 23

Banque de Marches et D'Arbitrage
109 rue du Faubourg St-Honoré
75008 Paris
Tel: 45 63 04 43

Coficoba (Art 69)
14 bd Malesherbes, 75008 Paris
Tel: 47 42 37 60

Compagnie Bancaire Transactions (CBT)
2 rue de la Trinité
75009 Paris
Tel: 47 38 83 00

Compagnie Bancaire
5 avenue Kléber, 75016 Paris
Tel: 45 25 25 25

Financiere Cardif-Fidif Banque
2 rue de la Trinité
75009 Paris
Tel: 47 38 87 42

Financiere Kleber (art 99)
5 avenue Kléber, 75016 Paris
Tel: 45 25 25 25

Compensation Vendome
52 av Champs-Elysées
75008 Paris
Tel: 75008 Paris

Finacor (art 99)
52 av Champs Elysées
75008 Paris
Tel: 40 74 15 15

Peter SACB (art 69)
52 av Champs-Elysées
75008 Paris
Tel: 40 74 15 15

GMAT
53 rue de Chateaudun
75009 Paris
Tel: 42 80 80 88

Credit Industriel et Commercial de Paris
66 rue des Victoires
75009 Paris
Tel: 42 80 80 80

Sté de bourse
Rondeleux SA
20 rue Drouot, 75009 Paris
Tel: 40 22 68 00

IFITEC
49 avenue de l'Opéra
75002 Paris
Tel: 47 42 15 47

Credit Lyonnais
19 bd des Italiens
75002 Paris
Tel: 42 95 80 85

Banque Internationale de Gestion et de
Tresorerie
46 avenue Kléber, 75116 Paris
Tel: 45 01 51 40

Options Futures
3/5 rue Saint-Georges
75009 Paris
Tel: 42 85 27 22

Banque du Batiment et des Travaux
Publics
253 bd Pereire, 75382 Paris, Cedex 17
Tel: 47 54 75 75

Sté de bourse
J Francois-Dufour
J-L Kervern SA
116 rue de Réaumur, 75002 Paris
Tel: 42 36 44 60

Banque de Neuflize Schlumberger
Mallet
3 avenue Hoche, 75008 Paris
Tel: 47 66 61 11

Dianergy
Immeuble Cotentin
90 bd Pasteur, 75015 Paris
Tel: 43 23 30 30

Segespar Futures
Tour Maine Montparnasse
33 av du Maine, 75755 Paris
Tel: 43 23 30 30

Sté de bourse Bertrand
Michel SA
7 rue de la Bourse, 75002 Paris
Tel: 42 61 52 60

Sté de bourse Yves
Soulie SA
17 rue de Provence, 75009 Paris
Tel: 45 23 00 93

Societes de Bourse

Auboyneau Labouret Ollivier & Cie
23 bd Poissonnière
75008 Paris
Tel: 42 33 21 80

Bacot Allain Farra SA
13 rue la Fayette
75009 Paris
Tel: 40 16 30 30

Boscher SA
28 rue Drouot
75009 Paris
Tel: 40 22 15 15

Patrick du Bouzet SA
10 cité Rougemont
75009 Paris
Tel: 40 22 19 92

J Cheuvreux B de Virieu SA
2 rue de Choiseul
75002 Paris
Tel: 42 61 80 08

Jean de Cholet Gilles Dupont & Cie
3 rue de Gramont
75002 Paris
Tel: 42 61 83 22

B de Compiegne
G Augustin-Normand SA
92 rue de Richelieu
75002 Paris
Tel: 42 96 66 16

Courcoux Bouvet SA
5 rue Gaillon
75002 Paris
Tel: 40 17 50 00

Dufour Lacarriere Pouget SA
8 rue Lavoisier
75008 Paris
Tel: 42 66 02 30

X Dupont F Denant SA
42 rue N-D des Victoires
75002 Paris
Tel: 42 21 25 25

Fauchier Magnan Durant Des Aulnois
SA
75 rue de Richelieu
75002 Paris
Tel: 40 15 25 25

A Ferri B Ferri C Germe
53 rue Vivienne, 75002 Paris
Tel: 40 41 42 43

Finacor Bourse
52 av Champs-Elysées
75008 Paris
Tel: 40 74 15 15

B Gorgeu J J Perquel M Krucker & Cie
29 rue du Louvre, 75001 Paris
Tel: 40 26 34 50

Mayaux du Tilly & Cie
19 rue de Provence
75009 Paris
Tel: 42 46 82 76

Legrand Legrand & Cie
7 rue Bergère, 75009 Paris
Tel: 47 70 72 90

Leven Chaussier SA
63 rue Sainte-Anne
75002 Paris
Tel: 42 61 51 19

Massonaud, Fontenay SA
8 rue du Sentier
75002 Paris
Tel: 40 39 56 00

Meeschaert Rousselle & Cie
16 bd Montmartre
75009 Paris
Tel: 42 46 72 64

Societe Oddo & Cie
Pascal et Philippe Oddo
31 rue St-Augustin
75002 Paris
Tel: 40 17 58 00

Didier Philippe & Cie
3 rue Taitbout
75009 Paris
Tel: 42 46 72 95

Jean-Pierre Pinatton SA
8 rue Auber, 75009 Paris
Tel: 40 17 52 00

Puget, Mahe SA
7 rue Drouot, 75009 Paris
Tel: 40 22 85 85

Schelcher Prince SA
5/7 rue St-Augustin
75009 Paris
Tel: 42 96 16 16

Sellier SA
12 rue d'Uzès
75002 Paris
Tel: 42 33 51 01

Wolff Goirand & Cie
10 rue d'Uzès
75002 Paris
Tel: 40 41 37 37

Patrice Wargny SA
9 rue du 4 septembre
75002 Paris
Tel: 42 96 60 83

Negociàteurs Courtiers

Banques

Banque Europeenne de Tokyo (ACG –
Fimat)
4–8 rue Sainte-Anne
75001 Paris
Tel: 42 61 58 55

Caisse de Gestion Mobiliere
(ACG – Interfutur)
6 rue des Petits-Pères
75002 Paris
Tel: 40 20 20 00

Establissements de L'Article 99 de la Loi Bancaire

Rafe SA
(ACG: Banque Federative du Credit Mutuel)
16 pl de la Madeleine
75008 Paris
Tel: 42 66 03 04
42 66 26 31

Trifutures
(ACG : Caisse des depots et Consignations)
13 bd Haussmann
75009 Paris
Tel: 48 24 85 44

Establissements de L'Article 69 de la Loi Bancaire

Grel
(ACG - Interfutur)
11 av Delcassé
BP 625 - 75367 Paris
Cedex 08
Tel: 42 89 27 27

Jacques Pollak et Cie
(ACG : Midland Bank SA)
30 rue de Gramont
75002 Paris
Tel: 42 61 84 06

Societes de Bourse

Goy Hauvette SA
(ACG - Bred)
142 rue Montmartre
75002 Paris
Tel: 42 33 44 56

Magnin Cordelle & Cie
(ACG : Securite Futures)
89 rue la Boëtie
75008 Paris
Tel: 45 63 13 13

Jean Claude Melendes SA
(ACG - Carr Futures International)
10 rue du 4-septembre
75002 Paris
Tel: 42 96 60 22

Meunier de la Fourniere
Michelez le Febvre & Cie
(ACG - Carr Futures International)
40 rue N-D des Victoires
75002 Paris
Tel: 42 33 61 96

Michel Nouailhetas & Cie
(ACG - Nord Futures)
88 rue Vivienne
75002 Paris
Tel: 42 61 53 62

Jean Saintoin Xavier Roulet SA
(ACG - Carr Futures International)
36 rue du Louvre
75001 Paris
Tel: 40 39 17 17

Liste de Comissionnaires Agrees

Bauche Termé
4 rue Jean Nicot
75007 Paris
Tel: 45 51 76 70

Compagnie Francaise du Sucre et des Produits du Sol (CFS)
18 ave Matignon
75008 Paris
Tel: 42 66 92 22

Debayser, Wiart & Desbief (DWD)
27-29 rue Chateaubriand
75008 Paris
Tel: 45 63 17 44

Debman SA
27-29 rue Chateaubriand
75008 Paris
Tel: 45 63 11 80

Etlafric (France)
15 rue de la Banque
75002 Paris
Tel: 42 60 32 32

General Cocoa (France)
15 rue du Louvre
75001 Paris
Tel: 42 33 94 12

Goldschmidt Conseil & Associes (GCA)
149 rue Saint Honoré
75001 Paris
Tel: 42 60 33 11

Luc Terme SA
15 rue du Louvre
75001 Paris
Tel: 42 33 71 39

Node Langlois Matieres Premieres
8 rue Cambacérès
75008 Paris
Tel: 42 65 86 49

Nouvelle Primateria
36 ave Hoche
75008 Paris
Tel: 45 63 11 28

Pacol SA
56 ave Victor Hugo
75116 Paris
Tel: 45 01 54 74

Societe Anonyme LB
336 rue Saint Honoré
75001 Paris
Tel: 42 60 01 62

Sucres & Denrees Terme
133 av des Champs Elysées
75008 Paris
Tel: 47 23 55 77

Sucre Union SA
27-29 rue Chateaubriand
75008 Paris
Tel: 45 63 17 33

Debayser Wiart et Desbief SA
27-29 rue Chateaubriand
75008 Paris
Tel: 45 63 16 88

Uni Termé
137 rue du FG St Honoré
75008 Paris
Tel: 45 62 31 31

Societe Nouvelles des Maiseries de la
Mediterranee
4 rue Montesquieu
75001 Paris
Tel: 40 20 75 00

Hong Kong

The Chinese Gold and Silver Exchange Society

Algarve Gold Merchant Co
Rm 701-5 Shell House
24-28 Queen's Rd, C
Hong Kong
Tel: 5 8107939

BM Co
8B Valiant Comm Bldg
22-24 Prat Ave, Tsimshatsui
KLN, Hong Kong
Tel: 3 690121

C & C Co
Rm 403, Far East Exchange Bldg
8 Wyndham St, Hong Kong
Tel: 5 217277

C C Tsan & Co
165 Un Chau St, G/F
Sham Shui PO
KLN, Hong Kong
Tel: 5 220614

Campbell Bullion Co
1/F Maxwell Industrial Bldg
350 Kwun Tong Rd, Kwun Tong
Kowloon, Hong Kong
Tel: 3 7991111

Champion Co
Rm 904 Tai Sang Bank Bldg
130 Des Voeux Rd, C
Hong Kong
Tel: 5 458288

Charleswin Co
Rm 1501 Tung Ning Bldg
125-127 Connaught Rd, C
Hong Kong
Tel: 5 441055

Cheerful Bullion Co
Rm 2105 World-Wide House
19 Des Voeux Rd, C
Hong Kong
Tel: 5 236131

Cheong Fat
Rm 2104 Far East Consortium
Blgd, 121 Des Voeux Rd, C
Hong Kong
Tel: 5 454321

Cheong Kee
1 Water St, 5/F, Flat J
Sai Ying Poon
Hong Kong
Tel: 5 474059

Cheong On Fat
Rm 903, 156-157 Connaught Rd
C, Hong Kong
Tel: 5 448286

Cheow Seng Gold Dealer
Rm 1312 Shun Tak Centre
200 Connaught Rd, C
Hong Kong
Tel: 5 494196

Cheung Kee Bullion Trading Co
90 Waterloo Rd 9/F
Flat A, KLN, Hong Kong
Tel: 5 222066

Cheung Shun
77 Bonham Strand E
Hong Kong
Tel: 5 448601

Cheung's Gold Dealers
Rm 1901-6, Bank Centre
636 Nathan Rd
KLN, Hong Kong
Tel: 3 323711

Chief Co
15 Cochrane St, 7/F
Hong Kong
Tel: 5 449931

China Merchants Bullion Co
5/F Union Bank Bldg
59-65 Queen's Rd C
Hong Kong
Tel: 5 251041, 5 860455

Chow Sang Sang
Chow Sang Sang Bldg
229 Nathan Rd, KLN
Hong Kong
Tel: 3 663874

Chow Tai Fook
31/F New World Tower
16-18 Queen's Rd, C
Hong Kong
Tel: 5 243166

Chuen Kee
36/F Connaught Centre
Hong Kong

Chun Tak
B1-3 3/F 21 Yuk Lan Rd
Yau Yat Chuen, KLN
Hong Kong
Tel: 3 802739

Chung Hing Gold Dealer
Flat B 26/F Hing Hon Bldg
26 King's Rd, Hong Kong
Tel: 5 663564

Chung Wah Gold Traders Co
Unit A 7/F Caineway Mansion
128-132 Caine Rd
Hong Kong
Tel: 5 464716

Cosmos Rich Co
15/F Gold & Silver Comm
Bldg, 12-18 Mercer St
Hong Kong
Tel: 5 448330

Dao Heng
4/F Dao Heng Bldg
7-19 Bonham Strand East
Hong Kong
Tel: 5 447141

Dat Cheong Gold & Silver Co
7/F St George's Bldg
2 Ice House St, Hong Kong
Tel: 5 252701

David Gold Dealer
Rm 904-5 Hang Seng Bank
Tsimshatsui Branch Bldg
18 Carnavon Rd, KLN, Hong Kong
Tel: 3 7221717

Deak & Co
Rm 804 West Tower
Bond Centre, Queensway Central
Hong Kong
Tel: 5 266111

Diamount Bullion Co
Rm 503 Far East Consortium
Blg, 121 Des Voeux Rd, C
Hong Kong
Tel: 5 237270

Dollar Gold Co
230 G/F, FA Yuen St
Kowloon, Hong Kong
Tel: 3 974333

Extensive Co
Edko Tower, 12/F
32 Ice House St
Hong Kong
Tel: 5 261850

Far East (HK) Co
Rm 1405 Western Central Bldg
48 Des Voeux Rd, W
Hong Kong
Tel: 5 480 458

Fat Lee Co
6/F, Nam Pak Hong Bldg
22 Bonham Strand W
Hong Kong
Tel: 5 437351

Fau Tak
Flat F, 7/F, 30 Johnston Rd
Hong Kong

Fidelity Co
45/F, Sun Hung Kai Centre
Harbour Rd, Wanchai
Hong Kong
Tel: 5 8325314

Foo Kee & Co
13 Hiller St, 3/F
Hong Kong
Tel: 5 455333

Fook Lung
10/F, Blk F
60 Cloud View Rd
Hong Kong
Tel: 5 719338

Fook Tai Co
Rm 905-8 New World Tower
18 Queen's Rd, C
Hong Kong
Tel: 5 251001

Forex Fix Gold Dealers
Rm 2402 New World Tower
Queen's Rd, C
Hong Kong
Tel: 5 8401388

Fu Hang
Rm 702 Far East Exchange Bldg
8 Wyndham St, Hong Kong
Tel: 5 231525

Global Gold Co
Rm 703 Gold & Silver Comm Bldg
12-18 Mercer St
Hong Kong
Tel: 5 8541778

Gobon Investment Co
Rm 3607 Shun Tak Centre
200 Connaught Rd C
Hong Kong
Tel: 5 497132

Golden Eagle Bullion Co
Rm 2205 Arion Comm Centre
2 Queen's Rd, W
Hong Kong
Tel: 5 442060

Goldlion Gold Traders
Rm 1420 Central Bldg
Pedder St, Hong Kong
Tel: 5 8151333

Goldlion Co
15 Sze Shan St, Yau Tong Bay
KLN, Hong Kong
Tel: 3 400111

Hai Lung Co
Rm 607 Malbourne Plaza
33 Queen's Rd, C
Hong Kong
Tel: 5 239924

Hang Fong
16/F, Wong Hse
26-30 Des Voeux Rd, W
Hong Kong
Tel: 5 497576

Hang Fook
10/F, Flat B, Man Hing Bldg
79-83 Queen's Rd, C
Hong Kong
Tel: 5 240631

Hang Seng
77 Des Voeux Rd, C
Hong Kong
Tel: 5 8255111

Hang Shing
7/F 151-155 Queen's Rd Central
Hong Kong
Tel: 5 8151133

Hang Tai Gold Dealer
2/F, 84 Morrision Hill Rd
Hong Kong
Tel: 5 754455

Hang Yick
6/F, World Wide Hse
19 Des Voeux Rd, C
Hong Kong
Tel: 5 255977

Hing Cheong Gold Dealer
Blk B, 14/F, Hillier Comm
Bldg, 89-91 Wing Lok St
Hong Kong
Tel: 5 447331

Hing Fung Co
12/F, Diamond Exchange Bldg
20 Ice Hse St
Hong Kong
5 217222

Hing Hop
G/F, 18-20 Des Voeux Rd, W
Hong Kong
Tel: 5 408998

Hing Yep Gold Dealers
22/F, Euro Trade Centre
13-14 Connaught Rd Central
Hong Kong
Tel: 5 254422

Hon Hing Hong
23/F, Relaty Bldg
71 Des Voeux Rd, C
Hong Kong
Tel: 5 8456722

Hop Sing Gold Co
25/F Flat A1, Elizabeth Hse
Tower A, 250 Gloucester Rd
Hong Kong
Tel: 5 8935143

Hsing Lung Co
Rm 2502 Admiralty Centre
Tower 1, 18 Harcourt Rd
Hong Kong
Tel: 5 273715

Hung Tak
Rm 702 Gold & Silver Comm Bldg
12-18 Mercer St
Hong Kong
Tel: 5 438060

Hung Wai Gold Traders
Rm 1712-4 Melbourne Plaza
33 Queen's Rd Central
Hong Kong
Tel: 5 210578

J A Livermore Bullion Co
20/F, Admiralty Centre
Tower 2, Harcourt Rd
Hong Kong
Tel: 5 284938

Ka Wah
6/F, Hang Seng Bank Bldg
77 Des Voeux Rd, C
Hong Kong
Tel: 5 8468111

Kai Tak Co
Rm 1108 Lane Crawford Hse
70 Queen's Rd, C
Hong Kong
Tel: 5 263992

Kam Fook
Kai Fat Bldg, 6/F, Flat B
45 Connaught Rd, W
Hong Kong
Tel: 5 493070

Kam Kee Gold Co
Flat A, 21/F, Man On Comm Bldg
12 Jubilee St
Hong Kong
Tel: 5 457945

Kam Tat Gold Co
Room 1707 Beverley Comm
Centre, 87-105 Chatham Rd
Tsim Sha Tsui, KLN, Hong Kong
Tel: 3 661211

Kin Shing
Rm 702, 12 Mercer St
Hong Kong
Tel: 5 438060

King Fook
30-32 Des Voeux Rd, C, G/F
Central, Hong Kond
Tel: 5 235111

King Hing Co
Rm 1001 Admiralty Centre
Tower 2, Harcourt Rd
Hong Kong
Tel: 5 291020

King Lung Gold Traders
Suite 1308, Two Exchange Square
8 Connaught Place
Central, Hong Kong
Tel: 5 249341

King Sang Gold Dealer
Rm 1303 Gold & Silver Comm Bldg
12-18 Mercer St
Hong Kong
Tel: 5 414848

King Shing
30-32 Des Voeux Rd, C, G/F
Hong Kong
Tel: 5 235111

Kingly Gold Co
9/F, Wing's Bldg
110 Queen's Rd, C
Hong Kong
Tel: 5 8152223

Kui Shing Gold Trader
Rm 1501 Wing Hang Bank Bldg
161 Queen's Rd, C
Hong Kong
Tel: 5 421128

Kung Lee
5 Li Yuen St, W, 5/F
Hong Kong
Tel: 5 7907646

Kung Yue
Rm 600, 12 Queen's Rd, C
Hong Kong

Kwong Cheung Co
G/F, 29 Po On Rd
Sham Shui Po, Kowloon
Hong Kong
Tel: 3 7205241-4

Kwong Fat
Rm 1001 Far East Exchange Bldg
8 Wyndham St
Hong Kong
Tel: 5 241135

Lai Kee Gold Co
61 Bonham Strand, E
Hong Kong
Tel: 5 443102

Lam Tai Shing Gold Dealer
244-246 Cheung Sha Wan Rd
G/F, KLN, Hong Kong
Tel: 3 7205125

Lee Cheong Gold Dealer
Rm 705-706 Wing On Hse
71 Des Voeux Rd, C
Hong Kong
Tel: 5 213106

Lee On
Flat C, 8/F, Wing Cheong Bldg
19 Jervois St, Hong Kong
Tel: 5 440941

Lee Sang Co
Room 501, Tin Fook Hong Bldg
77 Jervois St, Hong Kong
Tel: 5 444138

Lee Shing
12 Mercer St, 3/F
Hong Kong
Tel: 5 439093

Legarleon Gold Traders
Suite 1506, Tower 1, Exchange Square
8 Connaught Place
Central, Hong Kong
Tel: 5 262061

Li Kee Hong
4/F, Sing Pao Centre
8 Queen's Rd, C
Hong Kong
Tel: 5 8451188

Loong Shing Co
Rm 603, 6/F
12-18 Mercer St
Hong Kong
Tel: 5 431064

Lotus Gold & Silver Co
17/F, Grand Bldg
15-18 Connaught Rd, Central Hong
Kong
Tel: 5 266647

Loy Hing Gold Dealer
42 Bonham Strand, E
Hong Kong
Tel: 5 441395

Luen Fat
Rm 601, 12-18 Mercer St
Hong Kong
Tel: 5 433092

Luen Hing Co
40-41 Connaught Rd, W, 1/F
Hong Kong
Tel: 5 410797

Luen On Kam Ho
Flat A & B, 8/F
205 Wing Lok St, W
Hong Kong
Tel: 5 435780

Luen Thai Co
Room 524 Man Yee Bldg
Des Voeux Rd, Central
Hong Kong
Tel: 5 266994 (3 Lines)

Malahon Bullion Co
5 & 6/F, Malahon Centre
10–12 Stanley St
Hong Kong
Tel: 5 8680628

Man Cheong
2 Ko Shing St
Hong Kong
Tel: 5 484913

Man Fat & Co
33/F, Connaught Centre
Connaught Rd, C, Hong Kong

Man Hing Co
14/F, 243–247 Des Voeux Rd, Central
Hong Kong
Tel: 5 448075

Man Loong Co
Rm 1201 Pacific House
20 Queen's Rd, C, Hong Kong
Tel: 5 257289

Man Shing Co
315 Nathan Road
2/F, Front Door, KLN
Hong Kong
Tel: 3 327609

Man Sun
Rm 905–908 New World Tower
18 Queen's Rd, C, Hong Kong
Tel: 5 251001

Manin Hing Co
9/F, Union Bank Bldg
59–65 Queen's Rd, C
Hong Kong
Tel: 5 248461

Mansion House Bullion Co
8/F, China Bldg
29 Queen's Rd, C
Hong Kong
Tel: 5 8431431

Maryloone Gold Dealers
10A Bowen Rd
Hong Kong
Tel: 5 263389

Ming Fung Gold Trader
2/F, 178–180 Queen's Road, C
Hong Kong
Tel: 5 455300

Ming Hing
2 Ko Shing St
Sai Ying Poon
Hong Kong
Tel: 5 484913

Ming Tai Co
22 Des Voeux Rd, West
Hong Kong
Tel: 5 406138

Nam Wah
45 Des Voeux Rd, C
Hong Kong
Tel: 5 8268333

National
4/F Pedder Bldg
12 Pedder St
Hong Kong
Tel: 5 227131

O & S Bullion Co
Rm 2106 Wing On Hse
71 Des Vouex Rd, C
Hong Kong
Tel: 5 259268

On Lung Gold & Silver Co
G/F, Central Mansion
276 Queen's Rd, C
Hong Kong
Tel: 5 439512

Pak Kai Gold Co
G/F 591 Shanghai St
KLN, Hong Kong
Tel: 3 951272

Pak Lok Co
Rm 1001, 10/F, Silvercord
Tower 2, 30 Canton Rd
Tsim Sha Tsui, KLN
Hong Kong
Tel: 3 7233631

Pennant Bullion Co
Rm 605–6 Leader Comm Bldg
54 Hillwood Rd
KLN, Hong Kong
Tel: 3 671165/3 671166

Po Fung Bullion Co
Suite 1102-1103, Two Exchange Square
8 Connaught Place
Hong Kong
Tel: 5 215451

Po Sang
71 Des Voeux Rd
1/F, Central, Hong Kong
Tel: 5 8436111

Po Tai Bullion Co
Flat D, 22/F
Wing Cheong Comm Bldg
19-25 Jervois, Hong Kong
Tel: 5 433080

Po Tung Gold Trader
3/F, Kayamally Bldg
22 Queen's Rd, Central
Hong Kong
Tel: 5 235733

Poly Enterprises
Rm 808, Yu Sung Boon Bldg
111 Des Voeux Road, C
Hong Kong
Tel: 5 412389

Profit Mark Bullion Co
Rm 902 Houston Centre
63 Mody Road, Tst, East
Kowloon, Hong Kong
Tel: 3 7396212

Sai Shing
Rm 2206 Wing On House
71 Des Voeux Rd, C
Hong Kong
Tel: 5 255777

San Fu & Co
2001-3 Far East Consortium
Bldg, 20/F, 121 Des Voeux
Rd, C, Hong Kong
Tel: 5 8532132/5 458813

Sang Fat Cheung
Rm 1302 Nan Dao Comm Bldg
359-361 Queen's Road, C
Hong Kong
Tel: 5 8151928

Seapower Bullion Co
17/F, Bank of East Asia Bldg
10 Des Voeux Road, C
Hong Kong
Tel: 5 8474888

Shui Cheong
138 Wing Lok St, W, 7/F
Hong Kong
Tel: 5 456907

Shui Fung Hong
16/F, Malahon Centre
10-12 Stanley St
Central, Hong Kong
Tel: 5 8682345

Shun Kai Bullion Co
Rm 1401 Hung Tak Bldg
106-108 Des Voeux Rd, C
Hong Kong
Tel: 5 456708

Shun Lee Gold Traders Co
Room 301-2, 3/F
93 Wing Lok St
Hong Kong
Tel: 5 420323

Shun Loong Co
Rm 2502 Admiralty Centre
Tower 1, 18 Harcourt Rd
Hong Kong
Tel: 5 200111

Sing Lung Gold Trader Co
c/o Asean Express Finance (HK)
Co Ltd, 710 Wing On House
71 Des Voeux Rd, C, Hong Kong
Tel: 5 264394

Sinovest Precious Metals Co
Rm 2201-4 Vicwood Plaza
199 Des Voeux Rd, C
Hong Kong
Tel: 5 456637

Solid Commodities Co
Units 1905-6 19/F
Vicwood Plaza, 199 Des Voeux Rd, C,
Hong Kong
Tel: 5 456563

South China Bullion Co
9/F & 10/F, BCC House
10 Queen's Rd, C
Hong Kong
Tel: 5 8456386

Standard Bullion
Rm 2108 Edinburgh Tower
Landmark, Central
Hong Kong
Tel: 5 8108098

Sui Cheung Gold Daeler
14/F, Wing Lung Bank Bldg
45 Des Voeux Rd, C
Hong Kong
Tel: 5 8107171

Sun Hing
3/F Admiralty Centre
18 Harcourt Rd
Hong Kong
Tel: 5 8225678

Sun Hung Kai
3/F Admiralty Centre
18 Harcourt Rd
Hong Kong
Tel: 5 8225678

Sun Kwong Co
Rm 6A, Kimley Comm Bldg
142–146 Queen's Rd, C
Hong Kong
Tel: 5 446664

Sun Kwong Lee
4/F, Dao Heng Bldg
7–19 Bonham Strand, East
Hong Kong
Tel: 5 447141

Sun Wing Yuen Bullion Co
Rm 2503–4 International Bldg
141 Des Voeux Rd, C
Hong Kong
Tel: 5 413821/6

Sunnymen & Co
Flat B, 29/F, Jubilee Garden
Block 7 Sha Tin, NT
Tel: 0 6060898

Sze Lee
3 Bonham Strand, E
Hong Kong
Tel: 5 440201

Tah Hsin Gold Dealer
Rm 601A Wah Ying Cheong
Central Bldg, 158–164 Queen's Rd
C, Hong Kong
Tel: 5 423046

Tai Fat
Flat A, 7/F, Nam Pak Hong Bldg
24 Bonham Strand, W
Hong Kong
Tel: 5 446515

Tai Heng
130 Des Voeux Rd, C
Hong Kong
Tel: 5 445011

Tai Lam
82 Jervois St, G/F
Hong Kong
Tel: 5 438031

Tai Lee Gold Traders
Rm 601, Hua Chiao Comm Bldg
88–98 Des Voeux Rd, Central
Hong Kong

Tai Loy Gold Dealer
22/F, Room 3 Pak Po Lee Comm
Centre, 1A Sai Yeung Choi St
Kowloon, Hong Kong
Tel: 3 327283/3 7107671

Tai Sang
130 Des Voeux Rd Central
Hong Kong
Tel: 5 445011

Tai Yau
16/F Tak Shing House
20 Des Voeux Rd Central
Hong Kong
Tel: 5 229001

Tak Sang Gold Smith
49 Chung On St, G/F
Tsuen Wan, N T, Hong Kong
Tel: 0 426955

Tak Shun
Rm 802, Cosmopolitan Bldg
10 Stanley St
Hong Kong

Tak Sum Gold Co
Rm 1003 Wah Ying Cheong
Central Bldg, 158–164 Queen's Rd
C, Hong Kong
Tel: 5 434203

Tak Wo
Flat B, 5/F
58 Bonham Strand, E
Hong Kong
Tel: 5 442993

Tang Kee
G/F, Pedder Bldg
12 Pedder St
Hong Kong
Tel: 5 221792

The Sun
17-19/F, The Sun House
90 Connaught Rd Central
Hong Kong
Tel: 5 458766

Thomson Bullion Co
5/F, Hutchison Hse
10 Harcourt Rd, Hong Kong
Tel: 5 211661

Tin Fook
12/F, 12-18 Mercer St
Hong Kong
Tel: 5 422109

Tse Sui Luen
Blk B, G/F, Summit Bldg
30 Man Yue St, Hunghom
KLN, Hong Kong
Tel: 3 334221

Universal (Investment) Co
Room 504
Mong Kok Commercial Centre
16 Argyle St, KLN, Hong Kong
Tel: 3 944693

Uptrend Bullion Co
324 Castle Peak Rd, M/F
Kowloon, Hong Kong
Tel: 3 618172

Upyear Gold Dealer
15/F, Euro Trade Centre
13-14 Connaught Rd, C
Hong Kong
Tel: 5 211238

Vanroy Gold Traders
Rm 1005-6, 664 Nathan Rd
KLN, Hong Kong
Tel: 3 960195

Wah Tai Co
Rm 1703 Tai Sang Comm Bldg
24-34 Hennessy Rd, Hong Kong
Tel: 5 276121

Wai Chong Co
Room 1009 Lane Crawford House
70 Queen's Rd, C, Hong Kong
Tel: 5 212141

Wang Fung Co
59 Des Voeux Rd, C
Chung Nam House, 8/F
Hong Kong
Tel: 5 254465

Wayfoong Bullion Co
5/F, Hutchison House
10 Harcourt Rd
Hong Kong
Tel: 5 2116611

Whitehall Bullion Co
2D Conway Mansion
29 Conduit Rd
Hong Kong
Tel: 5 401411

Wing Hang Ho
161 Queen's Rd, C, Hong Kong
Tel: 5 8525111

Wing Lung
45 Des Voeux Rd, C
Hong Kong
Tel: 5 8268333

Wing On Gold Dealer
31/F, Bank of America Tower
12 Harcourt Rd
Hong Kong
Tel: 5 238118

Wing Shing Loong
63 Bonham Strand, E
Hong Kong
Tel: 5 440853

Wing Wah
6/F, Hang Seng Bank Bldg
77 Des Voeux Rd, C
Hong Kong
Tel: 5 8468111

Wing Wah Co
Rm 1501-2 Sin Hua Bank Bldg
2-8 Wellington St
Central, Hong Kong
Tel: 5 254521-7

Wu Leung Lee Gold Dealer
18/F, Wing Tuck Comm Centre
177–183 Wing Lok St, W
Hong Kong
Tel: 5 418111

Yan Tai
Flat F, 7/F, Hoi Sing Mansion
Sing Fai Terrace, Taikoo Shing
Hong Kong
Tel: 5 686506

Yan Yan & Co
Rm 1601 Yu Sung Boon Bldg
107–111 Des Voeux Rd, C
Hong Kong
Tel: 5 443180

Yat Lung
12/F, Diamond Exchange Bldg
20 Ice Hse St, Central
Hong Kong
Tel: 5 217222

Yau Hang Ho
Rm 2201-3 Far East Consortium Bldg
113–123 Des Voeux Rd
Central, Hong Kong
Tel: 5 449912

Yau Hing
12/F, Winner Mansion
697 Nathan Rd
KLN, Hong Kong
Tel: 3 967513

Yau Lee Hoo
Flat A, 5/F, The Sun House
181 Des Voeux Rd, Central
Hong Kong
Tel: 5 451788

Yau Seng
Rm 507 Gold & Silver Comm Bldg
12–18 Mercer St
Hong Kong
Tel: 5 411035

Yau Wing Gold Dealers
16/F, Wong House
26 Des Voeux Rd, W
Hong Kong
Tel: 5 497576

Yee Fi Co
2/F, Mainslit Bldg
42 Stanley St
Hong Kong
Tel: 5 221165

Yick Hing Bullion Co
19/F, Wah Kwong Regent Centre
88 Queen's Rd, C
Hong Kong
Tel: 5 8101555

Yorkwell Investment Co
Room 1108 Sincere Bldg
173 Des Voeux Rd, Central
Hong Kong
Tel: 5 451494

Yue Sang Ho
71 Des Voeux Rd, C, 1/F
Hong Kong
Tel: 5 8436111

Yuen Chow Bullion Co
20/F, Wah Kwong Regent Centre
88 Queen's Rd, C
Hong Kong
Tel: 5 8101555

Yuen Yee Co
Rm 901, 12 Mercer St
Hong Kong
Tel: 5 440362

Yuet Kee Gold Dealers
Flat B1, 43 Blue Pool Rd
Hong Kong
Tel: 5 216159

India

Bangalore Coffee Board

Members

Allansons Pvt Ltd
Allana House, 4 Barrow Rd, PO Box
997
GPO Bombay 400039
Tel: 240576/240590
Telex: 011 3317/4849/5348

All India Coffee & Produce Merchants
Association
Pandeshwar, Bangalore 1
Tel: 24344
Tel: 0842 267

Brooke Bond India Ltd
Brooke House, PO Box 187
No 9 Shakesponre Sarani

Brooke Bond India Ltd
Coffee Division, 6th Floor
9-1 Mahalakshmi Chambers, PO Box
5021
Bangalore 560001
Tel: 55974/562505

Brooke Bond India Division
Corporate Office, Mahalakshmi
Chambers
9-2 MG Rd, Bangalore 560001
Tel: 55974/562505
Telex: 0845 806 KORA IN

Chande Exports (P) Ltd
1st Floor, Indian Express Bldg
Bangalore 560001
Tel: 72400/28181
Telex: 845 480 CEPL/845 780 CEPL

Coffee Exporters Association
45-1 Palace Rd, Bangalore 563001
Tel: 71427/73520
Telex: 0845 609/8396

W T Craig Jones (Exports)
107 Andrews Bldg, Mahatma Gandhi Rd
Bangalore 560001
Tel: 576590
Telex: 0845 468 AB SEAJ

East India Coffee Exporters Pvt Ltd
No 19, 2nd Floor, 'Shrunagae', 12-12A
Mahatma Gandhi Rd, Bangalore 560001
Tel: 51506
Telex: 845 8301

Emdee Exports
No 60 Rajamahal Vilas Extension
Bangalore 560006
Tel: 31318
Telex: 645

Food Specialities Ltd
Nestle House, M-5A Connaught Circus,
PO Box 611
New Delhi 110001
Tel: 353270
Telex: 31 2580 FSL IN

General Commodities Ltd
PO Box 2476, 16 Pollock St, Calcutta
700001
Tel: 26 5891

D C Ghose & Co (Agents) Private Ltd
Bombay Company's Bldg, 1st Floor
Willingdon Island, Cochin 682003
Tel: 6497/6168
Telex: 0885 439

Indian Products Ltd
604A Queens Corner, 3 Queens Rd
Bangalore 560001
Tel: 28687
Telex: 845 8385 MJ BG IN

IVP Ltd
Shashimanth N, Redij Marg, Ghorupdeo
Bombay 400038
Tel: 8729631/34
Telex: 5152 IVPL IN

Kotak & Co
Navasari Bldg, 249 Dr D N Rd
Bombay 400061
Tel: 263331
Telex: 011 2466 KIK IN

Kothari Exports Corp
604 Regent Chambers, 208 Nariman
Point
Bombay 400021
Tel: 235135/240427
Telex: 011 2026 KCPC IN

Kothari Oil Products Co
604 Regent Chambers, 6th Floor
208 Nariman Point, Bombay 400061
Tel: 235292/240427
Telex: 011 2026 A/B KOPC IN

Madhu Jaynathi Pvt Ltd
604A Queens Corner, 3 Queens Rd
Bangalore 560001
Tel: 812 28687
Telex: 845 8385 MJBG IN

MSP Exports (Coffee Division of MSP
Spices Pvt Ltd)
34-2 Cunningham Rd, Bangalore
560002
Tel: 75497/74640
Telex: 0845 665 MSP IN

Multitrade (India) Ltd
8 Mangos Lane, Calcutta
Tel: 235879
Telex: 11 4090 SHAH IN

Nandan Exports
44 Palace Rd, Bangalore 560001
Tel: 73444/29087
Telex: 0845 8092 ABC IN

Omega Exports
PO Box 651, Cochin 682003
Tel: 69038
Telex: 0885 640 OMEGA IN

Ramesh Enterprises (Coffee Division of
Ramesh Exports Pvt Ltd)
45 Palace Rd, Bangalore 560001
Tel: 71427/73520
Telex: 0845 609 CAFE

State Trading Corp of India Ltd
Chandrakirah, 2nd Floor, 10A Kasturba
Rd
Bangalore 560001
Tel: 51121/51122
Telex: 0845 713

A Tosh & Sons Pvt Ltd
Tosh House, PO Box 605, Willingdon
Island
Cochin 682008
Tel: 6373
Telex: 0885 607

The United Coffee Supply Co Ltd
Coffee Export Division, 5-6 4th Main
Rd
New Tharagupet, Bangalore 560002
Tel: 607337
Telex: 0845 202 AMCO IN

United Planters Association of Southern
India
Glenview, Coonoor

Ireland

Irish Futures and Options Exchange

Agricultural Credit Corp Plc
ACC House
Upper Hatch St
Dublin 2

Algemene Bank Nederland (Ireland) Ltd
121-122 St Stephen's Green
Dublin 2

Allied Irish Banks Plc
Bankcentre
Ballsbridge
Dublin 4

Allied Irish Investment Managers Ltd
Carrisbrook House
Pembroke Rd
Dublin 4

An Bord Bainne (Services) Ltd
Grattan House
Lr Mount St
Dublin 2

Anglo Irish Bank Corp Plc
Stephen Court
18-21 St Stephen's Green
Dublin 2

The Bank of Ireland
91 Pembroke Rd
Dublin 4

Banque Nationale de Paris (Ireland) Ltd
111 St Stephen's Green West
Dublin 2

Bloxham Maguire
9-12 Fleet St
Dublin 2

Citibank NA
St Stephen's Green
Dublin 2

Davy Futures Ltd
Davy House
49 Dawson St
Dublin 2

Gandon Securities Ltd
60-63 Dawson St
Dublin 2

Goodbody James Capel
(Financial Futures) Ltd
5 College Green
Dublin 2

Hibernian Insurance Co Ltd
Hibernian House
Haddington Rd
Dublin 4

Industrial Credit Corp Plc
32-34 Harcourt St
Dublin 2

Investment Bank of Ireland Ltd
26 Fitzwilliam Place
Dublin 2

Irish Life Assurance Co
Irish Life Centre
Middle Abbey St
Dublin 2

Irish Telecommunications Investments
Plc
Merrion House
Dublin 4

National Irish Bank Ltd
27 College Green
Dublin 2

NCB Stockbrokers Ltd
Ferry House
48-53 Lr Mount St
Dublin 2

Riada & Co
28 Grafton St
Dublin 2

Shield Life Insurance Co Ltd
Blackrock Hall
Frascati Rd
Blackrock
Co Dublin

Trinity Bank Ltd
Woodchester House
Golden Lane
Dublin 8

Ulster Bank Ltd
33 College Green
Dublin 2

Appendix 1

Board of Exchange

Chairman:
Dermot Desmond, National & City
Brokers
John Kearney, Allied Irish Banks
Coleman Lydon, Bank of Ireland
Brian O'Loughlin, Irish Life
John Corrigan, Allied Irish Investment
Managers
Frank Shanley, Riada
Martin Wilson, Ulster Bank
Diarmuid Bradley, IFOX
Kieran Luddy, IFOX

Membership

Banks
Allied Irish Banks
Bank of Ireland
Ulster Bank
National Irish Bank
Citibank
Banque Nationale de Paris
Algemene Bank Nederland
Industrial Credit Corp
Anglo Irish Bank
Trinity Bank
Agricultural Credit Corp

Fund Managers
Allied Irish Investment Managers
Investment Bank of Ireland
Irish Life Assurance Co
Shield Life Insurance

Stockbrokers
National & City Brokers
Riada
Goodbody James Capel
Davys
Bloxham Maguire

Treasury
Hibernian Insurance
Gandon Securities
Bord Bainne
ITI Plc

Appendix 2

IFOX Staff

Chief Executive, Diarmuid Bradley
Operations Director, Kieran Luddy
Financial Controller, Patricia Morris
Guarantee & Compliance Officer,
Michael Whelan
Software Development Team: Iain
Ballesty, Marie O'Sullivan Greene, Denis
Nagle
Clearing System, Dymphna McHugh
Secretary, Brenda Maguire

Japan

Kobe Rubber Exchange

Daikyo Shohin Co Ltd
15-2 1-chome, Nishi-Nakajima
Yodogawa-ku, Osaka 532

Eguchi Shoji Co Ltd
2-5 2-chome, Koraibashi, Chuo-ku
Osaka 541

Fujichu Co Ltd
3-7 2-chome, Funakoshi-cho
Higashi-ku, Osaka 540

Hiro Shoji Co Ltd
10-14 1-chome, Awaza
Nishi-ku, Osaka 550

Hokushin Shohin Co Ltd
2-1 3-chome, Nishi-Azabu
Minato-ku, Tokyo 106

Hoteiya Rubber Co Ltd
3-8 5-chome, Kami-kita
Hirano-ku, Osaka 547

Imex Co Ltd
11-7 2-chome, Sakae, Naka-ku
Nagoya 460

C Itoh & Co Ltd
1-3 4-chome, Kita-Kyutaro-machi
Chuo-ku, Osaka 541

Kanetsu Shoji Co Ltd
11-5 1-chome, Nihonbashi-Kakigaracho
Chuo-ku, Tokyo 103

Kasho Co Ltd
3-7 8-chome, Isogami-dori
Chuo-ku, Kobe 651

Kobayashi Yoko Co Ltd
15-5 1-chome, Nihonbashi-Kakigara-cho
Chuo-ku, Tokyo 103

Kobe Gomutori Daiko Kaisha Ltd
49 Harima-cho, Chuo-ku, Kobe 650

Kojima Shoji Co Ltd
4-9 2-Chome, Kita-Kyuhoji-machi
Chuo-ku, Osaka 541

Kometsune Co Ltd
45 1-chome, Shiga-Hondori
Kita-ku, Nagoya 462

Kyoei Bussan Co Ltd
6-1 1-chome, Hacchobori
Chuo-ku, Tokyo 104

Marubeni Corp
5-7 2-chome, Honmachi, Chuo-ku
Osaka 541

Marugo Shoji Co Ltd
4-11 2-chome, Koraibashi, Chuo-ku
Osaka 541

Mitsui & Co Ltd
3-33 2-chome, Nakanoshima
Kita-ku, Osaka 530

Nichimen Corp
11-1 3-chome, Nihonbashi
Chuo-ku, Tokyo 103

S Nishida & Co Ltd
1-27 1-chome, Kitahama
Chuo-ku, Osaka 541

Nomura Trading Co Ltd
4.-5 1-chome, Bingo-machi
Chuo-ku, Osaka 541

Okachi & Co Ltd
7-29 3-chome, Sakae
Naka-ku, Nagoya 460

Okato Shoji Co Ltd
2-11 3-chome, Honmachi
Chuo-ku, Osaka 541

Okura Shoji Co Ltd
7-2 6-chome, Nishi-Tenma
Kita-ku, Osaka 530

Osaka Oishi Shoji Co Ltd
5-24 2-chome, Chuo-Senba
Chuo-ku, Osaka 542

Osaka Oroshi-Iryou Co Ltd
1-10 2-chome, Koraibashi
Chuo-ku, Osaka 541

Orient Boeki Co Ltd
24-30 5-chome, Watanabe-dori
Chuo-ku, Fukuoka 810

Orion Koeki Co Ltd
113-1 Higashimachi, Chuo-ku
Kobe 650

Santomi & Co Ltd
49 Harima-cho, Chuo-ku
Kobe 650

Sanyo Trading Co Ltd
6-2 3-chome, Hirano-machi
Chuo-ku, Osaka 541

Seibu Kanetsu Bussan Co Ltd
1-7 2-chome, Kita-Kyuhoji-machi
Chuo-ku, Osaka 541

Seiyu Shoji Co Ltd
4-23 2-chome, Chuo-Senba
Chuo-ku, Osaka 542

Sumitomo Corp
1-28 1-chome, Sakaemachi-dori
Chuo-ku, Kobe 650

Taisei Commodity Co Ltd
2-7 2-chome, Honmachi
Chuo-ku, Osaka 541

Taisei Koeki Kaisha Ltd
7-4 1-chome, Nihonbashi
Chuo-ku, Tokyo 103

Taiyo General Inc
12-7 8-chome, Ginza
Chuo-ku, Tokyo 104

Tayama & Co Ltd
3-3 1-chome, Minami-Honmachi
Chuo-ku, Osaka 541

Tokyo General Corp
9-9 1-chome, Kitahama
Chuo-ku, Osaka 541

Yamasan Shokai Co Ltd
10-14 1-chome, Awaza
Nishi-ku, Osaka 550

Yutaka Shoji Co Ltd
5-28 2-chome, Kyutaro-machi, Chuo-ku,
Osaka 541

Associate Members

Alcan Far East (Pte) Ltd
111 North Bridge Rd
#10-04/05 Peninsula Plaza
Singapore 0617

Cargill Commodity Trading (Pte) Ltd
435 Orchard Rd, #22-00
Wisma Atria, Singapore 0923

Centrotrade Commodities (Pte) Ltd
10 Collyer Quay, #07-07
Ocean Bldg, Singapore 0104

Dexin Enterprise (Pte) Ltd
108 Middle Rd #03-00
Bright chambers, Singapore 0718

Hecht, Heyworth & Alcan Ltd
Myrtil House, 70 Clifton St
London EC2A 4SP, UK

Joo Cheong Co (Pte) Ltd
42 Middle Rd
Singapore 0718

Kautschuk-Gesellschaft mbH
Reuterweg 14, D-6000 Frankfurt/M
F R Germany

Lam Seng Rubber Co (Pte) Ltd
2 Alexandra Rd, #05-02B
Delta House, Singapore 0315

Marubeni America Corp
200 Park Ave, New York
NY 10166 USA

Nordmann, Rassmann GMBH & Co
Kajen 2, 2000 Hamburg 11
FR Germany

Pacol Ltd
Latham House, 16 Minories
London EC3N 1NA, UK

Singapore Tong Teik (Pte) Ltd
3 Shenton Way, #15-01
Shenton House, Singapore 0106

Sin Huat Rubber Co (Pte) Ltd
141 Cecil St, #07-01/04
Tung Ann Assn Bldg
Singapore 0105

The Maebashi Dried Cocoon Exchange
Commodity Commission Merchants

ACE Koeki Co Ltd
1-26-26 Higashi Shibuya-ku
Tokyo

Daiwa Tsusho Co Ltd
2-5-1 Sadae Naka-ku, Nagoya-city

Fuji Shohin Co Ltd
1-8-6 Muromachi Nihonbashi Chuo-ku
Tokyo

Hokushin Bussan Co Ltd
1-9-2 Kayaba-cho Nihonbashi Chuo-ku
Tokyo

Hokushin Shohin Co Ltd
3-2-1 Nishiazabu Minato-ku, Tokyo

Japan Silk Selling Federation of
Agricultural Co-operative Association
5-57 Kitanakadori Naka-ku
Yokohama-city

Kanetsu Boeki Co Ltd
1-11-5 Kakigara-cho Nihonbashi
Chuo-ku
Tokyo

Kanetsu Shoji Co Ltd
1-11-5 Kakigara-cho Nihonbashi
Chuo-ku
Tokyo

Kawano Shoji Co Ltd
3-3-19 Chiyoda-machi Maebashi-city
Gunma Pref

Kobayashi Yoko Co Ltd
1-15-5 Kakigara-cho Nihonbashi
Chuo-ku
Tokyo

Kohwa Shoji Co Ltd
1-13-15 Kayaba-cho Nihonbashi
Chuo-ku
Tokyo

Marushizu Shoji Co Ltd
1-1-8 Honmachi Nihonbashi Chuo-ku
Tokyo

Mashita Shoji Co Ltd
1-1-4 Shibuya Shibuya-ku, Tokyo

Meiji Bussan Co Ltd
1-1-23 Ningyo-cho Nihonbashi
Chuo-ku
Tokyo

S Nishida & Co Ltd
2-77 Kitahama Higashi-ku
Osaka-city

Okachi & Co Ltd
3-7-29 Sakae Naka-ku, Nagoya-city

Sanwardo Boeki Co Ltd
4-6-1 Odorinishi Chuo-ku
Sapporo-city

Shinnihon Shohin Co Ltd
3-14-13 Ginza Chuo-ku, Tokyo

Taichi Shoji Co Ltd
1-13-13 Kayaba-cho Nihonbashi
Chuo-ku
Tokyo

Taiyo General Co Ltd
8-12-7 Ginza Chuo-ku, Tokyo

Tokyo General Co Ltd
3-9-6 Kyobashi Chuo-ku, Tokyo

Yamabun Sangyo Co Ltd
2-5-12 Iwamoto-cho Chiyoda-ku
Tokyo

Yamanashi Shoji Co Ltd
2-60-6 Hamacho Nihonbashi Chuo-ku
Tokyo

Yunion Boeki Co Ltd
1-6-10 Ningyo-cho Nihonbashi
Chuo-ku
Tokyo

Yutaka Shoji Co Ltd
1-16-12 Kakigara-cho Nihonbashi
Chuo-ku
Tokyo

**Member of the Maebashi Dried Cocoon
Exchange**

Abe Seishi Co Ltd
56 Reizancho Dategun Fukushima Pref

Daiichi Shohin Co Ltd
2-16-8 Dogenzaka Shibuya-ku, Tokyo

Eiko Kigyo Co Ltd
1-28-10 Takada baba Shinzyuku-ku
Tokyo

Fujichu Corp
2-48 Funakoshicho Higashi-ku
Osaka

Gunsan Co Ltd
785 Fuzioka Fuzioka-city Gunma Pref

Iida Co
5-20-10 Tateishi Katsushika-ku
Tokyo

Isibashi Kiito Co Ltd
1-banchi Yamashitacho Naka-ku
Yokohama

Jyoumou Nenshi Co Ltd
370 Rokkumachi Maebashi Gunma Pref

Katakura Kougyo Co Ltd
3-1-2 Kyobashi Chuo-ku
Tokyo

Kawamura Co Ltd
3-15-6 Nakamachi Kiriu Gunma Pref

Kohoku Bussan Co Ltd
3-2-1 Nishiazabu Minato-ku, Tokyo

Kojima Co Ltd
4-40 Minaminakadori Naka-ku
Yokohama

Kumagaya Sanshi Co Ltd
2,253 Hirado Ohaza Kumagaya

Marudai Seishi Co Ltd
1-12-22 Kokuryomachi Maebashi
Gunma Pref

Nikko Shohin Co Ltd
1-38-12 Kakigaracho Nihonbashi
Chuo-ku
Tokyo

Ohno Silk Reeling Co
3-15-6 Jyotomachi Maebashi Gunma
Pref

Okato Shoji Co Ltd
3-24 Honmachi Higashi-ku, Osaka

Sanki Shoji Co Ltd
1-19-9 Kakigaracho Nihonbashi
Chuo-ku
Tokyo

Sanshi Kyodo Co Ltd
5-25-2 Kaigandori Naka-ku, Yokohama

Sekiguchi Silk Reeling Co
536 Sekinemachi Maebashi Gunma Pref

Shigeo Kishi
1-12-2 Asahi-cho Maebashi Gunma Pref

Shoei Co Ltd
1-2-1 Nishiki-cho Kanda Chiyoda-ku
Tokyo

Takasaki Seishi Co Ltd
450 Namiecho Takasaki Gunma Pref

Teruo Adachi
1,058 Iizukamachi Takasaki Gunma Pref

Tomio Kishi
1-6-11 Omotecho Maebashi Gunma
Pref

Toyo Rex Co Ltd
1-1-16 Saga Koto-ku, Tokyo

Yamazen Shoji Co Ltd
1-9-9 Kakigaracho Nihonbashi
Chuo-ku, Tokyo

The Tokyo Commodity Exchange

(*Codes:* p = precious metals – gold, silver, platinum; r = rubber; cy = cotton yarn; wy = woollen yarn)

ACE Koeki Co Ltd
26-26 Higashi 1-chome, Shibuya-kum
Tokyo 150
Tel: 03 406 4649
Fax: 03 499 6514
(p),(r),(cy),(wy)

Asahi Trust Co Ltd
1-8 Nihonbashi-Honcho 1-chome
Chuo-ku, Tokyo 103
Tel: 03 279 5021
Fax: 03 241 0121
(p),(r),(cy)

Central Shoji Co Ltd
7-9 Nihonbashi-Kakigaracho 1-chome
Chuo-ku
Tokyo 103
Tel: 03 666 1161
Fax: 03 664 1175
(p),(r),(cy),(wy)

C Itoh & Co Ltd
5-1 Kita Aoyama 2-chome, Minato-ku
Tokyo 107
Tel: 03 497 3915
Fax: 03 497 7953
(p)

Dai-Ichi Shohin Co Ltd
16-8 Dogenzaka 2-chome, Shibuya-ku
Tokyo 150
Tel: 03 476 0811
Fax: 03 476 0819
(p),(r),(cy),(wy)

Daiki Sangyo Co Ltd
Nagoya Center Bldg 2-13, Nishiki 2-chome
Naka-ku, Nagoya 460
Tel: 052 201 6311
Fax: 052 201 6318
(cy),(wy)

Daikyo Shohin Co Ltd
15–2 Nishi-Nakajima 1-chome
Yodogawa-ku, Osaka 532
Tel: 06 304 5071
Fax: 06 304 6196
(p),(r),(cy),(wy)

Daiwa Shohin Co Ltd
8–3 Higashi Nihonbashi 2-chome
Chuo-ku Tokyo 103
Tel: 03 862 0181
Fax: 03 862 0540
(p)

Daiwa Trading Co Ltd
9–3 Kita-Ichijo-Nishi, Chuo-ku
Sapporo, Hokkaido 060
Tel: 011 231 8211
Fax: 011 221 8752
(cy),(wy)

Daiwa Precious Metals Co Ltd
Matumoto Ginza Bld 11–13, Ginza 3-chome
Chuo-ku, Tokyo 104
Tel: 03 543 8011
Fax: 03 543 8070

Daiwa Trading Corp
5–1 Sakae 2-Chome, Naka-ku
Nagoya 460
Tel: 052 201 5251
Fax: 052 201 5250
(r)

Doi Shoji Co Ltd
8–5 Sakae 2-chome, Naka-ku
Nagoya 460
Tel: 052 201 2101
Fax: 052 211 1779
(r),(cy),(wy)

Eguchi Shoji Co Ltd
53 Koraibashi 2-chome, Chuo-ku
Osaka 541
Tel: 06 231 7671
Fax: 06 226 0716
(p),(r),(cy),(wy)

Fuji Shohin Co Ltd
8–6 Nihonbashi-Muromachi 1-chome
Chuo-ku, Tokyo 103
Tel: 03 270 2211
Fax: 03 270 2298
(r),(cy),(wy)

Fujichu Shoji Co Ltd
48 Funakoshicho 2-chome, Chuo-ku
Osaka 540
Tel: 06 942 2131
Fax: 06 947 0676
(p),(r),(cy),(wy)

Hirako (Japan) Inc
31–8 Taito 4-chome, Taito-ku
Tokyo 110
Tel: 03 835 3686
Fax: 03 835 1955
(p)

Hiro Shoji Co Ltd
10–14 Awaza 1-chome, Minato-ku
Tokyo 106
Tel: 06 533 2151
Fax: 06 533 2810
(p),(r),(cy),(wy)

Hokushin Bussan Co Ltd
0–2 Nihonbashi-Kayabacho 1-chome
Chuo-ku, Tokyo 103
Tel: 03 668 8111
Fax: 03 668 4417
(p),(r),(cy),(wy)

Hokushin Shohin Co Ltd
2–1 Nishi-Azabu 3-chome, Minato-ku
Tokyo 106
Tel: 03 403 3111
Fax: 03 479 2704
(p),(r),(cy),(wy)

Kanematsu-Gosho Ltd
14–1 Kyobashi 2-chome, Chuo-ku
Tokyo 104
Tel: 03 562 8695
Fax: 03 562 7557
(r)

Kanetsu Shoji Co Ltd
11–5 Nihonbashi-Kakigaracho 1-chome
Chuo-ku, Tokyo 103
Tel: 03 662 0111
Fax: 03 668 0808
(p),(r),(cy),(wy)

Kanetsu Trading Co Ltd
11–5 Nihonbashi-Kakigaracho 1-chome
Chuo-ku, Tokyo 103
Tel: 03 668 8111
Fax: 03 639 2518
(p),(r),(cy),(wy)

Kasho Co Ltd
14-9 Nihonbashi 2-chome, Chuo-ku
Tokyo 103
Tel: 03 276 7641
Fax: 03 278 8684
(r)

Kinsho-Mataichi Corp
24-1 Nihonbashi Shinkawa 1-chome
Chuo-ku, Tokyo 103
Tel: 03 297 7142
Fax: 03 297 7387
(p)

Kobayashi Yoko Co Ltd
15-5 Nihonbashi-Kakigaracho 1-chome
Chuo-ku, Tokyo 103
(p),(r),(cy),(wy)

Kojima Shoji Co Ltd
39 Kita-Kyuhoujicho 2-chome, Chuo-ku
Osaka 541
Tel: 06 262 2912
Fax: 06 264 0379
(r),(cy)

Kometsune Co Ltd
45 Shigahondori 1-chome, Kita-ku
Nagoya 462
Tel: 052 981 3571
Fax: 052 911 1321
(p)

Kowa Shoji Co Ltd
13-15 Nihonbashi-Kayabacho 1-chome
Chuo-ku, Tokyo 103
Tel: 03 661 1821
Fax: 03 661 5789
(p),(r),(cy),(wy)

Kyoei Bussan Co Ltd
6-1 Hachobori 1-chome, Chuo-ku
Tokyo 104
Tel: 03 553 4151
Fax: 03 553 4160
(p),(r),(cy),(wy)

Mashita Shoji Co Ltd
1-4 Shibuya 1-chome, Shibuya-ku
Tokyo 150
Tel: 03 407 8271
Fax: 03 499 5467
(r)

Marubeni Corp
4-2 Otemachi 1-chome, Chiyoda-ku
Tokyo 100
Tel: 03 282 2111
Fax: 03 282 7456
(p),(r)

Marumura Shoji Co Ltd
11-26 Nishiki 3-chome, Naka-ku
Nagoya 460
Tel: 052 231 7341
Fax: 052 203 5609
(p)

Meiji Bussan Co Ltd
1-23 Nihonbashi-Ningyocho 1-chome
Chuo-ku, Tokyo 103
Tel: 03 666 2511
Fax: 03 666 9280
(p),(r),(cy),(wy)

Mitsubishi Corp
6-3 Marunouchi 2-chome, Chiyoda-ku
Tokyo 100-86
Tel: 03 210 3759
Fax: 03 210 3994/3999
(p)

Mitui & Co Ltd
2-1 Otemachi 1-chome, Chiyoda-ku
Tokyo 100
Tel: 03 285 3393
Fax: 03 285 9915
(p),(r)

Million Trading Co Ltd
8-20 Marunouchi 1-chome, Naka-ku
Nagoya 460
Tel: 052 202 4111
Fax: 052 202 4055
(p),(cy)

Naruoka Co Ltd
3-61 Asakusa 2-chome, Taito-ku, Tokyo
111
Tel: 03 843 6911
Fax: 03 845 5745
(r)

Nichimen Corp
13-1 Kyobashi 1-chome, Chuo-ku
Tokyo 104
Tel: 03 277 5111
Fax: 03 271 6294
(p)

Nihon Koeki Co Ltd
4-4 Nishi-Shinjuku 7-chome, Shinjuku-
ku
Tokyo 160
Tel: 03 369 1171
Fax: 03 369 8902
(r),(cy),(wy)

Nissho-Iwai Corp
4-5 Akasaka 2-chome, Minato-ku
Tokyo 107
Tel: 03 588 2917
Fax: 03 588 4827
(p)

Nomura Trading Co Ltd
15 Bingocho 1-chome, Chuo-ku
Osaka 541
Tel: 06 268 8353
Fax: 06 273 7664
(r)

Oishi Shoji Co Ltd
14-30 Sakae 3-chome, Naka-ku
Nagoya 460
Tel: 052 241 1556
Fax: 052 241 5734
(p)

Okachi & Co Ltd
7-29 Sakae 3-chome, Naka-ku
Nagoya 460
Tel: 052 261 3311
Fax: 052 262 6717
(p),(r),(cy),(wy)

Okato Shoji Co Ltd
13-9 Shinkawa 2-chome, Chuo-ku
Tokyo 104
Tel: 03 553 0711
Fax: 03 552 1169
(p),(r),(cy),(wy)

Okayasu Shoji Co Ltd
53 Kitahama 2-chome, Chuo-ku
Osaka 541
Tel: 06 222 0001
Fax: 06 227 0119
(p)

Okura Shoji Co Ltd
Umeshin-Higashi Bldg
7-2 Nishi-Tenma 6-chome, Kita-ku
Osaka 530
Tel: 06 362 8681
Fax: 06 362 8689
(p)

Sanki Shoji Co Ltd
19-9 Nihonbashi-Kakigaracho 2-chome
Chuo-ku
Tokyo 103
Tel: 03 667 5251
Fax: 03 664 0050
(p)

Sanko Shokuhin Co Ltd
16-7 Nihonbashi-Kakigaracho 2-chome
Chuo-ku, Tokyo 103
Tel: 03 669 5901
Fax: 03 639 4044
(p)

Sanward Trading Inc
Sapporo Akigin Bldg 6-1
Oodorinishi 4-chome, Chuo-ku
Sapporo, Hokkaido 060
Tel: 011 221 5311
Fax: 011 222 6406
(r),(cy),(wy)

Seiyu Shoji Co Ltd
10-11 Nihonbashi-Horidomecho 1-
chome
Chuo-ku
Tokyo 160
Tel: 03 663 5711
Fax: 03 669 0410
(p),(r),(cy),(wy)

Shinnihon Kishi Co Ltd
4-1 Honmachi 4-chome, Chuo-ku
Osaka 541
Tel: 06 271 2153
Fax: 06 264 0545
(p)

Shinnihon Shohin Co Ltd
14-13 Ginza 3-chome, Chuo-ku
Tokyo 104
Tel: 03 543 8181
Fax: 03 545 4624
(r),(cy),(wy)

Sumitomo Corp
Sumisho Nishikicho Bldg 11-1
Kandanishikicho 3-chome, Chiyoda-ku
Tokyo 100-91
Tel: 03 296 3203
Fax: 03 294 6176

S Nishida Co Ltd
77 Kitahama 2-chome, Chuo-ku
Osaka 541
Tel: 06 202 4541
Fax: 06 231 9158
(p),(r)

Sunrise Trading Corp
19-4 Higashi-Ikebukuro 1-chome
Toshima-ku, Tokyo 170
Tel: 03 988 7351
Fax: 03 985 9007
(p),(r),(cy),(wy)

Taichi Shoji Co Ltd
13-13 Nihonbashi-Kayabacho 1-chome
Chuo-ku, Tokyo 103
Tel: 03 668 9351
Fax: 03 668 0013
(p),(r),(cy),(wy)

Taiheiyo Bussan Co Ltd
11-2 Nihonbashi-Kakigaracho 1-chome
Chuo-ku, Tokyo 103
Tel: 03 668 1451
Telex: 03 668 1455
(cy),(wy)

Taisei Commodity Co Ltd
10-1 Honmachi 2-chome, Chuo-ku
Osaka 530
Tel: 06 264 2181
Fax: 06 264 2191
(p),(r),(cy),(wy)

Taisei Stamps & Coins Co Ltd
Ohno Bldg 19-8 Kyobashi 1-chome
Chuo-ku, Tokyo 104
Tel: 03 562 0711
Fax: 03 564 1255
(p)

Taiyo General Corp
12-7 Ginza 8-chome, Chuo-ku
Tokyo 104
Tel: 03 545 6111
Fax: 03 546 0236
(p)

Tokai Koueki Co Ltd
31 Suemoridori 3-chome
Chigusa-ku Nagoya 464
Tel: 052 752 2201
Fax: 052 751 1741
(cy),(wy)

Toyoka Shoji Co Ltd
28-4 Nihonbashi-Kakigaracho 1-chome
Chuo-ku, Tokyo 103
Tel: 03 668 0651
Fax: 03 668 0667
(r)

Tokyo General Corp
9-6 Kyobashi 3-chome, Chuo-ku
Tokyo 104
Tel: 03 535 6111
Fax: 03 535 6162
(p),(r),(cy),(wy)

Tokyo Medex Corp
3-6 Kamikawabatamachi, Hakata-ku
Fukuoka 812
Tel: 092 281 7641
Fax: 092 281 6986
(p)

Toyo Menka Kaisha Ltd
14-27 Akasaka 2-chome, Minato-ku
Tokyo 104
Tel: 03 588 6977
Fax: 03 588 6949
(p)

Union Trading Co ltd
6-10 Nihonbashi-Ningyocho 1-chome
Chuo-ku, Tokyo 103
Tel: 03 668 2331
Fax: 03 639 3690
(p),(r),(cy),(wy)

Yamabun Sangyo Co Ltd
5-12 Iwamotocho 2-chome, Chiyoda-ku
Tokyo 100
Tel: 03 865 8611
Fax: 03 865 8046
(r),(cy),(wy)

Yamanashi Shoji Co Ltd
60-6 Nihonbashi-Hamacho 2-chome
Chuo-ku, Tokyo 103
Tel: 03 664 0221
Fax: 03 664 0585
(p),(r)

Yamatane Bussan Co Ltd
1-1 Nihonbashi-Ningyocho 1-chome
Chuo-ku, Tokyo 103
Tel: 03 667 7011
Fax: 03 667 4962
(p),(r),(cy),(wy)

Yamazen Shoji Co Ltd
No 8 Wakoh Bldg 9–9 Nihonbashi-
Kakigaracho
1-chome, Chuo-ku, Tokyo 103
*Tel:*03 667 4361
Fax: 03 667 8071
(r),(cy),(wy)

Yutaka Shoji Co Ltd
16–12 Nihonbashi-Kakigaracho 1-chome
Chuo-ku, Tokyo 103
Tel: 03 667 5211
Fax: 03 666 6125
(p),(r),(cy),(wy)

Yamasan Shokai Co Ltd
10–14 Awaza 1-chome, Nishi-ku
Osaka 550
Tel: 06 543 2118
Fax: 06 533 2394
(p)

Associate Members of the Precious Metals Division

Ayrton Metals Ltd
30 Ely Place, London EC1N 6RT
UK

Balfour Maclaine Futures Inc
Wall St Plaza, New York
NY 10005, USA

The Chase Manhattan Bank NA
1 Chase Manhattan Plaza
New York, NY 10081, USA

Credit Suisse
Paradeplatz 8, PO Box 590
8021 Zurich, Switzerland

Deak International Trading Ltd
804 West Tower, Bond Centre
89 Queensway, Central, Hong Kong

Degussa AG
PO Box 11 05 33, D-6000
Frankfurt/M 11, West Germany

Derby Metals Ltd
15/F Jardine House
1 Connaught Place, Hong Kong

Drexel Burnham Lambert Trading Corp
2 Executive Drive, Fort Lee
New Jersey 07024, USA

E D & F Man International Ltd
Sugar Quay, Lower Thames St
London EC3R 6DU, UK

Engelhard Metals Corp
70 Wood Ave, South Iseiln
New Jersey 08830, USA

Gerald Metals Inc
High Ridge Park, Stamford
CT 06904, USA

J Aron & Co
85 Broad St, New York
NY 10004, USA

Kleinwort Benson Australia Ltd
2nd Floor, Kleinwort Benson House
55 Harrington St, Sydney 2000
Australia

Macquarie Bank Ltd
Level 26, 20 Bond St, Sydney
NSW 2000, Australia

Mase Westpac Ltd
5 Lloyds Ave, London EC3N 3DB
UK

MG Commodity Corp
17 Ballindamm, D-2000 Hamburg 1
West Germany

Mocatta Commercial Ltd
Mocatta House, 4 Crosby Square
London EC3A 6AQ, UK

Morgan Guaranty Trust Co of New York
c/o Hong Kong Office
23rd floor, Edinburg Tower
15 Queens Rd Central
Hong Kong

Morgan Stanley Hong Kong
Commodities Ltd
Suite 4008, Two Exchange Square
Hong Kong

N M Rothschild & Sons Ltd
New Court, St Swithin's Lane
London EC4P 4DU, UK

Prudential-Bache Securities Inc
100 Gold St, New York
NY 10292, USA

Republic National Bank of New York
452 Fifth Ave, New York
NY 10018, USA

Rudolf Wolff & Co Ltd
Plantation House
31–35 Fenchurch St
Longon EC3M 3DX, UK

Sharps Pixley Inc
200 Park Ave, New York
NY 10166, USA

Shearson Lehman Hutton Bullion (Asia)
Ltd
Level 38, One Pacific Place
88 Queensway, Hong Kong

Sun Hung Kai Bullion Co Ltd
3rd Floor, Admiralty Centre
18 Harcourt Rd, Hong Kong

Swiss Bank Corp
Aeschenplatz 6, 4002 Basle
Switzerland

Triland Metals Ltd
Bow Bells House, Bread St
London EC4M 9BQ, UK

Sumitomo Corp (UK) Ltd
107 Cheapside, London EC2V 6DQ
UK

Sumitomo Corp of America
345 Park Ave, New York
NY 10154, USA

Union Bank of Switzerland
Bahnhofstrasse 45, CH-8021
Zurich, Switzerland

Members

All Enterprise Co Ltd

Asahi Chemical Laboratory Co Ltd

Bear Co Ltd

Bridgestone Co Ltd

Chigasaki Woolen Spinning & Weaving
Co Ltd

Chogin Co Ltd

Chori Co Ltd

Chubu Dai-ichi Shohin Co Ltd

Chugai Kogyo Co Ltd

Chuo Shohin Co Ltd

Dah Chong Hon (Japan) Ltd

Daiei Sogyo Co Ltd

Daisen Shoji Co Ltd

Daito Woolen Spinning & Weaving Co
Ltd

Daiwabo Co Ltd

Dowa Kogyo Co Ltd

Eguchi Co Ltd

Eikoh Kigyo Co Ltd

Four Nine Co Ltd

Fuji Spinning Co Ltd

Fujitomi Co Ltd

Fukutani Co Ltd

Fukuwa Gomu Co Ltd

Furukawa Co Ltd

Gold Tokai Co Ltd

Gomi Sangyo Co Ltd

Maruni Shokusan Shokai & Co Ltd

Hirano Shoten

Hoei Shoji Co Ltd

Ichida Co Ltd

Ido Shoten Co Ltd

Iimori Shoten Co Ltd

Imex Co Ltd

Isemichi Co Ltd

Ito Shoji Co Ltd

Itoya Co Ltd

Iwasaki Shoji Co Ltd

Kagawa Tokei Shokai Co Ltd

Kanebo Cotton Yarn Co Ltd

Kanto Sugar Co Ltd

Kashisei Co Ltd

Kato Sansho Co Ltd

Kawachi Co Ltd

Kawano Shoji Co Ltd

Kawashima Co Ltd

Kikuchi Metal Co Ltd

Kikuya Pearl Co Ltd

Kitani Shoji Co Ltd

Kohoku Bussan Co Ltd

Kuniyasu Tokeiten

Kurabo Industries Co Ltd

Kushida Co Ltd

Kyodo Shohin Co Ltd

M Senda Shoten

Marugo-Shoji Co Ltd

Maruho Takara Shohin Co Ltd

Maruichi Shoten Co Ltd

Maruko Shoten

Marumoto Co Ltd

Maruume Co Ltd

Maruyo Seni Kogyo Co Ltd

Miki Shoji Co Ltd

Mitsubishi Metal Co Ltd

Mitsui Mining & Smelting Co Ltd

Mitukoshi Co Ltd

Murakami Kinzoku Sangyo Co Ltd

Nagahori Co Ltd

Nihon Mining Co Ltd

Nihon Nosanbutsu Co Ltd

Nikko Shohin Co Ltd

Nishida Co Ltd

Nishimura Co Ltd

Nisshin Spinning Co Ltd

Nisshin Boeki Co Ltd

Nittetsu Mining Co Ltd

Nitto Boeki Co Ltd

Nitto Boseki Co Ltd

Noguchi Shoji Co Ltd

Nomi Co Ltd

Olympic Gold Gallery Co Ltd

Onishi Shoji Co Ltd

Orient Boeki Co Ltd

Orion Koeki Co Ltd

Osaka Oishi Shoji Co Ltd

Osaka Oroshi Iryo Co Ltd

Otobe Beikoku Co Ltd

Ozawa Tokeiten Co Ltd

Saibo Co Ltd

Saikai Shoji Co Ltd

Sakata Tokei Boeki Co Ltd

Sanchu & Co Ltd

Sanyo Trading Co Ltd

Seibu Kanetsu Bussan Co Ltd

Shikibo Ltd

Shinei Shoji Co Ltd

Shinko Shoji Co Ltd

Sumitomo Metal Mining Co Ltd

Sunmenard Co Ltd

Suzuki Shoten Co Ltd

T Kobayashi Shoten Co Ltd

Tachikawa Co Ltd

Taisei Koeki Co Ltd

Taiyo Bussan Co Ltd

Tamurakoma Co Ltd

Tayama Co Ltd

Teikoku Seni Co Ltd

Toko Shotori Daiko Co Ltd

Toho Rayon Co Ltd

Tokei Hoseki No Ito Co Ltd

Toyobo Co Ltd

Toyo Lex Co Ltd

Toyoshima & Co Ltd

Toyota Tsusho Co Ltd

Tsutsui Shoten Co Ltd

Ueno Co Ltd

Ueno & Co

Unitika Ltd

Yagi Co Ltd

Yamacho Co Ltd

Yamadai Shoji Co Ltd

Yamago Shoji Co Ltd

Yamasa Shoji K K

Yokohama Rubber Co Ltd

Yoshida Kogyo Co Ltd

Yoshizawa Goro Shoten Co Ltd

The Tokyo Grain Exchange

Members

ACE Koeki Co Ltd
26-26 Higashi 1-chome, Shibuya-ku
Tokyo 150
Tel: 03 406 4649

Central Shoji Co Ltd
7-9 Kakigaracho 1-chome, Nihonbashi
Chuo-ku, Tokyo 103
Tel: 03 666 1161

Daiichi Shohin Co Ltd
16-8 Dougenzaka 2-chome, Shibuya-ku
Tokyo 150
Tel: 03 476 0811

Daiki Sangyo Co Ltd
2-13 Nishiki 2-chome, Naka-ku
Nagoya 460
Tel: 052 201 6311

Daikyo Commodities Co Ltd
15-2 Nishinakajima 1-chome,
Yodogawa-ku
Osaka 532
Tel: 06 304 5071

Daiwa Shohin Co Ltd
2-8-3 Higashinihonbashi, Chuo-ku
Tokyo 103
Tel: 03 862 1081

Daiwa Tsusho Co Ltd
5-1 Sakae 2-chome, Naka-ku
Nagoya 460
Tel: 052 201 5251

Doishoji Co Ltd
8-5 Sakae 2-chome, Naka-ku
Nagoya 460
Tel: 052 201 2101

Eguchi Shoji Co Ltd
2-5 Kouraibashi, 2-chome, Chuo-ku
Osaka 541
Tel: 06 231 7671

Fujichiu Corp
3-7 Funakoshicho 2-chome, Chuo-ku
Osaka 540
Tel: 06 942 2131

Fuji Shohin Co Ltd
8-6 Muromachi 1-chome, Nihonbashi
Chuo-ku, Tokyo 103
Tel: 03 270 2211

Fujitomi Co Ltd
1 1-chome Minami-Ichijyo, Nishi
Chuo-ku, Sapporo
Tel: 011 251 4261

Hokushin Bussan Co Ltd
9-2 Kayabacho 1-chome, Nihonbashi
Chuo-ku, Tokyo 103
Tel: 03 668 8111

Hokushin Shohin Co Ltd
2-1 Nishiazabu 3-chome, Minato-ku
Tokyo 106
Tel: 03 403 3111

Kanetsu Boeki Co Ltd
11-5 Kakigaracho 1-chome, Nihonbashi
Chuo-ku, Tokyo 103
Tel: 03 668 1711

Kanetsu Shoji Co Ltd
11-5 Kakigaracho 1-chome, Nihonbashi
Chuo-ku, Tokyo 103
Tel: 03 662 0111

Kobayashi Yoko Co Ltd
15-5 Kakigaracho 1-chome, Nihonbashi
Chuo-ku, Tokyo 103
Tel: 03 669 4111

Kometsune Corp
45 Shigahondori 1-chome, Kita-ku
Nagoya 462
Tel: 052 981 3571

Kowa Shoji Co Ltd
13–15 Kayabacho 1-chome, Nihonbashi
Chuo-ku, Tokyo 103
Tel: 03 661 1821

Kyoei Bussan Co Ltd
6–1 Hatchobori 1-chome, Chuo-ku
Tokyo 104
Tel: 03 553 4151

Maruho Takara Shohin Co Ltd
15–10 Ginza 3-chome, Chuo-ku
Tokyo 104
Tel: 03 543 8121

Maruichi & Co Ltd
7–1 Saga 1-chome, Koto-ku, Tokyo 135
Tel: 03 641 8411

Marumoto & Co Ltd
13–16 Awaza 1-chome, Nishi-ku
Osaka 550
Tel: 06 543 2511

Marushizu Shoji Co Ltd
1–8 Honcho 1-chome, Nihonbashi
Chuo-ku, Tokyo 103
Tel: 03 279 5021

Maruume Co Ltd
17–9 Kayabacho 2-chome, Nihonbashi
Chuo-ku, Tokyo 103
Tel: 03 664 8751

Mashita Shoji Co Ltd
1–4 Shibuya 1-chome, Shibuya-ku
Tokyo 150
Tel: 03 407 8271

Meiji Bussan Co Ltd
1–23 Ningyocho 1-chome, Nihonbashi
Chuo-ku, Tokyo 103
Tel: 03 666 2511

Million Trading Co Ltd
8–20 Marunouchi 1-chome, Naka-ku
Nagoya 460
Tel: 052 202 4111

Mitsui-Bussan Futures Ltd
8–3 Nihonbashi, Honcho 3-chome,
Chuo-ku
Tokyo
Tel: 03 660 6800

Nihon Koeki Co Ltd
4–4 Nishishinjuku 7-chome, Shinjuku-ku
Tokyo 160
Tel: 03 369 1171

Nihon Agricultural Products Co Ltd
10 Kitasanjonishi 1-chome, Chuo-ku
Sapporo, Hokkaido 060
Tel: 011 251 7156

S Nishida & Co Ltd
1–27 Kitahana 1-chome, Chuo-ku
Osaka 541
Tel: 06 202 4541

Okachi & Co Ltd
7–29 Sakae 3-chome, Naka-ku
Nagoya 460
Tel: 052 261 3311

Okato Shoji Co Ltd
2–11 Honmachi 3-chome, Chuo-ku
Osaka 541
Tel: 06 261 7671

Okayasu Shoji Co Ltd
3–8 Kitahama 2-chome, Chuo-ku
Osaka 541
Tel: 06 222 0001

Sanchu & Co Ltd
11–3 Saga 1-chome, Koto-ku
Tokyo 135
Tel: 03 643 5500

Sanki Shoji Co Ltd
19–9 Kakigaracho, 1-chome, Nihonbashi
Chuo-ku, Tokyo 103
Tel: 03 667 5251

Sanko Shokuhin Co Ltd
16–7 Kakigaracho, 2-chome, Nihonbashi
Chuo-ku, Tokyo 103
Tel: 03 669 5901

The Sansiao Trading Co Ltd
2–9 Nihonbashi, 3-chome, Chuo-ku
Tokyo 103
Tel: 03 275 1001

Seiyu Shoji Co Ltd
10–11 Horidomecho 1-chome,
Nihonbashi
Chuo-ku, Tokyo 103
Tel: 03 663 5711

Sunrise Trading
19-4 Higashiikebukuro 1-chome
Toshima-ku, Tokyo 170
Tel: 03 988 7351

Sunward Trading Inc
West 4 Odori Chuo-ku, Sapporo 060
Tel: 011 221 5311

Taichi Shoji Co Ltd
13-13 Kayabacho 1-chome, Nihonbashi
Chuo-ku, Tokyo 103
Tel: 03 668 9351

Taiheiyo Bussan Co Ltd
11-2 Kakigaracho 1-chome, Nihonbashi
Chuo-ku, Tokyo 103
Tel: 03 668 1451

Taisei Commodity Co Ltd
2-7 Honmachi 2-chome, Chuo-ku
Osaka 541
Tel: 06 264 2181

Taiyo General Corp
12-7 Ginsa 8-chome, Chuo-ku
Tokyo 104
Tel: 03 545 6111

Tokio Medex Corp
Shibuya 3-27-11 Shibuya-ku
Tokyo 150
Tel: 03 498 2234

Tokyo General Trading Corp
9-6 Kyobashi 3-chome, Chuo-ku
Tokyo 104
Tel: 03 535 6111

Tokyoto Chuo Foodstuff Cooperative
Union
16-16 Koamicho, Chuo-ku, Tokyo 103
Tel: 03 666 5141

Toyoka Shoji Co Ltd
28-4 Kakigaracho 1-chome, Nihonbashi
Chuo-ku, Tokyo 103
Tel: 03 668 0651

Toyolex Co Ltd
1-16 Saga 1-chome, Koto-ku
Tokyo 135
Tel: 03 642 4531

Union Trading Corp
6-10 Ningyocho 1-chome, Nihonbashi
Chuo-ku, Tokyo 103
Tel: 03 668 2331

Yamabun Sangyo Co Ltd
5-12 Iwamotocho 2-chome, Chiyodaku
Tokyo 101
Tel: 03 865 8611

Yamadai Shoji Co Ltd
13-5 Kayabacho 3-chome, Nihonbashi
Chuo-ku, Tokyo 103
Tel: 03 666 2211

Yamezen Shoji Co Ltd
9-9 Kakigaracho 1-chome, Nihonbashi
Chuo-ku, Tokyo 103
Tel: 03 667 4361

Yamanashi Shoji Co Ltd
60-6 Hamacho 2-chome, Nihonbashi
Chuo-ku, Tokyo 103
Tel: 03 664 0221

Yamasan Shakai Co Ltd
10-14 Awaza 1-chome, Nishi-ku, Osaka
550
Tel: 06 543 2118

Yamatane Bussan Co Ltd
1-1 Ningyocho 1-chome, Nihonbashi
Chuo-ku, Tokyo 103
Tel: 03 667 7011

Yutaka Shoji Co Ltd
16-12 Kakigaracho 1-chome,
Nihonbashi
Chuo-ku, Tokyo 103
Tel: 03 667 5211

General Members

Ajinomoto Co Ltd
5-8 Kyobashi 1-chome, Chuo-ku, Tokyo
Tel: 03 272 1111

Arai Shoji Co Ltd
17-2 Beniya-cho Hiratsuka-City 254
Kanagawa
Tel: 0463 23 2011

Dah Chong Hong (Japan) Ltd
Dah Chong No 2 Bldg Roppongi 5-18-2
Minato-ku, Tokyo
Tel: 03 582 0708

Daiei Sogyo Co Ltd
Sankyo Bldg, 2-2-11 Nipponbashi
Kayabacho Chuo-ku, Tokyo
Tel: 03 664 5471

Daisen Shoji Co Ltd
7-9 1-chome, Kakigaracho Nihonbashi
Chuo-ku, Tokyo
Tel: 03 666 7728

Emery Trading Co Ltd
No 5-13 1-chome, Matsugaoka
Chigasakishi
Kanagawa-Ken
Tel: 0467 86 6604

Fuji Shoji Co Ltd
1-3 Saga 1-chome, Koto-ku, Tokyo
Tel: 03 642 0045

Goko Bussan Co Ltd
7-13 Ningyocho 3-chome, Nihonbashi
Chuo-ku, Tokyo
Tel: 03 668 5161

Gomei Shoji Co Ltd
11-6 1-chome, Hatchobori Chuo-ku
Tokyo
Tel: 03 553 5011

Haruyuki, Iida
3-29-4 Hama-cho Nihonbashi
Chuo-ku, Tokyo 103
Tel: 03 666 9639

Hiro Shoji Co Ltd
1-10-14 Awaza Nishi-ku, Osaka
Tel: 06 533 2151

Hokuren Federation of Agricultural
Cooperatives
Sapporo-shi, Chuo-ku, Nishi1, Kita4, 3
Tel: 011 231 2111

Howa Shoji Co Ltd
11-3-405 Kakigaracho 1-chome
Nihonbashi
Tokyo
Tel: 03 669 7731

Honen Corp
Mitusi Seimei Bldg 2-3 1-chome
Otemachi, Chiyoda-ku, Tokyo
Tel: 03 211 6511

Ibaraki Pre Food Sale Coop
2-7-15 Shiraume, Mito City, Ibaraki
Tel: 0292 21 2161

Ichiro, Igarashi
Apt ITOH 708, 15-4 Ebisu-Nishi 1-
chome
Shibuya-ku, Tokyo 103
Tel: 03 461 8480

Ikutatsu Co Ltd
3-13-12 Nishi-Ichinoe, Edogawa-ku
Tokyo
Tel: 03 654 9176

Isemichi Co Ltd
2-9-9 Nihonbashi Chuo-ku, Tokyo
Tel: 03 281 6407

Ishikawa Co Ltd
8-5 2-chome, Ginza, Chuo-ku, Tokyo
Tel: 03 562 4411

Itabashi Ryokoku
42-11 Itabashi 1-chome, Itabashi-ku
Tokyo
Tel: 03 961 5211

C Itoh & Co Ltd
5-1 Kita-Aoyama 2-chome, Minato-ku
Tokyo
Tel: 03 497 6068

Iwasaki Seishichi Shoten Co
Chiyoda-ku Marunouchi 2-4-1, Tokyo
Tel: 03 201 1666

Josan Shoji Co Ltd
13-13 Higashioi 6-chome, Shinagawa-ku
Tokyo 140
Tel: 03 761 1310

Kasho Co Ltd
14-9 Nihonbashi 2-chome, Chuo-ku
Tokyo 103
Tel: 03 276 7623

Kawamitsu Bussan Co Ltd
1-2-17 Nihonbashi, Chuo-ku, Tokyo
Tel: 03 271 3334

Keio Shoji Co Ltd
Hakataekihigashi 2-9-1 Hakata-ku
Fukuokashi
Tel: 092 472 2191

Kitoku Co Ltd
7-2-22 Ginza Chuo-ku, Tokyo 104
Tel: 03 571 2181

Koami Co Ltd
1–7 Nihonbashi, Koamicho, Chuo-ku
Tokyo 103
Tel: 03 667 6211

T Kobayashi Shoten Ltd
Haniuda Bldg 7–6 2-chome, Kayaba-cho
Nihonbashi, Chuo-ku, Tokyo
Tel: 03 668 1271

Koichi Kuwako
15–13 Nagasaki 1-chome, Toshima-ku
Tokyo 171
Tel: 03 973 3456

Kokusen Co Ltd
776 Kozono, Ayase-City, Kanagawa
Tel: 0467 77 2355

Kondo Tokuji Co Ltd
17–13 1-chome, Shinkawa Chuo-ku
Tokyo 104
Tel: 03 555 8080

Koto Syokuryo Hanbai Kyodo Kumiai
8–13 Saga 1-chome, Koto-ku,Tokyo 135
Tel: 03 641 8401

Linore Oil Mills Co Ltd
15–8 3-chome, Nihonbashi Chuo-ku,
Tokyo
Tel: 03 273 5651

Marubeni Corp
4–2 Ohtemachi 1-chome, Chiyoda-ku
Tokyo
Tel: 03 282 2111

Maruha Shoji Co Ltd
3–18 Koamicho Nihonbashi, Chuo-ku
Tokyo
Tel: 03 667 0109

Marukin Shoji Co Ltd
8–2–503 Kakigaracho 1-chome
Nihonbashi
Chuo-ku, Tokyo
Tel: 03 669 4424

Maruma Co Ltd
43 Higashimatsushitacho, Kanda
Chiyoda-ku, Tokyo
Tel: 03 254 4813

Mashita Shoten Co Ltd
1–15 Saga 1-chome, Koto-ku, Tokyo
Tel: 03 641 8481

Matsudai, Aihara
4–15–3 Chome, Sekimachi, Kita
Nerima-ku, Tokyo
Tel: 03 667 1770

Mitsubishi Corp
3–1 Marunouchi 2-chome, Chiyoda-ku
Tokyo
Tel: 03 210 6522

Mitsui & Co Ltd
2–1 Otemachi 1-chome, Chiyoda-ku
Tokyo 100
Tel: 03 285 1111

Mizuno Shoji Co Ltd
7–10 Iidabashi 1-chome, Chiyoda-ku
Tokyo Sankyo Bldg 8F
Tel: 03 265 9038

Musashi Beikoku Oroshi Ltd
4–30 2–chome, Akebono-cho
Tachikawa-shi, Tokyo
Tel: 0425 26 0634

The National Federation of Rice
Marketing Co-operative Association
6–3 3-chome, Kojimachi Chiyoda-ku
Tokyo
Tel: 03 263 0311

Nichimen Corp
13–1 Kyobashi 1-chome, Chuo-ku
Tokyo 104
Tel: 03 277 8271

Nikko Oil Mills Co Ltd
Kowa Hitothubashi Bldg 3–5–1 Kanda
Nishiki-cho, Chiyoda-ku, Tokyo
Tel: 03 233 3961

The Nisshin Oil Mills Ltd
23–1 Shinkawa 1-chome, Chuo-ku
Tokyo 104
Tel: 03 555 6923

Nissho Bussan Kaisha Ltd
2–1–18 Nihonbashi, Chuo-ku, Tokyo
Tel: 03 273 1301

Nissho-Iwai Co Ltd
4–5 Akasaka 2-chome, Minato-ku, Tokyo
107
Tel: 03 588 3503

Nozawa Beikoku Oroshi KK
1–12–6 Noguchicho
Higashimurayama-shi, Tokyo
Tel: 0423 93 3211

Okazaki Shoten Co Ltd
5–6 Toyotomakita Nerima-ku, Tokyo
176
Tel: 03 992 0111

Okura & Co Ltd
3–6 Ginza 2-chome, Chuo-ku, Tokyo
104
Tel: 03 566 6611

Otsuka Shoten Co Ltd
1–32–2 Kakigaracho, Nihonbashi
Chuo-ku, Tokyo
Tel: 03 666 0883

Saikai Shoji Co Ltd
474–6 Teshigawara, Kamizato-Machi
Kodamagun, Saitama
Tel: 0495 33 1634

Sakae Shokai Co Ltd
3–17–2 Juso Higashi Yodogawa-ku,
Osaka
Tel: 06 304 5819

Sanki Shoji Co Ltd
2–1–7 Masago, ChibaCity, Chibaken
Tel: 0472 79 3611

Sanko Trading Co Ltd
2–16–7 Nihonbashi, Kakigaracho
Chuo-ku, Tokyo
Tel: 03 664 2491

Santama Syokuryo Oroshi
KyoudoKumiai
16–24 Shibazakicho 3-chome
Tachikawa-shi
Tokyo
Tel: 0425 27 1311

Sasagawa Ltd
PaRe Rowaiyal Nagatacho 901 9–8
Nagatacho
2-chome, Chiyoda-ku, Tokyo 100
Tel: 03 592 0056

Shin Nihon Shohin Co Ltd
14–13 3-chome, Ginza Chuo-ku, Tokyo
Tel: 03 543 8181

Shinozaki Shoji Co Ltd
2–16 Iwamotocho 2–chome, Chiyoda-ku
Tokyo
Tel: 03 865 2401

Showa Sangyo Co Ltd
Kamakuragashi Bldg 2–1 Uchi-Kanda
2-chome Chiyoda-ku, Tokyo
Tel: 03 257 2011

Sumida Shoji Co Ltd
1–8–13 Saga, Koto-ku, Tokyo 135
Tel: 03 642 1811

Sumitomo Corp
2–2 Hitotsubashi 1-chome, Chiyoda-ku
Tokyo
Tel: 03 296 2730

Taishin Co Ltd
Taishin Bldg 2–4–7 Nakayamate, dori
Chuo-ku, Kobe
Tel: 078 331 7944

Taiyo Bussan Kaisha Ltd
Siga Bldg 12–9 Kodemmacho
Nihonbashi, Chuo-ku, Tokyo
Tel: 03 666 8271

Taiyo Sangyo Co Ltd
Nishikawa Bldg 3–9 3-Chome
Nihonbashi
Chuo-ku, Tokyo
Tel: 03 273 6451

Taiyo Telephone Co Ltd
33–6 Takadanobaba 1-chome
Shinjuku-ku
Tokyo 160
Tel: 03 941 7151

Takanabe Shoji Co Ltd
8–4 Yoshino 2-chome, Fukushima-ku
Osaka
Tel: 06 451 7616

Tokoku Daiko Co Ltd
12–5 Kakigaracho 1-chome, Nihonbashi
Chuo-ku, Tokyo 103
Tel: 03 668 9882

Tokyoebisu Shokuryo Kyoudo Kumiai
19–10 Jinnan 1-chome, Shibuya-ku
Tokyo
Tel: 03 463 7911

Tokyo Hozon Shokuryo Co Ltd
4 Kobunacho 1-chome, Nihonbashi
Chuo-ku
Tokyo 103
Tel: 03 666 2471

Tokyo-Johoku Shokuryo Hanbai Co-Operative Union
2-45-1 Nishi-Nippori Arakawa-ku
Tokyo 116
Tel: 03 891 6181

Tokyo-Jonan-Shokuryo
4-1-23 Heiwajima-Ohta-ku, Tokyo
Tel: 03 763 2222

Tokyo-Yamate Shokuryo Hanbai kyodo Kumiai
19-6 Nishi-Shinjuku 1-chome
Shinjuku-ku
Tokyo
Tel: 03 342 4281

Tokyo Yoko Co Ltd
15-5 Nihonbashi, Kakigaracho 1-chome
Chuo-ku, Tokyo 103
Tel: 03 669 7139

Tomen Co Ltd
1-20 Akasaka 6-chome, Minato-ku
Tokyo 107
Tel: 03 588 6650

Toshin Co Ltd
14-1 Nihonbashi, Koamicho, Chuo-ku
Tokyo 103
Tel: 03 668 1111

Toshoku Ltd
4-3 Nihonbashi, Muromachi, 2-chome
Chuo-ku, Tokyo 107
Tel: 03 245 2211

Uchida Kogyo Co Ltd
1-5-4 Kaji-cho Chiyoda-ku, Tokyo
Tel: 03 251 4551

Wako Shokuryo Co Ltd
No 10-8 1-chome, Uchikanda Chiyoda-ku, Tokyo
Tel: 03 294 2201

Yamasa K K
2-21-1 Shinbashi Minato-ku, Tokyo
Tel: 03 573 6351

Yanai Sangyo Co Ltd
Kurosawa 2-855-Ome-shi, Tokyo
Tel: 0428 74 5200

Yoshiwara Oil Mill Ltd
Mituwa Ogawa Bldg 3-7-1 Kanda
Ogawacho
Chiyoda-ku, Tokyo
Tel: 03 291 2633

Yuasa Trading Co Ltd
No 25 Kowa Bldg, 8-7 Sanban-cho
Chiyoda-ku
Tokyo
Tel: 03 265 4026

Tokyo Sugar Exchange

Members 1

ACE Koeki Co Ltd
26-26 Higashi 1-chome, Shibuya-ku
Tokyo 150
Tel: 03 406 4649

Asahi Trust Co Ltd
1-8 Honcho 1-chome, Nihonbashi
Chuo-ku, Tokyo 103
Tel: 03 279 5021

Daiichi Shohin Co Ltd
16-8 Dogenzaka 2-chome, Shibuya-ku
Tokyo 150
Tel: 03 476 0811

Eguchi Shoji Co Ltd
11-7 Ginza 6-chome, Chuo-ku
Tokyo 104
Tel: 03 573 4711

Fukutani Co Ltd
27-5 Kakigara-cho 1-chome
Nihonbashi, Chuo-ku
Tokyo 103
Tel: 03 666 8411

Fuji Shohin Co Ltd
8-6 Muromachi 1-chome, Nihonbashi
Chuo-ku, Tokyo 103
Tel: 03 270 2211

Fujitomi Co Ltd
3-17 Okubo 1-chome, Shinjuku-ku
Tokyo 160
Tel: 03 200 1521

Hokushin Bussan Co Ltd
9-2 Kayaba-cho 1-chome, Nihonbashi
Chuo-ku, Tokyo 103
Tel: 03 668 8111

Hokushin Shohin Co Ltd
2-1 Nishi-Azabu 3-chome, Minato-ku
Tokyo 106
Tel: 03 403 3111

Izutsu Shokai Co Ltd
12-9 Koami-cho, Nihonbashi, Chuo-ku
Tokyo 103
Tel: 03 666 8451/5

Kanetsu Boeki Co Ltd
11-5 Kakigara-cho 1-chome
Nihonbashi, Chuo-ku
Tokyo 103
Tel: 03 668 1711

Kanetsu Shoji Co Ltd
11-5 Kakigara-cho 1-chome, Nihonbashi
Chuo-ku, Tokyo 103
Tel: 03 662 0111

Kanto Sato Co Ltd
7-4 Ningyo-cho 1-chome, Nihonbashi
Chuo-ku, Tokyo 103
Tel: 03 666 3935

Kabayashi Yoko Co Ltd
15-5 Kakigara-cho 1-chome, Nihonbashi
Chuo-ku, Tokyo 103
Tel: 03 669 3991

Kowa Shoji Co Ltd
13-15 Kayaba-cho 1-chome, Nihonbashi
Tokyo 103
Tel: 03 661 1821/2

Kyoei Bussan Co Ltd
6-1 Hatchobori 1-chome, Chuo-ku
Tokyo 104
Tel: 03 553 4151

Meiji Bussan Co Ltd
1-23 Ningyo-cho 1-chome, Nihonbashi
Chuo-ku, Tokyo 103
Tel: 03 666 2511

Meisho Trading Corp
4-17 Kyobashi 2-chome, Chuo-ku
Tokyo 104
Tel: 03 273 0291

Nihon Koeki Co Ltd
4-4 Nishi-Shinjuku 7-chome
Shinjuku-ku
Tokyo 160
Tel: 03 369 1171

Nikko Shohin Co Ltd
38-12 Kakigara-cho 1-chome
Nihonbashi
Chuo-ku, Tokyo 103
Tel: 03 668 1351

Nishikawa & Co Ltd
3-9 Nihonbashi 3-chome, Chuo-ku
Tokyo 103
Tel: 03 273 9572

Nisshin Cup Co Ltd
14-1 Koami-cho, Nihonbashi, Chuo-ku
Tokyo 103
Tel: 03 668 1111

Okachi & Co Ltd
12-5 Koami-cho, Nihonbashi, Chuo-ku
Tokyo 103
Tel: 03 667 7511

Okato Shoji Co Ltd
3-9 Shinkawa 2-chome, Chuo-ku
Tokyo 104
Tel: 03 553 0711

Okatsune Shoji Co Ltd
1-8 Honcho 3-chome, Nihonbashi
Chuo-ku, Tokyo 103
Tel: 03 241 3241

Oshima Shoten Co Ltd
1-3 Koami-cho, Nihonbashi, Chuo-ku
Tokyo 103
Tel: 03 666 1181

Sanchu & Co Ltd
11-3 Saga 1-chome, Koto-ku, Tokyo 136
Tel: 03 643 5500

Sanki Shoji Co Ltd
18-9 Kakigara-cho 1-chome, Nihonbashi
Chuo-ku, Tokyo 103
Tel: 03 667 5251

Sanko Shokuhin Co Ltd
16-7 Kakigara-cho 2-chome, Nihonbashi
Chuo-ku, Tokyo 103
*Tel:*03 669 6901

Seiyu Shoji Co Ltd
10-11 Horidome-cho 1-chome
Nihonbashi
Chuo-ku
Tokyo 103
Tel: 03 663 5711

Shinnihon Shohin Co Ltd
14–13 Ginza 3-chome, Chuo-ku, Tokyo
104
Tel: 03 543 8181

S Nishida & Co Ltd
1–6 Kayaba-cho 1-chome, Nihonbashi
Chuo-ku, Tokyo 103
Tel: 03 666 8587

Sugiyama Shoji Co Ltd
13–3 Koami-cho, Nihonbashi
Chuo-ku, Tokyo 103
Tel: 03 666 0121

Sanrise Trading Corp
19–4 Higashi-Ikebukuro 1-chome
Toshima-ku, Tokyo 170
Tel: 03 988 7351

Sunward Trading Inc
3–2 Shimomiyabi-cho, Shinjuku-ku
Tokyo 162
Tel: 03 260 0211

Taichi Shoji Co Ltd
13–13 Kayaba-cho 1-chome, Nihonbashi
Chuo-ku, Tokyo 103
Tel: 03 668 9351

Taisei Commodity Co Ltd
4–15 Akasaka 5-chome, Minato-ku
Tokyo 107
Tel: 03 585 9611

Taiyo Fishery Co Ltd
1–2 Otemachi 1-chome, Chiyoda-ku
Tokyo 100
Tel: 03 216 0811

Taiyo General Corp
12–7 Ginza 8-chome, Chuo-ku, Tokyo
104
Tel: 03 545 6111

Tokyo General Corp
9–6 Kyobashi 3-chome, Chuo-ku, Tokyo
104
Tel: 03 535 6111

Tokyo-To Chuo Foodstuff Cooperative
Society
16–16 Koami-cho Nihonbashi, Chuo-ku
Tokyo 103
Tel: 03 666 6141

Toyoka Shoji Co Ltd
28–4 Kakigara-cho 1-chome, Nihonbashi
Chuo-ku, Tokyo 103
Tel: 03 668 0651

Union Trading Corp
6–10 Ningyo-cho 1-chome, Nihonbashi
Chuo-ku, Tokyo 103
Tel: 03 668 2331

Yada Shoten Co Ltd
1–8 Higashi-Shinbashi 1-chome
Minato-ku
Tokyo 105
Tel: 03 571 9171

Yamabun Sangyo Co Ltd
5–12 Iwemoto-cho 2-chome, Chiyoda-ku
Tokyo 101
Tel: 03 865 8611

Yamatane Bussan Co Ltd
1–1 Ningyo-cho 1-chome, Nihonbashi
Chuo-ku
Tokyo 103
Tel: 03 667 1791

Yamato Sangyo Co Ltd
30–1 Kakigara-cho 1-chome, Nihonbashi
Chuo-ku, Tokyo 103
Tel: 03 667 1791

Yamazen Shoji Co Ltd
9–9 Kakigara-cho 1-chome, Nihonbashi
Chuo-ku
Tokyo 103
Tel: 03 667 4361

Yutaka Shoji Co Ltd
16–12 Kakigara-cho 1-chome
Nihonbashi, Chuo-ku
Tokyo 103
Tel: 03 667 5211

Yamasan Shokai Ltd
1–15 Ningyo-cho 3 chome, Nihonbashi
Chuo-ku, Tokyo 103
Tel: 03 668 9611

Members 2

C Itoh & Co Ltd
5–1 Kita-Aoyama 2-chome Minato-ku
Tokyo 107
Tel: 03 497 2121

Central Shoji Co Ltd
7-9 Kakigara-cho 1-chome, Nihonbashi
Chuo-ku, Tokyo 103
Tel: 03 666 1161

Daikyo Shohin Co Ltd
15-2 Nishi-Nakajima 1-chome
Yodogawa-ku
Osaka 532
Tel: 06 304 5071

Daito Seito Co Ltd
6-12 Matsue 4-chome, Edogawa-ku
Tokyo 132
Tel: 03 652 1266

Daiwa Commerce Co Ltd
5-1 Sakae 2-chome, Naka-ku, Nagoya
460
Tel: 052 201 3131

Daiichi Togyo Co Ltd
6-3 Muromachi 1-chome Nihonbashi
Chuo-ku
Tokyo 103
Tel: 03 279 6411

Dai-nippon Sugar Mfg Co Ltd
5-1 Marunouchi 1-chome, Chiyoda-ku
Tokyo 100
Tel: 03 271 0101

Ensuiko Sugar Refining Co Ltd
13-46 Daikoku-cho Tsurumi-ku
Yokohamashi
Kanagawa 230
Tel: 045 501 1251

Fujichu Corp
15-3 Ginza 7-chome, Chuo-ku
Tokyo 104
Tel: 03 545 8121

Fuji Seito Co Ltd
8-6 Nihonbashi 3-chome, Chuo-ku
Tokyo 103
Tel: 03 273 7481

Hokuren Nogyo Cooperative
4-1 Marunouchi 2-chome, Chiyoda-ku
Tokyo 100
Tel: 03 212 1911

Kasho Co Ltd
14-9 Nihonbashi 2-chome, Chuo-ku
Tokyo 103
Tel: 03 276 7611

Kojima Shoji Co Ltd
3-6 Ningyo-cho 1-chome Nihonbashi
Chuo-ku, Tokyo 103
Tel: 03 669 6161

Kohoku Bussan Co Ltd
2-1 Nishi-Azabu 3 chome, Minato-ku
Tokyo 106
Tel: 03 479 3790

Marubeni Corp
4-2 Otemachi 1-chome, Chiyoda-ku
Tokyo 100
Tel: 03 282 2111

Maruho Takara Shohin Co Ltd
15-10 Ginza 3-chome, Chuo-ku, Tokyo
104
Tel: 03 543 8121

Maruume Co ltd
17-9 Kayabe-cho 2-chome, Nihonbashi
Chuo-ku, Tokyo 103
Tel: 03 664 8751

Marusan Co Ltd
4-9 Kayaba-cho 1-chome, Nihonbashi
Chuo-ku, Tokyo 103
Tel: 03 668 0331

Mashita Shoji Co Ltd
1-4 Shibuya 1-chome, Shibuya-ku
Tokyo 150
Tel: 03 407 8271

Matsukan Co Ltd
12-6 Kinshi-cho 3-chome, Sumida-ku
Tokyo 130
Tel: 03-622 3136

Meiji Sugar Mfg Co Ltd
3-13 Kyobashi 2-chome, Chuo-ku
Tokyo 104
Tel: 03 281 3141

Mitsubishi Corp
6-3 Marunouchi 2-chome, Chiyoda-ku
Tokyo 100
Tel: 03 210 2121

Mitsui & Co Ltd
2-1 Otemachi 1-chome, Chiyoda-ku
Tokyo 100
Tel: 03 285 1111

Mitsui Sugar Co Ltd
8-3 Muromachi 3-chome, Nihonbashi
Chuo-ku, Tokyo 103
Tel: 03 663 3111

Nichimen Corp
13-1 Kyobashi 1-chome, Chuo-ku
Tokyo 104
Tel: 03 277 8224

Nozaki & Co Ltd
16-19 Ginza 7-chome, Chuo-ku
Tokyo 104
Tel: 03 542 9234

Nisshin Sugar Mfg Co Ltd
14-1 Koami-cho Nihonbashi, Chuo-ku
Tokyo 103
Tel: 03 668 1111

Nippon Beet Sugar Mfg Co Ltd
3-13 Kyobashi 2-chome, Chuo-ku
Tokyo 104
Tel: 03 281 2101

Nihon Sugar Refining Co Ltd
4-9 Kayaba-cho 1-chome, Nihonbashi
Chuo-ku, Tokyo 103
Tel: 03 667 7811

Nissho Iwai Corp
4-5 Adasaka 2-chome, Minato-ku, Tokyo
107
Tel: 03 588 2111

Nissho Iwai Foods Corp
23-14 Ueno 5-chome, Taito-ku, Tokyo
110
Tel: 03 837 7851

Niigata-Ken Sato Oroshi-Niuke Shogyo
Cooperative
37 Minami Bandai-cho 3-chome
Nilgata-shi
Niigata 950
Tel: 0252 44 9201

Oji Seito Co Ltd
11-12 Hon-Komagome 6-chome
Bunkyo-ku, Tokyo 113
Tel: 03 943 8521

Onishi Shoji Co Ltd
22-14 Nabe-cho Shimonoseki-shi
Yamaguchi 750
Tel: 0832 31 5155

Orient Trading Inc
24-30 Watanabe dori 5-chome, Chuo-ku
Fukuoka-shi, Fukuoka 8
Tel: 092 712 3111

Sasagawa Co Ltd
9-4 Koami-cho Nihonbashi, Chuo-ku
Tokyo 103
Tel: 03 667 0018

Shinko Sugar Co Ltd
4-15 Nihonbashi 3-chome, Chuo-ku
Tokyo 103
Tel: 03 201 9166

Taito Co Ltd
13-5 Honcho 4-chome Nihonbashi
Chuo-ku
Tokyo 103
Tel: 03 663 3851

Taiheiyo Bussan Co Ltd
11-2 Kakigara-cho 1-chome Nihonbashi
Chuo-ku
Tokyo 103
Tel: 03 663 1451

The Sansho Trading Co Ltd
2-9 Nihonbashi 3-chome, Chuo-ku
Tokyo 103
Tel: 03 275 1001

Toshin Sangyo Co Ltd
14-1 Koami-cho Nihonbashi, Chuo-ku
Tokyo 103
Tel: 03 668 1111

Toyo Lex Co Ltd
1-16 Saga 1-chome, Koto-ku
Tokyo 135
Tel: 03 642 4531

Toyo Sugar Refining Co Ltd
8-4 Koami-cho, Nihonbashi
Chuo-ku, Tokyo 103
Tel: 03 668 7871

Tokyo Totori Daiko Co Ltd
9-4 Koami-cho, Nihonbashi
Chuo-ku, Tokyo 103
Tel: 03 661 4776

Toshoku Ltd
4-3 Muromachi 2-chome, Nihonbashi
Chuo-ku, Tokyo 103
Tel: 03 245 2300

Tomen Co Ltd
14-27 Akawaka 2-chome, Minato-ku
Tokyo 107
Tel: 03 588 7111

Tohan Co Ltd
8-4 Koami-cho, Nihonbashi
Chuo-ku, Tokyo 103
Tel: 03 667 1461

Wako Shoji Co Ltd
8-16 Honcho 1-chome, Nihonbashi
Chuo-ku, Tokyo 103
Tel: 03 242 4741

Wada Sugar Refining Co Ltd
6-11 Kakigara-cho 1-chome
Nihonbashi, Chuo-ku, Tokyo 103
Tel: 03 666 4005

Kenya

East African Tea Trade Association

Kenya Buyers

Abbas Traders
PO Box 80240, Mombasa

HM Adam & Co
PO Box 98660, Mombasa

Afriqe Trading & Shipping Co Ltd
PO Box 82481, Mombasa

Al Emir Ltd
PO Box 81254, Mombasa

Alibhai Ramji (msa) Ltd
PO Box 80398, Mombasa

Almeta Import Export Co
PO Box 14828, Nairobi

MS Bawazir & Co Ltd
PO Box 80326

Belmont Trading Co Ltd
PO Box 44614, Nairobi

Bico Ltd
PO Box 84745, Mombasa

Brooke Bond Mombasa
PO Box 95105, Nairobi

Chai Exporters (K) Ltd
PO Box 84078, Mombasa

Clarke M J
PO Box 84321, Mombasa

Coastal Growers and Packers
PO Box 81189, Mombasa

Comterk Trading & Economic Con
PO Box 99530, Mombasa

Contea Ltd
PO Box 14678, Nairobi

Cristobol Investment Co
PO Box 43285, Nairobi

Davco Enterprises Ltd
PO Box 13073, Nairobi

Devchand Keshavji (K) Ltd
PO Box 80478, Mombasa

Down Town Traders Ltd
PO Box 49925, Nairobi

EA Tea Exporters Ltd
82339, Mombasa

El Nasr Export & Import
PO Box 30573, Nairobi

El Reza Tea Exports
PO Box 87563, Mombasa

Finlay James & Co Ltd
PO Box 72244, Nairobi

Green Gulf Enterprises
PO Box 67303, Nairobi

Gulleid Kenya Industries
PO Box 99296, Mombasa

MG Habib & Co
PO Box 87491, Mombasa

Hussein & Co
PO Box 80028, Mombasa

Inter Shipping Co Agencies
PO Box 85634, Mombasa

James Noble Tea Co Ltd
PO Box 84673, Mombasa

Jethbhai Enterprises Ltd
PO Box 81124, Mombasa

Juja Coffee Exports Ltd
PO Box 85039, Mombasa

Kegio Horticultural Growers Ltd
PO Box 56522, Nairobi

Kempak Agencies Ltd
PO Box 11023, Nairobi

Ken-U-Tan Exports ltd
PO Box 84384, Mombasa

Khaku Exports
PO Box 88265, Mombasa

Lipton Ltd
PO Box 83067, Mombasa

Louisa International Ltd
PO Box 31077, Nairobi

Lowe DJ Co Ltd
PO Box 86232, Mombasa

Mombasa Coffee Ltd
PO Box 88623, Mombasa

Mosbery Ltd
PO Box 81112, Mombasa

Oakdale Commodities Ltd
PO Box 78001, Nairobi

Petroleum Co of Central & EA Ltd
PO Box 48726, Nairobi

Phillips International Ltd
PO Box 90244, Mombasa

Plaza Investment Ltd
PO Box 40511, Nairobi

Prime Commodities Ltd
PO Box 49925, Nairobi

Prodex International Ltd
PO Box 56789, Nairobi

Rauf Coffee & Tea Exporters Ltd
PO Box 81672, Mombasa

Sea Air Forwarders Int Ltd
PO Box 83354, Mombasa

Seyffert & Co Ltd
PO Box 87759, Mombasa

Shriti Traders
PO Box 82668, Mombasa

Stansand (Africa) Ltd
PO Box 90683, Mombasa

Sun Trading Ltd
PO Box 61421, Nairobi

Tasty Tea Ltd
PO Box 43762, Nairobi

Unèximp Ltd
PO Box 30657, Nairobi

Unitea Ltd
PO Box 56789, Nairobi

Van Rees (GB) Ltd
PO Box 83835, Mombasa

Wanyo Ltd
PO Box 81336, Mombasa

Yamaani Chemical & Household Agen
PO Box 81747, Mombasa

Kenya Producers

African Highlands Produce Co
PO Box 72244, Nairobi

Brooke Bond Kenya Ltd
PO Box 42011, Nairobi

EA Coffee Plantations Ltd
94, Nandi Hills

Eastern Produce Africa Ltd
22, Nandi Hills

George Williamson Kenya Ltd
PO Box 42281, Nairobi

Kaimosi Tea Estates Ltd
PO Box 42281, Nairobi

Kapchorua Tea Co Ltd
PO Box 42281, Nairobi

Kapsumbeiwa Factory Co Ltd
PO Box 45560, Nairobi

Karirana Estates Ltd
PO Box 30345, Nairobi

Kenya Tea Development Authority
PO Box 30213, Nairobi

Kibwari Tea Estates Ltd
PO Box 40006, Nairobi

Kipkebe Ltd
PO Box 30572, Nairobi

Kipkoimet Tea Co
PO Box 45560, Nairobi

Koisagat Tea Estates Ltd
PO Box 53104, Nairobi

Mau Forest Ltd
PO Box 42281, Nairobi

Nandi Tea Estates Ltd
26, Nandi Hills

Ngorongo Tea Co
364, Kiambu

Nyambeni Tea Co
PO Meru

Siret Tea Co
PO Box 30572, Nairobi

Sotik Highlands Tea Estate
PO Box 72244, Nairobi

Sotik Tea Co
PO Box 72244, Nairobi

Subukia Tea Co Ltd
PO Box 43709, Nairobi

Tea Agents Ltd
PO Box 14827, Nairobi

Tinderet Tea Estates Ltd
PO Box 144, Songhor

Buyer Associates

African Commodities
PO Box 99436, Mombasa

Almurtaza Trading Co
PO Box 85643, Mombasa

Al Noor Feisal & Co
PO 14766, Nairobi

Alpha Coffee & Tea Trading Co Ltd
PO Box 83259, Mombasa

Anchor Africa Ltd
PO Box 63039, Nairobi

Aristocrats Coffee & Tea Ltd
PO Box 49729, Nairobi

Bario Exim Services
PO Box 50719, Nairobi

Bharat Industries Ltd
PO Box 48071, Nairobi

Big Tea (T) Ltd 99
PO Box 99682, Mombasa

Chai Ltd
PO Box 72889, Nairobi

Coffee Exporters (K) Ltd
PO Box 49443, Nairobi

Commercial Consortium Ltd
PO Box 59466, Nairobi

Dinkie Impex Ltd
PO Box 84112, Mombasa

EA Acceptances
PO Box 40310, Nairobi

EA Coffee Exporters Ltd
PO Box 97464, Mombasa

East Afro Expo Ltd
PO Box 43832, Nairobi

Economic Carriers
PO Box 86489, Mombasa

Esco Kenya Ltd
PO Box 43387, Nairobi

Freight Hauliers Ltd
PO Box 83388, Mombasa

Hashan SA (Africa) Ltd
PO Box 49000, Nairobi

Hydery Printers Ltd
PO Box 82576, Mombasa

International Freighters Ltd
PO Box 84358, Mombasa

Jakal Services Ltd
PO Box 86874, Mombasa

Kalidas Kanii (A) Ltd
PO Box 80939, Mombasa

Kengrains Ltd
PO Box 78008, Nairobi

Kenline Agencies Ltd
PO Box 56454, Nairobi

Kenya National Trading Corp
PO Box 30587, Nairobi

Lalit T Pandit Ltd
PO Box 45604, Nairobi

Malaika Coffee & Tea
PO Box 41921, Nairobi

Malde and Co
PO Box 41265, Nairobi

Mars Enterprises
PO Box 80038, Mombasa

Maziwa (K) Ltd
PO Box 49464, Nairobi

Meghji Kanji & Co Ltd
PO Box 43579, Nairobi

Meka Trading Co
PO Box 43579, Nairobi

Merali Devji & Sons Ltd
PO Box 80214, Mombasa

Moledina Commodities Ltd
PO Box 80324, Mombasa

Mwafrika Ltd
PO Box 81358, Mombasa

Pandit MA
PO Box 82680, Mombasa

Panji MA Bros Ltd
PO Box 82680, Mombasa

Purshottam Bhimji & Sons
PO Box 80545, Mombasa

Rashid Moledina & Co Ltd
PO Box 80324, Mombasa

Roshanali & Co (Msa) Ltd
PO Box 81486, Mombasa

Sagga Industries Ltd
PO Box 46951, Nairobi

Samar International
PO Box 84539, Mombasa

Sameer International
PO Box 85901, Mombasa

Shah Meghji & Hirji Ltd
PO Box 48162, Nairobi

Shantilal Pethraj & Co
PO Box 81239, Mombasa

Sunderji Naji Ltd
PO Box 80324, Mombasa

Tapya Holdings Ltd
PO Box 84396, Mombasa

Tea Sales EA Ltd
PO Box 72289, Nairobi

Trade Wings Ltd
PO Box 40583, Nairobi

United Food Products
PO Box 90002, Mombasa

Vohora Brothers Ltd
PO Box 72463

Wami International Ltd
PO Box 88369, Mombasa

Wanjohi Exporters
PO Box 39036, Nairobi

Wayne Ltd
PO Box 42844, Nairobi

Zubedi Tea & Produce Centre
PO Box 81264, Mombasa

Associate Members

Elgeyo Saw Mills (K) Ltd
PO Box 18043, Nairobi

Latif Wood Works
PO Box 81144 Mombasa

Vijay Investment Ltd
PO Box 99879, Mombasa

Warehouse Members

Bahari Transport Co Ltd
PO Box 81829, Mombasa

Combined Warehouses Ltd
PO Box 81862, Mombasa

Consolidated (Msa) Ltd
PO Box 90400, Mombasa

Etco Mombasa Ltd
PO Box 90631, Mombasa

Kenya Bonded Warehouses Co
PO Box 80522, Mombasa

Kenya Transit Trading Co
PO Box 90403, Mombasa

Mbaraki Port Warehouses
PO Box 80066, Mombasa

Mitchell Cotts Kenya Ltd
PO Box 90151, Mombasa

Multimodal Forwarders Ltd
PO Box 89003, Mombasa

Notco Mombasa Ltd
PO Box 90262, Mombasa

SGS (K) Ltd
PO Box 90264, Mombasa

Swife Ltd
PO Box 99434, Mombasa

Topaz Transport Co Ltd
PO Box 89051, Mombasa

Transami (K) Ltd
PO Box 90262, Mombasa

Brokers

Africa Tea Brokers
PO Box 81883, Mombasa

Anjeli Ltd
PO Box 75015, Nairobi

Combrok Ltd
PO Box 87411, Mombasa

Tea Brokers East Africa Ltd
PO Box 87296, Mombasa

Union Tea Brokers Ltd
PO Box 81120, Mombasa

Venus Tea Brokers
PO Box 99954, Mombasa

Tanzania Producers

Ambangulu Estates Ltd
PO Box 2667, Dar es Salaam

Balangai Estates
PO Box 27, Korogwe

Bombay Burmar Trading Co
PO Box 22, Soni

Brooke Bond Liebig (T) Co
PO Box 40, Mufindi

Dindira Tea Estates Ltd
PO Box 409, Tanga

Karimjee Jivanjee Estates
PO Box 4, Tanga

Luponde Tea Estates Ltd
PO Box 487, Tanga

Mufindi Tea Estates Ltd
PO Box 40, Mufindi

Tanzania Sisal Authority
PO Box 2663, Dar es Salaam

Tanzania Tea Authority
PO Box 2663, Dar es Salaam

Tukuyu Tea Estates Ltd
PO Box 2667, Dar es Salaam

Uganda Producers

Agricultural Enterprises Ltd
PO Box 7020, Kampala

Bhazma International
PO Box 1586, Kampala

Namutamba Tea Co Ltd
PO Box 4161, Kampala

Toro Mityana Tea Co Ltd
PO Box 6641, Kampala

Uganda Tea Authority
PO Box 4161, Kampala

Uganda Tea Growers Corp
PO Box 7157, Kampala

Uganda Buyers

Abdullahi Busulwa & Sons
PO Box 323, Kampala

Eagle Investments Ltd
PO Box 506, Jinja

Burundi Producer

Office du the Burundi
BP 2680, Bujumbura

Rwanda Producers

Office des Cultures Industrielles
du Rwanda, Dept The
BP 1344, Kingali

Societe d-Investment
BP 1136, Kingali

Zaire Producers

Plantations de Lubona SZRL
BP 398, Bukavu

Plantations Lever au Zaire
BP 8611, Kinshasa

Malaysia

Futures Clearing Corporation

(Keys: * = Suspended, # = Voluntary
Suspension, (FLR) = Non-Clearing
Member on the Floor)

Clearing Members

Drexcomm (M) Sdn Bhd
Lot 20.04, 20th Floor
Menara Promet
Jalan Sultan Ismail
50250 Kuala Lumpur
PO Box 12122
50768 Kuala Lumpur
Tel: 03 2436133
Telex: MA 32277/30668 DCOMM
Fax: 03 2437925

Fuji Malaysia Enterprise Sdn Bhd
15th Floor, Selangor Complex
Jalan Sultan
50000 Kuala Lumpur
Tel: 03 2305377/2305531
Telex: MA 30749 FUJIME
Fax: 03 2385030

Guan Soon Heng Futures Trading
Sdn Bhd
290 Jalan Raja Laut
50350 Kuala Lumpur
Tel: 03 2915233
Fax: 03 2915970

Kumpulan Guthrie Bhd
Wisma Guthrie
21 Jalan Gelenggang
Damansara Heights
PO Box 12516
50780 Kuala Lumpur
Tel: 03 2541644
Telex: MA 30346 GEALCO/30889
HILO
Fax: 03 2557934

Lam Soon Commodities Sdn Bhd
No 5 Jalan 205
PO Box 8
46050 Petaling Jaya
Selangor
Tel: 03 7912755
Telex: MA 37671 LAMVEG
Fax: 03 7912572

Maika Commodities (M) Sdn Bhd
3rd Floor Wisma Manickavasagam
No 1, Jalan Rahmat
Off Jalan Tun Ismail
50350 Kuala Lumpur
PO Box 11334
50742 Kuala Lumpur
Tel: 03 4427287/86/88/89/90
Telex: MA 33739 MAIKA
Fax: 03 4412990

MMC Commodities Sdn Bhd
Tingkat 37, Menara PNB
201A Jalan Tun Razak
PO Box 11133
50736 Kuala Lumpur
Tel: 03 2616000/2616064
Telex: MA 33772/33773 MMCM
Fax: 03 2610385

Manilal Holdings Sdn Bhd
3rd Floor Wisma MLS
32 Penang St
10200 Penang
Tel: 04 625070/624221
Telex: MA 40055 MANLAL

Multi-Purpose Commodity
Trading Sdn Bhd
Batu 7 Jalan Kajang, Puchong
43000 Kajang, PO Box 11453
50746 Kuala Lumpur
Telex: 03 9489811/9486811
Telex: MA 32422 MULMAR/33102
DUNEST
Fax: 03 9489998

Pro Futures Sdn Bhd
34–1 Jalan Tun Sambanthan 3
50470 Kuala Lumpur
Tel: 03 2749088/2749114
Telex: MA 31508 PROFU
Fax: 03 2749479

Sime Darby Futures Trading Sdn Bhd
4th Floor, Wisma Sime Darby
Jalan Raja Laut
Tel: 03 2930922
Telex: MA 30413 SIMECO
Fax: 03 2933602

Sunny Futures Sdn Bhd
3rd Floor, Wisma Merlin
Jalan Sultan Ismail
50250 Kuala Lumpur
Tel: 03 2434100
Telex: MA 21053 TOPCOM
Fax: 03 3313898

Union Rouse Eastern (M) Sdn Bhd
Suite 2.02, 2nd Floor
Wisma Song Pang Seng
Jalan Imbi
55100 Kuala Lumpur
Tel: 03 2432742/2432568
Telex: MA 30318 WYLTON

Non-Clearing Members

Ace Commercial Enterprise
Sdn Bhd (Flr)
Lot 34.4, 34th Floor, Menara Maybank
100 Jalan Tun Perak
50050 Kuala Lumpur
PO Box 12042
50766 Kuala Lumpur
Tel: 03 2328088
Telex: MA 30670 ACECOM
Fax: 03 2327380

Alcan Commodities (M) Sdn Bhd
19th Floor, Plaza Atrium
Lot 117, Lorong P Ramlee
PO Box 12094
50768 Kuala Lumpur
Tel: 03 2380066
Telex: MA 30479 ALGETA
MA 32450 ALRUB
Fax: 03 2380050

Ari, Gan & Din Sdn Bhd
Lot 316, 3rd Floor
Wisma HLA
Jalan Raja Chulan
50200 Kuala Lumpur
Tel: 03 2411711/2411722
Telex: MA 32870 ARIGAN

Bapema Trading Sdn Bhd
12th Floor, Menara Sambungan UMBC
Jalan Sulaiman
50000 Kuala Lumpur
Tel: 03 2747266/2747261
Telex: MA 30102 PEMA
Fax: 03 2747202

Biztech Sdn Bhd (FLR)
Room 701, 7th Floor
Pernas International
Jalan Sultan Ismail
50250 Kuala Lumpur
Tel: 03 2618588
Telex: MA 21298 YCEK L
Fax: 03 2618031

Boustead Estates Agency Sdn Bhd
7th Floor Wisma Boustead
71 Jalan Rija Chulan
50200 Kuala Lumpur
Tel: 03 2419044
Telex: MA 30442 BABEAL
Fax: 03 2419750

* Cayman Associates (Ipoh) Sdn Bhd
c/o Projects for Asia
(Management) Sdn Bhd
Room A 2nd Floor
57B–65B Jalan Veerasamy
30450 Ipoh, Perak
Tel: 05 260787

* Commodity Services (M) Sdn Bhd

* Commwell Sdn Bhd (FLR)
Suite 16A, 16th Floor
Office Tower, Kompleks Nagaria
Jalan Imbi
55100 Kuala Lumpur
Tel: 03 2385395/2485266
Telex: MA 30610 COMWELL

Comtra Sdn Bhd (FLR)
Room 509, 5th Floor
Lee Yan Lian Bldg
Jalan Tun Perak
50050 Kuala Lumpur
Tel: 03 2304777/80
Telex: MA 30125 COMTRA

Convest Sdn Bhd (FLR)
Lot 202, 2nd Floor, Wisma HLA
Jalan Raja Chulan
50200 Kuala Lumpur
Tel: 03 2488980
Telex: MA 20335 FUCOMM

Datuk Keramat Smelting Sdn Bhd
73 Jalan Datuk Keramat
PO Box 280
10150 Penang
Tel: 04 27171/27166
Telex: MA 40037 ESMELT
Fax: 04 375501

Discount House Sdn Bhd (FLR)
Lot 3.81-3.82 3rd Floor
Wisma Stephens
Jalan Raja Chulan
50200 Kuala Lumpur
Tel: 03 2426785/2434938
Telex: MA 32941 DHSBKL

Felda Marketing Corporation
10th Floor, Menara Boustead
69 Jalan Raja Chulan
50200 Kuala Lumpur
Tel: 03 2418387
Telex: MA 30219/30789 FELDA
Fax: 03 2439810

Felda Refinery Corporation
11th Floor, Menara Boustead
69 Jalan Raja Chulan
50200 Kuala Lumpur
Tel: 03 2419800/9814
Telex: MA 30219/30789 FELDA

Gan Teng Siew Realty Sdn Bhd
10th Floor Bangunan Yee Seng
15 Jalan Raja Chulan
50200 Kuala Lumpur
Tel: 03 2326751/2321629

Ganda Plantations Sdn Bhd
10th Floor Wisma Central
Jalan Ampang
50450 Kuala Lumpur
Tel: 03 2616522
Telex: MA 32206 EDIOIL
Fax: 03 2613217

General Edible Oil Sdn Bhd
5 & 6 Kawasan Perindustrian
Tanjung Kling, Tangga Batu
76400 Melaka
Tel: 06 511101/ 511102
Telex: MA 62876 GEOIL

General Oil Refining Sdn Bhd
Kamunting Industrial Estate
PO Box 74
34007 Taiping
Perak
Tel: 05 824961/824962
Telex: MA 44114 GENOIL

Golden Agricultural Oils Sdn Bhd
171–173 Mak Mandin
Industrial Estate
13400 Butterworth
Tel: 04 341411/341341
Telex: MA 40174 MAGRI

Green & Collier (M) Sdn Bhd (FLR)
7th Floor, Menara Boustead
69 Jalan Raja Chulan
50200 Kuala Lumpur
PO Box 12252
50772 Kuala Lumpur
Tel: 03 2429133
Telex: MA 30149 GRECOL
Fax: 03 2437668

Highlands & Lowlands Bhd
c/o Kumpulan Guthrie Bhd
21 Julan Gelenggang
Damansara Heights
50780 Kuala Lumpur
Tel: 03 2541644
Telex: MA 30346 GEALCO/30889
HILO
Fax: 03 2557934

Hock Tong Rubber Brokers (M)
Sdn Bhd
91 Jalan Ampang
50764 Kuala Lumpur
Tel: 03 2389171/2389161
Telex: MA 30402 HTRB

Holiday, Cutler, Bath Sdn Bhd (FLR)
4th Floor Menara Boustead
Jalan Raja Chulan
50200 Kuala Lumpur
Tel: 03 2418071/2418130
Telex: MA 30148 HOLDAY

Hundai Corp Sdn Bhd
23 Jalan Maju
PO Box 1527
96000 Sibu, Sarawak
Tel: 084 339700
Telex: MA 72369 HUNDAI

* Intracom (M) Sdn Bhd
Lot 6, Jln Perusahaan 2
Kawasan Perindustrian Bt Caves
68100 Batu Caves, Selangor
Tel: 03 6897246
Telex: MA 31258 PEGI

Intrafi (M) Sdn Bhd (FLR)
Lot 31.3, 31st Floor, Menara Maybank
100 Jalan Tun Perak
50050 Kuala Lumpur
Tel: 03 2307311
Telex: MA 21324 INTRAM
Fax: 03 2325324

Jomalina Sdn Bhd
Telok Panglima Garang
Industrial Estate
Batu 9 Jalan Banting-Kelang
Kuala Langat, PO Box 12709
50786 Kuala Lumpur
Tel: 03 3526301
Telex: MA 39616/39717 OILINA
Fax: 03 3526688

Joo Seng Rubber Co Sdn Bhd
14 Jalan Taiping
33000 Kuala Kangsar
Perak
Tel: 05 861006/861635
Telex: MA 44170 JSR

Kayjay Enterprise Sdn Bhd
No 8 Ground Floor
Jalan Dato Sulaiman
Taman Tun Dr Ismail
60000 Kuala Lumpur
Tel: 03 7180363/7180345

Keck Seng (M) Bhd
111 North Bridge Rd, #28-03
28th Floor, Peninsula Plaza
Singapore 0617
Tel: 02 3382828
Telex: RS 23353/20119 KSPALM
Fax: 02 3398503

Komodimas (M) Sdn Bhd (FLR)
17th Floor Wisma On-Tai
Letter Box 31
161-B Jalan Ampang
50450 Kuala Lumpur
Tel: 03 2610033
Telex: MA 21024 KOMMAS
Fax: 03 2616776

Kuala Lumpur Kepong Bhd
Wisma Taiko No 1
Jalan SP Seenivasagam
30000 Ipoh, Perak
Tel: 05 517844/519422
Telex: MA 44094/44324 TAIKO
Fax: 05 505312

Kumpulan Ladang-Ladang Trengganu
Sdn Bhd
102 & 102A Jalan Sultan Ismail
20200 Kuala Trengganu
Trengganu
Tel: 09 623209/623217
Telex: MA 51420 PEMIN

Kupak Sdn Bhd
Suite C, 18th Floor, Bgn Tabung Haji
201 Jalan Tun Razak
50400 Kuala Lumpur
Tel: 03 2611455
Telex: MA 32260/32790 KUPAK
Fax: 03 2619725

LPC Futures (M) Sdn Bhd (FLR)
Lot 1503, 15th Floor, Wisma HLA
Jalan Raja Chulan
50200 Kuala Lumpur
Tel: 03 2432677/2427089/2432715
Telex: MA 31129

Ladang Tai Tak (Kota Tinggi)
Sdn Bhd
21st Storey, UOB Bldg
1 Bonham St #21-01
Singapore 0104
Tel: 02 5356881/5356883
Telex: RS 23664 TAITAK

Lee Oil Mills Sdn Bhd
234 Jalan Kapar
PO Box 34
41700 Kelang
Selangor
Tel: 03 3426611
Telex: MA 39610 LEEOIL
Fax: 03 3421789

Lee Rubber (S'gor) Sdn Bhd
28th Floor Wisma Lee Rubber
Jalan Melaka
50100 Kuala Lumpur
Tel: 03 2912077
Telex: MA 32859 LEESEL
Fax: 03 2987948

* Lee Sin Cheong Holdings Bhd
7.03, 7th Floor, Komplek Selangor
Jalan Sultan
50000 Kuala Lumpur
Tel: 03 2382355/2382353
Telex: MA 33717 PACOM

Malayan Tin Smelting Co
Sdn Bhd
5th Floor Straits Trading Bldg
4 Leboh Pasar Besar
PO Box 10010
50700 Kuala Lumpur
Tel: 03 2984188/2984210
Telex: MA 30071 SWORD
Fax: 03 2937542

Malaysia Smelting Corp Bhd
27 Jalan Pantai
PO Box 2
12700 Butterworth
Tel: 04 342100/342251
Telex: MA 47566 TIMAH
Fax: 04 317405

Malaysian Rubber Development
Corporation Bhd
Bangunan MARDEC
Ulu Kelang, Selangor
PO Box 10546
50716 Kuala Lumpur
Tel: 03 4567055/4560959
Telex: MA 30950/30785 MARUB
Fax: 03 4574724

Marpro Oils & Grains Sdn Bhd (FLR)
Room 905, 9th Floor, Wisma HLA
Jalan Raja Chulan
50200 Kuala Lumpur
Tel: 03 2425311
Telex: MA 31229 MARPRO
Fax: 03 2423034

* Matthes & Porton (M) Sdn Bhd
2nd Floor Wisma SPS
32 Jalan Imbi
55100 Kuala Lumpur
Tel: 03 2427022/2426569
Telex: MA 30617/30057 MANDP
Fax: 03 2482563

Melaka Tong Bee Sdn Bhd
87 Jalan Kampong Hulu
75200 Melaka
Tel: 06 223346/223347
Telex: MA 62812 TONGBE

Merrill Lynch (M) Sdn Bhd
c/o PFA Corporate Services Sdn Bhd
19th Floor Bgn Arab-Malaysian
55 Jalan Raja Chulan
50200 Kuala Lumpur
Tel: 03 2380266
Telex: MA 30236 KCTAX

* Modern Commodities Traders (M)
Sdn Bhd (FLR)
Lot 2.8, 2nd Floor
Wisma Angkasa Raya
Jalan Ampang
50450 Kuala Lumpur
Tel: 03 2428077
Telex: MA 30569 MCICO
Fax: 03 2436971

Nalin Industries Sdn Bhd
17th Floor, UMBC Bldg
4 Julan Sultan Sulaiman
50000 Kuala Lumpur
Tel: 03 2329933
Telex: MA 31041/32827 OLIN
Fax: 03 2321215

Nikkei Futures Sdn Bhd
1501–1502, 15th Floor
Holiday Plaza (Office Tower)
Jln Datuk Sulaiman, Century Garden
80250 Johore Bahru
Tel: 07 226800 05
Telex: MA 60018 NIKKEI
Fax: 07 249805

North Malaya Commodities Sdn Bhd
No 23, Lebuh Chulia
10200 Penang
Tel: 04 628379/627424
Telex: MA 40271 HOCKBE

Okachi (M) Sdn Bhd (FLR)
5.05, 5th Floor, Menara MPPJ
46200 Petaling Jaya
Tel: 03 7579500
Fax: 03 7579509

Pacific Commodities Sdn Bhd
25th Floor, Wisma Lee Rubber
Jalan Melaka
50100 Kuala Lumpur
Tel: 03 2987111
Telex: MA 33230 PREASE

Pahang Enterprise Sdn Bhd
Suite 121, 1st Floor Johore Tower
No 15 Jalan Gereja
80100 Johore Bahru
Tel: 07 231633/231634
Telex: MA 60017 PENT

Palmex Industries Sdn Bhd
Wisma Palmex
Prai Industrial Complex
Lorong Perusahaan Satu
13609 Butterworth
Tel: 04 306766
Telex: MA 47107/47108 PALMCO
Fax: 04 398337

Pamol Plantations Sdn Bhd
A602 & 603, 6th Floor, West Wing
Wisma Tractors, 7 Jln SS16/1
Subang Jaya, 47500 Petaling Jaya
Selangor
Tel: 03 7336878
Telex: MA 36259 PAMPLA
Fax: 03 7336885

Pan Century Edible Oils Sdn Bhd
8th Floor Plaza MBF
Jalan Ampang
50450 Kuala Lumpur
Tel: 03 2617644/2617645
Telex: MA 30046 PANOIL
Fax: 03 2612324

Pasternak Baum (M) Sdn Bhd (FLR)
Suite 1205-1206 Wisma HLA
Jalan Raja Chulan
50200 Kuala Lumpur
Tel: 03 2481255/2424211
Telex: MA 31104/31105 PABMAL
Fax: 03 2433253

* Patel Holdings Sdn Bhd
No 6 Penang St
10200 Penang
Tel: 04 619421/617239
Telex: MA 40103 PATEL
Fax: 03 2939749

Perak Motor Company Sdn Bhd
86-88 Jalan Sultan Yussuf
30000 Ipoh, Perak
Tel: 05 512233/512234
Telex: MA 44180 YOW

Sabah Marketing Corp Sdn Bhd
1st & 2nd Floor, Wisma Perkasa
Jalan Gaya
PO Box 11501
88816 Kota Kinabalu, Sabah
Tel: 088 58211/58151 3
Telex: MA 80234/80238 SAMAKK
Fax: 088 211344

Sin Thye Management Sdn Bhd
No 107 Changkat Thambi
Dollah (1st Floor)
55100 Kuala Lumpur
Tel: 03 2488901/2427490

Socoil Corp Bhd
167 Jalan Kem
42000 Port Kelang
Selangor
Tel: 03 3686525/3686545
Telex: MA 39706 SOCOIL/38661
SOCORP
Fax: 03 3686546

Soctek Sdn Bhd
5th Floor, Wisma KLI
126 Jalan Bukit Bintang
55100 Kuala Lumpur
Tel: 03 2430211
Telex: MA 31209 STEKHO/32249
STEKKL
Fax: 03 2431123

* Sun Edible Oils Industries
Sdn Bhd
49 A&B, Jalan 1 Kawasan 16
Berkeley New Town Centre
41300 Kelang
Tel: 03 3411545/3411554
Telex: MA 38636 SUNMAL

Synn Edible Oils Sdn Bhd
1st Mile, Jln Kampung Dew
34700 Simpang
Taiping, Perak
Tel: 05 843536
Telex: MA 44117 SPO

Taiko Plantations Sdn Bhd
Wisma Taiko, No 1
Jalan SP Seenivasagam
30000 Ipoh
Perak
Tel: 05 517844/519422
Telex: MA 44324/44094 TAIKO
Fax: 05 505312

Transcommodities Futures (M) Sdn Bhd
Box 279, L5B4 1st Floor, Block B
Kuala Lumpur Plaza, Jln Bukit Bintang
55100 Kuala Lumpur
Tel: 03 2436611
Telex: MA 21066 TRANS
Fax: 03 2410441

Trans Pacific Corp Sdn Bhd
Lot 212, 2nd Floor Wisma HLA
Jalan Raja Chulan
50200 Kuala Lumpur
Tel: 03 2424536/2489146
Telex: MA 30827 CENCOR

Transworld Commodities (M) Sdn
Bhd
Lot 85 Jalan Portland
Tasek Industrial Estate
31400 Ipoh, Perak
Tel: 05 551055/551028
Telex: MA 44031 YLO

Union Rubber Brokers (M) Sdn Bhd
c/o Union Rubber Brokers Pte Ltd
122-B/C Robinson Rd
#04-00 Chiang Hong Bldg
Singapore 0106
Tel: 02 2238776
Telex: RS 24869 WYLTON

Unitata Bhd
Jendarata Estate
Teluk Intan
36000 Perak
Tel: 05 661511/661202
Telex: MA 44337/44338 BERTA

United Plantations Bhd
Jendarata Estate
Teluk Intan
36000 Perak
Tel: 05 661411
Telex: MA 44061 UNITED
Fax: 05 661876

Untung Commodities (M) Sdn Bhd
7.21, 7th Floor Wisma Central
Jalan Ampang
50450 Kuala Lumpur
Tel: 03 2612254/2615080
Telex: MA 33101 UNTUNG

* U-Vin Commodities Sdn Bhd

Kuala Lumpur Tin Market

Datuk Keramat Smelting Sdn Bhd
73 Jalan Datuk Keramat
PO Box 280
10150 Penang
Tel: 04 27166
Telex: MA 40037
Fax: 04 375501/03 2741854

H H Bhatt Sdn Bhd
90 Penang St
10750 Penang
Tel: 04 610326
Telex: MA 40269
Fax: 04 620125

Malaysia Mining Corp Bhd
Tingkat 32, Menara PNB
201A Jalan Tun Razak
50400 Kuala Lumpur
PO Box 11133
50736 Kuala Lumpur
Tel: 03 2616000
Telex: MA 31316
Fax: 03 261951

Malaysia Smelting Corp Sdn Bhd
27 Jalan Pantai
PO Box 2
12000 Butterworth
Tel: 04 342100
Telex: MA 47566
Fax: 04 317405

Mitsui & Co Ltd
17th Floor, Menara Promet
Jalan Sultan Ismail
50250 Kuala Lumpur
PO Box 12147
50768 Kuala Lumpur
Tel: 03 2418099
Telex: MA 30150
Fax: 03 2437992

MMC Marketing Sdn Berhad
Tingkat 32, Menara PNB
210A Jalan Tun Razak
50400 Kuala Lumpur
PO Box 10300
50710 Kuala Lumpur
Tel: 03 2616000
Telex: MA 33772
Fax: 03 2610385

Perangsang International Sdn Bhd
Tingkat 16, Plaza Perangsang
Persiaran Perbandaran
40000 Shah Alam
Tel: 03 5503999
Telex: MA 38669
Fax: 03 550997

Phibro (M) Sdn Berhad
IBG Plaza, Suite 15.01
15th Floor
Jalan Kampar
50400 Kuala Lumpur
Tel: 03 4419588
Telex: MA 31074
Fax: 03 4416840

Sinar Berlian Sdn Bhd
15th Floor, Pernas International
Jalan Sultan Ismail
50250 Kuala Lumpur
Tel: 03 2611255
Telex: MA 31112
Fax: 03 2612312

Thailand Smelting & Refining Co Ltd
7th Floor, Shell Bldg
No 10 Soonthornkosa Rd
Klongtoey
Bangkok 10110
Thailand
Tel: 0062 2490491
Telex: 0086 87324 SHELL TH
Fax: 00662 2498335

Toyota Tsusho (M) Sdn Bhd
Room 1404 Wisma Lim Foo Yong
No 86 Jalan Raja Chulan
50200 Kuala Lumpur
Tel: 03 2423366/2425622
Telex: MA 30419
Fax: 03 2425809

Trans-World Metals Ltd
224 Batu Ferringhi Rd
Batu Ferringhi
1110 Penang
Tel: 04 811489/811541

Netherlands

Brokers on the Amsterdam Pork and Potato Terminal Market

Makelaardij WM Kreeuwen BV
Postbus 3733
1001 AM Amsterdam
Tel: 020 24 88 97

Manager Intermedia BV
Postbus 10030
1001 EA Amsterdam
Tel: 020 27 03 01

Proterma BV
Postbus 10215
1001 EE Amsterdam
Tel: 020 26 76 35

G de Vries Termijnmarkt BV
Damrak 379
1012 ZJ Amsterdam
Tel: 020 20 50 01

Wegeterm BV
Postbus 47
3780 BA Voorthuizen
Tel: 020 24 88 81

W F Westermann & Co BV
Postbus 3445
1001 EA Amsterdam
Tel: 020 26 27 48

Van Zanten & Van Westen BV
Prins Hendrikkade 48
1012 AC Amsterdam
Tel: 020 26 22 06

Amsterdam Futures Clearing House and the Foundation

NLKKAS
Postbus 252
1000 AG Amsterdam
Tel: 020 5504390

Stichting Aardappeltermijnmarkt
Postbus 529
1000 AM Amsterdam
Tel: 020 38 22 39/38 22 58

Singapore

Singapore International Monetary Exchange Ltd

Clearing Members

ABC Futures & Bullion Pte Ltd
50 Raffles Place, #14-00 Shell Tower
Singapore 0104
Tel: 2242977
Telex: RS 28989 ABCSNG
Fax: 2250440

ACB Bullion & Futures Pte Ltd
60 Robinson Rd, #09-00
Singapore 0106
Tel: 2228222
Telex: RS 21911/23116 ASIACOM
Fax: 2253493

BA Futures, Inc
78 Shenton Way, #19-00
Singapore 0207
Tel: 3203389/2730710
Telex: RS 29159 BAFSIN
Fax: 3203390

BT Futures (Singapore) Ltd
50 Raffles Place, #26-01/06 Shell Tower
Singapore 0104
Tel: 2229191
Telex: RS 28626 BTCOFX
Fax: 2255552

Carr Futures International Pte Ltd
3 Shenton Way, #22-04 Shenton House
Singapore 0106
Tel: 2215377/5228
Telex: RS 43280 CARRS
Fax: 2244846

Chase Manhattan Futures Corp
50 Raffles Place, #08-00 Shell Tower
Singapore 0104
Tel: 5304478
Telex: RS 26051 CMFSIN/37619 CMFCSP
Fax: 5304477

Chemical Futures Inc
c/o Chemical Bank
50 Raffles Place, #32-01 Shell Tower
Singapore 0104
Tel: 2204944
Telex: RS 23022 CHEMBNK
Fax: 2249189

Citicorp Futures Ltd
5 Shenton Way, #26-02 UIC Bldg
Singapore 0106
Tel: 2259422
Telex: RS 29260 CITICF
Fax: 2258924

CL Alexanders Rouse (Pte) Ltd
1 Maritime Square, #11-09 World Trade Centre
Singapore 0409
Tel: 2788477
Telex: RS 22368 ROUSE
Fax: 2781500

CM & M Futures (Singapore) Pte Ltd
20 Collyer Quay, #11-03 Tung Centre
Singapore 0104
Tel: 2257322
Telex: RS 55102 CCMMSIN
Fax: 2257079

Continental First Options Inc
10 Collyer Quay, #20-06/08 Ocean Bldg
Singapore 0104
Tel: 5356466
Telex: RS 22030 CONSING
Fax: 5338329

Daiwa Futures Pte Ltd
6 Shenton Way, #39-01/02 DBS Bldg
Singapore 0106
Tel: 2203666
Telex: RS 21126 DAIWA
Fax: 2253797

DBS Trading (Pte) Ltd
6 Shenton Way, DBS Bldg
Singapore 0106
Tel: 2201111
Telex: RS 24850 DBSDEAL
Fax: 2257464

Drexel Burnham Lambert (S) Pte Ltd
5 Shenton Way, #22-08 ULC Bldg
Singapore 0106
Tel: 2251388
Telex: RS 23615 DREBUR
Fax: 2240542

Fulton Prebon Futures Clearing
(Singapore) Ltd
50 Robinson Rd, #15-00 MBN Bldg
Singapore 0106
Tel: 2230777
Telex: RS22939/20107 FULSING
Fax: 2249186

J P Morgan Futures Inc
6 Shenton Way, #30-01 DBS Bldg
Singapore 0106
Tel: 2251011
Telex: RS 22770 MFCSIN
Fax: 2259138

Merrill Lynch Futures (S) Pte Ltd
50 Raffles Place, #27-01 Shell Tower
Singapore 0104
Tel: 2210555
Telex: RS 21800 MERLEAP
Fax: 2253895

The Nikko Futures (Singapore) Pte Ltd
6 Battery Rd, #28-01 Standard
Chartered Bank Bldg
Singapore 0104
Tel: 2233390
Telex: RS 35089 NIKOMB
Fax: 2252854

Nomura Futures (Singapore) Pte Ltd
6 Battery Rd, #39-01 Standard
Chartered Bank Bldg
Singapore 0104
Tel: 2208766
Telex: RS 21198 SINGNOM
Fax: 2240966

OCBC Bullion & Futures Ltd
65 Chulla St, #11-00 OCBC Centre
Singapore 0104
Tel: 5357222
Telex: RS 24444 OCBCBU
Fax: 5326007

Ong First Chicago Futures Pte Ltd
76 Shenton Way, #10-00 Ong Bldg
Singapore 0207
Tel: 2239477
Telex: RS 24279 AURIC
Fax: 2239890

OUB Bullion & Futures Ltd
(Wholly owned subsidiary of Overseas
Union Bank Ltd)
1 Raffles Place, 15th Floor OUB Centre
Singapore 0104
Tel: 5338686
Telex: RS 22373 OUBANK
Fax: 5332208

Phillip Commodities (Pte) Ltd
95 South Bridge Rd, #11-17 South
Bridge Centre
Singapore 0105
Tel: 5351155
Telex: RS 20188 PILSEC
Fax: 5330593

Prudential-Bache Securities Asia Pacific
Ltd
5 Shenton Way, 26th Floor ULC Bldg
Singapore 0106
Tel: 2246122
Telex: RS 22107 BACHECO
Fax: 2245640

RCC Futures (Singapore) Ltd
143 Cecil St, #26-00 GB Bldg
Singapore 0106
Tel: 2240355/0077
Telex: RS 20066/20237 RNBSIN
Fax: 2251330

Refco (Singapore) Pte Ltd
20 Collyer Quay, #12-03 Tung Centre
Singapore 0104
Tel: 2253628
Telex: RS 40184 REFCTY
Fax: 2257373

Rothschild Bullion & Financial Futures
Pte Ltd
9 Battery Rd, #01-02 Straits Trading
Bldg
Singapore 0104
Tel: 5358311
Telex: RS 36269 NMRS
Fax: 5342407

Sasson Financial Futures Pte Ltd
1 Raffles Place, #43-01 OUB Centre
Singapore 0104
Tel: 5341966
Telex: RS 23475 SFFDLR
Fax: 5334889

Security Pacific Asia Futures Inc
1 Maritime Square, #09-37 World Trade
Centre
Singapore 0409
Tel: 2783434/4777
Telex: RS 42716/50446 SPAFI
Fax: 2786901/2242775

Shearson Lehman Hutton Pte Ltd
4 Shenton Way, #12-01/08 Shing Kwan
House
Singapore 0106
Tel: 2228366
Telex: RS 20212 SAES
Fax: 2247735

Standard Chartered Futures (S) Pte Ltd
6 Battery Rd, 5th Floor Standard
Chartered Bank Bldg
Singapore 0104
Tel: 2258888
Telex: RS 23019 SCBSIN
Fax: 2259136

Sung Hong Kai Bullion & Futures Pte
Ltd
20 Collyer Quay, #18-01 Tung Centre
Singapore 0104
Tel: 2247077
Telex: RS 20327 SHKSEC
Fax: 2228330

TLB Bullion & Futures Pte Ltd
63 Market Street, #03-00 Tat Lee Bank
Bldg
Singapore 0104
Tel: 5356811
Telex: RS 20647 TLGOLD
Fax: 5331043

UOB Bullion & Futures Ltd
1 Bonham St, UOB Bldg
Singapore 0104
Tel: 533898
Telex: RS 21539 TYEHUA
Fax: 5343028

Wardley-Thomson Futures Singapore Pte
Ltd
21 Collyer Quay, #20-02 Hongkong
Bank Bldg
Singapore 0104
Tel: 2254007
Telex: RS 22129 WTFSIN
Fax: 2249201

Winall Investments Pte Ltd
200 Cantonment Rd, #15-00 Southpoint
Singapore 0208
Tel: 2250367/0411
Telex: RS 36874 KIBPL
Fax: 2243040

Non-Clearing Members

Ascom Commodities Pte Ltd
63 Robinson Rd, #04-03 Afro-Asia Bldg
Singapore 0106
Tel: 2214433
Telex: RS 23081 ASCOM
Fax: 2245278

Baring Futures (Singapore) Pte Ltd
10 Collyer Quay, #06-05 Ocean Bldg
Singapore 0104
Tel: 5353688
Telex: RS 26881/2 BARSEC
Fax: 5325592

BOT Futures (Singapore) Pte Ltd
16 Raffles Quay, #01-06 Hong Leong
Bldg
Singapore 0104
Tel: 2208111
Telex: RS 24363 TOHBANK
Fax: 2244965

CIC Futures Pte Ltd
36 Robinson Rd, #11-01 City House
Singapore 0106
Tel: 2250333
Telex: RS 29070 CICSGP
Fax: 2244923

CRT Asia, Inc
1 Maritime Square, #09-44 World Trade
Centre
Singapore 0409
Tel: 2789412
Fax: 2789411

DKB Futures (Singapore) Pte Ltd
1 Raffles Place, #47-00 OUB Centre
Singapore 0104
Tel: 5332626
Telex: RS 21622 DKBSP
Fax: 5332190

Daiwa Bk Financial Futures Singapore
Pte Ltd
6 Shenton Way, #09-01 DBS Bldg
Singapore 0106
Tel: 2201791
Telex: RS 22123 DAIWABK
Fax: 2246840

DMT Futures (Asia) Pte Ltd
101 Cecil St, #22-11 Tong Eng Bldg
Singapore 0106
Tel: 2239066
Telex: RS 34138 DMTINT
Fax: 2249974

Diamond Futures (Singapore) Pte Ltd
20 Collyer Quay, #01-02 Tung Centre
Singapore 0104
Tel: 2205666
Telex: RS 21913/4 BISHIBK
Fax: 2254739

Discount Corp of New York Futures
Madison Plaza 2nd Floor, 200 West
Madison
Chicago, Illinois 60606
USA
Tel: 312 8761930
Telex: 023 3723282 DCNYFCGO
Fax: 312 3682281

The Fuji Futures (Singapore) Pte Ltd
1 Raffles Place, #20-00 OUB Centre
Singapore 0104
Tel: 5343500
Telex: RS 24670 FUJISP/24610
FUJIG N
Fax: 5327310

Golden Hope Commodities Pte Ltd
3 Phillip St, #08-01/03 Matterhorn
Bldg
Singapore 0104
Tel: 5325611
Telex: RS 34510 HOPE
Fax: 5322749

Goldman Sachs (Singapore) Pte Ltd
c/o Sidley & Austin
5 Shenton Way, #20-08 UIC Bldg
Singapore 0106
Tel: 2245000
Telex: RS 28754 USLAW
Fax: 2240530

IBJ Futures Pte Ltd
6 Shenton Way, #14-01 DBS Bldg
Singapore 0106
Tel: 2200133
Telex: RS 21880 KOGINPO
Fax: 2243702

J Ballas Futures Pte Ltd
9 Battery Rd, #19-06 Straits Trading
Bldg
Singapore 0104
Tel: 5353677/5324633
Telex: RS 21718 JBFPL
Fax: 5341313

Kidder, Peabody & Co Incorporated*
20 Exchange Place
New York, NY 10005
USA
Telex: 023 620455 KIDDER
Fax: 011 65 2730241

Kyowa Financial Futures (Singapore) Pte
Ltd
24 Raffles Place, #12-01/06 Clifford
Centre
Singapore 0104
Tel: 5354822
Telex: RS 22059 KYOWASP
Fax: 5331462

LTCB Futures (Singapore) Pte Ltd
65 Chulla St, #32-00 OCBC Centre
Singapore 0104
Tel: 5341977
Telex: RS 23813 LTCBSIN
Fax: 5326048

Macron Futures Pte Ltd
70 Anson Rd, #23-00 Apex Tower
Singapore 0207
Tel: 2212777
Telex: RS 55010 MARCON
Fax: 2212219

Mitsui Financial Futures (Singapore) Pte
Ltd
16 Raffles Quay, #01-04 Hong Leong
Bldg
Singapore 0104
Tel: 2209761
Telex: RS 21319 MITUI
Fax: 2250962

Mitsui Trust Futures (Singapore) Pte
Ltd
6 Shenton Way, #35-01 DBS Bldg
Singapore 0106
Tel: 2208553/8554
Telex: RS 23796 MITUITB/29653
MTBSPR
Fax: 2241669/2250605

Morgan Grenfell Asia Futures Pte Ltd
36 Robinson Rd, #13-01 City House
Singapore 0106
Tel: 2258080
Telex: RS 23147 MGASIA
Fax: 2252869

Okachi Futures Pte Ltd
138 Cecil St, #08-01 Cecil Court
Singapore 0106
Tel: 2255744/5745
Telex: RS 29333 OKACHI
Fax: 2244662

Panin Futures Pte Ltd
108 Middle Rd, #09-00 Bright
Chambers
Singapore 0718
Tel: 3368933
Telex: RS 34750 PANINS
Fax: 3380880

Rudolf Wolff & Co Ltd*
c/o Allen & Gledhill
36 Robinson Rd, #19-00 City House
Singapore 0106
Tel: 2251611/2711
Telex: RS 21600 GLEDHILL
Fax: 2248210

Saitama Financial Futures (Singapore)
Pte Ltd
1 Raffles Place, #41-00 OUB Centre
Singapore 0104
Tel: 5333334
Telex: RS 20371/69 SAIGIN
Fax: 5333244

Salomon Brothers Futures Pte Ltd
101 Thomson Rd, #16-03 Goldhill
Square
Singapore 1130
Tel: 2506088
Telex: RS 24374 PHIBRO
Fax: 2506124

Sanwa Futures (Singapore) Pte Ltd
50 Raffles Place, #25-01 Shell Tower
Singapore 0104
Tel: 2249822
Telex: RS 28573 SNWSGP
Fax: 2251444

SBCI Futures Inc*
6 Battery Rd, #35-01 Standard
Chartered Bank Bldg
Singapore 0104
Tel: 2242200
Telex: RS 24140 SINSUIS
Fax: 2247743

SIMBL Investments Pte Ltd
65 Chulla St, #47-01 OCBC Centre
Singapore 0104
Tel: 5353411
Telex: RS 28146 SIMBL
Fax: 5343917

Sin Huat Bullion (S) Pte Ltd
141 Cecil St, #07-01/04 Tung Ann
Association Bldg
Singapore 0106
Tel: 2233178/8118
Telex: RS 25133 SHGOLD
Fax: 2235675

Sing Bullion & Futures Pte Ltd
96 Robinson Rd, #02-00 SIF Bldg
Singapore 0106
Tel: 2219998/2259798
Telex: RS 20083 SING
Fax: 2253267

STB Financial Futures (Singapore) Pte
Ltd
5 Shenton Way, #02-16 UIC Bldg
Singapore 0106
Tel: 2249055
Telex: RS 20717 SMTRST
Fax: 2242873

Sumitomo Financial Futures (Singapore)
Pte Ltd
6 Shenton Way, #01-09 DBS Bldg
Singapore 0106
Tel: 2201611
Telex: RS 21656 SUMIBANK
Fax: 2259647

Taiyo Kobe Financial Futures
(Singapore) Pte Ltd
50 Raffles Place, #24-02 Shell Tower
Singapore 0104
Tel: 2227871
Telex: RS 23058 TAIKOSI
Fax: 2240754

Takugin Financial Futures (Singapore)
Pte Ltd
65 Chulla St, #48-01 OCBC Centre
Singapore 0104
Tel: 5332155
Telex: RS 24414 HTBSIN
Fax: 5334047

Tokai Financial Futures (Singapore) Pte
Ltd
24 Raffles Place, #22-01/06 Clifford
Centre
Singapore 0104
Tel: 5358222
Telex: RS 21848 TOKAIBK
Fax: 5325453

Tokyo Forex and Tullett (Futures) Pte
Ltd
10 Anson Rd, #16-11 International
Plaza
Singapore 0207
Tel: 2248077
Telex: RS 28571 KTD FX
Fax: 2241021

Union Bank of Switzerland*
50 Raffles Place, #38-01 Shell Tower
Singapore 0104
Tel: 2203622
Telex: RS 21549 UDS CH
Fax: 2241839

Wocom Commodities Pte Ltd
150 Cecil St, #16-00 Wing On Life Bldg
Singapore 0106
Tel: 2255988
Telex: RS 23278 WOLASCO
Fax: 2248890

Yamaichi Futures Pte Ltd
138 Robinson Rd, #20-01/21-01 Hong
Leong Centre
Singapore 0106
Tel: 2250688
Telex: RS 22571 YAMASP
Fax: 2250075

YTB Financial Futures (Singapore) Pte
Ltd
50 Raffles Place, #16-02 Shell Tower
Singapore 0104
Tel: 2237266
Telex: RS 33285 YTBCSI
Fax: 2244365

Commercial Associate Members
BP Singapore Pte Ltd*
BP House, 1 Pasir Panjang Rd
Singapore 0511
Tel: 4756633
Telex: RS 55788/21240 BEEPEE
Fax: 2737897/4759273

C Itoh International Petroleum Co
(Singapore) Pte Ltd
16 Raffles Quay, #13-01 Hong Leong
Bldg
Singapore 0104
Tel: 2255555
Telex: RS 21275/20401 CITOH
Fax: 2259809

Caltex (Asia) Ltd*
210 Jalan Buroh
Singapore 2260
Tel: 2651000
Telex: RS 21207 CALTEX
Fax: 2658489

Mobil Sales and Supply Corp*
18 Pioneer Rd
Singapore 2282
Tel: 6606000
Telex: RS 21327 MOBOIL
Fax: 2641693

Mitsul & Co Ltd*
16 Raffles Quay, #17-00 Hong Leong
Bldg
Singapore 1014
Tel: 3213111
Telex: RS 21331 MITSUI
Fax: 2243458/7289

Marubeni International Petroleum (S)
Pte Ltd*
16 Raffles Quay, #40-01A Hong Leong
Bldg
Singapore 0104
Tel: 2240466
Telex: RS 21245 MARBENI
Fax: 2215458

Mitsubish Corp*
138 Robinson Rd, #08-00 Hong Leong Centre
Singapore 0106
Tel: 2209111
Telex: RS 21266 MSK S'PORE
Fax: 2256047

Shell Eastern Petroleum (Pte) Ltd*
50 Raffles Place, Shell Tower
Singapore 0104
Tel: 2247777
Telex: RS 21251/21271 SHELL
Fax: 2240379

Singapore Petroleum Co Pte Ltd*
6 Shenton Way, #42-01 DBS Bldg
Singapore 0106
Tel: 2213166
Telex: RS 21430 SPC
Fax: 2213691

* Approval-in-Principal

United Kingdom

ICCH Members

ABB Futures (UK) Ltd
11a West Halkin St
London SW1X 8JL
Tel: 235 1389

Anglo Chemical Metals Ltd
E Section Ground Floor, Plantation House
5–8 Mincing Lane
London EC3M 3DX
Tel: 721 4000

Adequate Investment Co Ltd
15 F Chiyoda Bldgs
115 Chatham Rd
TST Kowloon
Hong Kong
Tel: 3 7239559

Amerex Futures Ltd
1st Floor, Albermarle House
1 Albermarle St
London W1X 3HF
Tel: 629 6668

Allied Irish Investment Bank Ltd
Futures Administration
12 Old Jewry
London EC2R 8DP
Tel: 606 3070

A J D Financial Services Ltd
60 Cornhill
London EC3V 3PD
Tel: 623 1782

Arbuthnot Latham Bank Ltd
131 Finsbury Pavement
Moorgate
London EC2A 1AY
Tel: 628 9876

Amalgamated Metal Trading Ltd
Ground Floor, Adelaide House
London Bridge
London EC4R 9DT
Tel: 626 4521

Australia & New Zealand Banking Group Ltd
55 Gracechurch St
London EC3V 0BN
Tel: 280 3100

Riggs A P Bank Ltd
21 Great Winchester St
London EC2N 2HH
Tel: 588 7575

Argus Corp
Phoenix House
18 King William St
London EC4N 7SA
Tel: 623 8949

Arbuthnot Stotler International Ltd
131 Finsbury Pavement
Moorgate
London EC2A 1AY
Tel: 280 8410

Astroline Corp
95 Walkers Brook Drive
Reading
Massachusetts 01867
USA
Tel: 6179421900

Baring Securities Ltd
Lloyds Chambers
1 Portsoken St
London E1 8DF
Tel: 621 1500

M C Brackenbury & Co Ltd
3rd Floor
19 St Mary-at-Hill
London EC3R 8EE
Tel: 623 7870

Banque Belge Ltd
4 Bishopsgate
London EC2N 4AD
Tel: 283 1080

Baring Brothers & Co Ltd
14th Floor
8 Bishopsgate
London EC2N 4AE
Tel: 283 8833

Prudential-Bache (Futures) Ltd
Ground Floor
9 Devonshire Square
London EC2M 4HP
Tel: 283 9166

Bank of Tokyo Capital Markets Ltd
6th Floor
20–24 Moorgate
London EC2R 6DH
Tel: 628 3000

C A & L Bell Commodities Corp Pty
Ltd
5th Floor
19 Great Winchester St
London EC2N 2BH
Tel: 588 1756

BDF Commodities Ltd
65 London Fruit Exchange
Spitalfields Market
65 Brushfield St
London E1 6EP
Tel: 377 6996

Billiton-Enthoven Metals Ltd
84 Fenchurch St
London EC3M 4BY
Tel: 480 7290

Brandeis (Brokers) Ltd
4 Fore St
London EC2P 2NU
Tel: 638 5877

Balfour Maclaine International (UK) Ltd
Europe House
World Trade Centre
London E1 9AA
Tel: 488 9592

Banque Nationale de Paris plc
Foreign Exchange Proc Futures
8–13 King William St
London EC4P 4HS
Tel: 626 5678

The Bank of Nova Scotia
Scotia House
33 Finsbury Square
London EC2A 1BB
Tel: 638 5644

B A Futures Inc
1 Watling St
London EC4P 4BX
Tel: 634 4491

BP Oil International Ltd
Britannic House
Moor Lane
London EC2Y 9BU
Tel: 920 8000

BP Oil UK Ltd
BP House
Breakspear Way
Hemel Hempstead
Herts HP2 4UL
Tel: 0442 232323

B T Futures Corp
Dashwood House
69 Old Broad St
London EC2P 2EE
Tel: 726 4141

Britannic Trading Ltd
Britannic House
Moor Lane
London EC2Y 9BU
Tel: 920 8000

The Bank of Tokyo Ltd
4th Floor
20–24 Moorgate
London EC2R 6DH
Tel: 638 1271

Bunge & Co Ltd
Bunge House
15–25 Artillery Lane
London E1 7HA
Tel: 247 4444

Barclays de Zoete Wedd Futures Ltd
2nd Floor
Minster House
12–18 Arthur St
London EC4R 9AB
Tel: 623 2323

Cater Allen Futures Ltd
1 King William St
London EC4N 7AU
Tel: 623 2070

Bozzo Commerce de Cafe SA
14 Rue Le Corbusier
Geneva CH – 1208
Switzerland
Tel: 022 47 43 11

Continentale en Afrikaanse
Handelsvereniging BV
'Continaf'
Prinsengracht 917–919
PO Box 3779
Amsterdam C, Holland
Tel: 225533

Cargill Investor Services Ltd
Staple Hall
Stone House Court
London EC3A 7AX
Tel: 283 5272

Christiania Bank 06 Kreditkasse
Lloyds Chambers
1 Portsoken St
London E1 8RU
Tel: 702 1390

Cadbury Ltd
P T W Shaw
Confectionery Finance Dept
Bournville
Birmingham B30 2LU
Tel: 021 458 2000

Charles Davis (Metal Brokers) Ltd
9–13 Fenchurch Bldgs
London EC3M 5HR
Tel: 702 9735

Chemical Bank
Chemical Bank House
180 Strand
London WC2R 1ET
Tel: 379 7474

Cerro Metals (UK) Ltd
Devonshire House
146 Bishopsgate
London EC2M 4JX
Tel: 377 8050

Citifutures Ltd
1st Floor
7 Birchin Lane
London EC3V 9DE
Tel: 234 2570

CGIC
69 Rue Ampere
75017 Paris
France
Tel: 42 570283

Continental Bank Nat Ass Ltd
1 King William St
London EC4 7AU

Charterhouse Bank Ltd
1 Paternoster Row
St Pauls
London EC4M 7DH
Tel: 248 4000

Credit Lyonnais Rouse Ltd
International House
1 St Katharines Way
London E1 9UN
Tel: 481 2121

James Capel C M & M (UK) Ltd
7 Devonshire Square
London EC2M 4HT
Tel: 621 0792

Chase Manhattan Futures (UK) Ltd
PO Box 16
Woolgate House
Coleman St
London EC2P 2HD
Tel: 726 7036

Lewis & Peat (Futures) Ltd
32 St Mary at Hill
London EC3R 8DH
Tel: 623 3111

Czarnikow Rionda Co Inc
58 Borough High St
London SE1 1XF
Tel: 407 6421

CRT Europe Inc
1-6 Lombard St
London EC3V 9DT
Tel: 220 7041

Credit Suisse First Boston Ltd
2a Great Titchfield St
London W1P 7AA
Tel: 322 4000

Continental UK Ltd
Southside
105 Victoria St
London SW1E 6QT
Tel: 828 7868

Czarnikow Futures Ltd
PO Box 602
66 Mark Lane
London EC3P 3EA
Tel: 480 9300

Daarnhouwer & Co Ltd
International House
World Trade Centre
St Katharines Way
London E1 9UN
Tel: 488 9151

Discount Corp of New York Futures
16 St Helens Place
London EC3A 6DE
Tel: 588 8283

Daiwa Europe Ltd
5 King William St
London EC4N 7AX
Tel: 548 8080

Dai-Ichi (Europe) Ltd
Durrant House
8-13 Chiswell St
London EC1Y 4TQ
Tel: 588 6075

Deak International Trading (UK) Ltd
6th Floor, Section B
Plantation House
5-8 Mincing Lane
London EC3M 3AR
Tel: 283 6362

The Dai-Ichi Kangyo Bank Ltd
DKB House
24 King William St
London EC4R 9DB
Tel: 283 0929

Drexel Burnham Lambert Ltd
Drexel Burnham House
1 Alie St
London E1 8DB
Tel: 325 9797

Den Norske Creditbank
20 St Dunstans Hill
London EC3R 8HY
Tel: 621 1111

Dresdner Bank AG
125 Wood St
London EC2V 7AQ
Tel: 606 7030

Dean Witter Futures Ltd
1 Appold St, 6th Floor
Broadgate 5
London EC2A 2AA
Tel: 480 8500

Elders Futures Inc
73 Cornhill
London
EC3V 3QQ
Tel: 929 4009

Energy Futures Ltd
130 Jermyn St
London SW1Y 4UJ
Tel: 403 0766

Elders Finance Group UK Ltd
73 Cornhill
London EC3V 3QQ
Tel: 929 4009

Entores (Metal Brokers) Ltd
1 Singer St
London EC2A 4BQ
Tel: 962 0933

First Chicago Futures Inc
First Chicago House
90 Long Acre
London WC2E 9RB
Tel: 240 7240

Fernstone Ltd
c/o Fordyce, Curry & Co
St Bartholomew Chambers
61 West Smithfield
London EC1A 9EA
Tel: 606 5711

S Figgis & Co (Broking) Ltd
53–54 Aldgate High St
London EC3N 1LU
Tel: 488 4511

F Murphy (Metals) Ltd
Brunswick St
Leicester LE1 2BA
Tel: 0533 29252

First Options of Chicago Ltd
Continental Bank House
162 Queen Victoria St
London EC4V 4BS
Tel: 860 5400

Frank Fehr & Co Ltd
Prince Rupert House
64 Queen St
London EC4 1ER
Tel: 248 5066

Fritz Kopp AG
Sempacherstrasse 5
Lucerne CH-6002
Switzerland
Tel: 4141 244422

The Fuji Bank Ltd
25–31 Moorgate
London EC2R 6HQ
Tel: 628 4477

First Continental Trading Inc
The Stock Exchange
Old Broad St
London EC4 1NH

Fulton Prebon Futures Ltd
34–40 Ludgate Hill
London EC4M 7JT
Tel: 248 3242

Geldermann Ltd
Plantation House
Mincing Lane
London EC3M 3DX
Tel: 623 9611

Gerald Ltd
Europe House
World Trade Centre
St Katharine By The Tower
London E1 9AA
Tel: 481 0681

GNI Wallace Ltd
Colechurch House
1 London Bridge Walk
London SE1 2SX
Tel: 378 7171

GNI Ltd
Colechurch House
1 London Bridge Walk
London SE1 2SX
Tel: 378 7171

Giles W Pritchard-Gordon (Futures) Ltd
11–15 Arlington St
St James
London SW1A 1RD
Tel: 408 0585

Goldman Sachs Futures Ltd
5 Old Bailey
London EC4M 7AH
Tel: 248 6464

J W Gaskell (Commodities) Ltd
81 London Fruit Exchange
London E1 6EP
Tel: 377 8966

Gill & Duffus London Ltd
St Dunstan's House
201 Borough High St
London SE1 1HW
Tel: 407 7050

Hambros Bank Ltd
41 Tower Hill
London EC3N 4HA
Tel: 480 5000

Hecht Heyworth & Alcan Ltd
Myrtil House
70 Clifton St
London EC2A 4SP
Tel: 377 8773

Hope Commodities Ltd
Long Lodge
267–269 Kingston Rd
Merton Park
London SW19
Tel: 543 3151

Hill Samuel Bank Ltd
100 Wood St
London EC2P 2AJ
Tel: 628 8011

Holco Trading Co Ltd
Sugar Quay
Lower Thames St
London EC3R 6DY
Tel: 623 1800

International Clearing Services Ltd
37 Lombard St
London EC3V 9PE
Tel: 283 7061

Imperial Coffee International Ltd
1 Marble Quay
St Katharine By The Tower
London E1 9UL
Tel: 481 1466

Hydro Aluminium A3
Drammensveun 134
Pont-baks 245 Skoyen
0212 OSLO 2 Norway

Irving Trust Co
46 Berkeley St
London W1X 6AA
Tel: 499 1234

IBJ International Ltd
Bucklersbury House
3 Queen Victoria St
London EC3N 8HR
Tel: 236 1090

Ixomex Ltd
49 Wigmore St
London W1H 9LE
Tel: 935 4455

J H Rayner (Futures) Ltd
Berisford Wing
1 Prescot St
London E1 8AZ
Tel: 481 9144

Jean Lion (Sugar) Ltd
Quay Level, Europe House
World Trade Centre
East Smithfield
London E1 9AA
Tel: 481 3755

G W Joynson & Co Ltd
14 Trinity Square
London EC3N 4AA
Tel: 702 1499

J P Morgan Futures Inc
7th Floor, Morgan House
1 Angel Court
London EC2R 7AE
Tel: 606 4321

KAS Clearing Agent Ltd
Suite 560
Salisbury House
London Wall
London EC2M 5NU
Tel: 588 6400

Kesperry Ltd
30–32 Tabard St
London SE1 4JU
Tel: 407 3572

Kleinwort Benson Ltd
T/A Kleinwort Grieveson Futures
PO Box 560
20 Fenchurch St
London EC3P 3DB
Tel: 623 8000

S N Kurkjian (Commodity Brokers) Ltd
Sakur Suite
4 Telfords Yard
6–8 The Highway
London E1 9PQ
Tel: 488 4616

A/S Torvald Klaveness Commodities
PO Box 182 Skoyen
Hovfaret 17
0212 Oslo 2
Norway
Tel: 010472503040

Lantic Sugar Ltd
5660 Ferrier St
Montreal
Quebec H4P 1M7
Canada
Tel: 514 342 5660

Lazmet Ltd
7th Floor
Roman House
Wood St
London EC2Y 5BA
Tel: 588 6155

LCF Ltd
3 Finsbury Square
London EC2A 1AD
Tel: 638 7943

DG Bank, Deutsche
Genossenschaftsbank
10 Aldersgate St
London EC1A 4XX
Tel: 726 6791

Louis Dreyfus Ltd
65 Kingsway
London WC2B 6TD
Tel: 242 4424

Louis Dreyfus Trading Ltd
65 Kingsway
London WC2B 6TD
Tel: 242 4424

Lit Futures Ltd
Level 2 Suite 7, International House
World Trade Centre
1 St Katharines Way
London E1 9UN
Tel: 481 1712

Lloyds Bank Financial Futures Ltd
2nd Floor, Faryners House
25 Monument St
London EC3R 8BQ
Tel: 283 1000

L M Fischel & Co Ltd
1 Marble Quay
St Katharine By The Tower
London E1 9UL
Tel: 481 1519

Lancom Ltd
2nd Floor, Trident House
Broad St
Bridgetown
Barbados
Tel: 809 436 3980

Marshall French & Lucas Ltd
Plantation House
31–35 Fenchurch St
London EC3M 3DX
Tel: 626 9151

Lewisohn & Marshall Ltd
7 Bedford Square
London WC1B 3RA
Tel: 323 2822

D B Mack Ltd
c/o S R Langler Esq
67 Burnwell Rd
Exning, Newmarket
Suffolk CB8 7DU
Tel: 0638 778211

E D & F Man International Ltd
Sugar Quay
Lower Thames St
London EC3R 6DU
Tel: 626 8788

Gilbert J McCaul (Overseas) Ltd
Bridge House
4 Borough High St
London SE1 9QZ
Tel: 378 1415

Mocatta Commercial Ltd
Mocatta House
4 Crosby Square
London EC3A 6AQ
Tel: 638 5789

Metdist Trading Ltd
Blossoms Inn
3–6 Trump St
London EC2V 8AR
Tel: 606 0463

Mocatta Futures Corp
1 World Trade Centre
Suite 2437
New York, NY10048
USA
Tel: 212 488 0600

Metallgesellschaft Ltd
4th Floor
Three Quays House
Tower Hill
London EC3R 6DS
Tel: 626 6763

Midland Bank plc
Financial Futures Unit Group Treasury
10 Lower Thames St
London EC3R 6AE
Tel: 260 0600

The Mitsui Bank Ltd
Ground & 1st Floor
6 Broadgate
London EC2M 2RQ
Tel: 638 3131

The Mitsui Trust & Banking Co Ltd
5th Floor
6 Broadgate
London EC2M 2TB
Tel: 638 0841

Merrill Lynch Futures Inc
Ropemaker Place
25 Ropemaker St
London EC2Y 9LY
Tel: 628 1000

MLPF & S (Brokers & Dealers) Ltd
Ropemaker Place
25 Ropemaker St
London EC2Y 9LY
Tel: 628 1000

Multitrade BV
PO Box 1485
1200 BL Hilversum
The Netherlands
Tel: 35 255441

E D & F Man (Cocoa) Ltd
Sugar Quay
Lower Thames St
London EC3R 6DU
Tel: 623 1800

Morgan Grenfell & Co Ltd
PO Box 481
20 Finsbury Circus
London EC2M 7HH
Tel: 256 6278

Moutafian Commodities Ltd
2-4 Eastcheap
London EC3M 1AL
Tel: 623 3311

Morgan Stanley International
Colegrave House
70 Berners St
London W1P 3AE
Tel: 709 3000

The Mitsubishi Bank Ltd
6 Broadgate
London EC2M 2FX

Muirpace Ltd
6 Lloyds Ave
London EC3N 3NX
Tel: 702 9776

The Nikko Securities Co (Europe) Ltd
55 Victoria St
London SW1H 0EU
Tel: 489 1551

New Japan Securities Europe Ltd
4 Fenchurch St
London EC3M 3AL
Tel: 626 7855

N M Rothschild & Sons Ltd
New Court
St Swithins Lane
London EC4P 4DU
Tel: 280 5000

Nomura International plc
Nomura House
24 Monument St
London EC3R 8AJ
Tel: 283 8811

National Westminster Financial Futures
Ltd
41 Threadneedle St
London EC2R 8AP
Tel: 920 5555

Pacol Futures Ltd
St Dunstan's House
201 Borough High St
London SE1 1JA
Tel: 407 4400

Philipp Brothers Futures Ltd
Victoria Plaza
111 Buckingham Palace Rd
London SW1W 0SL
Tel: 721 4000

Sharps Pixley Ltd
10 Rood Lane
London EC3M 8BB
Tel: 623 8000

PK English Trust Co Ltd
Carthusian Court
12 Carthusian St
London EC1M 6EB
Tel: 796 1200

Paine Webber International Futures Ltd
1 Finsbury Ave
London EC2M 2PA
Tel: 377 0055

UBS Phillips & Drew Futures Ltd
100 Liverpool St
London EC2M 2RH
Tel: 901 3333

The Royal Bank of Scotland plc
Futures & Options Settlements
Treasury Support Services
67 Lombard St
London EC3P 3DL
Tel: 623 4356

Marc Rich & Co Ltd
49 Wigmore St
London W1H 9LE
Tel: 935 4455

Rionda (London) Ltd
58 Borough High St
London SE1 1XF
Tel: 407 6421

REFCO Inc
c/o REFCO International
Europe House
World Trade Centre
London E1 9AA
Tel: 488 3232

Alan J Ridge & Breminer Ltd
1st Floor
19-21 Great Tower St
London EC3R 5AQ
Tel: 623 2161

Rionda Futures Ltd
58 Borough High St
London SE1 1XF
Tel: 407 6421

Rowntree Mackintosh (Ingredients) Ltd
The Cocoa Works
York YO1 1XY
Tel: 0904 653071

c/o SOPAD SA
17-19 Quai du President Paul Doumer
92414 Courbevoie
France
Tel: 334 3100

Republic National Bank of New York
30 Monument St
London EC3R 8NB
Tel: 860 3000

Refco Overseas Ltd
Europe House
World Trade Centre
London E1 9AA
Tel: 488 3232

Rayner Brokerage Ltd
Berisford Wing
1 Prescot St
London E1 8AY

Redpath Industries Ltd
Comtrad Division
95 Queens Quay East
Toronto, Ontario M5E 1A3
Canada
Tel: 416 366 3561

Rucker & Slann Ltd
7 Seax Way
Southfields
Laindon
Essex SS15 6SL
Tel: 0268 417711

Rudolf Wolff & Co Ltd
Second Floor, D Section
Plantation House
31-35 Fenchurch St
London EC3M 3DX
Tel: 626 8765

Shearson Lehman Hutton Inc
5th Floor
1 Broadgate
London EC2M 7HA
Tel: 601 0011

Swiss Bank Corp
Swiss Bank House
1 High Timber St
London EC4V 3SB
Tel: 329 0329

Saudi International Bank
99 Bishopsgate
London EC2M 3TB
Tel: 638 2323

Scandinavian Bank Group plc
Scandinavian House
2–6 Cannon St
London EC4M 6XX
Tel: 236 6090

Sime Darby Commodities Ltd
Hibernia Chambers
London Bridge
London SE1 9QX
Tel: 403 1234

Spection Futures Ltd
11 Grosvenor Place
London SW1X 7HH

Safic Alcan (Futures) Ltd
Myrtil House
70 Clifton St
London EC2A 4SP

Seio Commodities Traders (HK) Ltd
Room 1011
New World Tower
16–18 Queens Rd Central
Hong Kong
Tel: 8525262141

Shearson Lehman Hutton Commodities
Ltd
5th Floor
1–2 Broadgate
London EC2M 7HA
Tel: 601 0011

Sanwa International Ltd
PO Box 245
1 Undershaft
London EC3A 8BR
Tel: 623 7991

Salomon Brothers International Ltd
Futures and Options Level 3
111 Buckingham Palace Rd
London SW1W 0SB
Tel: 721 2432

The Sumitomo Trust & Banking Co Ltd
62–63 Threadneedle St
London EC2R 8BR
Tel: 628 5621

Socomex Futures Ltd
5th Floor
10 Old Jewry
London EC2R 8DU
Tel: 606 9091

Finat (UK) Ltd
Warnford Court
29 Throgmorton St
London EC2N 2AT
Tel: 628 6018

Sogemin (Metals) Ltd
4th Floor
98 Cannon St
London EC4N 6EN
Tel: 621 0330

Instituto Bancario San Paulo Di Torino
9 St Pauls Churchyard
London EC4 8AB
Tel: 82 27800

SOPAD SA
17–19 Quai Du President Paul Doumer
92414 Courbevoie
France
Tel: 334 3100

W G Spice & Co Ltd
Sugar Quay
Lower Thames St
London EC3R 6DU
Tel: 623 1800

South African Sugar Association
1st Floor
Sugar Quay
Lower Thames St
London EC3R 6LR
Tel: 626 1844

Standard Chartered Bank
22 Billiter St
London EC3A 2BE
Tel: 280 7500

Henry Stephens & Sons (London) Ltd
Henry Stephens House
12 Minories
London EC3N 1BJ
Tel: 488 4754

The Sanwa Bank Ltd
PO Box 36
Commercial Union Bldg
1 Undershaft
London EC38 8LA
Tel: 282 5252

Sucden (UK) Ltd
5 London Bridge St
London SE1 9SG
Tel: 378 6322

The Taiyo Kobe Bank Ltd
Commercial Union Bldg
1 Undershaft
London EC3A 8TB
Tel: 621 1430

Tokyo Commodity Ltd
16/F Parkview Commercial Bldg
9-11 Shelter St
Causeway Bay
Hong Kong
Tel: 5777136

Tardivat International SA
137 Rue de Faubourg Saint Honore
75008 Paris
France
Tel: 562 3131

Theobroma NV
PO Box 12200
100 AE
Amsterdam ZO
Tel: 3120 5675911

The Tokai Bank Ltd
99 Bishopsgate
London EC2M 3TA
Tel: 283 8500

Thomson McKinnon Futures Ltd
Greenly House
40 Dukes Place
London EC3A 5HJ
Tel: 626 1511

Tullett & Tokyo (Futures and Traded
Options) Ltd
Cable House
54-62 New Broad St
London EC2M 1JJ
Tel: 895 9595

Triland Metals Ltd
Bow Bells House
Bread St
London EC4M 9BQ
Tel: 248 0126

Truxo Ltd
87 Worship St
London EC2A 2BE
Tel: 247 3411

Tardivat Futures Ltd
Suite 6, Free Trade Wharf
350 The Highway
London E1 9DH
Tel: 265 8155

Tate & Lyle International
(Division of Tate & Lyle Industries Ltd)
Sugar Quay
Lower Thames St
London EC3R 6DQ
Tel: 626 6525

The United Bank of Kuwait plc
3 Lombard St
London EC3V 9DT
Tel: 626 3422

Unidaf
103 Boulevard de Strasbourg
BP 247
76600 Le Havre
France
Tel: 225 7690

Union Discount Futures Ltd
39 Cornhill
London EC3V 3NU
Tel: 623 1020

Unidaf Trading Co Ltd
3rd Floor
6-7 St Mary at Hill
London EC3R 8EE
Tel: 623 1991

V Berg & Sons Ltd
112 Union St
London SE1 0NL
Tel: 928 9000

Woodhouse Drake and Carey
(Commodities) Ltd
Three Quays
Tower Hill
London EC3R 6EP
Tel: 623 7575

S G Warburg Futures & Options Ltd
4th Floor North
1 Finsbury Ave
London EC2M 2PA
Tel: 606 1066

Warenhandelsgesellschaft 'Corinth'
MBH
16 Grosse Bleichen
2000 Hamburg 36
West Germany
Tel: 4940340521

Wallace Smith Interfutures
Division of British Trusts Association
Ltd
77 London Wall
London EC2N 1AB
Tel: 638 6444

Westpac Banking Corp
Wallbrook House
23 Wallbrook
London EC4N 8LD
Tel: 626 4500

Yamaichi International (Europe) Ltd
Finsbury Court
111–117 Finsbury Pavement
London EC2A 1EQ
Tel: 628 2271

Yasuda Trust Europe Ltd
1 Liverpool St
London EC2M 7NH
Tel: 256 6188

International Petroleum Exchange

Floor Member Companies

Amerex Futures Ltd
1st Floor
Albermarle House
1 Albermarle St
London W1X 3HF
Tel: 01 629 6668
Telex: 296673
Fax: 01 493 4406

Samuel Banner & Co Ltd
59–61 Sandhills Lane
Liverpool L5 9XL

Cargill Investor Services Ltd
Staple Hall
Stone House Court
London EC3A 7AX
Tel: 01 283 5272
Telex: 885453
Fax: 01 929 4885

CL-Alexanders Rouse Ltd
International House
1 St Katharine's Way
London E1 9UN
Tel: 01 481 2121
Telex: 8950831
Fax: 01 480 5865

CRT Europe Inc
1–6 Lombard St
London EC3V 9AA
Tel: 01 220 7041
Telex: 946172
Fax: 01 929 3529

Czarnikow Futures Ltd
PO Box 602
66 Mark Lane
London EC3P 3EA
Tel: 01 480 9460
Telex: 885012
Fax: 01 480 9500

Dean Witter Futures Ltd
1 Appold St
6th Floor
Broadgate 5
London EC2A 2AA
Tel: 01 480 8500
Telex: 925380
Fax: 481 8440

Drexel Burnham Lambert Ltd
Drexel Burnham House
1 Alie St
London E1 8DB
Tel: 01 325 9797
Telex: 884845
Fax: 01 325 9431/9799

Elders Futures Inc
73 Cornhill
London EC3V 3QQ
Tel: 01 929 4009
Telex: 929115
Fax: 01 929 3706

Falcon Brokers & Investments SA
16 rue de Hesse
1211 Geneve 11
Switzerland

Fernstone Ltd
c/o Messrs, Fordyce, Curry & Co
St Bartholomew Chambers
61 West Smithfield
London EC1A 9EA
Tel: 01 606 5711

Gerald Ltd
Europe House
World Trade Centre
St Katharine By The Tower
London E1 9AA
Tel: 01 481 0681
Telex: 884377
Fax: 01 480 7369

Gill & Duffus London Ltd
St Dunstan's House
201 Borough High St
London SE1 1HW
Tel: 01 407 7050
Telex: 887162
Fax: 01 403 7050

GNI Wallace Ltd
Colechurch House
1 London Bridge Walk
London SE1 2SX
Tel: 01 378 7171
Telex: 884962
Fax: 01 407 3848

Goldman Sachs Futures Ltd
5 Old Bailey
London EC4M 7AH
Tel: 01 248 6464
Telex: 887902
Fax: 01 489 2911

Hope Commodities Ltd
Long Lodge
267–269 Kingston Rd
Merton
London SW19 3NW
Tel: 01 543 3151
Fax: 946656

LCF Ltd
3 Finsbury Square
London EC2A 1AD
Tel: 01 638 7943
Fax: 01 638 4060

LIT Futures Ltd
International House
1 St Katharine's Way
London E1 9UN
Tel: 01 481 1712
01 480 5854 (Night)
Telex: 886583
Fax: 01 488 4791

E D & F Man
Sugar Quay
Lower Thames St
London EC3R 6DU
Tel: 01 626 8788
Telex: 885431
Fax: 01 621 0149

E D & F Man International Ltd
Sugar Quay
Lower Thames St
London EC3R 6DU
Tel: 01 626 8788
Telex: 885431
Fax: 01 621 0149

Merrill Lynch Pierce Fenner & Smith
(Brokers & Dealers) Ltd
Ropemaker Place
25 Ropemaker St
London EC2Y 9LY
Tel: 01 628 1000
Telex: 8811047
Fax: 01 867 2867
also at
International House
World Trade Centre
1 St Katharine's Way
London E1 9UN

Mocatta Commercial Ltd
4 Crosby Square
London EC3A 6AQ
Tel: 01 638 5789
Telex: 887419
Fax: 01 256 7750
or 01 256 8200

Moutafian Commodities Ltd
2–4 Eastcheap
London EC3M 1AL
Tel: 01 623 3311
Telex: 886953

Muirpace Ltd
6 Lloyds Ave
London EC3N 3NX
Tel: 01 702 9776
Telex: 886309
Fax: 01 480 6115

Muirpace Holdings Ltd
6 Lloyds Ave
London EC3N 3NX
Tel: 01 407 8940
Telex: 886309
Fax: 01 480 6115

Philipp Brothers Futures Ltd
Victoria Plaza
111 Buckingham Palace Rd
London SW1W 0SL
Tel: 01 721 4000
Telex: 883801/2
Fax: 01 222 4299

Prudential-Bache (Futures) Ltd
9 Devonshire Square
London EC2M 4HP
Tel: 01 283 9166
Telex: 883251
Fax: 01 626 6785

J H Rayner (Futures) Ltd
Berisford Wing
1 Prescot St
London E1 8AZ
Tel: 01 481 9144
Telex: 883461

Refco Overseas Ltd
Europe House
World Trade Centre
East Smithfield
London E1 9AA
Tel: 01 488 3232
Telex: 887438
Fax: 01 480 7069

Rudolf Wolff & Co Ltd
2nd Floor D Section
Plantation House
31–35 Fenchurch St
London EC3M 3DX
Tel: 01 626 8765
Telex: 885034
Fax: 01 626 3939

Shearson Lehman Hutton Inc
14 Wall St
12th Floor
New York
NY 10048
USA
One Broadgate
London EC2M 7HA
Tel: 01 601 0011
Telex: 888881
Fax: 01 260 2999

Sucden (UK) Ltd
5 London Bridge St
London SE1 9SG
Tel: 01 378 6322
Telex: 883780
Fax: 01 378 6556

Thomson McKinnon Futures Ltd
Greenly House
40 Duke's Place
London EC3A 5HJ
Tel: 01 626 1511
Telex: 884562
Fax: 01 929 3338

Woodhouse Drake & Carey
(Commodities) Ltd
Three Quays
Tower Hill
London EC3R 6EP
Tel: 01 623 7575
Telex: 886271
Fax: 01 929 4343

United City Merchants Plc
Fourth Floor
2 Albert Gate
London SW1X 7JU
Tel: 01 245 9081
Telex: 8953507
Fax: 01 235 4382

The London Futures and Options Exchange

Codes: (c) = cocoa; (co) = coffee; (s) = sugar

AML Futures
c/o Donaldson Lufkin & Jenrette
140 Broadway
New York
USA
Tel: 212 312 2000
(co)

Alan J Ridge & Breminer Ltd
19–21 Great Tower St
London EC3R 5AQ
Tel: 01 623 2161
(co)

B L Oxley & Co Ltd
c/o R C L Oxley Esq
Newbridge International Ltd
39 Hatton Garden
London EC1N 8BX
(s)

Burgon Hall Ltd
4 Burgon St
London EC4V 5DR
Tel: 01 248 8121
(s)

CL-Alexanders Rouse Ltd
International House
1 St Katharine's Way
London E1 9UN
Tel: 01 481 2121
(c) (co) (s)

Cadbury Ltd
PO Box 12
Bournville
Birmingham B30 2LU
Tel: 021 458 2000
(c)

Cargill Investor Services Ltd
Staple Hall
Stone House Court
London EC3A 7AX
Tel: 01 283 5272
(c) (co)

Cargill UK Ltd
3 Shortlands
London W6 8RT
Tel: 01 741 9090
(c)

Czarnikow Futures Ltd
66 Mark Lane
London EC3P 3EA
Tel: 01 480 9300
(c) (co) (s)

Czarnikow Holdings Ltd
66 Mark Lane
London EC3P 3EA
Tel: 01 480 9300
(s)

Daarnhouwer & Co Ltd
International House
World Trade Centre
1 St Katharine's Way
London E1 9UN
Tel: 01 488 9151
(c)

Dean Witter Futures Ltd
1 Appold St
6th Floor
Broadgate 5
London EC2A 2AA
Tel: 01 480 8500
(c)

Drexel Burnham Lambert Ltd
Drexel Burnham House
1 Alie St
London E1 8DB
Tel: 01 325 9797
(c) (co) (s)

E D & F Man (Cocoa) Ltd
Sugar Quay
Lower Thames St
London EC3R 6DU
Tel: 01 623 1800
(c)

E D & F Man International Ltd
Sugar Quay
Lower Thames St
London EC3R 6DU
Tel: 01 626 8788
(co) (s)

E D & F Man Ltd
Sugar Quay
Lower Thames St
London EC3R 6DU
Tel: 01 626 8788
(s)

Frank Fehr & Co Ltd
Prince Rupert House
64 Queen St
London EC4R 1ER
Tel: 01 248 5066
(c) (co)

G W Joynson & Co Ltd
14 Trinity Square
London EC3N 4AA
Tel: 01 702 1499
(c) (co)

GNI Ltd
Colechurch House
1 London Bridge Walk
London
Tel: 01 378 7171
(c)

GNI Wallace Ltd
1 London Bridge Walk
London SE1 2SX
Tel: 01 378 7171
(c) (co) (s)

Geldermann Ltd
Plantation House
Mincing Lane
London EC3M 3DX
Tel: 01 623 9611
(c)

Gilbert J McCaul (Overseas) Ltd
Bridge House
4 Borough High St
London SE1 9QZ
Tel: 01 378 1415
(c)

Gill & Duffus London Ltd
St Dunstan's House
201 Borough High St
London SE1 1HW
Tel: 01 407 7050
(c) (co) (s)

Hecht Heyworth & Alcan Ltd
Myrtil House
70 Clifton St
London EC2A 4SP
Tel: 01 377 8773
(c)

Henry Stephens & Son (London) Ltd
Henry Stephens House
12 Minories
London EC3N 1BJ
Tel: 01 488 4754
(c) (co)

Holco Trading Co Ltd
Sugar Quay
Lower Thames St
London EC3R 6DU
Tel: 01 623 1800
(c) (co)

Holiday Cutler Bath Ltd
c/o Deloitte Haskins & Sells
PO Box 207
128 Queen Victoria St
London EC4P 4JX
Tel: 01 236 6500
(co) (s)

J Aron & Co (UK) Ltd
7th Floor
8–10 New Fetter Lane
London EC4A 1DB
Tel: 01 489 5501
(co)

J H Rayner Futures Ltd
Berisford Wing
1 Prescot St
London E1 8AY
Tel: 01 481 9144
(c) (co) (s)

Jean Lion (Sugar) Ltd
Quay Level
Europe House
World Trade Centre
East Smithfield
London E1
Tel: 01 481 9367
(s)

LCF Ltd
Europe House
World Trade Centre
London E1 9AA
Tel: 01 265 0561
(c) (co) (s)

L M Fischel & Co Ltd
1 Marble Quay
St Katharine by the Tower
London E1 9UL
Tel: 01 481 1519
(c) (co)

LIT Futures Ltd
International House
No 1 St Katharines Way
London E1 9UN
Tel: 01 481 1712
(c) (co) (s)

Lonconex Ltd
Aldwych House
71-91 Aldwych
London WC2B 4HN
Tel: 01 242 8888
(c) (s)

Marshall French & Lucas Ltd
Plantation House
31-35 Fenchurch St
London EC3M 3DX
Tel: 01 623 7451
(c) (co)

Merrill Lynch Pierce Fenner & Smith
(Brokers & Dealers) Ltd
Ropemaker Place
25 Ropemaker St
London EC2Y 9LY
Tel: 01 628 1000
(c) (co)

Moutafian Commodities Ltd
2-4 Eastcheap
London EC3M 1AL
Tel: 01 623 3311
(c) (co) (s)

Muirpace Ltd
6 Lloyds Ave
London EC3N 3NX
Tel: 01 702 9976
(c)

Pacol Futures Ltd
Latham House
16 Minories
London EC3N 1NA
Tel: 01 488 2333
(c) (s)

Paterson Commodities Ltd
19-21 Great Tower St
London EC3R 5AQ
Tel: 01 895 8765
(c)

Philipp Brothers Futures Ltd
Victoria Plaza
111 Buckingham Palace Rd
London SW1W 0SL
Tel: 01 721 4000
(c) (co) (s)

Prudential-Bache (Futures) Ltd
Ground Floor
9 Devonshire Square
London EC2M 4HP
Tel: 01 283 9166
(c) (co)

Refco Overseas Ltd
5th Floor
Europe House
World Trade Centre
London E1 9AA
Tel: 01 488 3232
(c) (co) (s)

Rionda Futures Ltd
58 Borough High St
London SE1 1XF
Tel: 01 407 6421
(s)

Rowntree Mackintosh (Ing) Ltd
York YO1 1XY
Tel: 0904 653071
(c)

Rudolf Wolff & Co Ltd
Plantation House
31–35 Fenchurch St
London EC3M 3DX
Tel: 01 626 8765
(c) (co) (s)

S Figgis & Co (Broking) Ltd
53–54 Aldgate High St
London EC3N 1LU
Tel: 01 488 4511
(c)

S N Kurjian (Commodity Brokers) Ltd
4 Telfords Yard
6–8 The Highway
London E1 9BG
Tel: 01 488 4616
(c)

Shearson Lehman Hutton Inc
1 Broadgate
London EC2M 7HA
Tel: 01 601 0011
(c) (co)

Sime Darby Commodities Ltd
Hibernia Chambers
London Bridge
London
Tel: 01 403 1234
(c)

Socomex Futures Ltd
7th Floor
10 Old Jewry
London EC2R 8DU
Tel: 01 606 9091
(c) (co)

Sucden (UK) Ltd
5 London Bridge St
London SE1 9SG
Tel: 01 378 6322
(c) (co) (s)

Tardivat Futures Ltd
Suite No 6
Free Trade Wharf
350 The Highway
London E1 9DH
Tel: 01 265 8155
(c) (co)

The Nestle Co Ltd
St George's House
Croydon
Surrey CR9 1NR
Tel: 01 686 333
(c)

Transcontinental Affiliates Ltd
Aldwych House
71–91 Aldwych
London WC2B 4HN
Tel: 01 242 8888
(s)

Truxo Ltd
87 Worship St
London EC2A 2BE
Tel: 01 247 3411
(co)

Unidaf Trading Co Ltd
6 St Mary at Hill
London EC3R 8EE
Tel: 01 623 1991
(co)

United City Merchants Plc
4th Floor
2 Albert Gate
London SW1X 7JU
Tel: 01 245 9081
(c) (s)

V Berg & Sons Ltd
112 Union St
London SE1 0NL
Tel: 01 928 9000
(c)

W G Spice & Co Ltd
Court Mills
Hook, Nr Basingstoke
Hants RG27 9JD
Tel: 0256 722206
(c)

Wilson Smithett & Cope Ltd
PO Box 50
32 St Mary at Hill
London EC3R 8LT
Tel: 01 623 3111
(c) (co)

Woodhouse Drake & Carey
(Commodities) Ltd
Three Quays
Tower Hill
London EC3R 6EP
Tel: 01 623 7575
(c) (co) (s)

Fox Options
Authorised Floor Memberships

Mr A J Dickinson
AJD Futures Ltd
Cornhill House
60 Cornhill London EC3

Mr S Hicks
LIT Futures Ltd
International House
1 St Katharine's Way
London E1 9UN

Mr Culme-Seymour
V Berg & Sons Ltd
112 Union St
London SE1 0NL

Mr P J Gamble
CL Alexanders Rouse Ltd
International House
1 St Katharine's Way
London E1 9UN

Mr J Yuill
CRT Europe Inc
1–6 Lombard St
London EC3V 9AA

Mr J C F Parry
Capcom Financial Services Ltd
9–13 St Andrew St
London EC4A 3AE

Mr R Wands
Cargill Investor Services Ltd
Staple Hall
Stone House Court
London EC3A 7AX

Mr P Thompson
Czarnikow Futures Ltd
66 Mark Lane
London EC3P 3EA

Mr M Fox-Andrews
Drexel Burnham Lambert Ltd
Drexel Burnham House
1 Alie St
London E1 8DB

Mr P Fletcher
GNI Wallace Ltd
Colechurch House
1 London Bridge
London SE1 2SX

Mr G Perske
Gerald Ltd
Europe House
World Trade Centre
St Katharine-by-the-Tower
London E1 9AA

Mrs E Holder
Hope Commodities Ltd
Long Lodge
267–269 Kingston Rd
Merton Park
London SW19 3NW

Ms L Booth
E F Hutton & Co (London) Ltd
c/o Shearson Lehman Hutton Inc
1 Broadgate
London EC2M 7HA

Mr J D C Biggs
E D & F Man (International) Ltd
Sugar Quay
Lower Thames St
London EC3R 6DU

The Managing Director
Marshall French & Lucas Ltd
Plantation House
31–35 Fenchurch St
London EC3

Mrs C A Langham
Merrill Lynch Pierce Fenner & Smith
(Brokers & Dealers) Ltd
Merrill Lynch House
Ropemaker Place
25 Ropemaker St
London EC2Y 9LY

Mr R Legg
Mocatta Commercial Ltd
Mocatta House
4 Crosby Square
London EC3A 6AG

517

Mr J Woodcock
Muirpace Ltd
6 Lloyds Ave
London EC3N 3NX

Mr J Brackley
Prudential Bache (Futures) Ltd
9 Devonshire Square
London EC2M 4HP

Mr T Truscott
J H Rayner (Futures) Ltd
Berisford Wing
1 Prescot St
London E1 8AY

Mr B Nolan
Refco Overseas Ltd
Europe House
World Trade Centre
London E1 9AA

Mr S Hubbard
Alan J Ridge & Breminer Ltd
19-21 Great Tower St
London EC3R 5AQ

Mr I S Anderson
Rudolf Wolff & Co Ltd
2nd Floor
D Section
Plantation House
31-35 Fenchurch St
London EC3M 3DX

Mr P Lynch
Shearson Lehman Hutton Inc
1 Broadgate
London EC2M 7HA

Mr A Rapley
Socomex Futures Ltd
10 Old Jewry
London EC2R 8DU

Mr M Overlander
Sucden (UK) Ltd
5 London Bridge St
London SE1 9SG

Mr R D Wallis
Truxo Ltd
87 Worship St
London EC2A 2BD

Mr J Patterson
Woodhouse Drake & Carey
(Commodities) Ltd
Three Quays
Tower Hill
London EC3R 6EP

**The London International Financial
Futures Exchange (LIFFE)**

MBR Members Details Report

AJD Futures Ltd
Cornhill House
60 Cornhill
London EC3
Tel: 01 623 1782

AOT (London) Ltd
c/o 37 Lombard St
London EC3V 9PE
Tel: 01 588 2004
Telex: 265704

Adams Viner Mosler (UK) Ltd
48 Limerston St
London SW10 0HH
Tel: 01 352 8512

Adrian Bone (Financial Futures) Ltd
c/o Box 'ABF'
LIFFE Ltd
Royal Exchange
London EC3V 3PJ
Tel: 01 623 0383

Al-Mal International Ltd
3 Saint James's Square
London SW1Y 4JU
Tel: 01 930 9575
Telex: 262192 ALMAL G
Fax: 839 3849

Alexanders Discount Futures Ltd
65 Cornhill
London EC3V 3PP
Tel: 01 626 5467
Telex: 883126
Fax: 01 623 1116

Allied Irish Investment Bank Plc
Bankcentre Britain
Belmont Rd
Uxbridge UB8 1SA
Middlesex
Tel: 0895 72222
Telex: 925657
Fax: 0895 39444

Amalgamated Metal Trading Ltd
Ground Floor
Adelaide House
London Bridge
London EC4R 9DT
Tel: 01 626 4521
Telex: 888704 AMTRAD G
Fax: 01 623 3982

Amoptions (Financial Futures) Ltd
1-2 Royal Exchange Bldgs
London EC3V 3LD
Tel: 01 929 0351
Telex: 934560

Andy Martin Futures Ltd
8 Whitby Ave
Ingrave
Brentwood
Essex CM13 3NT
Tel: 0277 811153

Anthony Paul Caton
Cross Stream
Whitmore Vale
Grayshott
Surrey GU26 6JB
Tel: 01 621 0780

Arbuthnot Latham Bank Ltd
131 Finsbury Pavement
Moorgate
London EC2A 1AY
Tel: 01 628 9876
Telex: 885970 ARBLDN G

Arbuthnot Stotler International Ltd
131 Finsbury Pavement
Moorgate
London EC2A 1AY
Tel: 01 628 9876
Telex: 22441 ABSI G
Fax: 01 280 8524

Argus Corp
7th Floor
Phoenix House
18 King William St
London EC3N 7SA
Tel: 01 623 8949

Australia & New Zealand Banking
Group Ltd
55 Gracechurch St
London EC3V 0BN
Tel: 01 280 3100
Telex: 8812741 ANZBK L G

BA Futures Incorporated
1 Watling St
London EC4P 4BX
Tel: 01 634 4491
Telex: 885172 BAFTRS G
Fax: 01 634 4317

BT Futures Corp
1 Appold St
Broadgate
London EC2A 2HE
Tel: 01 726 4141
Telex: 883341 BANTR G

Babcock & Brown (Financial Futures)
Ltd
Lower Ground Floor
3 Finsbury Square
London EC2A 1AD
Tel: 01 628 6115
Telex: 8953271 AML BB
Fax: 01 628 6942

Baguley Futures Ltd
Deramore House
Chalk Lane
Hyde Heath
Amersham, Bucks HP6 5SA
Tel: 01 860 5400

Balfour Maclaine International (UK) Ltd
Europe House
World Trade Centre
London E1 9AA
Tel: 01 488 9592
Telex: 889031 BALMAC G

Bank of Scotland
International Division
Treasury Department
55 Old Broad St
London EC2P 2HL
Tel: 01 628 8060
Telex: 893389 BOSLIF G

Bank of Tokyo Capital Markets Ltd
6th Floor
20-24 Moorgate
London EC2R 6DH
Tel: 01 628 3000
Telex: 883254
Fax: 01 256 9842

Banque Belge Ltd
4 Bishopsgate
London EC2N 4AD
Tel: 01 283 1080
Telex: 886604 BELBNK G

Banque Nationale de Paris Plc
PO Box 416
8–13 King William St
London EC4P 4HS
Tel: 01 895 7070
Telex: 883412 BNPLNB G
Fax: 01 929 0310

Banque Paribas Capital Markets Ltd
33 Wigmore St
London W1H 0BN
Tel: 01 355 2000
Telex: 296723/23707

Barclays de Zoete Wedd Futures Ltd
Ebbgate House
2 Swan Lane
London EC4R 3TS
Tel: 01 623 2323
Telex: 892667 BZWFUT G
Fax: 01 623 8601

Barclays de Zoete Wedd Futures Trading
Ltd
Ebbgate House
2 Swan Lane
London EC4R 3TS
Tel: 01 623 2323
Telex: 8812124 BZW G

Baring Brothers & Co Ltd
8 Bishopsgate
London EC2N 4AE
Tel: 01 283 8833
Telex: 883622 BB LDN G

Baring Securities Ltd
Lloyds Chambers
1 Portsoken St
London E1 8DF
Tel: 01 621 1500
Telex: 887741
Fax: 01 623 1012

Bomac Futures Ltd
65 Princes Ave
Woodford Green
Essex IG8 0LW
Tel: 01 505 2771

Bruce Pollock
c/o BMP Wertpapiere & Optionen
Bahnhofstrasse 52
CH-8022 Zurich
Switzerland
Tel: USA 312 786 2594

Butler Harlow (Financial Futures) Ltd
4th Floor
Adelaide House
London Bridge
London EC4R 9HN
Tel: 01 623 5222
Telex: 919410 MAACTS O

CRT Europe Inc
1–6 Lombard St
London EC3V 9DT
Tel: 01 220 7041
Telex: 946172 CRTOPS G

CL-Alexanders Rouse Ltd
International House
1 St Katharine's Way
London E1 9UN
Tel: 01 481 2121
Telex: 8950831 RWLLTD

Capcom Financial Services Ltd
Ground Floor
9–13 St Andrew St
London EC4A 3AE
Tel: 01 583 0164
Telex: 945055 CAPCOM G

Cargill Investor Services Ltd
Staple Hall
Stone House Court
London EC3A 7AX
Tel: 01 283 5272
Telex: 885453 CARGIL G
Fax: 01 929 4885

Cater Allen Futures Ltd
1 King William St
London EC4N 7AU
Tel: 01 283 7432
Telex: 929445 CAFL G

Charterhouse Bank Ltd
1 Paternoster Row
London EC4M 7DH
Tel: 01 248 4000
Telex: 884276 CB LDN G

Chase Manhattan Futures (UK) Ltd
PO Box 16 Woolgate House, 1st Floor
Coleman St
London EC2P 2HD
Tel: 01 726 7036
Telex: 8958831

Chemical Bank
180 The Strand
London WC2R 1EX
Tel: 01 379 7474
Telex: 24159 CEMBK G

Christiania Bank og Kreditkasse
Lloyds Chambers
1 Portsoken St
London E1 8RU
Tel: 01 702 1390
Telex: 8812511
Fax: 10 481 1860

Citifutures Ltd
1st Floor
7 Birchin Lane
London EC3V 9DE
Tel: 01 234 2570
Telex: 884174 CITIFT G

Commonwealth Bank of Australia
8 Old Jewry
London EC2R 8ED
Tel: 01 600 0822
Telex: 883864 CTBALN G
Fax: 01 726 2622

Continental Illinois Nat Bank & Trust
Co of Chicago
Continental Bank House
162 Queen Victoria St
London EC4V 4BS
Tel: 01 236 7444
Telex: 883620 CONTINOIS LDN
Fax: 01 860 5303

Crawley Futures Ltd
15 Sara Court
Albermarle Rd
Beckenham
Kent
Tel: 01 623 0244 (TNT)

Credit Suisse First Boston Ltd
2A Great Titchfield St
London W1P 7AA
Tel: 01 322 4662/4
Telex: 892131 CSFBG
Fax: 01 322 4170

Cresvale Ltd
4 Battlebridge Lane
London SE1 2JB
Tel: 01 357 6400
Telex: 8953714 CRESLO G
Fax: 01 357 7539

Czarnikow Futures Ltd
66 Mark Lane
London EC3P 3EA
Tel: 01 480 9300
Telex: 885011 CZAKOW G
Fax: 01 480 9416

DG Bank Deutsche Genossenschaftsbank
10 Aldersgate St
London EC1A 4XX
Tel: 01 726 6791
Telex: 886647 DG LDN

Dai-Ichi Europe Ltd
Durrant House
8–13 Chiswell St
London EC1Y 4TQ
Tel: 01 588 6075
Telex: 8813944/5 ICHILD G
Fax: 01 588 2644

Daiwa Europe Ltd
PO Box 72
5 King William St
London EC4N 7AX
Tel: 01 548 8080
Telex: 919495 DAIFUT G
Fax: 01 548 8640

David Morgan Futures Ltd
c/o Box 'MFF'
LIFFE Ltd
Royal Exchange
London EC3V 3PJ
Tel: 01 623 0525

Dean Murray Futures Ltd
49 Pert Cottages
Sandringham Gardens
Barkingside
Essex
Tel: 01 623 0244 (TNT)

Dean Witter Futures Ltd
1 Appold St
6th Floor, Broadgate 5
London EC2A 2AA
Tel: 01 480 8500
Telex: 925380
Fax: 01 956 1247

Degeld Options Ltd
c/o Box 'DGL'
LIFFE Ltd
Royal Exchange
London EC3V 3PJ

Den norske Creditbank Plc
20 St Dunstan's Hill
London EC3R 8HY
Tel: 01 621 1111
Telex: 887654 DNCLDN

Deutsche Bank AG
6 Bishopsgate
London EC2P 2AT
Tel: 01 283 4600
Telex: 884547 DEUTBK G
Fax: 01 626 1377

Dingwall Main (Near East) Ltd
International House, Level 2
1 St Katharine's Way
London E1 9UN
Tel: 01 488 2400
Telex: 884015 DINGMN G

Diocrest Ltd
c/o Box 'HSR'
LIFFE Ltd
Royal Exchange
London EC3V 3PJ
Tel: 01 623 0252

Discount Corp of New York Futures
16 St Helen's Place
London EC3A 6DE
Tel: 01 588 8283
Telex: 887610 DISLON G
Fax: 01 588 0016

Douglas Fisher
Blackbarn House
Pages Lane
Harold Wood
Essex RM3 0NL
Tel: 01 623 0507

Dresdner Bank AG
Dresdner Bank House
125 Wood St
London EC2V 7AQ
Tel: 01 606 7030
Telex: 887613 DRESBK G
Fax: 01 726 2394

Drexel Burnham Lambert Ltd
Drexel Burnham House
1 Alie St
London E1 8DB
Tel: 01 325 9797
Telex: 884845 DREBUR G
Fax: 01 325 9911

E D & F Man International Ltd
Sugar Quay
Lower Thames St
London EC3R 6DU
Tel: 01 626 8788
Telex: 885431 EDFMAN G

EXCO Futures Ltd
Sherborne House
119 Cannon St
London EC4N 5AY
Tel: 01 623 4040
Telex: 887198
Fax: 283 8450

Eastern Capital Futures Ltd
2nd Floor
Walsingham House
35 Seething Lane
London EC3N 4AH
Tel: 01 488 1761
Telex: 255680 ECAP LG

Elders Finance Group UK Ltd
73 Cornhill
London EC3V 3QQ
Tel: 01 929 4009
Telex: 929620
Fax: 01 929 3706

First Chicago Futures Inc
First Chicago House
90 Long Acre
London WC2E 9RB
Tel: 01 240 7240
Telex: 887716 FNBCLK G

First Continental Trading Ltd
Suite 2200
30 S Wacker Drive
Chicago, Illinois 60606
USA
Tel: 0101 312 559 8895
Telex: 510 600 2243
Fax: 01 628 1293

First Options of Chicago Ltd
Continental Bank House
162 Queen Victoria St
London EC4V 4BS
Tel: 01 860 5400
Fax: 01 860 5101

Fulton Prebon Futures Ltd
34-40 Ludgate Hill
London EC4M 7JT
Tel: 01 248 3242
Telex: 8954252 FULTON G
Fax: 01 236 2372

GNI Ltd
Colechurch House
1 London Bridge Walk
London SE1 2SX
Tel: 01 378 7171
Telex: 884962 INTER G

GNI Wallace Ltd
Colechurch House
1 London Bridge Walk
London SE1 2SX
Tel: 01 378 7171
Telex: 884962 INTER G

GNP Commodities Incorporated
30 South Wacker Drive
Suite 900
Chicago, Illinois 60606
USA
Tel: USA 312 930 7800
Telex: 23 206188 GNP CGO

Gedon Hertshten
48 Argaman
Ramat Efal
Israel
Tel: 010 9723355553

Geldermann Ltd
4th Floor
Plantation House
Mincing Lane
London EC3M 3DX
Tel: 01 623 9611
Telex: 8950781 GELDER G

Gerald Ltd
Europe House
World Trade Centre
St Katharine by the Tower
London EC1A 7LD
Tel: 01 481 0681
Telex: 884377

Gerrard & National Ltd
33 Lombard St
London EC3V 9BQ
Tel: 01 623 9981
Telex: 884104 GERNAT G
Fax: 01 623 6173

Gill & Duffus Ltd
St Dunstan's House
201 Borough High St
London SE1 1HW
Tel: 01 407 7050
Telex: 887162 GILDUF G

Girobank Plc
10 Milk St
London EC2V 8JH
Tel: 01 600 6020
Telex: 885700 GIROH G

Goldman Sachs Futures Ltd
5 Old Bailey
London EC4M 7AH
Tel: 01 248 6464
Telex: 934431 ARON UK

Gourlay Wolff Futures Ltd
116 Borough High St
London SE1 1LB
Tel: 01 403 0582
Telex: 886926 GWLOND G

Gover Horowitz & Blunt Ltd
Grosvenor Gardens House
35-37 Grosvenor Gardens
London SW1W 0BS
Tel: 01 630 7777
Telex: 8953671 GHBCO G

Hambros Bank Ltd
41 Tower Hill
London EC3N 4HA
Tel: 01 480 5000
Telex: 884637
Fax: 01 702 4424

Harris Futures Corp
Bucklersbury House
1st Floor
3 Queen Victoria St
London EC4N 8EL
Tel: 01 248 0364
Telex: 190204

Henning-Krajewski Trading Inc
141 West Jackson Blvd
Suite 1920
Chicago, Illinois 60604
USA
Tel: 0101 312 341 7815
Fax: 0101 312 341 7801

Hill Samuel Bank Ltd
100 Wood St
London EC2P 2AJ
Tel: 01 628 8011
Telex: 888822 HSAMUK G
Fax: 01 606 6681

International Clearing Services Ltd
37 Lombard St
London EC3V 9PE
Tel: 01 283 7061
Telex: 265704
Fax: 01 283 2659

International Option Investment Ltd
c/o ICS Ltd
37 Lombard St
London EC3V 9PE
Tel: 01 283 7061
Telex: 2657044

Irving Trust Co
46 Berkeley St
London W1X 6AA
Tel: 01 499 1234
Telex: 883265/6

J H Rayner (Futures) Ltd
Berisford Wing
1 Prescot St
London E1 8AY
Tel: 01 481 9144
Telex: 883461 RAYMAR G

J Henry Schroder Wagg & Co Ltd
120 Cheapside
London EC2V 6DS
Tel: 01 382 6220
Telex: 888681 SWFOEX G

J P Morgan Futures Inc
Morgan House
1 Angel Court
London EC2R 7AE
Tel: 01 606 4321
Telex: 8955711 MFCLO G

James Capel CM & M (UK) Ltd
7 Devonshire Square
London EC2M 4HT
Tel: 01 621 0792
Telex: 919968 CMMLDNG
Fax: 01 621 0567

John Jackson
34 Camden Rd
Bexeley
Kent DA5 3NU
Tel: 0322 522197

John Massey
33 Durlston Rd
London E5 8RP
Tel: 01 806 4265

Julius Baer International Ltd
Bevis Marks House
Bevis Marks
London EC3A 7NE
Tel: 01 623 4211
Telex: 887272 BAER G

Kas Clearing Agent Ltd
Suite 560
Salisbury House
29 Finsbury Circus
London EC2M 5NU
Tel: 01 588 6400
Fax: 01 528 8829

Kesperry Ltd
30–32 Tabard St
London SE1 4JU
Tel: 01 407 3572
Telex: 8951464 KESPRY G

Kevin G Thomas
c/o First Options of Chicago
1–2 Royal Exchange Bldgs
London EC3V 3LD
Tel: 01 860 5400

Kidder Peabody International Ltd
107 Cheapside
London EC2V 6DD
Tel: 01 480 8200
Telex: 884694 KPSEC G

Kleinwort Benson Ltd
(trdg as K'wort G'son Futures)
PO Box 560
20 Fenchurch St
London EC3P 3DB
Tel: 01 623 8000
Telex: 888531 KLNWRT G

Kreider Futures Ltd
c/o Box 'KDL'
LIFFE Ltd
Royal Exchange
London EC3V 3PJ
Tel: 01 256 8757/8931

Kyte Futures Ltd
13 Gordon Ave
Stanmore
Middlesex
HA7 3QE
Tel: 01 954 7661

LCF Ltd
Europe House
World Trade Centre
London E1 9AA
Tel: 01 265 0561
Fax: 01 265 1980

LIT Futures Ltd
International House
World Trade Centre Level 2
1 St Katharine's Way
London E1 9UN
Tel: 01 481 1712
Telex: 887275 LITEUR G
Fax: 01 480 7615

Lloyds Bank Financial Futures Ltd
Faryners House
25 Monument St
London EC3R 8BQ
Tel: 01 283 1000
Telex: 9413559 LMB FFG

M C Brackenbury & Co Ltd
19 St Mary-at-Hill
London EC3R 8EE
Tel: 01 623 5701
Telex: 883304 MCB G
Fax: 01 623 7806

MGA (London) Ltd
Suite No 528
Salisbury House
London Wall
London EC2M 5SH
Tel: 01 638 8381

Madoff Securities International Ltd
43 London Wall
London EC2M 5TB
Tel: 01 374 0898
Telex: 947639

Manufacturers Hanover Ltd
7 Princes St
London EC2P 2EN
Tel: 01 600 4585
Telex: 884901 MANLTD G
Fax: 01 489 9337

Mark C Stanton
c/o First Options of Chicago
3rd Floor
1–2 Royal Exchange Bldgs
London EC3P 3LD
Tel: 01 860 5400

Merrill Lynch Pierce Fenner & Smith
(B & D) Ltd
2nd Floor
Ropemaker Place
25 Ropemaker St
London EC2Y 9LY
Tel: 01 628 1000
Telex: 8811047 MERLYN G

Midland Montagu Futures/Div Midland
Bank Plc
Midland Bank plc
Fin Futures Unit, Gp Treasury
10 Lower Thames St
London EC3R 6AE
Tel: 01 283 7074
Telex: 8955467 MIDFTC G

Million Trading Co Ltd
4-3-10 Toranomon
Minato-Ku
Tokyo
105 Japan
Tel: 03 436 2311
Telex: 0242 2515

Minat Incorporated
Flat No 1
79 Harcourt Terrace
London SW10
Tel: 01 283 7922

Morgan Grenfell & Co Ltd
5th Floor
20 Finsbury Circus
London EC2M 7HH
Tel: 01 826 7323
Telex: 8953511
Fax: 01 826 6045

Morgan Stanley International
Colegrave House
70 Werners St
London W1P 3AE
Tel: 01 709 3000
Telex: 8812564
Fax: 01 709 3921

Morgan Sussex Ltd
c/o Box 'MSL'
LIFFE Ltd
Royal Exchange
London EC3V 3PJ
Tel: 01 623 0533

Muirpace Ltd
6 Lloyds Ave
London EC3N 3NX
Tel: 01 702 9776
Telex: 886309 MURPCE G
Fax: 480 6115

N M Rothschild & Sons Ltd
PO Box 185
New Court
St Swithin's Lane
London EC4P 4DU
Tel: 01 280 5000
Telex: 888031 NMR B G

National Westminster Financial Futures
Ltd
41 Threadneedle St
London EC2R 8AP
Tel: 01 920 5543
Telex: 8952881 NWBIFF G

New Japan Securities Europe Ltd
4 Fenchurch St
London EC3M 3AL
Tel: 01 626 7855
Telex: 883066 NJELDN G
Fax: 01 929 4637

Nippon Kangyo Kakumaru (Europe) Ltd
5th Floor
Garden House
18 Finsbury Circus
London EC2M 7AT
Tel: 01 638 4871
Telex: 886221 KANGYO G

Nomura International Ltd
Nomura House
24 Monument St
London EC3R 8AJ
Tel: 01 283 8811
Telex: 883119 NOMURA G

O'Connor Securities Ltd
Level 16
City Tower
40 Basinghall St
London EC2V 5DE
Tel: 01 374 4545
Fax: 01 628 9528

Okasan International (Europe) Ltd
5 Devonshire Square
London EC2M 4YD
Tel: 01 626 1682
Telex: 8811131

P C Barnett
c/o Box 'PCB'
LIFFE Ltd
Royal Exchange
London EC3V 3PJ
Tel: 01 929 0351

PK English Trust Co Ltd
4 Fore St
London EC2Y 5EH
Tel: 01 628 66263
Telex: 8814900

Paine Webber International Futures Ltd
1 Finsbury Ave
London EC2M 2PA
Tel: 01 377 0055
Telex: 297361 PWINT G

Panmure Gordon Financial Futures Ltd
9 Moorfields Highwalk
London EC2Y 9DS
Tel: 01 638 4010
Telex: 883832 PANGOR G

Prudential-Bache (Futures) Ltd
9 Devonshire Square
London EC2M 4HP
Tel: 01 283 9166
Telex: 928413 BACHE G

R P Martin Futures Ltd
4 Deans Court
London EC4V 5AA
Tel: 01 600 8691
Telex: 8952865 MARTIN G

Refco Incorporated
c/o Refco Overseas Ltd
5th Floor, Europe House
World Trade Centre
London E1 9AA
Tel: 01 488 3232
Telex: 887438 REFCO G
Fax: 01 480 7069

Refco Overseas Ltd
5th Floor, Europe House
World Trade Centre
London E1 9AA
Tel: 01 488 3232
Telex: 887438 REFCO G
Fax: 01 480 7069

Republic National Bank of New York
30 Monument St
London EC3R 8NB
Tel: 01 860 3000
Telex: 889217
Fax: 01 623 2866

Resource Trading Group
c/o Gerald Ltd
World Trade Centre
St Katharine by the Tower
London E1 9AA
Tel: 01 481 0681
Telex: 884377
Fax: 01 480 7369

Riggs AP Bank Ltd
PO Box 141
21 Great Winchester St
London EC2N 2HH
Tel: 01 588 7575
Telex: 888218 BANKAP G
Fax: 01 920 9457

Robert Dekker Ltd
Kas Clearing Agent Ltd
Salisbury House
London Wall
London EC2M 5NU
Tel: 01 588 6400
Telex: 01 528 8829

Robert Fleming & Co Ltd
25 Copthall Ave
London EC2R 7DR
Tel: 01 638 5858
Telex: 297451 FLEDGE G

Rudolf Wolff & Co Ltd
2nd Floor D Section
Plantation House
31-35 Fenchurch St
London EC3M 3DX
Tel: 01 626 8765
Telex: 885034

S & W Futures Ltd
c/o Box 'S&W'
LIFFE Ltd
Royal Exchange
London EC3V 3PJ
Tel: 01 623 0502

S Aikin Futures Ltd
c/o Box 'SEL'
LIFFE Ltd
Royal Exchange
London EC3V 3PJ
Tel: 01 860 5400
Telex: 934560 FOCLTD G

S G Warburg Futures & Options Ltd
1 Finsbury Ave
London EC2M 2PA
Tel: 01 606 1066
Telex: 8952485

Socden (UK) Ltd
5 London Bridge St
London SE1 9SG
Tel: 01 378 6322
Telex: 883780 COMFIN G

Salomon Brothers International Ltd
Victoria Plaza
111 Buckingham Palace Rd
London SW1W 0SB
Tel: 01 721 2000
Telex: 886441 SALBRO G

Sanwa International Ltd
PO Box 245
1 Undershaft
London EC3A 8BR
Tel: 01 623 7991
Telex: 887132

Saudi International Bank
99 Bishopsgate
London EC2M 3TB
Tel: 01 638 2323
Telex: 8812261 SAUDI G

Scandinavian Bank Group plc
Scandinavian House
2-6 Cannon St
London EC4M 6XX
Tel: 01 236 6090
Telex: 889093 SBL BK G

Shearson Lehman Hutton Inc
5th Floor
One Broadgate
London EC2M 7HA
Tel: 01 601 0011
Telex: 888881 SAE LON G
Fax: 01 260 2999

Societe Generale
PO Box 513
60 Gracechurch St
London EC3V 0HD
Tel: 01 626 1201
Telex: 888077 SOCGEN G

Socomex Ltd
10 Old Jewry
London EC2R 8DU
Tel: 01 606 9091
Telex: 8814835

Standard Chartered Bank
IBD Financial Futures
22 Billiter St
London EC3A 2BE
Tel: 01 280 6347
Telex: 885951 SCBL G

Swiss Bank Corp
Swiss Bank House
1 High Timber St
London EC4V 3SB
Tel: 01 329 0329
Telex: 88 7434 SBCOG
Fax: 01 329 8700

The Bank of Nova Scotia
Scotia House
33 Finsbury Square
London EC2A 1BB
Tel: 01 638 5644
Telex: 885188 BNSLDN G

The Bank of Tokyo Ltd
4th Floor
20-24 Moorgate
London EC2R 6DH
Tel: 01 628 7337
Telex: 884673
Fax: 01 588 0836

The Bank of Yokohama Ltd
40 Basinghall St
London EC2V 5DE
Tel: 01 628 9973
Fax: 887995 HAMAGI G

The Chuo Trust & Banking Co Ltd
Dealing Room, 10th Floor
Woolgate House
Coleman St
London EC2R 5AT
Tel: 01 726 6050
Telex: 8812700 CHUOLN G

The Dai-Ichi Kangyo Bank Ltd
DKB House
24 King William St
London EC4R 9DB
Tel: 01 283 0929
Telex: 884042/885521
Fax: 01 929 3319

The Daiwa Bank Ltd
PO Box 70
Commercial Union Bldg
St Helen's, 1 Undershaft
London EC3A 8JJ
Tel: 01 623 8200
Telex: 886569 DIWABK G
Fax: 01 623 2718

The Fuji Bank Ltd
25–31 Moorgate
London EC2R 6HQ
Tel: 01 628 4477
Telex: 886352 FUJIBK G

The Hokkaido Takushoku Bank Ltd
Garrard House
31–45 Gresham St
London EC2V 7ED
Tel: 01 606 8961
Telex: 888840 TAKULD G

The Industrial Bank of Japan Ltd
Bucklersbury House
14 Walbrook
London EC4N 8BR
Tel: 01 236 8310
Telex: 885393 IBJLFX G

The Kyowa Bank Ltd
Princes House
93–95 Gresham St
London EC2V 7NA
Tel: 01 606 8795
Telex: 885452 KYOWA G

The Long Term Credit Bank of Japan
Ltd
18 King William St
London EC4N 7BR
Tel: 01 623 9511
Telex: 885305 LTCBLD G

The Mitsubishi Bank Ltd
Atlas House
1 King St
London EC2V 8LQ
Tel: 01 606 6644
Telex: 8958931 BISHIBK G

The Mitsubishi Trust & Banking Corp
24 Lombard St
London EC3V 9AJ
Tel: 01 929 2323
Telex: 887208 MTBCLN G
Fax: 01 929 1905/6

The Mitsui Bank Ltd
Ground and 1st Floor
6 Broadgate
London EC2M 2RQ
Tel: 01 638 3131
Telex: 888519 MTUIBK G

The Mitsui Trust & Banking Co Ltd
5th Floor
6 Broadgate
London EC2M 2TB
Tel: 01 638 0841
Telex: 920280
Fax: 01 588 6910

The Nikko Securities Co (Europe) Ltd
55 Victoria St
London SW1H 0EU
Tel: 01 799 2222
Telex: 884717 NIKOSE G
Fax: 01 222 3605

The Nippon Credit Bank Ltd
City Tower
40 Basinghall St
London EC2V 5DE
Tel: 01 638 6411
Telex: 893273 NCBLDN G

The Royal Bank of Scotland Plc
Treasury Division
67 Lombard St
London EC3P 3DL
Tel: 01 623 4356
Telex: 885571 RBSFXA

The Saitama Bank Ltd
London Branch
30 Cannon St
London EC4M 6XH
Tel: 01 248 9421
Telex: 886400 SINGIN G
Fax: 01 248 3862

The Sanwa Bank Ltd
Commercial Union Bldg
1 Undershaft
London EC3A 8LA
Tel: 01 283 5252
Fax: 888350 SANBKL G

The Sumitomo Bank Ltd
Temple Court
11 Queen Victoria St
London EC4 4TA
Tel: 01 236 4761
Telex: 888174 SUMTFX G
Fax: 01 236 0049

529

The Sumitomo Trust & Banking Co Ltd
62–63 Threadneedle St
London EC2R 8BR
Tel: 01 628 5621
Telex: 888924 SMITR G

The Taiyo Kobe Bank Ltd
Commercial Union Bldg
1 Undershaft
London EC3A 8TB
Tel: 01 621 1430
Telex: 883513/884521
Fax: 01 621 1870

The Tokai Bank Ltd
99 Bishopsgate
London EC2M 3TA2
Tel: 01 283 8500
Telex: 887375 TOKAIL G
Fax: 01 626 0020

The Toyo Trust & Banking Co Ltd
Bucklersbury House, 5th Floor
83 Cannon St
London EC4N 8AJ
Tel: 01 236 4020
Telex: 885619 TYTBRL G

The United Bank of Kuwait Plc
3 Lombard St
London EC3V 9DT
Tel: 01 626 3422
Telex: 888441 BANKUW G

Thomson McKinnon Futures Ltd
Greenly House
40 Dukes Place
London EC3A 5HJ
Tel: 01 626 1511
Telex: 884562 TOMKIN G
Fax: 01 929 3338

Tubby Financial Futures Ltd
c/o Box 'M&T'
LIFFE Ltd
Royal Exchange
London EC3V 3PJ
Tel: 01 929 3909

Tullett & Tokyo (Futures & Traded
Options) Ltd
Bucklersbury House
2nd Floor
83 Cannon St
London EC4
Tel: 01 895 9595
Telex: 884045 TULRIL G
Fax: 01 248 3662

UBS Phillips & Drew Futures Ltd
100 Liverpool St
London EC2M 2RH
Tel: 01 901 1292
Telex: 92 3333 UBSPDW
Fax: 01 901 2345

Union Discount Futures Ltd
39 Cornhill
London EC3V 3NU
Tel: 01 623 1020
Telex: 262220 UDISEC G

Van Lessen Richardson & Co Ltd
Headland House
7–9 Solebay St
London E1 4PW
Tel: 01 790 2023
Telex: 885009 VLRCO G

Venetsianos Kakkavas
68 Fitzgeorge Ave
London W14
Tel: 01 581 2303

Wallace Smith Interfutures/Div Br
Trusts Assoc Ltd
77 London Wall
London EC2N 1AB
Tel: 01 638 6444
Telex: 887379 WST GIL G
Fax: 01 588 1413

Westdeutsche Landesbank Girozentrale
51 Moorgate
London EC2R 6AE
Tel: 01 638 6141
Telex: 887984 WESTLB G

Westpac Banking Corp
Walbrook House
23 Walbrook
London EC4N 8LD
Tel: 01 626 4500
Telex: 888641 WBANK G
Fax: 01 623 9428

Williams de Broe Futures Ltd
PO Box 515
6 Broadgate
London EC2M 2RP
Tel: 01 588 7511
Telex: 893277G
Fax: 01 588 4970

Woodhouse Drake & Carey
(Commodities) Ltd
Three Quays
Tower Hill
London EC3R 6EP
Tel: 01 623 7575
Telex: 886271

Yamaichi International (Europe) Ltd
Finsbury Court
111–117 Finsbury Pavement
London EC2A 1EQ
Tel: 01 638 5599
Telex: 887414 YSCLDN G
Fax: 01 374 8485

Yasuda Trust Europe Ltd
1 Liverpool St
London EC2M 7NH
Tel: 01 256 6188
Telex: 915192 YTELTDG
Fax: 01 374 0831

London Jute Association

Bunge & Co Ltd
Bunge House
St Mary Axe
London EC3

Bunzl & Biach (British) Ltd
215 Marsh Rd
Pinner
Middlesex
HA5 5NE

Louis Dreyfus & Co Ltd
65 Kingsway
London WC2B 6TD

J C Duffus & Co (London) Ltd
St Clare House
30–33 Minories
London EC3N 1LN

East Indian Produce Co Ltd
Works Rd
Letchworth
Herts

Douglas Fraser & Sons Ltd
61–2 London Fruit Exchange
Brushfield St
London E1 6EP

The Frindon Trading Co Ltd
64 Queen St
London EC4

Jainex International Ltd
24 Southwark St
London SE1

J Mackenzie Stewart & Co Ltd
78–84 Bell St
Dundee DD1 1HW

Sethia Enterprises Ltd
2 Eyre St Hill
London EC1R 5ET

Sidlaw Yarns
Manhattan Works
Dundonald St
Dundee DD3 7PY

Wigglesworth & Co Ltd
Wigglesworth House
69 Southwark Bridge Rd
London SE1 0NG

R E B Willcox Ltd
18–25 Eldon St
London EC2M 7LA

London Metal Exchange

Associate Trade Clearing Members

Marc Rich & Co Ltd
49 Wigmore St
London W1H 9LE
Tel: 01 935 4455

Associate Broker Members

M C Brackenbury & Co Ltd
53 Monument St
19 St Mary-at-Hill
London EC3R 8EE
Tel: 01 623 5701

Gourlay Wolff Futures Ltd
116 Borough High St
London SE1 1LB
Tel: 01 403 0582

G W Joynson & Co Ltd
14 Trinity Square
London EC3N 4AA
Tel: 01 702 1499

Associate Trade Members

AM & S Europe Ltd
PO Box 237
1 Redcliff St
Bristol BS99 7EA
Tel: 0272 215491

Amalgamated Metal Corp plc
Adelaide House
London Bridge
London EC4R 9DT
Tel: 01 626 4521

Amari International plc
Amari House
52 High St
Kingston
Surrey KT1 1HN
Tel: 01 549 6122

Astra Metals Ltd
Northway House
High Rd
Whetstone
London N20 9LP
Tel: 01 446 4381

Ayrton & Partners Ltd
Friendly House
34 Galena Rd
London W6 1AA
Tel: 01 748 1258

BICC Cables Ltd
PO Box 1
Prescot
Merseyside L34 5SZ
Tel: 051 430 2000

Billiton UK Ltd
190 Strand
London WC2R 1DT
Tel: 01 257 5900

Thomas Bolton & Johnson Ltd
PO Box 1
Froghall
Stoke-on-Trent ST10 2HF
Tel: 0538 752241

Chile Copper Ltd
101–102 Centre Block
Bush House
Aldwych
London WC2B 4QU
Tel: 01 240 0221

Chloride Metals Ltd
Thorpe
Wakefield
West Yorkshire WF3 3BS
Tel: 0532 823811

Coe & Clerici Srl
Via Martin Piaggio
17–16122 Genoa
Italy
Tel: 010 3910 54891

Cookson Industrial Materials Ltd
Crescent House
Newcastle-Upon-Tyne NE99 1GE
Tel: 091 261 0161

Elders Exsud Ltd
247 Tottenham Court Rd
London W1P 0BU
Tel: 01 782 0011

'HIRSCH' Kupfer-und Messingwerke GmbH
Postfach 20 05 21
4050 Monchengladbach 2
West Germany
Tel: 010 49 21 66 2981

IMI plc
c/o IMI Refiners Ltd
James Bridge Copper Works
Darlaston Rd
Walsall WS2 9SJ
Tel: 0922 721292

INCO Ltd
PO Box 44
Royal Trust Tower
Toronto-Dominion Centre
Toronto
Canada M5K 1N4
Tel: 0101 416 7511

Jacob Metals Ltd
Clareville House
25–27 Oxendon St
London SW1Y 4EL
Tel: 01 930 6953

Leopold Lazarus Ltd
Gotch House
20–34 St Bride St
London EC4A 4DL
Tel: 01 583 8060

Lewis & Peat (Metals) Ltd
PO Box 50
32 St Mary-at-Hill
London EC3R 8LT
Tel: 01 623 3111

Lonconex Ltd
Aldwych House
71–91 Aldwych
London WC2B 4HN
Tel: 01 242 8888

Memaco Services Ltd
Zimco House
16–28 Tabernacle St
London EC2A 4BN
Tel: 01 588 6433

Metal Distributors (UK) Ltd
Binani House
35 Paul St
London EC2A 4JU
Tel: 01 628 8331

Metdist Ltd
Blossoms Inn
3–6 Trump St
London EC2V 8AR
Tel: 01 606 0463

Noranda Sales Corp Of Canada Ltd
New Zealand House
Haymarket
London SW1Y 4TH
Tel: 01 839 7601

Norddeutsche Affinerie
Aktiengesellschaft
Alsterterrasse 2
D-2000 Hamburg 36
West Germany
Tel: 010 49 40 441961

Philipp Brothers Ltd
Victoria Plaza
111 Buckingham Palace Rd
London SW1W 0SL
Tel: 01 721 4000

Philipp & Lion Ltd
Chapel Court
Chapel Place
Rivington St
London EC2A 3DQ
Tel: 01 628 3060

Pirelli General plc
PO Box 4
Western Esplanade
Southampton SO9 7AE
Tel: 0703 634366

Possehl Erzkontor GmbH
Postfach 1633
D-2400 Lubeck 1
West Germany
Tel: 010 49 451 1480

Primary Industries (UK) Ltd
Carrier House
1–9 Warwick Row
London SW1E 5ER
Tel: 01 834 6767

Richmond Metal Co Ltd
Dellbow Rd
North Feltham Trading Estate
Feltham
Middlesex TW14 0SQ
Tel: 01 890 0981

Richmond Metal Trading Ltd
Dellbow Rd
Feltham
Middlesex TW14 0SQ
Tel: 01 890 0981

Sherritt Metals Marketing Co
PO Box 28
Commerce Court West
Toronto
Ontario
Canada M5L 1B1
Tel: 0101 416 366 0236

David L Threlkeld & Co Inc
The Carriage House
41 South Main St
Randolph VT 05060
USA
Tel: 0101 802 728 4471

Associate Broker Clearing Members

ABB Futures (UK) Ltd
11a West Halkin St
London SW1X 8JL
Tel: 01 235 1389

Balfour Maclaine International (UK) Ltd
Europe House
World Trade Centre
London E1 9AA
Tel: 01 488 9592

C A & L Bell Commodities Corp Pty
Ltd
Level 28, Nauru House
80 Collins St
Melbourne 3000
Australia
Tel: 010 61 36 543677

CL-Alexanders Rouse Ltd
International House
1 St Katharine's Way
London E1 9UN
Tel: 01 481 2121

CRT Europe Inc
1-6 Lombard St
London EC3V 9DT
Tel: 01 220 7041

Dean Witter Futures Ltd
6th Floor
1 Appold St
Broadgate 5
London EC2A 2AA
Tel: 01 480 8500

Geldermann Ltd
Plantation House
Mincing Lane
London EC3M 3DX
Tel: 01 623 9611

GNI Ltd
Colechurch House
1 London Bridge Walk
London SE1 2SX
Tel: 01 378 7171

LIT Futures Ltd
International House
1 St Katherine's Way
London E1 9UN
Tel: 01 481 1712

E D & F Man International Ltd
Sugar Quay
Lower Thames St
London EC3R 6DU
Tel: 01 626 8788

Merrill Lynch Pierce Fenner & Smith
(Brokers & Dealers) Ltd
Ropemaker Place
25 Ropemaker St
London EC2Y 9LY
Tel: 01 628 1000

F Murphy (Metals) Ltd
Brunswick St
Leicester LE1 2BA
Tel: 0533 29252

Paine Webber International Futures Ltd
1 Finsbury Ave
London EC2M 2PA
Tel: 01 377 0055

Prudential-Bache (Futures) Ltd
9 Devonshire Square
London EC2M 4HP
Tel: 01 283 9166

J H Rayner (Futures) Ltd
Berisford Wing
1 Prescot St
London E1 8AY
Tel: 01 481 9144

Sucden (UK) Ltd
5 London Bridge St
London SE1 9SG
Tel: 01 378 6322

Thomson McKinnon Futures Ltd
Greenly House
40 Duke's Place
London EC3A 5HJ
Tel: 01 626 1511

Ring Dealing Members

Amalgamated Metal Trading Ltd
Ground Floor
Adelaide House
London Bridge
London EC4R 9DT
Tel: 01 626 4521

Anglo Chemical Metals Ltd
'E' Section Ground Floor
Plantation House
5-8 Mincing Lane
London EC3M 3DX
Tel: 01 721 4000

Billiton-Enthoven Metals Ltd
84 Fenchurch St
London EC3M 4BY
Tel: 01 480 7290

Brandeis (Brokers) Ltd
4 Fore St
London EC2P 2NU
Tel: 01 638 5877

Cerro Metals (UK) Ltd
Devonshire House
146 Bishopsgate
London EC2M 4JX
Tel: 01 377 8050

Charles Davis (Metal Brokers) Ltd
9-13 Fenchurch Bldgs
London EC3M 5HR
Tel: 01 702 9735

Deak International Trading (UK) Ltd
'B' Section 6th Floor
Plantation House
5-8 Mincing Lane
London EC3M 3AR
Tel: 01 283 6362

Drexel Burnham Lambert Ltd
Drexel Burnham House
1 Alie St
London E1 8DB
Tel: 01 325 9797

Entores (Metal Brokers) Ltd
No 1 Singer St
London EC2A 4BQ
Tel: 01 962 0933

Gerald Ltd
Europe House
World Trade Centre
St Katharine by the Tower
London E1 9AA
Tel: 01 481 0681

Lazmet Ltd
7th Floor
Roman House
Wood St
London EC2Y 5BA
Tel: 01 638 3181

Metallgesellschaft Ltd
4th Floor
Three Quays
Tower Hill
London EC3R 6DS
Tel: 01 626 4221

Metdist Trading Ltd
Blossoms Inn
3-6 Trump St
London EC2V 8AR
Tel: 01 606 8321

Mocatta Commercial Ltd
Mocatta House
4 Crosby Square
London EC3A 6AQ
Tel: 01 638 5789

Refco Overseas Ltd
Europe House
World Trade Centre
East Smithfield
London E1 9AA
Tel: 01 488 3232

Sharps Pixley Ltd
10 Rood Lane
London EC3M 8BB
Tel: 01 623 8000

Shearson Lehman Hutton Commodities Ltd
One Broadgate
London EC2M 7HA
Tel: 01 601 0011

Sogemin (Metals) Ltd
4th Floor
98 Cannon St
London EC4N 6EN
Tel: 01 621 0330

Triland Metals Ltd
Bow Bells House
Bread St
London EC4M 9BQ
Tel: 01 236 5551

Rudolf Wolff & Co Ltd
'D' Section 2nd Floor
Plantation House
31–35 Fenchurch St
London EC3M 3DX
Tel: 01 626 8765

The Tea Brokers' Association of London

Full Members

Haines & Co (London) Ltd
Central House
32–66 High St
Stratford
London E15 2PD
Tel: 555 4227/8

Thompson, Lloyd & Ewart
Sir John Lyon House
Upper Thames St
London EC4V 3LU
Tel: 248 6631

Geo White & Co
84 Middlesex St
London E1 7EZ
Tel: 247 1161/4

Wilson, Smithett & Co
Sir John Lyon House
Upper Thames St
London EC4V 3LS
Tel: 236 0611

Associate Members

J W Clark & Co
Brooks House
48 Upper Thames St
London EC4V 3LJ
Tel: 248 6685

Percy Moss & Co Ltd
Sir John Lyon House
Upper Thames St
London EC4V 3NA
Tel: 236 3715/6

United States of America

Kansas City Board of Trade

Class A Members

(Symbols Denote: * Lessor ** Lessee)

Allen, William R Jr
Union Equity Cooperative Exchange
PO Box 3408, Enid
OK 73702
Tel: 405 233 5100

Andres, Robert R Jr
Prudential-Bache Securities Inc
4800 Main, Suit 333A, Kansas City
MO 64112
Tel: 816 756 2922

Artigas, Jose J
Prudential-Bache Securities Inc
4800 Main, Suite 333A, Kansas City
MO 64112
Tel: 816 756 2922

Attebury, Sam L
Attebury Grain Inc
PO Box 2707, Amarillo
TX 79105
Tel: 806 335 1639

Balthazor, Roland E
Staley Commodities Intl Inc
4800 Main, Suite 300 Kansas City
MO 64112
Tel: 816 561 0610

Barker, James T
International Multifoods Corp
4800 Main, Suite 258, Kansas City
MO 64112
Tel: 816 931 2875

Barre, J J
Term Commodities
PO Box 10924, Shawnee Mission
KS 66210
Tel: 913 345 2111

Bartlett, Paul D Jr
Bartlett & Co
4800 Main, Suite 600, Kansas City
MO 64112
Tel: 816 753 6300

Barton, Breck
Cargill Inc
4800 Main, Suite 530, Kansas City
MO 64112
Tel: 816 756 0587

Batte, Robert E
Bunge Corp
300 Southwest Blvd, Kansas City
KS 66103
Tel: 913 236 6500

Baumgartner, J F
Simonds-Shields-Theis Grain Co
4800 Main, Suite 401, Kansas City
MO 64112
Tel: 816 561 4155

Benschoter, Bruce A
Bunge Corp
300 Southwest Blvd, Kansas City
KS 66103
Tel: 913 236 6500

Berg, Robert
Bartlett Futures Inc
4800 Main, Suite 460, Kansas City
MO 64112
Tel: 816 753 6300

Bisang, Frank A
Garnac Grain Co Inc
PO Box 59, Kansas City
MO 64141
Tel: 913 661 6100

Blake, Michael J
Individual
3948½, West 50th St, Edina
MN 55424
Tel: 612 929 5372

Bosley, Jim Jr
Wolcott & Lincoln Inc
4800 Main, Suite 565, Kansas City
MO 64112
Tel: 816 753 6750

** Bradley, Harold
Individual
6409 W 125th St, Overland Park
KS 66209
Tel: 913 491 6572

Burdett, Thomas V
ADM Milling Co
4800 Main, Suite G-29, Kansas City
MO 64112
Tel: 816 491 9400

Carmody, Philip J
Lincoln Grain Inc
1900 W 47th Pl, #406,
Shawnee Mission, KS 66205
Tel: 816 677 1414

Carter, John L
Individual
4800 Main, Suite 200, Kansas City
MO 64112
Tel: 816 753 7800

Carter, John Mark
Continental Grain
PO Box 419036, Kansas City
MO 64141
Tel: 816 756 2550

Cernich, Thomas G
T G Cernich Corp
4800 Main, Suite 260, Kansas City
MO 64112
Tel: 816 756 0011

Crawford, David P
Individual
4800 Main, Suite 203, Kansas City
MO 64112
Tel: 816 531 3430

Daly, Paul Russ
Cargill Inc
4800 Main, Suite 530, Kansas City
MO 64112
Tel: 816 756 0587

Dawson, Ronald L
Simonds-Shields-Theis Grain Co
4800 Main, Suite 401, Kansas City
MO 64112
Tel: 816 561 4155

Dean, R L
Seaboard Corp
PO Box 2972, Shawnee Mission
KS 66201
Tel: 913 676 8800

Deardoff, Harold L
Garvey Elevators Inc
Box 1948, Hutchinson
KS 67504
Tel: 316 662 5411

DeBruce, Paul E
DeBruce Grain Inc
PO Box 10670, Gladstone
MO 64118
Tel: 816 436 8182

Deeds, Craig N
C Deeds Inc
4800 Main, Suite 241, Kansas City
MO 64112
Tel: 816 753 0448

Dolan, Robert F Jr
Shearson Lehman Brothers Inc
440 S LaSalle, Suite 2200, Chicago
IL 60604
Tel: 312 207 5459

Doudrick, Robert W
Louis Dreyfus Corp
PO Box 10924, Overland Park
KS 66210
Tel: 913 345 2111

Dreher, David B
Individual
4800 Main, Suite 565, Kansas City
MO 64112
Tel: 816 753 6750

Easton, Robert G
Commodities Trading Corp Ltd
CN 850, Princeton
NJ 08542
Tel: 609 924 6500

Edelblute, Gregory F
Union Equity Coop Exchange
4800 Main, Suite 455, Kansas City
MO 64112
Tel: 816 931 6210

Engelbrecht, Earl D
BC Christopher Securities Inc
4800 Main, Suite 100, Kansas City
MO 64112
Tel: 816 932 7135

Epling, H R
Geisel Grain Co (Inc)
4800 Main, Suite 204, Kansas City
MO 64112
Tel: 816 753 4466

Erlichson, Jan P
PO Box 30285, Kansas City
MO 64112
Tel: 913 236 4396

Erwin, Dennis M
Individual
4800 Main, Suite 565, Kansas City
MO 64112
Tel: 816 753 6750

Evans, S D Sr
Evans Grain Co
PO Box 1520, Salina
KS 67402
Tel: 913 827 4484

Farmer, W Mike
Individual
4800 Main, Suite 239, Kansas City
MO 64112
Tel: 816 756 1866

Farnen, James F
Frank J Farnen & Co Inc
4800 Main, Suite 501, Kansas City
MO 64112
Tel: 816 531 5528

Farnen, William W
Frank J Farnen & Co Inc
4800 Main, Suite 501, Kansas City
MO 64112
Tel: 816 531 5528

Felts, Cornelius B Jr
Garvey Elevators Inc
PO Box 9600, Fort Worth
TX 76107
Tel: 817 335 5881

Findlay, William A Jr
WAF Inc
4800 Main, Suite 565, Kansas City
MO 64112
816 753 6750

Fjeldheim, Richard H
Merrill Lynch Futures Inc
141 W Jackson, Room 380, Chicago
IL 60604
Tel: 312 347 6505

Fielschmann, Kenneth M
Geisel Grain Co
4800 Main, Suite 204, Kansas City
MO 64112
Tel: 816 753 4466

Fleming, William A
Union Equity Coop Exchange
4800 Main, Suite 455, Kansas City
MO 64112
Tel: 816 931 6210

Frank, Richard
Richard Frank Group
4800 Main, Suite 236, Kansas City
MO 64112
Tel: 816 931 2062

Frost, James A
Continental Grain Co
PO Box 419036, Kansas City
MO 64141
Tel: 816 756 2550

Fujioka, Isao
Toshoku America Inc
551 Fifth Ave, New York
NY 10176
Tel: 212 661 5400

Geiger, Michael C
Scoular Grain Co
4800 Main, Suite 274, Kansas City
MO 64112
Tel: 816 756 1474

Geisel, Joseph S Jr
Geisel Grain Co
4800 Main, Suite 204, Kansas City, MO
64112
Tel: 816 753 4466

Getter, Henry I
Wolcott & Lincoln Inc
4800 Main, Suite 565, Kansas City
MO 64112
Tel: 816 753 6750

Gibson, Daniel L
Wolcott & Lincoln Inc
4800 Main, Suite 565, Kansas City
MO 64112
Tel: 816 753 6750

Gibson, David W
Wolcott & Lincoln Inc
4800 Main, Suite 565, Kansas City
MO 64112
Tel: 816 753 6750

Gound, John C
Staley Commodities Intl Inc
4800 Main, Suite 300, Kansas City
MO 64112
Tel: 816 561 0610

Graverson, John R
Continental Grain Co
PO Box 419036, Kansas City
MO 64141
Tel: 816 756 2550

Greenwood, James
Individual
4800 Main, Suite 326, Kansas City
MO 64112
Tel: 816 531 2253

Gregg, Joseph P
Morrison-Gregg Grain Co
4800 Main, Suite 458, Kansas City
MO 64112
Tel: 816 931 7756

Grismore, Steve D
E F Hutton & Co Inc
4800 Main, Suite 356, Kansas City
MO 64112
Tel: 816 756 2905

Gwin, John D
International Multifoods Corp
Multifoods Tower, Box 2942
Minneapolis, MN 55402
Tel: 612 340 3300

Hale, H D
ADM Milling Co
4800 Main, Suite G-29, Kansas City
MO 64112
Tel: 816 491 9400

Hansen, Hal T
Cargill Investor Services Inc
141 W Jackson, Chicago
IL 60604
Tel: 312 435 8300

Hansen, R Parker
Individual
14720 Village Drive, Olathe
KS 66062
Tel: 913 782 6212

Harrington, John R
The Pillsbury Co
4800 Main, Suite 230, Kansas City
MO 64112
Tel: 816 753 1605

Hartzell, Richard B
Individual
4800 Main, Suite 260, Kansas City
MO 64112
Tel: 816 765 0011

Haw, C L W
National Farms Inc
4800 Main, Suite 246, Kansas City
MO 64112
Tel: 816 753 4501

Hay, William W
The Pillsbury Co
Pillsbury Center, Suite 3526
Minneapolis, MN 55902
Tel: 612 330 4819

Heerman, Kenneth A
ADM Milling Co
4800 Main, Suite G-29, Kansas City
MO 64112
Tel: 816 491 9400

Herrick, Robert C
Shay Grain Co
4800 Main, Suite 358, Kansas City
MO 64112
Tel: 816 531 5320

Hesemann, Harold F
Geisel Grain Co
4800 Main, Suite 204, Kansas City
MO 64112
Tel: 816 753 4466

Hills, Donald E Jr
General Mills Inc
4800 Main, Suite 363, Kansas City
MO 64112
Tel: 816 753 2200

Hirsch, John A
Garvey Elevators Inc
PO Box 1948, Hutchinson
KS 67504-1948
Tel: 316 662 5411

House, Dale M
Lincoln Grain Inc
1900 West 47th Pl #406
Shawnee Mission, KS 66205
Tel: 913 677 1414

House, Harold E
Wolcott & Lincoln Inc
4800 Main, Suite 565, Kansas City
MO 64112
Tel: 816 753 6750

Inactive
Smoot Grain Co
4800 Main, Suite G-29, Kansas City
MO 64112
Tel: 816 931 7144

** Jennings, E Shannon
8024 Granada, Prairie Village
KS 66208
Tel: 913 648 0670

Johnson, Lawrence N
Individual
600 E 65th St, Kansas City
MO 64131
Tel: 816 361 2815

Johnson, Wayne N
J Lynch & Co
9200 Indian Creek Parkway, Suite 180
Overland Park, KS 66210
Tel: 913 451 4400

Johnson, Horace W
Barnes & Co
480 Main, Suite 262, Kansas City
MO 64112
Tel: 816 756 3450

Jordan, James B
Union Equity Coop Exchange
4800 Main, Suite 455, Kansas City
MO 64112
Tel: 816 931 6210

540

Joyce, John W
Staley Commodities Intl Inc
4800 Main, Suite 300, Kansas City
MO 64112
Tel: 816 561 0610

Katoh, Motoaki
Sumitomo Corp of America
345 Park Ave, 14th Floor, New York
NY 10154
Tel: 212 207 0809

Kearney, John J
Individual
4800 Main, Suite 335, Kansas City
MO 64112
Tel: 816 753 6750

King, J R
James R King & Co
4800 Main, Suite 200, Kansas City
MO 64112
Tel: 816 341 9485

Kingan, Terrence R
Shay Grain Co
4800 Main, Suite 358, Kansas City
MO 64112
Tel: 816 531 5320

Kiszka, Wayne A
Paine Webber Inc
208 S LaSalle, Suite 1900, Chicago
IL 60604
Tel: 312 580 8204

Knadle, Richard D
Bartlett & Co
4800 Main, Suite 600, Kansas City
MO 64112
Tel: 816 753 6300

LaPiana, Don
Cargill Investor Services Inc
4800 Main, Suite 251, Kansas City
MO 64112
Tel: 816 531 3888

Latshaw, John
International Trading Association Inc
3 Dunford Circle, Kansas City
MO 64112
Tel: 816 283 7301

Lewi, Serge B
Louis Dreyfus Corp
24 Richmond Hill Ave, Stamford
CT 06904
Tel: 203 357 8444

Littleton, Glen E
Individual
4800 Main, Suite 266, Kansas City
MO 64112
Tel: 816 931 6852

Lock, John P
Bunge Corp
300 Southwest Blvd, Kansas City
KS 66103
Tel: 913 236 6500

Lottie, Raymond F
General Mills Inc
4800 Main, Suite 363, Kansas City
MO 64112
Tel: 816 753 2200

Mack, Kevin
Geldermann Inc
One Financial Plaza, Chicago
IL 60605
Tel: 312 341 7700

Mandl, L Michael
Individual
4800 Main, Suite 335, Kansas City
MO 64112
Tel: 816 753 6750

Mandl, Richard L
The Pillsbury Co
4800 Main, Suite 230, Kansas City
MO 64112
Tel: 816 753 1605

Mantini, Dana R
Individual
4800 Main, Suite 335, Kansas City
MO 64112
Tel: 816 753 6750

Marquardt, Rock Dean
Union Equity Cooperative Exchange
4800 Main, Suite 455, Kansas City
MO 64112
Tel: 816 931 6210

Matthies, Silas L
General Mills Inc
Box 15003, Commerce Station,
Minneapolis, MN 55415
Tel: 612 540 3309

Mayer Estate, Robert J
c/o Alan H Hammerman
640 N LaSalle St, Suite 390, Chicago
IL 60610
Tel: 312 642 1322

McGinley, Conan
Individual
4800 Main, Suite 203, Kansas City
MO 64112
Tel: 816 753 7800

Merrill, Fred L
Cereal Food Processors Inc
PO Box 20, Kansas City
MO 64141
Tel: 913 262 1121

Merrill, Scott
Individual
4800 Main, Suite 232, Kansas City
MO 64112
Tel: 816 753 7800

Mesker, David W
A G Edwards & Sons Inc
One North Jefferson Ave, St Louis
MO 63103
Tel: 314 289 3000

Miller, John Dwaine
Individual
4800 Main, Suite 565, Kansas City
MO 64112
Tel: 816 753 6750

Miller, John H
Continental Grain Co
PO Box 419036, Kansas City
MO 64141
Tel: 816 756 2550

Miller, Richard D
Individual
15521 Overbrook Ln, Stanley
KS 66224
Tel: 913 897 2505

Mollner, Laurence
Dean Witter Reynolds Inc
150 S Wacker Drive, Chicago
IL 60606
Tel: 312 984 4205

Moneymaker, Richard A
Bunge Corp
300 Southwest Blvd, Kansas City
KS 66103
Tel: 913 236 6500

Mooney, Dixon B
Individual
8341 Cedar, Prairie Village
KS 66207-1817
Tel: 913 432 3395

Morrison, Roger F
ConAgra Inc
One Central Park Plaza, Omaha
NE 68102
Tel: 402 346 8004

Moyer, Jan R
Garvey International Inc
5755 S Hoover, Wichita
KS 67209
Tel: 316 522 4871

Murphy, Kevin
Individual
4800 Main, Suite 260, Kansas City
MO 64112
Tel: 816 753 7800

Myers, A H Jr
Myers & Co Inc
4800 Main, Suite 110, Kansas City
MO 64112
Tel: 816 931 8517

Newton, Anthony H
Nabisco Brands Inc
100 River Rd, East Hanover
NJ 07936
Tel: 201 503 2000

Nutt, David W
J W Nutt Co Inc
PO Box 798, N Little Rock
AR 72115
Tel: 501 376 0431

Nygaard, Terrence W
Individual
10905 W 120th St, Overland Park
KS 66213
Tel: 913 897 4129

O'Brien, Greg
Individual
12401 Horton, Overland Park
KS 66209
Tel: 816 753 7800

Odell, Thomas
Individual
4800 Main, Suite 565, Kansas City
MO 64112
Tel: 816 753 7800

Ohashi, Nobuo
Mitsui Grain Corp
10 S Wacker Dr, Suite 1965, Chicago
IL 60606
Tel: 312 993 5700

Olson, Lynn B
Continental Grain Co
PO Box 419036, Kansas City
MO 64141
Tel: 816 756 2550

Overman, Charles R
C R Overman Inc
4800 Main, Suite 241, Kansas City
MO 64112
Tel: 816 931 5144

Owens, Cynthia A
Bartlett Futures Inc
4800 Main, Suite 460, Kansas City
MO 64112
Tel: 816 753 6300

Pappan, William L
Individual
4800 Main, Suite 565, Kansas City
MO 64112
Tel: 816 753 6750

Pearson, Dodd J
Drexel Burnham Lambert Inc
4800 Main, Suite 357, Kansas City
MO 64112
Tel: 816 931 0313

Polonyl, Albin S
A S Polonyi Co
4800 Main, Suite 200, Kansas City
MO 64112
Tel: 816 931 6785

Porter, Daniel
Geldermann Inc
4800 Main, Suite 249, Kansas City
MO 64112
Tel: 816 931 7620

Presler, Martin
Smith Barney, Harris Upham & Co
333 W 34th St, 9th Floor, New York
NY 10001
Tel: 212 399 6000

Punke, Douglas
Cargill Inc
4800 Main, Suite 530, Kansas City
MO 64112
Tel: 816 756 0587

Ramsbottom, Nile D
Purina Mills Inc
1401 S Hanley Rd, St Louis
MO 63144
Tel: 314 768 4178

Richardson, George T
Richardson Greenshields/Canada Ltd
One Lombard Place, 30th Floor
Winnipeg, Canada R3BOY1
Tel: 204 934 5858

Rickel, E J
Rickel Inc
4800 Main, Suite 430, Kansas City
MO 64112
Tel: 816 561 5912

Riley, Kevin
CRT Services
4800 Main, Suite 204, Kansas City
MO 64112
Tel: 816 753 7800

Risko, Kathleen M
Bartlett Futures Inc
4800 Main, Suite 460, Kansas City
MO 64112
Tel: 816 753 6300

Romain, Edward D
Romain Grain Co
4800 Main, Suite 240, Kansas City
MO 64112
Tel: 816 531 6780

Rosevear, Robert A
Individual
11055 Cedar Pkwy, Suite 112
Overland Park, KS 66211
Tel: 913 491 6680

Ryan, Timothy J
Australian Wheat Board
630 Fifth Ave, Suite 467, New York
NY 10111
Tel: 212 307 6090

Sanderson, Phyllis M
Geldermann Inc
4800 Main, Suite 249, Kansas City
MO 64112
Tel: 816 931 7620

Saunders, Harold E, Jr
E F Hutton & Co Inc
4800 Main, Suite 356, Kansas City
MO 64112
Tel: 816 756 2905

Schlunk, Karl H
Alfred C Toepfer Intl Inc
2 Federal Plaza, 52 Duane St, New York
NY 10007
Tel: 212 425 0119

Schorie, John M
Individual
4800 Main, Suite 565, Kansas City
MO 64112
Tel: 816 753 6750

Schram, Daniel C
J Lynch & Co Inc
9200 Indian Creek Parkway, Suite 180
Overland Park, KS 66210
Tel: 913 451 4400

Schultz, Bradford A
The Pillsbury Co
PO Box 1160, St Joseph
MO 64505
Tel: 816 238 4507

Schwendiman, Larry C
Continental Grain Co
PO Box 419036, Kansas City
MO 64141
Tel: 816 756 2550

Searcy, Donald E, Jr
Staley Commodities Intl Inc
4800 Main, Suite 300, Kansas City
MO 64112
Tel: 816 561 0610

Shay, D H
Shay Grain Co
4800 Main, Suite 358, Kansas City
MO 64112
Tel: 816 531 5320

Shay, R Morgan
Shay Grain Clearing Co
4800 Main, Suite 358, Kansas City
MO 64112
Tel: 816 531 5320

Shouse, M Blair
Cargill Inc
4800 Main, Suite 530, Kansas City
MO 64112
Tel: 816 756 0587

Sidie, Jay D
ADM Investor Services
4800 Main, Suite G-29, Kansas City
MO 64112
Tel: 816 931 7144

Siegel, Matthew A
Individual
4800 Main, Suite 565, Kansas City
MO 64112
Tel: 816 753 7800

Sigourney, David F
Lincoln Grain Inc
1900 W 47th Pl, #406,
Shawnee Mission, KS 66205
Tel: 913 677 1414

Sims, William W
Ralston Purina Co
Checkerboard Square, St Louis
MO 63164
Tel: 314 982 2293

Smalley, Steven A
Cargill Inc
4800 Main, Suite 530, Kansas City
MO 64112
Tel: 816 756 0587

Smith, Chris N
The Smoot Grain Co
4800 Main, Suite G-29, Kansas City
MO 64112
Tel: 816 931 7144

Sosland, Morton I
Sosland Publishing Co
PO Box 29155, Shawnee Mission
KS 66201
Tel: 816 236 7300

Sparks, Willard R
Refco Inc
889 Ridge Lake Blvd, Memphis
TN 38119
Tel: 901 766 4600

Stettler, Hans P
Garnac Grain Co Inc
PO Box 59, Kansas City
MO 64141
Tel: 913 661 6100

Stolle, James R
International Multifoods Corp
Multifoods Tower, Box 2942
Minneapolis, MN 55402
Tel: 612 340 6676

Stone, H Franklin
Geldermann Inc
4800 Main, Suite 249, Kansas City
MO 64112
Tel: 816 931 7620

Stout, John T Jr
Dixie Portland Flour Mills Inc
PO Box 17236, Memphis
TN 38117
Tel: 901 761 1105

Stover, Roger B
Individual
4800 Main, Suite 335, Kansas City
MO 64112
Tel: 816 753 6750

Sullivan, James P
Barnes & Co
4800 Main, Suite 262, Kansas City
MO 64112
Tel: 816 756 3450

Sullivan, John J
Individual
4800 Main, Suite 249, Kansas City
MO 64112
Tel: 816 932 7000

Sweet, Richard L
Cargill Inc
4800 Main, Suite 530, Kansas City
MO 64112
Tel: 816 756 0587

Swisher, Charles H Jr
ADM Milling Co
4800 Main, Suite G-29, Kansas City
MO 64112
Tel: 816 491 9400

Teetor, Norman L
Union Equity Coop Exchange
4800 Main, Suite 455, Kansas City
MO 64112
Tel: 816 931 6210

Theis, Stephen O
Simonds-Shields-Theis Grain Co
4800 Main, Suite 401, Kansas City
MO 64112
Tel: 816 561 4155

Theis, Willis C Sr
Simonds-Shields-Theis Grain Co
4800 Main, Suite 401, Kansas City
MO 64112
Tel: 816 561 4155

Theis, Willis C Jr
S-S-T Clearing Co Inc
4800 Main, Suite 401, Kansas City
MO 64112
Tel: 816 561 4155

Thompson, Charles L
Merrill Lynch Futures Inc
801 W 47th St, Kansas City
MO 64112
Tel: 816 932 9781

Thompson, David C
Garnac Grain Co Inc
PO Box 59, Kansas City
MO 64141
Tel: 913 661 6100

Thompson, Wanda A
B C Christopher Securities Co
4800 Main, Suite 100, Kansas City
MO 64112
Tel: 816 932 7000

Tinberg, Richard W
Individual
4800 Main, Suite 243, Kansas City
MO 64112
Tel: 816 931 7620

Uhlmann, R Hugh
The Uhlmann Co
PO Box 419410, Kansas City
MO 64141
Tel: 816 221 8200

Unger, Jeffrey J
Refco Inc
4800 Main, Suite 328, Kansas City
MO 64112
Tel: 816 531 8084

Vaughn, Mark B
Index Futures Group Inc
222 W Adams, Suite 1249, Chicago
IL 60606
Tel: 312 207 5700

Vetsch, Kurt
Individual
10204 Mowhawk Lane, Leawood
KS 66206
Tel: 816 753 7800

Vogel, David J
Whitehall Clearing Corp, Futures Div
1 Financial Square, 14th Floor
New York, NY 10006
Tel: 212 804 3494

Wallace, Randall O
Farmers Commodities Corp
1900 Swift, Suite 209, N Kansas City
MO 64116
Tel: 816 842 1399

Wands, Hayden
Bartlett & Co
4800 Main, Suite 600, Kansas City
MO 64112
Tel: 816 753 6300

Warner, Jay Ryan
Cargill Inc
4800 Main, Suite 530, Kansas City
MO 64112
Tel: 816 756 0587

Wells, Bryce C
Drexel Burnham Lambert Inc
4800 Main, Suite 357, Kansas City
MO 64112
Tel: 816 931 0313

West, Michael A
Cargill Investor Services Inc
4800 Main, Suite 251, Kansas City
MO 64112
Tel: 816 531 3888

Wheeler, Eugene O
Wheeler Brothers Grain Co Inc
PO Box 29, Watonga
OK 73772
Tel: 405 623 7223

Wholf, Morrice E
Bunge Corp
300 Southwest Blvd, Kansas City
KS 66103
Tel: 913 236 6500

Williams, Richard M
Wolcott & Lincoln Futures Inc
4800 Main, Suite 565, Kansas City
MO 64112
Tel: 816 753 6750

Wilson, Robert L
Bartlett & Co
4800 Main, Suite 600, Kansas City
MO 64112
Tel: 816 753 6300

Zalewski, Gearold L
GLZ Inc
11903 Fuller, Grandview
MO 64030
Tel: 816 753 7800

Zalewski, Gearold L, Jr
Individual
4800 Main, Suite 565, Kansas City
MO 64112
Tel: 816 753 6750

Class B Members

(Symbols Denote: * Lessor ** Lessee)

Adams, Michael K
Wolcott & Lincoln Inc
4800 Main, Suite 565, Kansas City
MO 64112
Tel: 816 753 6750

Anderson, Robert
Individual
5015 Sunset Drive, Kansas City
MO 64112
Tel: 816 561 3430

Attebery, Kevin
T G Cernich Corp
4800 Main, Suite 260, Kansas City
MO 64112
Tel: 816 756 0011

Azar, Frederick
Individual
2301 W 121st St, Leawood
KS 66209
Tel: 816 753 7800

Balthazor, Roland E
Individual
4800 Main, Suite 300, Kansas City
MO 64112
Tel: 816 561 0610

Baur, Kent
Individual
235 Appletree Court, Apt 5, Columbia
MO 65203
Tel: 816 753 6750

Beck, Randy D
Refco Inc
4800 Main, Suite 328, Kansas City
MO 64112
Tel: 816 531 8084

Bellatti, Robert M
Individual
PO Box 30100, Kansas City
MO 64112
Tel: 816 753 6750

Bomstad, Michael
Barnes & Co
4800 Main, Suite 262, Kansas City
MO 64112
Tel: 816 756 3450

Bumgarner, Nora J
Individual
5812 N Cypress, Kansas City
MO 64119
Tel: 816 753 7800

Cranor, Timothy W
Cereal Food Processors Inc
PO Box 20, Kansas City
MO 64141
Tel: 913 262 1121

Dance, Jeff
Individual
4300 NW 79th Terrace, Apt 16
Kansas City, MO 64151
Tel: 816 587 6464

Davis, William
Individual
8004 Belinder, Leawood
KS 66206
Tel: 816 753 7800

DiCapo, Jack
SL Holding Co
2510 Grand, Suite 904, Kansas City
MO 64108
Tel: 816 753 7800

Dow, Paul J
Dow-Purcell Co
2041 W 84th Terrace, Leawood
KS 66206
Tel: 913 888 5491

Flynn, James
Individual
4800 Main, Suite 565, Kansas City
MO 64112
Tel: 816 753 6750

Friess, Helga
4800 Main, Trade Floor, Kansas City
MO 64112
Tel: 816 753 7800

Gavin, James
Individual
4800 Main, Suite 565, Kansas City
MO 64112
Tel: 816 753 6750

Gerfen, Warren L
Individual
4800 Main, Suite 260, Kansas City
MO 64112
Tel: 913 753 7800

Goldman, David
Individual
1212 No Hercules Ave, Clearwater
FL 33575
Tel: 813 461 3000

Halford, Christopher
Susquehanna Investment Group
4800 Main, Suite 262, Kansas City
MO 64112
Tel: 816 753 7800

Halperin, Scott A
Halperin Brothers Futures
575 W Madison, #4201/Tower 2
Chicago IL 60606
Tel: 816 561 3430

Hook, Steven R
Individual
10612 W 115th St, Overland Park
KS 66210
Tel: 913 371 2020

Hoppes, David
Hoppes-Clothier
1714 E 11th St Winfield
KS 67156
Tel: 913 642 1157

Inactive
Duck Brothers Inc
949 Caledonia St, Philadelphia
PA 19128
Tel: 215 963 7000

Inactive
Murlas Commodities
200 W Adams, Suite 1500, Chicago
IL 60606
Tel: 312 236 6970

Inactive
Wolcott & Lincoln Inc
4800 Main, Suite 565, Kansas City
MO 64112
Tel: 816 753 6750

James, Louis
Individual
4800 Main, Suite 260, Kansas City
MO 64112
Tel: 816 753 7800

Jones Estate, Stanley T
c/o Robert A Andrews Spec Adm
8650 West 95th St, Overland Park
KS 66212
Tel: 913 341 5005

Kitzmiller, Richard W
Individual
3509 West 71st St, Prairie Village
KS 66208
Tel: 913 362 7804

Klaehre, Igor
Individual
4800 Main, Suite 200, Kansas City
MO 64112
Tel: 816 753 7800

Kreamer, James B
Individual
3708 E Roanoke Drive, Kansas City
MO 64111
Tel: 816 561 2677

Leftridge, Gary
Individual
12607 W 70th Terrace
Shawnee Mission, KS 66216
Tel: 816 753 7800

Loftis, Barbara Ann
S-S-T Clearing Co Inc
4800 Main, Suite 401, Kansas City
MO 64112
Tel: 816 561 4155

Lorenson, Richard D
Individual
2485 E North St, Salina
KS 67401
Tel: 913 823 6036

Malone, Michael
A S Polonyi Co
4800 Main, Suite 200, Kansas City
MO 64112
Tel: 816 931 6785

Mann, David
Wolcott & Lincoln Inc
4800 Main, Suite 565, Kansas City
MO 64112
Tel: 816 753 6750

Mateski, John J Jr
Individual
15 East 52nd St, Kansas City
MO 64112
Tel: 816 753 7800

McGovern, Timothy F
Individual
4800 Main, Suite 200, Kansas City
MO 64112
Tel: 816 931 6875

Miller, Herbert
Individual
2026 W 63rd St, Mission Hills
KS 66208
Tel: 913 362 2804

Murphy, Timothy
Individual
4800 Main, Suite 260, Kansas City
MO 64112
Tel: 816 756 0065

Nagels, Earl L
Individual
4551 W 107th St, Suite 333
Overland Park, KS 66207
Tel: 913 648 6333

Neville, James
SL Holding Co
1009 W 69th Terrace, Kansas City
MO 64113
Tel: 816 753 7800

Norris, Paul
T G Cernich Corp
4800 Main, Suite 260, Kansas City
MO 64112
Tel: 816 753 7800

Overman, James E
Individual
4800 Main, Suite 565, Kansas City
MO 64112
Tel: 816 753 7800

Paulsen, James R
Individual
445 W 63rd St, Kansas City
MO 64113
Tel: 816 753 7800

Pearson, Scott
Individual
111 Antioch, Overland Park
KS 66209
Tel: 913 262 7286

Ricklefs, John L
Individual
8731 N Boone, Kansas City
MO 64155
Tel: 816 436 4671

Riley, Kevin
CRT Services Inc
4800 Main, Suite 204, Kansas City
MO 64112
Tel: 816 753 7800

Roberts, Wayne
Individual
3681 South Orchard Rd, Littleton
CO 80121
Tel: 816 753 7800

Roper, Rudolph J
Great Plains Trading
4800 Main, Suite 565, Kansas City
MO 64112
Tel: 816 753 6750

** Roufa, Sheldon
Individual
10983 Granada, Suite 100
Overland Park, KS 66211
Tel: 913 345 8300

Schreiber, Gail
Refco Inc
4800 Main, Suite 328, Kansas City
MO 64112
Tel: 816 531 8084

Sifers, Steve
Individual
4800 Main, Suite 565, Kansas City
MO 64112
Tel: 816 753 6750

Simmons, Michael
Individual
10600 Farley, Overland Park
KS 66212
Tel: 913 888 0867

Snyder, Willard B
Individual
c/o Security Bank of KC, PO Box 1297
Kansas City, KS 66117
Tel: 913 621 8458

Starr, Sarah L
Staley Commodities Ltd
4800 Main, Suite 300, Kansas City
MO 64112
Tel: 816 561 0610

Suwara, Ernest E
Individual
4800 Main, Suite 200, Kansas City
MO 64112
Tel: 816 753 7800

Walters, Max E
Individual
4800 Main, Suite 235, Kansas City
MO 64112
Tel: 816 756 2616

Weisenborn, Brent M
Individual
707 Minnesota Ave, Suite 602
Kansas City, KS 66101
Tel: 913 371 2020

Werntz, Randall
Individual
4800 Main, Suite 565, Kansas City
MO 64112
Tel: 816 753 7800

Williams, John
Intermarket Trading Inc
PO Box 30341, Kansas City
MO 64112
Tel: 816 756 1014

Willoughby, Sam
T G Cernich Corp
4800 Main, Suite 260, Kansas City
MO 64112
Tel: 816 756 0011

Willoughby, Sam
T G Cernich Corp
4800 Main, Suite 260, Kansas City
MO 64112
Tel: 816 756 0011

Firms and Corporations Represented by Members

**(Clearing Members represented by §
Futures Commission Merchants by #)**

§ ADM Investor Services
4800 Main, Suite G-29, Kansas City
MO 64112
Tel: 816 931 7144

ADM Milling Co
4800 Main, Suite G-29, Kansas City
MO 64112
Tel: 913 491 9400

A G Edwards & Sons Inc
One North Jefferson Ave, St Louis
MO 63103
Tel: 314 289 3000

Alfred C Toepfer Intl Inc
2 Federal Plaza, 52 Duane St, New York
NY 10007
Tel: 212 425 0119

§ A S Polonyi Co
4800 Main, Suite 200, Kansas City
MO 64112
Tel: 816 931 6785

Attebury Grain Inc
PO Box 2707, Amarillo
TX 79105
Tel: 806 335 1639

Australian Wheat Board
630 Fifth Ave, Suite 467, New York
NY 10111
Tel: 212 307 6090

§ Barnes & Co
4800 Main, Suite 262, Kansas City
MO 64112
Tel: 816 756 3450

§ Bartlett & Co
4800 Main, Suite 600, Kansas City
MO 64112
Tel: 816 753 6300

§ Bartlett Futures Inc
4800 Main, Suite 460, Kansas City
MO 64112
Tel: 816 753 6300

B C Christopher Securities Inc
4800 Main, Suite 100, Kansas City
MO 64112
Tel: 816 932 7000

§ Bunge Corp
300 Southwest Blvd, Kansas City
KS 66103
Tel: 913 236 6500

C Deeds Inc
4800 Main, Suite 241, Kansas City
MO 64112
Tel: 816 753 0448

§ Cargill Inc
4800 Main, Suite 530, Kansas City
MO 64112
Tel: 816 756 0587

§ Cargill Investor Services Inc
141 W Jackson, Chicago
IL 60604
Tel: 312 435 8300
4800 Main, Suite 251, Kansas City
MO 64112
Tel: 816 531 3888

§ Cereal Food Processors Inc
PO Box 20, Kansas City
MO 64141
Tel: 913 262 1121

Commodities Trading Corp Ltd
CN 850, Princeton
NJ 08542
Tel: 609 924 6500

ConAgra Inc
One Central Park Plaza, Omaha
NE 68102
Tel: 402 346 8004

§ Continental Grain
PO Box 419036, Kansas City
MO 64141
Tel: 816 756 2550

CRT Services
4800 Main, Suite 204, Kansas City
MO 64112
Tel: 816 753 7800

Dean Witter Reynolds Inc
150 S Wacker Drive, Chicago
IL 60606
Tel: 312 984 4205

DeBruce Grain Inc
PO Box 10670, Gladstone
MO 64118
Tel: 816 436 8182

Dixie Portland Flour Mills Inc
PO Box 17236, Memphis
TN 38117
Tel: 901 761 1105

Dow-Purcell Co
2041 W 84 Terrace, Leawood
KS 66206
Tel: 913 888 5491

§ Drexel Burnham Lambert Inc
4800 Main, Suite 357, Kansas City
MO 64112
Tel: 816 931 0313

Duck Brothers Inc
949 Caledonia St, Philadelphia
PA 19128
Tel: 215 963 7000

§ E F Hutton & Co Inc
4800 Main, Suite 356, Kansas City
MO 64112
Tel: 816 756 2905

Evans Grain Co
PO Box 1520, Salina
KS 67402
Tel: 913 827 4484

§ Farmers Commodities Corp
1900 Swift, Suite 209, N Kansas City
MO 64116
Tel: 816 842 1399

Frank J Farnen & Co Inc
4800 Main, Suite 501, Kansas City
MO 64112
Tel: 816 531 5528

§ GLZ Inc
11903 Fuller, Grandview
MO 64030
Tel: 816 753 7800

§ Garnac Grain Co Inc
PO Box 59, Kansas City
MO 64141
Tel: 913 661 6100

Garvey Elevators Inc
Box 1948, Hutchinson
KS 67504
Tel: 316 662 5411
PO Box 9600, Fort Worth
TX 76107
Tel: 817 335 5881

Garvey International Inc
5755 Hoover, Wichita
KS 67209
Tel: 316 522 4871

§ Geisel Grain Co
4800 Main, Suite 204, Kansas City
MO 64112
Tel: 816 753 4466

§ Geldermann Inc
One Financial Plaza, Chicago
IL 60605
Tel: 312 341 7700
4800 Main, Suite 249, Kansas City
MO 64112
Tel: 816 931 7620

§ General Mills Inc
4800 Main, Suite 363, Kansas City
MO 64112
Tel: 816 753 2200
Box 15003, Commerce Stat
Minneapolis, MN 55415
Tel: 612 540 3309

Great Plains Trading
4800 Main, Suite 565, Kansas City
MO 64112
Tel: 816 753 6750

Halperin Brothers Futures
731 S Plymouth Court, #613, Chicago
IL 60605
Tel: 312 427 6063

Hoppes-Clothier
1714 E 11th St, Winfield
KS 67156
Tel: 913 642 1157

§ Index Futures Group Inc
222 W Adams, Suite 1249, Chicago
IL 60606
Tel: 312 207 5700

Intermarket Trading Inc
PO Box 30341, Kansas City
MO 64112
Tel: 816 756 1014

§ International Multifoods Corp
4800 Main, Suite 258, Kansas City
MO 64112
Tel: 816 931 2875
Multifoods Tower, Box 2942
Minneapolis, MN 55402
Tel: 612 340 3300
612 340 6676

International Trading Association Inc
3 Dunford Circle, Kansas City
MO 64112
Tel: 816 283 7301

J Lynch & Co
9200 Indian Creek Pkway, Suite 180
Overland Park, KS 66210
Tel: 913 451 4400

J W Nutt Co Inc
PO Box 798, N Little Rock
AR 72115
Tel: 501 376 0431

James R King & Co
4800 Main, Suite 200, Kansas City
MO 64112
Tel: 816 341 9485

§ Lincoln Grain Inc
1900 W 47th Place, #406
Shawnee Mission, KS 66205
Tel: 816 677 1414

Louis Dreyfus Corp
PO Box 10924, Overland Park, KS
66210
Tel: 913 345 2111
24 Richmond Hill Ave, Stamford
CT 06904
Tel: 203 357 8444

§ Merrill Lynch Futures Inc
141 W Jackson, Room 380, Chicago
IL 60604
Tel: 312 347 6505
801 W 47th St, Kansas City
MO 64112
Tel: 816 932 9781

Mitsui Grain Corp
10 S Wacker Dr, Suite 1965, Chicago
IL 60606
Tel: 312 993 5700

§ Morrison-Gregg Grain Co
4800 Main, Suite 458, Kansas City
MO 64112
Tel: 816 931 7756

Murias Commodities
200 W Adams, Suite 1500, Chicago
IL 60606
Tel: 312 236 6970

§ Myers and Co Inc
4800 Main, Suite 110, Kansas City
MO 64112
Tel: 816 931 8517

Nabisco Brands Inc
100 River Rd, East Hanover
NJ 07936
Tel: 201 503 2000

National Farms Inc
4800 Main, Suite 246, Kansas City
MO 64112
Tel: 816 753 4501

§ C R Overman Inc
4800 Main, Suite 241, Kansas City
MO 64112
Tel: 816 931 5144

§ Paine Webber Inc
208 S LaSalle, Suite 1900, Chicago
IL 60604
Tel: 312 580 8204

§ The Pillsbury Co
4800 Main, Suite 230, Kansas City
MO 64112
Tel: 816 753 1605
Pillsbury Center, Suite 3526
Minneapolis, MN 55902
Tel: 612 330 4819
PO Box 1160, St Joseph
MO 64505
Tel: 816 238 4507

§ Prudential-Bache Securities Inc
4800 Main, Suite 333A, Kansas City
MO 64112
Tel: 816 756 2922

Purina Mills Inc
1401 S Hanley Rd, St Louis
MO 63144
Tel: 314 768 4178

Ralston Purina Co (Checkerboard
Grain)
Checkerboard Square, St Louis
MO 63164
Tel: 314 982 2293

§ Refco Inc
889 Ridge Lake Blvd, Memphis
TN 38119
Tel: 901 766 4600
4800 Main, Suite 328, Kansas City
MO 64112
Tel: 816 531 8084

§ Richard Frank Group
4800 Main, Suite 236, Kansas City
MO 64112
Tel: 816 931 2062

Richardson Greenshields/Canada Ltd
One Lombard Place, 30th Fl, Winnipeg
Canada R3B 0Y1
Tel: 204 934 5858

§ Rickel Inc
4800 Main, Suite 430, Kansas City
MO 64112
Tel: 816 561 5912

Romain Grain Co
4800 Main, Suite 240, Kansas City
MO 64112
Tel: 816 531 6780

SL Holding Co
2510 Grand, Suite 904, Kansas City
MO 64108
Tel: 816 753 7800

§ S-S-T Clearing Co Inc
4800 Main, Suite 401, Kansas City
MO 64112
Tel: 816 561 4155

Scoular Grain Co
4800 Main, Suite 274, Kansas City
MO 64112
Tel: 816 756 1474

Seaboard Corp
PO Box 2972, Shawnee Mission
KS 66201
Tel: 913 676 8800

§ Shay Grain Clearing Co
4800 Main, Suite 358, Kansas City
MO 64112
Tel: 816 531 5320

Shay Grain Co
4800 Main, Suite 358, Kansas City
MO 64112
Tel: 816 531 5320

Shearson Lehman Brothers Inc
440 S LaSalle, Ste 2200, Chicago
IL 60604
Tel: 312 207 5459

§ Simonds-Shields-Theis Grain Co
4800 Main, Suite 401, Kansas City
MO 64112
Tel: 816 561 4155

Smith Barney, Harris Upham & Co
333 W 34th St, 9th Floor, New York
NY 10001
Tel: 212 399 6000

§ The Smoot Grain Co
4800 Main, Suite G-29, Kansas City
MO 64112
Tel: 816 931 7144

Sosland Publishing Co
PO Box 29155, Shawnee Mission
KS 66201
Tel: 816 236 7300

§ Staley Commodities Intl Inc
4800 Main, Suite 300, Kansas City
MO 64112
Tel: 816 561 0610

Staley Commodities, Ltd
4800 Main, Suite 300, Kansas City
MO 64112
Tel: 816 561 0610

Sumitomo Corp of America
345 Park Ave, 14th Floor, New York
NY 10154
Tel: 212 207 0809

Susquehanna Investment Group
4800 Main, Suite 262, Kansas City
MO 64112
Tel: 816 753 7800

§ T G Cernich Corp
4800 Main, Suite 260, Kansas City
MO 64112
Tel: 816 756 0011

§ Term Commodities
PO Box 10924, Shawnee Mission
KS 66210
Tel: 913 345 2111

Toshoku America Inc
551 Fifth Ave, New York
NY 10176
Tel: 212 661 5400

The Uhlmann Co
PO Box 419410, Kansas City
MO 64141
Tel: 816 221 8200

§ Union Equity Cooperative Exchange
PO Box 3408, Enid
OK 73702
Tel: 405 233 5100
4800 Main, Suite 455, Kansas City
MO 64112
Tel: 816 931 6210

WAF Inc
4800 Main, Suite 565, Kansas City
MO 64112
Tel: 816 753 6750

Wheeler Brothers Grain Co Inc
PO Box 29, Watonga
OK 73772
Tel: 405 623 7223

Whitehall Clearing Corp Futures Div
1 Financial Square, 14th Floor
New York, NY 10006
Tel: 212 804 3494

§ Wolcott & Lincoln Futures Inc
4800 Main, Suite 565, Kansas City
MO 64112
Tel: 816 753 6750

§ Wolcott & Lincoln Inc
4800 Main, Suite 565, Kansas City
MO 64112
Tel: 816 753 6750

Appendices

Appendix 1: Glossary of Commodity Market Terms

Actuals: Physical commodities, also commodities readily available. The commodity itself as opposed to a futures contract.

Afloats: Commodities on board, ready to sail.

Arbitrage: Purchase of contract in one market while simultaneously selling the same amount in another to take advantage of price or currency differentials.

At-the-money: An option with an exercise price equal or near to the current underlying futures price.

Backwardation: When the spot or nearby prices are higher than those for future delivery months. Usually caused by delays in shipment thus creating shortages in available supplies. Opposite of *contango*.

Basis/basis grade: Difference between cash price and futures price.

Basis price: Agreed price between buyer and seller of an option at which the option may be taken up. Also called 'striking price' or 'exercise price'.

Basis quote: Offer/sale of cash commodity as a difference above or below a futures price.

Bear: Person expecting a decline in prices.

Bear market: A market in which prices are declining.

Best orders: These are buy or sell orders executed by the broker at what is considered to be the best price.

Bid: An offer to purchase at a specified price.

Borrowing: Purchase of a nearby delivery date and simultaneous sale of a forward date. Used mainly on the London Metal Exchange.

Broker: Establishes contact between buyer and seller, for a fee. In the US, floor dealing members of futures markets are frequently called brokers.

Bull: Person expecting a rise in prices.

Bull market: A market in which prices are rising.

Buy in: To cover, offset or close out a short position.

Buying basis: Difference between cost of a cash commodity and a future sold as a hedge. See *selling basis*.

Buy on close: To buy at the end of a trading session at a price within the closing range.

Buy on opening: To buy at the beginning of a trading session at a price within the opening range.

Call option: An option that gives the holder the right to enter a long futures position at a specific price, and obligates the seller to enter a short futures position at a specific price, should the option be exercised.

C & F: Cost and freight.

Carrying: General term covering both *borrowing* and *lending*.

Carrying costs: Costs connected with warehouse storage, insurance, etc. Sometimes includes interest and estimated changes in weight.

Cash market: Market for the physical commodity.

Cash price: In the US the price of the physical commodity; on the London Metal Exchange the spot price.

Certified stocks: Supplies rated as deliverable.

CIF: Cost, insurance and freight (included in the price).

Clearances: Aggregate shipments of a commodity made by sea on a specified date.

Clearing house: An adjunct to a futures exchange through which transactions executed on the floor are settled using a process of matching purchases and sales. A clearing organization is also charged with the proper conduct of delivery procedures and the adequate financing of the entire operation.

Commission: The one time fee charged by a broker to a customer when a position is liquidated either by offset or delivery.

Commission house: A company which trades on behalf of clients for a commission. The commission house only handles clients' business and does not trade on its own account.

Commodity Futures Trading Commission (CFTC): A US regulatory agency which exercises control over US commodity futures market trading.

Commodity Price Index: Index, or average, of commodity price movements.

Contango: A situation where prices are higher in the forward delivery months than in the nearby delivery month. Opposite of *backwardation*. Normally in evidence when supplies are adequate or in surplus. The contango reflects either wholly or in part the costs of holding and financing.

Contract: An agreement to buy or sell a specified amount of a particular commodity. The contract details show the amount and grade of the product and the date on which the contract will mature and become deliverable, if not previously liquidated.

Contract grades: That which is deliverable on a futures contract. Basic contract grade is the one deliverable at par. There may be more than one basic grade.

Contract month(s): The month(s) in which futures contracts may be satisfied by making or accepting a delivery.

Contract weights: Deliverable weights of contract as shown on warehouse receipts.

Cover: The balancing of an open position by buying or selling in the market.

Day order/trading: Order valid throughout trading hours during day on which it is placed.

Day trading: Establishing and liquidating the same position or positions within one day's trading.

Delivery: There are three types of delivery: 'current'—delivery during the present month; 'nearby'—delivery during the nearest active month; 'distant'—delivery in a month further off.

Delivery date: Date on which the commodity must be delivered to fulfil the terms of the contract.

Delivery notice: The written notice given by the seller of his intention to make delivery of a commodity to settle a futures contract.

Delivery points: Locations designated by futures exchanges to which the commodity may be physically delivered.

Delivery price: Price fixed by clearing house at which futures deliveries are invoiced. Also price at which a commodities futures contract is settled when deliveries are made.

Deposit: Sum of money required by the broker from his client, usually 10 per cent of the value of the contract, to justify opening of a futures position.

Differentials: Premiums paid for grades better than basic grade or discounts allowed for grades below basic grade.

Double option: An option which gives the buyer or person taking the option the right either to buy from or sell to the seller of the option or the person who gives it, at the *basis price*.

Expiration date: The last day that an option may be exercised.

First notice day: The first day on which notices are issued indicating delivery in a specific delivery month.

FOB: Free on board.

Futures: A term used to designate all contracts covering the purchase and sale of physical commodities or financial instruments for future delivery on a commodity exchange.

Good Till Cancelled Order (GTC): Order which is valid at any time during market hours until executed or cancelled by the client.

Hedge: The purchase or sale of a futures contract as a temporary substitute for a transaction to be made at a later date. Usually it involves opposite positions in the cash market and the futures market at the same time.

In-the-money: A situation where the market price of a futures contract is higher than the exercise price of a call, or lower than the exercise price of a put.

Job lot: Unit of trading smaller than the regular contract unit.

Kerb trading: Unofficial trading when the market has closed. The term 'kerb' dates from the time when dealers continued trading on the kerb outside the exchanges after they had closed.

Last trading day: The final day under an exchange's rules during which trading may take place in a particular delivery futures month. Positions which have not been closed by the last trading day must be fulfilled by making or taking delivery of the physical commodities or financial instruments.

Lending: Sale of a nearby delivery date coupled with the simultaneous purchase of a more distant date (LME term).

Limit order: An order given to a broker by a customer which has restrictions upon its execution. The customer specifies a price and the order can only be executed if the market reaches or betters that price.

Limit price: Largest permitted price fluctuation in a futures contract during a trading session, as fixed by the contract market's rules. Also known as 'maximum price fluctuation'.

Liquidation: Any transaction that offsets or closes out a long or short position. See *buy in*.

Locals: Small, private individual traders on US exchanges, whose activities provide liquidity.

Long: An open purchased futures contract. Buying forward on the market.

Long hedge: The purchase of a futures contract in anticipation of actual purchases in the cash market.

Maintenance margin: A sum, usually smaller than, but part of, the original margin, which must be maintained on deposit at all times. If a customer's equity in any futures position drops to, or under, the maintenance margin level, the broker must issue a *margin call* for the amount of money required to restore the customer's equity in the account to the original margin level.

Margin: A cash amount of funds that must be deposited with the broker for each futures contract as a guarantee of fulfilment of the contract. Also called *security deposit*.

Margin call: A commodity broker's request to a client for additional funds to secure the original deposits.

Mark to market: The daily adjustment of an account to reflect profits and losses.

Minimum price fluctuation: Set by the rules of the exchange, this is the minimum unit by which the price of a commodity can fluctuate per trade.

Nearby delivery: The nearest active month of delivery on a futures market.

Nominal price: Price quotations on futures period in which no actual trading took place.

Notice day: A day on which notices of intent to deliver pertaining to a specified delivery month may be issued. See *delivery notice*.

Offer: Indicates a willingness to sell a futures contract at a given price.

Offset: Liquidation of a long or short position by the opposite transaction: the sale offsets a long position; the purchase offsets a short position.

Open contracts: Contracts which have been bought or sold without the transaction being completed by subsequent sale or purchase, or by making or taking actual delivery of the commodity.

Open interest: Number of open futures contracts—unliquidated purchases or sales.

Open outcry: Trading conducted by calling out *bids* and *offers* across a *ring* or a *pit* and having them accepted.

Option: An option is a method of trading a futures market with a predetermined maximum risk. For the payment of a premium, the buyer may purchase the right to buy or sell a commodity or financial instrument at a specified price within a specified time limit.

Original margin: The margin needed to cover a specific new position.

Out-of-the-money: A situation where the market price of a futures contract is below the exercise price of a call, or above the exercise price of a put.

Pit: Place where futures are traded on the floor of the commodity exchange. Also known as *ring*.

Point: Minimum price unit in which a commodity price is quoted.

Position trader: Someone who takes long or short position in futures markets in consequence of an opinion that prices are about to advance or decline.

Premium: The excess of one futures contract price over that of another or over the cash market price.

Put option: Gives the buyer (or taker) of the option, in exchange for the premium which he pays, the right to decide at a later date whether or not to sell to the seller (or grantor) at the price (*basis* or striking price) agreed at the time the premium was paid. The right may be exercised at any point from the purchase of the option up to the *expiration date* (the date on which the option expires).

Rally: An upward movement of prices following a decline. Also known as a 'recovery'.

Ring: Space on trading floor where futures are traded. Also known as the *pit*.

Scalper: One who trades for small gains. This trader normally establishes and liquidates a position quickly, usually within the same day.

Security deposit—initial: A cash amount of funds that must be deposited with the broker for each contract as a guarantee of fulfilment of the futures contract. It is not considered as part payment or purchase.

Selling basis: Term meaning that the buying basis is increased to include costs and profits.

Short: One who has sold a futures contract to establish a market position and who has not yet closed out this position through an offsetting purchase; the opposite of a *long*.

Short hedge: The sale of a futures contract(s) to eliminate or lessen the possible decline in value of ownership of an approximately equal amount of the actual physical commodity or financial instrument.

Spot: Term denoting immediate delivery for cash as distinct from future delivery.

Spot month: The first month in which delivery can take place and for which a quotation is made on the futures market.

Spread: Refers to a simultaneous purchase and sale of futures contracts for the same commodity or instrument for delivery in different months or in different but related markets.

Squeeze: Pressure on a delivery date which results in the price of that date becoming firmer in relation to other dates.

Stop loss order: An order which can be fulfilled only when the price has reached the level specified by the client. As soon as the price has been traded, the order is executed at the next obtainable price. There is no guarantee that the order will be executed at the level specified in the original order.

Straddle: The simultaneous buying and selling of the same commodity on the same market.

Tender: To offer for delivery against futures.

Tenderable grades and staples: These are grades and staples deliverable to settle a futures contract.

Terminal market: Usually synonymous with commodity exchange or futures market, especially in the UK. Also used to signify principals' market as opposed to brokers' market.

Tick: Refers to a change in price, either up or down.

Transferable notice: A notice signifying the intention to make actual delivery. This is given by the seller of a futures contract, usually specifying a day about one week hence.

Volume: The number of transactions in a futures contract made during a specified period of time.

Warehouse receipt: A receipt for a commodity given by a licensed or authorized warehouseman and issued as a tender on futures contracts.

Wet barrels: Oil trading term signifying delivery of a product rather than the transfer of a tanker receipt.

Appendix 2: World Time Zones

Standard Times at Noon Greenwich Mean Time

Accra	12.00	Damascus	14.00	Ottawa	07.00
Adelaide	21.30	Darwin	21.30	Panama	07.00
Algiers	13.00	Delhi	17.30	Paris	13.00
Amman	14.00	Djakarta	20.00	Peking	20.00
Amsterdam	13.00	Dublin	12.00	Perth	20.00
Ankara	14.00	Gibraltar	13.00	Prague	13.00
Athens	14.00	Helsinki	14.00	Quebec	07.00
Auckland	24.00	Hobart	22.00	Rangoon	18.30
Baghdad	15.00	Hong Kong	20.00	Rawalpindi	17.00
Bangkok	19.00	Istanbul	14.00	Reykjavik	12.00
Beirut	14.00	Jerusalem	14.00	Rio de Janeiro	09.00
Belgrade	13.00	Karachi	17.00	Rome	13.00
Berlin	13.00	Kuala Lumpur	20.00	San Francisco	04.00
Berne	13.00	Lagos	13.00	Santiago	08.00
Bombay	17.30	Leningrad	15.00	Sofia	14.00
Bonn	13.00	Lima	07.00	Singapore	19.30
Brisbane	22.00	Lisbon	13.00	Stockholm	13.00
Brussels	13.00	Luxemburg	13.00	Sydney	22.00
Bucharest	14.00	Madras	17.30	Tehran	15.30
Budapest	13.00	Madrid	13.00	Tokyo	21.00
Buenos Aires	09.00	Melbourne	22.00	Toronto	07.00
Cairo	14.00	Mexico City	06.00	Tunis	13.00
Calcutta	17.30	Montevideo	08.30	Vancouver	04.00
Canberra	22.00	Moscow	15.00	Vienna	13.00
Cape Town	14.00	Nairobi	15.00	Warsaw	13.00
Caracas	08.00	New York	07.00	Washington	07.00
Chicago	06.00	Nicosia	14.00	Wellington	24.00
Copenhagen	13.00	Oslo	13.00	Winnipeg	06.00

Note to World Time Zones map

The earth turns one complete revolution in 24 hours. The surface of the earth is divided into 24 time zones, each of 15° longitude or 1 hour of time. In 24 hours it turns through 360°. The times shown are the standard times on land and sea when it is 12.00 hours on the Greenwich Meridian.

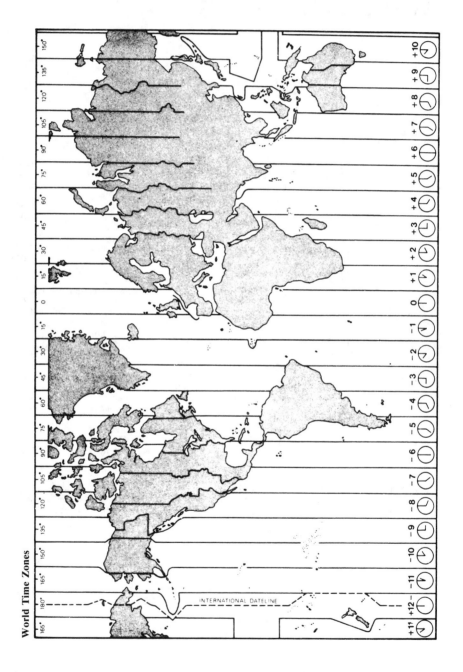

World Time Zones

Appendix 3: Conversion Tables

Mass	Long tons	Metric tons	Short tons	Pikuls	Kilograms	Pounds	Ounces troy	Pennyweights	Grains
Long ton		1.016	1.120	16.8	1,016	2,240			
Metric ton	0.984		1.102	16.535	1,000	2,204.5			
Short ton	0.893	0.907		15.00	907	2,000			
Pikul	0.0595	0.0605	0.067		60.48	133.33			
Kilogram	0.00098	0.0001	0.0011	0.0165		2.2045	32.150	642.83	15,431.5
Pound	0.0004	0.0004	0.0005	0.0075	0.4536		14.583	291.6	7,000
Ounce troy					0.03112	0.0686		20.00	480.0
Pennyweight					0.00015				24.00

Area	Hectares	Acres	Square Kilometres	Square Miles	Square Metres	Square Feet
Hectare	—	2.471	0.01	0.004	10,000	—
Acre	0.405	—	0.004	0.0015	4,046.86	
Square Kilometre	100.0	247.1	—	0.386	—	—
Square Mile	259.0	640.0	2.590	—	—	—
Square Metre	10,000	4,046.86	—	—	—	10,764
Square Foot	—	—	—	—	0.093	—

Volume	Barrels	Imperial Gallons	US Gallons	Kilolitres	Cubic Feet	Cubic Metres
Barrel	—	34.973	42	0.159	5.614	0.1589
Imperial Gallon	0.028	—	1.201	0.004	0.1605	0.0045
US Gallon	0.0238	0.833	—	0.003	0.134	0.0037
Kilolitre	6.289	219.97	264.17	—	—	—
Cubic Foot	0.178	6.2288	7.4805	—	—	0.028
Cubic Metre	6.289	219.97	264.17	—	35.315	—

Appendix 4:

Average monthly dollar/sterling rate

	Jan	Feb	March	April	May	June	July	August	Sept	Oct	Nov	Dec	Average
1970	2.3999	2.4042	2.4056	2.4059	2.4033	2.3976	2.3903	2.3877	2.3845	2.3870	2.3899	2.3903	2.3955
1971	2.4047	2.4170	2.4182	2.4175	2.4183	2.4179	2.4182	2.4342	2.4709	2.4915	2.4937	2.5267	2.4441
1972	2.5703	2.6030	2.6178	2.6093	2.6117	2.5814	2.4415	2.4502	2.4425	2.3968	2.3518	2.3456	2.5018
1973	2.3558	2.4418	2.4778	2.4825	2.5174	2.5743	2.5402	2.4742	2.4163	2.4260	2.3890	2.3171	2.4510
1974	2.2263	2.2738	2.3369	2.3906	2.4117	2.3876	2.3869	2.3445	2.3146	2.3310	2.3271	2.3271	2.3382
1975	2.3603	2.3917	2.4172	2.3680	2.3185	2.2807	2.1833	2.1133	2.0852	2.0548	2.0499	2.0208	2.2203
1976	2.0276	2.0257	1.9455	1.8476	1.8156	1.7710	1.7863	1.7819	1.7309	1.6401	1.6370	1.6787	1.8073
1977	1.7127	1.7100	1.7172	1.7195	1.7188	1.7193	1.7221	1.7403	1.7436	1.7703	1.8203	1.8550	1.7485
1978	1.9338	1.9405	1.9103	1.8507	1.8175	1.8366	1.8940	1.9419	1.9593	1.9740	1.9905	1.9950	1.9203
1979	2.0030	2.0040	2.0351	2.0759	2.0541	2.1029	2.2495	2.2326	2.2005	2.1472	2.1308	2.1966	2.1190
1980	2.2676	2.2908	2.1982	2.2146	2.2913	2.3460	2.3570	2.3470	2.3970	2.3880	2.4370	2.3585	2.3246
1981	2.3920	2.3680	2.2190	2.2450	2.1410	2.0705	1.9805	1.8060	1.8360	1.8510	1.9000	1.9043	2.0300
1982	1.8900	1.8500	1.8065	1.7700	1.8121	1.7600	1.7300	1.7277	1.7120	1.7000	1.6300	1.6178	1.7505
1983	1.5700	1.5300	1.4900	1.5418	1.5700	1.5495	1.5277	1.5027	1.4990	1.4955	1.4630	1.4380	1.5200
1984	1.4081	1.4382	1.4560	1.4365	1.3905	1.3773	1.3210	1.3139	1.2595	1.2300	1.3032	1.1800	1.3445
1985	1.1278	1.0900	1.1369	1.2410	1.2517	1.2802	1.3784	1.3838	1.3669	1.4212	1.4411	1.4454	1.2970
1986	1.4282	1.4308	1.4679	1.4959	1.5204	1.5015	1.5030	1.4866	1.4724	1.4295	1.4242	1.4303	1.4659
1987	1.5059	1.5258	1.5939	1.6299	1.6678	1.6287	1.6105	1.5962	1.6448	1.6597	1.7742	1.8275	1.6387
1988	1.8035	1.7559	1.8288	1.8759	1.8702	1.7843	1.7054	1.6989	1.6835	1.7347	1.8066	1.8278	1.7813
1989	1.7779	1.7549	1.7154	1.7009	1.6332	1.5530	1.6212	1.5990	1.5720	—	—	—	1.6586

With thanks to: National Australian Bank Group, London.

INDEX

567